SELECT SPECIMENS OF THE THEATRE OF THE HINDUS

SELECT SPECIMENS OF THE THEATRE OF THE HINDUS

TRANSLATED FROM ORIGINAL SANSKRIT

IN TWO VOLUMES

HORACE HAYMAN WILSON

VOL. I

Third Edition

GYAN

Published by

Gyan Publishing House
5, Ansari Road
Daryaganj, New Delhi-110002
Phone: 011-47034999, 9811692060
E-mail: books@gyanbooks.com

Distribution Network
gyanbooks.com
India, USA, Canada, UK, Australia, France

ISBN : 978-81-212-3992-9 (Set)
ISBN : 978-81-212-4905-8 (HB)
First Published, 1871

2nd Impression 2020

Printed at: Gyan Press, Delhi.

The book at your disposal is the edition of an old book originally published long back. The Text quality of this book may not be at par as compared to our other books but many readers approached us to reprint this important book so that it could satiate their hunger. We request all the readers of this book to help us to improve its quality by providing the necessary text of those pages which are not properly visible. Your valuable support in this case will be highly appreciated and acknowledged and our future readers will be benefitted immensely.

TO

HIS MOST GRACIOUS MAJESTY

GEORGE THE FOURTH,

AS

THE PATRON OF ORIENTAL LITERATURE,

THIS ATTEMPT

TO FAMILIARISE HIS BRITISH SUBJECTS

WITH

THE MANNERS AND FEELINGS

OF THEIR FELLOW-SUBJECTS IN THE EAST,

IS

MOST RESPECTFULLY INSCRIBED

BY

THE TRANSLATOR.

CALCUTTA, 16*th* *May* 1827.

ADVERTISEMENT TO THE SECOND EDITION.

UPON the first publication of the Specimens of the Theatre of the Hindus, I stated explicitly the object which I had proposed to myself in the translation, and explained it to be my ambition to secure to the Hindu Theatre a place in English literature. It was not my purpose to furnish the student of Sanskrit with a class-book, and I did not, therefore, attempt to render the text word for word or line for line. At the same time I expressed my belief, that few translations of the same class could pretend to greater fidelity, as nothing had been added, little omitted, and the expressions of the original had been adhered to as closely as the genius of the two languages, and my own command of either, would allow. To this character of accuracy I can now more confidently lay claim, as in preparing the present edition for the press, I have carefully compared the translation with the text, and corrected those mistakes which inadvertence, interruption, and erroneous, or undecipherable manuscripts, had led me, as I formerly stated I anticipated they would lead me, to commit. Since the publication of my translation also, the original Sanskrit plays have been printed and published in Calcutta, under the authority of the Committee of Public Instruction ; the edition was prepared from my manuscripts, collated with others belonging to the Sanskrit College and to different individuals, by Jaya Gopála Tarkálaṁkára, the professor of Sanskrit literature in the college; and although the work may present a few typographical errors and some questionable readings, it is upon the whole a highly creditable specimen of unassuming editorial erudition and care. It is with this printed edition that I have compared my translation, and some alterations have been rendered necessary by following the reading there adopted, when it differed from that of the manuscripts which I originally employed.

OXFORD, 15*th December* 1834.

ADVERTISEMENT TO THE THIRD EDITION.

THE third Edition of the "Select Specimens of the Theatre of the Hindus" is a literal reprint, generally page for page, of the second Edition, after a careful correction of typographical and analogous errors which, in the latter, had been overlooked. The orthography for the transliteration of Sanskrit words in Roman characters is, in the present edition, the same as that adopted by Professor Wilson in his later writings, and adhered to, throughout, in the previous volumes of his "Works."

THE PUBLISHERS.

May 15, 1871.

ADVERTISEMENT TO THE THIRD EDITION

CONTENTS OF VOL. I.

ERRATA

VOL. I.

Page xl.	line 21,	*instead of*	*khangas*, *read* *khángas*.	
lxx.	13,	,,	Hanuman- *read* Hanúman-	
	15,	,,	Viddhá-Śálábhanjiká, *read* Viddha-Śála-bhanjiká.	
	24,	,,	Śárada- *read* Śáradá-	
15,	33,	,,	Kánda, *read* Káńḍa.	
27,	18,	,,	Duhśásana, *read* Duḥśásana.	
59,	16,	,	*víná*, read *víńá*.	
109,	24,	,,	its, *read* it's.	
116,	4 *infra*	,,	Márkandeya, *read* Márkaṅḍeya.	
	5 ,,	,,	Chandipáth, *read* Chaṅḍípáṭha.	
193,	3 ,,	,,	Tillottamá, *read* Tilottamá.	
260,	5 ,,	,,	Védhaka, Réchaka, *read* Vedhaka, Rechaka.	
317,	5	,,	Vasishtha, *read* Vasishṭha.	

VOL. II.

Page 65,	line 2, *infra*,	*instead of*	143 *read* 148.
121,	1, ,,	,,	MÁLATI, *read* MÁLATÍ.
144,	12, ,,	,,	divided it into, *read* divided into.
363,	1,	*instead of*	NAṬAKA, *read* NÁṬAKA.
375,	1,	,,	MURÂRI- *read* MURÁRI-
390,	1,	,,	DUTÁNGADA, *read* DÚTÁNGADA.
393,	1,	,,	MADHÂVA, *read* MÁDHAVA.
395,	1,	,,	ABHIRAMÀMAŃI, *read* ABHIRÁMAMAŃI.

PREFACE.

MANY years have elapsed since the translation of *Śakuntalá*, by Sir William Jones, announced to the literary public of the western world that the Hindus had a national drama, the merits of which, it was inferred from those of the specimen published, might render it worthy of further investigation.

Notwithstanding the expectation thus excited, the subject has received little subsequent illustration. The translation of the *Prabodha-Chandrodaya*, or "Rise of the Moon of Intellect," by the late Dr. Taylor of Bombay, throws more light upon the metaphysics than the drama of the Hindus; and the account given of the *Málati Mádhava* in the Asiatic Researches, by Mr. Colebrooke, was subordinate to the object of his essay on *Sanskrit* and *Prákrit* prosody, and was unlikely to fall in the way of general readers. These two contributions, therefore, to the elucidation of Hindu dramatic literature, have added but little to the notice secured for it by the publication of *Śakuntalá*.

The objects for which an ancient dialect may be studied are its philology and its literature, or the arts and sciences, the notions and manners, the history and belief of the people by whom it was spoken. Particular branches of composition may be preferably cultivated for the due understanding of each of these subjects, but there is no one species which will be found to embrace so many purposes as the dramatic. The dialogue varies from simple to elaborate, from the conversation of ordinary life to the highest refinements of poetical taste. The illustrations are drawn from every known product of art, as well as every observable phenomenon of nature. The manners and feelings of the people are delineated, living and breathing before us, and history and religion furnish the most important and interesting topics to the bard. Wherever, therefore, there exists a dramatic literature, it must be pre-eminently entitled to the attention of the philosopher as well as the philologist, of the man of general literary taste as well as the professional scholar.

Independent, however, of the claims to notice which the Hindu theatre possesses, upon principles that equally apply to the dramatic literature of every nation, it may advance pretensions to consideration on its own account, connected both with its peculiar merits and with the history of the stage.

Neither of the dramas hitherto published, *Śakuntalá* or the *Prabodha-Chandrodaya*, can be considered to convey an accurate notion of the Hindu theatre. Each is but the species of its own genus. The latter belongs to the metaphysical, the former to the mytho-pastoral class of Sanskṛit plays; but these two varieties are far from representing every class and order. Their wide dissimilarity might lead us to anticipate the extensive range of the theatre to which they belong, and to infer that where such striking distinctions were to be found, others less decidedly marked must prevail. The inference would be justified by the fact, and the Hindu theatre affords examples of the drama of domestic, as well as of heroic life; of original invention as well as of legendary tradition.

At the same time, there are many peculiarities belonging to the Hindu theatre which it is necessary that we should know, before we can safely delineate the history, or propose the theory of the drama. Hitherto the views of all writers upon the subject have been circumscribed by the practice which alone was open to their observation, and their speculations have been grounded upon the narrow basis which the dramatic literature of classical antiquity supplied. To this must now be superadded the conclusions that are to be derived from the dramatic compositions of the Hindus.

The theatrical representations of modern Europe, however diversified by national features, are the legitimate offspring of the classical drama. Widely as the mysteries and moralities differed from the plays of Æschylus or Aristophanes, they emanated from the only schools where those writers were read, and the cultivation of the cloister, unembued with the animation of social life, produced no worthier harvest than those crude and absurd compositions. Such as they were, however, they formed the connecting link between the ancient and the modern theatre, and allied the compositions of Shakespeare, Lope de Vega, and Racine, with the songs of Bacchus and the monologues of Thespis.

Whatever may be the merits or defects of the Hindu drama, it may be safely asserted that they do not spring from the same parent, but are unmixedly its own. The science of the Hindus may be indebted to modern discoveries in other regions, and their mythology may have derived legions from Paganism or Christianity, but it is impossible that they should have borrowed their dramatic compositions from the people either of ancient or modern times. The nations of Europe possessed no dramatic literature before the fourteenth or fifteenth century, at which period the Hindu drama had passed into its decline. Mohammedan literature has ever been a stranger to theatrical writings, and the Mussulman conquerors of India could not have communicated what they never possessed. There is no record that theatrical entertainments were ever naturalised amongst the ancient Persians, Arabs, or Egyptians; and the Hindus, if they learned the art from others, can have been obliged alone to the Greeks or to the Chinese. A perusal of the Hindu plays will show how little likely it is that they are indebted to either, as, with the exception of a few features in common which could not fail to occur, they present characteristic varieties of conduct and construction which strongly evidence both original design and national development.

The Hindu theatre belongs to that division of dramatic composition which modern critics have agreed to term romantic, in opposition to what some schools have been pleased to call *classical.* This has not escaped the observation of one of the first dramatic critics of any age, and Schlegel observes, "The drama of *Śakuntalá* presents, through its oriental brilliancy of colouring, so striking a resemblance, upon the whole, to our romantic drama, that it might be suspected the love of Shakespeare had influenced the translator, if other orientalists had not borne testimony to the fidelity of his translation." The present collection will afford ample evidence to the same effect.

Hindu dramatists have little regard for the unities of time and place; and if by unity of action be meant singleness of incident, they exhibit an equal disdain for such a restriction. At the same time, as we shall subsequently see, they are not destitute of systematic and sensible rules, and they are as unfamiliar with the extravagance of the Chinese drama, as with the severe simplicity of Grecian tragedy.

There is one peculiarity in the Hindu theatre which remarkably distinguishes it from that of every other people. Although there is little reason to doubt that the Sanskṛit language was once a spoken tongue in some parts of India, yet it does not seem probable that it was ever the vernacular language of the whole country, and it certainly ceased to be a living dialect at a period of which we have no knowledge.

The greater part of every play is written in Sanskŕit. None of the dramatic compositions at present known can boast perhaps of a very high antiquity, and several of them are comparatively modern; they must, therefore, have been unintelligible to a considerable portion of their audiences, and never could have been so directly addressed to the bulk of the population, as to have exercised much influence upon their passions or their tastes.

This circumstance, however, is perfectly in harmony with the constitution of Hindu society, by which the highest branches of literature, as well as the highest offices in the state, were reserved for the privileged tribes of Kshattriyas and Brahmans. Even amongst them, however, a small portion could have followed the expressions of the actors so as to have felt their full force; and the plays of the Hindus must therefore have been exceedingly deficient in theatrical effect. In some measure, this deficiency was compensated by peculiar impressions; and the popularity of most of the stories, and the sanctity of the representation, as well as of the Sanskŕit language, substituted an adventitious interest for ordinary excitement. Still the appeal to popular feeling must have been immeasurably weakened; and the affectation or reality of scholarship, as at the Latin plays of Ariosto, or the scholastic exhibitions of Westminster, must have been a sorry substitute for universal, instantaneous, and irrepressible delight.

Besides being an entertainment appropriated to the leading or learned members of society, the dramatic entertainments of the Hindus essentially differed from those of modern Europe in the unfrequency of their representation. They seem to have been acted only on solemn or public occasions. In this respect they resembled the dramatic performances of the Athenians, which took place at distant intervals, and especially at the spring and autumnal festivals of Bacchus, the last being usually preferred, as the city was then filled with strangers, its tributaries and allies. According to Hindu authorities, the occasions suitable for dramatic representations are the lunar holidays, a royal coronation, assemblages of people at fairs and religious festivals, marriages, the meeting of friends, taking first possession of a house or a town, and the birth of a son. The most ordinary occasion, however, of a performance was, as will be seen, the season peculiarly sacred to some divinity.

Amongst the Athenians, also, a piece was never performed a second time, at least under the same form; and it is clear that the Hindu plays are written with a view to but one specific representation. At other times, and in other places, probably, successful dramas were repeated both in Greece and India; but this was a distant and accidental, and not, as with us, an immediate and anticipated consequence of success.

As the plays of the Hindus were only occasionally enacted, we can readily comprehend why they should be so much longer than our dramatic writings, and why they should be so few. The Hindu plays do not, like the Chinese, it is true, afford employment for ten days, but they sometimes extend, as we shall see, to ten acts, and those none of the shortest, and they must have occupied at least five or six hours in representation. With respect to their number, Sir William Jones was undoubtedly misinformed, when he was led to suppose that the Indian theatre would fill as many volumes as that of any nation in ancient or modern Europe. Many pieces, no doubt, are lost, and others are scarce; but it may be doubted whether all the plays that are to be found, and those of which mention is made by writers on the drama, amount to many more than sixty. We may form a tolerably accurate estimate of the extent of the Hindu theatre by the fact, that no more than three plays are attributed to each of the great masters of the art, Bhavabhúti and Kálidása; a most beggarly account, when contrasted with the three hundred and sixty-five comedies of Antiphanes, or the two thousand of Lope de Vega.

Although, however, the plays of the Hindus must have been less numerous than those of any of the nations of highest repute in theatrical literature, yet they must have existed in some number, to have offered the multiplied classes into which they have been divided by their critics, and which exhibit at least no want of variety. It may also be observed, that the dramatic pieces which have come down to us are those of the highest order, defended by their intrinsic purity from the corrosion of time. Those of an inferior description, and which existed sometimes apparently in the vernacular dialects, may have been more numerous and popular, and were more, strictly speaking, national. Traces of these are still observable in the dramatised stories of the *Bhanrs* or professional buffoons, in the *Játras* of the Bengalis, and the *Rásas* of the western provinces. The first is the representation of some ludicrous adventure by two or three performers, carried on in extempore dialogue, usually of a very coarse kind, and enlivened by practical jokes not always very decent. The *Játra* is generally the exhibition of some of the incidents in the youthful life of Kríshńa, maintained also in extempore dialogue, but interspersed with popular songs. The mistress of Kríshńa, Rádhá, his father, mother, and the Gopís, are the ordinary *dramatis personæ*, and Nárada acts as buffo. The Rása partakes more of the ballet, but it is accompanied also with songs, whilst the adventures of Kŕishńa or Ráma are represented in appropriate costume, by measured gesticulations. The Hindus have a strong relish for these diversions, but the domination under which they so long pined, and which was ever so singularly hostile to public enjoyments of a refined character, rendered theatrical representations infrequent, and induced a neglect of dramatic literature. Plays, however, continued to be written and performed to the latest periods, especially in the west and south of India, where Hindu principalities still subsisted. Performances also seem to have been exhibited at Benares in recent times, and we have one piece which was written, and possibly represented in Bengal, but a very few years ago. All the modern compositions, however, are of a mythological and sectarial character, and are intended to celebrate the power of Kŕishńa or of Śiva. They are also discriminated from older writings by the predominance of narrative, and by wire-drawn common-place descriptions of the periods of the day or the season of the year, of the rising and setting of the sun or moon, of the scorching heats of the summer or the reviving influence of spring. There is no attempt at incident beyond the original story, and many of the subjects for action, which the legend affords, are thrown into dull and tiresome dialogue. These defects are, indeed, to be found occasionally in several of the earlier pieces, but to a limited extent, whilst they form the substance of all later compositions.

When the art of theatrical composition had passed its zenith, and began to exhibit symptoms of decay, the same fate befell it in India which it encountered in other countries, and criticism usurped the authority of creation. Plays gave way to theories, and system-mongers took the place of dramatists and poets. Indian criticism, however, has been always in its infancy. It never learned to connect causes and effects; it never looked to the influence exercised by imagination or passion in poetry; it never, in short, became either poetical or philosophical. Technicalities were the only objects within its comprehension, and it delighted to elicit dogmatical precepts from the practice of established authors. The question of the "unities" is quite within the sphere of the Indian critic, had the poets ever descended to their observance. Some approach, as observed above, has been made to this important theme, but a text was wanted for its due appreciation. In the absence of this, and of loftier discussion, the critics of the Hindu school set themselves to classify plays, persons, and passions, until they wove a complicated web out of very spider-like materials. The distinctions thus multiplied are curious in themselves, and of some value for the record they afford of the compositions whence they are derived, and it has been thought advisable, therefore, to annex a view of the system, assigning to it a distinct section, as it can have little to attract or entertain general readers.

ON THE

DRAMATIC SYSTEM OF THE HINDUS.

1. THE AUTHORITIES OF THE HINDU DRAMATIC SYSTEM.

THE invention of dramatic entertainments is usually ascribed by Hindu writers to a *Muni*, or inspired sage, named *Bharata;* but, according to some authorities, they had a still more elevated origin, and the art having been gathered from the *Vedas* by the god *Brahmá*, was by him communicated to the *Muni*. The dramatic representations first invented consisted of three kinds: *Náťya*, *Nŕitya*, and *Nŕitta;* and these were exhibited before the gods by the *Gandharbas* and *Apsarasas*, the Spirits and Nymphs of *Indra's* heaven, who were trained by Bharata to the exhibition. S'iva added to these two other styles of performance, the *Táńđava* and *Lásya*.

Of these different modes of representation, only one, the *Náťya*, is properly the dramatic, being defined to be gesticulation with language. The *Nŕitya* is gesticulation without language, or pantomime; and the *Nŕitta* is simple dancing. The *Táńđava* and *Lásya*, which appear to be grafts upon the original system, are merely styles of dancing; the former so named from *Tańđu*, one of S'iva's attendants, whom the god instructed in it; whilst the *Lásya*, it is said, was taught by Párvatí to the princess Ushá, who instructed the *Gopís* of Dwáraká, the residence of her husband, in the art: by them it was communicated to the women of Suráshťra, and from them it passed to the females of various regions.

In these legends, as well as in the radical purport of the three original terms, we observe the intimate connexion between the idea of dancing and dramatic representation, which no doubt subsisted in the classical drama. The dances of the Chorus were no less important than their songs, and the arrangement of the ballet was as much the task of the author as the invention of the plot.

The attribution of dramatic performances to Bharata is no doubt founded upon his having been one of the earliest writers, by whom the art was reduced to a system. His *Sútras*, or aphorisms, are constantly cited by commentators on different plays, and suggest the doctrines which are taught by later authors : but, as far as has been ascertained, the work of Bharata has no existence in an entire shape, and it may be sometimes doubted whether the rules attributed to him are not fabricated for the occasion. This is not of much importance, as there are scarcely any debatable points in the technicalities of the drama, and the aphorisms, whether genuine or not, conform to the principles generally recognised in the standard authorities : a short notice of the principal of which will not perhaps be thought misplaced in this stage of the inquiry.

One of the best and earliest existing treatises on dramatic literature is the *Daśa-Rúpaka*, or description of the ten kinds of theatrical composition, of which the term *Rúpaka*, that which has a form, is the most appropriate designation. This work is exclusively devoted to dramatic criticism. It consists of a Text and a Gloss, with examples. The Text is the composition of Dhananjaya, the son of Vishńu, who styles Munja his patron, and who consequently wrote in the eleventh century, by which time, therefore, the dramatic art of the Hindus was complete, or rather was in its decline. The Gloss might be thought to be by the same hand as the text, the author being Dhanika, the son of Vishńu ; agreeing in the patronymic, and differing little in the name. Amongst his illustrations, however, a number of passages are cited from the *Ratnávalí*, a play written in the beginning of the twelfth century, which is rather incompatible with the author of the *Daśa-Rúpaka's* having written in the eleventh. There is also another difficulty in the title of the commentator, who calls himself an officer of a different prince, Maharája S'rímad Utpala Rája Mahásádhyapála, the chief usher, or minister of the illustrious Utpala Rája. Whether *Utpala* be the name of a prince or a country is uncertain, but in neither case can it apply to Munja or Bhoja. The date of the Gloss must therefore remain undetermined, although as the work is but rarely met with, it is no doubt of some antiquity. Ranga-náth, a commentator on the *Vikrama* and *Urvasí*, cites a comment on the *Daśa-Rúpaka* by a writer named Páńi (Páńi virachita Daśa Rúpaka ťíkáyám), which, if found, may tend to throw some light upon the history of this work.

The *Saraswatí Kańťhábharańa* is a work ascribed to Bhoja Rája. It treats generally of poetical or rhetorical composition, in five books, the last of which comprehends many of the details peculiar to dramatic writing. The examples quoted are from a variety of poems and plays, and they offer the same difficulty, as to the accuracy of the attribution, as the *Daśa-Rúpaka*, by including illustrations from the *Ratnávalí*. We might expect the plays of Kálidása and Bhavabhútí to be quoted, and we have no grounds for suspecting any anachronism in the examples derived from the *Mudrá-Rákshasa* and *Veńí Sanhára:* but Bhoja must have reigned some years later, or Harsha some years earlier, than has been hitherto believed on scarcely disputable grounds, for a composition of the one to be cited by the other. There is a commentary on this work by Ratneśwara Mahopádhyáya, but he takes no notice of the author.

The *Kávya-Prakáśa* is also a work on rhetorical composition in general, and is an authority of great repute, as well as the preceding. It is divided into ten sections, in different portions of which are scattered such details relating to dramatic writings as are common to them and other poems, illustrated, as in the preceding, by extracts from the most celebrated poems, which, however, are never named, either in this or in many other works of the same class. It is necessary, therefore, to be able to identify the passages from previous reading, to derive from these treatises that information respecting Sanskrit literary history which they are capable of affording. The author of the *Kávya-Prakáśa* is Mammaťa-Bhaťťa, a Cashmirian, and the work is prior to that next described, although subsequent to the *Ratnávalí*, and may be about five centuries old.

The *Sáhitya-Darpańa* is also a work of great merit and celebrity, on poetical writing, in ten sections, of which the sixth is mostly appropriated to theatrical technicalities. The quotations from the different plays are specified, and all the principal pieces in the present collection are named, besides several of which copies are not procurable. The date of the work is not known, but it is comparatively modern, and subsequent to the *Kávya-*

Prakáśa. One manuscript of it exists, which was copied, according to the date, in Saka 1426, or A.D. 1504. It is the work of a Bengali pandit of the medical caste, Viswanátha-Kavirája, the son of Chandra-S'ekhara, and is especially current as an authority in Bengal. According to universally-received tradition, the author lived beyond the Brahmaputra, in the district of Dacca.

The *Sangíta-Ratnákara*, as the name implies, treats more especially of singing and dancing than of dramatic literature. It furnishes, however, some curious notices of theatrical representation and gesture. It is the work of S'árngi-Deva, the son of Sorhala, the son of Bháskara, a Cashmirian pandit, who sought his fortunes in the south. His grandson is patronised by a prince named Sinhala-Deva, but of what time or place he does not inform us. It is clear, however, that he wrote between the twelfth and fifteenth centuries, as he names Bhoja amongst his predecessors in the science; and a comment on his own work was written by Kallinátha, by desire of Praud'ha, or Pratápa Deva king of Vijayanagar, from A.D. 1456 to 1477.

Amongst the works which treat generally *de Arte Poeticá*, and which are exceedingly numerous, some of the principal are, the *Kávyádarśa* by Dandin, the author of the *Daśa-Kumára*, and supposed to be contemporary with Bhoja; the *Kávyálankára Vŕitti*, by Vámana-Áchárya; the *Kuvalayánanda*, an enlargement of the *Chandráloka* of Jayadeva, by Apyaya Díkshita, who was patronised by Kŕishńa Ráya, sovereign of Vijayanagar about 1520; the *Alankára Sarvaswa* of Bháma; the *Rasa-Gangádhara* of Jagannátha Pandita Rája, and the *Alankára-Kaustubha* by Kavi Karńapúraka, a Vaishńava Gosain, who illustrates all his rules by verses of his own, relating to the loves of Kŕishńa and Rádhá, and the pastimes of the deity with the Gopís of Vrindávana.

Besides the general systems, there are several treatises on the passions and emotions which poetry is intended to depicture or excite, as the *Śŕingára-Tilaka* of Rudra-Bhat'ťa; and the *Rasa Manjárí* and the *Rasa Tarangińí* of Bhánu-Dat'ťa. The latter comprises a number of rules, which are quoted as those of Bharata.

In addition to the information derivable from these sources, as to the system or history of the Hindu drama, the commentaries by which several of the plays are accompanied furnish important accessions to our knowledge of both. With respect also to the latter, we have in the *Bhoja-Prabandha* and *Śárngdhara-Paddhati*, two satisfactory guides for the verification of the writers prior to their respective dates. Of the *Bhoja-Prabandha* I have given an account elsewhere, and have seen no reason to alter the opinion there expressed. The *Śárngdhara-Paddhati* is a similar catalogue of earlier writers written by S'árngdhará, the grandson of Rághava-Deva, the spiritual guide of Hammíra, prince of Sákambharí, in the beginning of the fourteenth century. This work is consequently not later than the end of the fourteenth or the beginning of the fifteenth century, and determines within that limit the existence of the writers it names, several of whom are included amongst the dramatic authors, as we shall have hereafter occasion to notice.

These different authorities, it might be thought, would afford a tolerably distinct and accurate view of the dramatic literature of the Hindus, and will no doubt convey quite sufficient for our purpose. The brevity and obscurity, however, of the technical definitions, the inconceivable inaccuracy of the manuscripts, and the little knowledge of the subject which the pandits generally possess, have rendered the taste of interpreting them laborious and painful, to an extent of which readers accustomed to typographic facilities can form no adequate conception.

---

2. Different Kinds of Dramatic Entertainments.

The general term for all dramatic compositions is *Rúpaka*,—from *rúpa*, form,—it being their chief object to embody characters and feelings, and to exhibit the natural indications of passion. A play is also defined, a Poem that is to be seen, or a Poem that is to be seen and heard.

Dramatic writings are arranged in two classes, the *Rúpakas* properly so termed, and the *Uparúpakas*, the minor or inferior *Rúpakas* "le théâtre du second ordre," although not precisely in the same sense. There are ten species of the former, and eighteen of the latter class.

Rupakas.

1. The *Náṭaka*, or the Play *par excellence*, comprises all the elements of a dramatic composition, and its construction, there-

fore, is fully explained in the original systems, before any notice is taken of the inferior varieties. This method is perhaps the most logical, and obviates the necessity of some repetition; but in an inquiry of the present description, the first point to determine appears to be, what the dramatic amusements of the Hindus really were, before we examine their constituent parts.

Specimens of the *Náťaka* are not wanting to illustrate its technical description, and we can therefore follow the original authorities with entire confidence. It is declared to be the most perfect kind of dramatic composition. The subject should always be celebrated and important. According to the *Sáhitya-Darpańa*, the story should be selected from mythological or historical record alone; but the *Daśa-Rúpaka* asserts that it may be also fictitious or mixed, or partly resting on tradition, and partly the creation of the author. The practice of the early writers seems to have sanctioned the latter rule, and although they adopted their plots from sacred poems or *Puráńas*, they considered themselves at liberty to vary the incidents as they pleased. Modern bards have been more scrupulous. The restriction imposed upon the selection of the subject is the same as that to which the French theatre so long submitted, from whose tragic code all newly-invented topics were excluded, in supposed imitation of the Greek theatre, in which however the *Flower of Agathon*, founded altogether upon fiction, was an early and popular production.

Like the Greek tragedy, however, the *Náťaka* is to represent worthy or exalted personages only, and the hero must be a monarch, as Dushyanta; a demigod, as Ráma; or a divinity, as Křishńa. The action, or more properly the passion, should be but one, as love or heroism. The plot should be simple, the incidents consistent; the business should spring direct from the story as a plant from its seed, and should be free from episodical and prolix interruptions. The time should not be protracted, and the duration of an act, according to the elder authority, should not exceed one day; but the *Sáhitya-Darpańa* extends it to a few days, or even to one year. When the action cannot be comprised within these limits, the less important events may be thrown into narrative, or may be supposed to pass between the acts; or they may be communicated to the audience by one of the actors, who holds the character of an interpreter, and explains to the persons of the assembly whatever they may require to know, or what is not conveyed to them by the representation; a rather awkward contrivance to supply the deficiencies of the piece, but one that would sometimes be useful to insinuate the plot into the audiences of more polished communities. The diction of a *Náťaka* should be perspicuous and polished. The piece should consist of not fewer than five acts, and not more than ten.

In many of these characteristics, the *Náťaka* presents an obvious analogy to the tragedy of the Greeks, which was, "the imitation of a solemn and perfect action, of adequate importance, told in pleasing language, exhibiting the several elements of dramatic composition in its different parts, represented through the instrumentality of agents, not by narration, and purifying the affections of human nature by the influence of pity and terror." In the expansion of this definition in the "Poetics," there are many points of affinity, and particularly in the selection of persons and subjects; but there are also differences, some of which merit to be noticed.

With regard to the Unities, we have that of action fully recognised, and a simplicity of business is enjoined quite in the spirit of the Greek drama. The unity of place is not noticed, as might have been expected from the probable absence of all scenic embellishment. It was impossible to transport the substantial decorations of the Grecian stage from place to place, and therefore the scene was the same throughout; but where everything was left to the imagination, one site was as easily conceivable as another, and the scene might be fancied, one while a garden, and another while a palace, as well as it could be imagined to be either. The unity of time is curiously modified, conformably to a principle which may satisfy the most fastidious; and "the time required for the fable elapses invariably between the acts." In practice there is generally less latitude than the rule indicates, and the duration of an act is very commonly that of the representation, or at most "one course of the sun," the night elapsing in the interval. In one piece, the *Uttara-Ráma-Charitra*, indeed, we have a more extensive period, and twelve years are supposed to pass between the first and second acts. This was the unavoidable consequence of the subject of the play, and affords an analogy to the licence of the romantic drama.

Another important difference from the classical drama, and from that of most countries, is the total absence of the distinction between Tragedy and Comedy. The Hindu plays confine themselves neither to the "crimes nor to the absurdities of mankind;" neither "to the momentous changes, nor lighter vicissitudes of life;" neither "to the terrors of distress nor the gaieties of prosperity." In this respect they may be classed with much of the Spanish and English drama, to which, as Schlegel observes, "the terms Tragedy and Comedy are wholly inapplicable, in the sense in which they were employed by the ancients." They are invariably of a mingled web, and blend "seriousness and sorrow with levity and laughter." They never offer, however, a calamitous conclusion, which, as Johnson remarks, was enough to constitute a Tragedy in Shakespeare's days; and although they propose to excite all the emotions of the human breast, terror and pity included, they never effect this object by leaving a painful impression upon the mind of the spectator. The Hindus, in fact, have no Tragedy; a defect that subverts the theory that Tragedy necessarily preceded Comedy, because in the infancy of society the stronger passions predominated, and it was not till social intercourse was complicated and refined, that the follies and frivolities of mankind afforded material for satire. The theory is evidently more ingenious than just, for a considerable advance in refinement must have been made before plays were written at all, and the days of Æschylus were not those of the fierce and fiery emotions he delineates. In truth, however, the individual and social organisation of the native of India is unfavourable to the development of towering passion; and whatever poets or philosophers may have insinuated to the contrary, there is no doubt that the regions of physical equability have ever been, and still are, those of moral extremes.

The absence of tragic catastrophe in the Hindu dramas is not merely an unconscious omission; such catastrophe is prohibited by a positive rule, and the death of either the hero or the heroine is never to be announced. With that regard, indeed, for decorum, which even Voltaire thought might be sometimes dispensed with, it is not allowed in any manner "*ensanglanter la scène*," and death must invariably be inflicted out of the view of the spectators. Attention to *bienséance* is carried even to a further extent, and a number of interdictions are peculiar to the system of the Hindus. The excepted topics of a serious nature are, hostile defiance, solemn imprecations, exile, degradation, and national calamity; whilst those of a less grave, or comic character, are biting, scratching, kissing, eating, sleeping, the bath, inunction, and the marriage ceremony. Dramatic writers, especially those of a modern date, have sometimes violated these precepts; but in general the conduct of what may be termed the classical drama of the Hindus is exemplary and dignified. Nor is its moral purport neglected; and one of their writers declares, in an illustration familiar to ancient and modern poetry, that the chief end of the theatre is to disguise, by the insidious sweet, the unpalatable but salutary bitter, of the cup.

The extent of the Hindu plays is another peculiarity in which they differ from the dramatic writings of other nations; and even the *Robbers, or Don Carlos*, will suffer in the comparison of length. The *Mrichchhakaťí* would make at least three of the plays of Æschylus. In actual representation, however, a Hindu play constituted a less unreasonable demand upon the patience of an audience than an Athenian performance, consisting at one sitting of three Tragedies and a Farce. If the Hindu stage exhibited a long play, it exhibited that alone.

The compositions of the first class, or *Náťakas*, are comparatively frequent, and some of them are amongst the best specimens of the art. *Śakuntalá*, the *Mudrá-Rákshasa*, the *Veńí Sanhára*, *Anargha-Rághava*, and several others, belong to this order. The first is well known by the version of Sir William Jones; a translation of the second, and some accounts of the rest, will be found in the present collection.

2. The second species of *Rúpaka* is the *Prakaraňa*, which agrees in all respects with the *Náťaka*, except that it takes a rather less elevated range. The fable is to be a pure fiction drawn from real life in a reputable class of society, and the most appropriate subject is love. The hero may be of ministerial rank, or a Brahman, or a merchant of respectability. The heroine may be a maid of family, or a courtesan. In the former case, the *Prakaraňa* is termed *Śuddha*, or pure; in the latter,

Sankírńa, or mixed. By the *Veśyá*, or courtesan, however, we are not to understand a female who has disregarded the obligations of law or the precepts of virtue, but a character reared by a state of manners unfriendly to the admission of wedded females into society, and opening it only at the expense of reputation to women, who were trained for association with men by personal and mental acquirements to which the matron was a stranger. The *Veśyá* of the Hindus was the *Hetera* of the Greeks. Without the talents of *Aspasia*, or profligacy of *Lais*, the *Vasantasená* of the first piece in this collection is a gentle, affectionate being, who, with the conventions of society in her favour, unites, as the *Hetera* often did, "accomplishments calculated to dazzle, with qualities of the heart which raise her above the contempt that, in spite of all precaution, falls upon her situation." The *Mrichchhakatí*, and *Málatí-Mádhava*, belong to the class of *Prakarańas*.

3. The *Bháńa*, according to the technical definition, is a monologue in one act, in which the performer narrates dramatically a variety of occurrences as happening either to himself or others. Love, war, fraud, intrigue, and imposition, are appropriate topics, and the narrator may enliven his recitation by a supposititious dialogue with an imaginary interlocutor. The language must be polished, and music and singing should precede and close the performance. The example quoted is the *Lílámadhukara*, but the only specimen met with is the *Śárada Tilaka*, of which some account is given in the following pages. It is not impossible that ventriloquism assisted to give effect to the imaginary dialogue, as the art is not unknown in India.

4. The *Vyáyoga* is a dramatic representation of some military transaction, in which no part of the interest is derived from female participation; the sentiment of love is consequently excluded from it, and it admits of no comic intermixture. It is restricted to one act, one action, and a duration of one day, and the hero should be a warrior or demigod. The *Sáhitya-Darpańa* names the *Saugandhikáharańa* as an example, the *Daśa-Rúpaka* specifies the *Jámadagnya-Jaya*, the latter alluding either to the defeat of Kártavíryárjuna, or to the subjugation of the military tribe by the Brahmanical hero Paraśu-Ráma, the son of Jamadagni. The subject of the former would seem to be the rape of a princess named Saugandhiká, only that the

interest springing from such an event would contravene the rule that relates to female exclusion, and it may refer to the conflict between Vasishṫha and Viśwámitra for the all-bestowing cow. The *Dhananjaya-Vijaya* belongs to this class.

5. The *Samavakára* is the dramatic representation of some mythological fable in three acts; the business of the first is to occupy about nine hours; the second, three and a half; and the third, an hour and a half. The story of the piece relates to gods and demons, although mortals may be introduced. There is no individual hero, or the heroes may be as many as twelve, as Kŕishńa and other divinities. The metre is that most usually employed in the *Vedas*, or the verses termed *Ushnih* and *Gáyatrí*. Although love may be touched upon, heroism should be the predominant passion; and the acts of enmity may be exhibited, both covert and avowed, such as ironical commendation and open defiance. Tempests, combats, and the storming of towns, may be represented, and all the pride and pomp of war, as horses, elephants, and cars, may be introduced. The example quoted, but which no longer exists in its dramatised form, is the *Samudra Mathana*, the Churning of the Ocean: a splendid subject for spectacle if well managed. We may doubt the success of the Hindu mechanicians in representing the mountain and the snake, the churning-staff and rope, or the agitations of the mighty main, from which sprang the personifications of health and beauty, and the beverage of immortality: this was, in all probability, clumsily contrived; but the gods and demons were well dressed and better acted, and with the patronage of a Rájá, the conflicts between the hosts of heaven and hell for the goddess of beauty and the cup of ambrosia, were no doubt got up with no want of numbers or of splendour. This entertainment must have been popular, as it was addressed more to the eye than the ear. As a mere spectacle it still exists, and in the western provinces the history of Ráma is represented in the dramatic form at the *Daśahara* on a vast, if not a magnificent scale. The followers of the contending chiefs, Ráma and Rávańa, amount sometimes to several hundreds: the battlements of Lanká, though of less durable materials, are of vast extent, and the encounters that take place are more like the mimic evolutions of real armies than a dramatic exhibition. It is scarcely necessary to add, that it occurs in the open air, usually

in a spacious plain, and with a want of order that ruins its dramatic effect. The most pleasing, as the best-conducted parts of the business, are the processions. The entry of Ráma and Sítá into Benares, in the year 1820, formed a richly picturesque and interesting scene.*

6. The *Ḍima* is a drama of a similar but more gloomy character than the last, and is limited to the representation of terrific events, as portents, incantations, sieges, and battles. It comprehends four acts. The hero should be a demon, demigod, or deity. The example named is the *Tripuradáha*, the destruction of the demon Tripura by S'iva, and conflagration of the three cities over which he ruled, and whence he derived his appellation.

7. The *Íhámṛiga* is a piece of intrigue in four acts, in which the hero is a god or illustrious mortal, and the heroine a goddess. Love and mirth are the prevailing sentiments. The heroine may be the subject of war or stratagem, and the devices of the hero may end in disappointment, but not in death. The example named is the *Kusumaśekhara-Vijaya*.

8. *Anka*. This is considered by some to be a piece in one act, but by others to be a supplementary act, serving as an introduction to a drama, or a more fully winding up of the story. The pathetic style should predominate: the hero may be a mortal; the subject should be well known. The example named is the *Śarmishṭhá-Yayáti*. A piece, termed *Yayáti-Charitra*, occurs amongst those noticed hereafter; but that is a *Náṭaka*, and cannot therefore be here intended.

9. The *Víthi* is something similar to the *Bháṅa*: it is in one act, and may be performed by one actor, though the *Daśa-Rúpaka* admits of two. In either case it is a love-story carried on in comic dialogue, consisting of equivoque, evasion, enigma, quibble, jest, repartee, wilful misconstruction and misapplication, ironical praise, extravagant endearment, and jocose abuse. It is not very different, perhaps, in character from the *Fabulæ Attellanæ* of the Tuscans.

10. The *Prahasana* is a farcical or comic satire, and might be thought to have originated, like the old comedy, from the

* In Prinsep's Illustrations of Benares, part iii., are interesting representations of this scene and one which precedes it, the capture of Lanká.

Phallic Hymn. Unlike the Aristophanic comedy, however, it is not levelled at the many-headed mob, but in general at the sanctified and privileged orders of the community, as Ascetics, Brahmans, men of rank and wealth, and princes. The vices satirised in the two latter are those which emanate from an abuse of riches rather than of power, and are those of low luxury, not tyrannic despotism: the objects of satire in the former are sensuality and hypocrisy. It is in their extreme indelicacy that they resemble, although perhaps they scarcely equal, the Greek comedy; but they have not its redeeming properties, exuberant gaiety and brilliant imagination: they have some causticity and humour, but they are deficient in the high merits of poetry and wit. The *Hásyárńava*, *Kautuka-Sarvasva*, and *Dhúrta-Nartaka*, are existing specimens of this class of dramatic representation. According to the technical definitions of our authorities, the *Prahasana* is a drama in one act, intended to excite laughter. The story should be fictitious, and the hero may be an Ascetic, a Brahman, a king, or a rogue. The *dramatis personæ* are to be composed of courtiers, menials, mendicants, knaves, and harlots: the inferior persons are to speak low Prákŕit, or a local dialect.

This terminates the first class of dramas: the second order is more numerous. It will be necessary to repeat the list, but it will not be essential to offer any detailed enumeration, as they tend to confirm what the foregoing remarks will have already suggested, that the Hindu writers multiply species very gratuitously, and make distinctions where no difference is discernible. In general, also, the descriptions will not admit of any illustration, as, except in the two first instances, the pieces cited as examples are not known to exist.

Uparupakas.

1. The *Náťiká* is of two kinds, bearing an affinity in subject and personages, severally, to the *Náťaka* and *Prakarańa*: in the latter case it is also termed *Prakarańiká*. The only difference from these forms is the length, the *Nátiká* being restricted to four acts. The *Ratnávalí*, of which a translation is given, is a *Náťiká*.

2. The *Troťaka* may consist of five, seven, eight, or nine

acts: the business is partly human, partly celestial, as in the *Vikrama and Urvaśí.*

3. The *Goshthí* is a piece in one act, with a *dramatis personæ* of nine or ten male, and five or six female characters. The subject is love. The example named is the *Raivata-madaniká.*

4. The *Saṫṫaka* is a marvellous story in any number of acts, but the language is to be wholly Prákṙit. The *Karpúra-Manjarí* is an example of the class.

5. The *Náṫyarásaka* consists chiefly of dancing and singing, and the subjects are love and mirth. It is in one act. The *Narmavatí* and *Vilásavatí* are cited as specimens.

6. The *Prasthána* is on the same subjects as the last, but the characters are of the lowest description: the hero and the heroine are slaves, and their associates outcasts. Song, music, and dancing, are its chief ingredients: it is in two acts. The *Śṙingára-Tilaka* is an example. The appropriation of a specific drama to a particular class of people is highly characteristic of the social system of the Hindus.

7. The *Ullápya* is in one act; the subject mythological—the sentiments are love, mirth, and pathos: the dialogue is interspersed with songs. The example named is the *Deví-Mahádeva.* This presents some analogy to the satiric drama of the Greeks, which was taken from mythology or heroic poetry, and differed chiefly from the Tragedies, which it followed, in a more lively strain and greater brevity, as well as in the introduction of songs and dances by Silenus and the Satyrs.

8. The *Kávya* is a love-story in one act, interspersed with poetical stanzas and musical airs. The *Yádavodaya* is an example.

9. The *Prenkhaṅa* is in one act, treating of war and dissension. The hero is of inferior rank, as in the *Báli Badha.*

10. The *Rásaka* is a comic entertainment in one act, with five characters. The hero and heroine are of elevated rank: the latter is of suitable merit, the former a fool. The *Aneká-múrtta* is a specimen.

11. The *Sanlápaka* is a drama in one, three, or four acts, the hero of which is a heretic. The subjects are controversy, deceit, violence, and war. The *Máyákápálika* is cited as an example; and possibly the *Prabodha-Chandradodaya,* the meta-

physical drama translated by the late Dr. Taylor, comes under this species.

12. *Śrígadita* is an entertainment in one act, in which the goddess Śrí, the goddess of prosperity or fortune, is introduced, or is imitated by the heroine. It is partly recited, and partly sung. An example of it is named the *Kríd́árasástala.*

13. The *Śilpaka* is in four acts. The scene is laid in a place where dead bodies are burned: the hero is a Brahman, and the confidant or *Pratinayaka* an outcast. Marvels and magic constitute the leading business of the piece. The *Kanakávatí-Mádhava* is an example cited; and to borrow an illustration from the dramatic literature of Europe, we might class the *Freyschütz* under this head.

14. The *Vilásiká* or *Lásiká* is an entertainment in one act, of which love is the subject, and the general strain is comic or farcical. No example is cited.

15. The *Durmalliká* is a comic intrigue in four acts, in each of which the friends of the hero and himself successively lead the business. The specimen named is the *Vindumatí.*

16. The *Prakarańiká* is here considered as a distinct class; but, as observed under the first head, this is usually considered only a variety of the *Nát́iká.*

17. The *Hallíśa* is an entertainment of singing and dancing, chiefly in one act, represented by one male and eight or ten female performers. The example named is the *Keliraivataka;* and the operatic ballets of Europe may afford some notion of the class.

18. The *Bháńiká* is a comic piece in one act. It is not very clearly defined, but it seems to be something like the piece which, after undergoing various migrations from *Le Dépit Amoureux* of Molière, ended in the farce of *Lovers' Quarrels*—a representation of unfounded jealousies and mutual reproaches. The *Kámadattá* is the specimen named.

All these varieties are clearly reducible to but two, differing according to the loftier or lowlier tone of the composition, the more serious or comic tenor of the subject, and the regularity or irregularity of the construction. We might also conveniently transfer to them the definitions of the European stage, and class them under the heads of Tragedy, Comedy, Opera, Ballet, Burletta, Melodrama, and Farce. Their technical distribution is, however, very unimportant; and the enumeration of the distinctions, as originally recognised, is a matter of little interest, except as it conveys a satisfactory proof of the extent to which dramatic literature was once cultivated by the Hindus.

From this general sketch of the varieties of the Hindu Theatre, we shall now proceed to examine what in their notions constituted a play; under the heads of its Dramatic Arrangement; the Conduct of the Plot; the Characters of the Drama; the objects of Dramatic Representation and the means by which they were effected, or the Diction and Scenic Apparatus.

---

3. Dramatic Arrangement.

In the Hindu drama every piece opens with a prelude or induction, in which the audience are made acquainted with the author, his work, the actors, and such part of the prior events as it is necessary for the spectators to know. In its propitiation of the audience, and reference to past occurrences, it is analogous to the prologue of ancient and modern times, and, as far as spoken in character, accords with what have been termed the Prologues of Euripides, and those of Plautus. Being in dialogue, however, it is more correctly the induction of the old Comedy, which, although considered "out of date" by Beaumont and Fletcher, was not unfrequent amongst their contemporaries, as in *Cynthia's Revels*, the *Returne from Parnassus*, and especially the *Malcontent of Marston*, in which the interlocutors are the actors. The *Faust* of Goethe affords a specimen of an induction in the present day. In the Hindu theatre, however, the actors of the prelude were never more than two, the manager and one of his company, either an actor or actress, and it differs from the similar preliminary performances of other people by leading immediately into the business of the drama.

The first part of this introduction is termed the *Púrva-ranga*, and agreeably to Hindu prejudices, and the religious complexion of the occasions on which performances were represented, opens with a prayer, invoking in a benedictory formula the protection of some deity in favour of the audience. This is termed the *Nándí*, or that which is the cause of gratification to men and gods. This benediction may consist of one, two, or three stanzas. The elder writers rarely exceed two, but those of later date extend the *Nándí* to three or four, and in one instance, the *Veńí-Sanhára,* we have as many as six. Occasionally a short prayer is added to the benediction, or even substituted for it.

It does not very distinctly appear by whom the *Nándí* was spoken, for the general stage direction, *Nándyanté Sútradháraḱ,* "at the end of the *Nándí* the *Sútradhára,*" seems to imply that it was not recited by this individual, the manager or conductor, the person who holds the thread or regulation of the business; but an aphorism of Bharata is cited, which says, "Let the *Sútradhára* recite the *Nándí* in a tone neither high nor low." If, however, he does not enter until it is recited, he must perform the recitation behind the scenes. Another text is cited from Bharata, which says, "Having read the *Nándí,* let the *Sútradhára* go off and the *Sthápaka* enter." And the *Sangíta-Kalpataru* has, "Let the *Sútradhára,* or some other person entering on the stage, pronounce the *Nándí.*" The commentator on the *Mudrá-Rákshasa* observes, therefore, "that it is equally correct to supply the ellipse after *Nándyante* by either *paṫhati* 'reads,' or *praviśati* 'enters:' in the former case the *Sútradhára* reciting the *Nándí* and then continuing the induction; in the latter, the benediction being pronounced by a different individual." It seems not unlikely that it was the intention of the original writers, although the commentators may not have understood it, to discriminate between the real and assumed personage of the *Sútradhára,* who spoke the benediction in his own character or as a Brahman, which he must have been, and then carried on the dialogue of the prelude as the manager of the theatrical corps. The *Sútradhára* was expected to be a man of no inferior qualifications; and according to the technical description of him, "he was to be well versed in light literature, as narrative, plays, and poetry: he should be familiar with various dialects; acquainted with the customs of different classes and the manners of various people, experienced in dramatic details, and conversant with different mechanical arts."

The prayer is usually often followed by some account of the author of the piece, which is always in a strain of panegyric, very different from the self-dispraising tone adopted by European dramatists, although no doubt more sincere. The induction must in most cases have been the work of the author of the play, but it may sometimes have been the composition of another hand. The introduction of the *Mrichchhakaťí* notices the death of the individual to whom the play is ascribed. In some places, the mention of the author is little more than the particularisation of his name.

The notice of the author is in general followed by a complimentary appeal to the favour of the audience, in a style with which we are perfectly familiar, and the manager occasionally gives a dramatic representation of himself and his concerns, as in the *Mrichchhakaťí* and *Mudrá-Rákshasa*, in a dialogue between him and one of his company, either an actor or an actress, who is termed the *Páripárświka*, or associate. The dialogue sometimes adverts to occurrences prior to the story of the piece, as in the *Uttara-Ráma-Charitra*, where the manager and actor are supposed to be inhabitants of Ayodhyá, and describe the departure of Ráma's guests, as if they had just witnessed it. In the *Veńí-Sanhára*, too, it should appear that they are inmates of the Páńďava camp; and in the *Mudrá-Rákshasa* the manager appears as an inhabitant of Páťaliputra. In other preludes the connexion is less immediate. In that of *Śakuntalá* the actress sings a song descriptive of the hot season, for the amusement of the audience; and in *Málatí and Mádhava* the manager and his companion declare the characters they are to play. In every case, however, the conclusion of the prelude, termed the *Prastávaná*, prepares the audience for the entrance of one of the dramatic personages, who appears either by simply naming him, as in *Śakuntalá*, where the manager abruptly exclaims, "Here comes the king Dushyanta," or by uttering something he is supposed to overhear, and to which he advances to reply, as in the *Mrichchhakaťí* and *Mudrá-Rákshasa*.

The piece, being thus opened, is carried on in the manner with which the theatres of Europe are familiar, or the division of scenes and acts.

The scene may be considered to be marked, as in the French drama, by the entrance of one character and the exit of another, for in general the stage is never left empty in the course of the act, nor does total change of place often occur. The rule, however, in this respect, is not very rigidly observed, and contrivances have been resorted to, to fill up the seeming chasm which such an interruption as a total change of scene requires, and to avoid that solecism which the entrance of a character, whose approach is unannounced, is considered.

Of these, two are personages: the interpreter and introducer; the *Vishkambhaka* and *Praveśaka.* These are members of the theatrical company, apparently, who may be supposed to sit by, and upon any interruption in the regular course of the piece, explain to the audience its cause and object. The *Vishkambha,* it is said, may appear at the beginning, in the middle, or at the end of an act: the *Praveśaka,* it is said, only between the acts. But this is contradicted by the constant practice, for in every place the *Praveśaka* indicates a change of scene. The duty of the *Praveśaka* was probably of a very simple nature, and he merely announced the change of scene and approach of a certain character. The *Vishkambha* had a more diversified duty, and besides filling up all the blanks in the story, he was expected to divert the audience by his wit and repartee, like the Arloquino Intromezzo, or the clowns of the Elizabethan period of our stage. The clumsiness of these supplementary performers seems not to have escaped the notice of the Hindu dramatists, and they are sometimes interwoven with the piece, as in the *Veńí-Sanhára,* where a scene between two goblins, who are seeking their banquet upon the field of battle, is considered to be chiefly intended to connect the business of the drama, and prepare the audience for the death of Drońa, which they behold and describe; and the description of the combat between Lava and Chandraketu, in the *Uttara-Ráma-Charitra,* by the two spirits of air, is a similar and still happier substitute for an interpreter. The employment of the *Vishkambha* and *Praveśaka* is indicated by a simple naming of them, and what either is to do or say is left to the person who fills the character.

The act, or *Anka,* is said to be marked by the exit of all the personages: a definition which is equally applicable to the practice of the French theatre. Of the duration of the act we have already spoken, and it will have been seen in the enumeration of the different species of theatrical compositions, that the number of acts varies from one to ten. The *Hanuman-Náťaka* indeed has fourteen; but it will be seen by the abstract account of that drama, that it is a poem rather than a play, or at most a piece of patchwork, in which the fragments of an old play have been eked out by poetic narrative, and connected by the interposition of extraneous and undramatic matters. The precise division of Hindu plays into acts is a feature which serves to discriminate them from the Greek compositions, in which the division into acts was unknown, the only distinctions recognised being those of prologue, episode, and exode, regulated by the intervening songs of the chorus, to which we find nothing parallel in the regular plays of the Hindus. The division into acts appears to have been an arrangement invented by the Romans, from whom we can scarcely suspect the Hindus to have derived it.

The first act, or the *Ankamukha*, corresponds to the exposition, prologue, or protasis of the ancient theatre, and furnishes a clue to the subject of the whole story. This is in general ably done ; as, for instance, in the *Mudrá Rákshasa*, the whole business of the last act of which is the development of contrivances intimated in the first. The first act of *Málatí and Mádhava* is entirely devoted to this object, with a minuteness of detail that is rather tedious, and reminds us of Puff's apology in the *Critic* for the language of the first scene of his play : "I was obliged to be plain and intelligible in the first scene, because there was so much matter of fact in it."

The ensuing acts carry on the business of the story to its final development in the last; and in general the Hindu writers are successful in maintaining the character of their exode, the business being rarely completed before the concluding act. The piece closes as it began, with a characteristic benediction or prayer, which is always repeated by the principal personage, and expresses his wishes for general plenty and happiness.

---

4. Conduct of the Plot.

The business of every piece is termed its *Vastu;* its substance or thing, the *pragma* or *res*.

It is of two kinds, principal and secondary, or essential and episodical.

Every business involves five elements, the *Víja*, *Vindu*, *Patáká*, *Prakarí*, and *Kárya*.

The *Víja*, or the seed, is the circumstance from which the

business arises. The policy of the prime minister in the *Ratnávalí* is the seed, or remote cause, of the Rája's obtaining the princess.

The *Vindu*, which literally means a drop, is the unintentional development of some secondary incident, which furnishes a clue to the event—as when Ratnávalí learns accidentally that she has beheld the person of the Rája Vatsa, she recollects she was designed by her father to be his bride, which after a due course of interruption she becomes.

Patáká, a banner, perhaps intended to signify embellishment, an episode.

Prakarí, an episodical incident, or an event of limited duration and subordinate importance, in which the principal characters bear no part.

Kárya, is the end, or object, which being effected, the whole is effected, as the marriage of Vatsa and Ratnávalí.

The end or object of the business admits of five conditions: Beginning, Promotion, Hope of Success, Removal of Obstacles, Completion.

The series or combinations of incidents, the *Sandhis*, by which an object is ultimately attained, are also five.

The *Mukha* is the opening or preparatory course of incidents, by which the train of events to be afterwards developed is first sprung. Thus in *Málatí and Mádhava*, the hero and heroine have been thrown in each other's way by seeming accident, but in fact by the devices of their friends; and this lays the foundation of their love, and the occurrences of the play.

The *Pratimukha* is the metabasis, or secondary event, calculated to obstruct or promote the catastrophe, as the suspicion entertained by the queen, Vásavadattá, of her husband's love for Ságariká.

The *Garbha* is the covert prosecution of purpose, giving way in appearance to impediments, but in reality adhering to the original intention.

Vimarsha is the peripateia, in which an effect is produced contrary to its intended cause, or change in the course of the story, by which expectation is baffled, and an unforeseen reverse ensues. S'akuntalá, by her marriage with Dushyanta, has attained the summit of her desires, when she incurs the displeasure of

Durvásas, and is in consequence separated from the recollection of her lord.

The *Upasanhŕiti* or *Nirvahańa*, is the catastrophe, or that to which all tends and in which all terminates.

This course assigned for the fable will be perhaps more intelligible if we apply the divisions to a drama of our own. In *Romeo and Juliet*, the ball at the house of Capulet may be considered the *Mukha*: the *Pratimukha* is the interview with Juliet in the garden: the *Garbha* is Juliet's apparent assent to the marriage with Paris: the *Vimarsha* is the despair of Romeo, consequent on a contrivance intended to preserve Juliet's faith. The catastrophe needs no elucidation.

Each of these divisions in the Hindu system comprehends a number of subdivisions, Angas, or members, to follow the description of which would be to exhaust any patience except Hindu. It will be therefore sufficient to observe, that they comprehend a variety of dramatic incidents, which the theatre of every nation abundantly presents, and which, in fact, have no limits but imagination and dramatic effect. The Hindus enumerate sixty-four; or twelve *Mukhángas*, twelve *Pratimukhangas*, thirteen *Garbhángas*, thirteen *Vimarshángas*, and fourteen *Nirvahańángas*. We may cite one of each as an example.

Yukti is a *Mukhánga*: it means the connexion of purpose and result. Yogandharáyańa has introduced Ságariká to the queen, merely to put her in the way of the Rája, that he may see and love her. The business of the piece is founded on the result. We might say that the wager of Iachimo and Posthumus, and the visit of the former to the court of Cymbeline, was an illustration of this element.

Parisarpa, a *Pratimukhánga*, implies the progressive narration of events. The Chamberlain relates in the *Veńí-Sanhára*, the death of Bhíshma and destruction of the Kauravas by Kŕishńa, as consequent upon the death of the son of the latter, Aniruddha. The description of the successive encounters of Macbeth and Banquo with the King of Norway and rebellious Thanes, by the bleeding soldier, is an instance of this variety.

Of the *Garbhángas*, *Abhútáharańa*, may be understood to signify misprision of loss or evil. Thus when, in the *Veńí-Sanhára*, the messenger proclaims that Aswatthâman has been slain by

Kŕishńa, it is supposed that the prince has fallen, but it turns out that the death of an elephant so named is intended. Thus Juliet first interprets the nurse's grief for Tybalt's death as occasioned by the death of Romeo.

One of the *Vimarshángas* is *Dyuti*, provoking to combat, as in the scene between Arjuna and Bhíma, in the *Veńí-Sanhára*. Examples of this are common enough in every dramā. The scene between Dorax and Sebastian, in *Don Sebastian*, and that between Stukely and Lewson in *The Gamester*, are amongst the most powerful in the English language.

One of the members of the catastrophe is *Grahańa*, referring to a purpose held in view throughout. Thus Bhíma reminds Draupadí that she had been forbidden by him to tie up her dishevelled hair, as he had vowed to do it for her, when he had slain those who had subjected her to the indignity of untying the fillet which had bound it. The avowal made by Zanga, in the concluding scene of *The Revenge*, of the feeling by which he has been animated to destroy Alonzo, may be held to be illustrative of this variety.

We shall not pursue these technicalities any further. It is clear from what has been stated, that considerable artifice must have been employed by the Hindu dramatists, in the construction of their fable, to authorise such a complicated subdivision of its details.

---

5. Characters of the Drama.

Every description of composition has its appropriate hero and heroine, and in the ample range of the Hindu drama, every class of society contributes its members to support these personages. The hero may be a god or demigod, or a mortal, in the higher kinds of composition: he is drawn, in the latter case, from mythology, history, or fable, or is the creation of the author. As love enters largely into the business of the Hindu theatre, the attributes of the hero are defined with reference to his fitness for feeling and inspiring passion, and he is to be represented young, handsome, graceful, liberal, valiant, amiable, accomplished, and well-born. The chief technical classification of the *Náyaka*, or hero, is into *Lalita*, gay, thoughtless, and good-humoured; *Śánta*, gentle and virtuous; *Dhírodátta*, high-spirited, but temperate and firm; *Udátta*, ardent and ambitious. These are again subdivided, so as to make forty-eight species; and by considering them as diversified by mortal, semi-divine, or celestial origin, are multiplied to a hundred and forty-four kinds. It must be rather difficult for a writer to observe, amidst such a multiplicity, the rule laid down for his delineation of the manners of his hero: for whatever individual he adopts, he must take care to make him consistent with himself, and not to give him qualities incompatible with his organisation. Thus it is said that it is incongruous to ascribe liberality to the demon Rávańa; to unite piety and pride in the son of Jamadagni; and to accuse the high-minded Ráma of compassing the death of Bali by fraud. These blemishes, when they occur in the original legend, should be kept out of view by the dramatist. Some allowance, however, is made for "lover's perjuries," and a prince and hero may compromise his credit for dignity and veracity, in concealing from a jealous bride his *égaremens de cœur*.

Equal minuteness has been displayed in specifying the classes of *Náyikás* or heroines; and the extent to which females are partakers of scenic incident, affords an interesting picture of the relations of that sex in Hindu society. In the *Nátakas* and *Nátikás* we have the nymphs of heaven, the brides of demigods, the wives of saints, and female saints themselves, and the deified woods and rivers; in the plays of pure fiction, we have princesses and courtesans; and in the pieces of intrigue, the different inmates of the harem. The first class of females is the legitimate creation of poetry and mythology, the others are portraits from social life. The introduction of the unmarried female of high birth into the lighter scenes of common life, is an accession to which ancient comedy was a stranger. The unmarried girl of family is never introduced in person in the scenes of Plautus and Terence. In *Málatí and Mádhava*, we have Málatí and her friend Madayantiká; and in the *Ratnávalí*, Ságariká and the other damsels of the interior of the palace. It may be suspected, however, that the former piece presents a purer specimen of Hindu manners than the latter. It seems probable that the princes of India learnt the practice of the rigid exclusion of women in their harems from the Mohammedans, and that previously, although they were subject to many restrictions, they were allowed to go freely into public on public occasions, they were present at dramatic performances, they formed the chief part at bridal processions, they were permitted to visit the temples of the gods, and to perform their ablutions with little or no privacy in sacred streams; which last-named privileges they still retain, and to which Mohammedan women have no similar right. Even in later times, the presence of men other than a husband or a son, was far from prohibited in the inner apartments; and in the *Ratnávalí*, the minister of Vatsa, with his chamberlain and the envoy from Ceylon, are admitted to the audience of the Rájá in the presence of the queen and her attending damsels. In what may be considered heroic times, queens and princesses seem to have travelled about where and how they pleased; and in the *Uttara-Ráma-Charitra*, Sítá is sent to live by herself in the forests, and the mother of Ráma comes with little or no parade to the hermitage of Válmíki

Although, however, the social restraints to which females were subjected, under the ancient Hindu system, were of a very different nature from those which Mohammedanism imposes, and were in all probability even less severe than those which prevailed in many of the Grecian states, they did no doubt operate to such an extent as to preclude women from taking any part in general society. This was more particularly the case with unmarried women; and we learn from several of the dramas, that it was a part of virtuous breeding for a virgin to decline conversation with a man, even with a lover. Thus Ságariká in the *Ratnávalí*, and Málatí in *Málatí and Mádhava*, can with difficulty be prevailed upon to address the objects of their affection. They answer to every question by proxy, and do not even trust their voices to their female companion above a whisper, when those they adore are present. Unmarried women, therefore, we may infer, might be in company with men and might hear their addresses, but would have violated decorum if they had ventured to reply. No restraint of the nature was imposed upon married women. S'akuntalá appears in the public court of Dushyanta and pleads her own cause; and Vásavadattá, in the *Ratnávalí*, enters unreservedly into communication with her father's envoy. The married ladies of the lighter pieces, indeed, exercise their wit upon their husband's particular confidant and friend, the Vidúshaka, and the queen of Agnimitra and her foster sister Mekhalá, indulge themselves in practical jokes at Cháráyańa's expense.

The want of opportunity thus afforded to Hindu youth to appreciate the characters and dispositions of those to whom they were affianced, might be supposed to have subjected them to subsequent disgust and disappointment at home, and consequently compelled them to seek the gratification derived from female society elsewhere. Such has been the reason assigned for a similar practice amongst the Greeks. It may be doubted, however, whether this want of previous acquaintance was in any way the cause of the effect ascribed to it, for the practice was very universal, and disappointment could not have universally occurred. In all probability, it occurred less often than it does in European society, in which so much pains are taken to embellish talent, and in which conventional good breeding conceals defects. The practice rather originated in what was considered to be the perfection of female virtue. "She was the best of women of whom little could be said, either in the way of good or harm : she was educated to see as little, to hear as little, and inquire as little as possible, and the chief purposes of her married life were to perpetuate her race, and regulate the economy of the household." Her maximum of merit consisted in the assiduity with which she nursed her children and controlled her servants, and whilst thus devoted "to suckle fools and chronicle small beer," she might be a very useful, but certainly could not be a very entertaining companion.

The defective education of the virtuous portion of the sex, and their consequent uninteresting character, held out an inducement to the unprincipled members, both of Greek and Hindu society, to rear a class of females, who should supply those wants which rendered home cheerless, and should give to men hetæra or female friends, and associates in intellectual as well as in animal enjoyment. A courtesan of this class inspired no abhorrence: she was brought up from her infancy to the life she professed, which she graced by her accomplishments, and not unfrequently dignified by her virtues. Her disregard of social restraint was not the voluntary breach of moral, social, or religious precepts : it was the business of her education to minister to pleasure, and in the imperfect system of the Greeks, she committed little or no trespass against the institutes of the national creed or the manners of society. The Hindu principles were more rigid; and not only was want of chastity in a female a capital breach of social and religious obligations, but the association of men with professed wantons was an equal violation of decorum, and, involving a departure from the purity of caste, was considered a virtual degradation from rank in society. In practice, however, greater latitude seems to have been observed; and in the *Mṙichchhakaṫí*, a Brahman, a man of family and repute, incurs apparently no discredit from his love for a courtesan. A still more curious feature is, that his passion for such an object seems to excite no sensation in his family nor uneasiness in his wife, and the nurse presents his child to his mistress, as to its mother; and his wife, besides interchanging civilities (a little coldly, perhaps, but not compulsively), finishes by calling her "sister," and acquiescing therefore in her legal union with her lord. It must be acknowledged that the poet has managed his story with great dexterity, and the interest with which he has invested his heroine prevents manners so revolting to our notions from being obtrusively offensive. No art was necessary, in the estimation of a Hindu writer, to provide his hero with a wife or two, more or less, and the acquisition of an additional bride is the ordinary catastrophe of the lighter dramas.

Women are distinguished as being *Swakíyá*, *Parakíyá*, and *Sámányá*—or the wife of an individual himself, the wife or daughter of another person, and one who is independent. Each of these is distinguished as *Mugdhá*, *Prauḋhá*, and *Pragalbhá*, or youthful, adolescent, and mature; and of each of these, again, there are many varieties, which it is needless to specify. We may observe, however, to the honour of the Hindu drama, that the *Parakíyá*, or she who is the wife of another person, is never to be made the object of a dramatic intrigue: a prohibition that would have sadly cooled the imagination and curbed the wit of Dryden and Congreve.

The incidental characters or conditions of a *Náyiká* are declared to be eight:—

1. The *Swádhínapatiká* is devoted to her husband.

2. The *Vásakasajjá* is a damsel full dressed in expectation of her lover.

3. The *Virahotkaṅṫhitá* mourns the absence of her lord.

4. The *Khaṅḍitá* is mortified by detecting a lover's infidelity.

5. The *Kalahántaritá* is overcome with grief or anger at real or fancied neglect.

6. The *Vipralabdhá* is disappointed by her lover's failing his appointment.

7. The *Proshitabhartriká* is a female whose husband or lover is in a foreign country.

8. The *Abhisáriká* is a female who goes to meet her lover, or sends to seek him.

The *Alankáras*, the ornaments or graces of women, and with which the *Náyiká* should be delineated by the dramatic or poetic writer, are said to be twenty. Many of these are palpable enough: such as *Śobhá*, brilliancy or beauty, and youth; *Mádhurya*, sweetness of disposition; *Dhairya*, steady attachment, &c. But there are some which, as characteristic of the Hindu system, may perhaps merit specification. *Bháva* is a slight personal indication of natural emotion. *Háva* is its stronger expression, as change of colour; and *Helá* is the decided manifestation of feeling. *Lílá* is mimicry of a lover's manner, language, dress, &c., for his diversion, or that of female companions. *Vilása* is the expression of desire evinced in look, act, or speech. *Vichchhitti* is neglect of dress and ornaments through mental agitation. *Vibhrama* is the wrong application of personal embellishments occasioned by hurry and anxiety. *Kilakinchita* is mixed sensation, as the conflict between joy and grief, tenderness and resentment. *Moṫṫáyita* is the silent expression of returned affection. *Kuṫṫamita* is the affected repulse of a lover's endearments. *Vikṙita* is the suppression of the sentiments of the heart through bashfulness; and *Lalita* is the conviction of triumphant charms, and the sentiment of gratified love, as expressed by elegance of attire and complacency of deportment.

The *dramatis personæ*, with the exception of the hero and heroine, form the *anga* or the body of the characters. Of these the following are distinguished :—

The *Píthamarda* is the friend and confidant of the hero, and sometimes the hero of a secondary action interwoven with the principal. Such is the case in the *Málatí and Mádhava*, in which the love of Makaranda for Madayantiká proceeds parallel with that of Mádhava for Málatí.

Another person of primary rank is the *Pratináyaka*, the counterpart and antagonist of the hero. Such is Rávańa as opposed to Ráma, and Duryodhana to Yudhishthira.

Each of these may have his courtiers, ministers, officers, companions, and dependants; but there are two individuals, termed specifically the *Viťa* and the *Vidúshaka*, that are peculiar in some degree to the theatre of the Hindus.

The character of the *Viťa* is not very easily understood. It is necessary that he should be accomplished in the lighter arts, particularly poetry, music, and singing, and he appears indiscriminately as the companion of a man or woman, although, in the latter case, the female is the courtesan. He is generally represented on familiar and easy, and yet dependent, terms with his associate, and evinces something of the character of the Parasite of the Greek comedy, but that he is never rendered contemptible. It does not appear that he professes to teach the arts he practises, although it is not impossible that such was his employ, and that he was retained about the person of the wealthy and dissipated, as a kind of private instructor as well as entertaining companion. In lexicons, the person indicated by the *Viťa* is a despicable being, of whose character no vestiges occur in the theatrical picture.

As Schlegel observes, every theatre has its buffoon, and the *Vidúshaka* plays that part in the theatre of the Hindus. He is the humble companion, not the servant, of a prince or man of rank; and it is a curious peculiarity, that he is always a Brahmin. He bears more affinity to Sancho Panza, perhaps, than any other character in western fiction, imitating him in his combination of shrewdness and simplicity, his fondness of good living, and his love of ease. In the dramas of intrigue, he exhibits some of the talents of Mercury, but with less activity and ingenuity, and occasionally suffers by his interference. In the *Mrichchhakaťi* he is further distinguished by his morality and his devotion to his friend. This character is always lively, and sometimes almost witty, although in general his facetiousness does not take a very lofty flight. According to the technical definition of his attributes, he is to excite mirth by being ridiculous in person, age, and attire.

The *Náyiká*, or heroine, has always her companion and confidante, and the most appropriate personage to fill this capacity is a foster sister. Where queens are the heroines, a favourite damsel discharges this duty. Female devotees play a leading part in several dramas as well as novels, and in that case are usually described as of the Bauddha sect. In the *Vrihat-Kathá* these pious ladies are usually painted in very unfavourable colours; but in *Málatí and Mádhava,* the old priestess, or rather ascetic, is represented as a woman of profound learning and sound morals, the instructress and friend of men who hold the highest offices in the state, and the instrument selected by them to secure the happiness of their children.

The subordinate characters of both sexes are derived from every class of society; and even the *Cháńdálas* find a place in the comedies of fiction. A strange enumeration is given of the male characters admissible as tenants of the interior of palaces, or Eunuchs, Mutes, Dwarfs, Foresters, and Barbarians. The attendance of females on the persons of kings is another national peculiarity, especially as it appears from the *Mudrá-Rákshasa,* that this practice was not confined to the inner apartments; for Chandragupta, although he does not appear in public so attended, goes thus accompanied from one palace to another.

---

6. Objects of Dramatic Representation.

The purposes that are to be aimed at in dramatic composition are described as the same with those of poetic fiction in general: they are to convey instruction through the means of amusement; and, with this view, they must affect the minds of the spectators with the sentiments which they express. These sentiments are termed by the Hindus, *Rasas,* tastes or flavours, and they imply both the quality as inherent in the composition, and the perception of it as recognised by the reader or spectator. The *Rasas,* however, are considered usually as effects, not causes, and they are said to come from the *Bhávas,* conditions of the mind or body, which are followed by a corresponding expression in those who feel, or are supposed to feel them, and a corresponding impression on those who behold them. When these conditions are of a permanent or perdurable description, and produce a lasting and general impression, which is not disturbed by the influence of collateral or contrary excitements, they are, in fact, the same with the impressions: as desire or love, as the main object of the action is both the condition of the chief character, and the sentiment with which the spectator is filled. When the conditions are incidental and transitory, they contribute to the general impression, but are not confounded with it. They may, indeed, be contrary to it in their essence, without weakening or counteracting it; as a hero may, for public reasons, abandon his mistress without foregoing his love, and may perform acts of horror even in furtherance of his passion.

The *Bhávas* are therefore divided into *Sthdyin* or lasting, and *Vyabhichárin*, transitory or incidental. There are also other divisions, which we shall proceed to notice.

The *Stháyi-Bhávas*, or permanent conditions, are, according to some authorities, eight; according to others, nine.

1. *Rati* is desire for any object, arising from seeing or hearing it, or having it present to the recollection.

2. *Hása* is laughter or mirth, distinct from the laughter of scorn.

3. *Śoka* is sorrow at separation from a beloved object.

4. *Krodha* is the resentment of injurious treatment.

5. *Utsáha* is high-mindedness, or that feeling which prompts valour, munificence, or mercy.

6. *Bhaya* is the fear of reproach.

7. *Jugupsá* is aversion, or disgust; the emotion which attends seeing, touching, or hearing of anything offensive.

8. *Vismaya* is the emotion produced by seeing, touching, or hearing of anything surprising.

9. *Śánta* is not always included in this enumeration: it implies that state of mind which contemplates all human events as transitory and insignificant.

Before adverting to the *Vyabhhichári-Bhávas*, we must notice the other divisions, as they are essential accompaniments of both them and the *Stháyi-Bhávas*. The *Bhávas* are distinguished as *Vibhávas*, *Anubhávas*, and *Sáttwika-Bhávas*.

The *Vibhávas* are the preliminary and accompanying conditions which lead to any particular state of mind or body, and the *Anubhávas* are the external signs which indicate its existence.

The *Sáttwika-Bhávas* are the involuntary expressions of emotion natural to a living being—as *Stambha*, paralysis; *Sweda*, perspiration; *Románcha*, erection of the hair of the body; *Swaravikára*, change of voice; *Vepathu*, trembling; *Varńavikára*, change of colour; *Aśru*, tears; and *Pralaya*, immobility or helplessness. These, as the results of emotion, are the same with the *Anubhávas*.

The *Vyabhichári-Bhávas* are the most numerous; and in order to give a more accurate notion of them, as well as of this part of the system, we shall implicitly follow the guidance of the native authorities.

1. *Nirveda*, self-disparagement; *Vibhávas*, dissatisfaction with the world and desire to acquire holy knowledge; *Anubhávas*, tears, sighs, and appearance of mental dejection.

Example.—"Wandering round the world only wearies the wise, the abundance of learning engenders controversy, the notice of the great yields but humiliation, and the looks that gaze upon the lotus face lead only to the pangs of parting. Náráyańa was not propitiated at Prayága by me of little wisdom." (*Rasa-Tarangińí.*)

2. *Gláni*, debility, inability to endure; *Vibhávas*, long sorrow, excess in exercise or pleasure, hunger and thirst; *Anubhávas*, inactivity, change of colour, and trembling of the limbs.

Example.—"Long and bitter sorrow withering her heart, like the tender bud of the lotus cut from its stem, has shrunk up her delicate frame, as the soft leaf of the *ketakí* is shrivelled by autumnal heat." (*Saraswatíkańťhábharańa*, from the *Uttara-Ráma-Charitra.*)

3. *Śanká*, apprehension of encountering what is not desired, or doubt of obtaining what is wished; *Vibhávas*, another person's aversion or individual misconduct; *Anubhávas*, trembling, anxious looks and manner, concealment.

Example.—"She shrinks from every gaze, suspecting that her secret is discovered. If she observe two of her companions in conversation, she thinks they are talking of her; and if they laugh, she thinks herself the object of their mirth." (*Daśa-Rúpaka*, from the *Ratnávalí.*)

4. *Asúyá*, intolerance of another's superiority, and attempt to humiliate him; *Vibhávas*, irascibility, baseness; *Anubhávas*, angry expression, recapitulation of defects.

Example.—"The praise of the enemy of Madhu, pronounced in the assembly by the son of Páńdu, was insupportable to the Chedi monarch, for the mind of the arrogant cannot brook another's praise" (*Sáhitya-Darpańa*, from *Mágha.*)

Some writers consider *Írshyá* as synonymous with *Asúyá:* but one authority distinguishes it as a variety, and restricts the former to jealousy or intolerance of attention or respect shown to a rival, as,

Example.—"Go, shameless wretch, to her to whom you have transferred your homage, the crimson tincture of whose feet you wear as the embellishment of your forehead." (*Saraswatíkańthábharańa.*)

5. *Mada*, intoxication, extravagant joy, and forgetfulness of sorrow; *Vibhávas*, drinking, &c.; *Anubhávas*, unsteadiness in movement, indistinctness of utterance, drowsiness, laughing, weeping.

Example.—"The tongue tastes the liquor, and our existence is wholly unprofitable: all the faculties are overwhelmed by the unreality of a shadow." (*Rasa-Tarangińí.*)

6. *Śrama*, weariness; *Vibhávas*, bodily exertion or excessive indulgence; *Anubhávas*, perspiration, languor, &c.

Example.—"There you reclined your form in repose upon my bosom, for vainly had my endearments sought to give relief to those tender limbs, beautiful in rest, and delicate as the soft fibres of the lotus stem, when wearied by the lengthened way." (*Daśa-Rúpaka*, from the *Uttara Ráma-Charitra.*)

7. *Álasya*, indolence, aversion to activity; *Vibhávas*, weariness, luxuriousness, pregnancy, meditation; *Anubhávas*, tardy and reluctant motion, stooping, yawning, becoming of a darker complexion.

Example.—"The daughter of the mountain, when heavy with her pleasing burden, was unable to prevent Hara from carrying off her necklace with her hands, and languidly raised her eye in smiles upon his theft." (*Rasa-Tarangińí*, from the *Kumára-Sambhava.*)

8. *Dainya*, the depression of indigence and pain; *Vibhávas*, desertion, neglect, contempt; *Anubhávas*, hunger, thirst, ragged apparel, wretchedness of appearance.

Example.—"The husband, old and blind, reclines upon the platform; the dwelling is in ruins, and the rainy season is at hand. There are no good tidings of the son, and as the matron anxiously preserves the last drop of oil in the fragment of a broken jar, she looks at her pregnant daughter-in-law, and weeps." (*Daśa-Rúpaka.*)

9. *Chintá*, painful reflection, the absorption of the mind in unpleasant recollection; *Vibhávas*, the loss or absence of a desired object; *Anubhávas*, tears, sighs, change of colour, feverish heat.

Example.—"Whom do you think of, gentle and lovely maiden, as you lean your cheek upon your hand, around whose wrists the lotus fibre twines its cooling bracelet? from those long lashes drop a stream of pearly tears, to weave a lengthened necklace, far more bright than Hara's radiant smile." (*Daśa-Rúpaka.*)

10. *Moha*, perplexity, distraction, not knowing what is to be done or left undone; *Vibhávas*, terror, impetuosity, painful recollection; *Anubhávas*, giddiness, falling on the ground, insensibility.

Example.—"I know not whether this be pain or pleasure that I feel; whether I wake or sleep, whether wine or venom spread through my frame; thy touch has confounded all my faculties, and now I shake with cold, and now I burn with inward heat." (*Daśa-Rúpaka*, from the *Uttara-Ráma-Charitra.*)

11. *Smŕiti*, recollection; *Vibhávas*, the effort to remember, association of ideas; *Anubhávas*, contracting or drawing up the eyebrows, &c.

Example.—"Is this Maináka that stops my way through the air? Whence is this audacity? Has he forgotten how he shrank from the thunderbolt of Indra?—Is it Tárkshya that thus presumes, who ought to know me, Rávana, the equal of his lord?—No, it is Jaťáyu—oppressed by years, he comes to court his death." (*Daśa-Rúpaka*, from the *Hanuman-Náťaka.*)

12. *Dhŕiti*, concentration or repose of the mind, fortitude or content; *Vibhávas*, knowledge, power; *Anubhávas*, calm enjoyment, patient suffering.

Example.—"We are contented here with the bark of trees; you are happy in affluence: our satisfaction is equal, there is no difference in our conditions. He alone is poor whose desires are insatiable; but when the mind is satisfied, who can be called poor, who can be termed rich?" (*Dasa-Rúpaka*, from the *Śatakas* of *Bhartŕihari.*)

13. *Vríďá*, shame, shrinking from praise or censure; *Vibhávas*, conscious impropriety, disgrace, defeat; *Anubhávas*, casting down the eyes, hanging down the head, covering the face, blushing.

Example.—"The eyes of Arjuna, suffused with starting tears, are fixed in sad dejection upon his bow; inflamed with rage, he mourns the death of Abhimanyu, slain by an unworthy enemy, but burns still more with shame to think it yet unrevenged! 'Alas, alas, my son!' are words that are swelling in his throat, but not suffered to find their way." (*Saraswatikańťhábharańa*, from the *Vеńí-Sanhára.*)

14. *Chapalatá*, unsteadiness, haste, repeatedly changing from

one thing to another; *Vibhávas*, envy, hatred, passion, joy; *Anubhávas*, angry looks, abuse, blows, following one's own inclination.

Example.—"When he heard that Ráma had taken up his bow, and announced with delight his expectation of the coming contest, after he had thrown a bridge over the sea and advanced to Lanká, the many hands of Rávańa dropped their shafts, as might be inferred from the rattling of the bracelets, which had been almost burst with exultation at the commencement of the war." (*Rasa-Tarangińí*, from the *Hanuman-Náťaka.*)

15. *Harsha*, joy, mental exultation; *Vibhávas*, meeting with a lover or friend, the birth of a son, &c.; *Anubhávas*, horripilation, perspiration, tears, sobbing, change of voice.

Example.—"The matron to whose arms her lord returns in safety from the dangers of a journey over desert lands, wipes from her eyes the starting tear of joy as she thinks of the perils of the way. She brushes with her mantle from the faithful camel's loaded hair the heavy sand, and fills his mouth with handfuls of his favourite fodder." (*Daśa Rúpaka.*)

16. *Ávega*, agitation or flurry, arising from unexpected or unpleasant events; *Vibhávas*, the approach of a friend or enemy, the occurrence of natural phenomena, and the proximity of imminent danger; *Anubhávas*, slipping, falling, tumbling, haste, inability to move, &c.

Example.—"Haste, haste, my arms!—Quick!—Caparison my steed!—Where is my sword? Bring me my dagger! Where is my bow, and where my mail? Such were the cries that echoed through the mountain caves, when, startled from their slumbers by the dream that thou hadst shown them, the enemy awoke in alarm." (*Daśa-Rúpaka*, from a play or poem of the author's own, which he has not named.)

17. *Jaďatá*, loss of faculty or activity, incapacity for every kind of business; *Vibhávas*, seeing, hearing, or encountering anything agreeable or disagreeable in excess; *Anubhávas*, silence, fixed look, apathetic indifference.

Example.—"1*st Rákshasa.* By whom have those mighty demons been slain, by Triśiras, Khara, and Dúshańa commanded?

"2*d Rákshasa.* By the ferocious warrior Ráma.

"1*st Rákshasa.* By him alone?

"2*d Rákshasa.* Who could believe it that did not see it? Amidst the din of battle, the numbers of our host were strewed headless corses on the plain, and plunging herons burrowed in the hollow of each severed neck.

"*1st Rákshasa.* If he be such as you describe, what can such as I attempt?" (*Daśa-Rúpaka*, from the *Udátta-Rághava.*)

Example.—"When the monkey chiefs heard from Hanumat, upon his return, that they would be unable to cross the expanded bed of the ocean, they laughed at his report; but when they reached the shore, and first beheld the vast and ever-tossing main, they stood to gaze upon it like figures in a picture." (*Rasa-Tarangińí*, from the *Hanuman-Náťaka.*)

18. *Garba*, arrogance, holding one's self superior to all men; *Vibhávas*, opinion of family, beauty, rank, and strength; *Anubhávas*, disrespect, frowns, freedoms, laughter, acts of prowess.

Example.—"Whilst I bear arms, what need of others' swords: that which cannot be accomplished by my falchion must be impossible for all." (*Saraswatíkańťhábharańa*, from the *Mahábhárata.*)

19. *Visháda*, despair of success, anticipation of misfortune; *Vibhávas*, failure in acquiring wealth, fame, or offspring, and their loss; *Anubhávas*, sighing, palpitation, abstraction, anxious search for friends or patrons, &c.

Example.—"Táraká, what is this? Gourds sink in the stream, and stones are buoyant. The glory of the mighty monarch of the Rákshasas is effaced, and the child of a mortal triumphs. I have lived to see my kinsmen slain; the feebleness of age forbids the discharge of my functions. What now is to be done?" (*Daśa-Rúpaka*, from the *Víra-Charitra.*)

20. *Autsukya*, impatience; *Vibháva*, expectation of a lover; *Anubhávas*, uneasiness, lassitude, sighs.

Example.—"The first watch is spent in agreeable diversions; the second, in weaving a wreath of lotus flowers, *champakas, ketakas, jasmines;* the third, in adjusting the golden bracelet, and chain, and ear-rings, and zone. But how, pretty damsel, is the last watch of the day to be passed?" (*Rasa-Tarangińí.*)

21. *Nidrá*, drowsiness, contraction of the mental faculties, or recession of their properties from the organs of sense; *Vibhávas*, fatigue of body or mind; *Anubhávas*, relaxation of the muscles, twinkling of the eyes, yawning, dosing.

Example.—"Still echo in my heart those gentle love-inspiring words my fawn-eyed maid breathed to-day, half indistinct and half articulate, when her eyes twinkled with drowsiness." (*Daśa-Rúpaka.*)

22. *Apasmára*, possession, demoniac or planetary influence; *Vibhávas*, impurity, solitude, excessive fear or grief, &c.; *Anu-*

bhávas, trembling, sighing, foaming, lolling out the tongue, falling on the ground in convulsions.

Example.—"When he beheld the Lord of Waters, furious and foaming, clinging to the earth and tossing high his mighty waves like arms, he thought him one possessed." (*Daśa-Rúpaka*, from *Mágha*).

23. *Supta*, sleep; *Vibháva*, sleepiness; *Anubhávas*, closing of the eyes, immobility, and hard breathing.

Example.—"As the eyes of the foe of Mura close, and the breath plays upon his quivering lip, in the bowers on the Yamuná's bank, one smiling damsel steals away his robe, another the gem from his ear, and a third the golden bracelets from his arms." (*Rasa-Tarangiñí.*)

24. *Vibodha*, the unfolding of the faculties, waking; *Vibháva*, dissipation of drowsiness; *Anubhávas*, rubbing the eyes, snapping the fingers, shaking the limbs.

Example.—"May the glances of Hari preserve you, when he extends his dripping limbs, designing to quit his discus, pillow, and serpent couch amidst the ocean, and averts his half-opening eyes, red with long slumber, from the blaze of the lamps, set with gems." (*Saraswatíkañṭhábharaña*, from the *Mudrá-Rákshasa*.)

25. *Amarsha*, impatience of opposition or rivalry; *Vibhávas*, discomfiture, disgrace; *Anubhávas*, perspiration, redness of the eyes, shaking of the head, abusive language, blows.

Example.—"Shall the sons of Dhṛitaráshṭra go unpunished, and I survive? They have set fire to our dwelling, offered us poison for food, assumed our state, seized upon our wealth, and sought our lives, and have laid violent hands upon the robe and tresses of our common bride." (*Saraswatíkañṭhábharaña*, from the *Veñí-Sanhára*.)

26. *Avahitthá*, disguise, attempted concealment of sentiments by personal acts; *Vibhávas*, modesty, turpitude, importance; *Anubhávas*, acting, looking, and speaking in a manner foreign to the real object.

Example.—"Whilst thus the divine sage spoke, the beauteous Parvatí, standing by his side, held down her head with shame, and pretended to count the leaves of the lotus in her hand." (*Daśa-Rúpaka*, from the *Kumára-Sambhava*.)

27. *Ugratá*, sternness, cruelty; *Vibhávas*, promulgation of fault or crime, theft, evil disposition; *Anubhávas*, reviling, abusing, beating.

Example.—"Is not my unrelenting spirit known to all the world? One and twenty times did I destroy the martial race, and hewed to pieces the very infants in the womb; nor desisted till I had allayed the fires of a father's wrath, by ablution in the reservoir of blood which I had promised to his ghost." (*Daśa-Rúpaka*, from the *Víra-Charitra.*)

28. *Mati*, apprehension, mental conclusion ; *Vibháva*, study of the Sástras ; *Anubhávas*, shaking the head, drawing up the brows, giving instruction or advice.

Example.—"Assuredly she is fit to be a Kshattriya's wife, for my mind feels her worthy of my love. The dictates of the soul are in all doubtful points the authority of the virtuous." (*Saraswatíkańthábharańa*, from *Śakuntalá.*)

29. *Vyádhi*, sickness ; *Vibhávas*, vitiation of the humours, effect of heat or cold, influence of the passions ; *Anubhávas*, appropriate bodily symptoms.

Example.—"Her kindred are in tears, her parents in sorrowful abstraction, her friends are overcome with melancholy, her associates with affliction : the hope to her that to-day or to-morrow her sufferings will cease is despair to others, but she participates not in the pain of separation from the world." (*Daśa-Rúpaka.*)

30. *Unmáda*, absence of reflection or restraint : *Vibhávas*, loss of a beloved or desired object, reverse of fortune, morbid action or possession ; *Anubhávas*, talking incoherently, laughing, weeping, or singing without cause.

Example.—"Vile Rákshasa, forbear ; whither wouldst thou bear my beloved ! Alas ! it is no demon, but a cloud. It is the bow of Indra, not the weapon of a distant foe ; the rain-drops beat upon me, not hostile shafts ; and that gleam of golden radiance is the lightning, not my love." (*Daśa-Rúpaka*, from *Vikrama and Urvaśí.*)

31. *Marańa*, death ; *Vibhávas*, expiration, wounds, injuries ; *Anubhávas*, falling on the ground, immobility.

Example.—"The female fiend, pierced through the heart by the resistless shafts of the blooming Ráma, poured through the nostrils a torrent of blood, and sought the dwelling of the lord of life." (*Sáhitya-Darpańa*, from the *Raghu-Vaṁśa.*)

32. *Trása*, fear without cause ; *Vibhávas*, hearing frightful sounds, seeing alarming objects ; *Anubhávas*, immobility, trembling, perspiration, relaxed muscles.

Example.—"As the fish played about their knees, the nymphs of heaven, their glances wild with terror and striking their hands together, looked upon each other fearfully." (*Saraswatíkańthábharańa*, from the *Kiráta.*)

33. *Vitarka*, consideration, discussion ; *Vibháva*, the percep-

tion of doubtful circumstances; *Anubhávas*, shaking the head, raising the eyebrows, &c.

Example.—"Has this been contrived by Bharata, misled by ambition, or has the second queen effected it through female levity? Both these notions must be incorrect. The prince is the hero's youngest brother; the queen, his parent and his father's wife. It is clear, therefore, that this unhappy event is the work of destiny." (*Daśa-Rúpaka.*)

This concludes the list of *Vyabhichári-Bhávas*, or incidental conditions, according to the best treatises on this subject; and as they assert, to the elementary rules of Bharata, in which they are enumerated. They are in many cases subtilised and subdivided in a manner which it is unnecessary here to notice. Their judicious delineation gives to poetic and dramatic composition its flavour or taste.

The *Rasas*, it is expressly stated, are so termed, from the analogy between mental and physical impressions. The conception of love or hatred, as derived from a drama, is fitly compared to the notion which such substances as may be sweet or saline convey of saltness or sweetness. The idea is not peculiar to Hindu literature; and the most polished nations of Europe agree in the employment of a term of similar literal and metaphorical import, as *taste*, *gusto*, *gout*, *geschmack*. A similar application of terms is traceable in Latin and Greek; and, as Addison observes, "this metaphor would have not been so general, had there not been a conformity between the mental taste and that sensitive taste which gives us a relish of every savour."

The *Rasas* reside in the composition, but are made sensible by their action on the reader or spectator. In the first case, they may be identified with the permanent conditions or *Bhávas*. It is more usual, however, to regard them as distinct—as the effects of the Bhávas and not of one nature with them. Their due appreciation depends upon the sensitiveness of the critic; but a spectator, who deserves the name, is defined by Bharata to be "one who is happy when the course of the drama is cheerful, melancholy when it is sorrowful, who rages when it is furious, and trembles when it is fearful," or, in a word, who sympathises with what he sees.

The *Rasas* are eight, according to Bharata: according to

some authorities there are nine. They are *Śṙingára*, love; *Hásya*, mirth; *Karuńá*, tenderness; *Raudra*, fury; *Víra*, heroism; *Bhayánaka*, terror; *Bíbhatsa*, disgust; and *Adbhuta*, wonder—the ninth is *Śánta*, or tranquillity. The serious part of this list is much more comprehensive than the Greek tragic *Rasas* of terror and pity; but, as anticipated by the Hindu critics, the whole might be easily extended. In reply to this, however, they say, that all other impressions may be classed under some of these, as paternal fondness comes under the head of tenderness, and avarice is an object of mirth; and the same argument may be urged in favour of the limitations of Aristotle. The fewer the classes, however, the more subtle is the ingenuity required to squeeze all the species into them, and so far the Hindu theory has an advantage over the Greek.

Śṙingára, or love, is a very leading principle in the drama of the Hindus: it is not, however, an indispensable ingredient, and many plays are wholly exempt from any trace of it. The love of the Hindus is less sensual than that of the Greek and Latin comedy, and less metaphysical than that of French and English tragedy. The loose gallantry of modern comedy is unknown to the Hindus, and they are equally strangers to the professed adoration of chivalric poetry: but their passion is neither tame nor undignified. It is sufficiently impassioned to be exempt from frigidity, and it is too tender to degrade the object of the passion; whilst, at the same time, the place that woman holds in society is too rationally defined for her to assume an influence foreign to her nature; and the estimation in which human life is held, is too humble, for a writer to elevate any mortal to the honours of a divinity. The condition of lovers is described as threefold: they may be in possession of each other's affections, and personally united; their passion may not have been mutually communicated, and their union not have taken place; and they may have been united and subsequently separated from each other. The first is called *Sambhoga*, the second *Ayoga*, and the third *Viprayoga*: or these kinds are reduced to two, and *Sambhoga* expresses successful, and *Vipralambha* unsuccessful love. The causes and consequences and modifications of these conditions are the subjects of much subtle definition, which it is not necessary to prosecute. Abundant illustration of the manner in which the passion is treated will be found in the following pages.

Víra is the *Rasa* of heroism; and heroic magnanimity is evinced in three ways: munificence, clemency, and valour. Where the latter is displayed, it must be calm, collected, and dispassionate: any indication of violence belongs to a different taste. The *Víra Charitra* affords an example of this *Rasa*, and the calm intrepidity of its hero presents a very favourable contrast to the fury of a Tydides, or the arrogance of a Rinaldo.

Bíbhatsa is the feeling of disgust inspired by filthy objects, or by fetid odours, or by low and virulent abuse. It is not the subject, it is believed, of any entire drama, but many scenes of this description occur, as the resort of Mádhava to the place of cremation, and the dialogue of the two demons in the *Veńí Saḿhára.*

Raudra is the sentiment of furious passion, expressed by violent gesticulation, threatening language, and acts of personal aggression. Examples of it occur only in detached characters, as in *Paraśuráma*, *Rávańa*, and *Duryodhana.*

Hásya is mirth arising from ridicule of person, speech, or dress, either one's own or another's, and engenders laughter of various intensity: as *Smita*, which is only the expansion of the eyelids; *Hasita* displays the teeth; *Vihasita* is characterised by a gentle exclamation: *Upahasita* exhibits tears; in *Apahasita* the tears flow in excess; and *Atihasita* is "laughter holding both his sides." The two first kinds of merriment are the genteelest; the two next are rather vulgar, but pardonable; the two last are absolutely low, or "the vulgar way the vulgar show their mirth."

The *Adbhuta Rasa* is the expression of the marvellous. Wonder is the prevailing characteristic produced by uncommon objects, and indicated by exclamation, trembling, and perspiration, &c.

The *Bhayánaka* is the taste of terror: it is induced by awful occurrences, and exhibited by trembling, perspiration, dryness of mouth, and indistinctness of judgment.

Karuńá is pity or tenderness excited by the occurrence of misfortunes: it is inspired by sighs and tears, mental unconsciousness or aberration, and is suitably illustrated by the delineation of depression, exhaustion, agony, and death.

The *Śánta Rasa* is very consistently excluded from dramatic composition, although it is allowed a place in moral or didactic poetry. It implies perfect quiescence, or exemption from mental excitement, and is therefore uncongenial to the drama, the object of which is to paint and inspire passion. The advocates for its exclusion suggest a compromise, and transfer it from the persons of the play to the audience, who are thus fitted for the impressions to be made upon them. It is highly proper, it is urged, that they should exhibit the *Śánta Rasa*, and sit in silent attention, their tempers perfectly passive, and their hearts free from every external influence.

Conformably to the genius of mythological classification, the *Rasas* are by some authorities considered to be personified of various hues, and subject to the influence of different divinities, as follows :—

Śŕingára, ...	black, subject to	Vishńu.
Hásya, ...	white, ...	Ráma.
Raudra, ...	red, ...	Rudra.
Víra,...........	red, ...	Śakra.
Karuńá, ...	gray, ...	Varuńa.
Bhayánaka, ...	black, ...	Yama.
Bíbhatsa, ...	blue, ...	Mahákála.
Adbhuta, ...	yellow, ...	Brahmá.

The arrangement appears, however, to be modern, and little recognised.

The combinations of the *Rasas* with each other, their modifications, and the manner in which they are affected by the intermixture of the different *Bhávas*, furnish the Hindu writers on the subject with ample opportunity to indulge their passion for infinite minutiæ. It may be observed, however, that this rage for subtile subdivision is most remarkable in writers of recent date, and the oldest works as the *Daśa-Rúpaka* for instance, are contented with a moderate multiplication of definitions. As to the dramatic writers themselves, they might possibly have been influenced in some degree by theoretical principles, and in the example of one of the most celebrated, *Bhavabhúti*, we have his three pieces severally appropriated, like Miss Baillie's plays of the Passions, to distinct emotions: *Málatí and Mádhava*, to the *Śringára Rasa*, or love; the *Víra Charitra* to heroism, or the *Víra Rasa;* and the *Uttara-Ráma-Charitra* to the *Karuńá Rasa*, or tenderness. We have no reason to think, however, that he, or any of the elder writers, troubled themselves about trifles, or knew or regarded the multiplied laws which have been derived from their practice. It is not so much to illustrate the plays themselves, that the foregoing picture of the system founded on them has been sketched, as to afford a view of the theatrical criticism of the Hindus, and a notion of their mode of theorising. We cannot now question that they had a theory, which has been elaborated with great diligence, if not with much success, and which, although it comprises many puerilities, is not wholly a stranger to just principles or refined taste.

As connected with the *Rasas*, we may notice one more division, which is less liable than the preceding to the charge of unnecessary trifling; it rather affects the construction than the objects of the drama, but as part of the means by which its purposes are effected, may not be inconveniently noticed here. According to Bharata's aphorisms, there are four *Vrittis*, which may be rendered Styles of Dramatic Representation, implying the general character of the dialogue and incidents, and which are severally appropriate to different *Rasas* or passions. They are termed *Kauśikí, Sáttwatí, Árabhatí*, and *Bhárati*. The three first are suited respectively to the *Śringára, Víra*, and *Raudra Rasas:* the last is common to all. The three first chiefly concern the incidents and situations: the latter regards the dialogue, and signifies merely appropriate and elegant language. The discovery of a lady's love, by her having painted a picture of her lover, which she vainly endeavours to conceal from a friend, is an incident in the *Kauśikí*, or playful and pleasing style. Inspiring dread of treachery by fabricated documents or suppositious proofs belongs to the *Sáttwatí*, the grave and serious style; and combat, tumult, magic, and natural portents, are occurrences in the style termed *Árabhatí*, the awful and appalling.

7. Diction.

The language of the Hindu theatre offers many peculiarities, but they can scarcely be fully detailed without citing the original passages, and could only be duly appreciated by students of the Sanskŕit language. It will be sufficient for our purpose, therefore, to advert to the principal characteristics.

According to the original aphorism of Bharata, "the poet is to employ choice and harmonious terms, and an elevated and polished style, embellished with the ornaments of rhetoric and rhythm." The injunction has not been disregarded, and in no department of Hindu literature are the powers of the Sanskŕit language more lavishly developed. In the late writers, the style is generally so painfully laboured as to be still more painfully read; but in the oldest and best pieces, the composition, although highly finished, is not in general of difficult apprehension. The language of Kálidása is remarkably easy; so is that of Bhavabhúti, in the *Uttara-Ráma-Charitra.* In his other two plays, and especially in *Málatí and Madháva,* it is more elaborate and difficult. The *Mŕichchhakatí* presents fewer difficulties than any of the whole series. The *Murári-Náṫaka* is one of the most unintelligible.

The ordinary business dialogue of the Hindu dramas is for the greater part in prose, but reflections or descriptions, and the poetical flights of the author, are in verse. Every one of the many kinds of Sanskŕit metre is employed on the latter occasion, from the *Anushṫubh* to the *Dańḋaka,* or verse of four lines of eight syllables each, to that which contains any number of syllables from twenty-seven to one hundred and ninety-nine. Bhavabhúti occasionally indulges in this last metre; Kálidása seldom, if ever. His favourite form appears to be the *Áryá* or *Gáthá;* but none of the poets confine themselves to a particular description. The first thirty-five stanzas of *Śakuntalá* exhibit eleven kinds of metre; and in the scene quoted from *Málatí and Mádhava* by Mr. Colebrooke, in his Essay on Sanskŕit and Prákŕit Prosody, in the tenth volume of the Asiatic Researches, we have the like number, or eleven varieties, for the greater part of the most complex description. That this diversity of composition enhances the difficulty of understanding the Hindu plays may be admitted, but it likewise adds to the richness and melody of the composition. It is impossible to conceive language so beautifully musical, or so magnificently grand, as that of many of the verses of Bhavabhúti and Kálidása.

Another peculiarity of the Hindu plays is their employing different forms of speech for different characters. This is not, like the *patois* of the French comedies, or the Scotch of English dramas, individual and occasional, but is general and invariable. The hero and the principal personages speak Sanskŕit, but women and the inferior characters use the various modifications of that language which are comprehended under the term Prákŕit. As observed by Mr. Colebrooke, in regard to this mixture of languages, the Italian theatre presents instances in the prose comedies of Ruzzanti; and the coincidence is noticed by Mr. Walker, with reference to Sir William Jones's remarks, prefixed to his translation of *Śakuntalá*. But these five-act farces, the notion of which was probably borrowed from the *Pœnulus* of Plautus, hold but an insignificant place in the dramatic literature of Italy, and the employment of the Venetian and Bergamask dialects by Goldoni is only like the use of those of Somersetshire or Yorkshire on the English stage, except that it is rather more prominent and frequent. In no theatre, however, have we a mixture of languages exactly analogous to that invariable in the drama of the Hindus.

"*Prákŕit,*" Sir William Jones observes (Preface to *Śakuntalá*), "is little more than the language of the Brahmans melted down, by a delicate articulation, to the softness of Italian :" in which he is quite correct, as far as the Prákŕit spoken by the heroine and principal female personages is concerned. Mr. Colebrooke, however, more correctly intimates, that the term *Prákŕit* is of a more comprehensive nature, and is properly applicable to all the written and cultivated dialects of India. It may be doubted, however, if it is usually understood in this sense, and the term is applied in the *Prákŕit* grammars to a variety of forms, which agree only in name with the spoken dialects. Thus the *Mágadhí*, by which name may be considered that dialect which is more ordinarily understood by *Prákŕit*, is very different from the vernacular language of Magadh or Behar. The

Śaurasení is by no means the same with the dialect of Mathura and Vrindavan, and the *Maháráshtrí* would be of little avail in communicating with the Mahrattas, or people of *Mahárásht́ra.* The other species enumerated are equally incapable of identification with the dialects to which they might be supposed to refer.

According to the technical authorities, the different dialects employed are these:—The heroine and principal female characters speak *Śaurasení;* attendants on royal persons speak *Mágadhí;* servants, Rajputs, and traders, *Arddha*—half or mixed *Mágadhí.* The *Vidúshaka* speaks the *Práchí*, or eastern dialect; rogues use *Ávantiká*, or the language of Ougein; and intriguers that of the Dekhan or Peninsula. The dialect of *Báhlíka* is spoken by the people of the north, and *Dráviḋa* by the people of the Coromandel coast. The individuals named *Śakas* and *Śakáris* speak dialects of their own; and cowherds, outcasts, and foresters, use their respective forms of speech. Even the imps of mischief have their appropriate jargon, and the *Piśáchas* or goblins, when introduced on the stage, speak a dialect of Prákŕit termed *Paiśáchí.*

If these directions were implicitly followed, a Hindu play would be a polyglot that few individuals could hope to understand. In practice, however, we have rarely more than three varieties, or Sanskŕit, and a Prákŕit more or less refined. In point of fact, indeed, there is little real difference in the several varieties of Prákŕit: they all agree in grammatical structure, and in the most important deviations from Sanskŕit, and only vary in their orthoepy, the lower kinds employing the harshest letters and rudest combinations. The words are essentially the same in all, and all are essentially the same with Sanskŕit, the difference affecting the pronunciation and spelling rather than the radical structure, and tending generally to shorten the words, and substitute a soft for a hard, and a slurred for an emphatic articulation. Thus *lavańa*, salt, becomes *lońa;* *mayúra*, a peacock, becomes *mora;* *madhúka*, a kind of tree, becomes *mahwa;* *purusha*, a man, is *puriso;* *śrigála*, a jackal, is *śidla;* *yauvana*, youth, is *jovańa;* and *bhavati* becomes *hodi.* Prákŕit is also averse to some forms of conjunct consonants, and either changes them to a simple reduplication or omits one of them: as *nagna*, naked, becomes *ṅagga; vatsa*, a child, *bachchha;* and *chandra*, the moon, *chanda*. In the aspirated letters, the aspirate alone is usually retained: as *gahîra*, for *gambhîra*, deep; *sahá*, for *sabhá*, an assembly. These will be sufficient to characterise the general nature of the changes by which Sanskṛit becomes Prákṛit, and which will sufficiently prove their identity. At the same time, in long and complicated sentences, the affinity is not always so obvious as it might be supposed, and the occurrence of Prákṛit offers a difficulty in the perusal of Sanskṛit plays which is not readily overcome without the aid of a commentary, in which the passages are always translated into Sanskṛit. Prákṛit admits of most of the prosody of Sanskṛit, and a due proportion of it is always written in varied metre. Its grammatical construction is marked by some peculiarities, such as the want of a dual number and dative case, and the employment of but one conjugation. The lower species are especially characterised by a disregard of grammatical concords, and the use of a common termination for every modification of gender, number, and person.

There is one question of some interest attaching to the construction of the Prákṛit, which merits a fuller inquiry than has been yet given to it, and on which this is not the place to dilate. Does it represent a dialect that was ever spoken? or is it an artificial modification of the Sanskṛit language, devised to adapt the latter to peculiar branches of literature? The latter seems to be the most likely; for there would be no difficulty in the present day in writing it, although it is no longer spoken, and highly-finished specimens are to be found in plays which are modern productions. The *Vidagdha-Mádhava*, for instance, consists more than half of high Prákṛit, and it was written less than three centuries ago. On the other hand, many of the modifications are to be found in the spoken dialects of Hindustan, and the rules of Prákṛit grammar account for changes which without such aid it is difficult to comprehend. The simplification of the grammatical construction, by the disuse of the dual number and the reduced number of verbal conjugations, looks also like the spontaneous substitution of practical to theoretic perfection in actual speech, and may tempt us to think the Prákṛit was once a spoken tongue. The subject is interesting, not only in a philological, but in a historical view;

for the sacred dialects of the Bauddhas and the Jainas are nothing else than Prákŕit, and the period and circumstances of its transfer to Ceylon and to Nepaul are connected with the rise and progress of that religion which is professed by the principal nations to the north and east of Hindustan.

---

8. Scenic Apparatus.

The Hindus never had any building appropriated to public entertainments; they could not, therefore, have had any complicated system of scenery or properties. It appears from several of the dramas, that in the palaces of kings there was a chamber or hall known as the *Sangíta-Śálá*, the music saloon, in which dancing and singing were practised and sometimes exhibited; but there is no reference to any separate edifice for such purposes, open to the public, either gratuitously or at a charge, and such an institution would be foreign to the state of society in the East, which in many respects certainly was not advanced beyond that of the Middle Ages in Europe, when minstrels and mimes were universally strollers, and performed in the halls of baronial castles, or in booths at fairs. In England, even, there appears to have been no resident company of players, or permanent theatre, earlier than the reign of Elizabeth. Companies of actors in India must have been common at an early date, and must have been reputable, for the inductions often refer to the poets as their personal friends, and a poet of tolerable merit in India, under the ancient regime, was the friend and associate of sages and kings. The Hindu actors were never apparently classed with vagabonds or menials, and were never reduced to contemplate a badge of servitude as a mark of distinction. As to theatrical edifices, the manners of the people, and the nature of the climate, were adverse to their existence, and the spacious open courts of the dwellings of persons of consequence were equally adapted to the purposes of dramatic representation and the convenience of the spectators. We should never forget, in speaking of the Hindu drama, that its exhibition, as has been noticed in the preface, was not an ordinary occurrence, or an amusement of the people, but that it was part of an occasional celebration of some solemn or religious festival.

The writers on dramatic systems furnish us with no information whatever on this part of our subject, with one exception, and in the *Sangíta-Ratnákara*, alone, have we any allusion to the place in which performances were held. The description there given, indeed, rather applies to a place for the exhibition of singing and dancing; but it was, no doubt, the same with that in which dramatic representations took place, and the audiences were similarly composed on both occasions. The description is not very precise, but the following is the purport.

"The chamber in which dancing is to be exhibited should be spacious and elegant. It should be covered over by an awning, supported by pillars richly decorated and hung with garlands. The master of the house should take his seat in the centre, on a throne: the inmates of the private apartments should be seated on his left, and persons of rank upon his right. Behind both are to be seated the chief officers of the state or household, and poets, astrologers, physicians, and men of learning, are to be arranged in the centre. Female attendants, selected for their beauty and figure, are to be about the person of the principal, with fans and chowris, whilst persons carrying wands are to be stationed to keep order, and armed men as guards are to be placed in different directions. When all are seated, the band is to enter and perform certain airs; after which the chief dancer is to advance from behind the curtain, and after saluting the audience, scattering at the same time flowers amongst them, she will display her skill."

The direction for the appearance of the dancer here indicates the separation of the performers from the audience by a screen or curtain; and of this frequent proofs are afforded, by the stage directions in different plays. The stage itself was termed *Ranga Bhúmi* or *Nepathya;* but the latter term is also applied to the "within," as sounds or exclamations off the stage are said to occur, in the *Nepathya*. We might infer the distinction, also, from the instructions of *praviśati* and *nishkkrámati*, "enter and exit," which are invariably given; but they admit the possibility, as was the case in the early French theatre, of the actors, continually in view of the audience throughout, coming forward and withdrawing as required, without ever disappearing. It is often said, however, where a character makes his appearance under the influence of hurry or alarm, that he enters *apatíkshe-*

peńa, with a toss of the curtain, throwing up or aside, apparently, the cloth suspended in the flat, instead of coming on regularly from the wing. It seems possible, also, that curtains were suspended transversely, so as to divide the stage into different portions, open equally to the audience, but screening one set of actors from the other, as if the one were within, and the other without a house or chamber. The first piece in the following collection often requires some such arrangement; unless, as is by no means unlikely, the whole was left to the imagination. It would appear, also, by the same piece, that part of the stage was raised, so as to form a terrace or balcony, as it was in Shakespeare's time in England.

The properties of the Hindu stage were, no doubt, as limited as the scenery, but seats, thrones, weapons, and cars with live cattle were used. The introduction of the latter is frequent, and could not always have been imaginary, being, as in the *Mŕichchhakatí* especially, indispensable to the business. Whether any contrivance was had recourse to, to represent the aërial chariots of the gods, is rather doubtful.

Costume was always observed, and various proofs occur of the personages being dressed in character. Females were represented in general by females; but it appears not to have been uncommon for men or lads to personate female characters, especially those of a graver character, like the Bauddha priestess in *Málatí and Mádhava.*

There is no want of instruction for stage business, and we have the "asides" and "aparts" as regularly indicated as in the modern theatre in Europe. Even German precision is not unfrequently affected, and the sentiment with which the speaker is to deliver himself particularised. In directions for passing from one place to another, much is evidently left to the imagination, and the spectator must eke out the distance traversed by his own conceptions. There is often much want of dexterity in this part of the business, and a very little ingenuity would have avoided the incongruities produced. The defect, however, is common to the early plays of all theatres, and in Shakespeare we find some very clumsy contrivances. Thus, in *Richard the Second*, the king orders the trumpets to sound, whilst the council apparently discusses what is to be done with Hereford and Norfolk; and without any further intervention, Richard commands the combatants, who as well as the king and the peers have been all the time on the stage, "to draw near and list, what with our council we have done."

These are the only notices that can be offered of the theatrical representations of the Hindus, and although scanty, leave no doubt of their general character. The Hindu stage, in fact, is best illustrated by those labours which have been so successfully addressed to the history of the stage in Europe, to which, prior to the sixteenth century, it may be considered precisely analogous, with the advantages of attention to costume and female personation. We must not extend this analogy, however, to the literary merits of the two theatres, as much of that of the Hindus may compete successfully with the greater number of the dramatic productions of modern Europe, and offers no affinity to the monstrous and crude abortions which preceded the introduction of the legitimate drama in the west.

LIST OF HINDU PLAYS.

---

* * Mṙichchhakaťí.
* Śakuntalá (translated by Sir William Jones).
* * Vikrama and Urvaśí.
* † Málaviká and Agnimitra.
* * Uttara-Ráma-Charitra.
* * Málatí and Mádhava.
* † Mahávíra-Charitra.
* † Veńí-Samhára.
* * Mudrá-Rákshasa.
* ‡ Udátta-Rághava.
* † Hanuman-Náťaka.
* * Ratnávalí.
* † Viddhá-Śálábhanjiká.
* ‡ Bála-Rámáyańa.
* † Prachańďa-Pánďava.
* ‡ Karpúra-Manjarí.
* ‡ Jámadagnya-Jaya.
* ‡ Samudra-Mathana.
* ‡ Tripuradáha.
* † Dhananjaya-Vijaya.
* ‡ Anargha-Rághava.
* † Śárada-Tilaka.
* † Yayáti-Charitra.
* ‡ Yayáti-Vijaya.
* || Yayáti and Śarmishthá.
* † Dútángada.
* † Mṙigánkalekhá.
* † Vidagdha-Mádhava.
* † Abhiráma-Mańi.
* † Madhuránirudhha.
* † Kamsa-Badha.
* † Pradyumna-Vijaya.
* † Śrídáma-Charitra.
* † Dhúrtta-Narttaka.
* † Dhúrtta-Samágama.
* † Hásyárńava.
* † Kautuka-Sarvaswa.
* Prabodha-Chandrodaya (translated by Dr. Taylor).
* || Rámábhyudaya.
* || Kunda-Málá.
* || Saugandhikáharańa.
* || Kusumaśekhara-Vijaya.
* || Raivata-Madaniká.
* || Narmavatí.
* || Vilásavatí.
* || Śṙingára-Tilaka.
* || Deví-Mahádeva.
* || Yádavodaya.
* || Báli-Badha.
* || Anekamurtta.
* || Mayakapáliká.
* || Kríďárasátala.
* || Kanakavatí-Mádhava.
* || Vindumatí.
* || Keliraivataka.
* || Kámadattá.
* ¶ Saukalpa-Súryodaya.
* ¶ Sudarśana-Vijaya.
* ¶ Vasantiká Parińaya.
* † Chitra-Yajna.

Those marked * are now translated, and some account is given of those marked †: the rest have not been procured.

Those marked ‡ are named in the *Daśa-Rúpaka*, and those marked || in the *Sáhitya-Darpańa*, as examples of the different kinds of dramatic composition. The three pieces marked ¶ were amongst the late Colonel Mackenzie's collection, and are known only in the south of India.

THE

MṘICHCHHAKAṪI,

OR

THE TOY-CART.

A Drama,

TRANSLATED FROM THE ORIGINAL

SANSKṘIT.

VOL. I.

PRELIMINARY NOTE.

THE uncertainty of the sounds to be given to the proper names that occur in the following pages will necessarily impair any satisfaction that their perusal may possibly afford. This difficulty may, however, be readily overcome by attention to a few simple rules.

The only letters to which any regard need be paid are the vowels *a*, *e*, *i*, and *u*.

A, *i*, and *u*, are distinguished as long or as short by an accent over the long vowel, as *a*, *á*; *i*, *í*; *u*, *ú*.

E, *i*, and *u*, whether long or short, are to be pronounced as in Italian, and so is the long or accented *á*.

The unaccented *a* has the sound of that letter in *adore*, *adorn*, *America*, or of *u* in *sun*. This is the most perplexing part of the system, but it rests on grounds that need not be detailed here. If written as pronounced, the names of the hero and heroine should be *Charooduttŭ* and *Vusuntusená*, instead of *Chárudatta*, *Vasantasená*.

The following recapitulation will afford a ready reference:

a short or unaccented, as *u* in *sun*;
á long or accented, as *a* in *far*;
e, as *a* in *care*;
i short or unaccented, as *i* in *kill*;
í long or accented, as *ee* in *keel*;
u short or unaccented, as *u* in *full*;
ú long or accented, as *oo* in *fool*.

It is also necessary to observe, that the syllable *ka* at the end of a proper name is an optional addition; thus *Chandana* and *Chandanaka*, *A'rya* and *A'ryaka*, are the same.

INTRODUCTION.

THE drama of which the translation is now published is a work of great interest, both in the literary and national history of the Hindus.

Although not named by the authority from which we have principally drawn our general view of the Hindu dramatic system, the *Daśa-Rúpaka*, it is unquestionably alluded to in the text of that work, and we may therefore feel assured that this play was written earlier than the tenth century; there is every reason to infer much earlier.

The introduction of the *Mṙichchhakaṫí* attributes the composition to a king named S'ÚDRAKA, and gives him a high character both in arms and letters: he lived, it is said, a hundred years and then burnt himself, leaving his kingdom to his son.

Over what kingdom S'ÚDRAKA ruled is not mentioned. The writer of the *Kámandakí* says it was *Avantí* or *Ougein;* tradition, especially in the *Dekhin,* includes him amongst the universal monarchs of India, and places him between CHANDRAGUPTA and VIKRAMÁDITYA, without specifying his capital. The late Col. Wilford (*As. Res.* vol. ix.) considers him the same with the founder of the *Ándhra* dynasty of *Magadha* kings, succeeding to the throne by deposing his master, the last of the *Kanwa* race, to whom he was minister; but these averments are very questionable. The circumstances are in fact attributed, it is said (p. 116), to a prince named BÁLIHITA, or S'IPRAKA, or SINDHUKA, or (p. 103) MÁHAKARŃI—and the identification of S'ÚDRAKA with either or all of these, rests upon chronological data by no means satisfactorily established. From these (p. 100) it appears, that the first *Ándhra* king of *Magadha* reigned 456 years earlier than the last, or PULIMAT, who, it is said, died A.D. 648 (p. 111), consequently the former reigned about A.D. 192. But it is stated, that in a work called the *Kumáriká-Khańda*, a portion of the *Skanda-Puráńa*, it is asserted that in the year of the *Kali* 3300—save 10—a great king would reign (it does not appear where) named S'ÚDRAKA. This date in our era is 190; the date of the first *Ándhra* king, as mentioned above. is 192; *therefore* S'ÚDRAKA must be that king: a deduction which may possibly be correct, but which depends too much upon the accuracy of a work very little known, and upon a calculation that yet requires to be revised, to be considered as decidedly invalidating the popular notion, that S'ÚDRAKA preceded VIKRAMÁDITYA, and consequently the era of Christianity, by a century at least.

The attribution of a play to a regal author is not a singular occurrence. The *Ratnávalí*, as will be hereafter noticed, is ascribed to a bard of like dignity: whether truly or not, whether the monarch was not rather the patron than the poet, is immaterial to the chronology of the drama; as, if the work of S'ÚDRAKA'S reign, it may be considered as the oldest extant specimen of the Hindu drama, and a composition of respectable antiquity. The play contains abundant internal evidence of an ancient date.

The style, though not meagre, is in general simple and unartificial, and of a day evidently preceding the elaborate richness of Hindu writing, not to speak of the fantastic tricks and abuses which began to disgrace Sanskŕit composition apparently in the ninth and tenth centuries. This may be considered a safe indication in a work of such pretence as one attributed to a regal bard; and although it could not be admitted alone as conclusive, yet, as associated with the name and date of S'ÚDRAKA, it is a strong confirmation of the latter, at least, being correct.

Another circumstance in favour of the antiquity of the drama is derived from a peculiarity in the language of one of the chief characters. SAḾSTHÁNAKA, the *Rája's* brother-in-law, affects literature, with which he has so little conversancy, that his citations of poetic personages and events are as erroneous as frequent. Now it is a remarkable circumstance that all his citations are from the *Rámáyańa* and *Mahábhárata*, and that he never alludes to the chief actors in the Pauráńik legends, as *Dhruva*, *Daksha*, *Prahláda*, *Bali*, &c. There can be no good reason why he should not cite from a *Puráńa* as well as from either of the poems which bear a similarly holy character, and it is not likely that the author of the drama, who was thoroughly familiar with the poems, should not have been acquainted with the *Puráńas* if they had existed, or been equally in circulation: we have great reason therefore to suspect that the *Mŕichchhakaťí* was written prior to the composition of the *Puráńas*, or at least before the stories they contain had acquired by their aggregation familiar and popular currency.

Peculiarities in manners contribute to a similar conclusion, and the very panegyric upon S'ÚDRAKA, specifying his voluntary cremation when arrived at extreme old age, praises him for an act proscribed in the *Kali*, or present period of the world. By all current legal authorities, except the texts of the most ancient, suicide is prohibited everywhere except at *Prayága*, and is there allowed only under certain circumstances. The prohibition may be disregarded, it is true, but such a breach of the law could not with any decency have been made the theme of public eulogium by a Brahman in the Sanskŕit language, and therefore the event most probably preceded the law.

The subject of the piece, the love of a respectable Brahman for a courtesan, is also in favour of a period of some remoteness, although it may be allowed to mark a state of social demoralisation, a decline from the purity of Hindu institutions; at the same time, it seems probable that the practice of antiquity, as regarded the intercourse of the sexes, was much more lax than it pretends to be in modern days. The laws of MANU recognise the cohabitation of a *Śúdrá* female with a Brahman, as an inferior kind of wife, or a handmaid. Now this association is prohibited in the *Kali* age, and its occurrence in the play, in which VASANTASENÁ, who may be supposed to be a *Śúdrá*, becomes the wife of CHÁRUDATTA, indicates a period anterior to the law prohibiting the marriage of a *Śúdrá* by a Brahman. The choice of such an event for the subject of a dramatic performance, renders it likely that such a prohibition could not have been then even contemplated.

The most unquestionable proof, however, of high antiquity, is the accuracy with which *Bauddha* observances are adverted to, and the flourishing condition in which the members of that sect are represented to exist. There is not only absolute toleration, but a kind of public recognition; the ascetic who renders such essential service to the heroine being recommended or nominated by authority, chief of all the *Vihárs* or *Bauddha* establishments of *Ujjayin.*

At what period could this diffusion and prosperity of the *Bauddha* faith have occurred, and when was it likely that a popular work should describe it correctly? Many centuries have elapsed since Hindu writers were acquainted with the *Bauddhas* in their genuine characters. Their tenets are preserved in philosophical treatises with something like accuracy, but any attempt to describe their persons and practices invariably confounds them with the *Jainas.* The *Mŕichchhakaṫi* is as yet the only work where the *Bauddhas* appear undisguised. Now we know from the Christian writers of the second century, that in their days the worship of *Butta* or *Buddha* was very prevalent in India. We have every reason to believe, that shortly after that time the religion began to decline, more in consequence of the rise and growth of the Jains, probably, than any persecution of the *Bauddhas;* and as it is clear that the drama was written in the days of their prosperity, it follows that we cannot fairly assign it a later date than the first centuries of the Christian era.

From the considerations thus stated, we cannot but regard

the *Mrichchhakati* as a work of considerable antiquity, and from internal evidence may very safely attribute it to the period when SÚDRAKA the sovereign reigned, whether that be reduced to the end of the second century after Christ, or whether we admit the traditional chronology, and place him about a century before our era.

The revolution in the government of *Ujjayin*, which forms an underplot in the piece, is narrated with so little exaggeration, that it is probably founded on fact. As the simple narrative of a simple event, it is the more entitled to our credence; and it is not at all unlikely that the Brahmans, offended by their sovereign PÁLAKA'S public disregard of them, brought about a change of the government, employing a hermit and a cow-boy, or young peasant, as their instruments. This plain story is not improbably the origin of the obscure allusions which exercised the industry of Colonel Wilford, and in which, and in the purport of the word *A'rya*, the name of the cowherd in the play, and in general acceptation a title of respect, he thought he could trace a reference to the history of Christianity in India.—(*As. Res.* vol. x., Essay on the Sacred Isles of the West.) There is also an *A'rya* of some renown in the history of *Cashmir*, whom the same learned and laborious, but injudicious writer, identified with *Śálivâhana.* The real character of that personage may now be more accurately appreciated.—(Essay on the History of Cashmir, *As. Res.* vol. xv. p. 84.)

The place which the *Mrichchhakati* holds in the dramatic literature of all nations will, however, be thought matter of more interest by most readers than its antiquity or historical importance. That it is a curious and interesting picture of national manners every one will readily admit; and it is not the less valuable in this respect, that it is free from all exterior influence or adulteration. It is a portrait purely Indian. It represents a state of society sufficiently advanced in civilisation to be luxurious and corrupt, and is certainly very far from offering a flattering similitude, although not without some attractive features. There will probably be more variety of opinion on its merits as a literary composition, and its title to rank with the more polished dramas of the West may be called in question by competent judges. As observed by the spirited translator of Aristophanes, it is no longer the fashion for translators to direct the taste of their readers, and they must be left to condemn or approve for themselves. I shall therefore refrain from any further observations on this head; and if, in imitation of high authority, I venture to subjoin my own sentiments by way of epilogue, I shall do so as briefly as possible, and without any hope to bias the judgment of the public.

DRAMATIS PERSONÆ.

OF THE PRELUDE.

MANAGER. ACTRESS.

OF THE PLAY.

MEN.

Chárudatta.—A *Brahman* of a wealthy and respectable family, reduced to poverty by his munificence, beloved by *Vasantasená.*

Rohasena.—The son of *Chárudatta,* a boy.

Maitreya.—A *Brahman,* the friend and companion of *Chárudatta,* the *Vidúshaka* or *Gracioso* of the piece, a character of mixed shrewdness and simplicity, with an affectionate disposition.

Vardhamána.—The servant of *Chárudatta.*

Samsthánaka.—The brother-in-law of the *Rájá,* an ignorant, frivolous, and cruel coxcomb.

The *Vita.*—The attendant, tutor, or parasite of the preceding.

Sthávaraka.—The servant of the Prince.

A'ryaka.—A cowherd and insurgent, finally successful.

Śarvilaka.—A dissipated *Brahman,* the friend of the preceding, in love with *Madaniká.*

The *Samváhaka.*—A man whose business it has been to rub and knead the joints, but who becomes a *Bauddha* mendicant or *Śramanaka.*

Máthura.—The keeper of a gaming-house.

Darduraka.—A Gambler.

Another Gambler.

Karnapúraka.—*Vasantasená's* servant.

The Judge.

The *Śreshtin*—or Provost.

The ***Káyastha.***—**Scribe or Recorder.**

Chandanaka } Captains of the Town Guard.
Víraka }

The *Viṫa*—or parasite attendant of *Vasantasená.*

Kumbhilaka.—A servant of *Vasantasená.*

Two *Cháńḋálas*—or Public Executioners.

Officers of the Court.

Women.

The Wife of *Chárudatta.*

Vasantasená.—A courtesan, in love with *Chárudatta*, and beloved by him: the object also of *Saḿsthánaka's* addresses.

The Mother of *Vasantasená.*

Madaniká.—The attendant of *Vasantasená*, belòved by *Śarvilaka.*

Radániká.—The servant of *Chárudatta's* house.

Persons spoken of.

Pálaka.—King of *Ujjayin.*

Rebhila.—A Musician.

The *Siddha* or Seer who has prophesied *A'ryaka's* triumph.

Passengers, Attendants, Guards, &c.

Scene, *Ujjayin*, the city and the suburbs.——Time, four days.

ACT I.

PRELUDE.

BENEDICTION.*

I. MAY that profound meditation of S'AMBHU † protect you! (*the audience*) which is intent on BRAHMAN, the absorbing end of every effort of abstract vision; as he contemplates with the eye of wisdom, spirit, in himself, detached from all material instruments; his senses being restrained by holy knowledge, as he sits ruminating with suspended breath, whilst his serpents coil with the folds of his vesture round his bended knees. ‡

* It is not said by whom this is uttered, and the Manager enters after it has been spoken.

† ŚAMBHU, a name of ŚIVA.

‡ This benediction alludes to the practices and notions of the *Pátanjala* modification of the *Sánkhya* philosophy, the *Yoga*, in which, by abstract meditation, *samádhi*, the fusion (*laya*) of individual with universal spirit, or *Brahman*, is to be effected, even in the body. Spirit is said to be detached from the instruments, *karańas*, the thirteen products of matter, or *mahat*, intellect; *ahankára*, consciousness; and the eleven organs of sense and action, which are enumerated amongst the categories of the *Sánkhya* system. The mode of effecting this union is by sitting in particular *ásanas*, or postures; one of which is sitting on the hams with a cloth fastened round the knees and back, the *paryanka-bandhana*, or, as here termed, the *paryanka-granthi*, the bed-binding or bed-knot; also by suppressions of breath as long as practicable, *pránávarodha;* by keeping the vision directed either on vacuity or inwardly, *śúnyekshańa;* and by preventing as vigilantly as possible the wanderings of the senses. That this form of devotion may boast of considerable antiquity is evident from its being described and commended in the *Mahábhárata*, and being the prevailing system in the *Puráńas*, especially those of a *Śaiva* character, in some of which the origin

II. May the neck of *Nílakańtha*,* which resembles a dark cloud in hue, and which is decorated by the entwining arms of *Gaurí*,† as brilliant as the lightning, be ever your protection.

Enter MANAGER.

Enough: delay not longer to gratify the curiosity of this assembly. Saluting, therefore, this gentle audience, I apprise them that we are prepared to enact the drama entitled the *Toy-Cart*.‡

There was a celebrated poet whose gait was that of an elephant, whose eyes resembled those of the *chakora*,§ whose countenance was like the full moon, and who was of stately person and profound veracity; chiefest of the *Kshattriya* race and distinguished by the appellation of ŚÚDRA: || he was well versed in the *Ŕig-* and *Sáma-Vedas*, in mathematical sciences, in the elegant arts, and the management of elephants.¶ By the favour of *Śiva* he enjoyed eyes uninvaded by darkness,

of the *Yoga* is ascribed to ŚIVA, who taught it in the person of ŚWETA, on the Himalaya mountains in the beginning of the *Kali* age. A peculiar and later modification of *Yoga* ascetism is manifest in the cavern temples and sculptures of Salsette, Elephanta, and Ellora.—See *As. Res.* vol. xvii. 183.

* A name of ŚIVA: the god with the dark-blue throat. The colour was the effect of the poison generated at the churning of the ocean which ŚIVA swallowed.

† The wife of ŚIVA.

‡ The term is literally *clay-cart*, a child's cart made of baked clay or earthenware, from *mŕid*, earth, and *śakaťí*, a little cart. It refers to a toy belonging to the child of Chárudatta, which, as will be hereafter seen, plays an important part in the drama. The equivalent *Toy-Cart* is most familiar to our language, and is less equivocal than the literal translation. The play is termed a *prakarańa*, the second species of drama.

§ The Greek partridge.

|| See the Introduction. The additional syllable *ka* is pleonastic.

¶ The *Hasti-śikshá*: it is an accomplishment curiously characteristic of national manners. The proficiency of the Indians in this art early attracted the attention of Alexander's successors; and natives of India were so long exclusively employed in this service, that the term Indian was applied to every elephant-driver, to whatever country he might belong.—*Schlegel, Indische Bibliothek.*

and beheld his son seated on the throne: after performing the exalted *Aśwamedha*,* having attained the age of a hundred years and ten days, he entered the fatal fire.† Valiant was he in war, and ready to encounter with his single arm the elephant of his adversary; yet he was void of wrath, eminent amongst those skilled in the *Vedas*, and affluent in piety: a prince was S'ÚDRAKA. In this drama, written by him, it is thus related.

In *Avanti* ‡ lived a young Brahman of distinguished

* The emblematic sacrifice of a horse: one of the most solemn rites of Hindus in ancient times.

† That the practice of terminating life whenever burdened with age or infirmity was held, if not meritorious, to be justifiable, we know from the authorities which declare it to be so no longer. The *Nirńaya-Sindhu*, and other treatises on Hindu law, enumerate suicide on account of protracted life amongst the acts prohibited in the present age. These works are, however, comparatively modern; and that the practice of voluntary cremation was observed long subsequent to the beginning of the *Kali* era, we know from classical authority. The stories told by Herodotus of the Indians who put their infirm or aged relations to death, originated probably in some indistinct accounts of this usage. Megasthenes asserts that there was no fixed rule on this subject, and intimates that the sages of India reprehended the practice. *Zarmanochagas* (*Śramanáchárya*) burnt himself at Athens, "after the custom of his country;" and *Calanus* (*Kalyáńa*) mounted the funeral pile at Pasargadæ in the presence of the astonished Greeks, who were at a loss to consider the act as that of a sage or a madman, and were never of a mood to imitate such a model. Whether the rite was founded on positive prescription we are not aware, but instances of it are given in works of the highest character and of a weight little inferior to the inspired codes. In the *Rámáyańa*, *Śarabhanga* the sage only delays his cremation until he has seen Ráma; after which, "having prepared the fire and offered oblations with the customary prayers, the pious and perfect *Śarabhanga* entered the flames."—*Árańya-Kánda*. The commentary on the drama states that the ceremony should be accompanied with the sacrifice called *sarvaswara*: it should probably be *sarvamedha*, prayers and oblations for universal success. The commentator is rather at a loss to explain how the author of the play announces his own death, and is disposed to ascribe it to his prophetic foresight acquired by astrological computation. There can be little doubt, however, that such part of these proems as relates to the personal history of the author is usually the work of another hand.

‡ The modern Ougein.

rank,* but of exceeding poverty; his name was CHÁRUDATTA. Of the many excellences of CHÁRUDATTA, a courtesan, VASANTASENÁ by name, became enamoured, and the story of their loves is the subject of king S'ÚDRAKA'S drama, which exhibits the infamy of wickedness, the villainy of law, the efficacy of virtue, and the triumph of faithful love.

(*Walks round the stage.*)

Hey! the boards are deserted:† where can all the actors have vanished? Ah, I understand. Empty is the house of the childless—empty is the heart of one that has no friends;‡ the universe is a blank to the blockhead, and all is desolate to the poor. I have been chanting and reciting until my eyes ache, the pupils twinkling with hunger, like the seeds of the lotus shrivelled in the hot weather by the rays of a scorching sun.§ I will call one of my wenches, and see if there be anything in the house for breakfast. What ho there—Here am I! But I had better talk to them in a language they can understand.‖—What ho—I say! What with long fasting and loud shouting my limbs are shrivelled like dry lotus stalks. It is high time to take myself home, and see what is prepared for my coming. This is my mansion—I will go in.

* The *Sárthaváha* of the Brahmans. In many of the Hindu cities the different classes of the community of every rank still acknowledge certain of their members as their hereditary headmen or provosts—such is the sense of *Śreshṫin* or *Seth*: the title in common use is *Chaudri* or *Sirdar*. It is also to be inferred from this title, that *Chárudatta*, though a Brahman by birth, is a merchant by occupation.

† The *Sangíta-śálá*, a hall or chamber for music, singing, and dancing.

‡ This passage occurs in the *Hitopadeśa* and *Panchatantra*, borrowed perhaps from the drama. The latter reads *hṙidayaṁśúnyam*, instead of *chiraśúnyam*: the metre allows of either, and the construction of the sentence evidently requires the former.

§ The expression is, *Kshudhá mama akshiṅí khaṫakhaṫáyete*, which may be rendered as in the text, but cannot be translated, for the verb is made from the noun with more regard to the sound than the sense.

‖ Or in *Prákṙit*, which is spoken always by the female characters; he accordingly proceeds in that dialect throughout the whole of the Prelude.

*Enters.**

Hey day !—Some new frolic is going on in this mansion of mine. The ground, like a young damsel fresh from her toilet, wears a *tilaka* † smeared with the discoloured water of the rice that has been boiled in the iron kettle, and is perfumed with most savoury smells. Verily, my hunger increaseth. What, in the name of wonder, have my people found a treasure—or from the promptings of my appetite do I fancy everything smacks of boiled rice? If there be no breakfast for me at home, this hunger will be the death of me. Yet everything puts on a new face : one hussy is grinding perfumes, another is stringing flowers : ‡ the meaning of all this must be inquired into. Come hither one of you.

Enter ACTRESS.

Act. Here am I, sir.

Man. Welcome, welcome.

Act. What are your commands?

Man. Hark ye, girl, I have been bawling myself both hoarse and hungry: is there anything in the house for me to eat?

Act. There is everything, sir.

Man. Indeed ; and what is there?

Act. For example—there is rice, dressed or undressed, sugar, curds ; in short, there is sustenance for a century §—so may the gods comply with all your desires.

* *Praviśya avalokya cha :* Having entered and looked round. How the entrance is managed we are rather at a loss to conjecture, as no change of scene was probably attempted. In the spacious hall, however, in which the piece was acted, one part of the stage was in all likelihood supposed to represent the exterior, the other the interior of the dwelling.

† Or *viśeshaka,* a mark with some coloured substance made in the middle of the forehead.

‡ The use of perfumes and garlands amongst the Hindus affords a parallel, both as an accompaniment to religious and convivial rites, to the usages of Athens and Rome.

§ *Ajjeńa attavvam rasáańam.* Literally, the drug that confers immortality is to be eaten by the master.

Man. Hark ye, my girl, is all this in my house, or do you jest?

Act. (*Apart.*) Oh, as he doubts, I will have a laugh at him. (*Aloud.*) Indeed and indeed, sir, there is all that I have mentioned—in the market.

Man. Ah, you hussy! May you be so disappointed. The deuce take you—you have hoisted me up like a ball on a turret top,* that I might tumble down again.

Act. Patience, sir, patience, I did but jest.

Man. Then what is the meaning of all this unusual preparation; this grinding of perfumes and stringing of chaplets? The ground is strewed with offerings of flowers of every dye.

Act. We hold a solemn fast to-day.†

Man. A fast, for what?

Act. That we may have a desirable master.‡

Man. In this world, or the next?

Act. Ah, in the next, to be sure.

Man. Here, gentles (*to the audience*), here is pretty usage: these damsels would engage a new manager in another world at my expense in this!

* The expression used does not seem to have been understood by the commentator. The words are, *varańila lambuo* (S. *varańda-lambuka*). The first is said to mean a long stick; the second, a column of clay fastened to one end of it, which, when raised mechanically to a given height, falls down by its own weight. A machine of this kind, a stick or bamboo resting on a fulcrum, with a weight at one end and a rope and bucket at the other, is used in some parts of India for drawing water. Or *varańda* is explained a lofty part of a building; *lambuka*, one part of it, which having been carried up to be attached to the top of the *varańda*, as a ball or pinnacle, falls down by accident. Neither of these explanations is very satisfactory, and the occurrence of such terms as these, of which the import must have been once familiar, but which is now uncertain, is a circumstance corroborative of the supposed antiquity of the composition.

† Every fast, when held as a religious observance on particular occasions, is a prelude to a feast.

‡ The Manager asks what is the name of the fast, every religious rite bearing its own appellation. The Actress replies, it is called the *Ahirúbabadi* or *Abhirúpapati*, which implies the meaning given in the text.

Act. Be appeased, sir. I have observed the fast, in order that I might have you again for my master in a future birth.

Man. That alters the case. But, pray, who directed you to hold this fast?

Act. Your particular friend, Chúrńavŕiddha.

Man. Oh, you son of a slave, I shall see you, Chúrńavŕiddha, some day or other, fast bound by king *Pálaka*, like the perfumed tresses of a new-married girl.

Act. Pardon us, dear sir; this fast was observed to secure the future felicity of our worthy Manager. (*Falls at his feet.*)

Man. Rise; enough. We must now consider by whom this fast is to be completed.

Act. We must invite some Brahman* of our own degree.

Man. Well, go, finish your preparations: I will seek the Brahman.

Act. I obey. [*Exit.*

MANAGER.

Alas! in such a flourishing city as *Ujjayin*, where am I to find a Brahman who is not of a superior rank to mine? (*Looking out.*) Yonder comes Maitreya, the friend of Chárudatta. I will ask him; he is poor enough. What, ho! Maitreya; condescend to be the first to eat in my house to-day.

MAITREYA (*behind the scenes*).

Call some other Brahman; I am particularly engaged.

Man. Food is provided; no enemy is in the way, and you shall have a present into the bargain.

Mait. (*Behind.*) I have already given you an answer. It is useless to disturb me.

Man. I shall not prevail upon him, and must therefore set off in quest of some other Brahman. [*Exit.*

* A Brahman should be invited to eat on these occasions before the household break their fast. The Manager and his family belong of course to the Brahmanical tribe.

(The Scene is supposed to represent a street on one side, and on the other the first court of Chárudatta's house: the outside of the house is also seen in the part next the street.)*

MAITREYA *enters the court with a piece of cloth in his hand.*

Truly, Maitreya, your condition is sad enough, and well qualified to subject you to be picked up in the street and fed by strangers. In the days of Chárudatta's prosperity, I was accustomed to stuff myself till I could eat no more, on scented dishes, until I breathed perfume; and sat lolling at yonder gateway, dyeing my fingers like a painter's, by dabbling amongst the coloured comfits, or chewing the cud at leisure like a high-fed city bull.† Now, in the season of his poverty, I wander about from house to house, like a tame pigeon, to pick up such crumbs as I can get. I am now sent by his dear friend Chúrńavŕiddha, with this garment that has lain amongst jasmine flowers till it is quite scented by them: it is for Chárudatta's wearing, when he has finished his devotions.—Oh, here he comes, he is presenting the oblation to the household gods.†

Enter CHÁRUDATTA *and* RADANIKÁ.

Chár. (With a sigh.)

Alas! how changed; the offering to the gods,

* We have already observed that it does not seem probable that the Hindus ever knew what scenes were, and that they substituted curtains for them. In the present case, the whole machinery might have been a curtain intersecting the stage at a right angle to the flat, one side being the interior, the other the exterior of Chárudatta's house.

† The Hindus are accustomed at marriages and other ceremonials to let loose a bull, who thenceforward rambles about at will without an owner. No person would presume to appropriate a stray animal of this kind, and many think it a merit to feed him. In large towns, where these bulls are most abundant, they are generally in good case, and numerous enough to be very much in the way, although they are rarely mischievous. They seem to know their privileged character, and haunt the market-places and shops with an air of independence. At Benares, they are proverbially abundant, and that city is famed for its *ránrh, sánrh,* and *sirhi,* or widows, bulls, and landing-places.

That swans and stately storks, in better time
About my threshold flocking, bore away,
Now a scant tribute to the insect tribe,
Falls 'midst rank grass, by worms to be devoured.*

(*Sits down.*)

Mait. I will approach the respectable Chárudatta. Health to you; may you prosper.

Chár. Maitreya, friend of all seasons, welcome; sit you down.

Mait. As you command. (*Sits down.*) This garment, perfumed by the jasmines it has lain amongst, is sent to you by your friend Chúrńavŕiddha, to be worn by you at the close of your devotions.

Chár. (*Takes it and appears thoughtful.*)

Mait. On what do you meditate?

Chár. My friend—

The happiness that follows close on sorrow,
Shows like a lamp that breaks upon the night:

* No house is supposed to be without its tutelary divinity, but the notion attached to this character is now very far from precise. The deity who is the object of hereditary and family worship, the *Kula-devatá*, is always one of the leading personages of the Hindu mythology, as Śiva, Vishńu, or Durgá, but the *Gŕiha-devatá* rarely bears any distinct appellation. In Bengal, the domestic god is sometimes the *śálagrám* stone, sometimes the *tulasí* plant; sometimes a basket with a little rice in it, and sometimes a water-jar—to either of which a brief adoration is daily addressed, most usually by the females of the family. Occasionally small images of Lakshmí or Chańdí fulfil the office, or should a snake appear he is venerated as the guardian of the dwelling. In general, however, in former times the household deities were regarded as the unseen spirits of ill, the ghosts and goblins who hovered about every spot, and claimed some particular sites as their own. Offerings were made to them in the open air, by scattering a little rice with a short formula at the close of all ceremonies to keep them in good humour. Thus, at the end of the daily ceremony, the householder is enjoined by Manu "to throw up his oblation (*bali*) in the open air to all the gods, to those who walk by day and those who walk by night."—3, 90. Such is the nature of the rite alluded to in the drama. In this light, the household gods correspond better with the *genii locorum* than with the *lares* or *penates* of antiquity.

But he that falls from affluence to poverty,
May wear the human semblance, but exists
A lifeless form alone.

Mait. What think you preferable then, death or poverty?

Chár. Had I the choice,
Death, and not poverty, were my election:
To die is transient suffering; to be poor,
Interminable anguish.

Mait. Nay, never heed. The loss of your wealth, lavished upon your kind friends, only enhances your merits; as the moon looks most lovely when reduced to the slender fragment that the draughts of the gods for half a month have left it.*

Chár. I do not, trust me, grieve for my lost wealth:
But that the guest no longer seeks the dwelling,
Whence wealth has vanished, does, I own, afflict me.
Like the ungrateful bees, who wanton fly
The elephant's broad front, when thick congeals
The dried-up dew,† they visit me no more.

Mait. The sons of slaves! your guest is ever ready to make a morning meal of a fortune: he is like the cow-boy, who, as if afraid of a gad-fly, drives his herds from place to place in the thicket, and sets them to feed always in fresh pasture.

Chár. 'Tis true.—I think not of my wasted fortune.
As fate decrees, so riches come and vanish.
But I lament to find the love of friends
Hangs all unstrung because a man is poor.

* The moon is supposed to be the reservoir of *amŕita* or ambrosia, and to furnish the gods and manes with the supply. "It is replenished from the sun during the fortnight of the increase. On the full moon the gods adore that planet for one night, and from the first day all of them, together with the *pitŕis* and *ŕishis,* drink one *kalá* or digit daily until the ambrosia is exhausted."—*Váyu-Puráńa.*

† At certain periods a thick dew exhales from the elephants' temples. The peculiarity, though known to Strabo, seems to have escaped naturalists ll lately, when it was noticed by Cuvier.

And then with poverty comes disrespect ;
From disrespect does self-dependence fail,
Then scorn and sorrow, following, overwhelm
The intellect ; and when the judgment fails
The being perishes ; and thus from poverty
Each ill that pains humanity proceeds.*

Mait. Ah well, it is but waste of thought to send it after the wealth-hunters ; we have had enough of this subject.

Chár. But poverty is aye the curse of thought.
It is our enemy's reproach ; the theme
Of scorn to our best friends and dearest kin.
I had abjured the world and sought the hermitage,
But that my wife had shared in my distress.
Alas, the fires of sorrow in the heart
Glow impotent ; they pain but burn not.
My friend, I have already made oblation
Unto the household gods—Go you to where
The four roads meet, and there present it
To the Great Mothers.†

Mait. Not I, indeed.

Chár. Why not?

Mait. Of what use is it? You have worshipped the gods: what have they done for you? it is labour in vain to bestow upon them adoration.

Chár. Speak not profanely. It is our duty.
And the gods
Undoubtedly are pleased with what is offered

* This passage occurs in the *Hitopadeśa,* with a slight variation.

† The *Mátŕi* is the personified energy of a divinity, and in a figurative sense the mother of gods and men. The Mátŕis are usually reckoned seven or eight, but in one enumeration they are made sixteen. The presentation of oblations to them as a regular and permanent rite is no longer known in Gangetic India. *Tántrika* ceremonies addressed to the sixteen Mátŕis are not uncommon, but the rite in the text appears to be a matter of course, and seems to take the place of that enjoined by Manu to the *Pitŕis,* the manes or progenitors. "Turning to the south, let him present all the residue of his oblations to the *Pitŕis.*"—3, 91.

In lowliness of spirit and with reverence,
In thought, and deed, and pious self-denial:
Go therefore and present the offering.

Mait. I will not go, indeed; send somebody else. With me every part of the ritual is apt to get out of its place, and, as in the reflection of a mirror, the right becomes left and the left right. At this time of the evening, too, the royal road is crowded with loose persons, with cut-throats, courtiers, and courtesans:* amongst such a set I shall fare like the unhappy mouse, that fell into the clutches of the snake which was lying in ambush for the frog.† I cannot go, indeed. Why not go yourself? You have nothing to do but to sit here.

Chár. Well, well—attend then whilst I tell my beads.

[*They retire.*

(*Behind the scenes.*) Stop, Vasantasená, stop!

Enter VASANTASENÁ *pursued by* SAḾSTHÁNAKA, *the King's brother-in-law, the* VIṬA,‡ *and his own Servant.*

Viṭa. Stop, Vasantasená, stop! Why, losing your gentleness in your fears, do you ply those feet so fast, that should be nimble only in the dance? You run along like the timid deer from the pursuing hunter, casting tremulous glances fearfully around.

Saḿs. Stop, Vasantasená, stop! Why do you thus scamper away, stumbling at every step? Be pacified, you are in no danger. With love alone is my poor heart inflamed; it is burnt to a cinder, like a piece of meat upon the blazing coals.

Ser. Stop, lady, stop! Why, sister, do you fly? She runs along like a pea-hen in summer with a tail in full feather,

* This, besides its general bearing, announces the approaching entrance of *Vasantasená* and her pursuers, agreeably to the rule, that no character is to enter without previous intimation.

† If we are to consider the antiquity of this play as established, this passage bears testimony to the early currency of apologues in India.

‡ The *Viṭa* is the companion and minister of the pleasures of *Saḿsthánaka*. See the remark made on this character in the introductory observations on the dramatic system of the Hindus, p, xlvii.

whilst my master follows her, like the young hound that chases the bird through the thicket.

Viťa. Stop, Vasantasená, stop! You tremble like the young plantain tree, whilst the ends of your red vesture wanton on the wind. The seeds of the red lotus are put to shame by your glowing eyes, and the bed of orpiment, when first penetrated by the axe, is rivalled by the complexion of your cheeks.

Saṁs. Stop, Vasantasená, stop! Why do you thus fly from a liking, a love, a passion which you inflame? My nights you deprive of rest, and you avoid me by day. It is unavailing: you will trip and tumble into my hands as *Kuntí* fell into those of *Rávańa.**

Viťa. Why, Vasantasená, do you grace my steps by leaving traces for them to obliterate? Like a snake from the monarch of the birds,† you glide away from me, but vain is your flight. I could outstrip the wind in such a chase, and shall I not overtake so delicate a fugitive?

Saṁs. Most worthy sir, I have invoked her by ten names. I have called her the taper lash of that filcher of broad pieces, *Káma;* the fish-eater, the figurante, the pug-nosed untamable shrew. I have termed her Love's dining-dish—the gulf of the poor man's substance—the walking frippery—the harlot—the hussy—the baggage—the wanton. I have addressed her by all these pretty names,‡ and yet she will have nothing to say to me.

* *Kuntí* is the mother of the *Páńđava* princes; *Rávańa,* the giant king of *Lanká*, destroyed by *Ráma.* The former is a character of the *Mahábhárata,* the latter of the *Rámáyańa.* There is no sort of connexion between the two, and instead of *Kuntí* it should have been *Sítá*, the wife of *Ráma,* whom *Rávańa* carried off. It may be here remarked, that this confusion of persons and events is invariably repeated by *Saṁsthánaka,* who thus evinces both his ignorance and pretension.

† *Garuđa,* the bird on which *Vishńu* rides, between whom and the serpent race is a deadly feud, originating in a dispute between their respective parents, *Kadrú* and *Vinatá,* the wives of *Kaśyapa.*

‡ To address a deity by a number of appellations is the readiest way to

Viṫa. Why, Vasantasená, do you fly us? The trembling pendants of your ears toss agitated against your cheeks, and make such music as the lute to a master's touch.* You fly like the female crane that starts away from the sound of thunder.

Saṁs. Your ornaments jingle to your paces as you run from us, as *Draupadí*† fled from *Ráma.*‡ But I shall have you; I will dart upon you like *Hanumat*§ upon *Subhadrá,*|| the lovely sister of *Viśwávasu.*¶

Ser. Relent, relent, be gracious to the prince's friend; accept the flesh and the fish. When they can get fish and flesh, the dogs prey not upon carrion.

Viṫa. What should have so strangely alarmed you? Believe me, you look like the guardian goddess of the city, as round your slender waist sparkles with starlike gems that tinkling zone, and your countenance is pale with terror.

Saṁs. As the female jackal is hunted by the dogs, so run you, and so we follow: you run along with your prey, and bear off from me both heart and pericardium.**

secure his good graces; so says the commentator. As to the names themselves, some latitude has been necessarily used in the translation, although an attempt has been made to convey some notion of their purport; the strain is not unlike that of our old comedies; the original is as follows: "*Bháve! Bháve! Eśá Ńáńaka-múśi-káma káśiká, Machchháśiká, Láśiká, Ńiśáśá, Kulańáśiká, Avaśiká, Kámáha-manjúśiká, Eśá veśabahú, Śuveśa-nilaá Veśangańá, Veśiá, Eśe śe daśa-ńámake mayi kale, Ajjá bi mam ṇechchhadi.*"

* Literally, such as is made by the touch of the *Viṫa* (*Viṫajana-nakha-ghaṫṫiteva víńá*), which indicates the particular art cultivated by this character.

† The wife of the *Páńḋavas* and heroine of the *Mahábhárata.*

‡ The hero of the *Rámáyańa.*

§ The monkey friend of *Ráma.*

|| The sister of *Kŕishńa,* carried off by *Arjuna,* as related in the *Mahábhárata.*

¶ This is probably intended for a blunder, instead of *Vásudeva. Viśwávasu* is the name of a demigod of an inferior order, one of the *Gandharbas,* or choristers of *Indra's* heaven.

** *Śaveṫṫhanaṁ me halaaṁ halanti,* "carrying off my heart and its envelopes," *veṫṫhanam* being the *Prákŕit* of *veshṫanam.*

Vas. (*Calling for her female attendants.*) What ho! Pallavá, Parabhŕitiká.

Saṁs. (*In alarm to the Viṫa.*) Eh, sir, sir! men, men!

Viṫa. Never fear.

Vas. Mádhaviká, what ho!

Viṫa. Blockhead; she is calling her servants.

Saṁs. What, her women?

Viṫa. To be sure.

Saṁs. Who is afraid? I am a hero—a match for a hundred of them.

Vas. Alas, alas! my people are not within hail: I must trust to myself alone for my escape.

Viṫa. Search about, search about.

Saṁs. Vasantasená, what is the use of your bawling there for bud and blossom, or all spring together!* Who is to preserve you when I pursue? What could *Bhímasena* † do for you, or the son of *Jamadagni*, ‡ or the son of *Kuntí*, § or *Daśakandhara* || himself? I would take them, like *Duḣśásana*, ¶ by their hair, and, as you shall see, with one touch of my well-sharpened sword off goes your head. Come, come, we have had enough of your running away. One who is desirous of dying cannot be said to live.

Vas. Good sir, I am only a weak woman.

Viṫa. True, therefore you may live.

Saṁs. True, you shall not die.

* Mistaking the names for *pallava*, a shoot, *mádhaviká*, a sort of creeper, and alluding to the latter's blossoming in the spring.

† The second of the sons of *Páńḋu*.

‡ *Paraśuráma*.

§ *Karńa*, or either of the *Páńḋava* princes.

|| *Rávańa*, the ten-headed sovereign of *Lanká*.

¶ One of the *Kaurava* princes, who dragged *Draupadí* by the hair into the public court; an act of bitter insult to the *Páńḋava* princes, in revenge of which *Bhíma* vowed he would never be appeased till he had drunk the aggressor's blood. In the war that ensued he killed *Duḣśásana*, and fulfilled his vow.

Vas. (*Apart.*) His very courtesy appals me. It shall be so. (*Aloud.*) Pray, sirs, why do you thus pursue me, or why address such language to me? Do you seek my jewels?

Viṫa. Fie, fie, what have we to do with your ornaments? Who plucks the blossoms of the creeper?

Vas. What is it, then, you require?

Saṁs. That I, who am a person of celestial nature, a mortal *Vásudeva*,* obtain your affections.

Vas. Get you gone; you talk idly.

Saṁs. (*Claps his hands and laughs.*) What think you of that, sir? Hear how this gentle damsel regards me: she bids me go and rest myself, no doubt, after my fatigue in running after her;† but I swear by your head and my feet,‡ that I have gone astray neither in town nor village, but have kept close to your heels all the way, by the which I am wearied.

Viṫa. (*Apart.*) The blockhead! he misapprehends the whole. (*Aloud.*) Why, Vasantasená, you act quite out of character: the dwelling of a harlot is the free resort of youth: a courtesan is like a creeper that grows by the road-side—her person is an article for sale, her love a thing that money will buy, and her welcome is equally bestowed upon the amiable and disgusting. The sage and the idiot, the Brahman and the outcast, all bathe in the same stream, and the crow and the peacock perch upon the branches of the same creeper. The Brahman, the Kshattriya, the Vaiśya, and all of every caste are ferried over in the same boat; and like the boat, the creeper, and the stream, the courtesan is equally accessible to all.

Vas. What you say may be just, but, believe me, merit alone, not brutal violence, inspires love.

* *Kṙishṅa.*

† *Vasantasená's* exclamation was *śántam*, an interjection of repugnance, or disgust. *Saṁsthánaka* assumes she said *śránta*, or *Prákṙit*, *śánta*, weary. The quibble is lost in the translation, but that is of no very great importance.

‡ A very affronting adjuration.

Saḿs. Sir, sir, the truth is, that the baggage has had the perverseness to fall in love with a miserable wretch, one Chárudatta, whom she met in the garden of *Kámadeva's* temple : he lives close by here on our left, so take care she does not slip through our fingers.

Viṫa. (*Aside.*) Confound the fool, he lets out everything he ought to conceal. In love with Chárudatta—humph ! no wonder ; it is truly said, pearls string with pearls : well, let it be so, never mind this simpleton. (*Aloud.*) What say you, is the house of Chárudatta on our left ? the deuce it is.

Saḿs. Very true, I assure you.

Vas. (*Aside.*) Indeed ! the house of Chárudatta so near ! These wretches have unintentionally befriended me, and promoted a meeting with my beloved.

Saḿs. Sir, sir, Vasantasená is no longer visible ; she is lost in the dark, like an ink-cake in a pile of black beans.

Viṫa. It is very dark, indeed ! The gloom cheats my eyesight of its faculty ; my eyes open only to be closed by it ; such obscurity envelops everything, as if the heavens rained lamp-black : sight is as unavailing as the service of a worthless man.

Saḿs. I must search for Vasantasená.

Viṫa. Indeed ! (*Aloud.*) Is there not anything by which you may trace her ?

Saḿs. What should there be ?

Viṫa. The tinkling of her ornaments ; the odour of her perfumes ; and the fragrance of her garland.

Saḿs. Very true ; I can hear with my nostrils the scent of her garland spreading through the darkness, but I do not see the sound of her ornaments.*

* So in the "Midsummer's Night's Dream"—

Bottom as Pyramus :

"I see a voice : now will I to the chink,
To spy an' I can hear my Thisby's face."

And in the same—

"Eye of man hath not heard, nor ear seen," &c.

Vita. (*Apart, in the direction of Vas.*) Very well, Vasantasená. True, you are hidden by the gloom of the evening, like the lightning between gathering clouds, but the fragrance of your chaplet, the music of your anklets, will betray you,—do you hear?

Vas. (*To herself.*) I hear and comprehend. (*Takes off her garland and the rings from her ankles.*) If I am not mistaken, the private entrance is in this direction: by carrying my hands along the wall—(*feels for the door*)—ah, it is shut.

Chár. (*Within the court.*) My prayer* is finished; now, Maitreya, go, present the offering to the divine mothers.

Mait. I tell you I will not go.

Chár. Alas it does embitter poverty—

That then our friends grow deaf to our desires,
And lend a keener anguish to our sorrows.
The poor man's truth is scorned: the tender light
Of each mild virtue languishes; suspicion
Stamps him the perpetrator of each crime
That others are the authors of: no man seeks
To form acquaintance with him, nor exchange
Familiar greeting or respectful courtesy.
If e'er he find a place in rich men's dwellings
At solemn festivals, the wealthier guests
Survey him with disdainful wonder; and
Whene'er by chance he meets upon the road
With state and wealth, he sneaks into a corner,
Ashamed of his scant covering, till they pass,
Rejoicing to be overlooked. Believe me,
He who incurs the guilt of poverty
Adds a sixth sin to those we term most heinous. †
In truth, I mourn e'en poverty for thee,

* Literally, *japa*—inaudible repetition of prayer.

† The five great sins in the Hindu code are—stealing gold, drinking spirituous liquors, murder of a Brahman, adultery with the wife of a spiritual teacher, and association with a person guilty of either of these crimes.

Whose cherished dwelling is this wasting frame,
And oft I sadly wonder what asylum,
When this shall be no more, shall then receive thee.

Mait. Ah! well, if I must go, I must; but let your maid Radaniká go along with me.

Chár. Radaniká, follow Maitreya.

Rad. As you command, sir.

Mait. Here, Radaniká, do you take the offerings and the lamp, while I open the back-door. (*Opens the door.*)

Vas. (*On the outside.*) Luckily for me, the door is opened: I shall now get in. Ah the lamp. (*Brushes it out with her scarf, and enters.*)

Chár. What was that?

Mait. Opening the door let in a gust of wind, which has blown the lamp out: never mind—go on, Radaniká. I will just step into the house and re-light the lamp, and will be with you again immediately.

Saṁs. (*On the outside.*) What can have become of Vasantasená!

Viṫa. Search, search.

Saṁs. So I do, but cannot find her—I have her. (*Lays hold of the Viṫa.*)

Viṫa. Blockhead, this is I.

Saṁs. Stand out of the way then. (*Lays hold of the servant.*) Now then I have caught her.

Ser. No, your honour has caught me.

Saṁs. Here then, this way, this way, here, master, servant, servant, master, here, here, stand here.* (*Lays hold of Radaniká by the hair as she comes out.*) Ha, ha! now I have her indeed. I detected her endeavouring to escape by the scent of the garland. I have her fast by the hair, as *Cháṅakya* caught *Draupadí.* †

* We may suppose that some display of practical wit took place here.

† *Cháṅakya* was a celebrated statesman and writer on politics: he was the minister of *Chandragupta*: it is needless to add, he could not possibly be connected with the story of *Draupadí.*

Viṫa. Very well, young lady, very pretty; running after honest men's sons, in the pride of youth, with your head full dressed with flowers; you are caught in the fact.

Saṁs. You are the young girl, I believe, that was caught by the hair of the head: now call, and cry, and scream, and curse, and abuse *Śiva, Śambhu, Śankara,* and *Íśwara.**

Rad. (*In alarm.*) Bless me, gentlemen, what do you mean?

Viṫa. How now! the voice is that of another person.

Saṁs. Oh, sir, your female can change her voice when she will, as the cat mews in a different key when she attempts to steal cream.

Viṫa. Such a difference can scarcely be, and yet it is possible. Yes, it may be she has been taught to disguise her voice in the way of her profession, both for the purposes of deception and the articulation of the gamut.

Enter MAITREYA.

Mait. How funnily the lamp burns: it goes flutter, flutter, in the evening breeze, like the heart of a goat just caught in a snare. (*Seeing Radaniká and the rest.*) Hey, Radaniká!

Saṁs. Holloa, master—a man.

Mait. What is all this?—it is not right; not right at all—although Chárudatta be poor, yet strangers are not to come into his house without leave.

Rad. See here; Maitreya, here 's disrespect to me.

Mait. Not you merely, but all of us. To me as well as you.

Rad. You, indeed—how can that be?

Mait. Why, have they been rude to you?

Rad. Rude indeed—to be sure, rude enough.

Mait. No, really.

Rad. Yes, really.

Mait. (*In wrath and taking up a stick.*) Then I will do for them: this is quite unbearable—every dog will bark in his own kennel, and why not a Brahman? With this dry bambu

* All names of ŚIVA.

staff, as crooked as our fortunes, will I batter that head of thine, thou abominable villain.

Vita. Patience, patience! worthy Brahman.*

Mait. (*To him.*) Eh! this cannot be the offender. (*Turns to Saṁsthánaka.*) Oh! here he is. Oh, you king's brother-in-law! you abominable miscreant! have you no decency? Do not you know that, notwithstanding the worthy Chárudatta be poor, he is an ornament to Ujjayin, and how dare you think of forcing your way into his house and maltreating his people? There is no disgrace in an untoward fate; disgrace is in misconduct; a worthless man of wealth is contemptible.

Vita. Worthy Brahman, pardon us, we mistook the person: we intended no affront, but looking for a female——

Mait. For her? (*Pointing to Radaniká.*)

Vita. Heaven forbid!—No, no, for a girl her own mistress, who has run away. Searching for her, we lighted upon this damsel, and committed an unintentional indecorum. We beg your pardon, and submit ourselves to whatever you may please to ordain. (*Gives his sword and falls at Maitreya's feet.*)

Mait. You are a man of sense; arise. I knew not your quality when I addressed you so roughly; now I am aware of it, I shall treat you with proper politeness.

Vita. You are entitled to our respect. I will only rise on one condition.

Mait. Declare it.

Vita. That you will say nothing to Chárudatta of what has chanced.

Mait. I will not say anything to him on the subject.

Vita. I will place your kindness, Brahman, on my head; armed with every excellence, you are invincible by arms.

Saṁs. What do you mean, my friend, by putting your hands together and falling at the feet of such a contemptible fellow?

* *Mahá-Bráhmaṅa*, great Brahman, is the term used; it is also an expression of contempt, and is applied to those Brahmans who officiate for Śúdras.

Viťa. I am afraid.

Saṁs. Of what?

Viťa. Of the eminent virtues of Chárudatta.

Saṁs. Very eminent, indeed, when they cannot afford his visitors a dinner.

Viťa. Never mind that; he has become impoverished by his liberality: like the lake in the summer which is exhausted by relieving the thirst of the travellers; in his prosperity he was kind to all, and never treated any one with disrespect.

Saṁs. Who is this slave, the son of a slave? Is he a warrior, a hero? Is he *Páńdu,** *Śwetaketu,*† the son of *Rádhá,*‡ *Rávańa,*§ or *Indradatta?*‖ Was he begotten on *Kuntí,* by *Ráma,* or is he *Áśwatthåman,*¶ *Dharmaputra,*** or *Jaťáyu?*††

Viťa. No, you wiseacre, I will tell you who he is: he is Chárudatta, the tree of plenty to the poor, bowed down by its abundant fruit. He is the cherisher of the good, the mirror of the wise, a touchstone of piety, an ocean of decorum, the doer of good to all, of evil to none, a treasure of manly virtues, intelligent, liberal, and upright; in a word, he only is worthy of admiration: in the plenitude of his merits he may

* The brother of *Dhŕitaráshťra,* and parent of the princes who are the heroes of the *Mahábhárata.* He was born of a fair complexion, whence his name, "The Pale." He left the kingdom of ancient Delhi to his brother, and retired to lead an ascetic life in the Himálaya mountains, where he died.

† *Śwetaketu* was a sage, the son of *Uddálaka,* and is mentioned in the *Mahábhárata.*

‡ *Rádhá* was the wife of the charioteer of *Duryodhana,* and bred *Karńa* as her son, after he was exposed on the banks of the Yamuná by his own mother.

§ *Rávańa* has already been noticed.

‖ *Indradatta* is a warrior in the *Mahábhárata.*

¶ *Áśwatthåman* is the son of *Drońa,* the military preceptor of the *Kaurava* and *Páńďava* princes; he fought in favour of *Dhŕitaráshťra.*

** The son of *Dharma,* the ruler of *Tartarus,* is the elder of the Páńďava princes *Yudhishťhira.*

†† This is a marvellous man-bird, the younger brother of *Sampáti*n and son of *Garuďa:* he attempted to rescue *Sítá* when carried off by *Rávańa,* and was slain by him.

be said to live indeed; other men merely breathe. So come, we had better depart.

Saṁs. What, without Vasantasená?

Viṭa. Vasantasená is lost.

Saṁs. How lost?

Viṭa. Like the sight of the blind, the health of the sick, the wisdom of the fool, and the prosperity of the sluggard; like the learning of the dull and dissipated, and the friendship of foes.

Saṁs. Well, I will not go hence until I recover her.

Viṭa. You may as well. Have you never heard the saying:

An elephant may be held by a chain,
A steed be curbed by his rider's art;
But even go hang, if you cannot gain
The only bond woman obeys—her heart.

You may as well, therefore, come away.

Saṁs. Go, if you please; I shall stay where I am.

Viṭa. Very well, I leave you. [*Exit.*

Saṁs. Let him go; who cares? (*To Maitreya.*) Now, you crow-foot pated pupil of mendicity, down with you.

Mait. We are cast down already.

Saṁs. By whom?

Mait. By destiny.

Saṁs. Get up then.

Mait. So we will.

Saṁs. When?

Mait. When fortune smiles.

Saṁs. Weep, weep.

Mait. So we do.

Saṁs. What for?

Mait. Our misfortunes.

Saṁs. Laugh, blockhead, laugh!

Mait. So we shall.

Saṁs. When?

Mait. When Chárudatta is again in prosperity.

Saṁs. Hark ye, fellow; do you carry a message from me

to the beggar Chárudatta. Say to him thus from me: A common wanton, hight Vasantasená, covered with gold upon gold, like the chief of a troop of comedians about to act a new play, saw you in the garden of *Kámadeva's* * temple, and took a fancy to you. Having put us to the trouble of using violence to secure her, she fled, and has taken refuge in your house. If you will give her up, and put her yourself into my hands without any litigation, her delivery shall be rewarded with my most particular regard; but if you will not put her forth, depend upon my eternal and exterminating enmity. Consider that a preserved pumpkin, a dried potherb, fried flesh, and boiled rice † that has stood for a night in the cold weather, stink when kept too long. Let him then not lose this opportunity. You speak well and distinctly; you must, therefore, speak my message so that I may hear you, as I sit in the upper terrace of my house, here adjoining. If you do not say what I have told you, I shall grind your head between my teeth, as I would a nut beneath my door. ‡

* The temple of *Kámadeva* makes a great figure in all the dramas and tales of the Hindus of any antiquity. There was always a garden or grove attached to it, to which no sanctity, however, seems to have been ascribed, as was to those of Albunea or Dodona: it was rather the Daphne of the Hindu religion, the resort of the young of either sex at public festivals, and the scene of many love adventures: although the reserve, to which Hindu women were always subjected in public, rendered it no school for the Daphnici Mores inspired by the shades of Antioch. All traces of the worship of *Kámadeva* have long since disappeared: his groves, indeed, could not possibly be frequented a moment after the intrusion of Mohammedan brutality.

† Allusion is made here to some circumstances of domestic economy, on which the Hindus of the present day can give no information, such cookery having long gone out of fashion, and no Dr. Kitchener having arisen in India to immortalise the culinary art. The stalk of the gourd, it is said, is covered with cow-dung to preserve it from insects. For the satisfaction of the curious the Prákŕit of the original follows: It is a verse in the *Upajáti* measure—"*Kakkáluká gochhaḍalittáreńá; Sáke a śukkhe; talide hu manśe; Bhatte a hemantialattiśiddhe; Líńe a bele ńa hu hodi páḍi.*"

‡ Literally, as the kernel of the wood-apple below a door.—*Kabála-tala-ppabiṭṭhaḿ kabiṭṭhaḿ guriaḿ via, maśtaaḿ de maḍamaḍáiśśam.*

Mait. I will deliver your message.

Saṁs. Is the worthy Viṫa really gone? (*To the servant.*)

Serv. He is, sir.

Saṁs. Then, let us follow him quick.

Serv. Please to take your sword.

Saṁs. No, carry it after me.

Serv. This is your honour's sword.

Saṁs. Ah, very well, give it me. (*Takes it by the wrong end.*) I bear it on my shoulder, sleeping in its pink sheath;* and thus go I home as a jackal retires to his lair, followed by the yell of all the dogs and bitches of the village. [*Exit.*

Mait. My good Radaniká, say nothing to Chárudatta about your having been insulted in this currish place, by that king's brother-in-law: he frets already about his affairs, and this business, I am sure, would double his vexation.

Rad. I am only Radaniká, Maitreya; I can hold my tongue.

Mait. Nay, nay, not so. [*They retire.*

Chár. (*Within the house, to Vasantasená.*) Radaniká, my boy Rohasena must have enjoyed the breeze long enough; he will be chilled by the evening dews; take him in, and cover him with this cloth.

Vas. (*Apart.*) He mistakes me for one of the servants. (*Takes the cloth and smells it.*) Scented with jasmine flowers! Ha, then, he is not all a philosopher.† [*Retires.*

Chár. Radaniká, carry Rohasena to the inner apartments.

Vas. (*Apart.*) Alas! my fortune gives me no admission to them.

Chár. What! No reply, Radaniká?—Alas! when a man has been unfortunate enough to have outlived his means, his best friends lose their regard, and old attachments change into dislike.

* Literally, of the colour of the flesh of the barkless radish.—*Ńivvakkalaṁ múlakapeśi vaṅńam.*

† Literally, his youth does not exhibit indifference.—*Aṅuddsiśaṁ se jovvanaṁ padiháсedi.*

Enter MAITREYA *and* RADANIKÁ.

Mait. Here, sir, is Radaniká.

Chár. Here—then who is this? Not knowing her, I have degraded her by the touch of my vestment.*

Vas. (*Apart.*) Degraded; no, exalted.

Chár. She looks like the waning moon, half hidden by autumnal clouds; fie, fie, another's wife; this is not a meet object for my regards.

Mait. (*Recognising Vasantasená.*) A wife indeed, a pretty wife! Why, sir, this is Vasantasená, a lady, who, having had the felicity of seeing you in the gardens of *Kámadeva's* temple, has taken it into her head to honour you with her affection.

Chár. (*Apart.*) Indeed; is this Vasantasená?

> What now avails it to return her love
> In my declining fortunes; let it sink
> Suppressed in silence, as a coward checks
> The wrath he dares not utter.

Mait. I have a message, too, from the king's brother-in-law.

Chár. What?

Mait. Thus he says:† "A common wanton, hight Vasantasená, covered with gold upon gold, like the chief of a troop of comedians about to act a new play, saw you in the garden of *Kámadeva's* temple, and took a fancy to you. Having put us to the trouble of violence to secure her"——

Vas. "Violence to secure her!" Oh, I am honoured by such words.

Mait. "She fled, and has taken refuge in your house. If you will give her up, and put her yourself into my hands with-

* This instances the great reserve that separated the virtuous part of the sexes amongst the Hindus. To have touched the wife of another with the hem of the garment was a violation of her person. In the *Rája-Tarangini* the present of a fine vest to the Queen of Cashmir, which had been stamped with the seal of the donor, the King of Ceylon, and so far seemed to belong to him, is said to have occasioned a war between the princes.

† Like the missions in Homer, the messages are always repeated *verbatim.*

out litigation, her delivery shall be rewarded with my most particular regard; but if you will not put her forth, depend upon my eternal and exterminating enmity."

Chár. (*With disdain.*) He is a fool.

(*To himself.*) She would become a shrine—

The pride of wealth
Presents no charm to her, and she disdains
The palace she is roughly bid to enter;
Nor makes she harsh reply, but silent leaves
The man she scorns, to waste his idle words.
Lady—I knew you not, and thus unwittingly
Mistaking you for my attendant, offered you
Unmeet indignity, I bend my head,
In hope of your forgiveness.

Vas. Nay, sir, I am the offender, by intruding into a place of which I am unworthy; it is my head that must be humbled in reverence and supplication.

Mait. Very pretty on both sides; and whilst you two stand there, nodding your heads to each other like a field of long grass, permit me to bend mine, although in the style of a young camel's stiff knees, and request that you will be pleased to hold yourselves upright again.

Chár. Be it so; no further ceremony.

Vas. (*Aside.*) How kind his manner, how pleasing his expression! But it is not proper for me to remain longer: let me think. It shall be so. (*Aloud.*) Sir, respected sir, if truly I have found favour in your sight, permit me to leave these ornaments in your house; it was to rob me of them, that the villains I fled from pursued me.

Chár. This house, lady, is unsuited to such a trust.

Vas. Nay, worthy sir, you do not speak me true. Men, and not houses, are the things we trust to.

Chár. Maitreya, take the trinkets.

Vas. You have obliged me.

Mait. Much obliged to your ladyship. (*Taking them.*)

Chár. Blockhead, this is but a trust.

Mait. (*To him apart.*) What if they should be stolen?

Chár. They will be here but a short time.

Mait. What she has given us is ours.

Chár. I shall send you about your business.

Vas. Worthy sir, I could wish to have the safeguard of this your friend's company to return home.

Chár. Maitreya, attend the lady.

Mait. Go yourself; you are the properest person; attending her graceful form as the stately swan upon his mate. I am but a poor Brahman, and should as soon be demolished by these libertines as a meat-offering in the market-place by the dogs.

Chár. Well, well, I will attend her, and for further security on the road let the torches be prepared.

Mait. What ho! Vardhamána—(*enter Servant*)—light the flambeaus.

Vardh. (*To him.*) You dunderhead, how are they to be lighted without oil?

Mait. (*Apart to Chárudatta.*) To say the truth, sir, our torches are like harlots; they shine not in poor men's houses.*

Chár. Never heed; we shall not need a torch.

Pale as the maiden's cheek who pines with love,
The moon is up, with all its starry train—
And lights the royal road with lamps divine,
Whilst through the gloom its milk-white rays descend,
Like streamlets winding o'er the miry plain.

(*They proceed.*) This, lady, is your dwelling.†

[*Vasantasená makes an obeisance, and exit.*

Come, my friend, let us return—

* The original contains a pun upon the word *Sneha*, which means oil or affection—the one has no love, the other has no oil.

† Either the space appropriated to the stage was more spacious than we can conceive, or this progress to a dwelling evidently intended to be remote must be left in a great measure to the imagination. On the Greek stage the characters were not unfrequently supposed to be advancing from some distance whilst the chorus was singing, and in the Latin comedy a character

The road is solitary, save where the watch
Performs his wonted round: the silent night—
Fit season only for dishonest acts—
Should find us not abroad.
As to this casket, let it be your charge
By night, by day it shall be Vardhamána's.

Mait. As you command. [*Exeunt.*

is often spoken of as near at hand some time before he takes part in the dialogue. On the Spanish stage a transit of a similar nature was performed, as in "Courtesy, not Love;" where the first part of the scene lies amongst rocks and woods, and presently, without any apparent change, we find one of the characters say—

"How heedlessly have we advanced,
Even to the palace gates: and see where stand
Ladies in the balcony."

—"Horæ Hispanicæ."—*Blackwood's Magazine*, No. C.

END OF THE FIRST ACT.

ACT II.

Scene—VASANTASENÁ'S HOUSE.*

Enter a Female Attendant.

I AM sent to Vasantasená with a message from her mother, I will therefore enter and deliver it to her. Ah, there she sits. She seems uneasy, I must approach her.

(*Vasantasená discovered seated,*† *Madaniká attending.*)

* The plan of this and subsequent scenes requires a similar arrangement as the first, or the stage to be divided transversely by a curtain, each being a double scene, or the inside and outside of the house. There might have not been even this ceremony, the characters whose business was over merely making way for the new comers, without leaving the stage, or being in any formal way separated from it. A case of this kind occurs in an old English play, *Monsieur D'Olive*, by Chapman, Act 3, Scene 1, where the Duke, Duchess, and train pass over the stage to see the Earl of Anne's unburied wife; pause and talk, yet take no notice of the Earl and his brother, who were in previous possession of the scene, and who remain on it when the rest depart, resuming their discourse as if nothing had occurred to interrupt them.

† In the original "enter seated," *ásanasthá praviśati*, a rather preposterous stage direction, but not without a parallel in the British drama. Thus in *The Pinner of Wakefield*: "Enter a shoemaker sitting upon the stage at work." In *'Tis pity She is a Whore*, Dodsley's edition, "Enter the Friar in his study, sitting in a chair." In the same piece, "Enter Giovanni and Annabella lying on a bed;" and in *The Lover's Melancholy*, "Enter Maleander on a couch." This sort of direction is constant in the old editions, and leaves it to be inferred that the characters had no alternative but to walk in and occupy the chair or bed, which latter the property man, as Malone observes, was ordered to thrust upon the stage when a bed-chamber was to be represented. The Greeks had some device for this purpose, although it does not appear very distinctly what. The Encyclema, as described by Julius Pollux, appears to have been a raised platform with a seat, and to have turned on a pivot, and the open side being made to face the audience, discovered the character sitting, as Euripides in the Acharnians and Sophocles in the clouds.

Vas. Well, girl, you must then——

Mad. Then—when—madam? You have given me no orders.

Vas. What said I?

Mad. You said, girl, you must then——

Vas. True.

Atten. (*Approaches.*) Madam, your mother desires that you will perform your ablutions and come to worship.

Vas. Tell my lady mother, child, that I shall not attend to-day; let the Brahman complete the ceremony.

Atten. As you command. [*Exit.*

Mad. Dear madam, affection, not malice, compels me to ask what you meant to say?

Vas. Why, Madaniká, what think you of me?

Mad. I should guess from your being so absent that you are in love.

Vas. Well said, Madaniká; you are a judge of hearts, it should seem.

Mad. Excuse me, but Love is a resistless god, and holds his holiday in the breast of youth: so tell me, what prince or courtier does my lady serve?

Vas. I pretend, Madaniká, to be a mistress, not a slave.

Mad. What young and learned Brahman, then, is it that you love?

Vas. A Brahman is to be venerated, not loved.

Mad. It must be a merchant then, rich with the collected wealth of the many countries he has visited.

Vas. Nay, Madaniká, it were very ill-advised to fix my affections on a trader to foreign lands. His repeated absence would subject me to a life of incessant grief.

Mad. Neither a prince nor a courtier, a Brahman nor a merchant; who then can he possibly be?

Vas. Madaniká, you were with me in the garden of *Kámadeva's* temple.

Mad. I was, madam.

Vas. Then why do you ask me, as if you knew nothing?

Mad. Ah! now I know—he in whose house you told me you had taken refuge.

Vas. How is he called?

Mad. He lives near the Exchange.*

Vas. I asked you his name.

Mad. His well-selected name is Chárudatta.

Vas. Right, Madaniká; right, girl, now you know all.

Mad. Is it so! (*Aside.*) But, lady, it is said that he is very poor.

Vas. I love him, nevertheless. No longer let the world believe that a courtesan is insensible to a poor man's merit.

Mad. Yet, lady, do the bees swarm in the mango-tree after it has shed its blossoms.

Vas. Therefore are they called wantons.†

Mad. Well, if he is the object of your affections, why not contrive an interview?

Vas. I have provided for it: the scheme must succeed; and although it is not easy to get access to him, yet it may be managed.

Mad. I suppose it was with this view that your ornaments were deposited in his hands?

Vas. You have a shrewd guess, wench. [*They retire.*

Scene—A Street, with an open Temple; noise behind.

Halloa, sirs, halloa! Yon gambler has lost ten *suvarńas*, and is running off without paying—stop him! stop him! Ah, I see you, there you go—stop! stop!

Enter the SAḾVÁHAKA *hastily.*‡

Curse on my gambling propensities; I am kicked by an ass, as it were by a she-ass just broke away from her first halter;

* *Seíthi-chattare paḋivasadi* or *Śreshíhi-chatware prativasati.* He lives in the street of the Seths, or principal merchants and bankers.

† The original is a pun on the word *madhukaras*, honey-makers or beggars.

‡ A person employed to knead and chafe the limbs. The stage direction for his entrance implies a curtain. He enters, as the manuscripts of this

I am picked up by a pike * like *Ghaṭotkacha* by the dart of *Karṅa*; † no sooner did I see the master of the table ‡ intent upon the writings, than I started. Now I have got away from them, where can I conceal myself? The gamester and

piece, both text and comment, have it, *apaṭákshepa*, which might be rendered not putting aside the curtain, breaking through it in some part, expressing hurry and fright; in other plays, however, the phrase is, more correctly, *apaṭíkshepa*, throwing up the curtain; from *apaṭí*, a screen, and *kshepa*, throwing.

* The sense of this passage is rather obscure, but there can be no doubt that puns are intended, and that *gaddahí* or *gardabhí*, meaning a she-ass, as well as *śakti*, a dart or pike, imply something else in this place; perhaps they signify the implements of play, cards, or dice. The commentator is evidently at a loss, but is inclined to consider them to mean coins, which is not impossible.

† The demon *Ghaṭotkacha* was killed by *Karṅa*, with a lance given him by *Indra*. The story is told in the *Máhabhárata*, and is translated in the 13th volume of the Asiatic Researches.

‡ The *Sabhika* is said in the *Mitákshará* to be a person who presides at houses where assemblies are held for purposes of gambling, and who provides the dice and all other materials. The *Agni-Puráṅa*, which in the law chapters is identically the same with the text of *Yájnyavalkya*, gives the following description of the *Sabhika's* duties and the laws of the gaming-table:— "The *Sabhika* is entitled to five per cent. on money won at play, whenever the sum exceeds one hundred; if it fall short of that amount, he is to receive ten per cent. In return for the protection of the king, he shall pay to the royal treasury a fixed proportion of his profits. It is his business to collect from the unsuccessful party whatever sums they may have lost, and transfer them to the winners; and it becomes him to do this civilly, and to adjust the payment on liberal and lenient terms. In all licensed gaming-houses, where the royal dues are regularly paid, the king should enforce the payment of all sums lost, but he should not interfere with gaming-houses of a different class. In all disputes, those who have been lookers-on are to be witnesses; and if any foul play or false dice be proved against a gambler, he shall be branded and banished the kingdom. The king shall appoint proper officers to attend at gambling-houses, and secure all dishonest characters; the same rules are applicable to cock-pits and other similar places, where animals are set to fight for wagers." The legal sanction thus given to gambling is very different from the sturdy and moral notions expressed by *Manu*, who directs kings to prohibit such practices in their dominions, and even to punish with death those who engage in them themselves or induce others to do so,—*Manu Saṁhitá*, ix. 221–224,—but regulations of either tendency are manifest indications of considerable progress in the vices of civilised society.

the master are at my heels. Here is an empty temple; I will walk backwards into it, and take my stand as its deity. (*Enters the temple.*)

Enter MÁTHURA, *the keeper of the Gaming-house, and the* Gambler.

Máth. Halloa, sirs! stop him, stop him.

Gam. Though you hide in hell, or take shelter with *Indra*, you shall not escape: *Rudra* himself cannot protect you. The keeper of the gaming-house is your only chance.

Máth. Whither, you deceiver of a courteous publican, have you flown. You are shaking with fear, every limb of you; I know it by your irregular footmarks, as your feet have slipped and stumbled over the ground, blackening your family and fame.

Gam. So far he has run, but here the track is lost.

Máth. Hey, the footmarks are all reversed. This temple had no image in it. Oh, the villain, he has walked backward into it.

Gam. Let us after him.

Máth. Agreed. (*Enter the temple, and signify in dumb show to each other the discovery of the Saṁvâhaka.*)

Gam. Is this image, think you, of wood?

Máth. No, it appears to me to be of stone. (*They shake and pinch the Saṁvâhaka.*) Never mind it, let us sit down and play out our game. (*They play.*)

Saṁ. (*Who gradually expresses an interest in watching the game.*) The rattling of the dice are as tantalising to a man without a penny, as the sound of a drum to a king without a kingdom. I shall not play, I know. Gambling is as bad as being pitched from the top of mount *Meru;* and yet, like the *Cöil's* song, the sound of the dice is really bewitching.

Gam. The throw is mine.

Máth. No, no, it is mine.

Saṁ. (*Forgetting himself and jumping off the pedestal.*) No, no, it is mine.

Gam. The man is taken.

Máth. (*Seizing the Saḿváhaka.*) Now, you scoundrel, we have you; where are the ten *suvarńas?**

Saḿ. I will pay them in the course of the day.

Máth. Pay them now.

Saḿ. Have patience, and you shall be paid.

Máth. I must be paid immediately.

Saḿ. Oh, dear, oh, lord, my head. (*Falls down as in a swoon. They beat him.*)

Máth. You are fast now in the gaming ring.†

Saḿ. (*Rising and expressing pain.*) It is very hard that you will not give me a little time; where am I to get the money?

Máth. Give me a pledge then.

Saḿ. Very well. (*Taking the Gamester aside.*) I tell you what, I will pay you half the money if you will forgive the rest.

Gam. Agreed.

Saḿ. (*to Máthura, aside.*) I will give you security for half the debt, if you cry quits for the other half.

Máth. Agreed.

Saḿ. (*To the Gamester aloud.*) You let me off half the debt?

Gam. I do.

* A *suvarńa* is a weight of gold which, according to different data, varies from 105 grains to 227. As the same with the *tola* in common use it should be 224½ grains; but the original authorities should perhaps be our guides in this place, and we may reckon the *suvarńa* at the lower weight of 105 grains. It may be estimated in value at about rupees 8·14, or 18s. 6d. It is here evidently intended to represent a coin as well as a weight, like our ancient penny and pound. It does not follow, because coins were weights, that therefore they could not be coins, and such an inference is contradicted by the history of all money. Pausanias probably made some such mistake when he asserted that "the Indians, although their country abounded with metals, had no coins." That they had coins is proved not only by the sense of the term *suvarńa* here, but by the probable sense of the words *gaddahí* and *śakti*, noticed above, and that of the *ńánaka* in page 25 (last note), which, according to the comment, means pieces bearing the figure of *Śiva*.

† Literally *júdiaramańḍalíe baddho si*. The meaning of *mańḍalí* here is no doubt technical, and its precise import is not understood.

Saṁ. And you give up half? (*To the Sabhika.*)

Máth. Yes, I do.

Saṁ. Then, good morning to you, gentlemen. (*Going.*)

Máth. Halloa, not so fast, where are you going?

Saṁ. See here, my masters—one has forgiven me one-half, and the other has let me off another half; is it not clear that I am quits for the whole?

Máth. Hark ye, my friend, my name is Máthura. I know a thing or two, and am not to be done in this way: so down directly with the whole sum.

Saṁ. Where am I to get it?

Máth. Sell your father.

Saṁ. Where is my father?

Máth. Sell your mother.

Saṁ. Where is she?

Máth. Sell yourself.*

Saṁ. Well, well, be pacified, take me upon the highway.

Máth. Come along. (*They proceed.*) What ho, good worthy friends; pray, some one buy me of this gambler for ten *suvarṅas.*

Passenger.† What noise is that?

Saṁ. I will be your servant, your slave. Gone, and no reply—well, try again: who buys, who buys; will no one buy me of this gambler for ten *suvarṅas?* He has passed and not said a syllable! Ah, luckless me, ever since the noble Chárudatta came to poverty, I prosper only in misfortunes.

Máth. Come, come—give me the money.

Saṁ. How should I give it? (*Falls and is dragged along by Máthura.*) Murder, murder! help—protect me.

* A creditor is authorised by the old Hindu law to enforce payment of an acknowledged debt by blows, the detention of the debtor's person, and compelling him to work in his service; this treatment of the *Saṁváhaka*, therefore, however barbarous, is perfectly legal.

† *Ákáśe* is the stage direction, a voice in the air; but this stage direction supposes a very thin company: none to act *mob.*

Enter DARDURAKA.

Gambling is to the gamester an empire without a throne; he never anticipates defeat, but levies tribute from all, and liberally disburses what he obtains; he enjoys the revenues of a prince, and counts the opulent amongst his servants; money, wife, friends, all are to be won at the gaming-table, and all is gained, all possessed, and all lost at play. Let me see: *Tray* carried off everything; *Deuce* set my skin crawling; *Ace* settled the point, and *Doublets* * dished me completely. Ha!

* The terms here used in the original are not familiar to the Hindus of the present day. They are *Tretá, Pávara, Nardita,* and *Kaía;* for these the commentary substitutes *Tíyá, Duá, Nádí,* and *Púrá,* or Three, Two, Ace, and Four. If correct, the game alluded to is a kind of Hazard: it is played upon a table or cloth with four compartments, called severally *Nádí, Duá, Tíyá,* and *Chouk* or *Púrá,* and by any number of players. Each stakes, upon one or other of the compartments, whatever sum the caster will set him in. The caster has sixteen cowries, which he shakes in his hands and throws on the ground; those that fall with the valve uppermost are counted, and according as they correspond to either of the divisions, that division sweeps the table. The mode of counting them refers to the favourite mode of telling off articles in India by four; and the numbers of one, two, &c., are not only those numbers simply, but the same in excess above four and its multiples; thus *Nádí* or Ace is counted by one, five, nine, or thirteen cowries; *Duá* or *Deuce,* by two, six, ten, and fourteen; *Tíyá* or *Tray,* by three, seven, eleven, and fifteen; and *Púrá,* by four, eight, twelve, and sixteen. There is reason to doubt, however, whether the commentator is correct, and the word *Nardita* presents some trace of the word *Nerd*—the game presented to the Indians by the Persians in exchange for chess; invented, according to *Firdusi,* by *Buzerjemehr*; but improved by him, according to other traditions noticed by the author of the *Burhankati.* The Arabic authorities quoted by Hyde refer it to *Shapur,* or his son *Ardeshir,* of the Sasanian dynasty; but, as he observes, the invention is more usually ascribed to Palamedes at the siege of Troy. It is undoubtedly an ancient game, and was probably familiarly known to all the eastern nations long before the time of *Nushirvan;* the Indians as well as others; and if they invented chess, they might very naturally have elaborated it out of this game, their *Chouper* or *Chaturanga,* a word which seems to be the original of *Shatreng* or *Shatrenj, Zatrikion, Echecs, Scacchi, Chess,* and which is applicable to the game as played with *four* bodies or armies. Sir William Jones was informed that Indian chess was so played; but there is no satisfactory proof of this, and it may be doubted whether any other game of tables than *Chouper* is traceable in Sanskṙit works.

here's my acquaintance, the keeper of the gaming-house, Máthura: I cannot avoid him, so I will wrap myself up so as not to be known. Eh! this vest is rather threadbare; it is embellished with sundry holes. It makes but a sorry covering, and looks best folded up. (*Folds up his uppercloth after examining it, and puts it under his arm.*) Never mind him; what can he do to me? I can stand with one foot on the ground, and the other in the air, as long as the sun is in the heavens.

Máth. Come, come; your money.

Saṁ. Whence is it to be got?

Dar. What is going on here?

Passen. This gambler is getting a thrashing from the *Sabhika*, and nobody will take his part.

Dar. Indeed! then I must interfere, I see. (*Approaches.*) Make way here; heigh, sirs: Máthura, that rogue, and the Saṁváhaka; the wretch, whose head is hanging below his heels at sunset, whose back is variegated with stripes and bruises, and whose legs are daily nibbled by the dogs; what has he, with his lank emaciated carcase, to do with gambling? I must appease Máthura. Good day, Máthura.

Máth. Good day, good day.

Dar. What are you at here?

Máth. This fellow owes me ten *suvarńas*.

Dar. A trifle, a trifle.*

Máth. (*Snatching Darduraka's ragged cloth from him.*) See here, my masters; here is a pretty fellow, in a ragged robe, to call ten *suvarńas* a trifle.

Dar. Why, you blockhead, how often do I stake ten *suvar-*

There is a striking resemblance between the *Páśas* of the Hindus and *Pessos* of the Greeks, the latter of which Hyde identifies with dice used in the *Nerdiludium.* Wodhull, the translator of Euripides, adopts the same version, and their authority is preferable to that of Pope, who renders it *Chess*, but makes it out something very different in his note on the passage.

* Literally, a morning meal, a breakfast, *Kalyavarttam.*

ńas on a throw. What is a man to do with his money? carry it in his waistband?* But you; you are villain enough, for the sake of ten *suvarńas*, to demolish the five senses of a man.

Máth. Keep your *suvarńas* for your morning meal, if you like: this is my property.

Dar. Very well; hear me! Give him other ten *suvarńas*, and let him play you for the whole.

Máth. How so?

Dar. If he wins, he shall pay you the money.

Máth. And if he lose?

Dar. Then, he shall not pay.

Máth. Go to; you talk nonsense. Will you give it? My name's *Máthura;* I am a cheat, and win other men's money unfairly: what then? I am not to be bullied by such a blackguard as you.

Dar. Whom do you call a blackguard?

Máth. You are a blackguard.

Dar. Your father was a blackguard. (*Makes signs to the Saḿvdhaka to escape.*)

Máth. You son of a slave! † are you not a gambler yourself?

Dar. Me? do you call me a gambler?

Máth. Enough, enough. Come, do you pay the ten *suvarńas.* (*To the Saḿváḥaka.*)

Saḿ. I will pay them to-day. [*Máthura drags him along.*

Dar. You villain! no one shall maltreat the poor in my presence.

[*Máthura gives the Saḿvdhaka a blow on the nose; it bleeds; the Saḿvdhaka, on seeing his blood, faints and falls on the ground. Darduraka approaches, gets*

* The natives of India commonly carry money tied up in one end of a cloth, which is bound round their loins, or sometimes thrown over their shoulders.

† *Gosávid-putta*, which the commentator explains *gańiká-* or *vésyá-putra:* this term of abuse is of all perhaps most widely disseminated, and in the languages of Spain and England is as native a in *Prákŕit.*

between him and Máthura, and a scuffle ensues: they pause.

Máth. You villain! you son of a slave! you shall suffer for this.

Dar. You fool! you have assaulted me on the king's highway; you shall see to-morrow, in court, whether you are to beat people in this manner.

Máth. Ah, ha! yes, yes, I shall see; depend upon it.

Dar. How so! how will you see?

Máth. How! why, so, to be sure. (*Thrusting his face forward.*)

[*Darduraka throws a handful of dust into his eyes; Máthura cries out with pain and falls; the Saṁváhaka recovers, and according to Darduraka's gesticulations makes his escape.*

Dar. Máthura is a man of some weight here, that's certain; I had better therefore take myself off. My friend S'arvilaka told me that a cunning man has prophesied to a cowherd, named Áryaka, that he shall be king, and people like myself are flocking to him accordingly: my plan is to join him with the rest. [*Exit.*

Scene—VASANTASENÁ'S HOUSE (*outside and inside*).

Enter the SAṀVÁHAKA, *wandering about.*

(*Interior.*) The door of this house is open; I will enter it. (*Enters and sees Vasantasená.*) Lady, I seek protection.

Vas. It is offered you; fear nothing. Madaniká, shut the door. What do you fly from?

Saṁ. A creditor.

Vas. Secure the door. (*To Madaniká.*)

Saṁ. (*To himself.*) She seems to be as much afraid of a creditor as myself; so much the better; he that takes a burthen suited to his strength will not slip by the way, nor perish in the thicket. My situation is duly known here, it seems.

Enter (outside of the House) MÁTHURA *and the* GAMBLER.

Máth. (*Rubbing his eyes.*) The money, I say; I will have the money.

Gam. Sir, whilst we were struggling with Darduraka, the other rogue has run off.

Máth. The villain! but I have flattened his nose for him; we shall track him by the blood.

Gam. He has entered here. (*Stops at Vasantasená's door.*)

Máth. The ten *suvarńas* are gone.

Gam. Let us complain to the prince.

Máth. In the meantime the scoundrel will come forth and escape. No; let us wait here; we shall have him yet.

Inside of the House.

Vas. (*Makes signs to Madaniká.*)

Mad. (*To the Saḿváhaka.*) My mistress, sir, wishes to know whence you are; who you are; what you are; and what you are afraid of.

Saḿ. I will tell you. I was born, lady, at Pátaliputra; I am the son of a householder, and follow the profession of a Saḿváhaka.

Vas. Were you trained to this effeminate occupation? *

Saḿ. I learnt the practice, lady, to get a livelihood.

Mad. So far so good. Proceed.

Saḿ. Whilst living in my father's house, I heard travellers talk of distant countries, and felt curious to visit them myself. Accordingly, I came to Ujjayin, where I entered into the service of a distinguished person, whose like for an engaging figure and courteous speech never yet acknowledged kindness or forgot offence—enough said; he only values his consequence as it enables him to do good and cherish all who seek his protection.

* She calls it a *sukumára-kalá*, a very soft art; perhaps not intending the exact sense which, in conformity with European ideas, is attached to it in the translation.

Mad. Who is this that so graces Ujjayin, having stolen the good qualities my lady loves?

Vas. Right, Madaniká, my heart suggests to me the same inquiry.

Mad. Proceed.

Saṁ. This gentleman having by his munificent bounty——

Vas. Lavished all his wealth.

Saṁ. How should your ladyship know? I have not yet told you this.

Vas. I need no telling: worth and wealth are rarely found together. The pool is full to the brim, whose water is unfit for drinking.

Mad. Oblige us with his name.

Saṁ. To whom is the appellation of that earthly moon unknown, entitled to universal eulogium? his habitation is near the Exchange; his name is Chárudatta.

Vas. (*Springs from her seat.*) Girl, girl, a seat. This house is yours, sir; pray be seated. A fan! wench—quick; our worthy guest is fatigued.*

Saṁ (*To himself.*) Such respect from the simple utterance of Chárudatta's name! Bravo! excellent Chárudatta! you in this world live; other men only breathe. (*Falls at Vasantasená's feet.*) Pray, lady, resume your seat.

Vas. (*Sitting down.*) Where is your wealthy dun?

Saṁ. He is truly wealthy, † who is rich in good acts, although he own not perishable riches. He who knows how to honour others, knows how his honour may be best deserved.

Vas. Proceed.

* This might be thought a little extravagant, but it is not without a parallel in European flattery, and from motives less reputable. Lewis XIV. having one day sent a footman to the Duke of Monbazon with a letter, the duke, who happened to be at dinner, made the footman take the highest place at his table, and afterwards accompanied him to the court-yard, because he came from the king.

† The connexion of the reply with Vasantasená's question turns upon the word *Dhanika*, which means a rich man as well as a creditor.

Saṁ. I was made by that gentleman one of his personal attendants; but in his reduced circumstances being necessarily discharged, I took to play, and by a run of ill-luck have lost ten *suvarṅas.*

Máth. (*Without.*) I am robbed! I am plundered!

Saṁ. Hear, lady, hear; those two gamblers are lying wait for me; what is your ladyship's will?

Vas. Madaniká, the birds are fluttering about and rustling in the leaves of the adjoining tree; go to this poor fellow's pursuers, and say to them that he sends them this jewel in payment.

Mad. As you command. [*Exit.*

Outside of the House.

Máth. I am robbed!

MADANIKÁ *enters by the side door unobserved.*

Mad. These two, by their casting such anxious looks up to the house, their agitation, their close conference, and the diligence with which they watch the door, must be the gambler and the keeper of the gaming-house. I salute you, sir.

Máth. Joy be with you, wench.

Mad. Which of you two is the master of the gaming-house?

Máth. He, my graceful damsel, whom you now address with pouting lip, soft speech, and wicked eye; but get you gone; I have nothing for you.

Mad. If you talk thus, you are no gambler. What! have you no one in your debt?

Máth. Yes, there is a fellow owes me ten *suvarṅas:* what of him?

Mad. On his behalf, my mistress sends—nay, I mistake—he sends you this bracelet.

Máth. Ha, ha! tell him I take this as a pledge, and that he may come and have his revenge when he will.

[*Exeunt severally.*

Inside of the House.

Enter MADANIKÁ.

They have gone away, madam, quite pleased.

Vas. Now, my friend, depart, and relieve the anxiety of your family.

Sam. If there be anything, lady, in which I can be of use to you, employ me.

Vas. There is a higher claim upon your service; you should still be ready to minister to him by whom you were once employed, and on whose account your skill was acquired.

Sam. The lady discards me; how shall I requite her kindness! (*Aloud.*) Lady, as I find my profession only begets disgrace, I will become a Bauddha mendicant;* I tell you my design, and beg you will keep it in your recollection.

Vas. Nay, friend, do nothing rashly.

Sam. I am determined, lady. (*Going.*) In bidding adieu to gambling, the hands of men are no longer armed against me: I can now hold up my head boldly as I go along the public road. (*A noise behind the scenes.*) What is the matter now?

(*Behind the scenes.*) Vasantasená's hunting elephant has broken loose.

Sam. I must go and see this furious beast;—yet why should I, as I purpose a pious life? [*Exit.*

A continued clamour without till KARŃAPÚRAKA *enters hastily.*

Kar. Where is my lady?

* Literally a *Śákya-śramańaka, śakkaśśamańaká.* The expression is rather remarkable, for it decides an important point in the religious history of the Hindus. The *Sarmanes* or *Germanes* of the days of *Alexander* have been supposed to be *Bauddha* ascetics only. Mr. Colebrooke, however, has shown that the term *Śramańa* is not restricted to the *Bauddha* sect, but is equally applicable to any ascetic; and although the probable original of *Śarmanes* and *Samanæans,* and usually expressing a *Bauddha,* it does not necessarily bear that import. This assertion is here confirmed, as the author thinks it necessary to add *Śákya* to *Śramańaka,* to imply a mendicant the follower of *Śákya Muni,* or last living *Buddha.*

Mad. You unmannerly fellow! what ails you? Cannot you see your mistress and address her fittingly?

Kar. Lady, I salute you.

Vas. Karńapúraka, you seem highly pleased with something; what is it?

Kar. You have lost a great deal to-day in not witnessing your humble servant's achievement.

Vas. What achievement?

Kar. Only hear. Your ladyship's fierce elephant Khuńťamoraka* killed his keeper and broke his chain; he then scoured off along the high road, making a terrible confusion. The people shouted and screamed, "Carry off the children, get up the trees, climb the walls, the elephant is coming!" Away went girdles and anklets; and pearls and diamonds were scattering about in all directions. There he was, plunging about in Ujjayin, and tearing everything to pieces with his trunk, his feet, and his tusks, as if the city had been a large tank full of lotus flowers. A mendicant came in his way; the elephant broke his staff, water-pot, and platter, sprinkled him with water from his trunk, and held him up between his tusks; all cried out, "The holy man will be killed."

Vas. Alas! alas!

Kar. Don't be alarmed; only hear. Seeing him thus at large, and handling the holy man so roughly, I, Karńapúraka, my lady's humblest slave, determined to rescue the mendicant and punish my gentleman; so I quickly snatched up an iron bar, and approaching him sidelong,† made a desperate blow at the animal.

Vas. Go on.

* The name of the elephant *Khuńťamoraka*, which is given in the text, is said to be a Mahratta compound, signifying the breaker of the post to which he is chained.

† *Vámachalańeńa júďa-lekkhaam ugghusia*, drawing a gaming-letter with the left foot, is the literal expression, the exact sense of which is not explained by the commentator.

Kar. Big as he was, like the peaks of Vindhya, I brought him down and saved the saint.

Vas. You have done well.

Kar. So everybody said, "Well done, Karńapúraka, well done!" for all Ujjayin, in a panic, like a boat ill-laden, was heaped on one spot, and one person, who had no great matter of dress to boast of himself, turning his eyes upwards, and fetching a deep sigh, threw his garment over me.

Vas. Does it smell of jasmines?

Kar. The smell of the elephant's frontal moisture is still in my nostrils; so I cannot tell how the garment smells.

Vas. Is there any name on it? see, see!

Kar. Here are letters; your ladyship will best be able to read them.*

Vas. (*Reads.*) Chárudatta! (*Throws the cloth round her with delight.*)

Mad. How well the garment becomes our mistress, does it not?

Kar. (*Sulkily.*) Yes, it becomes her well enough.

Vas. Karńapúraka, be this your recompense. (*Gives him an ornament.*)

Kar. (*Puts it to his head and bows.*) Now indeed the garment sets as it should do.

Vas. Where did you leave Chárudatta?

Kar. Going home, I believe, along this road.

Vas. (*To Madaniká.*) Quick, girl, quick; up on this terrace, and we may yet catch a glimpse of him. [*Exeunt.*

* The art of marking on linen was therefore known to the Hindus.

END OF THE SECOND ACT.

ACT III.

CHÁRUDATTA'S HOUSE (*outside and inside*).

Enter VARDHAMÁNA (*inside*).

A WORTHY kind master, even though he be poor, is the delight of his servants; whilst a morose haughty fellow, who has only his wealth to boast of, is a constant vexation. There is no changing nature; nothing can keep an ox out of a field of corn, nor stop a man who covets another's wife. There is no parting a gamester from the dice, and there is no remedy for an innate defect. My excellent master has gone to a concert. It is not quite midnight, I suppose. I need not expect his return yet awhile; I shall therefore take a nap in the hall. (*Sleeps.*)

Enter (*outside*) CHÁRUDATTA *and* MAITREYA.

Chár. Excellent, excellent indeed; Rebhila sang most exquisitely.

Although not ocean-born, the tuneful *viná* *
Is most assuredly a gem of heaven—

* The Hindu lute. A description of it may be seen in the first volume of the *Researches*; it is an instrument of much sweetness and compass, but little power. At the churning of the ocean by the gods and demons, various persons and articles were recovered from the deep; these are called *ratnas*, or gems, and the popular enumeration of them is fourteen—or *Lakshmí* the Goddess of Beauty, *Dhanwantari* the physician of the Gods, the *Apsarasas* or Nymphs of Indra's heaven, *Surá* the Goddess of Wine, the Moon, the Jewel worn by Krishńa, the all-bestowing Tree, the Cow of Abundance, the Elephant of Indra, his Steed, Poison, and Ambrosia: the other two are the Bow of Vishńu and his *Śankha*, or Shell; but they are not generally included in the Pauranic lists, and even the Bhágavata- and

Like a dear friend, it cheers the lonely heart,
And lends new lustre to the social meeting.
It lulls the pain that absent lovers feel,
And adds fresh impulse to the glow of passion.

Mait. Come, sir, let us get home.

Chár. In truth, brave Rebhila, 'twas deftly sung.

Mait. Now, to me, there are two things at which I cannot choose but laugh, a woman reading Sanskŕit, and a man singing a song: the woman snuffles like a young cow when the rope is first passed through her nostrils;* and the man wheezes like an old Pandit who has been repeating his bead-roll till the flowers of his chaplet are as dry as his throat: to my seeming it is vastly ridiculous.

Chár. What, my good friend, were you not pleased to-night with Rebhila's fine execution?—

Smooth were the tones, articulate and flowing
With graceful modulation, sweet and pleasing,
And fraught with warm and passionate expression;
So that I often thought the dulcet sounds
Some female, stationed covertly, must utter.
Still echoes in my ears the soothing strain,
And as I pace along, methinks I hear
The liquid cadence and melodious utterance.
The *víńá's* sweet notes, now gently undulating,
Now swelling high, now dying to a close—

Vishnu-Puráńa omit them. In one place the Padma-Puráńa gives but eleven, omitting the *Kaustubha* or gem of Kŕishńa; in another, the *Uttara-Khańda,* it enumerates nine, and the list is rather peculiar. It runs: Poison; the Goddess of Misfortune; the Goddess of Wine; Sloth; the Apsarasas; the Elephant of Indra; Lakshmí; the Moon; the Tulasí plant. The *Mahábhárata* specifies but nine; omitting the Cow and Tree of Plenty and the beauties of *Swarga.*

* The rein in draft-cattle is passed through the cartilaginous septum of the nose. The fashion seems to have been a European one in former times: thus *Iago* says of *Othello*—

"He will as tenderly be led by the nose,
As asses are."

Sporting awhile in desultory descant,
And still recurring to the tasteful theme.*

Mait. Come, my friend, the very dogs in the high road through the market-place are fast asleep; let us go home. See, see, the moon descends from his mansion in the skies, making his way through the darkness.

Chár. True have you said. From his high palace bowed,
And hastening to his setting, scantly gleams
The waning moon, amidst the gathering gloom;
In slender crescent, like the tusk's fine point,
That peers above the darkening wave, where bathes
The forest elephant.

Mait. Here we are at home. Holloa! Vardhamána, arise and open the door.

Vardh. (*Within.*) Hark, I hear Maitreya's voice: Chárudatta is returned; I must let him in. (*Opens the door.*) Sir, I salute you; you also Maitreya. Here are the couches ready spread; please you to repose. (*They enter and sit.*)

Mait. Vardhamána, tell Radaniká to bring water for the feet.†

Chár. Nay, nay, disturb not those who are asleep.

Vardh. I will bring water, and Maitreya here can wash your feet.

Mait. Do you hear, my friend, the son of a slave? he is to hold the water, and he sets me, who am a Brahman, to wash your feet.

* Some liberties have been here unavoidably taken with the text, for the precise force of several of the technical terms employed it is impossible to render without a familiarity with the musical theory of the Hindus, to which the translator makes no pretence. It is believed, however, that the deviation from their general tenor is not very excursive.

† Washing the feet upon a person's return home has always been the common practice of the oriental nations: it was equally the practice of the Greeks: thus *Philocleon* in the *Wasps*—

"Next my girl, sprightly nymph, brings her napkin and lymph,
Feet and ankles are quick in ablution."

Chár. Do you, Maitreya, hold the water; Vardhamána can perform the rest.

Vardh. Come then, worthy Maitreya, pour out the water. (*Vardhamána washes Chárudatta's feet, and is going.*)

Chár. Nay, Vardhamána, wash the feet of the Brahman.

Mait. Never mind; it is of little use; I must soon go tramping over the ground again, like a jackass.

Vardh. Most worthy Maitreya, you are a Brahman, are you?

Mait. To be sure I am; like the boa amongst serpents, so am I, a Brahman amongst Brahmans.

Vardh. I cry you mercy: that being the case, I will wash your feet. (*Does so.*) Now, Maitreya, this gold casket, of which I have had the charge by day, it is your turn to take care of. (*Gives it to him, and exit.*)

Mait. So; it is safe through the day. What! have we no thieves in Ujjayin, that no one could have carried off this vile pilferer of my rest: pray let me carry it into the court-yard.

Chár. Impossible, it has been left in trust;
And is not to be parted with to any
But the right owner; Brahman, take heed to it. (*Lies down.*)
Still do I hear the soothing strain.

Mait. Pray, sir, is it your intention to go to sleep?

Chár. Assuredly.
I feel the drowsy deity invade
My forehead, and descend upon my eyelids.
Sleep, like decay, viewless and variable,
Grows stronger in its triumph o'er our strength.

Mait. Very true, so let us go to sleep. (*They sleep.*)

Enter Śarvilaka (*outside*).

Creeping along the ground, like a snake crawling out of his old skin, I effect with slight and strength a passage for my cowering frame. (*Looking up.*) The sovereign of the skies is in his decline: 'tis well. Night, like a tender mother, shrouds with her protecting darkness those of her children whose prowess assails the dwellings of mankind, and shrinks from an encounter with the servants of the king. I have made a breach in the garden wall, and have got into the midst of the garden. Now for the house. Men call this practice infamous, whose chief success is gained from the sleep of others, and whose booty is won by craft. If not heroism, it is at least independence, and preferable to the homage paid by slaves. As to nocturnal attacks, did not *Aśwatthâman* long ago overpower in a night-onset his slumbering foes? * Where shall I make the breach? what part is softened by recent damp? where is it likely that no noise will be made by the falling fragments? where is a wide opening most practicable which will not be afterwards visible? in what part of the wall are the bricks old, and corroded by saline exudations? † where can I penetrate without encountering women? ‡ and where am I likely to light upon my booty? (*Feels the wall.*) The ground here is softened by continual sprinkling with water and exposure to the sun, and is crusted with salt. Here is a rat-hole. The prize is sure: this is the first omen of success the sons of *Skanda* have laid down. Let me see: how shall I proceed? The god of the golden spear § teaches four modes of breaching a house: picking out burnt bricks, cutting through unbaked ones, throwing water on a mud wall, and boring through one of wood. This wall is of baked bricks: they must be picked out, but I must give them a sample of my skill. Shall the breach be the lotus blossom, the full sun or the new moon, the lake, the

* This exploit forms the subject of a section of the *Mahâbhârata*, the *Sauptika-Parvan*.

† These considerations, and much of what follows, are agreeably to the Thief's Manual, which is said to exist in Sanskrit, or a work on the *Chaurya-Vidyâ*, the Science of Thieving, ascribed to *Yogâchârya*, who was taught the science by no less a person than the god *Kârttikeya*, resembling, in respect to the objects of this patronage, the Grecian Mercury.

‡ To be avoided either out of delicacy towards the sex or as a bad omen.

§ *Kârttikeya*.

swastika,* or the water-jar? It must be something to astonish the natives. The water-jar looks best in a brick wall;—that shall be the shape. In other walls that I have breached by night, the neighbours have had occasion both to censure and approve my talents. Reverence to the prince *Kárttikeya*, the giver of all good; reverence to the god of the golden spear; to *Bráhmańya*, the celestial champion of the celestials; the son of fire.† Reverence to *Yogáchárya*, whose chief scholar I am, and by whom well pleased was the magic unguent ‡ conferred upon me, anointed with which, no eye beholds nor weapon harms me. Shame on me! I have forgotten my measuring-line, —never mind, my Brahmanical thread will answer the purpose. This thread is a most useful appendage to a Brahman, especially one of my complexion: it serves to measure the depth and height of walls, and to withdraw ornaments from their position; it opens a latch in a door as well as a key, and is an excellent ligature for the bite of a snake. Let us take measure, and go to work: so, so—(*extracting the bricks*)—one brick alone remains. Ha! hang it; I am bitten by a snake—(*ties the finger with the cord*)—'tis well again,—I must get on. (*Looks in.*) How! a lamp alight! the golden ray streaming through the opening in the wall shows amidst the exterior darkness, like the yellow streak of pure metal on the touchstone. The breach is perfect; now to enter.§ There is no one. Reverence to *Kárttikeya*. (*Enters.*) Here are two men asleep; let me set the outer door

* A magical diagram so called.

† These are all epithets of *Kárttikeya*, who in his military character corresponds to the Grecian Mars. He seems to have lost his reputation as the patron of thieves, who more usually worship some of the forms of *Durgá*.

‡ *Yogarochaná*. *Yoga* here is abstract devotion, for the purpose of obtaining supernatural power. What the article is may be doubted, but *rochaná* may be rendered unguent.

§ He talks in the text, however, of sending in a deputy first; the term is *pratipurusha*, a pro-man or substitute: it is questionable, however, what is precisely meant here, especially as no further allusion is made to such a character: it is probably a slip of the author.

open to get off easily if there should be occasion; how it creaks! it is stiff with age; a little water will be of use. (*Sprinkles the floor.*) Nay, not so, it makes too much noise pattering on the ground. (*Supports the door with his back, and opens it.*) So far, so well. Now, are these true sleepers or only counterfeits? (*He tries them.*) They are sound: the breathing is regular and not fluttered; the eye is fast and firmly shut; the body is all relaxed; the joints are loose, and the limbs protrude beyond the limits of the bed. If shamming sleep, they will not bear the gleam of the lamp upon their faces. (*Passes the lamp over their faces.*) All is safe. What have we here? a drum, a tabor, a lute, pipes; and here are books. Why, zounds, I have got into the house of a dancer or a poet. I took it for the dwelling of some man of consequence, or I should have let it alone. Is this poverty, or only the show of poverty? fear of thieves, or dread of the king? Are the effects hid underground? Whatever is underground is my property. Let us scatter the seed, whose sowing leaves nothing undiscernible. (*Throws about seeds.*) The man is an absolute pauper, and so I leave him. (*Going.*)

Mait. (*Dreaming.*) Master, they are breaking into the house. I see the thief. Here, here! do you take care of the gold casket.

Śar. How! does he perceive me? does he mock me with his poverty? he dies. (*Approaching.*) Haply he dreams. (*Looking at Maitreya.*) Eh! sure enough, there is in the light of the lamp something like a casket wrapped up in a ragged bathing-gown; that must be mine. No, no; it is cruel to ruin a worthy man, so miserably reduced already. I will even let it alone.

Mait. (*Dreaming.*) My friend, if you do not take the casket, may you incur the guilt of disappointing a cow, and of deceiving a Brahman.

Śar. These invocations are irresistible: take it I must. Softly: the light will betray me. I have the fire-flapping insect to put it out. I must cast it into the lamp. (*Takes out the insect.*) Place and time requiring, let this insect fly. It hovers round the wick—with the wind of its wings the flame is extinguished. Shame on this total darkness, or rather shame on the darkness with which I have obscured the lustre of my race! how well it suits that S'arvilaka, a Brahman, the son of a Brahman, learned in the four *Vedas*, and above receiving donations from others, should now be engaged in such unworthy courses! And why? For the sake of a harlot, for the sake of Madaniká. Ah, well! I must even go on, and acknowledge the courtesy of this Brahman.

Mait. (*Half-awake.*) Eh, my good friend, how cold your hand is!

Śar. Blockhead! I had forgotten, I have chilled my hand by the water I touched; I will put it to my side. (*Chafes his left hand on his side and takes the casket with it.*)

Mait. (*Still only half-awake*). Have you got it?

Śar. The civility of this Brahman is exceeding! I have it.

Mait. Now like a pedlar that has sold all his wares, I shall go soundly to sleep. (*Sleeps.*)

Śar. Sleep, illustrious Brahman! May you sleep a hundred years! Fie on this love! for whose dear sake I thus bring trouble on a Brahman's dwelling—nay, rather call down shame upon myself; and fie! and fie! upon this unmanning poverty, that urges me to acts which I must needs condemn. Now to Vasantasená to redeem my beloved Madaniká with this night's booty. I hear footsteps; should it be the watch—what then?—shall I stand here like a post?—no, let S'arvilaka be his own protection. Am I not a cat in climbing, a deer in running, a snake in twisting, a hawk in darting upon the prey, a dog in baying man, whether asleep or awake? In assuming various forms am I not *Máyá* * herself, and *Saraswatí* † in the gift of tongues? A lamp in the night, a mule in a defile, a horse by land, a boat by water, a snake in motion, and a rock in

* The personification of illusion and unreality.

† The wife of *Brahmá*, and goddess of learning and the arts.

stability? In hovering about I compete with the king of birds, and in an eye to the ground, am keener than the hare. Am I not like a wolf in seizing, and like a lion in strength?

Enter RADANIKÁ.

Bless me! what has become of Vardhamána? He was asleep at the hall door, but is there no longer. I must wake Maitreya. (*Approaches.*)

Śar. (*Going to stab her.*) Ha! a woman! she is safe, and I may depart. [*Exit.*

Rad. Oh, dear me! a thief has broken into the house, and there he goes out at the door. Why, Maitreya! Maitreya! up, up, I say. A thief has broken into the house, and has just made his escape.

Mait. Eh, what do you say, you foolish toad? a thief made his escape?

Rad. Nay, this is no joke—see here.

Mait. What say you, hey, the outer door opened! Chárudatta, friend, awake! a thief has been in the house and has just made his escape.

Chár. This is not an hour to jest.

Mait. It is true enough, as you may satisfy yourself.

Chár. Where did he get in?

Mait. Look here. (*Discovers the breach.*)

Chár. Upon my word, a not unseemly fissure; the bricks are taken out above and below; the head is small, the body large: there is really talent in this thief.

Mait. The opening must have been made by one of two persons; by a novice, merely to try his hand, or by a stranger to this city; for who in Ujjayin is ignorant of the poverty of our mansion?

Chár. No doubt, by a stranger—one who did not know the condition of my affairs, and forgot that those only sleep soundly who have little to lose. Trusting to the external semblance of this mansion, erected in more prosperous times, he entered full of hope, and has gone away disappointed.

What will the poor fellow have to tell his comrades? I have broken into the house of the son of the chief of a corporation, and found nothing.

Mait. Really, I am very much concerned for the luckless rogue. Ah, ha! thought he, here is a fine house; now for jewels, for caskets. (*Recollecting.*) By the by, where is the casket? oh yes, I remember. Ha, ha! my friend, you are apt to say of me, that blockhead Maitreya! that dunderhead Maitreya! but it was a wise trick of mine to give the casket to you: had I not done so, the villain would have walked off with it.

Chár. Come, come, this jesting is misplaced.

Mait. Jesting—no, no; blockhead though I be, I know when a joke is out of season.

Chár. When did you give the casket to me?

Mait. When I called out to you, "How cold your hand is!"

Chár. It must be so. (*Looking about.*) My good friend, I am much obliged by your kindness.

Mait. Why: is not the casket stolen?

Chár. It is stolen.

Mait. Then what have you to thank me for?

Chár. That the poor rogue has not gone away empty-handed.

Mait. He has carried off what was left in trust.

Chár. How! in trust, alas! (*Faints.*)

Mait. Revive, revive, sir! though the thief has stolen the deposit, why should it so seriously affect you?

Chár. Alas! my friend, who will believe it stolen?

A general ordeal waits me. In this world
Cold poverty is doomed to wake suspicion.
Alas! till now, my fortune only felt
The enmity of fate; but now its venom
Sheds a foul blight upon my dearer fame.

Mait. I tell you what. I will maintain that the casket was never entrusted to us. Who gave it, pray? who took it? where are your witnesses?

Chár. Think you I can sanction thus a falsity?
No, no; I will beg alms, and so obtain
The value of the pledge, and quit its owner;
But cannot condescend to shame my soul
By utterance of a lie. [*Exit.*

Rad. I will go and tell my mistress what has happened. [*Exit.*

Scene—Another Room.

Enter the WIFE *of* CHÁRUDATTA *and* RADANIKÁ.*

Wife. But indeed is my lord unhurt? is he safe, and his friend Maitreya?

Rad. Both safe, madam, I assure you, but the ornaments left by the courtesan are stolen.

Wife. Alas, girl! what say you? My husband's person is unharmed: that glads me. Yet better had his person come to harm than his fair fame incur disparagement. The people of Ujjayin will now be ready to suspect that indigence has impelled him to an unworthy act. Destiny, thou potent deity, thou sportest with the fortunes of mankind, and renderest them as tremulous as the watery drop that quivers on the lotus leaves. This string of jewels was given me in my maternal mansion: † it is all that is left to us, and I know my husband, in the loftiness of his spirit, will not accept it from me. Girl, go call the worthy Maitreya hither. [*Exit.*

RADANIKÁ *returns with* MAITREYA.

Mait. Health to you, respected lady.

Wife. I salute you, sir. Oblige me by facing the east.

Mait. You are obeyed.

Wife. I pray you accept this.

Mait. Nay, not so.

* The close of the last scene, the present scene, and the first part of the ensuing, offer a favourable picture of the domestic character of the Hindus. Radaniká has been rather rapid in her communication.

† One of the sources of the wife's peculiar wealth over which the husband has no control.

Wife. I fasted on the *Ratnashashthí*,* when, as you know, wealth must be given to a Brahman. My Brahman had been provided elsewhere, and I beg therefore that, in his stead, you will accept this string of jewels.

Mait. Very well; I will go and state the matter to my friend.

Wife. Thanks, Maitreya; but take heed, do not put me to shame. [*Exit.*

Scene—The Hall. CHÁRUDATTA *discovered.*

Chár. Maitreya tarries long; in his distress I hope he does not purpose aught unfitting.

Enter MAITREYA.

Mait. Here am I, sir, and bring you this. (*Gives the string of jewels.*)

Chár. What is this?

Mait. The fruit borne by the excellence of a wife worthy of her husband.

Chár. Is this the kindness of the Brahman's wife?

Out on it!—that I should be reduced so low
As, when my own has disappeared, to need
Assistance from a woman's wealth. So true
It is, our very natures are transformed
By opulence: the poor man helpless grows,
And woman wealthy acts with manly vigour.—
'Tis false; I am not poor:—a wife whose love
Outlives my fortune; a true friend who shares
My sorrows and my joy; and honesty
Unwarped by indigence, these still are mine.
Maitreya, hie thee to Vasantasená,
Tell her the casket, heedlessly impledged,
Was lost by me at play, but in its stead
I do beseech her to accept these jewels.

* A vow is probably implied: the occasion is not at present in the ritual: the term *shashthí* implies it was some observance held on the sixth day of the lunar fortnight.

Mait. I will do no such thing. What! are we to part with these gems, the quintessence of the four oceans, for a thing carried off by thieves, and which we have neither eaten nor drank, nor touched a penny for?

Chár. Not so; to me, confiding in my care
And honesty, the casket was entrusted;
And for that faith, which cannot be o'ervalued,
A price of high amount must be repaid.
Touching my breast, I therefore supplicate,
You will not hence, this charge not undertaken.
You, Vardhamána, gather up these bricks
To fill the chasm again; we'll leave no trace
To catch the idle censure of men's tongues.
Come, come, Maitreya, rouse a liberal feeling,
Nor act in this a despicable niggard.

Mait. How can a pauper be a niggard? he has nothing to part with.

Chár. I am not poor, I tell thee, but retain
Treasures I prize beyond whate'er is lost.
Go then, discharge this office, and meanwhile
I hail the dawn with its accustomed rites. [*Exit.*

END OF THE THIRD ACT.

ACT IV.

VASANTASENÁ'S HOUSE.

Enter Female Attendant.

I am sent to the lady Vasantasená by her mother: oh, here she is, looking on a picture, and engaged in conversation with Madaniká.

Enter VASANTASENÁ *as described.*

Vas. But, Madaniká, is this a good likeness of Chárudatta?

Mad. Very good.

Vas. How do you know?

Mad. I conclude so, madam, from the affectionate looks which you bestow upon it.

Vas. How, wench, do you say this in the language of our profession?

Mad. Nay, madam, surely even one of us is not incapable of speaking truth.

Vas. The woman, wench, that admits the love of many men is false to them all.

Mad. Yet, madam, when the eyes and thoughts are intent but on one object, it is very unnecessary to inquire the cause.

Vas. But tell me, girl, do I not seem ridiculous to my friends?

Mad. Nay, not so, madam; a woman is secure of the sympathy of her companions.

Attendant *advances.*

Att. Madam, your mother desires you to ascend your litter and repair to the private apartments.

Vas. To meet my Chárudatta.

Att. The person, madam, who has sent the chariot has sent very costly ornaments.*

Vas. Who is he?

Att. Saḿsthánaka, the Rája's brother-in-law.

Vas. Begone, let me not hear him named.

Att. Forgive me, madam; I but deliver my message.

Vas. The message is odious.

Att. What reply am I to convey to your lady mother?

Vas. Tell her, if she would not have me dead, she must send me no more such messages.

Att. I shall obey. [*Exit.*

The Outside of the House—A Garden.

Enter Śarvilaka (*below*).

Śar. My course is like the moon's, and with the dawn
Declines its fading beams: my deeds have shamed
The lazy night, have triumphed over sleep,
And mocked the baffled vigilance of the watch.
Yet I am scant secure, and view with terror
Him who appears to track my rapid steps,
Or seems to hasten where I rest my flight.—
Thus guilty conscience makes me fear, for man
Is ever frightened by his own offences. †
'Tis for Madaniká's dear sake alone
I perpetrate this violence, as I shun
The leader and his train, avoid the mansion
A woman sole inhabits, or I stand
Still as the door-post, while the town-guard passes,
And with a hundred tricks thus make the night
As full of action as the busy day.

Vas. (*Within.*) Here, girl, take the picture, lay it on my couch; and here, bring me my fan.

* Literally, ornaments to the value of ten thousand *suvarńas.*

† It might be rendered, "Thus conscience does make cowards of us all." Taḿ sarvaḿ tulayati dúshito 'ntarátmá swair doshair bhavati hi śankito manushyaḣ.

Mad. I obey. [*Exit Madaniká.*

Śar. This is the dwelling of Vasantasená. (*Enters.*) Where can Madaniká be found?

MADANIKÁ *enters with the fan.*

Śar. Ah, here she comes, as graceful as the bride
Of love, and soothing to my burning heart
As sandal to the fevered flesh. Madaniká!

Mad. Eh! Śarvilaka? health to you. Whence do you come?

Śar. I will tell you.

Enter VASANTASENÁ (*above*).

Vas. (*Above.*) Madinaká tarries long; where can she be? (*Looks from the window.*) How! she is engaged in conversation with a man: her eyes are fixed intently upon him, and seem to quaff overflowing drafts of love; they appear to understand each other. He woos her probably to be his companion: well, be it so; never be genuine affection thwarted. I will wait her leisure.

Mad. Well, Śarvilaka, proceed. (*He looks cautiously round.*) Why do you thus examine the place? You seem alarmed.

Śar. I have a secret to entrust you with; are we alone?

Mad. Quite.

Vas. A secret! then I must not listen longer.

Śar. Tell me, Madaniká, what cost procures
Your manumission of Vasantasená?

Vas. He names me; the secret then regards me, and I must be a party in it; behind this window I can overhear him unobserved.

Mad. My lady has often declared, Śarvilaka, that she would liberate us all without price if she were her own mistress; but where is the wealth with which you are to purchase my freedom?

Śar. To tell you sooth, my poverty and love
Have urged me to an act of violence.

Vas. How has this act transformed his otherwise goodly appearance!

Mad. Ah! S'arvilaka, for a transitory enjoyment you have endangered two valuable things.

Śar. And what are they?

Mad. Your person and your reputation.

Śar. Silly girl! fortune favours force.

Mad. (*Ironically.*) Your conduct is without blame; the violence you have committed on my account is no doubt quite proper.

Śar. It may be venial, for I have not plundered
A lovely woman graced with glittering gems,
The blossoms of a creeper. I have not filched
A Brahman's gold, for purposes of piety
Collected, nor from the heedless nurse
Have I borne off the innocent babe for hire.
I have well weighed whate'er I have committed.
Apprise your mistress, then, these gems are hers,
That seem as they were made on purpose for her,
If she will yield you up, but let her keep them
Carefully concealed.

Mad. An ornament that must never be worn is but ill suited to my mistress. But come, let me see these trinkets.

Śar. Behold them.

Mad. I have certainly seen them before: where did you get them?

Śar. That concerns not you; ask no questions, but take them.

Mad. (*Angrily.*) If you can place no confidence in me, why seek to make me yours?

Śar. I was informed, then, that near the Bazar resided the chief of his tribe, one Chárudatta.

VASANTASENÁ *and* MADANIKÁ *both faint.*

Śar. Madaniká, revive! what ails the wench?
Her limbs are all unstrung, her looks are wild.
Why, girl, is this your love? is then so terrible
The thought to share your destiny with mine?

Mad. Avoid me, wretch! Yet stay, I dread to ask. Was no one hurt or murdered in that mansion?

Śar. I touch not one who trembles or who sleeps.
Unharmed by me were all in that abode.

Mad. In truth?

Śar. In very truth.

Vas. Do I yet live?

Mad. This is indeed a blessing.

Śar. (*With jealous warmth.*)
You seem to take strange interest in this business.
'Twas love of you that urged me to the act—
Me, sprung of virtuous and of pure descent.
Spurred by my passion, I have offered you
A life of credit and a faithful heart;
And this is my reward—to be reviled,
And find your cares devoted to another.
In vain the lofty tree of flowering youth
Bears goodly fruit, the prey of harlot birds.
Wealth, manhood, all we value, are consumed
By passion's fierce ungovernable fire.
Ah! what a fool is man, to place his trust
In woman or in fortune, fickle both
As serpent-nymphs! Be woman's love unwoo'd,
For humble love she pays with scorn. Let her
First proffer tenderness, and whilst it lasts
Be kind, but leave her as her fondness cools.
'Tis wisely said, for money woman weeps
And smiles at will, and of his confidence,
The man she trusts not, craftily beguiles.
Let then the youth of merit and of birth
Beware the wanton's charms, that baleful blow
Like flowers on charnel ground; the ocean waves
Are less unsteady, and the varying tints
Of eve less fleeting than a woman's fondness.
Wealth is her aim; as soon as man is drained
Of all his goods, like a squeezed colour bag,

She casts him off. Brief as the lightning's flash
Is woman's love. Nay, she can look devotion
To one man whilst another rules her heart,
And even whilst she holds in fond embrace
One lover, for his rival breathes her sighs.
But why expect what nature has withheld?
The lotus blooms not on the mountain's brow,
Nor bears the mule the burthen of the horse;
The grain of barley buds not into rice,
Nor dwells one virtue in the breast of woman.*
Fool that I was, to let that wretch escape;
'Tis not too late, and Chárudatta dies. (*Going.*)

Mad. (*Catching hold of him.*) You have talked a great deal of stuff, and are angry without rhyme or reason.

Śar. How, without reason?

Mad. These ornaments are in truth the property of Vasantasená.

Śar. Indeed!

Mad. And were left by her in deposit with Chárudatta.

Śar. For what purpose?

Mad. I will tell you. (*Whispers.*)

Śar. I am overcome with shame. The friendly branch
That gave me shadow when oppressed with heat,
My heedless hand has shorn of its bright leaves.

Vas. I am glad that he repents: he has acted without reflection.

Śar. What is to be done?

Mad. You are the best judge.

* In generalising some of these asperities the author is made to appear more of a misogynist than he really is; some of the aspersions are, however, addressed to the whole sex, and the application of the rest is not without countenance. The Hindu poets very rarely dispraise women; they almost invariably represent them as amiable and affectionate. In this they might give a lesson to the bards of more lofty nations, and particularly to the Greeks, who both in tragedy and comedy pursued the fair sex with implacable rancour. Aristophanes is not a whit behind Euripides, although he ridicules the tragedian for his ungallánt propensities.

Śar. Nay, not so.

Nature is woman's teacher, and she learns
More sense than man, the pedant, gleans from books.

Mad. I should advise you then, go and return these ornaments to Chárudatta.

Śar. And what if he deliver me up to justice?

Mad. There is no heat from the moon.

Śar. I heed not of his gentleness, and brave
Unshrinkingly the consequence of all
I dare to do—but this, this act I blush for;
And of such petty scoundrels as myself
How must the prince dispose? No—no,
We must devise some other means.

Mad. I have.

Vas. What can she suggest?

Mad. You shall pass yourself off as a messenger from Chárudatta, sent to restore these trinkets to my lady.

Śar. And what results?

Mad. You will be no thief; Chárudatta will sustain no loss, and my lady recover her own property.

Śar. This is downright robbery, carrying off my booty.

Mad. If you do not relinquish it, that will be much more like robbery.

Vas. Well said, Madaniká; you advise as a faithful friend.

Śar. I have gained much by asking your advice.
When there is no moon at night, 'tis difficult
To get a guide that may be safely followed.

Mad. Stay here,* whilst I give notice to my mistress.

Śar. Be it so.

Mad. (*Approaches Vasantasená.*) Lady, a Brahman attends you from Chárudatta.

Vas. How do you know his mission?

Mad. Do I not know my own affairs?

* In the original *Imassiṁ kámadevagehe*, in this dwelling of Kámadeva, a chamber or open porch probably, with the figure of the Hindu Cupid.

Vas. (*Smiling.*) Very true; let him advance, Madaniká.

[*She descends, and brings Śarvilaka forward as Vasantasená enters below.*

Śar. Lady, I salute you; peace be with you.

Vas. I salute you. Pray be seated. (*Sits.*)

Śar. The respected Chárudatta informs you, that as his house is very insecure, he is apprehensive this casket may be lost, and therefore begs you will take it back again. (*Gives it to Madaniká and is going.*)

Vas. Stay; I have a favour to request. Let me trouble you to convey to the worthy sender something from me.

Śar. (*Aside.*) Who the deuce is to give it to him? (*Aloud.*) What am I to take?

Vas. Madaniká.

Śar. I understand you not.

Vas. I understand myself.

Śar. What mean you?

Vas. The truth is, it was agreed between Chárudatta and me, that the person by whom he should send back these jewels should receive Madaniká as a present from me on his account: you are therefore to take this damsel, and thank Chárudatta for her. You understand me now.

Śar. (*Apart.*) She knows the truth; that is clear. No matter (*Aloud.*)

May all prosperity bless Chárudatta.
'Tis politic in man to nurture merit,
For poverty with worth is richer far
Than majesty without all real excellence.
Nought is beyond its reach; the radiant moon
Won by its worth a seat on *Śiva's* * brow.

Vas. Who waits? bring forth the litter.†

Śar. It attends. (*The carriage comes on.*)

Vas. My dear girl, Madaniká, ascend the litter; I have given you away: look at me well; do not forget me.

* The god *Śiva* wears the crescent moon as the ornament of his forehead.

† A small covered carriage on two wheels, drawn by oxen.

Mad. (*Weeping.*) I am discarded by my mistress. (*Falls at her feet.*)

Vas. Nay, wench, rise, it is now my place to stoop to you; go take your seat, and keep me ever in your recollection.

Śar. Lady, may every good attend you! Madaniká, with grateful looks survey your bounteous benefactress; bow your head in gratitude to her to whom you owe the unexpected dignity that waits upon the title and the state of wife.*

[*They salute* VASANTASENÁ *as she departs, and ascend the car.*

(*Behind.*)

Who hears? who hears? the Governor commands. In consequence of a reported prophecy, that the son of a cowherd, named Áryaka, shall ascend the throne, his majesty Pálaka has deemed it expedient to apprehend him, and detain him in confinement. Let all men therefore remain quietly in their houses, and entertain no alarm.

Śar. How! the king has seized my dear friend Áryaka, and I am thinking of a wife!

This world presents two things most dear to all men;
A friend and mistress; but the friend is prized
Above a hundred beauties. I must hence,
And try to liberate him. (*Alights.*)

Mad. Stay but a while, my dearest lord; consign me first to reputable friends, then leave me, if it must be so.

Śar. You speak my thoughts, love. Hark ye. (*To the servant.*) Know you the residence of Rebhila,
The chief of the musicians?

Serv. I do, sir.

* *Vadhúśabdávagunṫhana*, the covering of the title of wife. At the same time Madaniká is of course only a wife for the nonce, or rather of an inferior degree; an *amie de maison*, or a gentle concubine. In India these left-hand marriages are common amongst both Hindus and Mohammedans, and are considered by no means disreputable. It would be impossible to contract any other with a woman of Madaniká's past life and servile condition. On the ground of disparity of rank, left-hand marriages are still sanctioned in Germany, but they seem not essentially different from those here alluded to.

Śar. Convey my lady thither.

Serv. As you command.

Mad. I obey. Farewell. For my sake, be not rash.

[*Exit.*

Śar. Now then to rouse the friends of Áryaka,
Our kindred and associates—all who deem
The king has wronged their will, and all who trust
The prowess of their arms. We will redeem
Our chief from bonds, as by his faithful minister
*Udayana** was rescued.
This seizure is unjust, it is the deed
Of a most cowardly and treacherous foe;
But we shall soon release him from such grasp,
Like the fair moon from *Ráhu's* jaws set free.†

[*Exit.*

Vasantasená's Dwelling (inside).

Enter A Female Attendant, *meeting* VASANTASENÁ.

Att. Lady, you are fortunate, a Brahman from Chárudatta.

Vas. This is indeed a lucky day. Receive him with all

* *Udayana* or *Vatsa* is a celebrated character in Hindu fiction. He was the son of *Sahasránika* and grandson of *Śatánika*, who transferred the capital of Upper India from Hástinapur to Kausámbí. *Śatánika* was the son of *Janamejaya*, the great grandson of *Arjuna*. *Vatsa* was named *Udayana* from being educated on the Eastern or Udaya mountain by the sage *Jamadagni*. When arrived at maturity, he was decoyed into captivity by *Chańdasena*, king of Ujjayin. He was liberated by his minister *Yogandharáyańa*, and in his escape carried off *Vásavadattá*, the daughter of his captor. His adventures are recorded in the *Vásavadattá*, a poem by *Subhandhu*, and in the Vŕihat-Kathá. They have been translated from the latter and published in the *Calcutta Quarterly Magazine* for June 1824. All the parties will become more familiar to us hereafter, as *Vatsa* is the hero of the Ratnávalí, translated in the following pages.

† *Ráhu* is the ascending node, personified as the head of the Dragon, who is supposed, in the mythological astronomy of the Hindus, to seize upon the moon, and thus occasion eclipses. According to the *Mahábhárata*, *Ráhu* was one of the *Asuras*, or demons, who at the churning of the ocean crept amongst the gods and stole a draught of *amŕita* or ambrosia. The intruder was detected by the Sun and Moon, who pointing him out to Vishńu, that deity decapitated the demon: hence his immortality and his enmity to the planets.

respect; request him to enter, and call the Chamberlain* to attend him.

Att. As you command. [*Exit.*

Outside of the House.

Enter MAITREYA *and the* BANDHULA.

Mait. Here's honour! The sovereign of the *Rákhasàs*, *Rávańa*, travels in the car of *Kuvera*, obtained by the force of his devotions; but I, who am a poor Brahman, and no saint, yet I am conveyed about by lovely damsels.

Att. This is the outer door, sir.

Mait. A very pretty entrance, indeed. The threshold is very neatly coloured, well swept and watered; the floor is beautified with strings of sweet flowers; the top of the gate is lofty and gives one the pleasure of looking up to the clouds, whilst the jasmine festoon hangs tremblingly down, as if it were now tossing on the trunk of *Indra's* elephant.† Over the doorway is a lofty arch of ivory; above it again wave flags dyed with safflower, their fringes curling in the wind, like fingers that beckon me, "come hither." On either side, the capitals of the door-posts support elegant crystal flower-pots, in which young mango-trees are springing up. The door panels are of gold, stuck, like the stout breast of a demon, with studs of

* The word so rendered is *bandhula*, an explanation of which is offered in the text a little further on.

† This garland was the cause of very important events. According to the *Brahma-Vaivarta-Puráńa*, it was given to Indra by a choleric sage named *Durvásas*, who received it from a Vidyádharí: attaching little value to the gift, the god tossed it to his elephant, and the elephant threw it to earth. *Durvásas*, highly offended, pronounced that Indra and all the three worlds under his supremacy should be deprived of their *Śri*, fortune or prosperity: in consequence, the world fell into decay, sacrifices ceased, and the gods were enfeebled. Everything would have perished, if the goddess had not been recovered. To re-obtain her, the gods and demons, by the advice and with the aid of Vishńu, churned the ocean:—"Such mighty matters spring from trivial things."

adamant.* The whole cries "away" to a poor man, whilst its splendour catches the eye of the wisest.

Att. This leads to the first court.† Enter, sir, enter.

(*They enter the first Court.*)

Mait. Bless me! why here is a line of palaces, as white as the moon, as the conch, as the stalk of the water-lily—the stucco has been laid on here by handfuls; golden steps, embellished with various stones, lead to the upper apartments, whence the crystal windows, festooned with pearls, and bright as the eyes of a moon-faced maid, look down upon *Ujjayin.* The porter dozes on an easy-chair as stately as a Brahman deep in the Vedas; and the very crows, crammed with rice and curds, disdain the fragments of the sacrifice,‡ as if they were no more than scattered plaster. Proceed.

Att. That is the second court. Enter.

(*They enter the second Court.*)

Mait. Oh, here are the stables; the carriage oxen are in good case, pampered with *javasa*§ I declare; and straw and oil-cakes are ready for them; their horns are bright with

* The correctness of the comparison is more evident in the original, where the word *vajra* implies both a diamond and the thunderbolt of Indra, with which he pierces the breasts of his foes.

† The interior of the houses at Pompeii conveys some idea of an Indian house, which like them is a set of chambers, of one or two stories, surrounding a central unroofed square. A house of a superior description is merely denoted by the superior extent of this square, and by its comprising a set or series of them, as in the text. The several entrances were in representation left, we may presume, to the imagination of the audience; something after the fashion which Sir Philip Sydney describes: "Now you shall have three ladies walk to gather flowers, and then you must believe the stage to be a garden. By and by we hear news of shipwreck in the same place; then we are to blame, if we accept it not for a rock. Upon the back of that comes out a hideous monster with fire and smoke; and then the miserable beholders are bound to take it for a cave; while, in the meantime, two armies fly in, represented with swords and bucklers, and then what hard heart will not receive it for a pitched field."

‡ The last portion of the offering of rice, &c., thrown into the air for the spirits of ill, the *Bali,* of which notice was taken in the first scene.

§ A species of hedysarum.

grease. Here we have a buffalo snorting indignantly, like a Brahman of high caste whom somebody has affronted; here the ram* stands to have his neck well rubbed, like a wrestler after a match; here they dress the manes of the horses; here is a monkey tied as fast a thief;† and here the *mahauts*‡ are plying the elephants with balls of rice and *ghee*. Proceed.

Att. This, sir, is the third gateway.

(*They enter the third Court.*)

Mait. Oh, this is the public court, where the young bucks of *Ujjayin* assemble; these are their seats, I suppose—the half-read book lies on the gaming-table, the men of which are made of jewels. Oh, yonder are some old hangers-on, lounging about with many-coloured pictures in their hands, and skilled in the peace and war of love. What next?

Att. This is the entrance to the fourth court.

(*They enter the fourth Court.*)

Mait. Oh, ho! this is a very gay scene: here the drums, whilst beaten by taper fingers, emit, like clouds, a murmuring tone; there the cymbals beating time, flash as they descend like the unlucky stars § that fall from heaven. The flute here breathes the soft hum of the bee, whilst here a damsel holds the *víńá* in her lap, and frets its wires with her finger-nails, like some wild minx that sets her mark on the face of her offending swain: some damsels are singing, like so many bees intoxicated with flowery nectar; others are practising the graceful dance, and others are employed in reading plays and

* Rams in India are commonly trained to fight.

† Monkeys are kept in stables as a sort of scape-goats apparently: hence the Persian proverb current in Hindustan, "The misfortune of the stable on the head of the monkey:" *Bilai tavileh ber seri maimun.*—Roebuck's Proverbs.

‡ Elephant-driver; the Sanskrit is *Mahámátra*. The balls alluded to are the common food of the elephants.

§ The phrase is, the stars that have lost their virtue, *kshíńapuńyá táraká*. The notion is, that the stars are individuals raised to that honour for a time proportioned to the sum of their merits; this being exhausted, they descend to earth, often visibly, as in the case of shooting-stars.

poems.* The place is hung with water-jars, suspended to catch the cooling breeze. What comes next?

Att. This is the gate of the fifth court.

(*They enter the fifth Court.*)

Mait. Ah, how my mouth waters! what a savoury scent of oil and asafœtida! The kitchen sighs softly forth its fragrant and abundant smoke—the odours are delicious—they fill me with rapture. The butcher's boy is washing the skin of an animal just slain, like so much foul linen; the cook is surrounded with dishes; the sweetmeats are mixing; the cakes are baking. (*Apart.*) Oh that I could meet with some one to do me a friendly turn; one who would wash my feet, and say, eat, sir, eat. (*Aloud.*) This is certainly *Indra's* heaven; the damsels are *Apsarasas*, the *Bandhulas* are *Gandharbas.* Pray, why do they call you *Bandhulas?*

Att. We inhabit the dwellings of others and eat the bread of the stranger: we are the offspring of parents whom no tie connects: we exercise our indescribable merits in gaining men's money, and we sport through life as free and unrestrained as the cubs of the elephant.

Mait. What do we come to next?

Att. This is the sixth entry.

(*They enter.*)

Mait. The arched gateway is of gold and many-coloured gems on a ground of sapphire, and looks like the bow of *Indra*† in an azure sky. What is going forward here so busily? It is the jeweller's court: skilful artists are examining pearls, topazes, sapphires, emeralds, rubies, the lapis-lazuli, coral, and other jewels; some set rubies in gold, some work gold ornaments on coloured thread, some string pearls, some grind the lapis-lazuli, some pierce shells, and some cut coral. Here we have perfumers drying the saffron bags, shaking the musk bags, expressing the sandal-juice and compounding essences.

* Reading, *Nátyaṁ saśringáram.*

† The rainbow.

Whom have we here? fair damsels and their gallants, laughing, talking, chewing musk and betel, and drinking wine. Here are the male and female attendants, and here are miserable hangers-on—men that neglected their own families and spent their all upon the harlot, and are now glad to quaff the drainings of her wine-cup.

Att. This is the seventh court. Enter.

(*They enter the seventh Court.*)

Mait. This is the aviary—very handsome indeed! The doves bill and coo in comfort; the pampered parrot croaks like a Brahman *pańđit*, stuffed with curds and rice, chanting a hymn from the Vedas; the *Maina* * chatters as glibly as a housemaid issuing her mistress's command to her fellow-servants, while the *Kóil*,† crammed with juicy fruit, whines like a water-carrier. The quails fight; the partridges cry; the domestic peacock dances about delighted, and fans the palace with his gem-emblazoned tail, as if to cool its heated walls; the swans,‡ like balls of moonlight, roll about in pairs, and follow each graceful maid, as if to learn to imitate her walk, whilst the long-legged cranes § stalk about the court, like eunuchs on guard. I declare the lady lives here amongst the winged race as if she tenanted *Indra's* garden. Well, where do you go now?

Att. Enter, sir, the eighth court.

(*They enter.*)

Mait. Pray, who is that gentleman dressed in silken raiment, glittering with rich ornaments, and rolling about as if his limbs were out of joint?

Att. That, sir, is my lady's brother.

Mait. Humph—what course of pious austerity in his last life made him Vasantasená's brother? Nay, not so; for after

* The *Madanasárikà*, the talking Maina or Mainate, Indian Stare or Grakle (Gracula religiosa).

† The Indian cuckoo (Cuculus indicus).

‡ The *rájahańsa;* the term is also applied to the flamingo.

§ The *sárasa*, or Indian crane.

all, though smooth, bright, and fragrant, the *champa** tree that grows on funeral ground is not to be approached. And pray, who is that lady dressed in flowered muslin?†—a goodly person truly; her feet shining with oil thrust into a pair of slippers: she sits in state, high on a gorgeous throne.

Att. That is my lady's mother.

Mait. A portly old hag, indeed: how did she contrive to get in here? Oh, I suppose she was first set up here, as they do with an unwieldy *Mahádeva*, and then the walls were built round her.‡

Att. How now, slave? What! do you make a jest of our lady, affected, too, as she is with a quartan ague?

Mait. A what? O mighty Fever, be pleased to afflict me with a quartan, if such are its symptoms!

Att. You will die, slave.

Mait. No, hussey; better that this bloated porpoise, swelled up with wine and years, die; there will then be a dinner for a thousand jackals. But no matter; what do you know about it? I had heard of Vasantasená's wealth, and now I find it true; it seems to me that the treasures of the three worlds are collected in this mansion. I am in doubt whether to regard it as the dwelling of a courtesan or the palace of *Kuvera*.§ Where is your lady?

Att. She's in the arbour. Enter.

(*They enter the Garden.*)

Mait. A very lovely scene! the numerous trees are bowed down by delicious fruit, and between them are silken swings

* A handsome tree with fragrant blossoms (Michelia champac).

† *Phulla-pávâraa-páudá*, for *Pushpa-právâraka-právŕitá*, dressed in a garment of or with flowers, which the commentator explains to mean worked muslin: *Súkshma-sútra-pushpáńi kŕitrimáńi yatra bhavanti sa tathá pushpa-páta-prasiddhaK.* The cloth on which artificial flowers are worked in fine thread is well known as *Pushpapát*, flowered cloth.

‡ The stone emblems of this deity are sometimes of great bulk and weight.

§ The God of Wealth.

constructed for the light form of youthful beauty : the yellow jasmine, the graceful *málatí*,* the full-blossomed *malliká*,† the blue clitoria, spontaneous shed their flowers, and strew the ground with a carpet more lovely than any in the groves of *Indra* ; the reservoir glows with the red lotus blossoms, like the dawn with the fiery beams of the rising sun; and here the *aśoka*‡ tree, with its rich crimson blossoms, shines like a young warrior bathed with the sanguine shower of the furious fight. Where is your lady?

Att. Look lower, and you will see her.

Mait. (*Approaching Vasantasená.*) Health to you, lady.

Vas. (*Rising.*) Welcome, Maitreya ; take a seat.

Mait. Pray, keep you yours. (*They sit.*)

Vas. I hope all is well with the son of the *Sárthaváha*.§

Mait. Is all well with your ladyship?

Vas. Undoubtedly, Maitreya ; the birds of affection gladly nestle in the tree, which, fruitful in excellence, puts forth the flowers of magnanimity and the leaves of merit, and rises with the trunk of modesty from the root of honour. ||

Mait. (*Apart.*) Figurative indeed. (*Aloud.*) What else?

Vas. What brings you hither?¶

Mait. I will tell you :—Chárudatta presents his respects to you.

Vas. With respect I receive his commands.

Mait. He desires me to say, that he has lost your golden casket; it was impledged by him at play, and the keeper of

* Jasminum grandiflorum.

† Jasminum zambac.

‡ A tree with red blossoms, Jonesia asoka.

§ The head of his tribe.

|| This is a passage of a very unusual character in Sanskŕit composition, and is rather in the style of Persian than Indian writing : it has, however, more of the allegory than is common to Persian poetry, in which, though the metaphors follow one another without intermission, they are independent and unconnected.

¶ It is a singularity that so far in the scene Vasantasená speaks Sanskŕit.

the tables, a servant of the prince, is gone, no one knows whither.

Att. Lady, you are in luck; the grave Chárudatta turned gambler.

Vas. (*Apart.*) How? the casket has been stolen, and he says it was lost at play. Yet even in this I love him.

Mait. As the accident cannot now be helped, he requests, in lieu of the casket, you will accept this string of diamonds.

Vas. (*Apart.*) Shall I show him the ornaments? (*Considering.*) No, not so.

Mait. Will you not receive this equivalent?

Vas. (*Smiling.*) Why not, Maitreya? (*Takes and puts it to her heart.*) But how is this? do drops of nectar fall from the mango-tree after it has shed its blossoms? My good friend, tell that sad gambler, Chárudatta, that I shall call upon him in the evening.

Mait. (*Apart.*) So, so; she intends to get more out of him, I suppose. (*Aloud.*) I shall so inform him, madam. (*Apart.*) I wish he was rid of this precious acquaintance. [*Exit.*

Vas. Here, girl, take the jewels and attend me to Chárudatta.

Att. But look, madam, look! a sudden storm is gathering.

Vas. No matter.

Let the clouds gather and dark night descend,
And heavy fall unintermitted showers;
I heed them not, wench, when I haste to seek
His presence, whose loved image warms my heart.—
Take charge of these, and lightly trip along. [*Exit.*

END OF THE FOURTH ACT.

ACT V.

CHÁRUDATTA'S GARDEN.

Enter CHÁRUDATTA (*looking up*).

A HEAVY storm impends: the gathering gloom
Delights the peafowl* and distracts the swan, †
Not yet prepared for periodic flight;
And these deep shades contract with sad despondence
The heart that pines in absence. ‡ Through the air,
A rival *Keśava,* § the purple cloud
Rolls stately on, girt by the golden lightning,

* These birds are the invariable accompaniments of the rainy season, as observed in my translation of the Cloud Messenger. It is unnecessary to cite the parallel passages, as the idea recurs often enough in this act, in which all the commonplaces of Hindu poetry relating to the "Rains" are exhausted; a few of the repetitions have been purposely omitted.

† Rather the wild gray goose, which bird is supposed to migrate annually to the Himalaya mountains, particularly to the Mánasarovara Lake, whence it is termed Mánasaukas, the dweller of *Mánasa.* Mr Moorcroft, in his adventurous visit to this lake in 1812, found these birds in vast flocks along the beach and on the water; and concluded from what he saw that they were accustomed to frequent the lake and breed in the surrounding rocks, when the swell of the rivers of Hindustan and the inundation of the plains conceal their usual food.

‡ The time just previous to the commencement of the rainy season is the period at which Indian travellers may be expected home, not only because the weather is then favourable, but because after the rains have set in, the roads are broken up, and travelling becomes difficult and unpleasant. Hence the Hindu poets always speak of this season as one at which lovers, till then separated, meet again.

§ A name of Krishńa, *Crinitus,* alluding, as generally supposed, to his graceful tresses, but, according to the *Mahábhárata,* from his being an incarnation of one of the hairs of Vishńu.

As by his yellow garb, and bearing high
The long white line of storks, the God's pure shell :*
From the dark womb, in rapid fall descend
The silvery drops, and glittering in the gleam,
Shot from the lightning, bright and fitful, sparkle
Like a rich fringe rent from the robe of heaven.
The firmament is filled with scattered clouds,
And, as they fly before the wind, their forms,
As in a picture, image various shapes,
The semblances of storks and soaring swans,
Of dolphins and the monsters of the deep,
Of dragons vast, and pinnacles, and towers.
The spreading shade, methinks, is like the host
Of *Dhṙitarášhṫra* † shouting loud in thunder.
Yon strutting peacock welcomes its advance,
Like proud *Duryodhan*, vaunting of his might:
From its dread enmity, the *Kóil* ‡ flies,
Like luckless *Yudhishṫhira*, § by the dice
Bereaved of power, and scatter wild the swans,
Like the proscribed and houseless *Páńḋavas*,
Wandering from home and every comfort far,
Through paths untrod, till then, and realms unknown.
Maitreya long delays. Will not to-day
Apprise me of the issue of his visit? (*Retires.*)

Enter MAITREYA.

What a rapacious, mean wretch is this harlot! Scarcely a word did she say, but, without any ceremony, pounced upon the necklace. With all her pomp and parade, she could not say to me, my good friend, Maitreya, take a little refreshment; not

* The *śankha* or conch shell is borne by Vishńu in one of his hands.

† The father of *Duryodhana* and the other Kuru princes, whose war with their cousins, the sons of Páńḋu, is the subject of the *Mahábhárata*.

‡ The Indian cuckoo.

§ The eldest of the sons of Páńḋu, who with his brothers was banished from the realm of his forefathers and spent some time in the forests towards the South of India.

even so much as to offer me a draught of water—her wealth is positively all thrown away upon her. It is very true, there is no lotus that has not a stalk; no trader that is not a cheat; there is not a goldsmith that is not a thief; there never was a village meeting without a quarrel; and there never will be a harlot without rapacity: these are things that always go together. I shall therefore dissuade my worthy friend from his infatuation. Ha! yonder I see him in the garden. Health and prosperity to Chárudatta!

Chár. (*Comes forward.*) Welcome, my good friend; Maitreya, sit down.

Mait. I am seated. (*Sits.*)

Chár. Now, my friend, your news?

Mait. It is all over.

Chár. How so? does she refuse the proffered gems?

Mait. We have no such luck; she put her soft hands to her forehead, and then laid hold of the necklace.

Chár. Then, why do you complain?

Mait. Why? reason enough. We have made a pretty job of it; to lose a necklace worth the four seas, for a thing of little value, and one we neither ate, nor drank, and which a thief carried off.

Chár. You reason idly.

The pledge was here deposited in trust,
And for that trust a costly price was due.

Mait. I have another cause of complaint. She made signs to her damsels, and they covered their faces with their veils and made me their merriment. I beg, therefore, that you will desist from such unbecoming intercourse. A courtesan is like a thorn that has run into your foot; you cannot even get rid of it without pain; and it is indisputably true, that wherever a harlot, an elephant, a scribe,* a mendicant, a

* The *Káyastha* or *Kayth*, whose profession is writing and accounts. Men of this tribe were usually employed by the Hindu princes in the collection and record of their revenues, and their character for a spirit of extortion became proverbial. They appear to have been particularly obnoxious to the Brahmans.

spy, or a jackass, find admission, they are sure to do mischief.

Chár. Enough of this unmerited reviling.

My fallen fortunes are a sure protection.
The fiery steed bounds fleetly o'er the plain
Till fading breath retards his lagging course;
So man's desires first urge his heedless path,
But soon exhausted shrink into his bosom.
Believe me, friend, a female of this order,
A true wealth-hunter, troubles not the poor:
(*Apart.*) She, she, alone, bestows her love on merit.
(*Aloud.*) We are by wealth abandoned, and by her.

Mait. (*Apart.*) This love is the devil: he turns up his eyes and sighs from the very bottom of his heart. I see plainly my advice to him to conquer his passion only serves to confirm it. (*Aloud.*) She desired me to say, she intends paying you a visit this evening. I suspect she is not satisfied with the necklace, and intends to demand something more valuable.

Chár. Well, let her come; she shall depart contented.

Enter KUMBHILAKA, *Vasantasená's Servant.*

I wish every one to take notice, that the harder it rains, the more thoroughly do I get ducked, and the colder the wind that blows down my back, the more do my limbs shiver. A pretty situation for a man of my talents; for one who can play the flute with seven holes, the *víná* with seven strings, can sing like a jackass, and who acknowledges no musical superior, except perhaps *Tamburu** or *Nárada.*† Vasantasená sends me to Chárudatta's house. (*Advances.*) There is Chárudatta in the garden, and that dunderhead Maitreya with him. I must throw out a signal to him. (*Throws a clod of earth at Maitreya.*)

Mait. Holloa! who pelts me with a pellet, like a *kapittha*‡ tree in an orchard?

* An attendant upon *Kuvera*, and one of the chief *Gandharbas* or choristers of heaven.

† The son of Brahmá, the inventor of the Indian lute.

‡ The elephant or wood apple (Feronia elephantum).

Chár. It was probably thrown down in their sport by the pigeons that tenant the top of the garden wall.

Mait. Wait a while, you saucy son of a slave, and with this stick I will knock you off the wall, like a ripe mango from the tree.

Chár. Sit down, sit down; fright not the gentle bird, nor chase him from his mate.

Kum. The blockhead! he sees the pigeons and cannot see me. I must give him another salutation. (*Throws another clod.*)

Mait. Hey, again! (*Looks up.*) O Kumbhilaka! is it you? Wait a while, and I will come to you. (*Goes to the door.*) Come in; how fares it?

Kum. I salute you, sir.

Mait. And what brings you here in such foul weather?

Kum. She sent me.

Mait. And who is she?

Kum. She—she—she.

Mait. She—she—she! What are you sputtering about, like an old miser when things are dear? Who—who—who?

Kum. Hoo—hoo—hoo! What are you too-whooing about, like an owl that has been scared from a sacrifice? *

Mait. Speak out, man, intelligibly.

Kum. I will; but first I'll give you something to guess.

Mait. I shall give you a box of the ears, I believe.

Kum. Never mind that. In which season, pray, does the mango blossom?

Mait. In the season of *Grishma* † to be sure, you blockhead!

Kum. Blockhead yourself! it does no such thing.

Mait. Hey, how is that? I must ask my friend. Stop a moment. (*Goes to Chárudatta.*) Pray, sir, in which season does the mango blossom?

* In the original, Kumbhilaka says *Esá ká*, to which Maitreya replies, *ká, esá, ká*. Kumbhilaka's answer is, What are you barking about, like the lover of Indra's sacrifice (a dog)?

† The hot season.

Chár. Why, you simpleton, in *Vasanta.**

Mait. (*To Kumb.*) Why, you simpleton, the mango blossoms in *Vasanta.*

Kum. Very well. Now answer me one more question: Who guards wealthy towns?

Mait. Why, the town guard, to be sure.

Kum. No; that is not it.

Mait. No? Let me see. (*Aside.*) I must consult Chárudatta. Pray, sir, who guards wealthy towns?

Chár. The Sená† undoubtedly.

Mait. (*To Kum.*) The Sená undoubtedly.

Kum. Very well; now put your answers together; quick, quick!

Mait. Ha, I have it! Vasantasená.‡

Kum. She is here.

Mait. I must apprise my friend. Sir, we have a dun§ here.

Chár. Here? a dun in my house?

Mait. I do not know anything about the house, but there is one at the door. Vasantasená is arrived.

Chár. Nay, now you jest?

Mait. If you do not believe me, ask this fellow. Here, you Kumbhilaka!

Kum. (*Advancing.*) Sir, I salute you.

* Spring. It is necessary to keep the original words here, and in what follows.

† The army or military.

‡ This is sad quibbling, but may be vindicated by the example of much loftier genius; it is sufficient to show, also, that the regular charade—for it is nothing else—is neither of modern nor western invention. There is some further quibbling in the text. Maitreya puts his answer together *Sená Vasanta*, and the wit lies in punning and blundering on *parivartaya*, turn round or transpose, and *pada* a foot or an inflected word. The very term might be suspected of etymological affinity to the English "Pun," being *pahna*, the Prákŕit form of *praśna*, a question, Kumbhilaka commencing his *facetiœ* with *Ale, paṅhaṁ de daiśśam*, I will give you a question.

§ *Dhanika*, a creditor, a dun.

Chár. You are welcome; tell me, is Vasantasená here?

Kum. She is, sir.

Chár. Never be grateful message unrewarded; this for your pains. (*Gives him his garment.*)

Kum. (*Bows.*) I shall inform my mistress. [*Exit.*

Mait. Now, I hope you are satisfied. To come out in such weather; you can have no doubt what brings her.

Chár. I do not feel quite confident.

Mait. Depend upon it, I am right; the casket was worth more than the necklace, and she comes for the difference.

Chár. (*Apart.*) She shall be gratified. (*They retire.*)

(*Outside of the Garden.*)

Enter VASANTASENÁ *splendidly dressed, attended by the Vita, a female servant, and one carrying a large umbrella.**

Att. Lady, upon the mountain's brow, the clouds
Hang dark and drooping, as the aching heart
Of her who sorrows for her absent lord;
Their thunders rouse the peafowl, and the sky
Is agitated by their wings, as fanned
By thousand fans with costly gems inchased.
The chattering frog quaffs the pellucid drops
That cleanse his miry jaws. The peahen shrieks
With transport, and the *Nípa* freshly blooms.
The moon is blotted by the driving scud,
As is the saintly character by those
Who wear its garb to veil their abject lives;
And like the damsel whose fair fame is lost
In ever-changing loves, the lightning, true
To no one quarter, flits along the skies.

Vas. You speak it well, my friend: to me it seems—
The jealous night, as with the gloom she wantons,
Looks on me as a rival bride, and dreading
I may disturb her pleasures, stops my path
And bids me angrily my steps retrace.

* We have now an emulatively poetical description of the rainy season.

Att. Reply with courage, chide her to submission.
Vas. Reviling is the weakness of our sex,
And but of small avail,—I heed her not.
Let the clouds fall in torrents, thunder roar,
And heaven's red bolt dash fiery to the ground,
The dauntless damsel faithful love inspires,
Treads boldly on, nor dreads the maddening storm.
Vita. Like an invading prince, who holds his court
Within the city of his humbled foe,
Yon mighty cloud, advancing with the wind,
With store of arrowy shower, with thundering drums,
And blazing streamers, marches to assail
In his own heavens the monarch of the night.
Vas. Nay, nay, not so ; I rather read it thus :
The clouds, that like unwieldly elephants
Roll their inflated masses grumbling on,
Or whiten with the migratory troop
Of hovering cranes, teach anguish to the bosom.
The stork's shrill cry sounds like the plaintive tabor
To her who, while she wanders o'er its parchment,
Is lost in musings of her lord's return,
And every tone that hails the rainy season,
Falls on her heart like brine upon a wound.
Vita. Behold, where yonder ponderous cloud assumes
The stature of the elephant, the storks
Entwine a fillet for his front, and waves
The lightning, like a *chowri* o'er his head.
Vas. Observe, my friend, the day is swallowed up
By these deep shades, dark as the dripping leaf
Of the tamála tree, and, like an elephant
That cowering shuns the battle's arrowy sleet,
So shrinks the scattering ant-hill from the shower.
The fickle lightning darts such brilliant rays,
As gleam from golden lamps in temples hung,
Whilst, like the consort of an humble lord,
The timid moonlight peeps amidst the clouds.

Vita. There, like a string of elephants, the clouds
In regular file, by lightning fillets bound,
Move slowly at their potent god's commands.
The heavens let down a silver chain to earth.
The earth, that shines with buds and sheds sweet odours,
Is pierced with showers, like diamond-shafted darts
Launched from the rolling mass of deepest blue,
Which heaves before the breeze and foams with flame;
Like ocean's dark waves by the tempest driven,
And tossing high their flashing surge to shore.*

Vas. Hailed by the peafowl with their shrillest cries,
By the pleased storks delightedly caressed,
And by the provident swans with anxious eye
Regarded, yonder rests one threatening cloud
Involving all the atmosphere in gloom.

Vita. The countenance of heaven is close concealed,
By shades the lightning scant irradiates.
The day and night confusedly intermix,
And all the lotus eyes of either close,
The world is lulled to slumber by the sound
Of falling waters, sheltered by the clouds
That countless crowd the chambers of the sky.

Vas. The stars are all extinct, as fades the memory
Of kindness in a bad man's heart. The heavens
Are shorn of all their radiance, as the wife
Her glory loses in her husband's absence.
In sooth, I think the firmament dissolves:
Melted by Indra's scorching bolt it falls
In unexhausted torrents. Now the cloud
Ascends—now stoops—now roars aloud in thunder—
Now sheds its streams—now frowns with deeper gloom,
Full of fantastic change, like one new raised

* I have in this place, and in a few others, expanded the expression, in order to convey more accurately the idea intended by the simpler phraseology of the original.

By fortune's fickle favours.

Vita. Now the sky
With lightning flames, now laughs with whitening storks—
Now glows with *Indra's* painted bow, that hurls
Its hundred shafts—now rattles with his bolt—
Now loud it chafes with rushing winds, and now
With clustering clouds that roll their spiry folds
Like sable snakes along—it thickens dark,
As if 'twere clothed with vapours, such as spread
When incense soars in curling wreaths to heaven.

Vas. Shame on thee, cloud, that seekest to affright me
With thy loud threats, and with thy watery shafts
Wouldst stay my progress, hastening to my love.
Indra! I violate no vows to thee,
That thou shouldst thunder angrily reproof;
It ill becomes thee to obstruct my path.
Draw off thy clouds in pity to my passion,
If ever thou wert conscious of affection,
And for *Ahalyá** wore a husband's form.
Or be it so—rage on—still pour thy deluge,
And launch thy hundred-shafted bolt, in vain.
Thou canst not stop the faithful maid that flies
To lose her terrors in a lover's arms.
If the clouds roar—e'en be it so—it is
Their nature—all of man is ever savage.
But gentle lightning, how canst thou not know
The cares that agitate the female bosom?†

Vita. Enough—she now befriends us, like a lamp
That glows in *Indra's* palace, like a banner,
Whose white folds wave upon a mountain's brow,

* *Indra* having fallen in love with *Ahalyá*, the wife of the sage *Gautama*, and finding her not to be won to his purpose, deceived her by the Amphictryonic device of assuming her husband's shape.

† The clouds are male personifications, the lightning is a nymph.

Or like the gold cord on *Airávat's** breast,
She gleams and shows you where your lord resides.

Vas. Is this the mansion?

Vita. It is; I will anounce your coming.
Ho there! inform the worthy Chárudatta,
A lady at his door awaits; her locks
Are drenched with rain, her gentle nerves are shaken
By angry tempests, and her delicate feet
By cumbering mire and massy anklets wearied,†
She pauses to refresh with cooling streams.

Chár. (*To Maitreya.*) Hear you, my friend?

Mait. As you command. (*Opens the door.*)
Health to you, lady.

Vas. Sir, I salute you. (*To the Vita.*) Here, let the umbrella-bearer wait upon you.

Vita. (*Apart.*) A hint for me, I take it, to withdraw. I shall obey you. [*Exit.*

Vas. Now, good Maitreya, where is our gambler?

Mait. (*Apart.*) Gambler indeed! my friend is much honoured by the appellation. There he sits, madam, in the arbour.

Vas. In the arbour—is it dry?

Mait. Quite; there is nothing to eat or drink in it: enter, enter.

Vas. (*To her Servant.*) What shall I say?

Ser. Gambler, good evening to you.

Vas. Shall I be able?

Ser. Opportunity will give you courage.

Mait. Enter, lady, enter.

Vas. (*Enters, and approaching Chárudatta, throws flowers at him.*) Gambler, good evening to you.

Chár. (*Rising.*) Vasantasená!
Lady, believe me, every day has passed

* The elephant of *Indra.*

† It may be scarcely necessary to observe that heavy rings, usually of silver set with a fringe of small belts, are worn by Hindu ladies upon their ankles.

Most heavily, and sleepless dragged my nights,
But now your charms appear my cares are over,
And this glad evening terminates my sorrows.
Then welcome, welcome to my bower—be seated.

Mait. Take a seat, madam. (*They sit.*)

Chár. Maitreya, from the flowers that grace her ear
Surcharged with rain, the drops have trickled down
And bathed her bosom, like a young prince installed
The partner of imperial honours.* Haste and bring
A vest of finest texture to replace
This chilling robe.

Fem. Att. Stop, Maitreya, I will assist my mistress if you please. (*Does so.*)

Mait. (*To Chárudatta.*) Now, sir, shall I inquire the object of this visitation?

Chár. Do so.

Mait. And now, madam, may I ask what has brought you out, on such a vile, dark, rainy evening?

Att. Lady, here's a smart Brahman!

Vas. Nay, an able one, so call him.

Att. My mistress, sir, wished to be informed of the real value of the necklace that you brought her.

Mait. There, I said so. (*To Chárudatta.*)

Att. The reason why she wishes to know is that she has pledged it at play, and the keeper of the tables, being a servant of the prince's, is gone on some duty, and is not to be found.

Mait. Umph, tit for tat.

Att. Until he can be heard of, and the necklace be redeemed, be pleased to accept in lieu of it this golden casket. (*Gives him the casket stolen by Śarvilaka. Maitreya examines it.*) You examine it very closely; one would suppose you had seen it before.

* Therefore sprinkled with holy water.

Mait. It is very curious: the cunning of the workman beguiles my eyes.

Att. No, your eyesight is defective, it is the very same.

Mait. Indeed! my worthy friend, here is the gold casket again that was stolen from our house.

Chár. No, no, it is but a requital
Of our attempt to substitute a change
Of that entrusted to us; this is the truth,
Howe'er the casket may appear the same.

Mait. It is the same! I swear it, as I am a Brahman.

Chár. I am glad of it.

Mait. Shall I ask how they came by it?

Chár. Why not?

Mait. (*Whispers the Attendant.*) Is it so indeed?

Att. (*Whispers Maitreya.*) It is indeed.

Chár. What is?—why leave us out?

Mait. (*Whispers Chárudatta.*) This it is indeed.

Chár. (*To the Attendant.*) Is this indeed, my girl, the golden casket?

Att. It is the same, sir.

Chár. A pleasing speech with me should never go
Without fit recompense,—accept this ring. (*Looks at his hand; finds he has no ring; expresses shame.*)

Vas. How well he merits wealth.

Chár. (*Apart.*) How can that man be said to live, who lives
A pauper, and whose gratitude and wrath
Are barren both. The bird whose wings are clipped—
The leafless tree—the desiccated pool—
The desolate mansion, and the toothless snake—
Are all meet emblems of the hapless wretch
Whose festive hours no fond associates grace,
And brightest moments yield no fruit to others.

Mait. (*To him.*) Enough, enough, there is no good in fretting. (*Aloud.*) But, lady, I shall thank you to restore me my bathing-gown, in which the casket was wrapped at the time it was stolen.

Vas. And now, worthy Chárudatta, believe me, when the casket was stolen, it was quite unnecessary to send me this equivalent.

Chár. Had I not sent it, lady, who had trusted me?—
I and my wealth in most men's eyes are equal,
And poverty will ever be suspected.

Mait. A word, damsel; do you mean to take up your abode here?

Att. Fie, Maitreya, how you talk!

Mait. My good friend, the clouds are collecting again, and the heavy drops drive us from our easy seats.

Chár. 'Tis true, they penetrate the yielding clouds
As sinks the lotus stalk into its bed
Of plashy mire, and now again they fall
Like tears celestial from the weeping sky
That wails the absent moon.
The clouds, like *Baladeva's* vesture, dark,
Profusely shed a shower of precious pearls
From *Indra's* treasury—the drops descend
Rapid and rattling, like the angry shafts
From *Arjun's* quiver, and of like purity
As are the hearts of holy men.
See, lady, how the firmament, anointed
With unguent of the black tamála's hue,
And fanned by fragrant and refreshing gales,
Is by the lightning tenderly embraced,
As the loved lord whom fearlessly she flies to.

[*Vasantasená gesticulates affection, and falls into Chárudatta's arms.*

Chár. (*Embracing her.*)
Louder and louder still roar on, ye clouds!
To me the sound is music, by your aid
My love is blessed, my heart expands with hope.

Mait. (*As to the cloud.*) You foul-faced rascal, you are a worthless reprobate, to have so scared her ladyship by your lightnings.

Chár. Reprove it not, for let the rain descend,
The heavens still lour, and wide the lightnings launch
A hundred flames; they have befriended me,
And given me her for whom I sighed in vain.
Happy, thrice happy, they whose walls enshrine
The fair they worship, and whose arms enfold
Her shivering beauties in their warm embrace.
Look, love, the bow of Indra arches heaven;
Like outspread arms, extended with fatigue,
It stretches forth; the yawning sky displays
Its lightning tongue—its chin of clouds hangs low—
All woo us to repose—let us retire: the drops
Fall musical, and pattering on the leaves
Of the tall palm, or on the pebbly ground,
Or in the brook, emit such harmony
As sweetly wakens from the voice and lute. [*Exit.*

END OF THE FIFTH ACT.

ACT VI.

CHA'RUDATTA'S HOUSE,

Inside and Outside as before.

Inside.—Enter Female Servant.

Hey-day! does not my lady mean to rise this morning? I shall make bold to call her. Madam!

Enter VASANTASENA'.

Look, madam, it is day.

Vas. How! why the morning dawns as darkling as if it still were night.

Ser. It is morning to us, though it may be night to you, madam.

Vas. Where is your gambler?

Ser. Chárudatta, madam, having given his orders to Vardhamána, is gone to the old flower garden *Pushpakarańda.*

Vas. What orders gave he?

Ser. To get your litter ready.

Vas. Whither am I to go?

Ser. Whither Chárudatta is gone.

Vas. Very well, girl, I have scarcely yet beheld him; to-day will gratify me with his sight. What! did I find my way into the inner apártments?

Ser. Not only that, madam, but into every one's heart.

Vas. I fear me his family are vexed.

Ser. They will be vexed then only when——

Vas. When?

Ser. When you depart.

Vas. Then is it my place first to be afflicted. Here, girl, take this necklace to my respected sister,* and say from

* That is, to Chárudatta's wife.

me, I am Chárudatta's handmaid and your slave, then be this necklace again the ornament of that neck to which it of right belongs.

Ser. But, lady, Chárudatta will be displeased.

Vas. Go, do as I bid you; he will not be offended.

Ser. As you command. [*Exit, and returns presently.*

Madam, thus says the lady: you are favoured by the son of my lord; it is not proper for me to accept this necklace. Know that the only ornament I value is my husband.

Enter RADANIKÁ *and* CHÁRUDATTA'S CHILD.

Rad. Come along, my child, let us ride in your cart.

Child. I do not want this cart; it is only of clay—I want one of gold.

Rad. And where are we to get the gold, my little man? Wait till your father is rich again, and then he will buy you one: now this will do. Come, let us go and see Vasantasená. Lady, I salute you.

Vas. Welcome Radaniká. Whose charming boy is this? although so ill-attired, his lovely face quite fascinates me.

Rad. This is Rohasena, the son of Chárudatta.

Vas. (*Stretching out her arms.*) Come here, my little dear, and kiss me. (*Takes him on her lap.*) How like his father!

Rad. He is like him too in disposition. Chárudatta dotes on him.

Vas. Why does he weep?

Rad. The child of our neighbour had a golden cart, which this little fellow saw and wanted. I made him this of clay, but he is not pleased with it, and is crying for the other.

Vas. Alas, alas, this little creature is already mortified by another's prosperity. O fate! thou sportest with the fortunes of mankind, like drops of water trembling on the lotus leaf. Don't cry, my good boy, and you shall have a gold cart.

Child. Radaniká, who is this?

Vas. A handmaid purchased by your father's merits.

Rad. This is your lady mother, child.

Child. You tell me untruth, Radaniká; how can this be my mother when she wears such fine things?

Vas. How piteous a speech for so soft a tongue! (*Takes off her ornaments in tears.*) Now I am your mother. Here, take this trinket and go buy a gold cart.

Child. Away, I will not take it, you cry at parting with it.

Vas. (*Wiping her eyes.*) I weep no more. Go, love, and play. (*Fills his cart with her jewels.*) There go, get you a golden cart. [*Exit* RADANIKÁ *with* CHILD.

Outside.—Enter VARDHAMÁNA *with the litter.**

Radaniká, let the lady know the carriage waits for her at the private door.

Inside.—Enter RADANIKÁ.

Lady, the covered litter attends you at the back-door.

Vas. Stay a moment whilst I prepare myself.

Rad. Stay a moment, Vardhamána, the lady is not quite ready.

Var. And I have forgotten the cushions of the carriage. Wait till I bring them. These oxen are not steady enough to be left; I will drive back and return presently.

[*Exit with the car.*

Vas. (*Inside.*) Bring me my things, girl, I can put them on myself. (*Dressing.*)

Outside.—Enter STHÁVARAKA, *the Servant of Saḿsthánaka, with a carriage.*

I am ordered by the king's brother-in-law, my master, to take this vehicle with all speed to the old flower-garden, *Pushpakarańda.* Come up, come up. (*Looking.*) Why, the road is blocked with country carts. Holloa there! get out of

* A car of two wheels drawn by oxen and enclosed with curtains. The introduction of this kind of stage property is so constant and essential, that it must have been real, and shows that the place appropriated to the representation must have been level and spacious. It renders it probable that the open court within the house was the spot where the drama was exhibited.

the way. What says he, whose carriage is it? Saḿsthánaka's, the king's brother-in-law; quick, quick! clear the road. (*Drives on.*) Who should that be, that looked at me so curiously, and then stole off down another road, like an unlucky gambler that runs away from the table-keeper?* No matter; I must get on. Holloa you! out of the way there! What! Come and give you a turn of the wheel: it sticks, does it! It is very likely that the king's brother-in-law's man shall assist you to a twist of the wheel. Oh, it is a poor miserable rustic, and alone too. Well, I will lend you a hand. This is Chárudatta's postern door. I can leave the carriage here in the meantime so, stop there, I will be with you.

[*Exit, leaving the carriage at the door.*

Ser. (*Inside.*) I hear the wheels: the carriage is returned, madam.

Vas. Quick, quick! I feel strangely flurried;—open the door.

Ser. 'Tis done.

Vas. Go you to rest.

Ser. As you command. [*Exit.*

Vas. (*Goes forth and ascends Saḿsthánaka's carriage.*) My right eye twinkles;† never mind, meeting Chárudatta will prove it causeless. (*Draws the curtains.*)

Re-enter STHÁVARAKA.

I have helped him, and now have a clear road. (*Mounts and proceeds.*) Why, the vehicle is heavier than it was, or it appears so to me, because I am tired with helping yonder cart. No matter, I must proceed;—come up.

(*Behind the scenes.*)

Who ho, there, guards! look to it; be vigilant—sleep not at your posts; the cowherd has burst his bonds, slain his gaoler, and broken from his prison; he is now in flight—seize him! seize him!

* This is to prepare the entrance of *Áryaka*, who has just fled from prison.

† An unlucky omen for a woman, lucky for a man.

Sthá. Here's a precious uproar! I had better get clear of it.

[*Exit with the car.*

Enter ÁRYAKA *as in flight.*

I have swam thus far to shore, and from the wave
Of fell captivity, the tyrant Pálaka
Had plunged me into, once more have escaped.
Like a tame elephant from his stall broke loose,
I drag along with me my ruptured chain.
S'arvilaka, my friend, to thee I owe
My freedom and my life. Condemned to pine
In the dark dungeon, where the monarch's fears,
Awakened by the sage's prophecies,
Cast me to die, dragged from my humble home. (*Weeps.*)
What crime have I committed, to be sought
Thus like a venomous snake, to be destroyed!
If such my destiny, as is foretold,
In what consists my guilt? be fate accused—
Fate is a power resistless, and a king
Alike demands our homage. Who contends
With force superior? mine is to submit.
Yet for my life I fly—ah! whither now
Shall I find refuge? See, yon door invites me!
Some good man's gate is open, and like me
Its withered fortunes, for the bolt is broken,
And the broad valves are shattered and decayed:
It calls me kinsman, and it proves my friend.

VARDHAMÁNA *returning with Chárudatta's carriage* (*without*).
Come up, come up!

(ÁRYAKA *listening.*)

A carriage, and it comes this way.
If it should be a village car, not freighted
With passengers uncourteous, or a vehicle
For women, but its fair load not received,
Or be it travelling from the town, and fit
For decent occupancy—be it but empty
And unattended, and my fate befriends me.

Enter VARDHAMÁNA *with the carriage.*

What ho! Radaniká, I have got the cushions, and the car is ready: so inform the lady Vasantasená; tell her to ascend, that I may set off for *Pushpakarańdaka.*

Áry. It is a courtesan's, and travelling outwards;
'Tis fortunate—I mount. (*Advances.*)

Vard. (*Listening and hearing the ringing of Áryaka's chain.*) I hear the sound of the anklets, she is hear. Get up quick, lady; get up behind; the cattle are impatient, I must not leave them.

ÁRYAKA *ascends.*

Vard. The sound has ceased, and the carriage is heavier than it was: her ladyship must be seated, so here goes.

[*Exit with the car.*

Scene—Another Street.

Enter VÍRAKA, *Captain of the Watch, attended.*

Halloa! Jaya, Jayamána, Chandanaka, Mangala, Pushpabhadra, and the rest, follow quick, and we shall catch the villain, though he has broken his prison and the king's slumbers. Here, fall in; go you to the east gate, you to the west, you to the south, you to the north: on this pile of broken bricks, Chandanaka and I will stop and look about us. What ho, Chandanaka!

Enter CHANDANAKA *attended, in a bustle.*

What ho! Víraka, Viśalya, Bhímángada, Dańďakála, Dańďaśúra, quick, quick! never let the king's fortune move off into another family: away with you, search the streets, the roads, the gardens, the houses, the stalls, the markets, and let no suspicious corner pass unexamined;—away! (*Exeunt guard.*) Well, Víraka, what say you? will any one convey this runaway cowboy out of peril? Verily, whoever dares to carry him off whilst Chandanaka lives, had better have had at his birth the Sun in the eighth mansion, the Moon in the fourth, Venus in the sixth, Mars in the fifth, Jupiter in the sixth, and Saturn in the ninth.*

Vír. He must have had assistance, no doubt, valiant Chandanaka; but, by your heart, I swear that he escaped before dawn.

Enter VARDHAMÁNA *with the car and* ÁRYAKA *concealed.*

Chan. What ho, there! see, see, a covered litter passes along the high road; inquire whose it is and whither going.

Vír. What ho, driver! stop and answer. Whose vehicle is this; who is inside; and where are you going?

Var. The carriage belongs, sir, to the worthy Chárudatta; the lady Vasantasená is inside, and I am carrying her to the old flower-garden to meet Chárudatta there.

Chan. Let him pass.

Vír. Without inspection?

Chan. Undoubtedly.

Vír. On what surety?

Chan. Chárudatta's.

Vír. And who is Chárudatta, or who is Vasantasená, that the carriage is to pass free?

Chan. Do you not know who they are? If you know not Chárudatta and Vasantasená, you know not the moon and moonlight when you see them together in the skies. Who is there that is not acquainted with that moon of mildness, that lotus of merit, that liberator from sorrow, that pearl, the essence of the four oceans, Chárudatta? Both are of the highest respectability, the boast and pride of the city, the lovely Vasantasená and virtuous Chárudatta.

Vír. Phoo, phoo! I know them well enough, but in the discharge of my duty my own father must be a stranger.

Áryaka. (*In the car.*) Yon Víraka has ever been my foe,

* This appears to be the literal import of the passage; its astrological signification is not so clear. According to the commentary, these planetary conjunctions forbode severally pain, colic, fatuity, consumption, sorrow, and indigence.

Chandanaka my friend; the two are ill
Associated in a common duty.
One fire the marriage ceremony asks,
Another serves to light the funeral pile.*

Chan. Well, careful captain, high in the king's confidence, do you then look into the carriage, I will look to the cattle.

Vir. Nay, you are in command and confidence as well as I am; do you inspect it.

Chan. What I see is in fact seen by you.

Vir. Not only by me, but by the king himself.

Chan. Holloa, you! stop the car.

Áry. Unfortunately, I am discovered; I have no sword;
Like *Bhíma* then I must employ my hands;
Better to die than be again a captive.
Yet, hold, it is not yet despair.

CHANDANAKA *looks into the car.*

Áry. Protection:—I am at your mercy.

Chan. Fear not, who seeks protection will obtain it.

Áry. Fortune forsakes, tribe, family, and friends
Discard, and all men scorn the coward slave
Who fears to grant protection to the wretched.

Chan. How! Áryaka!

* Where a perpetual flame is maintained, it lights the fire round which the bride and bridegroom step at the marriage ceremony, and the funeral pile of either; but the household fire is preserved only by a particular sect, the *Agnihotras*, and the great body of the people have nothing of the kind. In this case they distinguish between the sources whence they obtain the kindling flame according to the purposes of its application, and the fire of the marriage rite is taken from the hearth of a respectable person, or from a fire lighted on some auspicious occasion, whilst for the funeral pile "any unpolluted fire may be used. It is only necessary to avoid taking it from another pile, or from the abode of an outcast, of a man belonging to the tribe of executioners, of a woman who has lately borne a child, or of any person who is unclean."—*Colebrook on the Religious Ceremonies of the Hindus: Asiatic Res.*, vii. 241. Notwithstanding these exceptions, it is the common practice of the Hindus of ordinary rank in the western provinces to procure fire from an outcast to light the funeral pile.

Like the poor bird that, flying from the hawk,
Falls in the fowler's net, art thou my prize,*
And, luckless wretch, appliest to me for aid?
He is in Chárudatta's car, his crime
Is none; Śarvilaka, to whom I owe
My own life, is his friend; but then—
My duty to the prince. What's to be done?
E'en be it so—I told him not to fear;
The words have passed my lips. I must befriend him,
Come on't what will: the succour once assured,
Must be extended, though the end be ruin.†

(*Returning.*) I have seen—Árya—Áryá Vasantasená, and she says right; it is indecorous to detain her on the road when she has an appointment with Chárudatta.

Vír. Excuse me, Chandanaka; I have some doubts in the matter.

Chan. How so?

Vír. You seem flurried, and it was with some indistinctness you call out first Árya, then corrected yourself, and said Áryá Vasantasená.‡ I have some strange misgivings.

Chan. Misgivings, indeed! why, you know, we of the South are not very nice in our articulation, and are apt to con-

* Another instance of the familiar use of apologues.

† The importance attached to the duty of affording protection to those who solicit it is repeatedly urged in the Hindu writings: thus in the Hitopadeśa:

"What even are called here great gifts, such as donations of land, gold, cattle, and food, are all inferior to the gift of protection, and he who affords succour to the helpless that fly to him for aid, obtains a reward equal to that of performing the *Aśwamědha* sacrifice, which confers the enjoyment of every desire."—*Hit.*

This feeling seems to have pervaded the heroic times both of Greece and Rome, and to have secured Adrastus an asylum at the court of Crœsus, and Coriolanus a refuge in the halls of Aufidius.

‡ The difference of masculine and feminine terminations, *Árya* and *Áryá*, the first being either the same with *Áryaka*, a name, or "the respectable," as applied to a man; the second means the same as applied to a woman.

found sounds. Being accustomed to speak the dialects of a number of barbarous and other outcast tribes,* it would be all the same to us, whether it was Árya or Áryá, masculine, feminine, or neuter.

Vír. Ah, well—I shall take a look myself: such are the prince's orders—he knows he can trust me.

Chan. And am I not trusted by him?

Vír. True, but I must obey his orders.

Chan. (*Apart.*) If it is known that the cowherd was seized in Chárudatta's carriage, *he* will be involved in the punishment. I must give my friend here a specimen of Carnatic eloquence. (*Aloud.*) Hark ye, Víraka, I have already inspected the carriage; why are you to inspect it again? who the deuce are you, I should like to know?

Vír. And who are you, pray?

Chan. I'll tell you: one entitled to your most profound respect: you should recollect your caste.

Vír. My caste, what is it then?

Chan. Oh, I do not wish to say.

Vír. Say, say if you like, and if you don't like it, leave it alone.

* The original specifies the countries, and the list is not only curious in itself, but it is worthy of remark, on account of the character of *Mlechchha* or barbarous tribes (that is to say, other than Hindu) being assigned to people who are chiefly, if not wholly, natives of Southern India. We might suppose that the nations of the Peninsula were not universally Hindus at the period when this play was written; they must, however, have received the religion, not only of the Vedas, but even of the Puráńas, before the Christian era, as the name of Cape *Comari* proves; so called, according to Arrian, from a temple dedicated to a goddess, or in fact to *Kumarí*, a name of *Párvatí* or *Umá*, the *virgin* bride of Śiva. The countries specified are *Khasa*, *Khattikhaďa*, *Kaďattha*, *Avilaka*, *Karńáta* (Carnatick), *Karńa*, *Právaraňa*, *Andhra* (Telingana), *Vida* (Virat or Berar), *Chola* (Coromandel), *Víńa*, *Barbara*, *Kherakhána*, *Mukha*, *Madhughála*. Most of these we cannot identify; they are very possibly distorted by the copyists. Their general application to the South is, however, not only indicated by the few which are recognisable, but by Chandanaka calling himself a *Dakhińatta* or Dakshińátya, a dweller of the South.

Chan. I do not wish to shame you: let it be; it is not worth while to break a wood apple.

Vír. Nay, I insist.

[*Chan. intimates by signs that Víraka is a Chamár, or worker in leather.*

Vír. It is false—I deny it.

Chan. You were wont to carry a dead jackal in your hand,* to replace dislocated joints, and to flourish a pair of shears; and you are now a general. A very pretty general!

Vír. You are a most high and mighty hero, no doubt, far above your real origin.

Chan. What was my origin?

Vír. Excuse me.

Chan. I defy you,—my caste is as pure as the moon.

Vír. No doubt; vastly pure, when your mother was a tabor, your father a kettle-drum, and your brother a tambourine;† but you—you are a general.

Chan. I a *Chamár*, I Chandanaka, a *Chamár;* mighty well, mighty well! Look, by all means.

Vír. Ho, driver! Stay till I inspect the car.

* Whose skin he is about to employ. The second attribute of this caste is rather derogatory to surgical science, if it be correctly rendered, which is not certain; the expression is *Purisánaṁ kuchcha gaṅthisaṅṭhabano—Purushánám kunchagranthisaṁsthápakaḥ;* the rectifier of men's crooked joints.

† Instruments covered with skins and made by out-castes. The expressions for the last are *Ḍummuha karaḍa-abhádá* (Durmukha-karaṭaka-bhrátá). *Karaṭa* has various meanings, one of which, a musical instrument, may apply, especially as the like designations are given to the parents. The chief difficulty is the not knowing what sort of instrument, but conformably to the main purport of the speech it must be a kind of drum. A consideration of some importance, however, is the possibility of *karaṭaka* being intended for the jackal of the *Hitopadeśa* so named. The animal is associated with the *Chamár* in the speech of Chandanaka, and a similar allusion may be intended here. How this would affect our speculations as to the date of the play is another question. It does not necessarily involve any difference of opinion, as the apologue may be of considerable antiquity, and prior to the Christian era. There is no doubt of its being widely diffused a few centuries subsequent.

(*Víraka approaches it; Chandanaka seizes him by the hair, drags him back, throws him down and kicks him.*)

Vír. (*Rising.*) What do you mean by this treatment of me?—but I will have vengeance. If I have not your head severed from your body, and your limbs quartered and exposed in the public place, I am not Víraka.* [*Exit.*

Chan. Away to the palace, or the court. Complain; I care not. Who will heed such a dog as you? (*To Vardhamána.*) Quick, and if any one stops you, say the carriage has been inspected by Víraka and Chandanaka. Lady Vasantasená, I give you this as a passport. (*Gives Áryaka a sword.*)

Áry. My right arm throbs as I receive the weapon.
Fortune is friendly to me. I am safe.

Chan. The Árya † will remember Chandana.
I ask not this for favour, but in love.

Áry. Fate has this day made Chandana my friend.
If the saint's prophecy should be fulfilled,
I will remember well how much I owe him.

Chan. May every deity ‡ befriend your cause;
And may your enemies before you fall,
Like *Śumbha* and *Niśumbha* by the wrath
Of the resentful goddess. § Drive on.

[*Exit Vardhamána with Car.*

* A rather unworthy mode of resenting the affront, especially the profession and rank of the speaker being considered: the affront itself is very unbecoming a hero and a general. The scene is a curious, and no doubt accurate, picture of manners amongst the Hindus.

† A title of respect.

‡ The original specifies the deities invoked, or *Siva, Vishnu, Brahmá,* the Sun and the Moon.

§ Durga, by whom the two demons, *Śumbha* and *Niśumbha,* were destroyed, as related in the fifth and following sections of the *Chandipáth,* a section of the *Márkandeya Puráńa;* also in the *Vámana* and other Puráńas. Agreeably to our notion of the priority of the play to the Puráńas, there should be other authority for the story, but it has not been found in the *Mahábhárata.*

Chan. (*Looking after it*). Ha! yonder I see my friend S'arvilaka follows the carriage. Well, may they prosper. Víraka will now to the prince and tell how he has been handled: I must collect my friends and relatives, and follow him without delay. [*Exit.*

END OF THE SIXTH ACT.

ACT VII.

THE GARDEN PUSHPAKARAŃḊA.

Enter CHÁRUDATTA *and* MAITREYA.

Mait. How bravely the old garden looks.

Chár. 'Tis true; like wealthy merchants are the trees
Who spread in clustering flowers the choicest wares;
Amongst them busily the bees are straying
To gather tribute for the royal hive.

Mait. Here is a fine block of stone; sit down on it.

Chár. (*Seated.*) Vardhamána tarries long.

Mait. I told him to make all possible haste.

Chár. Then why so tardy? Or the car rolls heavily;
Or it has broken down upon the way;
Or the old traces have been snapped; or lies
A tree across their path; or have they strayed
Another road, or are the beasts untractable?
Or have—oh, here he comes.

Enter VARDHAMÁNA *with the Car.*

Come up.

Áry. (*In the car.*)
Fled from the monarch's myrmidons, and cramped
By this vile fetter round my foot, I owe
My safety to this vehicle—where, like the cuckoo *
Nursed in a stranger nest, I find concealment.
Now, far beyond the city, I am safe.
Shall I alight, and seek to gain a refuge

* The Hindus believe that the *koil*, the Indian cuckoo, dep ts its eggs n the nest of the crow, and leaves them there to be hatched

Amidst the dark recesses of these groves,
Or shall I dare encounter with the owner
Of this befriending car? 'Twere far more grateful
To meet with Chárudatta, than to hear
His pity only as I darkling lurk
Among these shades. My new acquired liberty
Will yield him pleasure, and my wasted form
Will grow once more to vigour from the interview.

Var. This is the place :—what ho! Maitreya.

Mait. Welcome, Vardhamána; I have been looking out for you.

Var. Well, here I am; and so is Vasantasená.

Mait. But, you son of a slave, what has detained you so long?

Var. Do not be angry, Maitreya. I was obliged to go back to find the cushions which I had at first forgot.

Chár. Well, well.—Maitreya, assist Vasantasená to alight.

Mait. What! has she got fetters on her feet, that she cannot come down by herself? (*Goes to the car and looks in.*) Holloa! what have we here?* This is not Vasantasená—it is Vasantasena, I suppose.

Chár. Refrain your mirth, my friend; love ill-sustains
The least delay. I help her to alight. (*Rises.*)

Áry. Here comes the worthy Chárudatta;
Cheering his voice, and gentle is his aspect:
I need not fear.

Chár. (*Looking in.*) How! who is this?
His arms are like the elephant's vast tusks—
His breasts, his shoulders, brawny as the lion's—
His eyes are coppery-red and roll in anger—
How should a person of such goodly presence
Bear fetters on his limbs? Who art thou, say?

Áry. My name is *Áryaka*: to tend the herds

* The masculine form of the same noun, *Vasantasenus* est, non *Vasantasena.*

The duty I was born to; and to thee
I hither come, a suppliant for protection.

Chár. Art thou that *Áryaka*, our prince's fears
Dragged from his humble station to a prison?

Áry. The same.

Chár. Fate, that has brought thee hither, is thy friend.
My life I may resign, but cannot turn
Away from one who sues to me for refuge.
Vardhamána, remove those fetters.

Var. (*Obeys.*) The chains are off, sir.

Áry. (*To Chár.*) And chains more lasting by this aid imposed.

Mait. Then now pray take yourself off too. Come, my good friend, now this gentleman is at large, I think we had better get home as quick as we can.

Chár. Fie on thy speech! what need of haste?

Áry. Excuse* me, Chárudatta, that I mounted,
Nor sought permission first, into this car.

Chár. You have graced me by such courtesy.

Áry. Have I your leave to leave you?

Chár. It is yours.

Áry. I will descend.

Chár. Nay, friend, not so.
Your steps still labour from the weighty bond
So recently removed: besides, the car
Will unsuspected bear you on your way
Beyond our boundaries—pray keep your seat.

Áry. As you direct.

Chár. Auspicious be your way
To join your friends.

Áry. I hope I leave one here.

Chár. 'Tis one who hopes to be remembered by you
In other times.

Áry. Can I forget myself?

Chár. The gods protect your path.

* A very civil and nationally characteristic dialogue ensues.

Áry. It is to you
I owe my safety.

Chár. Not so, you owe it
To your bright fortunes.

Áry. Of the which, indeed,
I hold you as the cause.

Chár. But Pálaka
Must still be heeded; and around he sends
A numerous guard, who may detain your steps.
Use no delay; but with all speed depart.

Áry. To meet again. [*Exit.*

Chár. The deed that I have done will little please
The king, should it be known; and kings behold
Their subjects' actions by their spies. 'Twere well
To leave this spot at once. Maitreya, cast
The fetters deep into this ancient well. (*His eyes throbbing.*)
'Tis sad to miss a meeting with my love—
But that such chance to-day at least is hopeless
My left eye indicates; and without cause
A sudden languor creeps into my heart.
Let us leave this. (*Going.*) Ha, an evil omen!
A heretic * approaches us. (*Stops.*) Yet—hold—
Let him advance—we'll take another path. [*Exit.*

* A *Bauddha* mendicant or *Śramańaka.* Avoiding him is in harmony with the Brahmanical doctrine on this subject; at the same time, it is clear that the period of intolerance and persecution had not arrived, or he would not have so openly made his appearance in the presence of a Brahman. The Śramańaka is our old acquaintance the Samváhaka, see Act II.

END OF THE SEVENTH ACT.

ACT VIII.

SCENE THE SAME.

Enter the S'RAMAŃAKA, *or Bauddha mendicant, with a wet garment in his hand.*

S'RAMAŃAKA (*sings*).

BE virtue, friends, your only store,
And restless appetite restrain,
Beat meditation's drum, and sore
Your watch against each sense maintain;
The thief that still in ambush lies,
To make devotion's wealth his prize.

Cast the five senses all away,
That triumph o'er the virtuous will;
The pride of self-importance slay,
And ignorance remorseless kill:
So shall you safe the body guard,
And Heaven shall be your last reward.

Why shave the head and mow the chin
Whilst bristling follies choke the breast?
Apply the knife to parts within,
And heed not how deformed the rest:
The heart of pride and passion weed,
And then the man is pure indeed.

My cloth is heavy with the yet moist dye.* I will enter

* He has been staining it of a dull red, with the paste of an ochreous clay, commonly used for this purpose by *Sannyásins*, particularly now the *Śaivas*.

this garden belonging to the Rájá's brother-in-law, and wash it in the pool, and then I shall proceed more lightly. (*Does so.*)

(*Behind.*) What, ho! you rascally S'ramańaka, what are you doing there?

Śram. Alas, alas! here he is, Saḿsthánaka himself. He has been affronted by one mendicant, and whenever he meets another he sends him off with his nose slit like an ox. Where shall I fly to?—the lord *Buddha* be my refuge.

Enter SAḾSTHÁNAKA *with the* VIT́A, *his sword drawn.*

Saḿs. Stop, you vile vagabond, or off I take that head of thine, as they snap off the top of a red radish in a dram-shop.* (*Beats him.*)

Vit́a. Nay, nay, hold! beat not the poor wretch thus clad in the coloured garment of humility. This garden was intended by your excellency to be the seat of delight, and these trees were destined to afford shade and relief to the unsheltered; but now they are disappointed of their objects; they fail their promise, like the no longer hidden villainy of a scoundrel, and are only to be enjoyed at the risk of peril, like a new sovereignty disposed of before it is yet subdued.

Śram. Mercy, sir; be my protector, my saviour.

Saḿs. Hear him, the scoundrel, how he abuses me.

Vit́a. How so?

Saḿs. He calls me a *shaver.*†

* Where it is eaten as a relish to excite thirst and improve the flavour of the liquor.

† The original pun is *Upásaka*, which means a worshipper or a barber. It was not possible to retain the sense and the pun also: as it is, the attempt to preserve anything like a quibble is so bad, that it is not attempted to follow the original in two more specimens of this sort of wit, resting on the words *dhanya*, meaning prosperous or an atheist, and *puńya*, pious or a brick trough. The whole passage is this:—

" *Śra.* Sáadam, paśídadu ubáśake.

" *Śak.* Bháve bháve, pekkha pekkha, akkośadi mam.

" *Vit́.* Kim braviti.

" *Śak.* Ubáśaketti mam bhańádi; kim? Hagge ńábide.

" *Vit́.* Buddhopásaka! iti bhavantaḿ stauti.

Vita. Not so, he entreats you humbly.

Sams. And what are you doing here?

Śram. I was about to cleanse my garment in this pond.

Sams. Villain, was this superlative garden given to me by my sister's husband, the Rájá, for such a base purpose? Dogs drink here by day, and jackals by night: exalted in rank as I am, I do not bathe here, and shall you presume here to wash your foul and fetid rags;—but I shall make short work with you.*

Vita. In that case I suspect he will not have long followed the profession.

Sams. How so?

Vita. Observe: his head shines as if it had only been lately shaven; and his garment has been so little worn that there are no scars † on his shoulder. The ochry dye has not yet fully stained the cloth, and the open web, yet fresh and flaccid, hangs loosely over his arms.

Śram. I do not deny it, worthy sir; it is true I have but lately adopted the profession of a beggar.

Sams. And why so? why did you not become a beggar as soon as you were born, you scoundrel? (*Beats him.*)

Śram. Glory to Buddha.

Vita. Enough, enough! now let him go. (*To the Śram.*) Away with you.

Sams. Stop, stop! I must first ask leave.

Vita. From whom?

Sams. My own mind.

Vita. Well, he is not gone.

" *Śak.* Thunu, *śamanaká*, thunu.

" *Śra.* Tumaḿ dhańńe, tumaḿ puńńé.

" *Śak.* Bháve, dhańńe puńńetti maḿ bhanádi: kim? hagge śalávake, koshṫake kombhakále bá.

" *Viṫ.* Kánélímátah! nanu dhanyas twaḿ, puńyas twam: iti bhavantam stauti.

* *Tumam ekkapaláliam kalemi,*—I shall make you a man of one blow.

† Why they should be expected is very doubtful: the expression is *kálasya alpatayá cha chivarakŕitaḱ skandhe na játaḱ kińaḱ.*

Saṁs. My life, my heart, my chick, my child, shall this fellow go or stay? Very well, my mind says——

Viṭa. What?

Saṁs. He shall neither go, nor stay, nor move, nor breathe —let him fall down and be put to death.

Śram. Glory to Buddha! mercy, mercy!

Viṭa. Oh, let him go.

Saṁs. On one condition.

Viṭa. What is that?

Saṁs. He shall take all the clay of this pool out without muddying the water; or he shall make a pile of clean water and throw the mud aside.

Viṭa. Absurd! You might as well ask for skins of stone, and meat from trees. This world is sadly burthened with fools.

[*Śram. gesticulates imprecations.*

Saṁs. What does he mean?

Viṭa. He blesses you.

Saṁs. Speak my blessings.

Śram. Be as prosperous as you are pious.*

Saṁs. Begone! [*Exit Śram.*

Viṭa. Come, come, to other thoughts direct your mind;
Look round the garden; mark these stately trees,
Which duly, by the king's command attended,
Put forth abundantly their fruits and flowers,
And clasped by twining creepers, they resemble
The manly husband and the tender wife.

Saṁs. The ground is quite a picture, strewed with many-tinted flowers; the trees are bowed down with blossoms; the graceful creepers completely surmount even their tops; and the monkeys are sporting about like so many jack-fruits.†

Viṭa. Here let us take our seat.

Saṁs. I am seated. And now, my good friend, trust me,

* This is an interpolation, as in the original he retires after repeating his apparent imprecation, to which no words are attached.

† The large fruit of the Artocarpus integrifolia.

I cannot help thinking of Vasantasená : she holds her place in my heart, and rankles like the abuse of a blackguard.

Vita. (*Aside.*) To little purpose are these thoughts indulged :

So true it is—
The scorn of woman in ignoble breasts,
But adds fresh fuel to the scorching flame.
The manly heart disdain with scorn repays,
And soon subdues its unrequited passion.

Saṁs. What hour is it? That fellow Stháavaraka was ordered to be here early; what can be the reason he does not make his appearance? It is almost noon; I feel hungry, and it is impossible to think of walking at this time of day. The sun is now in mid-heaven, and looks as fierce as an angry ape; and the ground is as dry and shrivelled as *Gándhárí* looked when her hundred sons were slain.

Vita. 'Tis true : the cattle dozing in the shade
Let fall the unchamped fodder from their mouths;
The lively ape with slow and languid pace
Creeps to the pool to slake his parching thirst
In its now tepid waters; not a creature
Is seen upon the public road, nor braves
One solitary passenger the sun.
Perhaps the carriage from the heated track
Has turned aside, and waits a cooler hour.

Saṁs. Very likely, and I am left here to furnish a lodgment in my brains for the rays of the sun. The birds have all slunk into shelter amongst the branches, and passengers panting and breathing flame, are glad to mount the umbrella even in the shade. That fellow will not be here to-day; come let us amuse ourselves : I will give you a song.

(*He sings.*)

There, sir, what say you to that?

Vita. Say? That you are verily a *Gandharba.**

Saṁs. How should I fail being so; I make a practice of

* A chorister of *Swarga* or *Indra's* heaven.

taking asafœtida, cummin-seed, orris-root, treacle and ginger; my voice must necessarily be very *sweet.** I will give you another specimen. (*Sings.*)
There, what think you now?

Viṭa. That you are a very *Gandharba.*

Saṁs. I knew you would think so; but I take care to train myself suitably. I always feed upon meat presented to me by some of my slaves, and I have it fried in oil and ghee, and seasoned well with asafœtida and black pepper; that is your only diet for a sweet voice. Oh, that scoundrel, he will never arrive!

Viṭa. Have patience: he will soon be here. (*They retire.*)

Enter STHÁVARAKA *with the Car in which* VASANTASENÁ *is.*

Sthá. I am in a terrible fright; it is near noon; my master will be in a violent rage. Come up.

Vas. (*In the car.*) Alas! alas! that is not Vardhamána's voice. Who can it be? Whose vehicle is this? Has Chárudatta sent another car and servant to spare his own? Ha! my right eye throbs, my heart flutters, my sight is dim, everything forebodes misfortunes.

Saṁs. Master, the car is here.

Viṭa. How do you know?

Saṁs. Do you not hear a snorting like an old hog's?

Viṭa. You are right; here it is.

Saṁs. How, my good fellow, Sthávaraka, are you come at last?

Sthá. Yes, sir.

Saṁs. And the car?

Sthá. Here it is, sir.

Saṁs. And the oxen?

Sthá. Here they are.

Saṁs. And yourself?

Sthá. We are all together, your honour.

* He is, in fact, punning or blundering upon *gandha*, fragrance, and *Gandharba*, a singer of heaven.

Sams. Then drive in.

Sthá. Which way, sir?

Sams. Here, where the wall is broken.

Sthá. It is impossible, sir: it will kill the beasts, smash the car, and I shall get my neck broken into the bargain.

Sams. Do you recollect, sirrah, that I am the king's brother-in-law: be the cattle killed, I can buy others; let the car smash, I can have another made; and if you break your neck, I must hire another driver.

Sthá. That is very true, your honour; the loss will be mine; I shall not be able to replace myself.

Sams. I care not; drive in here, over the broken walls.

Sthá. Very well, sir, here goes. Break the car, go to pieces you and your driver; others are to be had, and I must report your fate to your master. (*Drives.*) How, all safe! There, sir, the carriage has come in.

Sams. You see what a lying rogue you are, and no mischief.

Sthá. Very true, sir.

Sams. Come, my friend, let us go to the car. You are my ever honoured teacher and master, precede: I know what is due to your dignity, ascend.

Vita. I comply.

Sams. Stop! stop! Did you make the carriage, pray? I am the owner of it, and shall therefore get in the first.

Vita. I did as you desired.

Sams. Very possibly; but you erred in not requesting me to precede.

Vita. Will your excellency be pleased to enter?

Sams. That is right. I shall ascend. (*Getting up, returns hastily, and lays hold of the Vita in alarm.*) Oh dear! I am a lost man; there 's a thief or a she-devil in the carriage! If a devil, we shall be robbed; if a thief, we shall be devoured alive!

Vita. Fear not; how should a she-devil get into a bullock carriage? It was nothing but the shadow of Sthávaraka, I dare say, which, your eyes having been dazzled with the glare, you saw indistinctly, and mistook for a living figure.

Saṁs. My poor Sthávaraka, are you alive?

Sthá. I rather think so, your honour.

Saṁs. There certainly is a woman in the car,—look yourself. (*To the Viṭa.*)

Viṭa. A woman! ha, ha!

Afraid to gaze upon the man of birth,
Who prides himself on my companionship,
They walk with downcast eyes, like shrinking cattle
That hang their heads against the driving rain.

Vas. Alas, that odious wretch, the Rája's brother!
What will become of me—unhappy girl!
A luckless seed my coming hither sows
In the parched soil of my disastrous fate.

Saṁs. That vile slave, not to have examined the carriage! —Come, master, look.

Viṭa. I am going.

Saṁs. Do jackals fly or crows run? Do men eat with their eyes and see with their teeth? So surely will I not stay here.

Viṭa. (*Looking in.*) How! can it be?
What brings the doe into the tiger's den?
Or does the cygnet fly the distant mate,
Though bright as autumn's moon, to wed the crow!
It is not well; or has your mother's will,
On gain intent, compelled you to come hither
To earn reluctant presents late despised?
You are by nature false, your fickle tribe,
I told you truly, ever are prepared
To yield their blandishments to those they scorn.

Vas. Believe it not of me—I was deceived,
Mistook the vehicle, and the fatal error
Has brought me hither. Oh, befriend—protect me!

Viṭa. I will befriend you; banish every fear.

I will beguile this blockhead. (*Descends.*)
There is indeed a devil in the car.

Saṁs. Indeed! how happens it she has not run off with you? If a thief, how is it she has not eaten you up?

Viṫa. Never mind.
Hence to Ujjayin a line of groves affords
Unbroken shade; let us walk there, 'twere better.

Saṁs. How so?

Viṫa. 'Twill yield us healthy exercise, and spare
The jaded cattle.

Saṁs. So be it. Come, Stháváraka, follow us with the carriage.—No, stop; I go on foot only before gods and Brahmans—I cannot walk along the road; I must get into the car, and then as I pass, the citizens will say to each other, There, that is he, his excellency the prince's most noble brother-in-law.

Viṫa. (*Apart.*) What is to be done? the case is critical,—
The remedy not obvious: yes, this were best.
(*Aloud to the prince.*) I did but jest. There is no female fiend.
Vasantasená has come here to meet you.

Vas. Ah me!

Saṁs. Am I not, master, a fine fellow, another *Vásudeva*?

Viṫa. Undoubtedly.

Saṁs. It is therefore that this unparalleled goddess waits upon me. I lately displeased her; I will now go and cast myself at her feet.

Viṫa. Well devised.

Saṁs. I go. (*Kneels to Vasantasená.*) Celestial Mother, listen to my prayers; behold me with those lotus eyes thus lowly at thy feet, and mark my hands uplifted thus to thy heavenly countenance. Forgive, most graceful nymph, the faults that love has urged me to commit, and accept me for thy servant and thy slave.

Vas. Away! your regard is my abhorrence. (*Spurns him with her foot.*)

Saṁs. (*Rising in great wrath.*) What! shall this head that bows not to the gods, this head that my mother caressed, be humbled to the ground, to be treated like a dead carcase by the jackals in a thicket? What ho! Stháváraka, where did you pick up this woman?

Sthá. Why, sir, to tell you the truth, some village carts blocked up the road near Chárudatta's garden; I got down to clear the way, and in the meantime left the carriage at his gate; I fancy she then came out of his house and ascended the car, mistaking it for another.

Saṁs. A mistake! Oh, then, she did not come here to seek me. Come down, madam, this carriage is mine. You come, I suppose, to meet that beggar's brat, the son of a higgler, and you take advantage of my cattle,—but turn out directly, I say.

Vas. That which you make my blame I make my boast;
As for the rest, whatever must be may be.

Saṁs. With these fair hands, armed with ten nails, and dexterous in inflicting punishment, I drag you from the carriage by the hair of your head, as *Jaṭáyu** seized upon the wife of *Báli.*†

Viṭa. Forbear, forbear, nor rudely thus invade
These graceful tresses. What destructive hand
Would roughly rend the creeper from the tree,
Or tear the blossom from the slender stem?
Leave her to me, I'll bring her from the car.

(*Goes and hands Vasantasená down.*)

Saṁs. (*Aside.*) The wrath that her disdainful treatment justly kindled is now more violent than ever: a blow! a kick! to be spurned! I am resolved,—she dies. (*Aloud.*) Master, if you have any relish for a mantle with a broad border and a

* *Jaṭáyu* is the name of a hero bird, the son of *Garuḍa* by *Śyenī*: he was slain by *Rávaṇa* in attempting to rescue *Sítá* when carried off by that demon.

† Here is a great confusion of persons; *Báli* carried off *Rumá*, the wife of *Sugríva*.

hundred tassels, or have any curiosity to taste a bit of delicate flesh, now is your time.

Viṭa. What mean you?

Saṁs. Will you oblige me?

Viṭa. In anything not unreasonable.

Saṁs. There is no more flavour of unreasonableness than of she-devils in it.

Viṭa. Well, speak on.

Saṁs. Put Vasantasená to death.

Viṭa. (*Stopping his ears.*)

Murder a young and unoffending female,
Of courteous manners and unrivalled beauty,
The pride of all *Ujjayin!* Where shall I find,
Believe you, a fit raft to waft my soul
Safe o'er the river of futurity?

Saṁs. I will have one made for you. Come, come, what have you to fear? In this lowly place, who shall see you?

Viṭa. All nature—the surrounding realms of space;
The genii of these groves, the moon, the sun,
The winds, the vault of heaven, the firm-set earth,
Hell's awful ruler, and the conscious soul—
These all bear witness to the good or ill
That men perform, and these will see the deed.*

Saṁs. Throw a cloth over her then, and hide her.

Viṭa. Fool! you are crazed.

Saṁs. And you are an old good-for-nothing dastardly jackal. Very well, I shall find some one else. Stháváraka shall do it. Here, Stháváraka, my lad, I will give you gold bracelets.

Sthá. Thank your honour, I will wear them.

Saṁs. You shall have a gold seat.

Sthá. I will sit upon it.

Saṁs. You shall have every dainty dish from my table.

* This passage is in fact from Manu, with a slight deviation only in the order.

Sthá. I will eat it; never fear me.

Saṁs. You shall be head over all my slaves.

Sthá. I shall be a very great man.

Saṁs. But attend to what I order.

Sthá. Depend upon me, in everything that may be done.

Saṁs. It may be done well enough.

Sthá. Say on, sir.

Saṁs. Kill this Vasantasená.

Sthá. Excuse me, sir, I brought her here.

Saṁs. Why, you villain, am I not your master?

Sthá. You are, sir; my body is yours, but not my innocence: I dare not obey you.

Saṁs. Of whom are you, my servant, to be afraid?

Sthá. Futurity.

Saṁs. And who is Mr. Futurity, pray?

Sthá. The requiter of our good and evil deeds.

Saṁs. And what is the return for good?

Sthá. Wealth and power like your honour's.

Saṁs. And what for evil?

Sthá. Eating, as I do, the bread of slavery; I will not do, therefore, what ought not to be done.

Saṁs. You will not obey me? (*Beats him.*)

Sthá. Beat me if you will, kill me if you will, I cannot do what ought not to be done. Fate has already punished me with servitude for the misdeeds of a former life, and I will not incur the penalty of being born again a slave.

Vas. Oh, sir, protect me. (*To the Vita.*)

Vita. Come, come, be pacified. (*To the prince.*)

Stháváraka is right; revolving fate
Has doomed him to a low and servile station,
From which he wisely hopes a life of virtue
Hereafter sets him free. Do you too think,
Though degradation wait not close on crime,
And many, obstinately foes to virtue,
Suffer not here the punishment they merit,
Yet destiny not blindly works. Though now

Her will gives servitude to him, to you
A master's sway; yet in a future being,
Your affluence may his portion be assigned,
And yours, to do submissively his bidding.

Saṁs. (*Apart.*) The old dastard, and this fool of a slave, are both afraid of futurity; but what shall I fear? I, who am the brother of a prince, and a man of courage as well as rank? (*To Sthávaraka.*) Begone, slave; retire into the garden, and wait apart.

Sthá. I obey, sir. (*To Vasantasená.*) Lady, fear not me. [*Exit.*

Saṁs. (*Tightening his girdle.*) Now, Vasantasená, die. (*Goes to seize her; the Viṭa stops him.*)

Viṭa. In my presence! (*Throws him down.*)

Saṁs. Ah, villain! would you kill your prince? (*Faints.*) Ah, you who have so long fed at my cost, do you now become my foe? (*Rising; apart.*) Let me think; this will do. I saw the old scoundrel give a signal. I must get him out of the way and then despatch her. (*Aloud.*) My good friend, how could you so mistake what I said? How could you suppose that I, born of so high a race,* should seriously purpose such an unworthy action? I merely used those menaces to terrify her into compliance.

Viṭa. Believe me, sir, it is of little import
To boast of noble birth, unless accord
The manners with the rank:—ungrateful thorns
Are most offensive in a goodly soil.

Saṁs. The truth of the matter is, that Vasantasená is

* The term used to designate his family importance in this place, and again in the ninth act, is *Mallaka-pramáṅam*. *Mallaka* is said by the Commentator to mean a leaf used to wrap up anything, and that the Śakára intends to say *samudra*, the ocean; but this seems very gratuitous. *Mallaka*, as synonymous with *malla*, is a very common name amongst the princes of the Dekhin, and perhaps the Śakára may intend to compare his family to theirs. It might be thought not impossible that the author intended to express the Arabic term *Melek*, a king; but how or when did this word find its way to India?

bashful in your presence: leave us by ourselves a little. That fellow Stháváraka, too, I am sure, intends to run away; go, bring him back, and I dare say when we are alone a little she will relent.

Viťa. (*Apart.*) It may be true that, valiant in my presence,
Vasantasená may continue still
To drive this fool to madness by denial.
Passion in privacy gains confidence.
I will consent to leave them for a while.
(*Aloud*). I shall retire and obey your orders.

Vas. (*Laying hold of his garment.*)
Oh, leave me not! I have no hope but you.

Vita. You have no cause for terror. Hear me, sir:
I leave Vasantasená as a pledge,
And safe expect her from your hands again.

Sams. Be assured of it, she shall be so accepted.

Viťa. In truth?

Samس. In truth.

Viťa. (*Apart.*) He may deceive me. I'll at first retire;
But so, that unobserved I may behold
His acts, and satisfy me of his purpose.

Sams. He is gone, and now she dies. But hold:—perhaps he juggles with me, the sly old fox, and now lies watch to see what I am doing: he shall meet his match; the deceiver be deceived. (*He gathers flowers and decorates himself.*) Come, Vasantasená, child, why so pettish? come, come.

Viťa. I see his love revives; I now may leave them. (*Departs.*)

Sams. I will give you gold, I will treat you tenderly, I will lay head and turban at your feet. Oh, if you still disdain me, and will not accept me as your slave, what have I to do longer with mankind?

Vas. Why should I hesitate? I spurn you;
Nor can you tempt me, abject wretch, with gold.
Though soiled the leaves, the bees fly not the lotus,
Nor shall my heart prove traitor to the homage
It pays to merit, though its lord be poor.

To love such excellence exalts my life,
And sheds a lustre on my humble lot.
And why should I forego it? Can I leave
The mango's stately stem to twine around
The low and worthless *dhák*?

Saṁs. What! dare you compare the beggar Chárudatta to a mango-tree, and me to the *dhák*,* not even a *kiṁśuka*!* Is it thus you treat me and cherish the recollection of Chárudatta?

Vas. How can I cease to think of one who dwells for ever in my heart?

Saṁs. We'll soon try that, and cut short your recollections and yourself together. Stop, you inamorata of a beggarly Brahman.

Vas. Delightful words! proceed, you speak my praise.

Saṁs. Let him defend you if he can.

Vas. Defend me! I were safe if he were here!

Saṁs. What! is he *Śakra*, or the son of *Báli—Mahendra*, or the son of *Rambhá—Kálanemi*, or *Subhandu—Rudra* or the son of *Dróńa—Jaťáyu—Cháńakya—Dhundhumára* or *Triśanku*?† If he were all these together, he could not aid you. As *Sítá* was slain by *Cháńakya*, as *Draupadí* by *Jaťáyu*, so art thou by me. (*Seizes her.*)

* They are both the same apparently; but from the former growing on arid and concary soils it is stunted and mean, whilst the latter grows to a respectable tree.

† Several of these have been named before. *Śakra* is a name of *Indra*, the king of the gods: the son of *Báli* is *Angada*, a fierce monkey chief, one of Ráma's confederates. *Mahendra* is another name of Indra. The son of *Rambhá* is a personage of whom no notice has been found elsewhere, unless it be a mistake for the son of *Rádhá*, *Karńa*. *Kálanemi* is a Daitya of some celebrity, and one of Rávańa's attendants. *Subhandhu* has not been identified. *Rudra* is a name of *Śiva*. The son of Dróńa is a celebrated hero in the *Mahábhárata* named *Aśwatthdman*. *Jaťáyu* is a fabulous bird killed by *Rávańa*. *Cháńakya* is a statesman, the minister of *Chandragupta*. *Dhundhumára* is the name of a king of Oude of the Solar line, properly called *Kuvalaydśwa*, but termed *Dhundhumára* from slaying a demon named *Dhundhu* who annoyed the Saint *Uttanka*. *Triśanku* is a prince of the same family, elevated to heaven during his life by the sage *Viśwámitra*. All these persons occur in the Mahábhárata or Rámáyańa.

Vas. Oh, my dear mother! Oh, my loved Chárudatta!
Too short and too imperfect are our loves—
Too soon I perish. I will cry for succour—
What! shall Vasantasená's voice be heard
Abroad? Oh, that were infamy! No more
But this. Bless, bless my Chárudatta.

Saṁs. Still do you repeat that name! Once more, now. (*Seizing her by the throat.*)

Vas. (*In a struggling tone.*) Bless my Chárudatta.

Saṁs. Die, harlot, die. (*Strangles her with his hands.*) 'Tis done, she is no more. This bundle of vice, this mansion of cruelty, has met her fate, instead of him whom she came in her love to meet. To what shall I compare the prowess of this arm? Destroyed in the fulness of her hopes, she has fallen like *Sítá* in the *Bhárata*. Deaf to my desires, she perishes in my resentment. The garden is empty; I may drag her away unperceived. My father and my mother, that *Draupadí*, as well as my brothers, may regret that they did not see the valiant actions of my mother's son.* The old jackal will be here again presently. I will withdraw and observe him.

Enter the VIṬA *and* STHÁVARAKA.

Viṭa. I have brought back Sthávaraka. Where is he? Here are foot-marks,—these are woman's!

Saṁs. (*Advances.*) Welcome, master: you are well returned, Sthávaraka.

Viṭa. Now render back my pledge.

Saṁs. What was that?

Viṭa. Vasantasená.

Saṁs. Oh, she is gone.

Viṭa. Whether?

Saṁs. After you.

Viṭa. She came not in that direction.

* This passage is in the original somewhat obscure. *Śevá vanchida-bháduke mama pidá, mádeva, śá Doppadí, je śé pekkhadi ńedísaṁ vavaśidaṁ puttáha śúlattaṅaṁ.*

Sams. Which way went you?

Vita. To the east.

Sams. Ah, that accounts for it; she turned off to the south.

Vita. I went south too.

Sams. Then, I suppose, she went north.

Vita. What mean you? I comprehend you not. Speak out.

Sams. I swear by your head and my feet,* that you may make yourself perfectly easy. Dismiss all alarm; I have killed her.

Vita. Killed her!

Sams. What! you do not believe me? Then look here, see this first proof of my prowess. (*Shows the body.*)

Vita. Alas, I die! (*Faints.*)

Sams. Hey-dey! is it all over with him?

Sthá. Revive, sir; it is I who am to blame: my inconsiderately bringing her hither has caused her death.

Vita. (*Reviving.*) Alas! Vasantasená,

The stream of tenderness is now dried up,
And beauty flies us for her native sphere.
Adorned with every grace, of lovely aspect,
Radiant with playfulness, alas! poor wench,
River of gentle feeling, isle of mirth,
And friendly refuge for all such as I am;
Alas! love's richest store, a mart exhaustless
Of exquisite delights, is here broke open.
This crime will amply be avenged. A deed
Done by such hands, in such a place committed,
Will bring down infamy upon the state,
And drive our guardian goddess from our city.
Let me reflect;—this villain may involve
Me in the crime—I will depart from hence.

[*The prince lays hold of him.*

Detain me not; I have already been
Too long your follower and friend.

* A very insulting oath.

Saṁs. Very likely, indeed. You have murdered Vasantasená, and seek to accuse me of the crime. Do you imagine I am without friends?

Viṭa. You are a wretch.

Saṁs. Come, come, I will give you money, a hundred *suvarṅas,* clothes, a turban. The consequence of abuse is common to all men.

Viṭa. Keep your gifts.

Sthá. Shame! shame!

Saṁs. Ha, ha, ha! (*Laughing.*)

Viṭa. Restrain your mirth. Let there be hate between us.

That friendship that confers alone disgrace
Is not for me; it must no more unite us.
I cast it from me, as a snapped
And stringless bow.

Saṁs. Come, good master, be appeased. Let us go bathe.

Viṭa. Whilst you were free from crime you might exact
My duty, but obedience to you now
Would but proclaim myself alike unworthy.
I cannot wait on guilt, nor, though I know
My innocence, have courage to encounter
Those speaking glances every female eye
Will cast abhorrent upon one who holds
Communion with a woman's murderer.
Poor, poor Vasantasená! may thy virtues
Win thee in after-life a happier portion;
And may the days of shame, and death of violence
That thou hast suffered in existence past,
Ensure thee honoured birth, the world's regard,
And wealth and happiness, in that to come. (*Going.*)

Saṁs. Where would you fly? In this, my garden, you have murdered a female; come along with me, and defend yourself before my brother-in-law. (*Seizes him.*)

Viṭa. Away, fool. (*Draws his sword.*)

Saṁs. (*Falls back.*) Oh, very well, if you are afraid, you may depart.

Viṭa. I am in danger here; yes, I will join
S'arvilaka and Chandana, and with them seek
The band that Árya has assembled. [*Exit.*

Saṁs. Go, fool, to death. Well, Stháváraka, my lad, what think you of this business?

Sthá. That it is most horrible.

Saṁs. How, slave, do you condemn me? With all my heart, be it so. Here, take these. (*Gives him his ornaments.*) I make you a present of them, that when I am full dressed, you may be suitably equipped to attend me: it is my command.

Sthá. These are too costly,—what am I to do with them, sir?

Saṁs. Take them, take them, and away with you. Conduct the carriage to the porch of my palace, and there wait my coming.

Sthá. I obey, sir. [*Exit.*

Saṁs. My worthy preceptor has taken himself off in alarm. As to the slave, as soon as I return I will put him in confinement; so my secret is safe, and I may depart without apprehension. Hold! let me be sure,—is she dead, or must I kill her again? no, she is safe. I will cover the body with my mantle. Stop! it bears my name, and will discover me. Well thought of,—the wind has scattered about a quantity of dry leaves; I will cover her over with them. (*Collects the leaves and piles them over Vasantasená.*) Now to the court, where I will enter an accusation against Chárudatta of having murdered Vasantasená for her wealth. Ingeniously devised! Chárudatta will be ruined; the virtuous city cannot tolerate even the death of an animal.* Now to my work. (*Going.*) Here comes that rascally mendicant again, and by the very road I was about to take; he owes me a grudge for threatening to slit his nose, and should he see me here, he will out of revenge come forward and tax me with this murder. How shall I avoid him? I can leap the broken wall here. Thus I fly, as the monkey

* This may imply the wide diffusion of Bauddha tenets.

Mahendra leaped through heaven, over earth and hell, from Hanumat* Peak to Lanká. (*Jumps down.*)

Enter the S'RAMAŃAKA *or Mendicant, as before.*

I have washed my mantle, and will hang it on these boughs to dry. No, here are a number of monkeys; I 'll spread it on the ground. No, there is too much dust. Ha! yonder the wind has blown together a pile of dry leaves; that will answer exactly; I 'll spread it upon them. (*Spreads his wrapper over Vasantasená and sits down.*) Glory to *Buddha!* (*Repeats the moral stanzas as above.*) But enough of this. I covet not the other world, until in this I may make some return for the lady Vasantasená's charity. On the day she liberated me from the gamester's clutches she made me her slave for ever. Holloa! something sighed amidst yon leaves! or perhaps it was only their crackling, scorched by the sun, and moistened by my damp garment. Bless me, they spread out like the wings of a bird. (*One of Vasantasená's hands appears.*) A woman's hand, as I live, with rich ornaments—and another; surely I have seen that hand before. It is, it is—it is the hand that once was stretched forth to save me. What should this mean! (*Throws off the wrapper and leaves, and sees Vasantasená.*) It is the lady Vasantasená; the devoted worshipper of *Buddha.* (*Vasantasená expresses by signs the want of water.*) She wants water: the pool is far away; what 's to be done? Ha! my wet garment. (*Applies it to her face and mouth and fans her.*)

Vas. (*Reviving.*) Thanks, thanks, my friend; who art thou?

Śram. Do you not recollect me, lady? You once redeemed me with ten *suvarńas.*

Vas. I remember *you;* aught else I have forgotten. I have suffered since.

Śram. How, lady?

Vas. As my fate deserved.

Śram. Rise, lady, rise; drag yourself to this tree: here,

* Hanumat is the monkey; Mahendra, the mountain.

hold by this creeper.* (*Bends it down to her; she lays hold of it and rises.*) In a neighbouring convent dwells a holy sister;† rest a while with her, lady, and recover your spirits: gently, lady, gently. (*They proceed.*) Stand aside, good friends, stand aside; make way for a young female and a poor beggar. It is my duty to restrain the hands and mouth, and keep the passions in subjection. What should such a man care for kingdoms? His is the world to come. [*Exit.*

* To a Bauddha ascetic female contact is unlawful. His observance of the prohibition, in spite of his gratitude and regard for Vasantasená, is a curious and characteristic delineation of the denaturalizing tendency of such institutions.

† The expression is *Edaśśiṁ vihále mama dhammabahiniá chiśṫadi.* Etasmin viháre mama dharmabhaginí tishṫati. Conventa for women are very characteristically Bauddha institutions: they did exist in the Burman empire till of late years, and are still to be met with in Nepaul and Tibet.

END OF THE EIGHTH ACT.

ACT IX.

THE HALL OF JUSTICE.

(Exterior and Interior.)

Enter OFFICER.

I AM commanded to prepare the benches in this hall for the judges. (*Arranges them.*) All is ready for their reception, the floor is swept, and the seats are placed, and I have only now to inform them all is ready. (*Going.*) Ha! here comes the king's brother-in-law, a worthless fellow; I will get out of his way. (*Retires.*)

Enter SAḾSTHÁNAKA, *splendidly dressed.*

I have bathed in limpid water and reposed in a shady grove, passing my time like a celestial chorister of elegant form, amidst an attendant train of lovely damsels, now tying my hair, then twisting it into a braid, then opening it in flowing tresses, and again gathering it into a graceful knot. Oh! I am a most accomplished and astonishing young prince, and yet I feel a vacancy, an interior chasm; such as is sought for by the fatal worm that works its darkling way through the human entrails. How shall I fill it up?—on whom shall I satiate my craving? Ha! I recollect; it is designed for the miserable Chárudatta. So be it. I will repair to the court, and cause an accusation to be registered against him, of the death of Vasantaseńá, asserting that he has robbed and murdered her. The court is open, I see. (*Enters.*) How! the seats are ready for the arrival of the judges. I shall wait their coming on this grass plot.

Doorkeeper. Here comes the Court; I must attend.

Enter the JUDGE, *with the* PROVOST *and* RECORDER * *and others.*

Crier. Hear, all men, the judge's commands.

Judge. Amidst the conflicting details of parties engaged in legal controversy, it is difficult for the judge to ascertain what is really in their hearts. Men accuse others of secret crimes, and even though the charge be disproved, they acknowledge not their fault, but, blinded by passion, persevere; and whilst their friends conceal their errors, and their foes exaggerate them, the character of the prince is assailed. Reproach indeed is easy, discrimination of but rare occurrence, and the quality of a judge is readily the subject of censure. A judge should be learned, sagacious, eloquent, dispassionate, impartial; he should pronounce judgment only after due deliberation and inquiry; he should be a guardian to the weak, a terror to the wicked; his heart should covet nothing, his mind be intent on nothing but equity and truth, and he should keep aloof the anger of the king.

Provost and Rec. The character of your worship is as free from censure, as the moon is from the imputation of obscurity.

Judge. Officers, lead the way to the seat of judgment.

Off. As your worship commands. (*They sit.*)

Judge. Now go forth, and see who comes to demand justice.

Off. By command of his honour the judge, I ask, who waits to demand justice?

Saṁs. (*Advancing.*) Oh, oh! the judges are seated. I

* The *Śreshthin*, the chief of the merchants, and *Káyastha* or Scribe. From the way in which they interfere, they seem to sit as joint-assessors or commissioners with the judge. This is a curious, and, as far as yet known, a solitary picture of the practical administration of Hindu law under Hindu government. It is not exactly, perhaps, according to rule: the number, three or more, is correct. The judge may be either a Brahman, a Kshatriya, or a Vaiśya, but the assessors should be Brahmans alone. Merchants, however, may be called in. The presence of the Káyastha, a man of mixed caste, as an assessor, is not in the books, although the Scribe is enumerated amongst the officers of the court.

demand justice; I, a man of rank, a *Vásudeva*, and brother-in-law of the Rája;—I have a plaint to enter.

Off. Have the goodness to wait a moment, your excellency, whilst I apprize the Court. (*Returns.*) So please your worship, the first plaintiff is his Majesty's brother-in-law.

Judge. The Rája's brother-in-law to proffer a plaint? An eclipse of the rising sun foreruns the downfall of some illustrious character: but there are other matters before us. Return and tell him his cause cannot come on to-day.

(*Officer returns to Saṁsthánaka.*)

Off. I am desired to inform your honour that your cause cannot be tried to-day.

Saṁs. How! not to-day? Then I shall apply to the King, my sister's husband. I shall apply to my sister, and to my mother, and have this judge dismissed, and another appointed immediately. (*Going.*)

Off. Stay one moment, your honour, and I will carry your message to the Court. (*Goes to the judge.*) Please your worship, his excellency is very angry; and declares if you do not try his suit to-day, he will complain to the royal family, and procure your worship's dismissal.

Judge. The blockhead has it in his power, it is true. Well, call him hither: his plaint shall be heard.

Off. (*To Saṁs.*) Will your excellency be pleased to enter; your plaint will be heard.

Saṁs. Oh, oh! first it could not be tried; now it will be heard; very well; the judges fear me: they will do what I desire. (*Enters.*) I am well pleased, gentlemen; you may therefore be so too, for it is in my hands to distribute or withhold satisfaction.

Judge. (*Apart.*) Very like the language of a complainant this! (*Aloud.*) Be seated.

Saṁs. Assuredly. This place is mine, and I shall sit where I please. (*To the Provost.*) I will sit here; no (*to the Recorder*), I will sit here; no, no (*puts his hands on the judge's head, and then sits down by his side*), I will even sit here.

Judge. Your excellency has a complaint?

Saṁs. To be sure I have.

Judge. Prefer it.

Saṁs. I will, in good time; but remember, I am born in a distinguished family. My father is the Rája's father-in-law; the Rája is my father's son-in-law; I am the Rája's brother; and the Rája is my sister's husband.

Judge. We know all this; but why dwell on family honours? Personal excellence is more important; there are always thorn-bushes in the fairest forests: declare therefore your suit.

Saṁs. This it is; but it involves no fault of mine. My noble brother-in-law, in his good pleasure, presented me, for my ease and recreation, the best of the royal gardens, the ancient *Pushpakaraṅḍaka.* It is my practice to visit it daily, and see it well swept and weeded, and kept in order; and having, as my wont, gone this day thither, what should I behold, but—I could scarcely believe my eyes—the dead body of a female!

Judge. Did you know the person?

Saṁs. Alas! too well. She was once our city's greatest pride. Her rich attire must have tempted some execrable wretch to beguile her into the lonely garden; and there, for the sake of her jewels, was the lovely Vasantasená strangled by his hands, not by me. (*Stops himself.*)

Judge. What neglect in the police! You heard the plaint, gentlemen; let it be recorded, including the words "not by me."

Rec. (*Writes it.*) It is done.

Saṁs. (*Apart.*) Vile carelessness! My heedlessness has plunged me into peril, like a man crossing a narrow bridge precipitately, who tumbles into the stream: it cannot now be helped. (*Aloud.*) Well, sagacious administrators of justice, you make a mighty fuss about a trifle. I was going to observe, not by me was the deed beheld. (*Puts his foot on the record, and wipes out the last part.*)

Judge. How, then, do you know the truth of what you have stated, that for the sake of her ornaments she was strangled by some person's hands?

Sams. I conclude so, for the neck was bare and swollen, and her dress rifled of its ornaments.

Prov. The case is likely enough.

Sams. (*Apart.*) Good; I am alive again.

Prov. Whom else do we require in this suit?

Judge. The case is twofold, and must be investigated both in relation to assertion and facts; the verbal investigation relates to plaintiff and respondent, that of facts depends upon the judge.

Prov. The cause then requires the evidence of Vasantasená's mother.

Judge. Undoubtedly. Officers, go and civilly call Vasantasená's mother into court.

Off. (*Exit Officer, and returns with the old woman.*) Come along, dame.

Moth. My daughter is gone to a friend's house. This old fellow comes and says to me: "Come along; his honour the judge has sent for you." I am ready to faint, and my heart flutters so.—Very well, sir, very well, sir, lead me to the court.

Off. Here we are;—enter. (*They enter.*)

Moth. Health and happiness to your worships!

Judge. You are welcome;—sit down. (*She sits.*)

Sams. Oh, old procuress, you are there, are you?

Judge. You are the mother of Vasantasená?

Moth. I am.

Judge. Where is your daughter?

Moth. At a friend's house.

Judge. The name of that friend?

Moth. (*Apart.*) Oh dear me, this is very awkward. (*Aloud.*) Surely, your worship, this is not a fit question for your worship to ask.

Judge. No hesitation;—the law asks the question.

Prov. and Rec. Speak out; the law asks the question; there is no impropriety in answering.

Moth. Why then, gentlemen, to say the truth, she is at the house of a very nice gentleman:—the son of Ságaradatta, grandson of the Provost Vinayadatta, whose own name is Chárudatta; he lives near the Exchange: my daughter is with him.

Saṁs. You hear, judges;—let this be registered. I accuse Chárudatta.

Prov. Chárudatta, her friend! he cannot be criminal.

Judge. The cause, however, requires his presence.

Prov. Certainly.

Judge. (*To the Scribe.*) Dhanadatta, write down that Vasantasená last went to Chárudatta's residence: this is the first step. Let me consider; how can Chárudatta be summoned hither? However, the law must be enforced. Officer, repair to Chárudatta, and say to him, the magistrate, with all due respect, requests to see him at his perfect convenience.

(*Officer goes out, and re-enters with Chárudatta.*)

Off. This way, sir.

Chár. The prince well knows my rank and character,
And yet thus calls me to his public court.
Haply he may have heard my car conveyed
The fugitive he feared beyond his reach,
Borne to his ear by some unfriendly spy.
Or haply—but away with fancies; soon
I learn the truth, arrived at the tribunal.

Off. This way, this way, sir.

Chár. What should this mean? his harshest note, yon crow
Responsive utters to his fellow's call,
With croak repeated. Ha! my left eye throbs;
What new misfortunes threaten?

Off. Proceed, sir, never fear.

Chár. Facing the sun, on yonder blighted tree,
The bird of evil augury is perched;
Ha! on my path, the black snake sleeping lies.

Rousen from his slumber, he unfolds in wrath
His spiry length, and threatening beats the ground
With bulk inflated, as he turns on me
His angry eyes, and from between his fangs
Protrudes his hissing tongue. I slip, yet here
No plashy mire betrays my heedless feet.—
Still throbs my left eye, and my left arm trembles;
And still that bird in flight sinistral cries,
To warn me of impending ill. Yes, death—
Terrible death awaits me. Be it so—
It is not mine to murmur against destiny,
Nor doubt that righteous which the gods ordain.

Off. This is the court, sir, enter.

Chár. (*Entering and looking round.*)

The prospect is but little pleasing.
The court looks like a sea;*—its councillors
Are deep engulphed in thought; its tossing waves
Are wrangling advocates; its brood of monsters
Are these wild animals—death's ministers—
Attorneys skim like wily snakes the surface—
Spies are the shell-fish cowering 'midst its weeds,
And vile informers, like the hovering curlew,
Hang fluttering o'er, then pounce upon their prey:
The beach, that should be justice, is unsafe,
Rough, rude, and broken by oppression's storms.

[*As he advances he knocks his head against the door-frame.*

More inauspicious omens! they attend
Each step I take; fate multiplies its favours.

* That the translator may not be thought to have had an English rather than an Indian court in his eye, he enumerates the terms of the original for the different members of which it is said to consist. *Mantrins*, councillors; *Dútas*, the envoys or representatives of the parties; the wild animals, death's ministers, are *Nágas* and *Aśwas*, elephants and horses employed to tread or tear condemned criminals to death; the *Cháras* are spies or runners; *Nándvásakas*, disguised emissaries or informers; and *Káyasthas* are scribes by profession, who discharge the duties of notaries and attorneys.

Judge. Chárudatta approaches. Observe him;—that face and form never gave shelter to causeless crime. Appearance is a test of character; and not only in man, but in elephants, horses and kine, the disposition never deviates from the perfect shape.*

Chár. Hail to the court; prosperity attend
The delegated ministers of justice.

Judge. Sir, you are welcome; officer, bring a seat.

Off. It is here; be seated, sir. (*To Chárudatta; he sits.*)

Saṁs. So, Mr. Woman-killer, you are here: very decorous this, indeed, to treat such a fellow with so much civility; but never mind.

Judge. Worthy Chárudatta, allow me to ask if any intimacy or connexion has ever subsisted between you and this woman's daughter?

Chár. What woman?

Judge. This. (*Showing Vasantasená's mother.*)

Chár. (*Rising.*) Lady, I salute you.

Moth. Son, long may you live!† (*Apart.*) This is Chárudatta, then; really my daughter has made a good choice.

Judge. Tell us, Chárudatta, were you ever acquainted with that courtezan? (*Chárudatta ashamed, hesitates.*)

Saṁs. Ah! he pretends to be vastly modest, or very much alarmed; it is merely a pretext to evade confessing his vicious courses: but that he murdered the woman for her wealth, the prince shall soon make manifest.

Prov. Away with this hesitation, Chárudatta: there is a charge against you.

Chár. Well, sirs, what shall I say? What if she were
A friend of mine? be youth accused, not habit.

Judge. Let me beg—no evasion, banish all reserve, speak the truth and act ingenuously: remember it is the law that calls upon you.

* This is literally translated, without any leaning to *Gall* or *Lavater*.

† Literally, long be *my* life: *chiraṁ me jíva.*

Chár. First tell me who is my accuser?

Sams. I am—I.

Chár. Thou! a mighty matter truly.

Sams. Indeed, you woman-killer! What! are you to murder such a woman as Vasantasená, and rob her of her jewels, and to think it will not be known?

Chár. Thou art crazed.

Judge. Enough of this; declare the truth: was the courtezan your friend?

Chár. She was, she was.

Judge. And where is Vasantasená now?

Chár. Gone.

Prov. Gone! how, whither, and how attended?

Chár. (*Apart.*) Shall I say she went privately? (*Aloud.*) She went to her own dwelling: what more can I say?

Sams. What more? Why, did you not accompany her to my princely garden; and did you not there, for the sake of her jewels, strangle her, with your own hands? How then can you say she is gone home?

Chár. Foul calumniator.*

No rain from heaven upon thy face descends,
Dark as the jay's unmoistened wing in showers.
These falsehoods parch thy lips, as wintry winds
Despoil the shrivelled lotus of its beauty.

Judge. (*Apart.*) I see it were as easy to weigh *Himálaya*, ford the ocean, or grasp the wind, as fix a stain on Chárudatta's reputation. (*Aloud.*) It cannot be, that this worthy man is guilty.

Sams. What have you to do with his defence?—let the case be tried.

Judge. Away, fool, is it not thus?—if you expound the *Vedas*† will not your tongue be cut out? if you gaze upon the mid-day sun, will you not lose your eye-sight? if you plunge

* The general sense of the passage is, "Your face is unwashed, dirty, foul with falsehood," a common oriental phrase here poetically expressed.

† Here we find the Brahminical notions enforced; such being the punishment of Śúdras who shall read and expound the *Vedas*.

your hand into flame, will it not be burnt? and think you that if you revile Chárudatta, the earth will not open and swallow you? This is Chárudatta—how can such a man have committed such a crime? He has exhausted in lavish munificence the ocean of his disregarded wealth, and is it possible that he, who was best among the best, and who has ever shown the most princely liberality, should have been guilty of a deed most hateful to a noble mind, for the sake of plunder?

Saṁs. I say again, it is not your province to undertake his defence; you are to try the cause.

Moth. I say the accusation is false. When in his distress my daughter intrusted a casket of jewels to his care, and it was stolen from him, even then he replaced it with a necklace of still greater value; and can he now, for the sake of wealth, have turned murderer? Oh, never! Alas! would that my daughter were here! (*Weeps.*)

Judge. Inform us, Chárudatta, how did she leave you—on foot or in a carriage?

Chár. I did not see her depart, and know not.

Enter Víraka *in haste.*

Now go I to the court, to tell them how I have been maltreated, kicked, and abused for keeping a good look-out after the runaway. Hail to your worships!

Judge. Ha! here is Víraka, the captain of the watch: what brings you hither, Víraka?

Vír. Hear me, your honour. Whilst engaged last night in quest of Áryaka, who had broke loose, we stopped a covered carriage: the captain, Chandanaka, looked into it, and I was going to do so too, when he prevented me, pulled me back, and cuffed and kicked me. I beg your honours will take proper notice of this business.

Judge. We will. Whose was the carriage, do you know?

Vír. The driver said it belonged to this gentleman, Chárudatta; and that it carried Vasantasená to meet him in *Pushpakaraṅḍaka.*

Saṁs. You hear, sirs!

Judge. Truly this spotless moon is threatened by the demon of eclipse; the limpid stream is sullied by the falling of the banks. We will inquire into your complaint, Víraka; in the meantime mount one of the messenger's horses at the gate; go to *Pushpakaraṅḍaka* with all speed, and bring us word whether the body of a murdered woman lies there.

Vír. I shall. (*Goes out, and presently returns.*) I have been to the garden, and have ascertained that a female body has been carried off by the beasts of prey.

Judge. How know you it was a female?

Vír. By the remains of the hair, and the marks of the hands and feet.

Judge. How difficult it is to discover the truth: the more one investigates, the greater is the perplexity. The points of law are sufficiently clear here, but the understanding still labours like a cow in a quagmire.*

Chár. (*Apart.*) When first the flower unfolds, as flock the bees
To drink the honeyed dew, so mischiefs crowd
The entrance opened by man's falling fortune.

Judge. Come, Chárudatta, speak the truth.

Chár. The wretch that sickens at another's merits,
The mind, by passion blinded, bent to ruin
The object of its malice, do not claim
Reply, nor any heed to what they utter,
Which from their very nature must be falsehood.
For me—you know me—would I pluck a flower,
I draw the tender creeper gently to me,
Nor rudely rob it of its clustering beauty.
How think you then?—could I with violent hands
Tear from their lovely seat those jetty locks,
More glossy than the black bee's wing, or how
So wrong my nature, and betray my love,
As with remorseless heart to blast in death
The weeping charms that vainly sued for mercy?

* Rather an undignified simile for a judge.

Saḿs. I tell you, judges, you will be held as the defendant's friends and abettors, if you allow him longer to remain seated in your presence.

Judge. Officer, remove him from his seat. (*Officer obeys.*)

Chár. Ministers of justice, yet reflect. (*Sits on the ground.*)

Saḿs. (*Apart.*) Ha, ha! my deeds are now safely deposited on another's head; I will go and sit near Chárudatta. (*Does so.*) Come, Chárudatta, look at me: confess; say honestly, "I killed Vasantasená."

Chár. Vile wretch, away! Alas! my humble friend,
My good Maitreya, what will be thy grief
To hear of my disgrace? and thine, dear wife,
The daughter of a pure and pious race?
Alas! my boy, amidst thy youthful sports
How little think'st thou of thy father's shame!
Where can Maitreya tarry? I had sent him
To seek Vasantasená, and restore
The costly gems her lavish love bestowed
Upon my child—where can he thus delay?

Outside—Enter MAITREYA *with Vasantasená's jewels.*

I am to return these trinkets to Vasantasená; the child took them to his mother; I must restore them, and, on no account, consent to take them back again. Ha! Rebhila; how now Rebhila, what is the matter? You seem agitated, what has chanced? (*Listening.*) Hey! what say you, my dear friend? summoned to the court? this is very alarming. Let me think:—I must go to him, and see what it means; I can go to Vasantasená afterwards. Oh, here is the court. (*Enters.*) Salutation to your worships! where is my friend?

Judge. There.

Mait. My dear friend, all happiness——

Chár. Will be hereafter.

Mait. Patience.

Chár. That I have.

Mait. But why so downcast? what are you brought here for?

Chár. I am a murderer—reckless of futurity—
Repaying woman's tender love with blood—
What else, let him declare.

Mait. What!

Chár. (*Whispers him.*) Even so.

Mait. Who says so?

Chár. (*To the Rája's brother-in-law.*)
Yon miserable man, the instrument
That destiny employs to work my fall.

Mait. Why not say she is gone home?

Chár. It recks not what I say; my humble state
Is not to be believed.

Mait. How, sirs! what is all this? Can he who has beautified our city with its chief ornaments, who has filled Ujjayin with gardens, and gates, and convents, and temples, and wells, and fountains,—can he, an utter reprobate, for the object of a few beggarly ornaments, have done such an iniquitous act? (*In anger.*) And you—you wretch, you king's brother-in-law, Samsthánaka,—you who stop at nothing, and are a stuffed vessel of everything offensive to mankind,—you monkey, tricked out with golden toys: say again before me, that my friend, who never plucked a flower roughly in his life, who never pulled more than one at a time, and always left the young buds untouched;—say that he has been guilty of a crime detestable in both worlds, and I will break thy head into a thousand pieces with this staff, as knotty and crooked as thy own heart.

Sams. Hear him, my masters. What has this crow-footpated hypocritical fellow to do with the cause between me and Chárudatta, that he is to break my head. Attempt it, if you dare, you hypocritical scoundrel. (*Mait. strikes him; a struggle ensues, in which Vasantasená's jewels fall from his girdle. Samsthánaka picks them up.*) See here, sirs! here,—here are the poor wench's jewels, for the sake of which yon villain murdered her.

[*The judges hang down their heads.*

Chár. (*To Mait.*) In an ill hour these jewels spring to light.
Such is my fate, their fall will lead to mine.

Mait. Why not explain?

Chár. The regal eye is feeble to discern
The truth amidst perplexity and doubt.
I can but urge—I have not done the deed,
And poverty like mine must hope to gain
Unwilling credence; shameful death awaits me.

Judge. Alas! Mars is obstructed and Jupiter obscured, and a new planet like a comet wanders in their orbits.

Prov. Come hither, lady (*to Vasantasená's mother*); look at this casket; was it your daughter's?

Moth. It is very like, but not the same.

Sams. Oh, you old baggage! your eyes tell one story and your tongue another.

Moth. Away, slanderer!

Prov. Be careful of what you say: is it your daughter's, or is it not?

Moth. Why, your worship, the skill of the workman makes it difficult to trust one's eyes; but this is not my daughter's.

Judge. Do you know these ornaments?

Moth. Have I not said? They may be different, though like: I cannot say more; they may be imitations made by some skilful artist.

Judge. It is true. Provost, examine them: they may be different, though like; the dexterity of the artists is no doubt very great, and they readily fabricate imitations of ornaments they have once seen, in such a manner, that the difference shall scarcely be discernible.

Prov. Are these ornaments your property, Chárudatta?

Chár. They are not.

Prov. Whose then?

Chár. This lady's daughter's.

Prov. How come they out of the owner's possession?

Chár. She parted with them.

Prov. Consider, Chárudatta, you must speak the truth. Truth alone is internal satisfaction; not to declare the truth is a crime; the truth is readily told; seek not to conceal it by a lie.

Chár. I do not know the ornaments; but this I know, they are now brought from my house.

Sams. You killed her in my garden first, and so obtained them; this prevarication is only to hide the truth.

Judge. Chárudatta, own the truth, or it must be my pleasure that heavy lashes fall upon that delicate frame.

Chár. Sprung from a race incapable of crime,
I have not shamed my sires—if you confound
The innocent with the guilty, I must suffer.
(*Apart.*) If I have lost indeed Vasantasená,
Life is a burden to me. (*Aloud.*) What avails it
To proffer further plea? be it acknowledged.
I have abandoned virtue, and deserved
Abhorrence here and punishment hereafter.
Let me be called a murderer, or what else
It pleases him (*to Sams.*) to declare.

Sams. She is killed: say at once, *I* killed her.

Chár. You have said.

Sams. You hear him: he confesses it; all doubt is removed by his own words: let him be punished. Poor Chárudatta!

Judge. Officer, obey the prince—secure the malefactor.

Moth. Yet, good gentlemen, hear me. I am sure the charge is false. If my dear daughter be slain, let him live, who is my life. Who are the parties in this cause? I make no complaint, and why then is he to be detained? Oh! set him at liberty.

Sams. Silence, you old fool! what have you to do with him?

Judge. Withdraw, lady. Officer, lead her forth.

Moth. My son, my dear son! (*Is forced out.*)

Sams. I have done the business worthy of myself, and shall now depart. [*Exit.*

Judge. Chárudatta, the business of proof it was ours to effect, the sentence rests with the prince. Officer, apprize the royal Pálaka, that the convicted culprit being a Brahman, he cannot according to Manu be put to death, but he may be banished the kingdom with his property untouched.

Off. I obey. (*Goes out and returns.*) I have been, and the king thus commands. Let the ornaments of Vasantasená be suspended to the neck of the criminal; let him be conducted by beat of drum to the southern cemetery, and there let him be impaled; that, by the severity of this punishment, men may be in future deterred from the commission of such atrocious acts.

Chár. Unjust and inconsiderate monarch.*

'Tis thus that evil councillors impel
The heedless prince into the scorching flames
Of fierce iniquity and foul disgrace;
And countless victims perish by the guilt
Of treacherous ministers, who thus involve
Both prince and people in promiscuous ruin!
My friend Maitreya, I bequeath to you
My helpless family; befriend my wife,
And be a second parent to my child.

Mait. Alas! when the root is destroyed, how can the tree remain?

Chár. Not so; a father lives beyond his death
And in his son survives; 'tis meet my boy
Enjoy that friendship which thou show'dst his sire.

Mait. You have ever been most dear to me, most excellent Chárudatta; I cannot cherish life deprived of you.

Chár. Bring my boy to me.

Mait. That shall be done.

* Possibly the political events described in this piece were not wholly matter of fiction, and Pálaka, leaning to the Bauddha doctrines, and disregarding Brahminical privileges, provoked the insurrection that is recorded in the drama.

Judge. Officer, lead him forth. Who waits there? Let the *Cháńḍálas* * be called. [*Exit with Court.*

Off. This way.

Chár. Alas, my poor friend! †

Had due investigation been allowed me,
Or any test proposed—water or poison,
The scales or scorching fire,‡ and I had failed
The proof, then might the law have been fulfilled,
And I deservedly received my doom.§
But this will be avenged: and for the sentence
That dooms a Brahman's death on the mere charge
Of a malicious foe, the bitter portion
That waits for thee, and all thy line, O king,
Is hell. Proceed—I am prepared. [*Exeunt.*

* Whose caste makes them public executioners.

† The following lines are uttered *ákáśe* or in the air, according to the original; that is, they are not spoken by any of the *dramatis personæ*. They are, however, so suitable to Chárudatta as to warrant a departure from the stage direction.

‡ The different modes of trial by ordeal.

§ Literally, the saw might have been applied to the body; *Krakachaṁ śaríre dátavyam*.

END OF THE NINTH ACT.

ACT X.

THE ROAD TO THE PLACE OF EXECUTION.

Enter CHÁRUDATTA *with two* CHÁŃḊÁLAS *as Executioners.*

1st Cháń. Out* of the way, sirs! out of the way! room for Chárudatta. Adorned with the *karavíra* † garland, and attended by his dexterous executioners, he approaches his end like a lamp ill-fed with oil.

Chár. Sepulchral blossoms decorate my limbs,
Covered with dust, and watered by my tears,
And round me harshly croak the carrion birds,
Impatient to enjoy their promised prey.

2d Cháń. Out of the way, sirs! what do you stare at? a good man whose head is to be chopped off by the axe of destiny? a tree that gave shelter to gentle birds to be cut down? Come on, Chárudatta.

Chár. Who can foresee the strange vicissitudes
Of man's sad destiny?—I little thought
That such a fate would ever be my portion,
Nor could have credited I should live to be
Dragged like a beast to public sacrifice,
Stained with the ruddy sandal spots and smeared
With meal—a victim to the sable goddess.‡
Yet as I pass along, my fellow-citizens

* The Prákŕit spoken by the Cháńḋálas is exceedingly rude and difficult; the commentator is often evidently at fault, and furnishes very imperfect and unsatisfactory interpretations: several passages have been accordingly omitted, but none of any importance.

† Sweet-scented oleander, or rose bay. *Nerium odorum.*

‡ This is an addition of the commentator: the text implies that he is equipped as a victim, but does not say to what deity.

Console me with their tears, and execrate
The cruel sentence that awards my death.
Unable to preserve my life, they pray
That heaven await me, and reward my sufferings.

1st Cháń. Stand out of the way—what crowd you to see? There are four things not to be looked at: *Indra* carried forth, the birth of a calf, the transit of a star, and the misfortune of a good man.* Look, brother Ahinta; the whole city is under sentence!—What! does the sky weep, or the thunderbolt fall without a cloud?

2d Cháń. No, brother Goha, not so; the shower falls from yonder cloud of women; yet though all the people weep, yet such is the throng, that their tears cannot lay the dust.

Chár. From every window lovely faces shed
The kindly drops, and bathe me with their tears.

1st Cháń. Here stop! strike the drum, and cry the sentence. —Hear ye, hear ye! This is Chárudatta, son of Ságaradatta, son of Provost Vinayadatta, by whom the courtezan Vasantasená has been robbed and murdered; he has been convicted and condemned, and we are ordered by king Pálaka to put him to death: so will his Majesty ever punish those that commit such crimes as both worlds abhor.

* This passage is not clear; the expression is *Inde paváhiante*, which seems to imply *Indrah praváhyamánań*. The oldest commentary translates it *Pravardhamána*, increasing, progressing; and supposes *Indra* put for his bow, the rainbow. It seems more probable, however, that the phrase alludes to some observance in honour of the deity which has fallen into disuse and is forgotten. Such, for example, as the *Śakradhwajotthána*, erection of a flag in honour of *Indra*, which, after being worshipped for some days, is directed to be removed privately at midnight, when all the people are asleep. (*Káliká-Puráńa.*) The paraphernalia and circumstances of a public execution, according to Hindu fashions, are interestingly described here; the scantiness of the official attendance shows that the people were as easily managed then as at any subsequent period. The character of the executioner corresponds precisely with that of the Roman Carnifex; and, in like manner, the place of execution is the public cemetery, or place of burning the dead. The criminal is dressed as a victim with very classical decorations.

Chár. Dreadful reverse—to hear such wretches herald
My death, and blacken thus with lies my fame:
Not so, my sires—for them the frequent shout
Has filled the sacred temple, where the crowd
Of holy Brahmans to the gods proclaimed
The costly rite accomplished: and shall I,
Alas! Vasantasená, who have drunk
Thy nectared tones from lips whose ruby glow
Disgraced the coral, and displayed the charms
Of teeth more pearly than the moon's chaste light,
Profane my ears with such envenomed draughts
Of infamy whilst yet my soul is free?

[*Puts his hands to his ears.*

1st Chán. Stand apart there—make way!

Chár. My friends avoid me as I pass, and, hiding
Their faces with their raiment, turn away.
Whilst fortune smiles each stranger is a friend,
But friends are strangers in adversity.

1st Chán. The road is now tolerably clear,—bring along the culprit.

(*Behind.*) Father! father!
My friend! my friend!

Chár. My worthy friends, grant me this one indulgence.

1st Chán. What! will you take anything of us?*

Chár. Disdain not my request. Though basely born,
You are not cruel, and a gentle nature
Ranks you above your sovereign. I implore you,
By all your future hopes, oh once permit me
To view my son, ere I depart to death!

1st Chán. Let him come.—Men, stand back, and let the child approach: here, this way.

Enter MAITREYA *with* ROHASENA.

Mait. Here we have him, boy, once more; your dear father, who is going to be murdered.

* That is, how can a *Brahman* condescend to accept anything from a *Cháńďála?* There is some bitterness in the question.

Boy. Father! father!

Chár. Come hither, my dear child. (*Embraces him and takes his hands.*)

These little hands will ill-suffice to sprinkle
The last sad drops upon my funeral pyre.
Scant will my spirit sip thy love, and then
A long and painful thirst in heaven succeeds.
What sad memorial shall I leave thee, boy,
To speak to thee hereafter of thy father?
This sacred string, whilst yet 'tis mine, I give thee.*
The Brahman's proudest decoration, boy,
Is not of gold nor gems; but this by which
He ministers to sages and to gods.
This grace my child when I shall be no more. (*Takes off his Brahmanical cord and puts it round his son's neck.*)

1*st Cháń.* Come, you Chárudatta, come along.

2*d Cháń.* More respect, my master; recollect, by night or day, in adversity or prosperity, fate holds its course, and puts men to trial. Come, sir; complaints are unavailing; and it is not to be expected that men will honour the moon when *Ráhu* has hold of him.

* The distinguishing mark of a man of the three superior classes is a cord worn over the left shoulder and under the right arm: it is imposed with much solemnity, and the investiture, with its accompanying formulæ, is considered to indicate the regeneration of the individual: whence his name *Dwija*, or twice-born. The rite is applicable to all the three superior castes, or the Brahman, Kshattriya, and Vaiśya, to each of whom the term *Dwija* is appropriate; although, as the two latter are considered to be extinct, it now signifies the Brahman only. The cord of the Brahman should be made of cotton, that of the Kshattriya of a kind of grass, and that of the Vaiśya of woollen thread. The investiture of the first should take place between the ages of five and sixteen; of the second, between six and twenty-two; and of the third, between eight and twenty-four. If delayed beyond the latter period the individual is considered degraded from his caste. An essential part of the ceremony is the communication of the *Gáyatrí* or holiest verse of the Vedas. It is communicable to all three, and is the following:—*Om*. Earth. Air. Heaven. Let us meditate on the supreme splendour of that divine Sun, who may illuminate our understanding.—*Om, bhúr bhuvaḱ swaḱ, tat savitur vareńyam bhargo devasya dhímahi, dhiyo yo naḱ prachodayát.*

Roha. Where do you lead my father, vile Cháńd́ála?

Cháń. I go to death, my child; the fatal chaplet
Of *Karavíra* hangs around my neck;
The stake upon my shoulder rests,* my heart
Is burdened with despair, as, like a victim
Dressed for the sacrifice, I meet my fate.

1*st Cháń.* Hark ye, my boy: they who are born *Cháńd́álas* are not the only ones; they who oppress the virtuous are *Cháńd́álas* too.

Roha. Why, then, want to kill my father?

1*st Cháń.* The king orders us; it is his fault, not ours.

Roha. Take and kill me; let my father go.

1*st Cháń.* My brave little fellow, long life to you!

Chár. (*Embracing him.*)
This is the truest wealth; love equal smiles
On poor and rich; the bosom's precious balm
Is not the fragrant herb, nor costly unguent—
But nature's breath, affection's holy perfume.

Mait. Come now, my good fellows, let my worthy friend escape: you only want a body,—mine is at your disposal.

Chár. Forbear, forbear!

1*st Cháń.* Come on! stand off! what do you throng to see? a good man who has lost his all and fallen into despair, like a gold bucket whose rope breaks and it tumbles into the well.

2*d Cháń.* Here stop: beat the drum, and proclaim the sentence. (*As before.*)

Chár. This is the heaviest pang of all; to think
Such bitter fruit attends my closing life.
And oh! what anguish, love, to hear the calumny,
Thus noised abroad, that thou wast slain by me!

[*Exeunt.*

* So condemned malefactors, according to the Roman code, bore their cross or gibbet to the place of execution.

SCENE II.—A ROOM IN THE PALACE.

STHÁVARAKA *discovered above, bound, listening to the drum and proclamation.*

How! the innocent Chárudatta to be executed, and I in chains still! I may be heard. What ho there! friends, hear me:—it was I, sinner that I am, who drove Vasantasená to the royal garden. There my master met us, and finding her deaf to his wishes, with his own hands strangled her. He is the murderer, not this worthy man.—They cannot hear me: I am too far off. Cannot I leap down?—it shall be so; better any chance than that Chárudatta should suffer. I can get out of this window and spring from the balcony: better I perish than Chárudatta, and if I die, heaven is my reward. (*Jumps down.*) I am not hurt, and fortunately my chain has snapped. Now, whence comes the cry of the Cháńd'álas:—ha! yonder,—I will overtake them. What ho there, stop! [*Exit.*

SCENE III.

Enter CHÁRUDATTA *as before—to them* STHÁVARAKA.

Sthá. What ho, stop!

1st Cháń. Who calls to us to stop?

Sthá. Hear me; Chárudatta is innocent. I took Vasantasená to the garden, where my master strangled her with his own hands.

Chár. Who comes rejoicing thus my latest hours,
To snatch me from the galling bonds of fate?
Like the full cloud, distent with friendly showers,
That timely hangs to save the dropping grain?
Heard you the words?—my fame again is clear.
My death I heeded not, I feared disgrace.
Death without shame is welcome as the babe
New-born. I perish now by hate
I ne'er provoked; by ignorance and malice—
I fall the mark of arrows dipped in venom,
And aimed at me by infamy and guilt.

1st Cháń. Hark ye, Stháváraka,—do you speak the truth?

Sthá. I do; and would have ere now proclaimed it: for fear of that I was chained, and shut up in one of the rooms of the palace.

Enter SAḾSTHÁNAKA (*above*).

I have had a most sumptuous regale in the palace here: rice, with acid sauce, and meat, and fish, and vegetables, and sweetmeats. What sounds were those I heard? The Cháńd'ála's voice, as harsh as a cracked bell, and the beat of the death-drum; the beggar Chárudatta is going to execution. The destruction of an enemy is a banquet to the heart. I have heard, too, that whoever looks upon the death of an adversary will never have bad eyes in his next birth. I will ascend the terrace of my palace and contemplate my triumph. (*Ascends.*) What a crowd has collected to see the execution of this miserable wretch! If so many flock to see him, what a concourse there would be to behold a great mań like myself put to death! He is dressed like a young steer. They are taking him to the south. What brings them this way, and why ceases the noise? (*Looks into the chamber.*) Hey! where is the slave Stháváraka? He has made his escape!—all my schemes will be ruined!—I must seek him. (*Descends.*)

Sthá. Here comes my master.

1st Cháń. Out of the way there! make room! Here he comes, like a mad ox, butting with the sharp horn of arrogance.

Saḿ. Room, room here! My boy Stháváraka, come you along with me.

Sthá. What, sir! are you not satisfied with having murdered Vasantasená, that you now endeavour to compass the death of the excellent Chárudatta?

Saḿ. I,—I,—a vessel of rich jewels, I murder a woman!

Crowd. Yes, yes, you murdered her; not Chárudatta.

Saḿ. Who says so?

Crowd. This honest man.

Saḿ. Stháváraka, my servant. (*Apart.*) He is the only

witness of my guilt. I have ill-secured him. It shall be so. (*Aloud.*) Hear ye, my masters: this is my slave; he is a thief, and for theft I punished and confined him: he owes me a grudge for this, and has made up this story to be revenged. Confess (*to Sthávaraka*), is it not so? (*Approaches and in an under-tone.*) Take this (*offers him a bracelet*); it is yours;—recall your words.

Sthá. (*Takes the bracelet and holds it up.*) See here, my friends, he bribes me, even now, to silence!

Saṁs. (*Snatches the bracelet.*) This is it; the very ornament I punished him for stealing; look here, Cháńḋálas: for pilfering from my treasury, which was under his charge, I had him whipped; if you doubt me, look at his back.

1st Cháń. It is very true; and a scorched slave will set anything on fire.

Sthá. Alas! this is the curse of slavery, to be disbelieved even when we speak the truth. Worthy Chárudatta, I can do no more. (*Falls at his feet.*)

Chár. Rise, thou who feelest for a good man's fall,
And com'st a virtuous friend to the afflicted.
Grieve not thy cares are vain. Whilst destiny
Forbids my liberation, all attempts
Like thine will profit nothing.

1st Cháń. As your honour has already chastised this slave, you should let him go.

Saṁs. Come, come. What is this delay, why do you not dispatch this fellow?

1st Cháń. If you are in such haste, sir, you had better do it yourself.

Roha. Kill me and let my father live.

Saṁs. Kill both; father and son perish together.

Chár. All answers to his wish. Return, my child,
Go to thy mother, and with her repair
To some asylum, where thy father's fate
Shall leave no stain on thee. My friend, conduct them
Hence without delay.

Mait. Think not, my dear friend, that I intend to survive you.

Chár. My good Maitreya, the vital spirit owes not
Obedience to our mortal will: beware
How you presume to cast that life away:
It is not thine to give or to abandon.

Mait. (*Apart.*) It may not be right, but I cannot bear to live when he is gone. I will go to the Brahman's wife, and then follow my friend. (*Aloud.*) Well, I obey; this task is easy. (*Falls at his feet, and rising, takes the child in his arms.*)

Saḿs. Holloa! did I not order you to put the boy to death along with his father? (*Chárudatta expresses alarm.*)

1*st Cháń.* We have no such orders from the Rája—away, boy, away. (*Forces off Maitreya and Rohasena.*) This is the third station, beat the drum, and proclaim the sentence. (*As before.*)

Saḿs. (*Apart.*) The people seem to disbelieve the charge. (*Aloud.*) Why, Chárudatta, the townsmen doubt all this; be honest; say at once, "I killed Vasantasená." (*Chárudatta continues silent.*) Ho! Cháńd́ála, this vile sinner is dumb; make him speak: lay your cane across his back.

2*d Cháń.* Speak, Chárudatta. (*Strikes him.*)

Chár. Strike! I fear not blows; in sorrow plunged,
Think you such lesser ills can shake my bosom?
Alone I feel the flame of men's reports,
The foul assertion that I slew my love.

Saḿs. Confess, confess!

Chár. My friends and fellow-citizens, ye know me.

Saḿs. She is murdered.

Chár. Be it so.

1*st Cháń.* Come; the execution is your duty.

2*d Cháń.* No; it is yours.

1*st Cháń.* Let us reckon. (*They count.**) Now, if it be my turn, I shall delay it as long as I can.

* They write or make marks or lines in various ways; such is the stage direction, but what is intended is not exactly known.

2d Cháń. Why?

1st Cháń. I will tell you:—my father, when about to depart to heaven, said to me, "Son, whenever you have a culprit to execute, proceed deliberately; never do your work in a hurry; for, perhaps, some worthy character may purchase the criminal's liberation; perhaps a son may be born to the Rája, and a general pardon be proclaimed; perhaps an elephant may break loose and the prisoner escape in the confusion; or, perhaps, a change of rulers may take place, and every one in bondage be set at large."

Sańs. (*Apart.*) A change of rulers!

1st Cháń. Come, let us finish our reckoning.

Sańs. Be quick, be quick! get rid of your prisoner. (*Retires.*)

1st Cháń. Worthy Chárudatta, we but discharge our duty; the king is culpable, not we, who must obey his orders: consider—have you anything to say?

Chár. If virtue yet prevail, may she who dwells
Amongst the blest above, or breathes on earth,
Clear my fair fame from the disastrous spots
Unfriendly fate and man's accusing tongue
Have fixed upon me—whither do you lead me?

1st Cháń. Behold the place, the southern cemetery, where criminals quickly get rid of life. See, where jackals feast upon one-half of the mangled body, whilst the other yet grins ghastly on the pointed stake!

Chár. Alas, my fate! (*Sits down.*)

Sańs. I shall not go till I have seen his death. How—sitting!

1st Cháń. What! are you afraid, Chárudatta?

Chár. (*Rising.*) Of infamy I am, but not of death.

1st Cháń. Worthy sir, in heaven itself the sun and moon are not free from change and suffering: how should we, poor weak mortals, hope to escape them in this lower world: one man rises but to fall, another falls to rise again; and the vesture of the carcase is at one time laid aside, and at another resumed:

think of these things, and be firm. This is the fourth station: proclaim the sentence. (*Proclamation as before.*)

Enter the SRAMAŃAKA *and* VASANTASENÁ.

Śram. Bless me, what shall I do? Thus leading Vasantasená, am I acting conformably to the laws of my order? Lady, whither shall I conduct you?

Vas. To the house of Chárudatta, my good friend;
His sight will bring me back to life, as the bright moon
Revives the leaflets of the drooping flower.

Śram. Let us get into the high road: here it is. Hey! what noise is this?

Vas. And what a crowd is here!—inquire the cause;
For all Ujjayin is gathered on one spot,
And earth is off its balance with the load.*

1*st Cháń.* This is the last station: proclaim the sentence. (*Proclamation as before.*) Now, Chárudatta, forgive us; all will soon be over.

Chár. The gods are mighty.

Śram. Lady! lady! they say here you have been murdered by Chárudatta, and they are therefore going to put him to death.

Vas. Unhappy wretch! that I should be the cause
Of so much danger to my Chárudatta.
Quick! lead me to him.

Śram. Quick, lady; worthy servant of *Buddha*, hasten to save Chárudatta. Room, good friends; make way.

Vas. Room! room! (*Pressing through the crowd.*)

1*st Cháń.* Remember, worthy Chárudatta, we but obey the king's commands; the sin is his, not ours.

Chár. Enough! perform your office.

1*st Cháń.* (*Draws his sword.*) Stand straight, your face

* This is rather extravagant, but less so than Lucan's apprehension that Nero after his apotheosis might occasion a somewhat similar accident:

"Ætheris immensi partem si presseris unam,
Sentiet axis onus, librati ponderi cœli
Orbe tene media."

upwards, and one blow sends you to heaven. (*Chárudatta obeys, the Cháńd́ála goes to strike, and drops his sword.*) How? I held the hilt firmly in my grasp! yet the sword, as unerring as a thunderbolt, has fallen on the ground! Chárudatta will escape; it is a sure sign. Goddess of the *Sahya* hills,* be pleased to hear me! If Chárudatta be yet set free, the greatest favour will be conferred upon the whole Cháńd́ála race.

2d *Cháń.* Come, let us do as we are ordered.

1st *Cháń.* Be it so. (*They are leading Chárudatta to the stake, when Vasantasená rushes through the crowd.*)

Vas. Forbear, forbear! in me behold the wretch
For whom he dies!

1st *Cháń.* Hey! who is this that with dishevelled locks and uplifted arms calls us to forbear?

Vas. Is it not true, dear, dearest Chárudatta? (*Throws herself on his bosom.*)

Śram. Is it not true, respected Chárudatta? (*Falls at his feet.*)

1st *Cháń.* Vasantasená! The innocent must not perish by our hands.

Śram. He lives! Chárudatta lives!

1st *Cháń.* May he live a hundred years!

Vas. I revive.

1st *Cháń.* Away! bear the news to the king; he is at the public place of sacrifice. (*Some go out.*)

Saṁs. (*Seeing Vasantasená.*) Alive still! Who has done this? I am not safe here, and must fly. [*Exit.*

1st *Cháń.* (*To the other.*) Hark ye, brother, we were ordered to put to death the murderer of Vasantasená: we had better therefore secure the Rája's brother-in-law.

2d *Cháń.* Agreed; let's follow him. [*Exeunt.*

Chár. Who thus, like showers to dying grain, has come
To snatch me from the uplifted sword and face
Of present death? Vasantasená,

* A form of *Durgá*, worshipped formerly in the *Vindhya* range, near Ougein.

Can this be she? or has another form
Like hers from heaven descended to my succour?
Am I awake, or do my senses wander—
Is my Vasantasená still alive?
Speeds she from spheres divine, in earthly charms
Arrayed again, to save the life she loved,
Or comes some goddess in her beauteous likeness?

Vas. (*Falls at his feet.*)
You see herself, the guilty cause that brought
This sad reverse upon thy honoured course.

Chár. (*Taking her up and looking at her.*)
My love, Vasantasená, is it thou?

Vas. That ill-starred wretch.

Chár. Vasantasená—can it—can it be?
And why these starting tears?—away with grief!
Didst thou not come, and like the wondrous power
That brings back life to its deserted source,*
Redeem triumphant from the grasp of death
This frame to be henceforward all thine own?
Such is the force of love omnipotent,
Who calls the very dead to life again!
Behold, my sweet, these emblems, that so late
Denoted shame and death, shall now proclaim
A different tale, and speak our nuptial joy—
This crimson vesture be the bridegroom's garb,
This garland be the bride's delightful present,
And this brisk drum shall change its mournful sounds
To cheerful tones of marriage celebration.

Vas. Ingenious ever is my lord's device.

Chár. Thy plotted death, dear girl, was my sad doing.
The Rája's brother has been long my foe;
And in his hate, which future doom will punish,
He sought, and partly worked his will, my fall.

Vas. Forbear, nor utter such ill-omened words.
By him, and him alone, my death was purposed.

* The mythological drug that restores the dead to life.

Chár. And who is this?

Vas. To him I owe my life:
His seasonable aid preserved me.

Chár. Who art thou, friend?

Śram. Your honour does not recollect me. I was employed as your personal servant: afterwards becoming connected with gamblers, and unfortunate, I should have been reduced to slavery, had not this lady redeemed me. I have since then adopted the life of a mendicant; and coming in my wanderings to the Rája's garden, was fortunately enabled to assist my former benefactress.

(*Behind.*) Victory to *Vríshabhaketu*,* the despoiler of *Daksha's* sacrifice! † glory to the six-faced scatterer of armies, the foe of *Krauncha!* ‡ Victory to Áryaka, the subjugator of his adversaries, and triumphant monarch of the wide-spread, mountain-bannered earth!

Enter ŚARVILAKA.

This hand has slain the king, and on the throne
Of Pálaka ascends our valiant chief,
Resistless Áryaka, in haste anointed.
Now to obey his first commands, and raise
The worthy Chárudatta far above
Calamity and fear. All is achieved—

* The deity whose emblem is a bull—*Śiva.*

† The *Prajápati* or patriarch *Daksha*, the son of *Brahmá*, married his daughter *Satí* to *Śiva*, but disgusted with the son-in-law, omitted to invite him to a solemn sacrifice at which all the gods and sages were assembled. *Satí*, in a fit of vexation, threw herself into the sacrificial flame; and in revenge of this, as well as the affront offered him, *Śiva* sent his attendant sprites, headed by *Vírabhadra* to disturb the rite. This they easily performed; bruising and mutilating the gods themselves. The legend seems to have been a favourite in the south of India at the period when the caves of Elephanta and Ellora were excavated, being elaborately sculptured on their walls. It is told in the *Mahábhárata*, omitting the burning of *Satí*, which seems to be a Pauráńik addition.

‡ *Kárttikeya*, the Hindu Mars. *Krauncha* is one of the confederates of the demon *Táraka*, against whom *Kárttikeya* led the gods and triumphed.

Of valour and of conduct destitute
The foe has fallen—the citizens behold
Well pleased the change, and thus has noble daring
Wrested an empire from its ancient lords,
And won a sway as absolute on earth
As that which *Indra* proudly holds in heaven.
This is the spot;—he must be near at hand
By this assemblage of the people. Well begins
The reign of Áryaka, if his first cares
Reap the rich fruit of Chárudatta's life.
Give way, and let me pass; 'tis he!—he lives!—
Vasantasená too!—my monarch's wish
Is all accomplished. Long this generous Brahman
Has mourned his sullied brightness like the moon
That labours in eclipse, but now he bounds
Again to honour and to happiness,
Borne safely o'er a boundless sea of troubles
By firm affection's bark, and favouring fate.
How shall I, sinner as I am, approach
Such lofty merit; yet the honest purpose
Is everywhere a passport. Chárudatta,
Hail, most worthy sir!

[*Joins his hands and raises them to his forehead.*

Chár. Who thus addresses me?

Śar. In me behold
The plunderer, that desperate forced his way
By night into your mansion, and bore off
The pledge intrusted to your care: I come
To own my fault and throw me on your mercy.

Chár. Not so, my friend, you may demand my thanks. (*Embraces him.*)

Śar. And further I inform you, that the king,
The unjust Pálaka, has fallen a victim,
Here in the place of sacrifice, to one
Who has avenged his wrongs and thine; to Áryaka,
Who ready homage pays to birth and virtue.

Chár. How say you?

Śar. That the fugitive,
Whom late your car conveyed in safety hence,
Has now returned, and in the place of offering
Slain Pálaka as a victim.

Chár. I rejoice
In his success—it was to you he owed
Escape from his confinement.

Śar. But to you
Escape from death; and to requite his debt
He gives to your authority in Ujjayin,
Along the *Veńá's* * borders, *Kuśávatí*—
A proof of his esteem and gratitude.

(*Without.*) Bring him along! bring him along! the Rája's villainous brother-in-law. (*Saṁsthánaka, his arms tied behind him, dragged on by the mob.*)

Saṁs. Alas, alas! how am I maltreated: bound and dragged along as if I were a restive ass, or a dog, or any brute beast. I am beset by the enemies of the state; whom can I fly to for protection?—yes, I will have recourse to him. (*Approaches Chárudatta.*) Preserve me. (*Falls at his feet.*)

Mob. Let him alone, Chárudatta; leave him to us; we'll dispatch him.

Saṁs. Oh, pray Chárudatta!—I am helpless, I have no hope but you.

Chár. Banish your terror: they that sue for mercy
Have nothing from their foes to dread.

Śar. Hence with the wretch!
Drag him from Chárudatta. Worthy sir,
Why spare this villain? Bind him, do you hear,
And cast him to the dogs; saw him asunder;
Or hoist him on the stake: dispatch, away.

* Neither Sir Charles Malet, nor Dr. Hunter, nor Sir J. Malcolm enable us to offer any account of this river or of *Kuśávatí*; we cannot therefore pretend to adjust their position. The river of Ujjayin is the *Śiprá*; whether it is ever called the *Veńá* we have no knowledge.

Chár. Hold, hold! may I be heard?

Śar. Assuredly.

Saṁs. Most excellent Chárudatta, I have flown to you for refuge; oh, protect me! spare me now, I will never seek your harm any more.

Mob. Kill him, kill him! why should such a wretch be suffered to live? (*Vasantasená takes the garland off Chárudatta's neck, and throws it round Saṁsthánaka's.*)

Saṁs. Gentle daughter of a courtezan, have pity upon me: I will never kill you again, never, never!

Śar. Give your commands, sirs, that he may be removed, and how we shall dispose of him.

Chár. Will you obey in what I shall enjoin?

Śar. Be sure of it.

Chár. In truth?

Śar. In very truth.

Chár. Then for the prisoner——

Śar. Kill him.

Chár. Set him free.

Śar. Why so?

Chár. An humbled foe, who prostrate at your feet
Solicits quarter, must not feel your sword.

Śar. Admit the law, then give him to the dogs.

Chár. Not so!
His punishment be mercy.

Śar. You move my wonder, but shall be obeyed.
What is your pleasure?

Chár. Loose him, and let him go.

Śar. He is at liberty. (*Unties him.*)

Saṁs. Huzza! I am again alive.

(*Without.*) Alas, alas! the noble wife of Chárudatta, with her child vainly clinging to her raiment, seeks to enter the fatal fire, in spite of the entreaties of the weeping crowd.

Enter CHANDANAKA.

Śar. How now, Chandanaka, what has chanced?

Chan. Does not your excellency see yon crowd collected on

the south of the royal palace? There the wife of Chárudatta is about to commit herself to the flames; I delayed the deed by assuring her that Chárudatta was safe;—but who in the agonies of despair is susceptible of consolation or confidence?*

Chár. Alas! my love, what frantic thought is this!
Although thy widowed virtues might disdain
The abject earth, yet, when to heaven transported,
What happiness canst thou enjoy, whilst yet
The husband's presence fails his faithful bride. (*Faints.*)

Śar. Out on this folly! we should fly to save
The dame, and he is senseless—all conspires
To snatch from our exertions this reward.

Vas. Dear Chárudatta, rouse thy fainting soul;
Haste to preserve her; want not firmness now,
Or all is unavailing.

Chár. Where is she?
Speak love! where art thou?—answer to my call.

Chan. This way, this way! [*Exeunt.*

Scene—The WIFE *of* CHÁRUDATTA, ROHASENA *holding her garment*, MAITREYA *and* RADANIKÁ—*The fire kindled.*

Wife. Loose me, my child! oppose not my desires,
I cannot live and hear my lord defamed.

Roha. Hold! my dear mother; think of me your child;
How shall I learn to live, deprived of you?

* The ancient commentary, the MS. of which consulted was dated above two centuries ago, cites a verse, stating that from this speech to that of *Śarvilaka*, "You are fortunate in your friends," the whole is an interpolation, the work of *Nílakańtha*, who considered that the author had not brought his characters together at the close with sufficient reason, and therefore devised the next scene. The cause assigned for the original defect seems rather an unaccountable one, "Through fear of sunrise;" but the phrase is a proverbial one, implying "finishing in a hurry." The passage is

"Yat súryodaya-bhayatań kavinochita-pátra-melanań na kŕitam,
Sundara-yuktibhir arachayad á-chandanokti Nílakańthas tat."

The style of the interpolation, although something different from that of the original, is ancient; and as the business and notions of the scene are genuinely Hindu, it has been retained in the translation.

Mait. Lady, forbear! your purpose is a crime:—our holy laws declare it sinful for a Brahman's wife to mount a separate pile.*

Wife. Better I sin than hear my husband's shame—
Remove my boy; he keeps me from the flames.

Rad. Nay, madam; I would rather give him help.

Mait. Excuse me: if you determine to perish, you must give me precedence; it is a Brahman's duty to consecrate a funeral fire.

Wife. What! neither listen to me! My dear child,
Remain to offer to your helpless parents
The sacred rites they claim from filial duty.
Alas! you know no more a father's care.

Chár. (*Coming forward and takes his Child in his arms.*)
His father still will guard him.

Wife. His voice! his form!—it is my lord, my love!

Rohá. My father holds me in his arms again! Now, mother, you are happy.

Chár. (*Embraces his Wife.*)
My dearest love, what frenzy drove thy mind
To seek destruction whilst thy lord survived?
Whilst yet the sun rides bright along the sky
The lotus closes not its amorous leaves.

Wife. True, my loved lord; but then his glowing kisses
Give her glad consciousness her love is present.

Mait. And do these eyes really see my dear friend once more? The wonderful effect of a virtuous wife! Her purpose of entering the fire has reunited her with her lord. Long life to Chárudatta.

Chár. My dear, my faithful friend. (*Embraces him.*)

Rad. Sir, I salute you. (*Falls at his feet.*)

Chár. Rise, good Radaniká. (*Puts his hand upon her shoulder.*)

Wife. (*To Vasantasená.*) Welcome, happy sister!

* This is still the law.

Vas. I now indeed am happy. (*They embrace.*)

Śar. You are fortunate in your friends.

Chár. To you I owe them.*

Śar. Lady Vasantasená, with your worth
The king is well acquainted, and requests
To hold you as his kinswoman.

Vas. Sir, I am grateful. (*Śarvilaka throws a veil over her.*)†

Śar. What shall we do for this good mendicant?

Chár. Speak, S'ramańaka, your wishes.

Śram. To follow still the path I have selected,
For all I see is full of care and change.

Chár. Since such is his resolve, let him be made
Chief of the monasteries of the *Bauddhas.*‡

Śar. It shall be so.

Śram. It likes me well.

Śar. Stháváraka remains to be rewarded.

Chár. Let him be made a free man;—slave no more.
For these Cháńd'álas let them be appointed
Heads of their tribe; and to Chandanaka
The power the Rája's brother-in-law abused
To his own purposes, be now assigned.§

Śar. As you direct: is there ought else?—command.

Chár. Nought but this.
Since Áryaka enjoys the sovereign sway,
And holds me as his friend;—since all my foes
Are now destroyed, save one poor wretch released,
To learn repentance for his former faults,

* The interpolation ends here.

† Marking thereby she is no longer a public character. The use of the veil in all oriental countries is well known, but its employment as in the text is a refinement upon its universal use. It seems, however, to have been understood as a type of the married condition by the early Christians, or as a sign of the subjection of woman to man. (See 1 Cor. xi. 10.) Amongst the Greeks the veil denoted a sacred and sacerdotal character.

‡ Literally, let him be made the master of the family (*Kulapati*) in the *Viháras* throughout the land.

§ The post is that of *Dańd́apálaka*, chief of the police, or Kotwal.

Since my fair fame again is clear, and this
Dear girl, my wife, and all I cherish most,
Are mine once more, I have no further suit
That asks for your indulgence, and no wish
That is not gratified. Fate views the world
A scene of mutual and perpetual struggle,
And sports with life as if it were the wheel
That draws the limpid waters from the well.
For some are raised to affluence, some depressed
In want, and some are borne a while aloft,
And some hurled down to wretchedness and woe.
Then let us all thus limit our desires:
Full-uddered be the kine; the soil be fertile;
May copious showers descend, and balmy gales
Breathe health and happiness on all mankind;
From pain be every living creature free,
And reverence on the pious Brahman wait;
And may all monarchs, prosperous and just,
Humble their foes and guard the world in peace.

[*Exeunt omnes.*

REMARKS ON THE TOY-CART.

THE preceding Drama cannot in equity be tried by laws with which the Author and his audience were unacquainted. If, therefore, it exceeds the limits of a play according to our approved models, we are not to consider it of disproportionate length; if it occasionally arranges the business of the stage after what we conceive an awkward fashion, we are not to pronounce it devoid altogether of theatrical ingenuity; and if it delineates manners repugnant to our social institutions, we are not to condemn them as unnatural or immoral. We must judge the composition after the rules laid down by Schlegel, and identify ourselves, as much as possible, with the people and the time to which it belongs.

Overlooking, then, those peculiarities which are clearly referable to age and country, it will probably be admitted, that the *Toy-Cart* possesses considerable dramatic merit. The action, if it want other unities, has the unity of interest; and proceeds with a regular, though diversified, march to its final development. The interest is rarely suspended, and in every case the apparent interruption is, with great ingenuity, made subservient to the common design. The connexion of the two plots is much better maintained than in the play we usually refer to as a happy specimen of such a combination:—the *Spanish Friar*. The deposition of Pálaka is interwoven with the main story so intimately, that it could not be detached from it without injury, and yet it never becomes so prominent as to divert attention from that to which it is only an appendage.

There is considerable variety of character amongst the

inferior persons of the Drama, and the two Captains of the Watch, and the two Cháńd'álas, are plainly discriminated. The superior characters are less varied, but they are national portraitures, and offer some singular combinations: the tenderness and devotion of Vasantasená seem little compatible with her profession, and the piety and gravity of Chárudatta still less so with his love. The master-piece of the play, however, is Saḿsthánaka, the Rája's brother-in-law. A character so utterly contemptible has perhaps been scarcely ever delineated: his vices are egregious; he is coldly and cruelly malicious, and yet he is so frivolous as scarcely to excite our indignation; anger were wasted on one so despicable; and without any feeling of compassion for his fate, we are quite disposed, when he is about to suffer the merited punishment of his crimes, to exclaim with Chárudatta, "Loose him, and let him go." He is an excellent example of a genus too common in every age in Asia, whose princes have been educated by sloth and servility, and have been ordinarily taught to cherish no principle but that of selfish gratification.

The music of Sanskŕit composition must ever be inadequately represented by any other tongue; of the language of the play it is therefore unnecessary to speak. With regard to the sentiments and conceptions of the author, they have been rendered as faithfully as was practicable, and it will possibly be conceded that they are wanting neither in beauty nor in truth.

VIKRAMA AND URVAŚÍ,

OR

THE HERO AND THE NYMPH.

A Drama,

TRANSLATED FROM THE ORIGINAL

SANSKṚIT.

INTRODUCTION.

THE drama of VIKRAMA AND URVAŚÍ is one of the three plays attributed to KÁLIDÁSA, already advantageously known to the western world as the author of *Śakuntalá.* The introductory observation of the Manager in the prelude is our evidence to this effect; and it is corroborated by the correspondence of these two compositions, in many of their characteristic merits and defects. The subject of each is taken from heroic mythology, and a royal demigod and nymph of more than human mould are the hero and heroine of either; there is the same vivacity of description and tenderness of feeling in both; the like delicate beauty in the thoughts, and extreme elegance in the style. It may be difficult to decide to which the palm belongs; but the story of the present play is perhaps more skilfully woven, and the incidents rise out of each other more naturally than in S'akuntalá, while, on the other hand, there is perhaps no one personage in it so interesting as the heroine of that drama.

Although, however, there is no reason to doubt that this play is the work of the same hand as that translated by Sir William Jones, the concurrence does not throw any further light upon the date or history of the author. We can only infer, from the observance of the same chaste style of composition, and the absence of any forced construction or offensive conceits, that they are both the production of a period anterior to the reign of BHOJA, when *his* KÁLIDÁSA, a man of fancy and taste, could descend to write a whole poem, the *Nalodaya,* for instance, in a strain of verbal paltering and a succession of jingling sounds.

The richness of the *Prákŕit* in this play, both in structure and in its metrical code, is very remarkable. A very great portion, especially of the fourth act, is in this language; and in that act also a considerable variety of metre is introduced; it is clear, therefore, that this form of Sanskŕit must have been highly cultivated long before the play was written, and this might lead us to doubt whether the composition can bear so remote a date as the reign of VIKRAMÁDITYA (56 B.C.) It is yet rather uncertain whether the classical language of Hindu literature had at that time received so high a polish as appears in the present drama; and still less, therefore, could the descendants have been exquisitely refined, if the parent was comparatively rude. We can scarcely conceive that the cultivation of *Prákŕit* preceded that of Sanskŕit, when we advert to the principles on which the former seems to be evolved from the latter; but it must be confessed that the relation between Sanskŕit and *Prákŕit* has been hitherto very imperfectly investigated, and is yet far from being understood.

The mythological notions of the author, as inferable from the benedictory stanzas opening all the three plays attributed to him, is rather adverse to a remote antiquity, as the worship of any individual deity as the Supreme Being, and with *Bhakti* or faith, appears to be an innovation in Hindu ritual and theology of a comparatively modern period. At the same time, the worship of *Śiva* undoubtedly prevailed in the Dekhin at the commencement of the Christian era, and VIKRAMÁDITYA, the patron of KÁLIDÁSA, is traditionally represented as devoted to *Śiva* and his consort.

It may be thought some argument for the comparative antiquity of the present drama, that it tells the story of PURÚRAVAS very differently from the Puráńas, in several of which it may be found. We may suppose, therefore, that the play preceded those works; as, had it been subsequently composed, the poet would either spontaneously, or in deference to sacred authority, have adhered more closely to the Pauráńik legend. The difference in the Puráńas also indicates that corruption of taste, which we cannot hesitate regarding as the product of more modern and degenerate days.

The loves of PURÚRAVAS and URVAŚÍ are related in various Puráńas. The following is the story as it appears in the *Vishńu Puráńa*, in which and in the *Padma*,* it is more fully and connectedly detailed than perhaps in any other composition of the same class.

URVAŚÍ, the *Apsaras*, or one of the nymphs of heaven so named, having incurred the displeasure of MITRA and VARUŃA, was sentenced by them to become the consort of a mortal, and in consequence of this curse she became enamoured of the king PURÚRAVAS, the son of BUDHA and ILÁ. Forgetting her celestial duties, and foregoing the delights of *Swarga*, she introduced herself to the monarch, and her charms did not fail to make an impression on his heart. She was delicately and symmetrically formed, was graceful in her gestures, and fascinating in her manners; her voice was music, her countenance was dressed in smiles, and her beauty was such as might enchant the world: no wonder, therefore, that PURÚRAVAS was at once inspired with fervent love. Confiding in his rank and renown, the king did not hesitate to propose a matrimonial alliance to the nymph of heaven; she was nothing loth, but had not the power to comply, without previously exacting the bridegroom's consent to two conditions. PURÚRAVAS hesitated not to accede to the stipulations.

URVAŚÍ had with her two pet-rams, creatures of heavenly and illusive natures, and one of her conditions was, that the king should take these animals under his own charge, and guard against their being ever carried away by fraud or force. The other stipulation was, that the nymph was never to behold the person of the king divested of his raiment. On the ready

* It is the subject also of a work of some length in *Telugu*, called the *Kavirája-manoranjanam*, or *Purúrava-charitram*, composed by Avyaya, the minister of a petty prince in the Dekhin, the Rája of Condavir. This story follows the *Puráńas*, but with some differences.

accession of PURÚRAVAS to these terms URVAŚÍ became his bride, and they dwelt together in the forest of *Chaitraratha*, near *Alaká*, the capital of *Kuvera*, for sixty-one years,* in perfect happiness and undiminished affection.

The absence of URVAŚÍ was very soon felt in the upper sphere, and the inhabitants of *Swarga* found their enjoyments stale and unprofitable, no longer heightened by the agreeable manners and entertaining society of the nymph. The whole body of *Apsarasas*, *Siddhas*, *Gandharbas*, and other tenants of Indra's heaven, regretted her loss, and determined to attempt her recovery as soon as the period of her exile, as denounced by the imprecation, should have expired. When this period arrived, they deputed some of the *Gandharbas* on the expedition, who undertook to bring about the violation of the terms on which the alliance of the king and the nymph depended. With this intent they entered the sleeping chamber of the monarch, and carried off one of the rams. The bleat of the animal woke URVAŚÍ, who echoed its cries with her lamentations, and aroused the prince. Apprehensive, however, of appearing before his bride undressed, PURÚRAVAS hesitated to pursue the thief, and thus incurred the angry reproaches of his spouse for his indifference to her loss. Presently the *Gandharbas* bore away the second ram, and the grief of URVAŚÍ was afresh excited; the king's indignation also could no longer be restrained, and, determined to pursue and punish the ravishers, he leaped naked out of bed, trusting that the darkness of night would screen him from the eye of his consort. This was what his enemies desired, and he was no sooner off the couch than a vivid flash of lightning revealed him to view, and put an end to his union with the nymph of *Swarga*. URVAŚÍ immediately disappeared, accompanying the *Gandharbas* to the halls of INDRA.

* This is, however, a mere moment in the extravagant duration of the ife of *Purúravas* according to the *Purúńas*: there is nothing of the kind in the play.

When PURÚRAVAS was conscious of his loss, his grief was so intense that it affected his intellects, and he long wandered frantic over the world in quest of his bride. After many years had elapsed he came to a lake in *Kurukshetra*, where he found several nymphs sporting on the bank; amongst them was URVAŚÍ. Recognizing her at once, he ran to her and with wild energy implored her return; the nymph, however, was no longer disposed, even if she had been permitted, to comply with his wishes, and was deaf to all his entreaties; and at last she succeeded in convincing him of the unreasonableness of his solicitations, and prevailed on him to resume his station, and the duties of a king, engaging on those terms to pay him an annual visit. PURÚRAVAS, however reluctantly, was compelled to submit, and returned sorrowfully but composed to his capital. His annual interviews with URVAŚÍ were punctually repeated, and the fruit of this intercourse was the birth of six sons,* A'YUS, DHÍMAT, AMÁVASU, VIŚWÁVASU, S'ATÁYUS, and S'RUTÁYUS, who were the progenitors of the lunar race of kings.

The occasional interviews with his bride granted to PURÚRAVAS were far from satisfying his desires, and he still sighed for the permanent enjoyment of her society. The *Gandharbas* at last, pitying his distress, engaged to promote his reunion with the nymph, and sent the king a brazier charged with fire, with which they directed him to perform a sacrifice in the forest, to attain the gratification of all his wishes. The king repaired to the woods, but reflecting that he had quitted URVAŚÍ in order to celebrate this rite, giving up the substance for the shadow, he returned to seek the nymph, leaving the vessel of fire in the thicket. Not finding his consort, he again directed his steps to the forest, but there the brazier was gone, and on the spot where it had stood, a *śamí* † and *aśwattha* ‡ tree

* All this part of the story, Urvaśí's loss and recovery, and the birth of Áyus, are totally different in the play.

† Mimosa suma.

‡ Religious fig.

had sprung up. After a little consideration PURÚRAVAS broke a branch from either tree, and carried them back to the palace, where, reciting the *Gáyatri* * and rubbing the sticks together, he generated fire with the friction: this primeval fire he divided into three portions, and with them he performed various sacrifices and oblations, until he obtained the rank of a *Gandharba*, and being elevated to the regions of *Swarga*, there enjoyed the constant society of his beloved URVAŚÍ.†

The latter circumstances of this legend seem to indicate the introduction of fire-worship into India by PURÚRAVAS, considered as a historical personage.‡ There may have been some old tradition to that effect, whence the *Pauráńik* writers derived the groundwork of their fable; but it is not noticed in the play, neither is any allusion made to it in the version of this story in another work in which it is found, the *Vŕihat-Kathá*, which differs in many particulars from both the play and the *Puráńa*. The story there, however, is very concisely narrated, and the author has clearly taken merely the personages and course of the fable from what was currently known, and given his own colouring to the incidents. It adds, therefore, nothing to the history of the narrative, and may be either anterior or subsequent to the forms in which it is now presented to English readers. Another authority, however, the *Matsya-Puráńa*, tells the story more agreeably to the tenor of the drama, as follows:

"When a year had elapsed, the divine *Tárá* bore a son of surpassing splendour, arrayed in celestial raiment of a yellow colour, and richly decorated with heavenly gems. From his youth he was versed in regal duties, and was so skilled in the

* The holiest verse of the *Vedas*.

† The play makes no allusion to these incidents, closing with the appearance of the elder son, Áyus.

‡ The three fires are: the *gárhapatya*, or perpetual fire maintained by a householder; the *áhavaníya*, or consecrated fire taken from the preceding and prepared for receiving oblations; and the *dakshińágni*, fire taken from either of the former and placed towards the south.

training of elephants that he taught the art, and acquired the appellation of *Gajavedhaka.* The gods being assembled at the mansion of her husband, *Vṙihaspati*, to perform the rites due to his birth, inquired of *Tárá* whose son he was, and with much reluctance she acknowledged the royal *Soma* was his father. *Soma* therefore took the boy, and named him *Budha*, and gave him dominion on the earth, and inaugurated him supreme over the world. *Brahmá* and the rest conferred upon him the dignity of a planetary power, and then took their departure.

"The holy *Budha* begot by *Ilá* a son, who performed by his own might a hundred *aśwamedhas.* He was named PURÚRAVAS, and was revered by all worlds. He worshipped *Vishńu* on the peaks of Himálaya, and thence became the monarch of the sevenfold earth. KEŚIN and myriads of *Daityas* fell before his prowess, and URVAŚÍ, fascinated by his personal graces, became his bride.

"*Virtue*, *Wealth*, and *Desire*, once paid this monarch a visit, curious to ascertain which of them held the first place in his esteem. The king received them with respect, but paid to *Virtue* his profoundest homage. *Wealth* and *Desire* were offended by the preference shown to their companion. *Wealth* denounced a curse upon him, that Avarice should occasion his fall; and *Desire* declared that he should be separated from his bride, and on that account suffer distraction in the forest of Kumára on the Gandhamádana mountain; but *Virtue* declared he should enjoy a long and pious life, that his descendants should continue to multiply as long as the sun and moon endured, and should ever enjoy the dominion of the earth. After this the divinities disappeared.

"PURÚRAVAS was in the habit of paying a visit to *Indra* every day. Having ascended his car, accompanying the Sun in his southern course, he beheld on one occasion the demon KEŚIN seize and carry off the nymphs *Chitralekhá* and URVAŚÍ. The king attacked the demon, and destroyed him with the shaft of *Váyu*, by which he not only rescued the nymphs, but established *Indra* on his throne, which the demon had endangered. For this service *Indra* repaid the monarch with his friendship, and gave him additional power, splendour, and glory.

"Having invited the king to a festival, at which was represented the celebrated story of *Lakshmí's* election of a husband, the invention of BHARATA, INDRA commanded MENAKÁ, RAMBHÁ, and URVAŚÍ to perform their respective parts. URVAŚÍ, who represented *Lakshmí*, being engrossed by admiration of the king, forgot what she had to enact, and thereby incurred the high displeasure of the sage, who sentenced her to separation from the prince on earth, and condemned her to pine fifty-five years transformed to a vine, until restored to the regrets of PURÚRAVAS. URVAŚÍ having made the king her lord, resided with him, and after the term of the curse had expired bore him eight sons: *Áyus*, *Dhṙitáyus*, *Aśwáyus*, *Dhanáyus*, *Dhṙitimat*, *Vasu*, *Divijáta*, and *Śátáyus*, all endowed with more than human power."

This story is evidently that of the play, although related less in detail, and with a few variations according to Pauráńik taste; but it is clear that it is either derived from a common source with the narration of the drama, or which is not improbable, that it has borrowed from the latter its general complexion. The nature of the relation which exists between the fiction as it appears in the drama, and in the *Puráńas*, our readers will be able to appreciate for themselves after perusal of the former.

DRAMATIS PERSONÆ.

OF THE PRELUDE.

MANAGER. ACTOR.

OF THE PLAY.

MEN.

Purúravas.—King of *Pratishṭhána.*
Áyus.—The son of *Purúravas.*
Máńavaka.—The *Vidúshaka* and confidential companion of the King.
Chitraratha.—King of the *Gandharbas,* the attendants on *Indra.*
Nárada.—The divine sage, the son of *Brahmá.*
Chamberlain.
A Forester.
Paila. } Two disciples of the sage *Bharata.*
Gálava. }

WOMEN.

Urvaśí.—An *Apsaras,* or nymph of *Indra's* heaven.
Chitralekhá.—Another nymph, her friend.
Sahajanyá. }
Rambhá. } Nymphs.*
Menaká. }

* According to the *Káśí-Khańda* there are thirty-five millions of these nymphs, but only one thousand and sixty are the principal. Of these, however, not more than five or six are the subject of Pauráńik or poetical narrations, or *Urvaśí, Menaká, Rambhá, Tillottamá,* and *Alambushá.* In their birth and denomination they offer some analogy to the goddess *Aphrodite:* like her they arose from the sea; and as her name is referred to *aphros,*

Auśinarí.—The queen of *Purúravas* and daughter of the king of *Káśí* or *Benares.*

Nipuńiká.—One of her attendants.

PERSONS SPOKEN OF.

Indra.—The chief of all the inferior deities, and sovereign of *Swarga* or Paradise.

Keśin.—A *Daitya* or Titan, an enemy of the gods.

Bharata.—A holy sage, the inventor of dramatic composition.

Guards.—Nymphs, &c.

SCENE in the First Act, the Peaks of the *Himálaya;* in the second and third, the palace of *Purúravas* at *Pratishíhána;* in the fourth, the forest of *Akalusha*; and in the fifth again, at the palace.

TIME, Uncertain.

"foam or spray," so that of the *Apsarasas* is from *ap* "water" and *saras* "who moves." Their origin is thus related in the first book of the *Rámáyańa*:—

"Then from the agitated deep upsprung
The legion of *Apsarasas*, so named
That to the watery element they owed
Their being. Myriads were they born, and all
In vesture heavenly clad, and heavenly gems:
Yet more divine their native semblance, rich
With all the gifts of grace, and youth, and beauty.
A train innumerous followed: yet thus fair
Nor God nor demon sought their wedded love:
Thus, *Rághava*, they still remain—their charms
The common treasure of the host of heaven."

PRELUDE.

Enter the MANAGER.

MAY that *Śiva** who is attainable by devotion and faith;† who is the sole male‡ of the Vedánta,§ spread through all space, to whom alone the name of Lord|| is applicable, and who is sought with suppressed breath¶ by those who covet final emancipation,** bestow upon you final felicity.

* The term used in the text is *Sthánu*, a name of ŚIVA, from *sthá* to stay or be, the existent or eternal.

† *Bhakti* faith, and *yoga* the practice of abstract meditation.

‡ The *ekapurusha*, the active instrument in creation.

§ The theological or metaphysical portion of the Vedas.

|| *Íśwara*, which is derived from *íś*, to have power, or *aś*, to pervade: in the latter case the vowel is changed.

¶ The exercise of *práńáyáma*, or breathing through either nostril alternately, and then closing both during the repetition mentally of certain formulæ.

** Inferior enjoyment in heaven is not an object of desire to the more enthusiastic of the Hindus, as it is but finite, and after its cessation the individual is born again in the world, and exposed to the calamities of a frail existence. The great aim of devotion is union with the supreme and universal spirit, in which case the soul no more assumes a perishable shape. The character of this benediction corresponds with that of *Śakuntalá* and the *Málavikágnimitra*, and all three indicate the author's belonging to that modification of the Hindú faith in which the abstract deism of the Vedánta is qualified by identifying the supreme, invisible, and inappreciable spirit with a delusive form, which was the person of *Rudra* or *Śiva*. It is of a more practical character, therefore, than pure *Vedántism*, and it is equally different from both the metaphysical and theistical *Sánkhya*. It is, in fact, the doctrine of the *Śaiva-Puráńas*. (See *As. Res.*, vol. xvii.) The Brahmans of the south and west are mostly of this sect; and whatever *Śankara-Swámin* may have taught, it is that of his descendants the *Dasnámi-Gosains* The sect is probably the oldest of all now existing in India.

Man. (*Looking off the stage.*) Ho! *Márisha*,* come hither.

Enter ACTOR.

Act. Here am I, sir.

Man. Many assemblies have witnessed the compositions of former dramatic bards:† I therefore propose to exhibit one not hitherto represented, the drama ‡ of *Vikrama* and *Urvaśí*.§ Desire the company to be ready to do justice to their respective parts.

Act. I shall, sir.

Man. I have now only to request the audience that they will listen to this work of *Kálidása* with attention and kindness, in consideration of its subject and respect for the author.||

* A term by which it is proper to address one of the principal performers.

† *Kálidása* is therefore not the oldest dramatic writer.

‡ The *Troṭaka*, a drama in five, eight, or nine acts, the characters of which are mixed, or heavenly and human. See the Introduction, p. xxxi.

§ Mr Lenz, in his very excellent edition and version of this play (Berlin, 1833), seems to think the title, *Urvaśí-vikrama*, *Urvasiæ incessus*, would be preferable to that of *Vikramorvaśí*, as the latter, if not a *Dwandwa* compound, is not capable of satisfactory translation, and if a *Dwandwa* compound, is not conformable to rule: the latter is matter of little moment with the poets; and that *Vikramorvaśí* is the author's reading, appears from the text. The addition of *náma*, *Vikramorvaśí náma troṭakam*, makes no difference, as indeed the commentator shows, who entitles his comment, *Vikramorvaśí-prakáśiká*, the explanation of the *Vikrama* and *Urvaśí*. With regard to the meaning of *Vikrama*, which is properly "heroism," it may be observed, that it is often used in a way where "king" or "hero" alone can be signified by it: thus *Vikramáditya* is as often called simply *Vikrama* as not. The traditions relating to him are termed the *Vikramacharitra*: the nine gems are said to be *ratnáni nava Vikramasya*. The word is applied also attributively, as *Dípakarńir iti khyáto rájábhúd rájya-vikramaḱ*: There was a king named *Dipakarńi*, the *Vikrama* of the realm. Here it might be thought equivalent to the Alexander or the Cæsar of his age, but it could not be so employed as a synonym of the Hindu Alexander himself, nor could it be so used in the universally-current (in India) title of the play. There can be no doubt, therefore, that by a poetic license *heroism* is here put for hero, and the compound is of the *Dwandwa* class, in despite of the grammarians.

|| The original may be so understood, although it is not quite clear.—Prańayishu dákshińyavaśád yadi vá sadvastu-purusha-bahumánat—śrińuta

(*Behind the Scenes.*)

Help, help ! if in the middle sky
A friend be found, to aid us fly !

Man. What sounds are these in the air, that like the plaintive bleat of lambs, break in upon my speech? Was it the murmur of the bee or *kôil's* distant song, or do the nymphs of heaven as they pass above warble their celestial strains? Ah, no ! it is the cry of distress. The fair creation of the saint, the friend of *Nara*, Urvaśí, has been carried off by a demon on her return from the halls of the sovereign of *Kailása*,* and her sisters are invoking some friendly power to their aid.

[*Exit.*

manobhir avahitaiḥ kriyám imám Kalidásasya. It is of little consequence, except that in the sense preferred it indicates the fame of the author to be established when this piece was written.

* *Kuvera*, the God of wealth, whose capital *Alaká* is supposed to be situated on mount *Kuvera*.

ACT I.

SCENE FIRST.

PART OF THE HIMÁLAYA RANGE OF MOUNTAINS.

Enter in the Air a Troop of Apsarasas or Nymphs of Heaven.

Nymphs. Help, help! if any friend be nigh,
To aid the daughters of the sky!

Enter PURÚRAVAS* *in a heavenly car, driven by his Charioteer.*

Pur. Suspend your cries; in me behold a friend,
Purúravas, returning from the sphere
Of the wide-glancing sun: command my aid,
And tell me what you dread.

Rambhá. A demon's violence.

Pur. What violence presumes the fiend to offer?

Menaká. Great king, it thus has chanced: we measured back
Our steps from an assembly of the gods

* *Purúravas* is a king of high descent, being sprung by his mother *Ilá* from the sun, and his father *Budha* from the moon, being the grandson of the latter and great grandson of the former. His origin is ultimately derived from Brahmá, thus:

BRAHMÁ.

Daksha. — Atri.
Aditi-Kaśyapa. — Soma.
Vivaswat, the sun.
Vaivaswata
Ilá. — Budha-Ilá.

Purúravas.

Held in *Kuvera's** hall. Before us stepped
The graceful Urvaśí, the nymph whose charms
Defeated Indra's stratagems† and shamed
The loveliness of *Śrí*,‡ the brightest ornament
Of heaven: when on our path the haughty *Dánava*,
Keśin, the monarch of the golden city,§
Sprang fierce and bore the struggling nymph away.

Pur. Which path pursued the wretch?

Sahajanyá. 'Tis yonder.

Pur. Banish your fears;
I go to rescue and restore your friend.

Rambhá. The act is worthy of your high descent.

Pur. Where wait you my return?

Rambhá. Here, on this peak.
The towering *Hemakúta*.||

Pur. (*To the Charioteer.*) Bend our course
To yonder point, and urge the rapid steeds
To swiftest flight. 'Tis done; before the car
Like volley'd dust the scattering clouds divide;
The whirling wheel deceives the dazzled eye,
And double round the axle seems to circle.
The waving chowrie on the steed's broad brow
Points backward, motionless as in a picture;
And backward streams the banner from the breeze
We meet—immovable.¶ We should outstrip

* The god of riches.

† See the note ‡ in page 201.

‡ The wife of *Vishńu*, goddess of prosperity and beauty.

§ *Hirańyapura* is the name in the text.

|| The golden or snowy peak.

¶ A very similar description, but less picturesque and just, occurs in the beginning of *Śakuntalá*, and the truth of it is rendered less striking by a loose translation. Sir William Jones translates Nishkampa-chámara-śikhá, "they tossed their manes," when it means "their manes and the chowries on their heads are unagitated," that is, they point against the wind without waving—a predicate much more indicative of a rapid advance against the breeze than the undulation of either. The chámara or chowrie, the white

The flight of *Vainateya*,* and must surely
O'ertake the ravisher. [*Exeunt.*

Rambhá. Now, sisters, on, and blithely seek
The golden mountain's glittering peak;
Secure the king extracts the dart
That rankles in each anxious heart.

Menaká. We need not fear.

Rambhá. Yet hard to quell,
The demon race.

Menaká. The brood of hell
Shall feel his prowess. Aid to bring
From mortal realms to *Swarga's* king—
He comes, and to his hand is given
Command o'er all the hosts of heaven. [*They proceed.*

Rambhá. Joy, sisters, joy, the king advances;
High o'er yon ridgy rampart dances
The deer-emblazoned banner. See
The heavenly car rolls on;—'tis he.

Enter PURÚRAVAS *in his car slowly;* URVAŚÍ *in the car fainting, supported by* CHITRALEKHÁ.

Chitral. Dear friend, revive.

Pur. Fair nymph, resume your courage.
Still wields the thunderer his bolt, and guards
The triple world from harm; the foes of heaven
Are put to flight:—why cherish this alarm
When its just cause is o'er? Unclose those lids—
The lotus opens when the night retires.

Chitral. Alas! her sighs alone declare her conscious.

Pur. Soft as the flower, the timid heart not soon
Foregoes its fears. The scarf that veils her bosom

bushy tail of the Tibet cow, fixed on a gold or ornamented shaft, rose from between the ears of the horse like the plume of the war horse of chivalry; the banner or banneret, with the device of the chief, rose at the back of the car; sometimes several little triangular flags were mounted on its sides.

* *Garuda*, the son of *Vinatá*.

Hides not its flutterings, and the panting breast
Seems as it felt the wreath of heavenly blossoms
Weigh too oppressively.

Chitral. Revive, my friend;
This weakness ill becomes a nymph of heaven.

Pur. Have patience; she recovers, though but faintly.
So gently steals the moon upon the night
Retiring tardily; so peeps the flame
Of evening fires through smoky wreaths; and thus,
The Ganges slowly clears her troubled wave,
Engulphs the ruin that the tumbling bank
Had hurled across her agitated course,
And flows a clear and stately stream again.*

Chitral. Awake, dear friend, the enemies of heaven
Are baffled in despair.

Urv. (*Reviving.*) By Indra's prowess.

Chitral. By prowess not inferior to *Mahendra's*:
By this most holy prince,† Purúravas.

Urv. (*Looking at Purúravas; then apart.*)
What thanks I owe the Dánava!

Pur. (*After looking at Urvaśí; then apart.*) What marvel,
The nymphs celestial blushed with humbled charms,
When, to rebuke their wantonness, the sage
Willed that this wondrous beauty should appear.
The creature of a sage!—it cannot be:
How could an aged anchoret,‡ grown old

* The idea in the last four lines is somewhat expanded, to convey more distinctly to European readers what one-fourth of their number would at once convey to those acquainted with the subject of the description. The original lines are exceedingly sweet and beautiful.

† He is always called a Rájarshi (Rája-Ŕishi or royal saint). In the classification of sages there are three orders; the Rájarshi, or kingly sage, such as JANAKA; the Brahmarshi, or Brahman sage, as VASISHŤHA; and the *Devarshi*, or divine sage, as NÁRADA.

‡ *Nara* and *Nárdyańa* were two saints, the sons of *Dharma* and *Ahiḿsá*: they devoted themselves to ascetic exercises which alarmed the gods, and

In dull devotion, and to feeling dead,
Conceive such matchless beauty—oh no! love
Himself was her creator, whilst the moon
Gave her his radiance, and the flowery spring
Taught her to madden men and gods with passion.

Urv. Where are our friends?

Chitral. The king will lead us to them.

Pur. Trust me, they mourn your loss; nor is it strange
That they, your friends, should miss you, when the eye
In whose delighted path you once have moved
Cannot but grieve to lose your lovely presence.

Urv. (*Apart.*) Delightful words! they fall like drops of nectar.
Nor wonder nectar from the moon should flow.
(*Aloud.*) Not less my eagerness to see again
The friends I love.

Pur. Behold them there! they keep
Their anxious watch on *Hemakúta's* brow,
And mark your coming, safe from the demon's grasp,
Like the bright moon emerging from eclipse.

Chitral. Why do you gaze on me, dear friend?

Urv. The same delight and pain my eyes imbibe as—

Chitral. Whose?

Urv. My friends.

Indra sent *Káma* and *Vasanta*, or love and spring, with the nymphs of heaven to inflame the sages with passion, and thus end their penance. *Náráyańa*, observing the gambols of the party, suspected their purpose. He invited them to approach, and treated them with so much civility, that they thought their object was attained. The sage, however, taking up a flower-stalk, placed it on his thigh, when a beautiful nymph appeared, the superiority of whose charms covered the nymphs of heaven with shame. *Náráyańa* then told them to return to Indra, and bear him a proof he needed not the company of beauty, in the present he made him of the new-born nymph, who accompanied the *Apsarasas* to *Swarga*, and was called *Urvaśí* from *úru* a thigh (*Vámana-Purána.*) The Commentator on the drama says, *Nara* and *Náráyańa* were *Avatáras*, descents or incarnations of *Arjuna* and *Krishńa.*

Rambhá. Attended by each brilliant star,
Like *Chandra** in his radiant car,
The king appears, and with him borne
Behold our sister nymphs return.

Menaká. For both the boons our thanks be poured:
The prince unharmed and friends restored.

Sahajanyá. Now, sister, see how hard to quell
By mortal might the sons of hell.

Pur. To yonder lofty mountain guide the car.
(*Apart.*) Not vain our journey hitherward: 'tis much
In the unsteady rolling of the chariot
But for a moment to have touched the form
Of this celestial nymph; the blissful contact
Shoots ecstasy through every fibre. Here (*aloud*)
Arrest our course. The maid's companion choir
Press on to her embrace, like flowery vines,
That bend to catch the beauty of the spring.

Chorus. Joy to the king. Propitious heaven
Has victory to his prowess given.

Pur. Behold in these my triumph!
[*Presenting Urvaśí and Chitralekhá.*

Urv. My dear, dear sisters, little did I hope
But late to feel once more this loved embrace.
[*Embraces them.*

Chorus. May countless ages blest survey
The mighty Purúravas' sway. [*A noise without.*

Charioteer. (*To the king.*)
Sire, from the east the rushing sound is heard
Of mighty chariots; yonder like clouds they roll
Along the mountain cliffs; now there alights
A chief in gorgeous raiment, like the blaze
Of lightning playing on the towering precipice.

Nymphs. Our king, great *Chitraratha.*

* Like the moon with the two stars of *Viśákhá*, one of the lunar asterisms containing two stars.

Enter CHITRARATHA, *the king of the Gandharbas** (*attended*).

Chitrar. Illustrious victor, friend of Indra, hail!

Pur. King of the heavenly quiristers, receive
The welcome of a friend.† What brings you hither?

Chitrar. When Indra learnt from Nárada the rape
Of this fair damsel by the *Daitya*, Keśin,
He bade me gather the *Gandharba* train
And hasten to her rescue. I obeyed;
But ere we marched, news of your triumph came
And stopped our progress. For your friendly aid
I bear you now our monarch's thanks, and more—
His wish to see you in the heavenly courts
Your worth has opened to your welcome visit.
This service is most dear to him. The nymph
Is now your boon—first given by *Náráyaṅa*
To grace the halls of *Swarga*—now redeemed
From hands profane by your resistless valour.

Pur. You rate the deed too high. Not mine the glory,
But his, the Thunderer's, from whom derived
The strength of those who conquer in his cause.
The very echo of the lion's roar,
As through the rocky rifts it spreads and deepens,
Appals the mighty elephant.

Chitrar. 'Tis well.
This modesty becomes your worth. Humility
Is ever found the ornament of valour.

Pur. Excuse me to the monarch. Other claims
Demand my distant presence; lead the nymph
Back to the king.

Chitrar. Your will shall be obeyed.

* The *Gandharbas* are the male attendants and choristers in the courts of *Śiva*, *Indra*, and *Kuvera*.

† The stage direction here is, "They shake hands:" "Parasparaṁ hastau spriśataḥ."

Urv. (*Apart to Chitralekhá.*)
Speak for me, my dear friend; my lips refuse
To bid adieu to my protector.—Speak.
Chitral. (*To the king.*)
Illustrious sir, my friend commands me ask
Your leave to carry back with her to heaven,
As one she dearly cherishes, your fame.
Pur. Farewell!—I trust ere long to meet again.

The GANDHARBAS *and* APSARASAS *ascend;* URVAŚÍ *loiters and pretends to be stopped.*

Urv. A moment pause! (*To Chitralekhá.*) Dear girl, this straggling vine
Has caught my garland—help me to get loose.
Chitral. No easy task, I fear—you seem entangled
Too fast to be set free: but come what may,
Depend upon my friendship.
Urv. Thanks, thanks,
Be mindful of your promise.
[*Chitralekhá employed in disengaging her.*
Pur. A thousand thanks, dear plant, to whose kind aid
I owe another instant, and behold,
But for a moment and imperfectly,
Those half-averted charms.
Charioteer. Come, royal sir,
Let us depart. The demon foes are hurled
Deep in the ocean wave—just punishment
For their rebellion against *Swarga's* king.
Now let the shaft, whose headlong force resembles
The blast of fate, sleep in its wonted quiver,
As cowers the snake within his gloomy covert.
[*They mount.*
Pur. Ascend the car.
Urv. Ah! me; ah! when again
Shall I behold my brave deliverer!
[*Departs with Chitralekhá and the nymphs.*

Pur. (*Looking after her.*)

What idle dreams does frantic love suggest!
What arduous tasks inspire! The beauteous nymph
Bears off my heart in triumph through the path
Her sire * immortal treads: so flies the swan
Through the mid air, charged with its precious spoil,
The milky nectar of the lotus stem.

[*Exit in his car.*

* *Nárâyańa* or *Vishńu*, according to the commentator.

END OF THE FIRST ACT.

ACT II.

The Garden of the Palace of Purúravas at Prayága (*Allahabad*).*

Enter Máńavaka, *the Vidúshaka.*

It is mighty inconvenient this, for a Brahman like myself, one so much sought after and subject to such frequent invitation, to be burthened with the king's secret! Going so much into company as I do, I shall never be able to set a guard upon my tongue. I must be prudent, and will stay here by myself in this retired temple, until my royal friend comes forth from the council chamber. (*Sits down and covers his face with his hands.*)

Enter Nipuńiká, *an Attendant on the Queen.*

The daughter of the king of Káśí † is quite sure, that since the king returned from the regions of the sun, he is no longer the same; he must have left his heart behind him,—what else can be the reason? I must try and find it out: if that crafty Brahman be in the secret, I shall easily get at it. A secret can rest no longer in his breast than morning dew upon the grass. Where can he be?—eh!—yes, there he sits deep in thought,

* It is also in other places called Pratishthána, and is described as at the confluence of the Yamuná and Ganges on the bank of the latter: it should seem, therefore, so late as the composition of this drama the ancient city still stood opposite to its present site. The ruins, according to Hamilton, are still to be seen at Jhusi on the left bank of the Ganges. (*Hamilton's Genealogies of the Hindus.*) Allahabad or Prayága was a holy place, having been the seat of *Bharadwája's* hermitage; but it never was a city until Akber made it one.

† The ancient name of Benares, which is recognizable in the Cassidia of Ptolemy.

like a monkey in a picture. Now to attack him, that is all I have to do. Árya * Máńavaka, I salute you!

Máń. Prosperity attend you. (*Apart.*) The king's secret is bursting forth at the mere sight of that hussy Nipuńiká. (*Aloud.*) Well, Nipuńiká, how is it you leave your music-practice † for the garden?

Nip. The queen has sent me to pay you a visit, sir.

Máń. And what may be her Majesty's commands?

Nip. She bids me say that she has ever esteemed you as her good friend, and that it is, therefore, with some surprise she finds you utterly indifferent to her present anxiety.

Máń. Why, what's the matter? Has my royal friend done anything to displease her?

Nip. Oh, that is not the point! My mistress knows the cause of his melancholy well enough; nay more, he let out the secret himself, and, in a fit of absence, addressed the queen by the very name of his new love.

Máń. (*Apart.*) Indeed! Oh, if his Majesty cannot keep his own secrets, why should I be plagued with them? (*Aloud.*) Why, what the deuce, Nipuńiká, did he call the queen?—Urvaśí?

Nip. And, pray, who is Urvaśí?

Máń. The nymph, the *Apsaras.* Ever since the king saw her, he has been out of his senses; he not only neglects her grace, but annoys me and spoils my dinner.

Nip. (*Apart.*) So, so; I have settled that matter, as I expected. (*Aloud.*) Well, I must return to the queen. What am I to say to her?

Máń. Tell her I am weary of attempting to cure my friend, the king, of this idle fancy of his. The only remedy is the sight of her lotus countenance.

Nip. You may depend upon me. [*Exit.*

The Warder. (*Without.*)

All hail to the monarch who toils through the day,

* A term of respect.

† *Sangída-vvdbára* for *Sangíta-vyápdra*: practice of music, singing, and dancing.

To shed o'er his subjects the light of his sway,
As travels unceasing the sun in his sphere
To chase from the universe darkness and fear.
The lord of lone splendour an instant suspends
His course at mid-noon ere he westward descends;
And brief are the moments our young monarch knows,
Devoted to pleasure or paid to repose.*

Máń. (*Listening.*) Ha! my royal friend has arisen from his seat, and is coming hither; I will await him.

* Frequent occasion will occur to notice the *Vaitálika*, a sort of poetical warder or bard, who announces fixed periods of the day, as dawn and evening, &c., in measured lines, and occasionally pours forth strains arising from any incidental occurrence. He here announces the arrival of the sixth hour or watch of the day, about two or three o'clock, in which alone he says the king can follow his own inclination. It appears, indeed, that the royal station was by no means a sinecure. The *Agni-Puráńa* lays down rules for the apportioning of the regal day; but the same are more fully detailed in the last story of the *Daśa-Kumára*, upon the authority of *Cháńakya*, the celebrated minister of *Chandragupta*, who is always cited as the author of the *Níti*, or Institutes of Government. From the *Daśa-Kumára* it appears that the day and night was each divided into eight portions, corresponding accordingly to one hour and a half, and they are thus disposed of: Day—first portion, the king being dressed is to audit his accounts; second, he is to pronounce judgment in suits appealed to him; third, he is to breakfast; fourth, he is to receive and make presents; fifth, to discuss political questions with his ministers and councillors; sixth, he is, as stated in the drama, his own master; seventh, he is to review the troops; eighth, he holds a military council. Night—first portion, the king is to receive the reports of his spies and envoys; second, he sups or dines; third, he retires to rest after the perusal of some sacred work; the fourth and fifth portions, or three hours, are allowed for sleep; in the sixth, he must rise and purify himself; in the seventh, he holds a private consultation with his ministers, and furnishes the officers of government with instructions; and the eighth is appropriated to the *Purohita* or priest, the Brahman and religious ceremonies, after which the business of the day is resumed. The author of the play has conformed to this distribution; bringing Purúravas from council at the sixth portion of the day. The precise hour depends upon the period of the year, the different portions being reckoned from sunrise. We may infer that the poet intends this to be about two P.M., as at the end of the act he makes the king describe the time as being past noon, when the heat is most oppressive; the sixth watch accordingly begins in the drama about one o'clock.

Enter PURÚRAVAS.

Pur. One glance sufficed; the unerring shaft of love
Laid bare the path, and gave a ready access
To that celestial nymph, to seat herself
Throned in my heart.

Máń. (*To himself.*) Ah! that is exactly what the poor daughter of *Káśirája* complains of.

Pur. (*To the Vidúshaka.*) You have kept my secret safe?

Máń. (*Apart.*) That baggage must have betrayed me! Why else should he ask the question?

Pur. (*Alarmed.*) How, you are silent?

Máń. Don't be alarmed; the fact is, that my tongue is so accustomed to the restraint I have put upon it, that I cannot answer off-hand even your inquiries.

Pur. 'Tis well! Now then for recreation—
What shall we do?

Máń. Pay a visit to the kitchen.

Pur. With what intent?

Máń. Why, the very sight of the savoury dishes in course of preparation will be sufficient to dissipate all melancholy ideas.

Pur. With you it may, for what you covet there
You may obtain; what my desires affect
Is hopeless! Where should I then seek diversion?

Máń. May I ask if the person of your Highness was not beheld by the lady Urvaśí?

Pur. What then?

Máń. Why, then, I should think her not quite so uncomeatable.

Pur. The fit compeer of beauty such as hers
Must needs be more than human.

Máń. What you say only adds to my surprise. What signifies madam Urvaśí's unrivalled beauty? Am I not equally without a peer, in ugliness?

Pur. Words cannot paint her every excellence.
Hear her, Máńavaka, described in brief.

Máń. I am all attention.

Pur. Her loveliness yields splendour to her ornaments,
Her purity gives fragrance to her perfumes ;
All the similitudes that poets use
To picture beauty, it were gross flattery
To them, to name with her surpassing charms.

Máń. This is mighty well ! but in the will-o'-the-wisp * fancy for such superhuman excellence, I should think your Majesty had taken the *chátaka* † for your model. Where, please you, shall we go ?

Pur. To melancholy moods the only solace
Is solitude ;—go onwards to the grove.

Máń. (*Apart.*) What absurdity ! (*Aloud.*) This way, sir ; here is the boundary of the grove, and the southern wind ‡ advances with due civility to meet you.

Pur. He comes to teach me, as he amorous sports
Amongst the blossoms of the *mádhaví* §
And dances frolic with the *kunda* ‖ flowers,
With all the impassioned fervour of desire
And graceful ingenuity of love—
I mark in him my pictured sentiments.

Máń. The only likeness I see is your mutual perseverance. But here we are ; please you to enter ?

Pur. Precede ! I fear my coming hither vain,
Nor yield these shades relief to my affliction—
Though with intent to gain tranquillity,
I seek these paths of solitude and peace ;
I feel like one contending with the stream,
And still borne backwards by the current's force.

Máń. Why entertain such feelings ?

* Literally, being desirous of the waters of the mirage.

† A bird said to drink no water but rain.

‡ During the hot weather the prevailing breeze in Hindustan is from the south.

§ A creeper with white flowers. ‖ A kind of jasmine.

Pur. How avoid them?

What I affect is of no light attainment:
The very thought presumption, and now love,
The five-armed god,* whose shafts already pierce me,
Call to his aid these passion-breathing blossoms,
The mango's fragrant flowers and pallid leaves,
Light wafted round us by the southern breeze.

Máń. Away with despondence! Be assured that in a little time *Ananga* † will be your friend, and help you to obtain your desires.

Pur. I take your words as ominous.

Máń. But now let your Highness notice the beauty of this garden, heralding, as it were, the presence of the spring.

Pur. I mark it well. In the *kuravaka*,

Behold the painted fingers of the fair
Red-tinted on the tip and edged with ebony;
Here the *aśoka* puts forth nascent buds
Just bursting into flowers, and here the mango
Is brown with blossoms, on whose tender crests
Scant lies the fragrant down; methinks I see
The pride of spring on either hand attended
By budding infancy and flowering youth.

Máń. The bower of jasmines yonder, with its slab of black marble, is studded thick with blossoms, and the bees crowd about them in heaps; it invites your Majesty to repose.

[*They enter the arbour.*

Pur. As you please.

Máń. Now, seated in this shade, you may dissipate your cares by contemplating the elegant plants around us.

Pur. How should I learn composure? As my eye

* The Hindu Cupid is armed with a bow strung with bees and five arrows, each tipped with a flower, and exercising peculiar influence on the heart.

† Love, the unembodied deity; having been once destroyed by *Śiva*, burnt to ashes by the fire of his eye, in resentment of *Káma's* aiming his darts at him.

Rests on the towering trees, and from their tops
Sees the lithe creeper wave, I call to mind
The graces that surpass its pendulous elegance.
Come, rouse your wit, and friendship may inspire
Some capable expedient to secure me
The object of my wishes.

Máń. Well, I will turn the matter over in my mind; but you must not disturb my cogitations by your sighs.

Pur. (*Feeling his eyes twinkle.*)
The moon-faced maid is far beyond my reach;
Then, why should love impart such flattering tokens!
They teach my mind to feel as if enjoyed
The present bliss, hope scarcely dares imagine.
[*They retire.*

Enter URVAŚÍ *and* CHITRALEKHÁ *in the air.*

Chitral. Tell me, dear girl, your purpose: whither go we?

Urv. Nay, tell me first, do you recall the promise
You made me jestingly upon the brow
Of *Hemakúta*, when your friendly hand
Detached my vesture from entangling thorns?
If it be still within your recollection,
You need not ask me whither we proceed.

Chitral. You seek the moon of monarchs, Purúravas.

Urv. Right, girl; though ill it argue of my modesty.

Chitral. Whom have you sent the envoy of your coming?

Urv. None, but my heart; that has long gone before me.

Chitral. But first consider.

Urv. Love impels me; how can I delay?

Chitral. I have no more to offer.

Urv. Assist me with your counsel, which way best
We may proceed, to meet with no impediment.

Chitral. There is no fear: the all-wise preceptor*
Of the immortals has imparted to you

* *Vríhaspati*, the planet Jupiter and teacher of the gods.

The spell that renders you invincible,
And mightier than the mightiest foe of heaven.*

Urv. My heart is confident, and yet my fears
Will sometimes bid me doubt.

Chitral. Behold where meet
Gangá and *Yamuná!* in the bright mirror
Of the broad waves, the palace of the king,
The crest-borne gem of *Pratishṫhána* views
Complacently its own reflected glory.

Urv. The scene in truth might tempt us to believe
The fields of heaven were here in prospect spread—
But where to find its lord, the pitying friend
Of all the helpless children of misfortune!

Chitral. Let us alight and hide us in this garden,

* In a former note on this passage some doubt was expressed as to its purport, the text being read "Abaráidam ńáma, siḿha-bandhaniḿ vijjam," explained by the commentator, "Aparájitáḿ náma śikhábandhaniḿ vidyám," the crest-binding science named the invincible. The term *aparájitá* occurs in "*Śakuntalá:* abaráidá ńáma suramahausí;" rendered by the late M. Chezy, "Cet amulette d'une nature toute divine, et célèbre sous le nom de l'invincible (*aparádjitá*)," and he has proposed to read the similar passage in this place, Siḿha-bandhana-vidyá, which he translates, "un talisman nommé *aparájitá*, capable d'enchaîner les lions." Mr. Lenz, following his authority, reads here, Siḿdha-bandhaní vidyá, "Leonum domandorum scientia." I am afraid that both are wrong. *Śikhá* is the explanation given by the commentator. The Prákŕit representative of this is *sihá*, as it occurs in the Calcutta edition, the dental being substituted for the palatal sibilant, by the rule in Vararuchi's Grammar Śashoḿ saḿ, as *ńisá* for *niśá*, and *h* for *kh*, by the rule *Kha-gha ṫha-dha-bhám haḱ;* as *suham* for *sukham:* so a little farther on we have *sihá-bharańa-bhúdam* for *śikhá-bharańa-bhútam*. Again, the word could not be *Siḿha* if it were even intended for the same Sanskŕit word signifying a lion. It would be *síha*, the *anuswára* being rejected, and the vowel made long, as in *sakka síha* for *śákya-siḿha*, according to the rule, Ítsiḿha-jihvayoścha, ex. for *siḿhaḱ, sího; jihvá, jíhá*. The only correction needed, therefore, was the elision of the *anuswára* reading, instead of *siḿhá, sihá*, the Prákŕit form of *śikhá*, as it occurs in the comment. Taming lions, as the faculty of a superhuman being, would need neither talisman nor drug, and the binding of the crest or braid of hair is an act of much more mystical importance in Hindu estimation: apparently the power is merely that of becoming invisible.

Whose groves may vie with Indra's, till we learn
Some news of him we seek.
Yonder I view him! [*They descend.*
He waits thy coming to display his beauty
With undiminished brightness, like the moon,
That newly risen, expects a while his bride
The soft moonlight, ere he put forth his radiance.

Urv. More graceful seems he than when first he met
My gaze.

Chitral. No doubt; come, let us approach.

Urv. No, hold a moment! let us conceal ourselves
In veiling mist,* and lurking thus unseen
About the arbour, we may overhear
What thoughts he utters in this solitude,
Communing with one only friend.

[*They become invisible to the king and the Vidúshaka.*

Máń. I have it; difficult as it is, I have hit upon a plan for securing you an interview with your charmer.

Urv. (*Behind.*) How! who! what female is so blest to be
The object of his anxious thoughts?

Chitral. Employ
Your meditation to discover her.

Urv. I fear too soon to know what may befall.

Máń. Did your Majesty hear me observe I had devised an expedient?

Pur. Say on; what is it?

Máń. This it is: let your Majesty cherish a comfortable nap; your union will then be effected by your dreams; or

* Being visible to the audience and invisible to individuals on the stage is a contrivance familiar to the plays of various people, especially our own, as the Ghost of Hamlet, that of Banquo, Ariel in the Tempest, and Angelo in the Virgin Martyr, who repeatedly enters invisible. The wardrobe of some of our old Comedians comprised a robe to walk invisible, which Gifford supposes was a dress of light gauzy texture. Something of the kind is used here apparently, as the stage directions are "covered with a veil," and "throwing aside the veil."

delineate a portrait of the lady Urvaśí, and recreate your imagination by gazing on her picture.

Urv. Be of good cheer, my heart!

Pur. I fear me both impracticable.

How can I hope to taste repose that dreams
Might give me Urvaśí, while fierce the shaft
Of *Káma** rankles in my breast! And vain
The task her blooming graces to portray;
The tears of hopeless love at every line
Would fill my eyes, and hide her beauties from me.

Chitral. You hear?

Urv. I do,—yet scarcely yet confide.

Máń. Ah well! my ingenuity extends no farther.

Pur. Cold and relentless; little does she know,
Or knowing, little heeds my fond despair.
Yet cannot I reproach the archer god,
Although, by giving to my hope such aim,
He tortures me with barren, wild desires.

Chitral. What say you now?

Urv. I grieve that he should deem me
Cold and unfeeling. I cannot now appear
Before I make these charges some reply:
I 'll make a *bhúrja* leaf,† and will inscribe
My thoughts on it, and cast it in his way.

[*She writes upon the leaf and lets it fall near the Vidúshaka, who picks it up.*

Máń. Holla! what is here, the slough of a snake dropped upon me to eat me up?

Pur. It is no snake-skin, but a leaf and something written on it.

Máń. No doubt the lady Urvaśí, unperceived, has overheard your lamentations, and sends this billet to console you.

* The Hindu Cupid.

† A kind of birch, the leaf of which is used as paper in some parts of Upper India, as that of the palm is in the Peninsula.

Pur. Hope dawns upon my passion. (*Reads the leaf.*) Your guess was right.

Máń. Oblige me, then, by letting me hear what is written.

Urv. Indeed! sir, you are curious.

Pur. (*Reads.*)

"Thou wrongst me, lord, to think I do not feel
Alike the pains that o'er thy bosom steal.
The breeze that softly floats through heavenly bowers,
Reclined upon my couch of coral flowers,
Sheds not on me its cool reviving breath,
But blows the hot and scorching gale of death:
O'er all my form the fevered venom flies,
And each bright bud beneath me droops and dies."

Máń. I hope you are pleased. You have now as much cause for rapture, as I should consider it to be civilly asked to dinner when I felt hungry.

Pur. How say you! cause for rapture? This dear leaf
Conveys indeed assurance most delightful:
Yet still I sigh to interchange our thoughts,
Met face to face, and eye encountering eye.

Urv. Our sentiments accord.

Pur. The drops that steal
Fast from my tremulous fingers may efface
These characters traced by her tender hand:
Take you the leaf, and as a sacred trust
With care preserve it.

Máń. Phoo! what matters it now? Since, by the assenting sentiments of the lady Urvaśí, your desire has borne flowers, will it not bear fruit?

Urv. Now, Chitralekhá, whilst I summon courage
To issue into view, do you appear,
And give the monarch notice of my purpose.

Chitral. I shall obey. (*Becomes visible.*) Hail, to the king!

Pur. Fair damsel, you are welcome; yet forgive me,
The less, your lovely friend comes not along:

The sacred streams before us show less stately
Until they flow in unison.

Chitral. Royal sir,
The cloud precedes the lightning.

Pur. Where is Urvaśí?
You are inseparable.

Chitral. She salutes the king,
And makes this her request.

Pur. Say, her command.

Chitral. Once, by the enemy of the gods assailed
And captive made, your valiant arm redeemed her.
Again in peril, she applies to you,
And claims your guardian shield against a foe
More formidable still, from *Madana*,*
Whom you have armed against her.

Pur. You tell me, gentle nymph, your fair friend pines
With amorous passion; but you do not see
The ardour that consumes this heart for her.
Alike our glowing flame: then quickly aid
Our union to cement, as close combines
Iron with iron,† when each fiery bar
With equal radiance glows.

Chitral. Appear, my friend!
The potent deity with like relentlessness
Afflicts the prince, and now to you I call
The herald of his sufferings.

Urv. Faithless friend,
Thus to desert me!

Chitral. It will soon be seen
Which merits best the title of deserter;
But now, be present.

Urv. (*Appearing.*) Triumph to the king!

Pur. The wish is victory,

* Another name of *Káma* or Cupid.

† The art of welding iron was, therefore, known to the Hindús.

When from the sovereign of the gods transferred
By lips celestial to a mortal monarch.*

[*Takes her hand and leads her to a seat.*

Máń. Fair lady, I am the Brahman of the king, and his friend, and so may claim some notice. (*Urvaśí bows to him smiling.*) Prosperity attend you.

A MESSENGER *of the Gods in the air.*

Mess. Ho, Chitralekhá! Urvaśí, repair
Swift to the palace of the Lord of air;
There your appointed duties to fulfil,
And give expression to the wondrous skill
Of Bharata, your master.† To the dome
Divine, the world's protecting rulers‡ come,

* That is, the customary wish with which Indra is addressed, when applied by you to a mortal, is in fact a boon to that effect. The words are, *Jaadu jaadu mahárão,* "May the great prince conquer."

† *Bharata* is the supposed inventor of dramatic composition.

‡ The *Lokapálas,* or guardians of the world, are sometimes confounded with the deities presiding over the different cardinal points; but this is not quite correct, and they are more properly the divinities who were appointed by *Brahmá* upon the creation of the world, to act as rulers over the different kinds of created things. The list occurs in several *Puráńas;* but the following is from the *Mahábhárata,* the *Harivaḿśa* portion.

Indra, sovereign of the three *Lokas,* or earth and the regions above and below.

Soma—of sacrifices, ascetic rites, the lunar and solar asterisms, Brahmans, and healing herbs.

Daksha—of the *Prajápatis,* the patriarchs or first-created and progenitors of mankind.

Varuńa—of the waters.

Vaiśwánara—of the *Pitŕis* or manes.

Váyu—of the *Gandharbas,* of unembodied element, of time and sound.

Mahádeva—of the *Mátŕis,* of the spirits of ill, of kine, of portents and planets, of infirmities and diseases, and of ghosts.

Vaiśravańa—of the *Yakshas, Rákshasas, Guhyakas,* of wealth and of all precious gems.

Śesha—of the entire serpent race.

Vásuki—of the *Nágas* or ophite tribes of *Pátála.*

Takshaka, younger brother of the *Ádityas*—of snakes.

Parjanya—of oceans, rivers, clouds, and rains.

Chitraratha—of the *Gandharbas.*

Eager to view the scene that genius fires,
That passion animates, and truth inspires.

Kámadeva—of the *Apsarasas*.

Nandi, the bull of *Śiva*—of all quadrupeds.

Hirańyáksha and *Hirańyakaśipu*—of the *Daityas*.

Viprachitti—of the *Dánavas*.

Mahákála—of the *Gańas* or *Śiva's* attendants.

Vŕitra—of the children of *Anáyusha*, the wife of *Twashtŕi*.

Ráhu—the son of *Simhiká*—of evil portents and prodigies.

Samvatsara—of the divisions of time, from the twinkling of an eye to the period of an age.

Suparńa—of birds of prey.

Garuḍa—of the winged race.

Aruńa—the brother of *Garuḍa*, was made by Indra ruler in the East.

Yama, the son of *Áditya*—in the South.

The son of *Kaśyapa*, *Amburája*—in the West.

Pingala, the son of *Pulastya*—in the North.

Having thus nominated the presiding spirits, various *Lokas* or districts were created by *Swayambhú*, as brilliant as the sun or fire, radiant as lightning, or chastely beaming as the moon, of various colours, movable at will, many hundreds of *yojanas* in extent, the fit abodes of the pious, exempt from sin and pain. Those Brahmans whose merit shines conspicuous are elevated to these regions, those who practise piety and worship devoutly, who are upright and benevolent, free from cupidity and cherishers of the poor.

Having thus distributed his sons, *Brahmá* departed to his own dwelling *Pushkara*. The deities rambled through the districts, and engaged in the charges respectively assigned them, being all cherished by *Mahendra*. The gods, with Indra at their head, as placed by *Swayambhú*, discharging their guardian duties obtained fame and heaven, and receiving their share of sacrifices enjoyed prosperity and happiness.

Some of the early sections of the *Káśi-khańḍa* of the *Skanda-Puráńa*, or from the 9th to the 23d, contain a description of the several *Lokas*, the cities or spheres of the different divinities, as they are traversed by *Śivaśarman* on his way from earth to the region of Śiva. He passes in this route the *Lokas* of the nymphs, of the sun, of *Indra*, *Agni*, *Nirŕita*, *Varuńa*, *Váyu*, *Kuvera*, of the *Gańas*, or attendants of *Śiva*, of *Soma*, of the lunar asterisms, of *Budha*, *Śukra*, *Bhauma*, *Guru*, and *Śani*, or the planets Mercury, Venus, Mars, Jupiter, and Saturn, of the seven *Ŕishis*, of *Dhruva*, the *Lokas*, called *Maharloka*, *Janaloka*, and *Tapoloka*, and that called *Satyaloka*, the abode of *Brahmá*, and *Vaikuńṭha* and *Kailása*, or the regions severally of *Vishńu* and *Śiva*. This disposition of the spheres, however, has evidently received a peculiar colouring from the Pauráńik cosmography, and the sectarial bias of the *Skanda-Puráńa*.

Chitral. Hear you, my friend? be speedy in your parting.

Urv. I cannot speak.

Chitral. My friend, great prince, requests
Permission to depart. She owes obedience
To heaven's high king, and dreads lest her delay
Incur his wrath.

Pur. Not mine to interrupt
The tasks your mighty Lord assigns. Farewell!
Do not forget me!

[*Urvaśí and Chitralekhá depart.*

Pur. (*To the Vidúshaka.*) She disappears! What else deserves my gaze?

Máń. Why, perhaps, this. (*Looking for the bhúrja leaf.*) (*Apart.*) Bless me, I have been so fascinated myself by the smiles of the lady Urvaśí, that the leaf with her billet upon it has unconsciously slipped out of my hands.

Pur. You were about to speak.

Máń. Yes, I was going to say, do not lose your fortitude. The nymph is firmly attached to you, and her going hence will not relax the attachment.

Pur. Of that I feel assured. The sighs that heaved
Her panting bosom as she hence departed,
Exhaled her heart, and lodged it in my bosom,
Free to dispose of it, although her person
Be forced to wait upon a master's will.*

Máń. (*Apart.*) I am all in a flutter lest he should ask me for that abominable leaf.

Pur. What shall console my eyes! Give me the leaf.

Máń. The leaf! dear me, it is not here!—it was a leaf of heaven, and must have gone after Urvaśí.

Pur. Heedless blockhead!

* Rowe is less daring, although in the *Rival Queens* he makes Alexander say something of this kind:

"*Alex.* (*To Statira.*) My fluttering heart, tumultuous with its bliss, would leap into thy bosom."

Máń. Let us search for it. Here, here!

[*They search for the leaf and retire.*

Enter in the foreground, AUŚÍNARÍ, *the* QUEEN, *with* NIPUŃIKÁ *and Attendants.*

Auśí. You saw his Highness, you are sure, Nipuńiká,
Entering the arbour with Máńavaka.

Nip. Why should your Majesty doubt my report?

Auśí. Well, let us seek him then, and unobserved,
Amidst these shades we may detect the truth.
But what is yon that meets us like a shred
Of some rent garment, floating on the wind?

Nip. A *bhojpatra* leaf;—there seem to be some marks like letters upon it; it is caught by your Grace's anklet. (*Picks it up.*) Will it please you read it?

Auśí. Glance o'er its tenor, and if not unfit
To meet our ear, peruse what there is written.

Nip. It looks like a memorial verse. Eh, no! now it strikes me, they must be lines addressed by Urvaśí to the king; this is some carelessness, now, of that blockhead Máńavaka.

Auśí. Read, I shall conceive its purport.

Nip. (*Reads the lines as above.*)

Auśí. Enough!—proceed; and with this evidence
We shall confound our nymph-enamoured swain.

They go round the arbour, the KING *and* MÁŃAVAKA *advance.*

Máń. Eh! is not that the leaf yonder on the mount, just on the edge of the garden?

Pur. Breeze of the south, the friend of love and spring,
Though from the flower you steal the fragrant down
To scatter perfume, yet why plunder me
Of those dear characters, her own fair hand,
In proof of her affection, traced? Thou knowest,
The lonely lover that in absence pines
Lives on such fond memorials.

Máń. No, I was mistaken; I was deceived by the tawny hue of the peacock's tail.

Pur. I am every way unhappy.

AUŚÍNARÍ *and her train advance.*

Auśí. Nay, my good lord,
I pray you be consoled, if, as I deem,
The loss of this occasion your distress.
[*Offering the leaf.*

Pur. (*Apart.*) The queen! (*Aloud.*) Madam, you are welcome.

Auśí. You do not think me so.

Pur. (*To the Vidúshaka apart.*) What is to be done?

Máń. I don't know: what excuse can a freebooter offer when he is taken in the fact?

Pur. This is no time to jest. (*Aloud.*) Believe me, madam,
This leaf was not the object of my search,
Nor cause of my anxiety.

Auśí. Excuse me,
If I suspect that your denial seeks
But to conceal the truth.

Máń. Your grace had better order dinner: that will be the most effectual remedy for his Majesty's bile.

Auśí. You hear, Nipuńiká, this most sage counsellor;
And how he would remove his friend's distress.

Máń. Why not, madam? Is not everybody put into good humour by a hearty meal?

Pur. Peace, blockhead! you but heighten my offence.

Auśí. Not yours the offence, my lord: 'tis mine, who tarry
Here, where my presence is not wished; 'tis soon
Removed. [*Going.*

Pur. Yet stay, I own myself to blame,—
Curb your resentment, that alone convicts me:
When monarchs are incensed it cannot be
But that their slaves are guilty. [*Falls at her feet.*

Auśí. Think me not
So light of purpose, as to be beguiled
By such assumed respect. You make, my lord,
An awkward penitent: I cannot trust you.

Nip. Come, madam, come!

[*The queen repels the king, and exit.*

Máń. Her Majesty has gone off in a hurry, like a river in the rains. You may rise. (*To the king, who has continued prostrate.*)

Pur. I might have spared myself the pains.
A woman is clear-sighted, and mere words
Touch not her heart. Passion must give them credit.
The lapidary, master of his craft,
With cold indifference eyes the spurious gem.

Máń. You care very little about this, I suppose; the eye that is dazzled with light cannot bear the lamp.

Pur. Not so. 'Tis true that Urvaśí engrosses
My heart, but Káśíràja's daughter claims
My deference; less indeed, that her contempt
Disdains my protestations, and this scorn
Will justify requital.

Máń. Well, let us have done with her Majesty, and think a little of a famished Brahman. It is high time to bathe and eat.

Pur. 'Tis past mid-day. Exhausted by the heat,
The peacock plunges in the scanty pool
That feeds the tall tree's root: the drowsy bee
Sleeps in the hollow chamber of the lotus
Darkened with closing petals: on the brink
Of the now tepid lake the wild duck lurks
Amongst the sedgy shade; and even here,
The parrot from his wiry bower complains,
And calls for water to allay his thirst. [*Exeunt.*

END OF THE SECOND ACT.

ACT III.

SCENE I.—THE HERMITAGE OF BHARATA.

Enter GÁLAVA* *and* PAILAVA,† *two of his disciples.*

Gál. Well, friend Pailava, what news? Whilst you were at *Mahendra's* palace with the Sage, I have been obliged to

* *Gálava* was a saint of some note, and is the hero of a long legend in the *Udyoga-Parvan* of the *Mahábhárata.* He there appears as the pupil of *Viśwámitra.* At the expiration of his studies he importuned his master to tell him what present he should make him. *Viśwámitra,* being out of humour, at last desired him to bring him eight hundred horses, each of a white colour, with one black ear. *Gálava* in his distress applied to *Garuḋa,* who was his particular friend, and with him repaired to *Yayáti,* king of *Pratishṫhána. Yayáti,* being unable to comply with the sage's wish, presented him his daughter *Mádhaví,* whom *Gálava* gave in marriage successively to *Haryaśwa,* king of Ayodhyá, *Divodása,* king of Káśí, *Uśinara,* king of Bhoja, and received from each, upon the birth of a son by her, two hundred of the steeds he was in quest of. These horses were originally a thousand in number. The saint *Ṙichika,* having demanded the daughter of *Gádhi,* sovereign of Kányakubja, as his wife, that prince, to evade the match, being afraid to decline it, required the steeds in question as a present in return. *Ṙichika* obtained them from the god of ocean, *Varuńa,* and transferred them to his father-in-law, by whose descendants six hundred were sold to different princes, and the rest given away to the Brahmans. *Gálava,* having procured the horses which were in possession of the kings, took them and the damsel, still by virtue of a boon a virgin, and presented them together to *Viśwámitra.* The sage received them and begot a son by her, *Ashṫaka,* to whom he resigned his hermitage and his stud, and retired to the woods: the place was thence called *Ashṫakapura.* The lady after this was reconducted by *Gálava* to her father, and he, in imitation of his preceptor, spent the rest of his days in solitary devotion.

† *Paila* is the name of a *Ṙishi,* by whom the *Ṙig-Veda* was arranged and subdivided into two portions. It is not certain that he is intended in this place by the name *Pailava,* although not unlikely.

stay at home to look after the holy fire. Were the immortals pleased with the specimen of our master's skill?

Pail. How could they choose but be pleased?—there was eloquence and melody for them. The drama was *Lakshmí's* choice of a lord;* the nymph Urvaśí quite lost herself in the impassioned passages.

Gál. There is something not quite right implied in your applause.

Pail. Very true, for unluckily Urvaśí stumbled in her part.

Gál. How so?

Pail. You shall hear. Urvaśí played *Lakshmí;* Menaká was *Váruní.* The latter says:—

> *Lakshmí*, the mighty powers that rule the spheres
> Are all assembled: at their head appears
> The blooming *Keśava.* Confess, to whom
> Inclines your heart?

Her reply should have been—To *Puru-shottama;* but instead of that—To *Purú-ravas*, escaped her lips.

Gál. The intellectual faculties are but the slaves of destiny. Was not the Sage much displeased?

Pail. He immediately denounced a curse on her, but she found favour with *Mahendra.*

Gál. How so?

Pail. The sentence of the Sage was, that as she had forgotten her part, so should she lose her divine knowledge. But when the performance was over, Indra observing her, as she stood apart, ashamed and disconsolate, called her to him.

* Or the *Lakshmí-Swayaṁvara.* It was common in the Hindu society of former times for princesses and women of rank to select a husband for themselves. The candidates for the hand of the lady were invited to her father's house, and after previous festivities for some days, were collected in a hall, round which the damsel passed and selected her future lord, by throwing a garland round his neck: the marriage rite was then celebrated as usual. The custom is the subject of much pleasing poetic description in the *Mahábhárata*, the *Naishadha*, and other works. A translation of the *Swayaṁvara* of *Draupadí* from the former is published in the *Calcutta Quarterly Magazine* for September 1825.

The mortal who engrossed her thoughts, he said, had been his friend in the hour of peril; he had aided him in conflict with the enemies of the gods, and was entitled to his acknowledgment. She must accordingly repair to the monarch, and remain with him till he beholds the offspring she shall bear him.

Gál. This was like *Mahendra;* he knows all hearts.

Pail. Come, come! we have been chattering here till it is almost the time when our preceptor performs his ablutions. Come, we have no time to lose; let us attend him.

[*Exeunt.*

SCENE II.—PART OF THE GARDENS OF THE PALACE.

Enter the CHAMBERLAIN.

As long as life is vigorous, man endures labour for the sake of procuring wealth; when farther advanced in age, his toils are lightened by the participation of his children; but for me, my strength is daily undermined and my body exhausted by this servitude. Waiting on women is the devil. I am now to find the king, and tell him that her Majesty, having dismissed all anger and resentment, is desirous of paying her homage to him this evening, for the completion of the vow in which she has engaged.* The close of the day is agreeable enough here in the palace. The peacocks nod upon their perches and the doves flock to the turret tops, scarcely distinguishable from the incense that flows through the lattices of the lofty chambers. The venerable servants of the inner apartment are all busily engaged in propitiatory rites, and substituting lamps for the offering of flowers that decorated the holy shrines throughout the day. Ah! here comes the prince, attended by the damsel train with flambeaux in their delicate hands: he moves like a mountain, around whose stately

* Obligations self-imposed are in constant practice amongst the Hindus. In this case, the queen has engaged to forego her ornaments and to hold a rigid fast until the moon enters a certain asterism.

skirts the slender *karńikára* spreads its brilliant blossoms. I will wait him here.

Enter PURÚRAVAS *and the* VIDÚSHAKA, *with female attendants** *carrying torches.*

So ends the day; the anxious cares of state
Have left no interval for private sorrow.
But how to pass the night: its dreary length
Affords no promise of relief.

Chamberlain. (*Advances.*) Glory to the king! So please your Grace, her Majesty expresses a wish to be honoured with your presence on the terrace of the pavilion of gems, to witness from it the entrance of the moon into the asterism Rohińí.

Pur. Go, my good friend, apprise her Majesty
She may dispose of us. [*Exit Chamberlain.*
What object, think you, that the queen, in truth,
Proposes by the vow she has assumed?

Máń. I suppose she repents of her pettishness, and wishes to be friends with you again. This is but an excuse to bring you to her presence, when she may efface the recollection of the indignity with which she treated you.

Pur. 'Tis very likely. Prudent wives full soon
Repent the scorn that urged them to repel
An humbled husband, and are glad to seek
Some fair pretext to win his love again—
We will indulge her Grace. On to the chamber.

Máń. 'Tis here. Ascend these steps of crystal, smooth shining as the waters of the Ganges. The pavilion of gems is particularly lovely when evening sets in. (*They ascend.*) The moon is just about to rise; the east is tinged with red.

* This might be supposed a copy of Mohammedan manners, but it is not necessarily so, having been the practice of the Hindus before the Christian era; for the king's person, when within the palace, used to be attended by women, his guards and other troops being stationed without the gates. Thus Strabo: "Regis corpus mulieres curant, ea quoque de parentibus emptæ, qui regem custodiunt, et reliquus exercitus manent extra portas." IV. 15.

Pur. 'Tis even so: illumined by the rays
Of his yet unseen orb, the evening glooms
On either hand retire, and in the midst
The horizon glows, like a fair face that smiles
Betwixt the jetty curls on either brow
In clusters pendulous. I could gaze for ever!

Máń. Ḥo! here he comes, the king of the Brahmans, as beautiful as a ball of almonds and sugar.

Pur. Oh, base similitude! Your thoughts, my friend,
Have rarely nobler prompter than your stomach.

[*Carries his hands to his forehead, and bows to the moon now risen.*

Hail, glorious lord of night! whose tempered fires
Are gleaned from solar fountains, but to yield
The virtuous fruit eternal, as they light
The flame of holy sacrifice, whose stores
Ambrosial serve but to regale the gods
And the immortal fathers of mankind—
All hail to thee! whose rising ray dispels
The glooms of eve, and whose pale crescent crowns
The glorious diadem of *Mahádeva.**

Máń. Enough, sir; your grandfather bids you, by me his interpreter, sit, that he may repose himself.

Pur. (*Makes the Vidúshaka sit, and then seats himself.*)
The splendour of the moon is light enough:
Remove the torches and command my train
Retire to rest.

* The first of these specifications refers to the astronomical facts of the moon's deriving its light from the sun, and by its positions forming the days of the lunar month, on which particular ceremonies are to be observed. In the latter case it is supposed to move in the *Mańḍala,* the sphere or orbit of the sun, and when in conjunction, as at the new moon or *Amávásyá,* funeral obsequies are specially to be celebrated. According to mythological notions also, the moon is the grand receptacle and storehouse of *amŕita* or ambrosia, which it supplies during the fortnight of its wane to the gods, and on the last day to the *Pitŕis* or deified progenitors. As personified, the moon is the father of *Budha* and grandfather of *Purúravas,* as already shown. The half-moon, as frequently noticed, is worn by *Śiva* upon his forehead.

Att. As you command. [*Withdraws with the torch-bearers.*

Pur. I think we may not yet expect the queen:
And now we are alone, I would impart
My thoughts.

Máń. Out with them; there is no appearance of her yet; and it is well to keep up your spirits with hope.

Pur. You counsel well. In truth, my fond desire
Becomes more fervid as enjoyment seems
Remote, and fresh impediments obstruct
My happiness—like an impetuous torrent,
That, checked by adverse rocks, a while delays
Its course, till high with chafing waters swollen,
It rushes past with aggravated fury.

Máń. There is one thing to be said: notwithstanding your anxiety has made you something thinner, it has rather improved than impaired your personal appearance. I argue from this that a meeting with the nymph is not very distant.

Pur. My right arm by its glad pulsation soothes
My grief, like you, with hope-inspiring words.

Máń. A Brahman's words, be assured, are never uttered in vain.

Enter above in a heavenly car URVAŚÍ *and* CHITRALEKHÁ: URVAŚÍ *in a purple dress with pearl ornaments.**

Urv. Now, my dear girl,
What say you? Do these purple robes become me,
Thus trimmed with pearls?

Chitral. I cannot think of words
To speak my admiration—only this,
Would I were Purúravas.

Urv. My dear friend,
I feel my strength desert me; bring him quickly,
Or quickly lead me to his royal palace.

* The text is, *Abhisárika-veśá*, in the garb of a woman who goes to meet her lover. The specification of the translation is from Urvaśí's first speech; the term is *níla*, which means dark-blue or black, most ordinarily the former.

Chitral. We are there. Behold it,
White gleaming in the moon-light, whilst below
The *Yamuná's* blue waters wash its foot;
Like the snow-tufted summits of *Kailása*,
Rising in radiance from their bosky base.
Advance.

Urv. One moment—exercise the power
Of meditative vision. Where is the king,
The master of my heart, and what employs him?

Chitral. (*Apart.*) I will rouse her fears.
I see him: in a fit solitude he waits
Impatiently the coming of the bride.

[*Urvaśí expresses despair.*

How, silly wench! what else would you desire
Should be his occupation?

Urv. Ah, my friend,
My fluttering heart is easily alarmed.

Chitral. In the pavilion of bright gems awaits
The king, his trusty friend alone attends him,
Let us thither.

Urv. Proceed.

[*They descend and leave the car.*

Pur. As spreads the moon its lustre, so my love
Grows with advancing night.

Urv. Ah me! I fear
Even yet to trust. Let us remain invisible,
And overhear their conference, till doubt
Be all dispersed.

Chitral. Be it as you will.

Máń. The rays of the moon are charged with ambrosia; do you find no benefit from them?

Pur. Small is their power, or that of aught, to mitigate
The pangs of love. Soft beds of fragrant flowers,
Sandal's cool unguent, strings of gelid pearl,
And these mild tempered rays, exhaust on me
In vain their virtue; nothing can allay

The fever of my heart. She, she alone,
The goddess I adore, or secret converse,
That ever speaks of her, can yield me rest.
These limbs that pressed her side, when on we drove
Through fields of ether, are still warm with life;
All else a lifeless load that burthens earth.

Urv. I need no more concealment. [*She advances hastily.*
Woe is me;
He deigns not to regard me.

Chitral. In your haste
You have forgotten to put off the veil
That screens you from his sight.

(*Behind.*) This way, your Grace.

[*All listen; Urvaśí throws herself into the arms of Chitralekhá.*

Máń. The queen is here! we had better be mute.

Pur. Assume the resemblance of indifference.

Urv. What shall we do?

Chitral. Remain invisible.
Not long her purposed stay: by her attire
She holds some sacred vow.

Enter the QUEEN, *with attendants bearing offerings; the Queen is dressed in white; flowers are her only ornaments.*

Queen. This union with the constellation yields
New brilliance to the lord of Rohińí.*

Att. Such effect attends your Grace's encounter with his Majesty.

Máń. (*To Purúravas.*) She comes, I imagine, to offer her benedictions; or under the resemblance of a solemn vow, she wishes to obliterate the recollection of the indignity with which she lately repelled your advances. Well, I think her Majesty looks very charming to-day.

Pur. In truth she pleases me. Thus chastely robed
In modest white, her clustering tresses decked

* The moon.

With sacred flowers alone,* her haughty mien
Exchanged for meek devotion; thus arrayed
She moves with heightened charms.

Queen. (*Advancing.*) Hail to the king!

Att. Hail to the king!

Pur. Madam, you are welcome. [*Leads her to a seat.*

Urv. (*Behind.*) She merits to be called divine;† the bride
Of heaven's great king‡ boasts not surpassing dignity.

Chitral. Your commendations speak you free from envy.

Queen. My gracious lord, I would perform a rite
Of which you are the object, and must beg you
Bear with the inconvenience that my presence
May for brief time occasion you.

Pur. You do me wrong;
Your presence is a favour.

Máń. May such inconvenience often befall me as to pronounce a benediction on like occasions.

Pur. (*To the queen.*) How call you your observance?

Nip. (*On the queen's turning to her.*) The conciliation of regard.§

Pur. Is it even so? Yet, trust me, it is needless
To wear this tender form, as slight and delicate
As the lithe lotus stem, with rude austerity.
In me behold your slave, whom to propitiate
Claims not your care; your favour is his happiness.

Urv. (*Smiling scornfully.*) He pays her mighty deference.

Chitral. So he should—
When the heart strays, the tongue is most profuse
Of bland professions to the slighted wife.

Queen. Not vain my vow, since it already wins me
My lord's complacent speech.

* Or with the blossoms of the holy *Dúrva* grass.

† *Deví*, or goddess, is one of the titles appropriate to the state of queen.

‡ *Śachí*, the wife of Indra.

§ *Pia-ppasádaná.*

Máń. Enough said on both sides; these civilities require no further reply.

Queen. Come, girls, the offerings, that I may present them

To the bright deity, whose rays diffuse
Intenser lustre on these splendid walls.

Att. Here are the perfumes, madam, here the flowers.

[*Gives them, and the queen goes through the usual form of presenting the Arghya or oblation of fruits, perfumes, flowers, &c.*

Queen. These cakes present Máńavaka, and these
Give to the chamberlain.

[*The attendant takes a tray of sweetmeats first to the Vidúshaka and then to the Kanchukin.*

Máń. Prosperity attend your Highness; may your fast prove fortunate.

Chamberlain. Prosperity to the queen!

Queen. Now, with your Grace's leave, I pay you homage.

[*Presents oblations to the king, bows, and falls at his feet, then rises.*

Resplendent pair who o'er the night preside,
Lord of the Deer-borne* banneret, and thou
His favourite, Rohińí†—hear and attest
The sacred promise that I make my husband.

* The car of the moon is decorated with a small flag on which a deer is represented.

† *Chandra*, or the moon, is fabled to have been married to the twenty-seven daughters of the patriarch *Daksha*, or *Aświní* and the rest, who are in fact personifications of the Lunar Asterisms. His favourite amongst them was *Rohińí*, to whom he so wholly devoted himself as to neglect the rest. They complained to their father, and *Daksha* repeatedly interposed, till finding his remonstrances vain, he denounced a curse upon his son-in-law, in consequence of which he remained childless and became affected by consumption. The wives of *Chandra* having interceded on his behalf with their father, *Daksha* modified an imprecation which he could not recall, and pronounced that the decay should be periodical only, not permanent, and that it should alternate with periods of recovery. Hence the successive wane and increase of the moon. (*Padma-Puráńa, Swarga Khańda*, Sec. II.) *Rohińí* in astronomy is the fourth lunar mansion, containing five stars, the principal of which is Aldebaran.

Whatever nymph attract my lord's regard,
And share with him the mutual bonds of love,
I henceforth treat with kindness and complacency.

Urv. Oh, my dear friend, how much these words assuage
The apprehensions of my heart.

Chitral. She is a lady
Of an exalted spirit, and a wife
Of duty most exemplary. You now
May rest assured, nothing will more impede
Your union with your love.

Máń. (*Apart to Purúravas.*) The culprit that escapes before his hand is cut off, determines never to run such a risk again. (*Aloud.*) What, then, is his Majesty indifferent to your Grace?

Queen. Wise sir, how think you? To promote his happiness
I have resigned my own. Does such a purpose
Prove him no longer dear to me?

Pur. I am not what you doubt me; but the power
Abides with you: do with me as you will.
Give me to whom you please, or if you please
Retain me still your slave.

Queen. Be what you list.
My vow is plighted—nor in vain the rite,
If it afford you satisfaction. Come,
Hence, girls, 'tis time we take our leave.

Pur. Not so:
So soon to leave me is no mark of favour.

Queen. You must excuse me, I may not forego
The duties I have solemnly incurred.

[*Exit with train.*

Urv. Why, girl, I doubt the Rájá still affects
His queen. So be it; it is now too late
For me to hope my heart can be reclaimed

Chitral. Away with doubt; you have no need to fear.

Pur. Is the queen far removed?

Máń. You may say whatever you wish, safely enough.

You are fairly given over by her, like a sick man by his physician.

Pur. I fear I am, by faithless Urvaśí.
Would she were here; and that the gentle music
Of her rich anklets murmured in my ears;
Or that her lotus hands, as with light step
She stole behind me, spread a tender veil
Before my eyes; that in this shady bower
She deigned descend spontaneous, or drawn hither
With welcome violence by some fair friend,—
Ha! the lovely daughter of *Náráyańa!*

[*Urvaśí has advanced behind the king and covers his eyes with her hands.*

Vid. How knows your Grace?

Pur. It must be Urvaśí,—
No other hand could shoot such ecstasy
Through this emaciate frame. The solar ray
Wakes not the night's fair blossom—that alone
Expands when conscious of the moon's dear presence.

Urv. (*Appearing.*) Joy to the king!

Pur. All hail, bright nymph of heaven!

[*Leads her to a seat.*

Chitral. (*Advancing.*) Be the king blest!

Pur. I feel I am already.

Urv. The queen, my friend, has just presented me
This pious prince, and therefore I approach
His person, as the object of my love.
You cannot say I claimed a part in him
Before the right was granted me.

Máń. What! were you here ever since sunset?

Pur. I have no purpose to dispute the claim.
But let me ask, if such assent were needed,
Who was it that first granted you permission
To rob me of my heart.

Chitral. My friend, I know,
Can proffer no reply—then let this be.

Now grant me my request; I must depart
To minister to *Súrya* at the term
Of the spring festival: till my return
Be careful that this nymph have never cause
To mourn the heaven she has resigned for thee.

Máń. Heaven, indeed! why should she ever think of such a place?—a place where they neither eat, nor drink, nor close their eyes even for a twinkle.*

Pur. The heaven of *Indra* is the eternal source
Of joy ineffable: it cannot be
The cares of Purúravas should efface
The memory of immortal bliss—
Yet, nymph, of this be confident, my soul
Shall know no other sovereign than your friend.

Chitral. 'Tis all I ask: be happy, Urvaśí,
And bid me now adieu!

Urv. (*Embracing her.*) Forget me not.

* The gods are supposed to be exempt from the momentary elevation and depression of the upper eyelid, to which mortals are subject, and to look with a firm unintermitted gaze. Hence a deity is termed *Animisha* and *Animesha*, one whose eyes do not twinkle. Various allusions to this attribute occur in poetry. When *Indra* visits *Sítá* to encourage her, he assumes at her request the mark of divinity—he treads the air, and suspends the motion of the eyelids (*Rámáyańa*). When *Agni*, *Varuńa*, and *Indra*, all assume the form of *Nala* at the marriage of *Damayantí*, she distinguishes her mortal lover by the twinkling of his eyes, whilst the gods are *stabdha-lochana*, fixed-eyed (*Mahábhárata*, *Nalopákhyána*). And when the *Aświní-Kumáras* practise the same trick upon the bride of *Chyavana*, she recognizes her husband by this amongst other indications (*Padma-Puráńa*). The notion is the more deserving of attention, as it is one of those coincidences with classical mythology which can scarcely be accidental. *Heliodorus* says: "The gods may be known by the eyes looking with a fixed regard, and never closing the eyelids;" and he cites Homer in proof of it. An instance from the Iliad which he has not noticed, may be cited perhaps as an additional confirmation, and the *marble eyes* of Venus, by which Helen knew the goddess, and which the commentators and translators seem to be much perplexed with, are probably the *stabdha-lochana*, the fixed eyes, of the Hindus, full, and unveiled even for an instant, like the eyes of a marble statue.

Chitral. That I should rather beg of you, thus blest
With one the only object of your wishes.
[*Bows to the king, and exit.*

Máń. Fate is propitious and crowns your Majesty's desires.

Pur. 'Tis true, I reach the height of my ambition.
The haughty canopy that spreads its shade
Of universal empire o'er the world;
The footstool of dominion, set with gems,
Torn from the glittering brows of prostrate kings,
Are in my mind less glorious than to lie
At Urvaśí's fair feet and do her bidding.

Urv. I have not words to speak my gratitude.

Pur. Now I behold thee thus! how changed is all
The current of my feelings—these mild rays,
Cool, vivifying, gleam; the shafts of *Madana*
Are now most welcome—all that was but late
Harsh and distasteful to me, now appears
Delightful by your presence.

Urv. I lament,
I caused my lord to suffer pain so long.

Pur. Nay, say not so! the joy that follows grief
Gains richer zest from agony foregone.
The traveller who faint pursues his track
In the fierce day, alone can tell how sweet
The grateful shelter of the friendly tree.

Máń. The moon is high; it were as well to go in.

Pur. Conduct the way: and, dearest, may the hours
With thee be still prolonged, as when, without thee,
They tardy brought the day.
[*Exeunt into the pavilion.*

END OF THE THIRD ACT.

ACT IV.*

SCENE—THE FOREST OF AKALUSHA ON THE ŚKIRTS OF GANDHAMÁDANA, ONE OF THE MOUNTAINOUS BARRIERS OF MERU.

Strains without.†

Soft voices low sound in the sky,
Where the nymphs a companion deplore,

* This act is without a parallel in any of the dramas yet met with. It is almost entirely in *Prákrit*, and the *Prákrit* is arranged not only in metrical forms peculiar to that language, but according to particular musical rhythm, as intended to be sung. Again, there are stage directions for the measure to which certain gesticulations are to be performed, so that it partakes both of the operatic and melo-dramatic character. The names of the airs and measures are not current in the present day, nor known to the Pańd́its; the explanations of them in the "*Ťiká*," or "Commentary on the Drama," are quoted usually from *Bharata*, whose rules no longer exist in a collective form. The manuscript, however, being full of errors, little assistance has been derived in this respect from the annotator; but his definitions of the airs seem to be extracted chiefly from the *Sangíta-Ratnákara*, from which authority it appears that this subject has yet been very insufficiently investigated, as the modifications of the six *Rágas* amounted to two hundred and sixty-four, with the whole of which we are yet unacquainted. *Soma* enumerates, according to Sir William Jones, nine hundred and sixty variations. A. R. III. 71.

In the former edition an attempt was made to explain in the notes the meaning of the terms employed in the text to indicate varieties of metre, melody, and gesticulation; but the subject is scarcely appropriate to a translation, and would more fitly accompany the Sanskŕit text. It has therefore, for the most part, been now omitted; and those who take an interest in it will find as much illustration as it perhaps admits, in the notes of the Calcutta edition of the text, and in the elaborate dissertation of Mr. Lenz in his edition of the same.

† The expression is *Ákshiptiká*, and as a musical term implies, *Air*, the adaptation of notes, or their names to poetical rhythm. *Bharata* adds, as cited by the commentator, it serves to introduce characters on the stage.

And lament, as together they fly,
The friend they encounter no more.
So, sad and melodious awakes
The plaint of the swan o'er the stream,
Where the red lotus blossoms, as breaks
On the wave, the day's orient beam.

Enter CHITRALEKHÁ *and* SAHAJANYÁ.

Chitral. (*Looking up.*)
The swans along the stream that sail
A fond companion's loss bewail—
With murmuring songs they soothe their grief,
Or find from tender tears, relief.

Sah. Now, Chitralekhá, what has chanced to cloud
Your countenance; it indicates your heart
Is ill at ease; what causes your distress?
Tell me, that I may share and soothe your sorrow.

Chitral. It is not all unknown to you. Engaged
Amidst our band in paying wonted service
To the all-seeing Sun, I have not shared
The vernal sports, my Urvaśí away.

Sah. This we all know, and know your mutual love.

Chitral. Whilst dwelling on her memory, anxious to learn
Some tidings of her, I employed my power
Of bringing absent objects to my view;
And by this art I learn what much alarms me.

Sah. Say on.

Chitral. The king, by Urvaśí's persuasions,
Resigned of late the reins of rule, and sought
With her the groves of *Gandhamádana.**

* The *Gandhamádana* mountain is one of the four boundary mountains enclosing the central region of the world, called *Ilávŕitta*, in which the golden mountain of the gods, or *Meru*, is situated. The *Puráńas* are rather at variance as to its position. According to the *Váyu* it lies on the West, connecting *Níla* and *Nishadha*, the North and South ranges. The *Vishńu-Puráńa* places it on the South, the Western mountain being there called *Vipula*. It has, however, a *Gandhamádana* to the West amongst

Sah. Amid such lovely scenes, the amorous pair
Would most enjoy each other's company.
What followed?

Chitral. Whilst wandering pleasantly along the brink
Of the *Mandákiní*, a nymph of air,
Who gambolled on its sandy shore, attracted
The monarch's momentary glance—and this
Aroused the jealous wrath of Urvaśí.

Sah. Ungenerous girl! although it proves her love,
Yet destiny is mightier.

Chitral. Thus incensed,
My friend disdainfully repelled her lord;
In sooth, her mind was darkened by the curse
The Sage erewhile denounced; and troubled thus,
She heedlessly forgot the law that bars
All female access from the hateful groves
Of *Kárttikeya*. Trespassing the bounds
Proscribed, she suffers now the penalty
Of her transgression, and to a slender vine
Transformed, there pines till time shall set her free.

Sah. How vain the hope to shun the will of fate!
What other cause could interrupt a love
So fervent.—Where is now the king?

Chitral. He roams,
Frantic with sorrow, through the wood, in search
Of his lost bride, nor night nor day desists
From the sad quest. These rising clouds that teach
Passion to pious sages, augur ill

he projecting branches or filaments of *Meru*. The *Bhágavata* places it on the East of *Meru*. The *Mahábhárata* agrees with the *Váyu-Puráńa*. The *Padma-Puráńa* is at variance with itself, and places it in one passage on the West, and in another describes it as on the East. According to this *Puráńa*, *Kuvera* resides on it with the *Apsarasas*, *Gandharbas*, and *Rákshasas*. The *Sítá*, alighting on its top, thence descends to the *Bhadráśwa-varsha*, and flows to the Eastern Sea.

For his alleviation—I much fear
There is but little hope of remedy—

[*Repeats the first stanza, "The swans along the stream that sail," &c.*

Sah. But think you there is no expedient then
To re-unite these lovers?

Chitral. There is but one.
The sacred gem that owes its ruby glow
To the bright tint of *Gaurí's** sacred feet,
Alone effects their union.

Sah. Let us hope it—
Their delicate forms endure not agony,
Violent and protracted, and the gods
Can surely never purpose such a pair
Should wholly perish—they will soon devise
Some means of their relief—to their high power
We leave them.—Come. The glorious sun reveals
His countenance; let us depart and pay
Our wonted adorations. (*Sings.*)

Amidst the lake, where the lotus shining,
Its flowers unfolds to the sunny beam,
The swan, for her lost companion pining,
Swims sad and slow o'er the lonely stream.

[*Exeunt.*

ANOTHER PART OF THE FOREST.

(*Strains without.*) †

AIR.

The lord of the elephant train
Now wanders afar from his mate,

* *Durgá* or *Párvati*, the bride of *Śiva.*

† Or in the text the *Praveśaka* the introducer—either a person on the stage or near it, who occasionally interposes to let the audience know who is coming when none of the characters perform that duty: the annunciation is in the same metre as the first, the *Ákshiptiká.*

And franticly comes, to complain
  To the woods of his desolate state.
Distraction his vigour consumes,
  As he plunges amidst the dark bowers,
While o'er his vast bulk sweetly blooms
  The garland of wild forest flowers.

Enter PURÚRAVAS *hastily, looking up to the heavens, his dress disordered, and his general appearance indicative of insanity.*

Hold, treacherous fiend, suspend thy flight, forbear—
Ah! whither wouldst thou bear my beauteous bride?
And now his arrows sting me—thick as hail
From yonder peak whose sharp top pierces heaven,
They shower upon me.

[*Rushes forward as to the attack—then pauses and looks upwards.*

AIR.

The lonely cygnet breasts the flood,
Without his mate, in mournful mood;
His ruffled plumage drooping lies,
And trickling tears suffuse his eyes.

It is no demon—but a friendly cloud;
No hostile quiver—but the bow of Indra:
The cooling rain-drops fall, not barbèd shafts,
And I mistake the lightning for my love.

[*Faints—then revives, and rising.*

AIR.

I madly thought a fiend conveyed
Away from me my fawn-eyed maid:
'Twas but a cloud that rained above
With the young lightning for its love.

Where can she bend her steps—or is she here
Invisible, in anger? If she seek
The skies, her love for me will soon revive.
Once mine again, not all the demon host

That brave the gods, should force her from my arms.
Alas! no more my gaze delighted dwells
Upon her loveliness—How sad the chance!
Fate heaps calamities with diligent malice
On those whom once misfortune has assailed.
Hence have I lost my love, when genial airs
And overshadowing clouds, veiling the day,
Had shed intenser rapture on her presence.

AIR.

Ye clouds whose ceaseless torrents shed
New glories through the gloomy air,
A while your angry showers forbear,
Nor burst upon this humbled head—
Give me to find my love, and then fulfil
Your wrath—Content, I bow me to your will.

Away with this humility—the wise
Call kings the lords of time—I will assert
My power, and bid the seasons stay their course.

AIR.

The tree of heaven invites the breeze,
And all its countless blossoms glow;
They dance upon the gale; the bees
With sweets inebriate, murmuring low,
Soft music lend, and gushes strong
The *kóil's* deep thick warbling song.

No, I will not arrest the march of time,
For all around behold my state apparelled—
The clouds expand my canopy—their lightnings
Gleam as its glittering fringe. Rich chowries wave
Of many-coloured hues from flowering trees.
The shrieking peafowl, clamorous in their joy,
Are the loud heralds of a sovereign's honours;
And those bright torrents, flashing o'er the brows
Of the tall mountains, are the wealthy streams,
Poured forth profuse from tributary realms.

Fie on it! what have I to do with pomp
And kingly pride? my sole sad business here
To thread the woods in search of my beloved.

AIR.

The monarch of the woods
With slow desponding gait
Wanders through vales and floods,
And rocks and forest bowers,
Gemmed with new springing flowers,
And mourns heart-broken for his absent mate.

Ah me! whatever I behold but aggravates
My woe. These bright and pendulous flowers,
Surcharged with dew, resemble those dear eyes
Glistening with starting tears. How shall I learn
If she have passed this way? The yielding soil,
Softened by showers, perchance may have retained
The delicate impression of her feet,
And show some vestige of their ruby tincture.*
Where in this lonely thicket may I hope
To gain some tidings of her? Yon proud bird,
Perched on the jutting crag, that stately stands
With neck outstretched and spreading tail, to tell
His raptures to the clouds, haply may give
Some kind intelligence.

AIR.

The royal elephant, the dread
Of all his rival foes,
With downcast eye and tardy tread,
Through tangled thickets goes;
To solitary grief a prey,
His loved companion far away.

* The soles being stained with the red juice of the *Mehndi*.

AIR.

I will speak to this peacock—Oh tell,
If, free on the wing as you soar,
In forest, or meadow, or dell,
You have seen the loved nymph I deplore—
You will know her, the fairest of damsels fair,
By her large soft eye, and her graceful air.

[*Advancing to the bird, and bowing.*

Bird of the dark-blue throat and eye of jet,
Oh tell me, have you seen the lovely face
Of my fair bride, lost in this dreary wilderness?
Her charms deserve your gaze. How! no reply?
He answers not, but beats a measure. How!
What means this merry mood? Oh yes, I know
The cause. He now may boast his plumage
Without a peer, nor shame to show his glories
Before the floating tresses of my Urvaśí.
I leave him, nor will waste a thought on one
Who feels no pity for another's woes.

[*Proceeds—Music.*

Yonder, amidst the thick and shady branches
Of the broad *jambu*, cowers the *kóil*—faint
Her flame of passion in the hotter breath
Of noon. She of the birds is wisest famed—
I will address her.

AIR.

Majestic as sails the mighty cloud
Along the dusky air,
The elephant cometh hither to shroud
In the thickets his despair.
From his heart all hope of delight is riven,
And his eyes with tears o'erflow,
As he roams the shades, where the sons of heaven
Descend to sport below.

AIR.

Say, nursling of a stranger nest,*
  Say, hast thou chanced my love to see,
Amidst these gardens of the blest,
  Wandering at liberty,
Or warbling with a voice divine
Melodious strains more sweet than thine?

[*Approaches, and kneels.*

Sweet bird—whom lovers deem Love's messenger,†
Skilled to direct the god's envenomed shafts
And tame the proudest heart; oh, hither guide
My lovely fugitive, or lead my steps
To where she strays.

[*Turns to his left, and as if replying.*

Why did she leave
One so devoted to her will? In wrath
She left me, but the cause of anger lives not
In my imagination; the fond tyranny
That women exercise o'er those who love them
Brooks not the slightest show of disregard.
How now! the bird has flown. 'Tis ever thus—
All coldly listen to another's sorrows.
Unheeding my affliction, lo, she speeds,
Intent on joy expected, to yon tree,
To banquet on the luscious juice the *jambu* ‡
From its now ripe and roseate fruit distils.
Like my beloved, the bird of tuneful song
Deserts me. Let her go—I can forgive her.

[*Proceeds.*

Ha!—on my right—amidst the wood I hear

* The *kóil*, like the cuckoo, is said to leave its eggs in the nests of other birds.

† Because the *kóil's* song is especially heard at the season of spring, the friend of love.

‡ The rose-apple, so denominated from its odour: it is, however, the *mahájambu* that is mentioned in the text.

A tinkling melody. 'Tis the sweet chime
My fair one's anklets echo to her footsteps.

AIR.

Through the woods the stately elephant strays,
And his glances despair express;
On his limbs the enfeebling malady preys,
And his steps are slow with distress;
In his eyes the starting tear-drops swell,
As his thoughts on his lost companion dwell.

Alas! the gathering of the clouds deceives
The swan, who hails rejoicingly the time
For periodic flight to *Mánasa.*
I hear his song of gladness, not the sound
Of tinkling anklets. Ere yet the troop begins
Its distant march I will address the chief.
Ho! Monarch of the tribes that breast the stream,
Forbear a while your course: forego the provender
Of lotus stems, not needed yet, and hear
My suit—redeem me from despair—impart
Some tidings of my love; 'tis worthier far
To render kindly offices to others
Than meanly labour for a selfish good.
Though bent on *Mánasa,* he gazes on me,
As if to own he had beheld my love.
Why seek to veil the truth? If my beloved
Was never seen by thee as graceful straying
Along the flowery borders of the lake,
Then whence this elegant gait?—'Tis hers—and thou
Hast stolen it from her, in whose every step
Love sports—thy walk betrays thee; own thy crime,
And lead me quickly to her. (*Laughs.*) Nay, he fears
Our royal power—the plunderer flies the king.

[*Proceeds—Music.*

Yonder I see the *chakwa** with his mate;
Of him I will inquire.

AIR.

In groves of tall trees with bright blossoms blooming,
And vocal with many sweet murmured tones,
The lord of the herd, whom grief is consuming,
Distracted, the loss of his mate bemoans.

AIR. *After a pause.*

Ah no, he replies, I taste, on the wing,
The joys of the cool returning spring,
And as each feather thrills with delight,
I mark not the fair that meet my sight.

Yet tell me—hast thou seen her? Know'st thou not
Who asks thy answer? The great king of day
And monarch of the night are my progenitors:
Their grandson I, and by their own free choice,
The lord of Urvaśí and of the earth.
How—silent! Thou might'st measure my affliction
By what thou feelest; all the air resounds
With thy incessant plaints, if, but a moment,
Thy fair companion nestling hides in sport
Amongst the lotus leaves, and flies thy view.
Alas! to one whom fate has cursed like me,
Nought is propitious; I will ask no more.

[*Proceeds—Music.*

How beautiful the lotus!—it arrests
My path and bids me gaze on it—the bees
Murmur amidst its petals—like the lip
Of my beloved it glows, when that has been
Somewhat too rudely sipped by mine, and sweetly
Protests against such violence—I will woo
This honey-rifler to become my friend.

[*Advances.*

* The *Chakraváka* or *Ruddy* goose: the birds are supposed to be separated through the night.

AIR.

Unheeding the cygnet at first,
His beak in the nectar of passion dips;
But fiercer and fiercer his thirst—
As deeper he sips.

Say, plunderer of the honeyed dew, hast thou
Beheld the nymph whose large and languid eye
Voluptuous rolls, as if it swam with wine?
And yet methinks 'tis idle to inquire;
For had he tasted her delicious breath,
He now would scorn the lotus. I will hence.

[*Proceeds.*

Beneath the shade of yon *kadamba* tree
The royal elephant reclines, and with him
His tender mate. I will approach—yet hold,
From his companion he accepts the bough
Her trunk has snapped from the balm-breathing tree,
Now rich with teeming shoots and juicy fragrance.

[*Advances, then pauses.*

He crushes it! I may proceed.

AIR.

King of the forest, whose sports have felled
The stateliest trees, the thicket's pride;
Oh, say, in these shades hast thou beheld,
More bright than the moon, my wandering bride?

[*Advancing a few paces.*

Chief of the mighty herd, say, hast thou seen
My love—like the young moon her delicate frame,
And with eternal youth her beauties glow;
Her voice is music—her long tresses wear
The jasmine's * golden hue. Hadst thou afar

* *Yúthiká-śavala-keśi*, having hair brown as the yellow *jasmine*, golden or *auburn*,—a very strange idea for a Hindu. It is said that in the west of India such hair is sometimes seen, but the prejudice in favour of ebon locks is so strong that it is considered a morbid affection of the hair, and the women dye and conceal it.

Beheld her charms, they must have fixed thy gaze.
Ha, he replies! That kind assenting roar
Conveys some intimation—oh repeat
The sound—consider that we should befriend
Each other, bound by various common ties.
Thou art the sovereign of the forest; me
They term the king of men. Thy bounty sheds
Thy frontal fragrance on the air; my wealth
On all is showered profuse. Amongst the bands
Of lovely nymphs, obedient to my will,
One only Urvaśí commands my love;
As thou hast chosen this, thy favourite,
From all the herd. Thus far our fates accord;
And never be the pangs of separation,
Such as distract my bosom, known to thee;
Propitious be thy fortunes. Friend, farewell.

[*Proceeds.*

What have we here? Deep in the mountain's breast
A yawning chasm appears: such shades are ever
Haunts of the nymphs of air and earth. Perchance
My Urvaśí now lurks within the grotto
In cool seclusion—I will enter. All
Is utter darkness. Would the lightning's flash
Now blaze to guide me—no, the cloud disdains,
Such is my fate perverse, to shed for me
Its many-channelled radiance. Be it so.
I will retire—but first the rock address.

AIR.

With horny hoofs and a resolute breast
  The boar through the thicket stalks;
He ploughs up the ground, as he plies his quest
  In the forest's gloomiest walks.

Say, mountain, whose expansive slope confines
The forest verge, oh tell me, hast thou seen
A nymph as beauteous as the bride of love,

Mounting with slender frame thy steep ascent,
Or wearied resting in thy crowning woods?
How—no reply! remote he hears me not—
I will approach him nearer.

AIR.

From thy crystal summits the glistening springs
  Rush down the flowery sides,
And the spirit of heaven delightedly sings,
  As among thy peaks he hides.
Say, mountain so favoured, have the feet
Of my fair one pressed this calm retreat?

Now, by my hopes, he answers! he has seen her—
Where is she?—say. Alas! again deceived—
Alone I hear the echo of my words,
As round the cavern's hollow mouth they roll
And multiplied return. Ah, Urvaśí! (*Faints.*)

[*Recovers, and sits as exhausted.*

Fatigue has overcome me. I will rest
Upon the borders of this mountain torrent,
And gather vigour from the breeze that gleans
Refreshing coolness from its gelid waves.
Whilst gazing on the stream, whose new swollen waters
Yet turbid flow, what strange imaginings
Possess my soul and fill it with delight!
The rippling wave is like her arching brow;
The fluttering line of storks, her timid tongue;
The foamy spray, her white loose-floating vest;
And this meandering course the current tracks,
Her undulating gait; all these recall
My soon-offended love—I must appease her.

AIR.

Be not relentless, dearest,
  Nor wroth with me for ever.
I mark where thou appearest
  A fair and mountain river.

Like *Gangá* proud thou showest,
From heavenly regions springing;
Around thee, as thou flowest,
The birds their course are winging.

The timid deer confiding,
Thy flowery borders throng;
And bees, their store providing,
Pour forth enraptured song.

AIR.

In the lowering east the king of the deep
Expects his coming bride;
His limbs are the clouds that darkly sweep
The skirts of the heaving tide;
And his tossing arms are the tumbling waves,
Where the gale o'er the heaving billows raves.

With rapture he dances, the lord of the main,
And proud in his state appears;
His steps are pursued by the monster train,
The deep sea darkness rears;
And the curlew, the swan, and glistening shell,
And the lotus, the monarch's glory swell.

The bellowing surges his fame resound,
And dash at the gates of heaven;
The sea with the sky they threat to confound,
But back with shame are driven;
For now the young rains are armed for their right,
And their prowess arrests old Ocean's might.*

[*Approaches, and bows.*

O nymph adored, what crime have I committed,
That thus you fly from one so wholly yours,
Who now implores your pity, and with terror

* This and the preceding verse are much expanded in the translation, in order to express their meaning; the first being very brief, and the second both brief and obscure.

Anticipates your loss? Relent—return—
This is not Urvaśí. She would not quit me
Even for the Ocean King. What's to be done?
Fortune crowns those who yield not to despair—
I'll back to where my love first disappeared.
Yonder the black deer couchant lies; of him
I will inquire. O antelope, behold,
The royal elephant *Airávata*,*
Scorched by the pangs of solitude, explores,
In search of his lost mate, the groves of *Nandana*;†
Whose close-embowering walks are resonant
With the glad *kóil's* song, as pleased he sips
The juicy nectar of the clustering blossoms.
How! he averts his gaze, as he disdained
To hear my suit! Ah, no!—he anxious marks
His doe approach him—tardily she comes,
Her frolic fawn impeding her advance.

AIR.

A nymph of heaven has left her sphere
To make a heavenly region here,
  And treads this sacred ground;
Her slender waist, her swelling hips,
Her languid eye, her ruby lips,
  With youth unfading crowned.
Oh tell me, through the tangled maze,
If wandering she has met thy gaze,
  Deer of the soft black eye,
Ere yet beneath the yawning brink
Of sorrow's gulph, immersed I sink?
  Befriend me, or I die—

[*Advances.*

Lord of the bounding herds, say, hast thou seen
My fair, whose large and languid eye resembles
That of thy tender mate? He heeds me not,

* The elephant of *Indra*.

† The garden of *Indra*.

But springs to meet his doe. Be happy both,
Though fate still adverse frowns on my desires.
[*Proceeds, and pauses.*

How now!—what stream of ruddy radiance breaks
Through the cleft rock? No flame could have survived
The fast descending torrents; 'tis perchance
Some sanguine fragment of the lion's feast.
No—'tis a gem—more roseate than the blush
Of the *aśoka* blossom, and the sun
Would grasp it with his beams—it pleases me,
And I will make it mine.

AIR.

With tearful eye and dejected gaze,
Despairing his love to meet,
All lonely the royal elephant strays
Through the forest's still retreat.

Why should I take the jewel? She whose brow,
Bound with *Mandára* fillet, best had worn
The costly gem is far—far from me—why
Should I distain the ruby with my tears?
[*Going—a voice in the air.*

Take up the gem, my son; its radiant red
The feet of *Hema's* holy daughter shed *
And wondrous virtue gave. Let it adorn
Thy hand, and thou wilt shortly cease to mourn
Thy absent bride—once more by this restored
To bless her sorrowing and lamented lord.

Pur. What voice is this! Descends some friendly sage
In pity of my griefs, or in some deer
Disguised, directs me thus? Seer, I obey
And thank thy holy counsel. Gem divine,
Restore me to my love, and I will bear thee

* *Gaurí* or *Párvatí;* the stone is fabled to have received its colour and virtues from contact with the soles of her feet stained with the red of the Mehndi (*Lawsonia inermis*).

High on my diadem, and hold thee ever
As dear as *Íśwara* his crescent moon.

[*Takes the gem and proceeds, then pauses.*

What means this strange emotion, as I gaze
Upon this vine? No blossoms deck its boughs;
Nipped by the falling rains, like briny tears,
That wash the ruddy freshness from the lips,
The buds have perished, and the mournful shrub
All unadorned appears to pine in absence;
No bees regale her with their songs; silent
And sad, she lonely shows the image
Of my repentant love, who now laments
Her causeless indignation. I will press
The melancholy likeness to my heart.

AIR.

Vine of the wilderness, behold
  A lone heart-broken wretch in me,
Who dreams in his embrace to fold
  His love, as wild he clings to thee.
And might relenting fate restore
  To these fond arms the nymph I mourn,
I'd bear her hence, and never more
  To these forbidden haunts return.

[*Goes to embrace the creeper, which is transformed to Urvaśí.**

What can this mean! through every fibre spreads
The conscious touch of Urvaśí—yet all
I deemed her charms deceived me—let me wake
And realise the vision or dispel it.
'Tis no deceit—'Tis she—my best beloved. [*Faints.*

Urv. (*In tears.*) Revive, my lord.

Pur. (*Reviving.*) Thy loss, dear love, has plunged my sinking spirit

* Or, "enters as it were in its very place," *Tataḥ praviśati tatsthána eva Urvaśí.*

Deep into dreariest gloom; but now thy sight
Arrests my soul, and calls me back to bliss.

Urv. I knew not of your woe, myself deprived
Of conscious being.

Pur. How! What mean you? Speak!

Urv. I will explain; but let me first implore
Forgiveness, that my causeless wrath has wrought
So sad a change in you.

Pur. Enough, enough;
You mine once more, all else is quite forgotten,
And every thought is ecstasy. But come,
Say how you cheered your time, your lord away?
For me—

AIR.*

I have sued to the starry-plumed bird,
And the *kóil* of love-breathing song;
To the lord of the elephant herd,
And the bee as he murmured along;
To the swan, and the loud waterfall,
To the *chakwa*, the rock, and the roe:
In thy search have I sued to them all,
But none of them lightened my woe.

Urv. To me, all news of my lamented lord
Came but in fond imaginings.

Pur. How thus?

Urv. In ancient days, the warrior god adopted
A cœnobite's observance; and for this,
Retiring to the woods that stud the vale
Of *Gandhamádana*, then called *Akalusha*,
He framed this law—

Pur. What law? Proceed!

Urv. The female that should rashly pass the bounds
Proscribed, and penetrate the forest shades,

* *Charchari.*

Should instant metamorphose undergo,
And to a twining shrub should be transformed,
Alone from such sad change to be redeemed
By the celestial gem, whose ruby glow
Is gleaned from *Gaurí's* foot. This law I broke.
Bewildered by the sage's imprecation,
I thoughtless plunged into the thicket's glooms
Shunned ever by the gods, and in a vine
My form and faculties a while were lost.

Pur. 'Tis all explained. No ordinary cause
I knew detained thee from me: thee, whose fears
Brooked not my momentary separation,
Even in thy dreams. The virtue of the gem,
As thou hast said, this day effects our meeting.
Behold it here!

Urv. The ruby of reunion:
This holy gem restores me to my nature.
[*Takes it and puts it respectfully to her forehead.*

Pur. A moment thus: let me behold thy brow,
Irradiated by this heavenly jewel,
Like the red lotus ere its buds expand.

Urv. The king delights to flatter me; but now
Let us return to *Pratishthána.* Long
The city mourns its absent lord, and I,
The cause of his departure, shall incur
The angry censures of the people. Come,
How will it please you travel?

Pur. Yonder cloud
Shall be our downy car, to waft us swift
And lightly on our way; the lightnings wave
Its glittering banners, and the bow of Indra
Hangs as its over-arching canopy
Of variegated and resplendent hues.

AIR.

The ardent swan his mate recovers,
  And all his spirit is delight:
With her aloft in air he hovers,
  And homeward wings his joyous flight.

[*Exeunt on the cloud—Music.*

END OF THE FOURTH ACT.

ACT V.

The Palace of Purúravas.

Enter Mánavaka.

At last, thank the fates, the king has returned with Madam Urvaśí from the groves of *Nandana*, the pleasant gardens of the Gods. My friend is once more attentive to his royal duties and the cares of state; yet he seems out of spirits. What should be the cause? Except the want of children, he has nothing to grieve for. This is a bustling day. The king and his queen have just performed their royal ablutions where the *Yamuná* and the Ganges meet: he must be at his toilet by this time, and by joining him I shall secure a share of the flowers and perfumes prepared for him.

(*Noise behind.*) The ruby! the ruby! A hawk, taking it for a piece of flesh, has borne away the ruby of reunion which had been taken out of its red palm-leaf case, and was being carried to the king for him to wear while absent from the nymph!

Mán. Here's a pretty piece of work! the jewel my friend so highly prized. Ho, here he comes, not yet attired. I will keep aloof.

Enter Purúravas *in haste, followed by the* Chamberlain, *a* Hunter,* *and attendants.*

Pur. Where is the winged thief that rashly courts
His own destruction, and presumes to violate
The dwelling of his sovereign?

* The *Védhaka*, in some copies *Réchaka*, explained a *Kiráta* a forester. The *Kirátas*, the mountaineer and savage tribes of India, were known to the ancients as the *Cirrhadæ* on the Coromandel coast. They appear to have been independent, but were tributary to the Hindu kings, or perhaps only rendered personal service.

Hunter. Yonder he goes, the golden chain of the jewel hanging from his beak.

Pur. I see him! As he rapid flies around
In airy rings, the whirling chain appears
To hem him in a fiery circle.
What's to be done?

Máń. (*Advancing.*) Punish him, to be sure; put the culprit to death.

Pur. Bring me my bow.

[*A female attendant* * *goes out and returns with a bow and arrows, which she gives to the king.*

'Tis now too late—he flies
Far to the south, beyond the arrow's reach.
Red as *aśoka* flowers, the precious gem
Graces the sky: with sullen fires it glows
Like angry Mars, bursting at intervals
Through the thick clouds that overhang the night.
My good *Tálavya* (*to the Chamberlain*), give command, the bird
Be tracked, and followed to his perch.

Cham. The king shall be obeyed. [*Exit.*†

Máń. Now please you sit; the thief will not be able to escape your power.

* A *Yavaní*, which is rather inexplicable. The Mohammedan princes had guards of African women in their harems, and the presence of female attendants in those of the Hindú sovereigns has also been adverted to; but the term *Yavana* has been applied by the later Hindús to the Mohammedans; and it is not likely that either Persian or Arabian women ever found their way into the inner apartments of Hindú princes, as personal attendants or guards. If, as has been supposed, *Yavanas* formerly implied Greeks, it is equally impossible that Greek women should have fulfilled such an office, as few could have found their way to India, or even to Bactria; and those would have been, it may be supposed, too highly valued by their countrymen to have been suffered to act as slaves to barbarians. Perhaps Tartarian or Bactrian women may be intended.

† There is evidently much more art in the conduct of the business in this piece than in the Toy Cart. The Chamberlain would there have been sent out, and would have returned immediately, in all probability, instead of any dialogue filling up the interval.

Pur. (*Sits.*) Were it an ordinary gem, its loss
Would move me not; but to lose this would vex me;
To it I owe reunion with my love.

Máń. Well, there is this comfort, as you have the lady, you are no longer in need of the jewel.

Enter the CHAMBERLAIN, *with an arrow and the jewel.*

Cham. Victory to your Grace! The bird, condemned by your Majesty's decree, has fallen, pierced by this shaft; the ruby is recovered. It has been cleansed with water; please you say to whom it shall be intrusted.

Pur. Ho, Forester! replace the gem
Safe in its casket.

Hunter. As your Majesty commands.

[*Exit the Kiráta or Forester.*

Pur. Know you to whom the shaft belongs?

Cham. There is a name inscribed upon it, your Grace, but my eye-sight cannot distinguish the characters.

Pur. Let me see them.

[*Takes the arrow, and expresses wonder and delight.*

Cham. With your Grace's leave I will now attend to other duties. [*Exit.*

Máń. What does your Majesty study so intently?

Pur. Listen—"The arrow of the all-subduing Áyus,
The son of Urvaśí and Purúravas."

Máń. Joy to your Grace! Fate has crowned your wishes.

Pur. How should this be? But for the interval
Of the *Naimisha** sacrificial rite,
My Urvaśí has always been with me.
I do recall, indeed, a transient period,
When her soft cheek was paler than the leaf

* The *Naimisheya* sacrifice is the great sacrifice performed at the *Naimisha* forest by the assembled sages, which lasted twelve years according to the *Mahábhárata*, a thousand according to the *Bhágavata.*

Cold-nipped and shrivelled, and her eloquent eye
Betrayed unwonted lassitude; aught else
I never noted.

Máń. Oh you must not suppose that the nymphs of heaven manage these matters like those of earth. No, no; they have the power to counteract all such appearances.

Pur. It may be so. Yet why this mystery?
Why keep from me all knowledge of my child?

Máń. Oh, there's no accounting for the fancies of celestial spirits.

Enter CHAMBERLAIN.

Cham. So please your Majesty, a saintly dame and a young lad from the hermitage of *Chyavana* * solicit admittance.

Pur. Let them enter—quick!

* *Chyavana* is the son of *Bhŕigu*, the son of *Brahmá*, by his wife *Pulomá*. A *Rákshasa*, or fiend, attempting to carry off *Pulomá*, the child was prematurely born, whence his name, from *chyu*, to fall from. Upon his birth his splendour was such as to reduce the insulter of his mother to ashes (*Mahábhárata Ádi-Parvan, Pulomá-Adhyáya*). The sage having adopted a life of ascetic devotion, was so immersed in abstraction that he became completely covered with the nests of white ants. *Sukanyá*, the daughter of king *Saryáti*, wandering in the forest, observed what she thought two lights in an ant-hill, and thrust in two blades of *kuśa* grass, which when withdrawn were followed by a flow of blood. Much alarmed, the princess repaired to her father and related what had happened. The king, conjecturing the truth, immediately went to the spot to deprecate the wrath of the *Ŕishi*, and pacified him by giving him the damsel in marriage. After being married some time, the *Aświní-Kumáras* passing by *Chyavana's* residence conferred upon him youth and beauty, in requital of which boons he gave them a share in the *soma* juice offered at sacrifices to the gods. The gods, with *Indra* at their head, opposed this grant, and *Indra* lifted up his hand to strike *Chyavana* dead with his thunderbolt, when the sage paralysed his arm. To appal the gods he created the demon *Mada*, intoxication personified, in terror of whom and of the power of the saint, the gods acceded to the participation of the *Aświní Kumáras* in divine honours. *Indra* was restored to the use of his arm, and *Mada* was divided and distributed amongst dice, women, and wine.—*Bhavishyat-Puráńa*, and the *Dána-dharma* section of the *Mahábhárata*.

Enter a TÁPASÍ *or Female Ascetic, and a Boy with a bow in his hand.*

Máń. Observe him, sir. That warrior lad must be the owner of the arrow; he is your perfect image.

Pur. May it prove so! My imperfect sight
Is dimmed with tears; my heart is overcome
With tenderness, and strong emotions crowd
My agitated mind; on all my limbs
A sudden tremor seizes. How I long
To clasp him to my bosom!

Cham. Here pause, most reverend lady.

Pur. (*Bowing.*) Hail, holy dame!

Táp. May fortune ever wait
The glorious line of Soma! (*Apart.*) Now, methinks,
The king has inward intimation given him
I bring him here his son. (*Aloud.*) Boy, pay your homage.

[*Áyus bows.*

Pur. May your years be many!

Áyus. (*Apart.*) If I dared listen to my heart, I should
Believe this were my father, I his son;
For what affection else would give a charm
To the endearments and embrace of age?

Pur. What brings thee to our presence, saintly dame?

Táp. Let the king hear. This princely youth, the son
Of Urvaśí, was for some cause confided,
Without your knowledge, to my secret care.
The ceremonies of his martial birth
The pious Chyavana has duly ministered,
Taught him the knowledge fitted to his station,
And lastly trained his growing youth to arms!*

* The original has *dhanurvidyá*, archery, which is always put for military science in general. That archery, however, was the predominant branch of the art among the Hindus, is evident from this use of the term, and from all descriptive accounts of heroic education. Ráma, his sons, the Páńdavas, Áyus, and all other princes, are represented in the *Rámáyańa*, *Mahábhárata*,

But now my charge expires, for an act
This day achieved, unfits him to remain
An inmate of the peaceful hermitage.

Pur. What act?

Táp. Whilst on his mission with the *Ŕishi's* sons,
To gather fuel, flowers, and holy grass
From the adjacent woods, he aimed a shaft
Against a hawk, new perched upon a tree
With his fresh prey, and took his felon life.
This deed of blood excludes him from our haunts,
And by the sage's orders I conduct him
Again to Urvaśí. I would see the queen.

Pur. Be seated, and meanwhile, Tálavya,
Apprise our queen, that we would see her here.

[*Exit Chamberlain.*

Come hither, boy. As the moon's silver ray
Affects the lunar gem, his presence sheds
Spontaneous joy, and through each fibre darts
The consciousness that I behold my son.

Táp. Obey your sire.

[*The Prince advances and prostrates himself. Purúravas raises and embraces him, and places him on the footstool of his throne.*

Pur. Salute your father's friend. Boy, fear not.

Máń. What should he fear? he has seen baboons enough in the hermitage.

Áyus. (*Smiling.*) Accept my homage, sir.

Máń. Fortune attend you ever!

Enter URVAŚÍ, *preceded by the* CHAMBERLAIN.

Cham. This way, your Grace.

Urv. (*Seeing Áyus.*) What youth is this, who, in the royal presence,

and all poems and plays, as making archery a principal part of their education, furnishing a remarkable analogy, in this respect, to the practice of the ancient Persians and Scythians.

Armed with the bow and quiver, honoured sits
Upon the golden footstool, whilst the king
Is fondly playing with his twisted tresses?
Ha! *Satyavatí* too! it is my son;
His growth outstrips my memory.

Pur. Behold your mother, boy: her gaze intent
Is fixed upon you, and her heaving bosom
Has rent its veiling scarf.

Táp. Haste to embrace her.

[*Áyus rises and goes to his Mother, who embraces him, then, after a pause,*

Urv. Hail, holy mother!

Táp. Ever may you know
Your lord's affection!

Áyus. Mother, accept my salutations.

Urv. (*Kisses him.*) My dear boy,
Be long your father's happiness and pride.
(*Advances.*) Glory to the king!

Pur. To the matron, honour!

[*Hands Urvaśí to a seat with him on the throne.*

Be seated all. [*They sit.*

Táp. The princely youth is perfectly accomplished
In all the science that becomes his rank,
And is of years and strength to bear the load
Of martial mail. Unfitted to the thoughts
And duties of the tranquil hermitage,
I yield him, therefore, in the royal presence,
Back to his mother's arms.

Urv. And I receive him
Most willingly: for it is no longer meet
He should disturb the quiet of devotion.
When he is satiate with his father's sight
He may revisit you; till then, farewell.

Pur. And bear my reverence to the holy sage.

Áyus. Will you not take me with you, *Satyavatí*?

Táp. No, my dear child: the labours of the student
Are all performed; 'tis time you enter now
On loftier duties,*

Áyus. Well, if it must be so,
Farewell; but send me here my favourite peacock.

Táp. I will; and boy, remember that you heed
Your father ever. Peace be unto all! [*Exit.*

Pur. Thus blessed, my love, with thee and with my son,
I envy not the happiness of Indra.†

Urv. Ah, me! [*Weeps violently.*

Pur. What means this sudden grief?
Why, when I contemplate with ecstasy
The proud perpetuation of my race,
Should these dear drops in swift succession spread
A pearly fillet on thy heaving bosom?

Urv. Alas, my lord! the name of *Swarga's* king
Brings to my memory a dread decree
By him denounced, which, happy in the sight
Of this loved boy, I had a while forgotten.
When for your love I gladly left the courts
Of heaven, the monarch thus declared his will:—
"Go, and be happy with the prince, my friend;
But when he views the son that thou shalt bear him,
Then hitherward direct thy prompt return."
'Twas fear of this that bade me keep concealed
My infant's birth, and instant I conveyed him
To *Chyavana's* retreat, entrusting him
To yonder pious dame to be instructed;
Such my pretext, in our most sacred lore.
The fated term expires, and to console
His father for my loss, he is restored.—
I may no longer tarry.

* Or literally, "You enter now the second order, that of the householder."

† Or, "I think myself, like *Indra* with *Paulomí* (his bride) and *Jayanta* (his son)."

Pur. Adverse fate
Is still intent to mar my perfect joy.
Scarce have I known the blessing of a son,
When my fair bride is snatched from my embrace.
The tree that languished in the summer's blaze,
Puts forth reviving, as young rain descends,
Its leafy shoots, when lo! the lightning bursts
Fierce on its top and fells it to the ground.

Máń. I see nothing left for this but to abandon the throne, assume the coat of bark, and betake yourself to the forests.*

Urv. But what remains for me, my task on earth
Fulfilled? Once gone, the king will soon forget me.

Pur. Dearest, not so. It is no grateful task
To tear our memory from those we love.
But we must bow to power supreme; do you
Obey your lord; for me, I will resign
My throne to this our son, and with the deer
Will henceforth mourn amidst the lonely woods.

Áyus. Excuse me, sire; my years are all unfit
For such a burthen; one so long upheld
By such exalted merits.

Pur. Fear it not.
The elephant cub † soon tames the forest herds;
The snake scarce hatched concocts the deadly poison;
Kings are in boyhood monarchs, and endowed
With powers inborn to rule the race of man:
Nature, not age, gives fitness. (*To the Chamberlain.*)
Tálavya, bid
Our ministers and priests be all prepared
For this our son's inauguration—speed!

* Such appears to have been a common practice with the princes of India, when satiate with years and power, or disgusted with the world.

† The young *gandhagaja* soon subdues other elephants, is the expression in the original. They are said to fly the odour of some particular excretion, whence the name of the animal.

Cham. I obey.

[*Exit sorrowfully, and all on the scene express grief.*

Pur. What sudden splendour breaks! whence are these flashes
Of lightning in a cloudless sky?

Urv. 'Tis Nárada.

Pur. His braided curls are of a golden dye;
His sacred cord, bright as the silver moon;
Around his neck are strings of heavenly pearl;
Like a celestial tree with glittering stem
He moves. Prepare we to receive him.

Urv. Here,
This offering of respect, gathered in haste,
Present the sage.

[*Gives the king some flowers.*

NÁRADA *descends.*

Nár. Triumph attend
The brave defender of this middle sphere!

Pur. (*Presenting the oblation.*) Reverence to the sage!

Urv. Accept my homage. [*Bows.*

Nár. Never be wife and husband disunited.

Pur. (*Apart.*) Oh, might this be! (*Aloud.*) Advance, my son, and pay
Your adoration to the holy seer.

Áyus. Áyus, the son of Urvaśí, presumes
To pay you homage. [*Bows to Nárada.*

Nár. May your days be many! King, attend:
The mighty Indra, to whom all is known,
By me thus intimates his high commands:—
Forego your purpose of ascetic sorrow.
The sages, to whose wisdom past and future
Are as the present, have foretold at hand
Hostilities in heaven, and the gods will need
Your prowess: then relinquish not your arms

And Urvaśí shall be* through life united
With thee in holy bonds.

Urv. These happy words
Extract a barbed arrow from my bosom.

Pur. Whatever Indra wills I shall obey.

Nár. 'Tis wisely said: he will not be unthankful.
The fiery element sustains the sun;
The sun returns his rays to nourish fire.

[*Looking upwards.*

Rambhá, appear, and bring the holy wave
Consigned by Indra to your charge, to consecrate
The prince's elevation to the throne,
As partner of the empire.†

[*Rambhá and other nymphs descend with a golden vase containing the water of the heavenly Ganges, a throne and other paraphernalia, which they arrange.*

Ram. All is prepared.

Nár. Prince, to your seat.

[*Nárada leads Áyus to the throne of Inauguration, takes the golden ewer from Rambhá, and pours water on the head of the prince.*

Rambhá, complete the rite.

[*Rambhá and the Apsarasas perform the rest of the ceremony.*)‡

Ram. Now, prince, salute your parents and the sage.

[*As Áyus bows to them respectively, they reply.*

Nár. Unvarying fortune wait upon thy reign!

Pur. My son, sustain the honour of your lineage.

Urv. My son, be still obedient to thy sire.

[*Chorus of bards without.*

* This is a very material variation in the story as told in the play and in the *Puráńas:* the passage *Tena na twayá śastraḿ sannyastavyam; iyaḿ cha Urvaśí yávadáyus távat sahadharmachárińí bhavishyati.*

† As *Yuvarája*, young king or Cæsar.

‡ The stage directions in the original are not more explicit, and the comment is silent.

Glory, all glory, on Áyus attending,
  Still in the son may the father we trace;
Justice and valour together extending
  The sway of his sceptre and fame of his race.
Son of the monarch the universe filling,
  Son of the God of the mist-shedding night,
Son of the sage,* whom the great Brahmá willing,
  Called with creation to life and to light.

Second Chorus.

Now bright o'er the regions the glories are gleaming,
  The sceptre and sway of the father have won,
And brighter than ever the radiance is streaming,
  Enhanced and confirmed by the fame of the son.
So Gangá descends from the peaks of the mountain
  That shine with the light of unperishing snows,
And mighty, meandering far from their fountain,
  In the breast of the ocean the waters repose.

Ram. (*To Urvaśí.*) No ordinary fate, dear sister, blesses you
  With such a son and lord.

Urv. I own my happiness.
  Come, my dear child, and offer to the queen,
  Your elder mother, filial homage.

Pur. Hold,
  One moment; we will presently together.

Nár. The splendours of your son's inauguration
  Bring to my memory the glorious time
  When *Mahásena* † was anointed chief
  Of all the heavenly hosts.

* Or the son of Purúravas, the son of *Budha*, the son of *Chandra* or the moon, the son of the sage *Atri*, one of the will-engendered sons of the creator *Brahmá*.

† *Kárttikeya*, the son of *Śiva*, who shortly after his birth was appointed general of the armies of heaven, against the *Daityas* or *Titans* under *Táraka*.

Pur. To you I owe
Such honour.

Ndr. Is there ought else Indra can do
To serve his friend?

Pur. To hold me in esteem
Is all I covet. Yet haply may this chance :—
May learning and prosperity oppose
No more each other, as their wont, as foes,
But in a friendly bond together twined,
Ensure the real welfare of mankind.*

[*Exeunt omnes.*

* A singular but characteristic concluding benediction. One copy adds a stanza desiderative of universal prosperity, but it does not occur in another. It may be here observed that the translation has been made from two copies of the text and one of the comment, all of them full of blunders. The sense has therefore often been made out conjecturally.

REMARKS

ON

THE HERO AND THE NYMPH.

If it was necessary to peruse the preceding drama with a liberal allowance for national peculiarities, it is equally requisite, in the present instance, to adapt our faith to the national creed, and to recognize, for poetical and dramatic purposes, the creations of the mythology of the Hindus.

In this respect, however, no very violent demand is made upon our imagination, as we have none of the monstrous extravagancies of the system forced upon our credulity. The intercourse of heroes and of goddesses is the familiar theme of our youthful studies, and the transformation of Urvaśí into a vine is not without abundant parallels in the metamorphoses of Ovid. The personages and situations of the superhuman portion of the drama are both elegant and picturesque; and the grouping of the nymphs upon the peaks of the Himálaya, or the descent of *Nárada* through the fields of ether, might be represented with as much beauty as facility by the machinery of the theatres of Europe.

There is also a peculiarity in the mythos of this drama, which identifies it with the dramatic compositions of antiquity. Trivial as the incidents may appear, unimportant as may be the loves of the hero and the heroine, both persons and events are subject to an awful control, whose interference invests them with a dignity superior to their natural level. Fate is the ruling principle of the narrative; and the monarch and the nymph, and the sovereign of the gods himself, are portrayed as subject to the inscrutable and inevitable decrees of destiny.

The simplicity of the story does not admit of much display of character, but the timid constancy of Urvaśí is not unhappily contrasted with the irresolute haughtiness of the queen. The poet, too, has shown himself not unacquainted with the springs of human feelings, and his observations on the relations of the sexes in domestic life are equally shrewd and just.

The chief charm of this piece, however, is its poetry. The story, the situations, and the characters are all highly imaginative, and nothing, if partiality for his work does not mislead the translator, can surpass the beauty and justice of many of the thoughts. To select one as an example were to disparage a number of other passages, and they may be left to the critical acumen and taste of the reader.

UTTARA-RÁMA-CHARITRA,

OR

CONTINUATION OF THE HISTORY OF RÁMA.

A Drama,

TRANSLATED FROM THE ORIGINAL

SANSKŔIT.

INTRODUCTION.

THE UTTARA-RÁMA-CHARITRA, or continuation of the history of RÁMA, is one of the three dramas attributed to BHAVABHÚTI, and the internal evidence of the composition fully corroborates the traditional appropriation. The style is equally vigorous and harmonious as that of the *Málatí* and *Mádhava;* several of the sentiments found in that play recur in this; and the general character of the two dramas, notwithstanding the difference of their subjects, offers many analogies. We have the same picturesque description and natural pathos in both.

The subject of the UTTARA-RÁMA-CHARITRA is, as the name implies, a continuation of the history of RÁMA, the prince of *Ayodhyá*, and comprises the events that occurred subsequent to the war which constitutes the subject of the *Rámáyańa.* It is taken from the last or supplementary section of that poem, one of the two principal poetical works of the Hindus not wholly mythological, and which have some pretensions to be included in the Epic class. It is, however, more correctly speaking, a continuation of a play by the same author, the *Víra-Ráma-Charitra,* in which the martial exploits of RÁMA, as described in the *Rámáyańa,* are dramatised. The date at which the *Uttara-Ráma-Charitra* was composed cannot be deduced, with certainty, from anything that occurs in the course of the play. It offers nothing, however, that is incompatible with the period at which the author is said to have flourished, or the eighth century, as will be noticed in the introduction to *Málatí* and *Mádhava.* The style is classical, and although elaborate, is not deformed by extravagant refinement. The thoughts are pure and undisgraced by conceits; and altogether the composition belongs to the era of good taste in Hindu writing, although in an advanced period, and upon the eve of its decline. But the most decided evidence of an early date is furnished by the allusions to the *Vedas*, and to some parts of the Hindu ritual which are not now familiarly known, and which there is reason to think have long fallen into disuse. The condition of the Hindu religion must have been very different, when this drama was composed, from any under which it has been observable for some centuries past.

The story of RÁMA has been communicated to European readers so fully in the writings of Jones, Wilford, Maurice, Ward, and Faber, as well as in the *Hindu Pantheon* of Moor, and in the translation of the two first books of the *Rámáyańa*, by the Rev. Messrs. Carey and Marshman, of Serampore, as well as probably by this time in the translation of the whole poem by A. W. Schlegel, that the events which precede the action of the following drama will be familiar to many of those who may peruse it. In order, however, to render it intelligible to those to whom the story may be unknown, a brief recapitulation of the previous adventures of its hero may not be superfluous. The author himself has not thought a preparation of this kind unnecessary even for a Hindu audience, as he has introduced, with some ingenuity, a summary sketch of the leading incidents of RÁMA'S earlier career. A reference to the notes accompanying that part of the drama will more fully explain the circumstances there alluded to, and supply some particulars of RÁMA'S adventures, not comprised in the following brief narrative.

The deities of the Hindu Pantheon by no means enjoy undisturbed possession of divinity, and they are obliged to contend for their own supremacy, or for the protection of the world, with various formidable races known as *Asuras, Daityas, Dánavas*, and *Rákshasas*, or different orders of Titanic and gigantic beings of superhuman strength and vitality, who, from the earliest periods,

Extruere montes ad sidera summa parabant,
Et magnum bello solicitare Jovem.

Of these, the *Rákshasas* bear the least of a celestial character, and belong to the malignant creations of ancient and modern fable, who to gigantic strength and stature unite particular hostility to man, and an appetite for human flesh. In the poetical mythology of the Hindus they are descended from BRAHMÁ through one of his will-born progeny, the sage and saint PULASTYA; but their numbers are every day augmented by the addition of the disembodied spirits of wicked men, condemned to this form for a season, in punishment of their crimes; and the class also comprehends sundry deformed and hideous bands, who are especially attached to the service of the god of wealth, and are supposed to keep watch over his treasures.

The first and most celebrated of the posterity of PULASTYA were RÁVAŃA and his brethren—

——propago
Contemtrix superum, sœvæque avidissima cædis,
Et violenta.

The half brother of KUVERA the god of wealth, RÁVAŃA, a *Rákshasa* with ten heads, dispossessed that deity of his capital *Lanká*, in which he seated himself, and thence spread terror, not only over the world, but throughout the heavens, compelling many of the subordinate divinities to perform the menial functions of his palace. To terminate these violences and alarms, VISHŃU was obliged to come down to earth, where he was born as RÁMA or RÁMACHAṆDRA, the eldest son of DAŚARATHA, a prince of the Solar dynasty and sovereign of *Ayodhyá* or *Oude*, by his wife KAUŚALYÁ. Other portions of the same deity animated the sons of DAŚARATHA, by his other wives, KAIKEYÍ and SUMITRÁ, the former of whom gave birth to BHARATA, and the latter to LAKSHMAŃA and S'ATRUGHNA. A number of the minor deities and the attendant spirits of heaven likewise assumed terrestrial shapes, and in the form of apes and bears became the warriors and allies of RÁMA.

Whilst yet a lad, the services of Ráma were solicited by the sage Viśwámitra to repel and slay the fiends, by whom the religious rites of himself and other pious individuals were interrupted. Ráma accordingly accompanied him, destroyed the *Rákshasí* or female fiend Táraká, and slew or chased other evil genii from the residence of the sages. On this occasion Viśwámitra transferred to Ráma and his descendants the command of the celestial weapons, or the power to wield the elements in war.

After these exploits, Viśwámitra conducted Ráma to *Mithilá*, the kingdom of Janaka, whose daughter Sítá, now marriageable, was to reward the prowess of the prince who should bend a bow, given to an ancestor of the monarch of *Mithilá* by the god S'iva. Ráma alone succeeded in the attempt, and snapped the bow asunder. The indignity thus offered to his tutelary divinity aroused the wrath of Paraśuráma, a previous incarnation of Vishńu, still upon earth, who, coming to *Mithilá* to defy and exterminate Rámachandra, was foiled by his junior, and obliged to return, humbled and in peace, to the retirement whence he had hastened on hearing of the bow's being broken. Ráma received the recompense of his vigour in the hand of Sítá; and at the same time Urmilá her sister, and Mándaví and S'rutakírtti, her cousins, were married to the other three sons of Daśaratha.

When Ráma approached to years of maturity, his father, by the advice of his ministers, and according to the wishes of his people, proposed to associate him in the government as *Yuvarájá*, young king, or Cæsar: a delegation of authority that seems to have been constant under the old political system of the Hindus, and traces of which have been preserved to the present day, in the petty Hindu states to the east of Bengal. Domestic intrigue, however, forced Daśaratha to forego his purpose, and to change the elevation of Ráma into exile. His second wife, Kaikeyí, instigated by the counsels of a female attendant, insisted upon the king's fulfilment of a promise which he had formerly made, and which, like the pledge of the gods of *Olympus*, was not to be recalled, whatever mischief might ensue. DAŚARATHA, when formerly wounded dangerously in battle, was preserved by the cares of KAIKEYÍ; in acknowledgment of which service he offered her two boons whenever she should demand them. These she now claimed,—the installation of her son BHARATA, and the banishment of RÁMA for fourteen years, and DAŚARATHA was forced to comply, although upon the departure of his son he expired with grief. BHARATA refused to accept the succession to the throne, and hastened after RÁMA to bring him back to the capital; but that prince, in veneration of his father's memory, determined to fulfil his injunction, notwithstanding his decease; and leaving BHARATA regent during his absence, repaired to the forests of Southern India, accompanied by his wife, and LAKSHMAŃA his brother.

Conformably to current traditions, and the evidence of names assigned to different places in the peninsula, RÁMA passed from *Ayodhyá* to the south-west, and first established himself near the sources of the *Godávarí* in the *Dańdaka* forest. On his journey, and during his residence in the thickets, he encountered and discomfited various members of the RÁKSHASA tribe, and amongst others maltreated S'ÚRPAŃAHKÁ, the sister of RÁVAŃA, requiting the tender sentiments with which he inspired her by cutting off her nose and ears. She first applied to her brothers, KHARA and DÚSHAŃA, who guarded the forests with numerous bands of RÁKSHASAS, to avenge her; but when they were slain in the quarrel by the sons of DAŚARATHA, she carried her complaints to RÁVAŃA in *Lanká*, and instigated him to resent the injuries that had been inflicted on her person, especially by inspiring him with a passion for SÍTÁ. In order to effect his purpose RÁVAŃA repaired to *Panchávatí*, the residence of RÁMA, with MARÍCHA, the son of TÁRAKÁ, who, transforming himself into a deer, beguiled RÁMA from his cottage in chase of the supposed animal. LAKSHMAŃA, by desire of SÍTÁ, going to look for his brother, she was left alone, on which RÁVAŃA, approaching her as an old mendicant, then discarded his disguise, and carried her off. On his way he was at first stopped by

JAṬÁYU, a mythological being, a chief of the winged tribes, and a friend of DAŚARATHA, who was speedily overcome and left mortally wounded, and RÁVAŃA effected his retreat to *Lanká* without further opposition.

On returning to his cottage and searching for his missing bride, RÁMA discovered the wounded JAṬÁYU, and before he expired, learned from him who was the ravisher of SÍTÁ, but not his residence; in quest of which, he plunged into the forests in the central part of the peninsula, and by the advice of a headless monster, whom he slew, repaired to the mountain *Ŕishyamúka* at the sources of the *Pampá* river, where SUGRÍVA, the monarch of the monkeys, held his court. On arriving at this spot, he found the monkey monarchy distracted by intestine divisions, and SUGRÍVA deprived of his wife and shorn of his authority by his brother BÁLI. RÁMA having formed an alliance with SUGRÍVA, engaged and killed BÁLI, and restored to his associate the supreme sovereignty over the baboons, and the capital *Kishkindhyá*. SUGRÍVA, in acknowledgment of this service, dispatched his principal monkeys in all directions to discover SÍTÁ, in which search HANUMAT was successful. The party he accompanied, headed by ANGADA, the son of BÁLI, proceeded southward to the sea, where they encountered SAMPÁTI the brother of JAṬÁYU, by whom they were apprised of the site of *Lanká* and the detention of SÍTÁ there by its ten-headed king. HANUMAT undertook to seek her there; and jumping across the arm of the sea, obtained access to the palace where SÍTÁ was confined, and an interview with that princess. Having thus ascertained the place of her existence, HANUMAT, after setting *Lanká* on fire, returned to RÁMA, and conveyed to him the information which he had been sent out to procure.

On receipt of this intelligence, RÁMA, accompanied by SUGRÍVA and an innumerable host of his monkey subjects, advanced to the point of the peninsula opposite to the northern extremity of Ceylon, where a passage across the channel by which that island is separated from the Coromandel coast was accomplished, by casting rocks and mountains into the sea, and thus constructing a bridge, the vestiges of which are said to be still visible in the reef of rocks which render the Straits of Manar impassable to vessels of burthen. At this point, RÁMA was joined by VIBHÍSHAŃA, the brother of RÁVAŃA, who having in vain counselled the restitution of SÍTÁ, and incurred by his advice the displeasure of the sovereign of *Lanká*, deserted his cause and went over to the enemy.

Having crossed the sea and encamped in the vicinity of the capital of RÁVAŃA, the baboon army was encountered by the monstrous bands in the service of *Lanká*, and a variety of engagements ensued, which, although attended by the occasional discomfiture of the assailants, ended in the utter defeat of the RÁKSHASAS, and the death of RÁVAŃA by the hands of RÁMA. Upon his fall SÍTÁ was recovered; but before being readmitted to her husband's embraces, she was compelled to vindicate her purity by undergoing the ordeal of fire. Having passed unhurt through the blazing pile, and being further justified by the oral testimony of BRAHMÁ and other gods, as well as the spirit of DAŚARATHA, her father-in-law, she was once more united to RÁMA, who, installing VIBHÍSHAŃA in the kingdom of *Lanká*, over which he is supposed still to reign, returned to *Ayodhyá*, where BHARATA gladly restored the sovereignty to his brother.

The incidents that immediately followed the return of RÁMA to his capital form the subject of the drama, and therefore require no notice in this place. The catastrophe is, however, differently brought about in the RÁMÁYAŃA and *Raghuvaṁśa*, a poetical account of RÁMA and his race, and closes in a different manner. RÁMA discovers his sons in consequence of their recital of the RÁMÁYAŃA at his sacrifice, and SÍTÁ, upon her innocence being recognised by the people, is suddenly carried off by the goddess of the earth, and disappears for ever. This *denouement* is very judiciously altered to her reunion with her sons and husband, in the play. RÁMA died soon after the disappearance of SÍTÁ, and divided his kingdom between his sons; but KUŚA, being the elder, and having established his capital at *Ayodhyá*, is regarded as the continuer of the line of RAGHU. The *Kachwáha Rájpúts* affect to derive their descent from KUŚA, whilst another *Rájpút* tribe, the *Bádkuja*, regard LAVA as the founder of their race.

DRAMATIS PERSONÆ.

MEN.

Ráma.—King of *Ayodhyá.*

Kuśa, }
Lava, } his twin sons.

Lakshmańa.—The brother of *Ráma.*

Chandraketu.—The son of *Lakshmańa.*

Válmíki.—A holy sage, the author of the *Rámáyańa,* and preceptor of *Kuśa* and *Lava.*

Janaka.—The father of *Sítá,* formerly king of *Mithilá,* now leading an ascetic life.

Śambúka.—An ascetic killed by *Ráma,* but appearing in his spiritual character.

Ashíávakra.—An ascetic.

Sumantra.—The charioteer of *Chandraketu.*

Durmukha.—An emissary employed by *Ráma.*

Saudhátaki, }
Bháńďáyana, } two of *Válmíki's* pupils.

A *Vidyádhara.*—A male spirit of air.

WOMEN.

Sítá.—The wife of *Ráma.*

Arundhatí.—A pious dame, the wife of the sage *Vasishtha* and guardian of *Sítá.*

Átreyí.—A pious dame, the wife of the sage *Atri.*

Kauśalyá.—The aged mother of *Ráma.*

Vásantí.—The guardian spirit of the forest of *Janasthána.*

Tamasá.—A river goddess.

Muralá.—The same.

A Vidhyádhari.—A female spirit of air.

CHARACTERS IN THE SCENE IN THE LAST ACT.

Gangá.—The goddess of the Ganges.

Príthiví.—The goddess of the earth.

Celestial spirits, guards, pupils, &c.

THE SCENE of the first Act is in the Palace of *Ráma* at *Ayodhyá;* of the second, in the forest of *Janasthána* along the *Godávarí:* in the rest of the piece it lies in the vicinity of *Válmíki's* hermitage at *Bithúr* on the Ganges.

An interval of twelve years occurs between the first Act and the remainder of the play. The time of each Act is that of representation.

PRELUDE.

Enter MANAGER.

Man. I praise the feet of the illustrious *Bhavabhúti.** We present this our salutation to the celebrated bards of old, and thus we obtain the divine goddess of eloquence,† who is a portion of the Supreme Spirit.

This being the festival of the glorious *Kálapriya-Nátha,*‡ I apprise you, sirs, that we purpose representing the *Uttara-Ráma-Charitra,* the composition of *Bhavabhúti,* entitled *Śrí-Kańtha,* of the race of *Kaśyapa,* and assimilated to an equality with *Brahmá* by the favour of *Saraswatí.*§ I act a native of *Ayodhyá,*|| and a stranger approaches——

This is the season of the inauguration of the renowned Ráma,

* The first sentence in this introductory benediction, *Śrí-kavirája-Bhavabhúti-charańáni naumi,* is not noticed by the commentator, and has been omitted in the Calcutta edition of the text, in consequence, no doubt, of its being considered, as it evidently is, the work of a different hand. The rest of the passage is of a peculiar character, but is probably part of the original composition.

† Or, literally, "We acquire divine ambrosial speech."

‡ The *Málatí* and *Mádhava* was composed for a similar festival.

§ The goddess of eloquence and wife of *Brahmá ;* the allusions to *Bhavabhúti's* family decent are explained in the *Málatí* and *Mádhava.*

|| *Ayodhyá* is the original of the name now given to a whole province or kingdom, *Awadh* or *Oude.* It was formerly confined to the capital, the kingdom bearing the designation of *Kośalá.* It was for many years the sovereignty of the princes of the Solar line. The remains of the ancient city are still to be seen at the town of Oude, situated on the banks of the Ghagra, seventy-nine miles from Lucknow and adjoining Fyzabad.

the threatening meteor of the race of *Pulastya*;* and the drum of rejoicing sounds unweariedly by night and day. But what should this mean; why are the public places to-day so silent and unfrequented?

Enter ACTOR.

Act. The monkey chiefs,† and friendly fiends, and all the warriors in alliance with the prince in the war of Lanká, have

* Intending especially the giant king of *Lanká*, *Rávańa*, and his brothers destroyed in the war with *Ráma*. *Rávańa* was the son of the sage *Viśravas*, by *Nikashá*, the daughter of *Sumáli*, a demon, who, observing the splendour of *Kuvera*, a son of the sage by his wife *Iravirá*, directed his daughter to propitiate the sage, that she also might have children by him. Having succeeded in obtaining the good graces of *Viśravas*, *Nikashá* had by him *Rávańa*, *Kumbhakarńa*, and *Vibhíshańa*, and a daughter, *Śúrpańakhá*.

Rávańa was engendered after the performance of a sacrifice with fire, in consequence of which he was born of an uncouth appearance, with ten heads and twenty arms. *Viśravas*, his father, was the son of *Pulastya*, one of the will-begotten sons of *Brahmá*. Although, therefore, a holy sage, he is often alluded to as the progenitor of the *Rákshasas*, of which race *Rávańa* and his brethren were such distinguished members (*Uttara-Rámáyańa* and *Padma Puráńa*). The *Bhágavata* agrees nearly with them, but names the mother of the *Rákshasas*, *Khumbhínasí*.

A very different legend is given in the *Vana-Parvan*, of the *Mahábhárata*. *Pulastya*, the son of *Brahmá*, begot *Kuvera*, who, by paying great attention to his grandfather, was made by him immortal, and appointed the god of wealth. His capital was *Lanká*, and the *Rákshasas* were his guards. His currying favour with *Brahmá* incensed his father, and *Pulastya* assumed the form of a holy sage, named *Viśravas*. To propitiate this wrathful manifestation of his father was *Kuvera's* next object, and with this view he gave him three *Rákshasís* as handmaids, *Pushpotkatá*, *Ráká*, and *Málini*. By the first *Viśravas* had *Kumbhakarńa* and *Rávańa*; by the second, *Khara*, and a daughter, *Śúrpańakhá*; and by *Málini*, *Vibhíshańa*.—We have a different account again in the *Linga-Puráńa* (ch. 63). *Pulastya* had by *Iravilá*, the daughter of *Třińavindu*, a son named *Viśravas*, who had four wives: *Devavarńiní*, the daughter of *Vřihaspati*; *Pushpotkatá*, and *Ráká* (or *Váká*), the daughters of the demon *Mályavat*, and *Nikashá*, the daughter of the demon *Śallaki*. By the first he had *Kuvera*, or *Vaiśravańa*; by the second, *Mahodara*, *Prahasta*, *Mahápárśwa*, and *Khara*, and *Karńanasí*, a daughter; by the third he had *Triśiras*, *Dúshańa*, and *Vidyujjihwa*, and *Śyámiká*, a daughter; and by the last, or *Nikashá*, the virtuous *Vibhíshańa*.

† *Ráma* was accompanied on his return to *Ayodhyá* by *Vibhíshańa*, the brother and successor of *Rávańa*, and by the monkey chiefs, *Sugríva*, *Anga-*

been dismissed to their several homes, as have the holy sages, assembled from various realms, whose reception has been hitherto the occasion of perpetual festivity.

Mana. True: and the mothers of *Rághava*,* under the guidance of Vasishtha,† and preceded by Arundhatí,‡ have departed to the dwelling of their son-in-law.

Act. I am a stranger here, you know; inform me who is this son-in-law?

Mana. The late king *Daśaratha*§ had a daughter named *Śántá*, whom he gave to king *Lomapáda* to adopt, and whom *Ŕishyaśŕinga*,|| the son of *Vibháńdaka*, espoused.¶ He now holds the ceremony of the twelve years' sacrifice,** and the elders have gone to assist at its celebration, leaving, with his

da, and *Hanumat.* They assisted at his coronation, and then returned to their dwellings in the *Dekhin* and *Lanká.*

* Or Ráma. The term is a patronymic, implying his being a descendant of *Raghu.* His mothers are the widows of his father *Daśaratha* : *Kauśalyá*, the mother of Ráma; *Sumitrá*, the mother of *Lakshmańa* and the youngest son, *Śatrughna*; and *Kaikeyí*, the mother of the third son, *Bharata.*

† The family priest of Ráma's race, the son of *Brahmá* in one birth, and of *Mitra* and *Varuńa*, or the sun and the sea, in another.

‡ Arundhatí is the wife of Vasishtha.

§ *Daśaratha*, the son of *Aja* and father of Ráma, was a distinguished prince of the Solar dynasty. Buchanan supposes him to have lived in the fifteenth century before the Christian era.

|| *Ŕishyaśŕinga*, the *deer-horned*, was born of a doe, and had a small horn on his forehead; whence his name.

¶ These circumstances are all narrated in the *Rámáyańa* at length.—Book 1, sections viii. ix. x. *Lomapáda* was king of Anga.

** This number offers some analogy to the visits of the gods to Ethiopia's blameless race; when

"Twelve days the powers indulged the genial rite."

Macrobius, however, would read this twelve hours, or the interval between sun-set and sun-rise, when Jove, as that planet, is below the horizon. It is true, the original leaves him at liberty to propose such a reading, as neither days nor hours are specified in this place. The return of the deities, however, is more specific.

Twelve *days* were passed, and now the dawning light
The gods had summoned to the Olympian height.

The same critic conceives, also, that some allusion may be made to the permission, the daughter of Janaka* at the capital. But come, time wears; let us go meet our friends at the palace, as was appointed.

Act. But tell me, in your opinion, has the title of *Most Pure* been very judiciously granted by the king to his bride?

Mana. Mind your own affairs; why talk upon improper subjects? Men are ever evil disposed towards the purity of words and women.

Act. Most maliciously true: especially as the calumnies insinuated against *Vaidehí*,† in consequence of her residence in the dwelling of the *Rákshasa*, were refuted by her passing the fiery ordeal.‡

signs of the zodiac.—(Sat. 1. xxiii. Somn. Scipion. lib. 2.) The number has very possibly some secret import, astronomical or mythological, both amongst the Hindus and Greeks.

* *Janaka* was king of Mithila, and a man of great piety and learning. He was the reputed father of Sítá, the wife of Ráma, having found her an infant in the earth, upon ploughing it for a sacrifice.

† Sítá bears the patronymic *Vaidehí* as the daughter of the king of *Videha.*

‡ After the recovery of Sítá from *Rávańa*, Ráma welcomed her coldly, and after intimating some suspicions unfavourable to her chastity, refused to receive her: on which Sítá determined to commit herself to the test of fire. Having entered the fire prepared for this purpose in the presence of the gods and of *Daśaratha*, the deceased father of Ráma, it proved innocuous, and *Agni*, its deity, restored Ráma his bride unhurt, and declared her purified by the ordeal she had undergone. *Daśaratha* also bore testimony to Sítá's virtue, and Ráma's doubts being thus dissipated, he joyfully received his bride (*Uttara-Rámáyańa.*) According to the *Brahma-Vaivarta-Puráńa*, Sítá herself was not carried off by *Rávańa*, her shadow or *chháyá* being substituted by *Agni* for her substance. It was this semblance, also, that entered the fire, in order to give *Agni* an opportunity of restoring the original to Ráma. The *Padma-Puráńa* (*Pátála Khańda*) dispenses with the ordeal, but brings forward *Agni, Váyu, Varuńa, Brahmá*, and *Daśaratha* to swear to Sítá's innocence; *Brahmá* further consoles Ráma by declaring it was necessary Sítá should have been carried off by *Rávańa*, as his rape of a virtuous woman was the only cause of destruction to which he was subject, agreeably to the curse denounced upon him by *Nala-Kuvera*, and the previous boon conferred upon him by *Brahmá*. In the *Uttara-Khańda* of the same *Puráńa*, she enters into the fire, as in the other authorities.

Man. Yet, should such reports as are still current reach the king, they will cause him great distress.

Act. The sages and the gods will provide for the best. Where is his Majesty? (*Listening.*) Oh, I hear Janaka, his father-in-law, has just left him to return to his own kingdom; and the king has quitted his seat of justice to repair to the inner apartments to console the queen.

[*Exeunt.*

ACT I.

SCENE I.—THE PALACE.

RÁMA *and* SÍTÁ *discovered.*

Droop not, dear Sítá; our respected friends
Have parted from us with no less reluctance
Than we have felt, but duty must be done.
To loftier claims must self-indulgence yield;
And they who venerate their household fire
Must bear the task such sacred charge imposes.*

Sítá. I know the truth of this, my dearest lord;
But still to separate from our nearest friends
And cherished kindred, cannot choose but grieve us.

Ráma. True, love—
But these, the sorrows of a feeling heart,
Are the sad portion of man's social life:
And, fearing them, the sage abandons all,
To quell desire, in solitary woods.

Enter ATTENDANT.

Att. Rámabhadra! (*Checking himself.*) Mahárája!

Ráma. (*Smiling.*) My worthy friend: I better love to hear
The name of Rámabhadra, from the mouths
Of those who were my father's followers.†
What is your message?

Att. Ashťávakra waits,
From *Ŕishyaśŕinga's* hermitage.

Sítá. What should delay his entrance?

* The maintenance of a perpetual fire implies also the observance of all the occasions on which sacrifices with fire are offered, and all those duties which a householder is enjoined.

† The mode here adopted of delineating Ráma's kindly disposition is very Shakespearian.

Enter the Ascetic ASHṬÁVAKRA.*

Ash. Health and peace to both!
Ráma. Respect await you, venerable sir!
Be seated.
Sítá. I salute you with respect;
And hold me highly honoured to receive
The pious kinsman of my sainted sister.
Ráma. No cares disturb my brother's holy peace,
Nor my respected sister's!
Sítá. Dwell we ever in their recollection?
Ash. Assuredly. They are well. Lady, to you
The sage Vasishṫha thus addresses him.
Thy mother is the all-sustaining earth;
Thy father is a king of no less fame
Than the primeval patriarchs; thy lord
Draws his proud lineage from the king of day,

* *Ashṭávakra* is the hero of a curious legend in the *Mahábhárata*. *Kahoḋa*, his father, was the pupil of *Uddálaka* and married his preceptor's daughter. He was so much addicted to study that he rather neglected his bride when far advanced in her pregnancy, and was rebuked for his conduct by his son yet unborn. The father indignantly pronounced that he should be born crooked, in punishment of his impertinence, and hence his name *Ashṭa*, eight (limbs), and *Vakra*, curved. *Kahoḋa* went to the great sacrifice of Janaka, king of *Mithilá*, soon after the birth of his son. To that festival came a seeming *Bauddha* sage, who, overcoming all his competitors in argument, had them thrown into the river. *Kahoḋa* venturing to encounter him suffered this fate. When Ashṭávakra was in his twelfth year he first heard of his father's mischance, and to revenge it, set off for the yet unfinished sacrifice, it being one of those already noticed as of twelve years' duration. Although young in age, the saint was mature in wisdom, and overcame his father's conqueror. When he insisted on his being thrown into the river, the supposed disputant declared himself to be the son of *Varuṅa*, the god of the same waters, who had commenced a similar sacrifice with that of Janaka, at the same time, and to secure the attendance of learned *Brahmans*, had adopted the expedient of sending his son to defeat them in disputation, and give them a subsequent ducking. The object being effected, they were dismissed with honour, and the parties separated mutually content. Ashṭávakra, by his father's instructions, bathed in the *Samangá* river, and by so doing was rendered perfectly straight. (*Máhábhárata, Vana-Parvan.*)—He was married to the daughter of the sage *Vadánya.*—(*Dána-Dharma.*)

And his illustrious house have ever owned
Our spiritual guidance. What alone remains?
That from thee spring an offspring to inherit
The conjoint honours of each glorious race?

Ráma. I thank the sage. In this imperfect world,
Man's tardy speech lags after things foregone;
But with the saints, the thoughts their lips express,
Precede, and presage sure, events to come.

Ash. Arundhatí and all the holy dames,
And S'ántá, bid thee well consider this:
Now there is hope of heirs, what must be done
Must be effected speedily.

Ráma. Declare it:
What must be done?

Ash. This *Ŕishyaśŕinga* tells me to impart.
Thou, queen,* art not ungentle. This, my son,
Is destined to secure thy happiness;
And I shall see thee bearing on thy lap
A smiling progeny.

Ráma. So may it be!
Is there aught else Vasishťha's wish ordains?

Ash. Attend.
The holy sacrifice absorbs our care,
And you, my son, are young in years and power.
Remember therefore that a king's true wealth,
His real glory, is his people's welfare.

Ráma. So *Maitrávaruńi* † has ever taught us:
And I am ready, pity, pleasure, love,
Nay, even Sítá, to resign, content,
If it be needful for the general good.

Sítá. In this my lord does honour to his race.

Ráma. Who waits? Attend upon the sage.

Ash. (*Rises and circumambulates them.*)
Behold the prince. [*Exit.*

* Or in the text *kaťhoragarbhá*, in reference to her protracted pregnancy.

† A name of Vasishťha, the son of *Mitra* and *Varuńa*.

Enter LAKSHMAŃA.

Laksh. Glory to Ráma!
Come, my most noble brother, on these walls
Behold a skilful artist has portrayed
Your story, as he learnt the tale from me.

Ráma. You have the skill
To dissipate our queen's uneasiness.
How far proceeds the tale, good brother?

Laksh. To where the queen
Was purified by flame.

Ráma. Most pure by birth,
She needed not the consecrated wave,
Nor sacred fire, to sanctify her nature.

Laksh. Daughter of sacrifice, respected Sítá,
Secure of a devotion that will cease
With life alone, forgive me.

Ráma. The base herd
Of men may censure rank and worth unheeded
But their foul calumnies do not deserve
By thee to be repeated. The flower that breathes
With nature's fragrance, on the brow should blossom,
Nor with contempt be trampled on the ground.*

Sítá. Come, let us see these paintings.

[*They rise and Exeunt.*

SCENE II.—THE GARDEN OF THE PALACE, WITH A PAVILION.

Enter LAKSHMAŃA, SÍTÁ, *and* RÁMA.

Laksh. Behold the picture! †

* This idea occurs in *Málati* and *Mádhava*.

† A long scroll in compartments, apparently fixed against a wall. Such pictures being panoramic representations of holy places usually, are still not uncommon, whilst the *Máhabhárata* and *Rámáyańa*, in illuminated and embellished portable scrolls, are very frequent. It is not uncommon, also, in the Western Provinces, to meet with a kind of fresco painting upon the walls of gardens, or enclosures of tanks, representing mythological or historical subjects.

Sítá. What are these that crowd
Around my lord, and seem to hymn his praises?
Laksh. They are the heavenly arms, that *Viśwámitra*,*
The holy sage from *Kuśa* sprung, the friend
Of all mankind, obtained from great *Kriśáśwa*,†

* *Viśwámitra* was born a prince in the Lunar dynasty. According to the *Rámáyańa* he was the fourth from *Prajápati*, but the *Bhágavata* makes him the fifteenth from *Brahmá*. They agree in calling him the son of *Gádhi*, who, according to the first, was the son of *Kuśanábha*, and according to the second, the son of *Kuśámba*. *Viśwámitra* was sovereign of Kanoj, and engaged in war with the sage *Vasishtha* for the possession of the all-bestowing cow. In this contest, the cow produced all sorts of forces, particularly *Mlechchhas*, or barbarians, by whose aid *Vasishtha* overcome his adversary. There can be little doubt that this legend is an allegorical account of a real transaction, and that by the cow we are to understand India, or the most valuable portion of it, for the sovereignty of which either two princes or two tribes, the *Bráhmans* and *Kshattriyas*, contended. One of the parties calling to their aid the barbarians, the Persians, and not impossibly the Greeks, triumphed by their means. *Viśwámitra* was born a sage, in consequence of his mother partaking of some charmed food prepared by the *Muni Ŕichika* for his wife, her daughter. After observing the superior might of the *Bráhmans*, he engaged in a course of austerities, to rise from the martial order in which he was born to that of the sacerdotal, and ultimately compelled *Brahmá* to grant him that elevation. (*Rámáyańa*, 1. Sect. 41-52, *Mahábhárata, Ádi-Parvan, Bhágavata*, ix. 15, &c.)

† Two sovereigns of the name of *Kriśáśwa* are traceable, one a king of *Ayodhyá*, the other of *Viśálá*. The position of the former in the Solar genealogy stands thus in Buchanan's authorities:

Bhágavata.	Vaḿśa-Latá.	Hari-Vaḿśa.
Nikumbha	Nikumbha	Nikumbha
Várhadaśwa	Várhadáśwa	Sanghátáśwa
Kriśáśwa	Kriśáśwa	Kriśáśwa
Senájit	Yuvanáśwa	Prasenajit
Yuvanáśwa		Yuvanáśwa.

But the *Vishńu-Puráńa* goes from *Nikumbha* to *Prasenajit* at once, omitting the two intermediate princes.

Kriśáśwa, the sovereign of *Viśálá*, is the son of *Saḿyama* and father of *Somadatta*, according to the *Bhágavata* and *Vaḿśa-Latá*. Buchanan is mistaken in supposing the former interposes a *Sahadeva* between him and *Saḿyama*. *Devaja* or *Devaka* is the son of *Saḿyama*, with *Kriśáśwa* or his brother. The mistake arises from considering *saha, with*, as part of the

And gave them to the prince to wage the fight
With that malignant demon *Táraká.**

Ráma. Pay reverence, Sítá, to the arms divine.
The ancient sages and the gods themselves
By penance for a thousand years endured,
Obtained the sight of these celestial arms,
Radiant and holy, for the wars of heaven.†

name. The text has, *Saṁyamád ásít Kriśáśwaḱ saha-Devajaḱ:* explained by the comment, *Devajena* or *Devakena sahitaḱ.*

Buchanan places the *Ayodhyá* prince in the eighteenth century before Christ, and the sovereign of *Viśálá* in the fourteenth; the latter is, therefore, made subsequent to Ráma, who is supposed by him to have flourished in the fifteenth.

Neither of these persons, however, appears to be the *Kŕiśáśwa* of the text, who is more probably a sage. One so named, a *Muni* or *Devarshi,* is said to have married two of the daughters of *Daksha, Jayá* and *Vijayá,* according to the *Rámáyańa,* but *Archi* and *Dhishańá* in the *Bhágavata.* He is also said to have been a writer on dramatic representation: whence an actor or a dancer is termed in the *Amara-Kosha, Kŕiśáświn.* Nothing further of him has been ascertained.

* A female fiend, the daughter of the *Yaksha Suketu,* and wife of the *Daitya Sunda.* She was changed into the form of a *Rákshasí,* after the death of her husband, by the curse of the sage *Agastya.* Having devastated the flourishing districts of *Malaja* and *Karusha,* and obstructing the sacrifices of the sages, *Viśwámitra* applied to Ráma for aid, and her destruction was his first exploit. (*Rámáyańa,* 1. Sec. 23-25.)

† These weapons are of a very unintelligible character. Some of them are occasionally wielded as missiles, but in general they appear to be mystical powers exercised by the individual: such as those of paralysing an enemy, or locking his senses fast in sleep, or bringing down storm and rain and fire from heaven. In the usual strain of the Hindu mythology, they are supposed to assume celestial shapes, endowed with human faculties, and in this capacity are alluded to in the text. The list of them, one hundred, is given in the first book of the *Rámáyańa,* and there also they are described as embodied, and address Ráma, saying, "Command us, Oh, *Rághava* of mighty arm—Here we are, Oh, chief of men, command us; what shall we do for thee?" The son of *Raghu* replied: "Depart all of you, and in time of necessity when called to mind, render me assistance. They then circumambulated Ráma, and having said, So be it, received his permission to depart, and went whence they came." The *Rámáyańa* calls them also the sons of *Kŕiśáśwa* and the sons of *Jayá* and *Vijayá,* the daughters of *Prajápati.* (*Rámáyańa,* 1. Sec. 20, 26, and 42.)

Sítá. (*Bowing.*) Receive my adoration.—

Ráma. They will aid
Thy children.

Sítá. I am grateful.

Laksh. There, the scene
Is changed to Mithilá.*

Sítá. Yes, I see my lord.
Dark as the deep blue lotus is his hue,
And strength and grace in every limb appear.
Paternal looks dwell wondering on his face,
Lovely with graceful curls, whilst high disdain
Swells every feature, as with force divine,
He snaps asunder the celestial bow.†

Laksh. See where your sire and the holy son
Of *Gautama*, the priest of Janaka,‡
Welcome Vasishťha and the rest who now
Become their kin!

Ráma. No wonder; for the alliance that united
Raghu with Janaka, could to none
Be else than pleasing, and where *Viśwámitra*
Himself was donor and receiver.

Sítá. A solemn scene, where gifts of kine secure
Auspicious destiny, and four bright youths
Are knit in marriage bonds with four fair maids.§

* The country north of the Ganges, between the *Gandaki* and *Kosi* rivers, comprehending the modern provinces of *Puraniya* and *Tirhut*. The remains of the capital founded by Janaka, and thence termed *Janakapur*, are still to be seen, according to Buchanan, on the northern frontier; at the *Janickpoor* of the maps.

† This bow originally belonged to *Śiva*, who wielded it victoriously against the other gods at *Daksha's* sacrifice, but without success, against *Vishńu*, on which he gave it to *Devaráta*, one of Janaka's ancestors, subsequent to whom it remained in the family. Like the bow of *Ulysses*, it was employed by Janaka to ascertain the strength of the candidates for his daughter's hand, none of whom were able to bend it; but it was broken with ease by Ráma. (*Rámáyańa*, 1. Sec. 52, 53, and 62.)

‡ *Śatánanda*, the son of *Gautama* and *Ahalyá*, and family priest of the king of *Mithilá*.

§ The sons of *Daśaratha* were *Ráma*, *Lakshmańa*, *Bharata*, and *Śa-*

I recognise you all;—and there—and then,
Am I.

Ráma. The season, too, is there recalled,
When the sage son of *Gautama*, thy hand,
With golden bands begirt, as if it were
The festival embodied, placed in mine.

Laksh. Behold the princess, and this is *Máńđaví*—
This *Śrutakírtti*—

Sítá. And the fourth—

Laksh. Why ask me?
You know that this is *Úrmilá.*
But here direct your eye—'tis *Bhárgava.**

Sítá. His look alarms me.

Ráma. Reverence to the saint.

Laksh. You should observe him well; for he, by Ráma—

Ráma. (*Interrupting.*)
Much else remains that more deserves attention.

Sítá. This modesty full well becomes my lord.

Laksh. Here we are in *Ayodhyá.*

Ráma. Ah! too well,
Too well does memory bring back the time,
When yet an honoured sire was alive,
Whilst yet a mother's love watched o'er our being;

trughna. At the time that Sítá was married to the former, the other daughter of Janaka, *Úrmilá*, was given to Lakshmańa, and the two other brothers were married to *Máńđaví* and *Śrutakírtti*, the daughters of *Kuśadhwaja*, the sovereign of *Sankáśya*, or, according to the *Agni Puráńa*, of *Káśí* or Benares, and brother of Janaka.

* The descendant of *Bhŕigu*, *Paraśuráma*, who was an incarnation of *Vishńu* for the destruction of the *Kshattriyas*. He was the son of *Jamadagni* the son of Ŕichíka, the son of *Bhŕigu* according to some, and grandson according to others. Being a disciple of *Śiva*, he was highly incensed at the presumption of *Rámachandra*, and intercepted him on his return, to punish him for breaking the bow of that deity. He was compelled, however, to acknowledge the superiority of the younger warrior; and after deprecating his anger, retired to a life of devotion on mount *Mahendra*.—(*Rámáyańa*, i. 72.) In the *Mahábhárata*, Ráma shoots arrows at him, and strikes him senseless.

When all was joy. Ah, me! those days are gone.
But here behold—see how the youthful bride,
Fair Sítá, wins maternal admiration:
Her smiling countenance resplendent shines
With youth and loveliness; her lips disclose
Teeth white as *jasmine* buds; her silky curls,
Luxuriant shade her cheeks, and every limb
Of slightest texture moves with natural grace,
Like moonbeams gliding through the yielding air.

Laksh. Here is the wretched *Mantharú.**

Ráma. (*Turning away.*)
Look here, love!—see the groves of *Śŕingavera*,†
Where from the monarch of the forest tribes
We met a friendly welcome.

Laksh. (*Apart.*) He avoids
The conduct of his step-dame. ‡

Sítá. And now behold assumed,
The braid of penance. §

Laksh. Yes: the task severe,
The elders of our race their state deposed,
In favour of their progeny adopted, ||
Was here by youth sustained; and opening life,
Content to languish in the forest's gloom.

* The confidential attendant of *Kaikeyí*, the second wife of *Daśaratha*, by whose instigations that princess opposed Ráma's accession to the throne, and insisted on his exile.

† *Śŕingavera* was a city on the north bank of the Ganges (or more properly a village, as the country on both sides of the Ganges was here a forest), inhabited by *Nishádas* or wild tribes, of whom *Guha* was the chief, by whose assistance Ráma, Lakshmańa, and Sítá were ferried over to the south bank of the Ganges, a day's march above its junction with the Jumna.

‡ Of *Kaikeyí.*

§ The *Jaťá*, or matted hair, assumed by Ráma and Lakshmańa on dismissing the royal chariot at the village of *Śŕingavera*, to indicate their entering upon a forest or ascetic life.—(Rám. ii. 40.)

|| It appears to have been customary for the ancient princes of the Hindus, when enfeebled by years, to transfer the crown to the successor and retire to a hermitage.

Sítá. Behold—the pure and sacred *Bhágírathí.**

Ráma. Goddess benign, who o'er the race of *Raghu*
Thy guardian care extendest, I salute thee!
Thy downward path *Bhagírath's* prayers propell'd,
And thy pure waves redeem'd his ancestry,
Reduced to ashes by the wrath of *Kapila*,
As through the bowels of the earth they sought
The steed escaped from *Sagara's* sacrifice.†
Deign, heavenly mother, to bestow thy care
On this thy daughter, and with emulous love,
Like chaste Arundhatí, her days defend.

Laksh. See, *Bharadwája's* ‡ hermitage, the road

* The Ganges, so named from having been brought down to earth by the devotions of king *Bhagíratha.*

† *Sagara*, purposing to perform an *Aśwamedha*, or sacrifice of a horse, set, as an essential part of the ceremony, the horse at liberty, who was carried off by one of the serpents of *Pátála*. The king directed his sons, by his wife *Sumati*, sixty thousand in number, to recover the steed. Their efforts, though unavailing, were enough to alarm the gods and demons, and to ensure their own destruction. After penetrating deep towards the subterraneous regions, they came upon the horse grazing near *Kapila*, an incarnation of *Vishńu* as a sage, whom the sons of *Sagara* challenged as the thief of the horse. *Kapila*, incensed, reduced them all to ashes with a blast from his nostrils. *Aḿśumat*, the son of *Asamanjas*, the son of *Sagara*, by his other wife, *Keśiní*, afterwards discovered the reliques of his uncles, and learned from *Garuda*, also their uncle, that the waters of the Ganges were necessary to procure them admission to heaven. Neither *Sagara* nor his successors, *Aḿśumat* and *Dilípa*, were able to effect the descent of Gangá, this being reserved for the son and successor of the latter, *Bhagíratha*. The austerities of this prince successively propitiating *Brahman*, *Umá*, and *Mahádeva*, the Ganges was, by their power, compelled to flow over the earth, following *Bhagíratha* to the sea, and thence to *Pátála*, where the ashes of his ancestors were laved by its waters. The Ganges was called *Bhágírathí*, in honour of the king, and the ocean termed *Ságara*, in commemoration of *Sagara* and his sons.—(Ráma, i. 35.)

‡ The accounts of this individual are rather obscure, but he was a Muni and expounder of the *Vedas*. In some places he is called the son of *Vŕihaspati*, and in the *Harivaḿśa* is said to have been adopted by *Bharata* as king of *Pratishṫhána*. In the *Rámáyańa* he appears as a sage residing at *Prayága*, or Allahabad, where a temple dedicated to him still exists. In the *Mahá-*

To *Chitrakúta*,* and the sable tree
That shades *Kálindí's* † borders.

Sítá. Does my lord
Recall these scenes to memory?

Ráma. Could it be,
That I should ever cease to recollect them?
I see you now, as on my breast reclined
And in my arms sustained, that delicate frame,
Exhausted with the long and weary way,
Sinks in o'erpowering slumber.

Laksh. Behold *Virádha*, ‡ who denies admission
To *Vindhya's* § thickets.

bhárata he is described as residing at Haridwára, and the father of *Droṅa*, the military preceptor of the *Páńḋava* and *Kaurava* princes. He is also the parent of *Arundhatí*, the wife of *Vasishṫha*.

* A mountain not far from the south bank of the Jumna, Ráma's first residence in his exile, and, according to the *Rámáyańa*, at that time the seat of *Válmíki's* hermitage. Many temples and establishments of *Vaishńava* ascetics exist at this spot, now called *Chitrakote*, and it is at different seasons a place of great resort.

† The *Kálindí* is the Jumna river, the daughter of *Kalinda*, a name of the sun. The tree should be the imperishable *Ber* tree, which has long been famed at *Allahabad*, and which is still represented by a withered stem in the cave of *Pátálapurí*, under-ground, but it should appear from the text that it grew in daylight, and the play probably preceded the construction of the cavern. There was, no doubt, a very ancient and venerable fig tree at Allahabad, perhaps for some centuries, for it is alluded to in various vocabularies as *Medini*, &c.; it is also described in the *Káśíkhańḋa*, and *Kúrma-Puráńa*. The first notice, however, is in the *Rámáyańa* (B. II. Sect. 41 and 42); Ráma, with his wife and brother resting under the shade of it after crossing the Jumna; so that not only was the tree in the open air, but it was on the opposite side of the river to that on which it is now traditionally venerated.

‡ A demon of formidable size and aspect, the son of *Kála* and *Śatahradá*, residing in *Dańḋakárańya*, and encountered by Ráma on his leaving the hermitage of Atri. Having seized Sítá, and threatened to devour the princes, he was attacked by them and slain by Ráma.—(*Rámáyańa*, B. III. Sect. 7, 8.)

§ The Vindhya mountains extend across Central India, and throw out branches behind Agra and Delhi to the north, and on the south to the extremity of the Peninsula.

Sítá. He is too horrible.
Mark where my lord collects the broad palm leaves,
And weaves a shade to screen me from the sun,
As to the forests of the south we travel.

Ráma. We come to where, amidst the southern forests,
By mountain brooks the holy sages dwell,
And here they spread their simple stores,* and cheer
The stranger guest with hospitable right.

Laksh. Amidst the thicket tall *Prasravańa*
Rears its dark brow, eternally with clouds
Invested, from whose watery stores, assembled
Within the echoing caverns, fair *Godávarí*
Bursts forth, and down the mountain wends her way
Through gloomy shades and thick entangling woods.

Ráma. Recall'st thou, love, our humble happy dwelling
Upon the borders of the shining stream,
Where every hour, in fond endearments wrapped,
Or in sweet interchange of thought engaged,
We lived in transport, not a wish beyond
Each other, reckless of the flight of time?

Laksh. See *Panchávatí* † next, and here behold
The demon *Śúrpańakhá.* ‡

Sítá. Ha, my dear lord,
Behold! (*As if alarmed.*)

Ráma. How now! afraid of separation?
'Tis but a picture, love.

Sítá. I cannot chuse,
But suffer terror at so vile a presence.

* Or, dress a handful of the *nivdra* or wild rice.

† The forest along the Godávarí.

‡ The sister of *Rávańa*, a female fiend of hideous form and sanguinary propensities. Having seen Ráma on the banks of the Godávarí, she offered herself as a bride to him, and on his refusal to Lakshmańa; but both rejecting her advances, she attempted to destroy Sítá, on which Lakshmańa by his brother's commands cut off her nose and ears. She fled to her brothers *Khara* and *Dúshańa*, and incited them to revenge her.—(*Rámay.* B. III. Sect. 23, 24.)

Ráma. The sad events that Janasthána * witnessed
Are once more present here.
Laksh. And here again,
The anguish which the craft of wicked fiends
And violence inflicted is renewed,
And the rude stone and adamantine rock
Dissolve in gentle pity, as they witness
The prince's sorrows in the lonely forest.
Sítá. Alas! that the delight of Raghu's race
For me should thus have suffered.
Laksh. Let us avert our thoughts
To subjects more auspicious. Here, observe
Displayed the valour of the great *Jatáyu*,
The ancient monarch of the winged tribes,
Of days coeval with a *Manu's* reign,
From *Kaśyapa* descended.† Here, extend
The forests of the west, where from the gloom
The headless sprite ‡ our devious path arrested.

* According to the comment, this place in the present age is called *Nasik*, situated on the Godávarí, not far from the Western Ghats, and a place of pilgrimage.

† *Jatáyu*, a bird of divine nature and descent and preternatural longevity, the son of *Garuda*, the son of *Kaśyapa*. He was the friend of *Daśaratha*, and on one occasion saved his life. That prince having gone to the ecliptic to rescue *Rohińí* from the hands of *Śani*, his carriage was consumed by a glance from the eye of the latter. *Daśaratha* falling was caught and sustained by *Jatáyu* on his expanded wings. When Sítá was carried off by *Rávańa*, *Jatáyu* attempted to stop him, but was slain by the *Rákshasa*.

‡ This *Kabandha* or headless monster is possibly the original of the anthropophagi of the East, and the "men whose heads do grow beneath their shoulders." He is described as vast as a mountain, of a sable hue, without legs; but with arms a league long, a formidable mouth in his belly, and a single eye of vast dimensions in his breast. He seized with his long arms both Ráma and Lakshmańa with an intention to devour them, but the princes extricated themselves by cutting off his arms. The monster then inquiring who they were, and being informed of their names and lineage, rejoiced in his mutilation as the means of freeing him from a form to which he had been metamorphosed from that of a handsome *Dánava*, the grandson of *Danu*, one of the wives of *Kaśyapa*, in consequence of the impre-

The mountain *Ŕishyamúka** see, and here
The dwelling of *Matanga.*†—This, the dame ‡
Whose life of penance now obtained reward.
Here are the sources of the *Pampá*,§ where
The grief of Ráma broke beyond restraint,
And fast descending tears at intervals
Concealed from view the beauties of the scene.||
Here mark the son of air, the monkey chief,
Of strength resistless and wide-wasting wrath.
The guardian of the world—the firm ally
Of *Raghu's* race—illustrious *Hanumat.*

cation of a *Ŕishi* named *Sthúlaśiras* as a punishment for his frightening the ascetics by assuming hideous shapes. The effects of the curse were produced by his defying *Indra*, who in the contest struck off his head and legs with his thunderbolt, but could not kill him, as he had obtained the boon of longevity from *Brahmá*. The appearance of Ráma was the term of his transformation, and his body being burnt by his desire, he recovered his original shape and returned to *Swarga*, previously directing Ráma to seek the residence of *Sugríva*. (*Rámáyańa*, III. 82, 83, 84.)

* This mountain, and the scenes in its vicinity alluded to, are said to be known by the same appellations in the neighbourhood of *Anagundi*, a part of the Dekhin, the maps of which are disgracefully defective. The mountain itself was the residence of the deposed monarch of the monkeys, *Sugríva*. It comprised, of course, the whole of the tract about the sources of the *Pampá*; but in the *Rámáyańa*, Ráma passes them before he comes to the dwelling of the monkey chief.

† On the ascent to the mountain occurs the forest of *Matanga*, or the *Meghaprabha* wood, in which the trees never wither and the flowers never fade. The saint and his disciples had long disappeared; but his hermitage had remained inaccessible to noxious or inimical beings, and the cooking utensils left by him, awaited, in perfect order, the arrival of Ráma, being destined for his accommodation.

‡ A *Śarari*, or female forester, named *Sravańá*, who had attended on *Matanga's* disciples, and whose ascension to *Swarga* was to be the reward of her acting as guide to Ráma.

§ A river rising in the *Ŕishyamúka* mountain, and flowing into the *Tungabhadra*, below *Anagundi*.

|| Not, however, before expatiating upon them at great length, at least in the *Rámáyańa*, *Árańyakáńda*, last section. The MSS. from which the translation was made differs here in many respects from the Calcutta edition.

Ráma. Reverence and glory to our hero friend!
Here let us pause, for every scene suggests
Heart-rending recollections.

Laksh. But a moment—
Regard the deeds incredible the hands
Of monkey warriors in their rage achieve.
Here view our triumph*—Now we close the scene.†

Sítá. My dearest lord, this picture has inspired
A foolish fancy;—may I give it utterance?

Ráma. Fear not to speak it, love.

Sítá. I long once more to wander through the shades ‡
Of the brown woods, and plunge amidst the wave
Of *Bhágírathí's* cool translucent stream.

Ráma. Lakshmańa!

Laksh. I understand you, and will order forth
The easy rolling car without delay;
As such desires the learned have declared
Should speedily be gratified.§ [*Exit.*

Sítá. But you will sure be with me, my good lord?

Ráma. Cruel! what need to ask your Ráma this?
Come, let us enter this pavilion, love.

Sítá. Most willingly; unusual lassitude
Creeps o'er my frame and woos me to repose.

Ráma. Recline on me, thy couch, and around my neck
Throw those dear arms, the lovely, living band
Of moon-gems melting in the lunar ray,
As weariness the pearly drops exhales.—

* The death of *Rávańa* and defeat of his troops, with the capture of *Lanká.*

† A few exclamatory sentences are henceforward omitted, and the description of the picture is compressed.

‡ Sítá's exposure required her own concurrence, which the desire she has just intimated affords. It is also ominous of what is to follow.

§ The term *dohada* usually signifies the desire of a pregnant woman, or longing, to which the Hindus attach equal importance as did the nations of Europe.

What can this mean? a sudden transport glows
In every nerve, shedding such strange emotion;
I know not whether it be pain or pleasure,
If poison parch my veins, or I have quaffed
The maddening wine-cup. Can such magic, hid
In this fair touch, thus overcome my nature?

Sítá. It is thy constant love; no charms of mine.

Ráma. Thy tender voice revives life's languid blossom;
And whilst its sound subdues each softening sense,
It comes like heavenly nectar on the ear,
And pours its balmy medicine on the soul.

Sítá. Dear flatterer, cease; here let us taste repose.

[*Looking round.*

Ráma. What seeks my Sítá? Be these arms thy pillow,
Thine, ever since the nuptial knot united us,
Thine, in the days of infancy and youth,
In lonely thickets and in princely palaces,
Thine ever—thine alone.

Sítá. True—true—my ever kind and cherished lord.

[*Sleeps.*

Ráma. Her latest waking words are words of love,
And nought of her but is most dear to me.
Her presence is ambrosia to my sight;
Her contact, fragrant sandal; her fond arms,
Twined round my neck, are a far richer clasp
Than costliest gems; and in my house she reigns
The guardian goddess of my fame and fortune.
Oh! I could never bear again to lose her.

Enter ATTENDANT.

Att. My lord, there waits—

Ráma. Who?

Att. Your personal attendant, Durmukha.

Ráma. He brings me word of what reports are spread
Amongst the citizens. Go, bid him enter.

[*Exit* ATTENDANT.

Enter DURMUKHA.*

Dur. (*To himself.*) How can I venture to communicate
The idle calumnies the giddy people
Invent against the queen?—No matter;
Unhappy that I am, it is my duty.

Sítá. (*In her sleep.*) Where art thou, dearest Ráma?

Ráma. She dreams that I have left her; or the view
Of our portrayed adventures has disturbed
Her gentle slumbers. Ah! how blest is he
Who ever dwells in long confirmed affection,
Alike in pleasure or in pain, whose heart
Reposes tranquilly in every fortune,
And on whose waning, as his budding life,
Love constant waits. Oh! how can fate be won
To grant such happiness?

Dur. Hail to the king!

Ráma. What hast thou to report?

Dur. The people are ill pleased; the general cry
Is, *Rámabhadra* disregards his subjects.

Ráma. What reason have they thus to think of me?
Declare what fault they charge me with.

Dur. 'Tis thus they talk. [*Whispers.*

Ráma. Shame on the vile traducer who assails
Domestic happiness! No common means
Redeem'd *Vaidehí*† from the former scourge
Of foul calumnious tongues; yet scandal foams,
Like a mad hound, with still o'erflowing venom.
What 's to be done? Alas! what choice remains?
The general good must be preferred. To that
My father sacrificed his son—his life—
And I must do my duty. Now it chances
As by the sage *Vasishtha* 'twas foretold.
My noble ancestors, the lofty race
That boast the sun their sire, have bequeathed

* The *kanchukin*, or chamberlain; an old Bráhman is the fittest person.

† Sítá.

A spotless reputation to my keeping;
And how shall I deserve the glorious charge
If calumny attach to aught that's mine?
Daughter of sacrifice! Fair child of earth!
Glory of Janaka's exalted race!
The loved of sages and their sainted dames!
Casket of Ráma's being! Cheering light
Of the dark forest-dwelling! Utterer
Of tender eloquence! Alas! what cause
Has rendered destiny thy ruthless foe?
All thy good deeds, distorted, turn to ill;
All thy munificence awards thee shame;
And whilst thou art about to give the world
A worthy lord, that world, ingrate, condemns
Thee to a widowed, solitary home.
Durmukha, go, bid Lakshmańa attend
To lead the queen to exile.

Dur. How so, my lord? must she, whose spotless fame
The flame has evidenced, in whom there live
The hopes of *Raghu's* line, be banished hence,
To please a thankless and malignant people?

Ráma. Nay, blame them not. No lack of love or honour
Towards the royal house, but adverse destiny
Instils these thoughts. And who, that witnessed not
The wondrous test of purity, could credit
Such marvels in a distant region wrought?
Go, then, and do our bidding.

Dur. Alas, poor queen! [*Exit*.

Ráma. Cruel task! I have become a savage.
The wife whose every hour since infancy
To me has been devoted, and whom all
Beloved by me have tenderly caressed,
I ruthlessly and fraudulent consign,
Like a domestic bird, to certain death.
Wretch that I am! why shall my touch impure
Pollute these charms? Hold me not thus—let loose

Your tender grasp, dear Sítá, from a man
Whom every crime degrades. You think you cling
Around the sandal's fragrant trunk, and clasp
The baleful poison-tree—let go—thus—thus.

[*Detaches himself and rises.*

What now is life?—a barren load; the world?—
A dreary, arid, solitary wild.
Where can I hope for comfort? Sense was given me
Only to make me conscious of affliction,
And firmly bound in an unyielding frame.
Departed sires! prophets and sages! all
Whom I have loved and honoured!* and all ye
Who have shown honour and regard for Ráma!
Celestial flame! auspicious parent, Earth!
To whom amongst ye dare I raise my voice?
What name may I invoke, nor wrong its sanctity?
Will ye not shrink from my solicitation
As from an outcast's touch; from me, who chase
My wife, the honour of my house, away,
And doom *Kat́horagarbhá*† to despair,
Like a dread offering to infernal fiends?

[*Bows down to Sítá's feet.*

Adored *Vaidehí!* for the last, last time,
Thy lovely feet exalt the head of Ráma.

(*Without.*) Help! help for the Bráhman tribe!‡

Ráma. How now!

Enter MESSENGER.

Mess. The assembled sages on the *Yamuná's* bank,
Disturbed amidst their ritual by *Lavańa*,§
The demon, fly to Ráma for protection.

* The original specifies the individuals.

† Sítá.

‡ The term is *abrahmańyam. Abrahmańyam* implying the absence of protection to the Bráhmans, and their incurring some distress.

§ The son of the *Asura Madhu*, by *Kumbhinasí* the daughter of *Viśravas* and sister of *Rávańa*. He inherited from his father a trident, presented by

Ráma. Still this profane intrusion! I will send
*Śatrughna** to chastise this impious son
Of *Kumbhinasí.* [*Going, looks back.*
Alas! my queen, what will become of thee?
Goddess divine! all-bearing Earth! protect
This, thine own daughter, at the solemn rite,
By thee brought forth,—the only stay of Janaka,
The sole remaining hope of *Raghu's* race.
[*Exit.*

Sítá. (*Waking.*) Oh, my loved husband! Ah! deceived
By evil dreams I call on him. How! gone!
Left me alone! asleep! well, well;
I will be very angry with thee, Ráma.
I will henceforth be mistress of myself;
Suppress my foolish fondness, and will learn
Henceforth to chide thee. Who attends? How now!

Enter DURMUKHA.

Dur. Prince Lakshmańa requests you will be pleased
To come and mount his chariot.

Sítá. I will come.
But gently, my good friend; the pleasing load
I bear, retards my steps. Accept my homage,
Gods of the race of *Raghu* and of Janaka,
Feet of my honoured lord, and all
Propitious saints, and ancestors revered.
[*Exeunt.*

Śiva to *Madhu*, the holder of which was invincible. *Śatrughna* subdued and slew him, by surprising him without his weapon. *Lavańa* was sovereign of *Mathurá*, to the government of which his conqueror succeeded. *Mathurá* was previously called *Madhuvana*, or *Madhupurí*, the grove or city of the demon *Madhu*.

* The youngest of his brothers.

END OF THE FIRST ACT.

ACT II.*

Scene—Janasthána Forest.

Enter Átreyí,† *a female ascetic.*

I see the genius of these groves approach.
She bears her flowery tribute.‡

Enter Vásantí, *the Dryad of Janasthána, with flowers, which she presents.*

Vás. Hail, holy dame! thy presence brings §
Delight to all our groves and springs:
Thy blessing and thy prayers be mine;
These fountains and these bowers are thine.
Here, in the tall tree's shade repose,
Where cool the limpid current flows,
And feast upon the blameless root,
Or pluck the overhanging fruit,—
The fitting fare of those who dwell
In silent grove, and hermit cell,—
And consecrate the calm retreat
With pious thoughts and converse sweet.

Átr. (*Takes the present.*)
Kindness of heart and gentleness of speech,
Modest demeanour, innocence of thought,

* An interval of twelve years has elapsed since the first Act.

† The wife of the sage *Atri*, more usually termed *Anasúyá*, the daughter of *Kardama Ŕishi.*

‡ She comes with an *arghya*, a present indicative of respect to a superior. It matters not of what it consists; and in this case is appropriately of flowers.

§ The conversation of mythological personages is so little attractive in general, that I have attempted to give it relief in this drama by a lighter measure, at the expense sometimes, perhaps, of close fidelity.

Unsullied nature, and devout associates,—
These are the charms and mystic powers of virtue,
And, with sincerity united, hallow
The grossness of existence. [*Sits.*

Vás. 'Tell me, venerable dame,
Who thou art, and what thy name?

Átr. Behold in me the wife of *Atri.**

Vás. Tell me, partner of the seer,
What thy holy purpose here?

Átr. Amidst these forests dwells the great *Agastya,*†
And many other holy teachers here
With him reside: from them I come to learn
The holy *Vedas*, having lately left
The lessons of Válmíki.‡

Vás. Yet wise, *Prachetas'*§ son, his mind
The deepest, darkest, truths can find,
And on him other sages wait,
Familiar with the laws of fate,
The books of *Brahm* were there made clear—
Why then this weary journey here?

Atr. I'll tell thee, spirit: in Válmíki's bower

* One of the will-born sons of *Brahmá*, and progenitor of the moon.

† Agastya was the son of *Mitra* and *Varuńa* conjointly, and born in a water-jar along with *Vasishtha.* Having commanded the *Vindhya* mountain to lie prostrate till his return, he repaired to the South of India, to *Kolapur*, where he continued to reside, and appears to have been mainly instrumental in introducing the Hindu religion into the Peninsula.

‡ The author of the *Rámáyańa*, settled at *Chitrakúta* at the time of Ráma's exile, but at this time at *Bithur.*

§ Válmíki was the son of *Varuńa*, the regent of the water, one of whose names is *Prachetas.* According to the *Adhyátma-Rámáyańa*, the sage, although a Bráhman by birth, associated in his youth with foresters and robbers. Attacking on one occasion the seven *Ŕishis*, they expostulated with him successfully, and taught him the *mantra* of Ráma reversed, or *Mára, Mára*, in the inaudible repetition of which he remained immovable for thousands of years, so that when the sages returned to the same spot, they found him still there, converted into a *valmíka*, or ant-hill, by the nests of the termites, whence his name of Válmíki.

What causes were there of delay and hindrance
To interrupt the weighty task. Attend.
Borne by some deity, two infant children,
Of more than common natures, at the hermitage
Arrived, and from their holy studies whiled
The gravest sages—nay, the very animals
Confessed the same surprising fascination.

Vás. Their names?

Átr. Kuśa and Lava were the names assigned
By their celestial guardian; and in proof
They were not of mere mortal race, they brought
Along with them the arms of heavenly fabric.
The sage received them; and with care paternal
Válmíki rears them. In their earliest years,
Except the sacred *Vedas*, they were taught
All sciences, and chief the use of arms;
But when they saw ten summers, he invested them,
After the kingly fashion, with the cord,*
And placed the Holy Scriptures in their hands.
Such is their aptness, they have far excelled
The oldest scholars, whose less active intellects
Toil after them in vain. The mind, alike
Vigorous or weak, is capable of culture,
But still bears fruit according to its nature.
'Tis not the teacher's skill that rears the scholar:
The sparkling gem gives back the glorious radiance
It drinks from other light, but the dull earth
Absorbs the blaze, and yields no gleam again.

Vás. 'Tis justly urged, and this compels
Thy feet to seek our saintly cells.

Átr. Another cause disturbed our pious studies—

* A thread worn by the three first orders of the Hindus over the left shoulder and under the right arm. It is imposed with much solemnity, as part of the ceremony of regeneration, whence the three castes are termed *Dwijas*, or twice-born. The thread of the military class is made of flax, and should be put on between the ages of ten and twenty-two.

The sage Válmíki in his noontide walk,
Along the *Tamasá*,* beheld a fowler
Strike to the ground one of a gentle pair
Of birds, that murmured love upon the bank.
Filled with affliction at the piteous sight,
The sage gave utterance to his wrath, and prompted
By the inspiring goddess,† thus proclaimed
His thoughts in unpremeditated verse:
"Hope not, barbarian, length of days to know,
Whose hand could deal so merciless a blow,
One of a harmless pair could thus destroy,
Consigned to death amidst the thoughts of joy."‡

Vás. 'Twas genius spoke, and first on earth
A heaven-descended art had birth.

Átr. The verse was scarcely uttered, when lo! *Brahmá*
Appeared before the sage, and thus addressed him:
"Thy spirit is awakened—now thou feelest
The present god, whose soul is eloquence.
Complete thy task—declare thy lofty strain,
The deeds of Ráma to the listening world.
This day, the new-born ray of heavenly knowledge
Breaks on thy sight, first poet amongst men."
This said, he disappeared. The sage obeyed,
And, first of mortals, sang, in measured strains,
The inspiration of the god who rules
O'er eloquence, the glorious deeds of Ráma.

Vás. To all the world the sacred tongue
Of gods and *Veds* shall hence belong.§

Atr. 'Tis true; and thus on our retired studies

* A small river near *Chitrakote*, commonly called the *Tonse*.

† *Saraswati* or *Váńí*, the goddess of speech and eloquence.

‡ The original here inserts the stanza of the *Rámáyańa* (I. 2, 18), which is there also stated to be the first *śloka*, or stanza, ever composed.

§ The literal expression is, *hanta, pańďitaḱ saṁsáraḱ*—Alas! the world is learned.

Profane intrusion may be apprehended.
Enough ! I now have rested. Friendly spirit,
Show me the way to great *Agastya's* dwelling.

Vás. The road through *Panchavatí* leads ;
And here across the stream proceeds.

Átr. The clear *Godávarí*—yonder extends
Prasravańa, whose high tops touch the clouds ;
This is the sacred forest, *Janasthána*,
And thou, if I mistake not, art Vásantí.

Vás. You speak my name.

Átr. These scenes suggest most painful recollections.
My poor child Jánakí, 'twas here thy fate
Once placed thee, and I think I see thee still,
Although, alas ! thy name is all that 's left
Of one who was so dear to me.

Vás. How, say you ! Does aught ill attend
The fortunes of my dearest friend ?

Átr. Not evil fortune only—evil fame. [*Whispers.*

Vás. Alas, alas ! relentless fate,
Is there no limit to thy hate ? [*Faints.*

Átr. Revive, my child ; be comforted.

Vás. Such, gentle Sítá, beauteous queen,
Thy destiny hath ever been.
Ah, Ráma ! but I will not chide—
Declare, Átreyí, what beside
Befell my hopeless friend, conveyed
By Lakshmańa to forest shade ?

Átr. It is not known.

Vás. But where, oh ! where
Was then Vasishťha's guardian care ?
Where was Arundhatí divine,
And all the chiefs of *Raghu's* line ?
The ancient queens ? were all content
To mark, unmoved, such sad event ?

Átr. The elders of the race had all repaired
To *Ŕishyaśringa's* hermitage—but late,

The twelve years' rite is finally effected.
They quit the hermit; but Arundhatí
Returns not to Ayodhyá whilst deprived
Of Sítá, and with her the queens agree.
'Twas, therefore, by *Vasishtha* counselled, they
Should for a while be tenants of those groves,
Where wise Válmíki and his pupils dwell.

Vás. And what doth Ráma?

Átr. He prepares
An *Aśwamedh**——

Vás. What female shares
The solemn rite? I fear him wed
To some new queen.

Átr. 'Tis idly said;—
A golden image of his cherished Sítá
The sacrifice partakes.

Vás. 'Tis well
He holds his faith; yet who can tell
Men's hearts? the purest comprehend
Such contradictions, and can blend
The force to bear, the power to feel,
The tender bud and tempered steel.

Átr. Already the pure steed, o'er whom the charms
By *Vámadeva* spoken are pronounced,
Is loosed to roam at will: his guards attend
According to the ritual. By the son
Of Lakshmańa, the noble Chandraketu,
Arrayed in mail, and with bright weapons armed,
From heavenly arsenals, the bands are led—
Scarce went they forth, when lo! a Bráhman brought
His son's dead body to the palace gate,
And called for succour to the Bráhman tribe.
Reflecting, when unseasonable death
Afflicts his people, that the monarch's faults

* The solemn sacrifice of a horse.

Must be the cause, full sorely Ráma grieved;
When to console him came a voice from heaven
Commanding him go forth and seek S'ambúka:
One of an outcast origin, engaged
In pious penance: he must fall by Ráma,
And then the Bráhman's son will live again.
This heard, the king assumed his arms, ascended
His car celestial, and he traverses
Even now the realms in quest of this ascetic.

Vás. Speed, Ráma, speed! the foe inhales
In these deep shades the healthful gales,
His only sustenance: but now,
Thy coming terminates his vow;
And thy blest steps shall spread around
New glories on this sainted ground!

Átr. Come, friendly spirit, haste we hence?

Vás. I lead. The sun, with glow intense,
Shoots through the sky, and drives to shade
The silent songsters of the glade.
Alone, amidst the loftiest boughs,
The dove repeats her tender vows;
Or wild fowl cry, as pleased they mark,
Their insect prey amid the bark.
By tangling branches overhead
A cooling gloom beneath is spread,
Where rests the elephant, reclining
Against the ancient trunk, or twining
His tusk around the branchy bower;
He scatters round a leafy shower
Of flowery buds, that falling seem
An offering to the sacred stream,
Whose crystal waters placid flow
Along the verdant shore below.

[*Exeunt.*

Enter RÁMA *in his car, with his sword drawn.*

Hand, thou hast done thy duty, and let fall

The sword of vengeance on the *Śúdra's* head,
To grant existence to the Bráhman's son.
This act was worthy him of whom thou'rt part.
Not such thy deed, when thrusting Sítá forth
To bear her burthen to the lonely woods.*

Enter S'AMBÚKA † *as a celestial spirit.*

Śam. Glory to Ráma! death's terrific king,
Awed by thy prowess, renders back to life
The Bráhman's son: the youth is with his sire.
To thee S'ambúka reverently bows,
For 'tis to thee he owes his present glories.
The death that is inflicted by the pious
Is but a passport to felicity.

Ráma. I joy in both events.
Long may you live a tenant of those realms
To which your penances have raised you; where
The pure and unimpassioned sages dwell,
And taste the bliss that recompenses virtue!

Śam. Not to my penance, but to thy benevolence
I owe this exaltation; yet I wrong
The force of my devotions, which have brought thee
In quest of such an abject worm as I.
Thou shouldst be sought out by the world, its great
And powerful defence; yet thou hast deigned
To quit Ayodhyá for the *Dańdak* forest,
And hither bend thy steps in search of me.

Ráma. And is this *Dańdaka?* do I once more
Behold the vast, the venerable shades,
Awful and dark with aged trees, and echoing
With roaring torrents from surrounding hills,
The haunt of pious seers, and holy pilgrims?

* The construction of the original is something different, and Ráma, according to the stage direction, striking at nothing, is lauded by unseen panegyrists. "This act is worthy of Ráma! now may the Bráhman's son revive."

† Having been killed by divine hands, he of course obtained deification.

Śam. This is the scene of thy triumphant prowess,
Where countless demons fell beneath thy sword,*
Hence *Janasthána's* timid denizens
Pass their calm days in undisturbed devotion.

Ráma. Lies *Janasthána* here?

Śam. Towards the south,
It skirts these thickets, through whose spacious bounds
Wander at will the monsters of the wild.
Fierce o'er the mountain stalks the ravenous tiger,
Or lurks in gloomy caves; through the thick grass
Curls the vast serpent, on whose painted back
The cricket chirps, and with the drops that dew
The scales allays his thirst. Silence profound
Enwraps the forest, save where babbling springs
Gush from the rock, or where the echoing hills
Give back the tiger's roar, or where the boughs
Burst into crackling flame, and wide extends
The blaze the dragon's fiery breath has kindled.

Ráma. I recognise the scene, and all the past
Rises to recollection. These drear shades
Appalled not Sítá, well content to brave
The forest gloom with Ráma at her side.
Such was her wondrous love, that cheerfully
She trod the wild. What wealth need man desire,
Who in the fond companion of his life,
Has one that shares his sorrows, and disperses
All anxious care with exquisite delight?

Śam. Dismiss such melancholy thoughts. Observe
The peafowl's glorious plumage, as he lights
Beneath yon copse—behold, through tufted grass,
Where come the trooping deer, bounding to covert,
Nor fear the gaze of man; there cooling fall
The sparkling torrents; as they flash beneath
The overhanging willows, or the boughs

* Or in the text 14,000 *Rákshasas*, besides the three principal, *Khara, Dúshańa,* and *Triśiras.*

Laden with fruit declining to the stream,
And vocal with innumerable choristers.
The she-bear growls along the flowery brink,
And from the incense-bearing tree, the elephant
Snaps the light branch, and all its gum exudes,
And breathes rich perfume through the balmy air.
I quit thee, lord, to visit, with thy leave,
Ere I ascend to heaven, *Agastya's* cell.

Ráma. Be thy path propitious!

[*Exit* SAMBÚKA.

'Twas here that long and happily I dwelt,
Ere other duties, and the cares of empire
Disturbed my tranquil joys. But such our lot—
Each various station has its proper claim.
The hermit's calm suits not the rank of king,
Nor kingly state the peaceful hermitage.
Scenes of repose, with lavish nature graced,
Haunts undisturbed of timid birds and deer,
Streams decorated with th' untrodden fringe
Of flowery blossoms and luxuriant creepers,
I know ye well. Yon distant wavy ridge,
Like a faint line of low-descending clouds,
Defines *Prasravańa*, whose lofty crest
Was once the vulture king, *Jatáyu's*, seat;
And from whose sides precipitously falls
The broad *Godávarí*. At the hill foot,
And on the margin of the stately wood,
Among dark trees, upon whose branches, bowed
Into the shining stream beneath, the birds
Sang sweet and oft, our leafy cottage stood.
And here is *Panchavatí*, long the witness
Of our contented stay, and the abode
Of Sítá's dearest friend, the fair Vásantí,
The kindly genius of these ancient shades.
Alas, how changed my fortune! Sad I pine
In lonely widowhood—affliction sheds

A deadly venom through my veins—despair,
Like a barbed arrow shot into my heart,
There sticks, and rankles in its cureless wound.
Let me beguile the hour, and try to lose
The memory of my sufferings, as I gaze
Once more on these dear scenes. Yet even they
Are not unchanged : where once the river flowed
A verdant bank extends ; and where the trees,
Close wove, denied admittance to the day,
An open champaign bares its breast to heaven.
Scarce could I deem the spot the same ; but still
The mighty landmarks tower aloft, and round
The same tall mountains mingle with the skies.
How may I dare to look upon these woods
Alone, without my love, with whom my days
Were once within their confines pass'd in peace
And happy converse in our humble dwelling !
Let me not think of this.

Śam. (*Returning.*) All hail to Ráma !
The seer *Agastya*, when he heard from me
Your presence in these wilds, thus speaks his wishes.
The tender *Lopámudrá* * and the saints
Who share our hermitage, will think it happiness
If, from thy heavenly car alighting, thou
Wilt for short season visit us. Then come,
Ere thou resume thy journey to Ayodhyá.

Ráma. Be it done.

* *Agastya* having seen his ancestors suspended by their heels in a pit, was told by them that they could only be extricated from their position by his begetting a son. In order to obtain a wife for this purpose, he made a girl of the most graceful parts of the animals of the forest, and gave her, without his privacy, to the king of *Vidarbha*, to be his daughter. She was named *Lopámudrá* from the distinctive beauties (*mudra*) of animals, as the eyes of deer, &c., being subjected to loss (*lopa*) in her superior charms. When marriageable, *Agastya* demanded her of her father, and, although sorely against his will, the king was obliged to consent to her becoming the wife of the sage. (*Mahábhárata, Vana-Parvan.*)

Bear with me, *Panchavatí*, that obeying
The pleasure of the sage, I still presume
To trespass on thy confines.

Śam. Here lies our path. Yonder is tall *Kraunchávat*,
Amidst the dark glens of whose wooded sides
The raven silent flits, and hoots the owl,
And whines through whistling caves the shrilly breeze :
And countless pea-fowl, with discordant shrieks,
Chase into sapless trunks and time-worn trees
The frightened snakes. Far to the south extends
The lofty range of hills, whose towering peaks
Are diademed with clouds ; whose central caverns
Roar loud with mighty waters, as from the earth
The springs of the *Godávarí* burst forth ;
And at whose base the sacred conflux blends,
In one broad stream, the loud, encountering torrents.

END OF THE SECOND ACT.

ACT III.

THE DAŃḊAKA FOREST CONTINUES.

Enter TAMASÁ *and* MURALÁ, *two river goddesses.*

Tam. How now, sister, whither bent?
Mur. By the holy matron sent,
Lopámudrá, charge of care
To *Godávarí* I bear.
Thus the matron bids me say:—
Ráma still through many a day,
Though exterior calmness screen
His sorrow, deeply mourns his queen;
And his declining form declares
The anguish that his bosom tears;
For soonest shall the soft heart perish
That loves a secret grief to cherish,
As gourds with coat of clay encased
Earliest into ripeness haste.
Brooding o'er his bosom's woes,
Ráma now desponding goes
Through the forest confines, where
Every object wakes despair.
Fond, he lingers on each spot,
Speaking of a happier lot,
When delightedly he strayed
With his Sítá through the shade.
Happiness for ever flown,
Now he weeps, and weeps alone;
And such sad despairing mood,
Nursed by gloom and solitude,
May to fierce distraction grow,
And the firmest mind o'erthrow.

Lest such hapless chance befall
Thou his sinking sense recall.
Moistened by thy gelid spray,
Cooling breezes round him play;
Balmy with the lotus bloom,
Shed the breeze its soft perfume:
So thy friendship shall dispense
Freshness on each fading sense.

Tam. 'Tis kindly done; but mightier art
To-day performs its surer part.

Mur. What art?

Tam. Attend: 'tis not unknown,
When Sítá, helpless and alone,
Left by Lakshmańa, deplored
Her hapless fate and cruel lord;
The sudden throes of nature came
Distracting o'er her tender frame,
And, wild with agony, she gave
Her beauties into Gangá's wave.

Mur. 'Tis true; and in the moment bore
Two lovely boys, whom to the shore,
Beneath the wave, the realms of shade,
The goddess of the stream conveyed:
And there with earth's great goddess, tended
With pious pains, till time had ended
The first and fond maternal care;
When Gangá took the nursling pair
To wise Válmíki's hermitage,
And gave them to the assenting sage.
Now, grown in strength and sense, appears
Each youth beyond his childish years,
Worthy his high imperial line,
The holy sage and nurse divine.

Tam. And now, throughout the regions flies
The fame, the fierce ascetic dies,

In *Janasthána's* drear domain
By *Rámabhadra's* falchion slain;
And Gangá from *Sarayú* hears
The news, and *Lopámudrá's* fears
For Ráma; and she hither speeds,
Pretending some domestic rite
That Sítá must fulfil, and leads
The princess to her husband's sight.

Mur. 'Twas wisely thought. Amidst affairs
Of empire, Ráma's private cares
Are scattered—but whilst thus he wends,
And grief alone his steps attends,
He feels his loss: but what device
To Ráma shall his queen entice?

Tam. 'Tis thus contrived: The queen of floods
Sends Sítá to these ancient woods
To gather flowers, and with them pay
Devotion to the god of day,
From whose bright loins the glorious race
Of *Raghu* their high lineage trace.
And homage, therefore, should be done
This day, to their great sire, the sun,
For that the lucky knot* has told
Twelve years their rapid course have rolled
Since, from the daughter of the earth,
Kuśa and Lava drew their birth.
Go forth, exclaimed the queen, my child,
Nor fear to tread the lonely wild:
For by my power a veiling cloud
Thy presence in these groves shall shroud
From spirits who o'er the wood preside,
And more from mortal eyes shall hide.

* The *Mangala-granthi*, literally rendered in the text. The expression alludes to the practice still in use amongst the Hindus, of making a knot every year of a person's life in the string or thread which is wound round the paper scroll on which the calculations of his nativity are inscribed.

By her command, too, I attend,
Her tender pupil to defend
From aught of harm, and hence am found
To-day upon this holy ground.

Mur. To *Lopámudrá* I depart,
The blissful tidings to impart.
But who comes here?

Tam. 'Tis Sítá : mark,
How lovely, through her tresses dark
And floating loose, her face appears,
Though pale and wan, and wet with tears.
She moves along like Tenderness
Invested with a mortal dress;
Or, like embodied Grief, she shines,
That sad o'er love in absence pines.

Mur. Bowed down by sorrow, see, she droops,
Like the soft lotus as it stoops
Its head, when some rude hand has broken
The slender stem. Those sighs betoken
A labouring heart, and withering care
With wasteful hand is busy there;
For every limb more fragile shows,—
So, when the sun of autumn glows,
The tender leaflet languid lies,
Shrinks in the scorching blaze, and dies.

[*Exit* MURALÁ.

Enter SÍTÁ (*as described*) *with flowers.*

Sítá. 'Tis very strange! Methought I heard the voice
Of my dear friend Vásantí once again.

(*Voices in the wood.*) The elephant is Sítá's, whom the queen
With her own tender hands is wont to feed:
And now he perishes—as to the stream
He with his mate repairs, a monstrous elephant,
Wild from the woods, approaches to assail him.

Sítá. Ah, my dear lord!—haste, haste thee to preserve
My favourite, my child, from death—the view

Of these familiar scenes suggests to me
Phrases alike familiar once—but now—
Ah me!—my husband— [*Faints.*

Re-enter TAMASÁ.

Tam. Revive, my child. [*Recovering her.*

Ráma. (*Without.*) Here, guider of the car—here stay our course.

Sítá. What voice was that? oh, it comes o'er my soul,
Like the low muttering of the thundercloud,
That promises refreshing dews to earth,
And calls me back to life!

Tam. What means this rapture?
Why such delight from inarticulate sounds,
Like the fond peahen at the muttered thunder?

Sítá. Sounds inarticulate, saidst thou?
To my enraptured ear it seemed
My dear lost lord had uttered the blest sounds.

Tam. It may be: for 'tis noised amongst mankind,
The subjugation of the ascetic *Śúdra*
Conducts the hero to this ancient forest.

Sítá. Thus pays he faithfully the lofty dues
Exacted by his station.—But he comes—
Do I again behold him?—Yes, 'tis he!
His gait declares him; but how pale and thin,
Like the fast waning moon in morning skies!
Oh, support me! [*Throws herself into the arms of Tamasá.*

Ráma. (*Rushing in.*)* Goddess adored!
Celestial daughter of *Videha's* kings! [*Falls fainting.*

Sítá. Ah me, ill-fated! See, his lotus eyes
Close at the sight of me! His deep distress
O'ermasters every sense! Oh save him! save him!
[*To Tamasá.*

* In the original, Ráma is supposed to fall behind the scenes, and Sítá goes out to him, when they are again discovered, or, in the language of the text, Enter Ráma fainted. Several speeches also, ruinous of the otherwise good stage effect, are omitted.

Tam. Dismiss your terrors—you can best restore him :
That gentle hand can bring him back to life.

Sítá. Say'st thou—

(*Kneels, takes one of Ráma's hands in one of hers, and applies the other to his forehead.*)

'Tis so—his spirits are recovering.

Ráma. What should this mean? the heavenly balm that wakes
The dead to life is poured into my heart ;
Or from the moon ambrosial dews descend,
Drop on my soul, and rouse me to existence.
Such is the power that well-known touch possesses
To change insensibility to life,
And cheer the chill of dark despair with hope.

Sítá. (*Withdrawing.*) Oh! this is too much for me.

Ráma. Why! was it not
My Sítá that restored me?

Sítá. Ah, my lord now seeks me.

Ráma. I will search.

Sítá. (*To Tamasá.*) I must not meet
His gaze uncalled. My lord will be displeased
That I approach him thus unbid.

Tam. Fear not ;
By *Bhagavatí's* powerful will enshrined,
You walk, unseen, e'en by the sylvan deities.

Ráma. Sítá! loved Sítá!—No, she is not here.
Where art thou flown—or was it but a dream?
Oft has my fancy anxiously explored
My Jánakí's retreat, and now, illusively,
It finds her in these shades.*

(*Behind.*) Help! help!
Or Sítá's elephant will be destroyed.

Ráma. My Sítá's favourite! Who dares molest
The animal she loved? [*Rises, and is going.*

* A few speeches that follow are here omitted ; and several subsequent passages have been also left out, as injurious to the interest of the scene.

Enter VÁSANTÍ.

Vás. The pride of *Raghu* in these honoured groves--
Hail, prince!

Sítá. My friend Vásantí.

Ráma. Do I see
My Sítá's dearest friend!

Vás. The same; but speed
To save the elephant. Cross the *Godávarí*,
Where Sítá's name gives virtue to the ford,
Leaving *Jaťáyu's* mountain on the right.

Sítá. Alas, *Jaťáyu!*
The forest is a waste deprived of thee!

Ráma. How many recollections do these names
Sadly recall!

Vás. No more delay; quick, follow me!

[*Exeunt* VÁSANTÍ *and* RÁMA.

Sítá. Tell me, dearest Tamasá, cannot, in sooth,
The wood nymphs see me?

Tam. Why should you doubt?
The might of Gangá far exceeds the power
Of every deity.

Sítá. Then let us follow
My lord and my dear friend. [*Exeunt.*

THE BANKS OF THE GODÁVARÍ.

Enter RÁMA *and* VÁSANTÍ, *and afterwards* SÍTÁ *and* TAMASÁ.

Ráma. Glory to *Godávarí!*

Vás. Now, prince, secure
The victory to him, whom as a child
Thy princess fondly cherished.

Ráma. Live and conquer!

Vás. 'Tis even thus—he triumphs o'er his foe.

Ráma. Fate, Sítá, has obeyed thee, and the elephant,
Whose sportive frolic pilfered from thine ears,

With trunk as flexile as the lotus fibres,
Their fragrant pendants, now in earliest youth
Defies the mighty monarch of the woods.
Nor less his tenderness than prowess. Mark
The arts he practises to gain the favour
Of his loved mate, as he imbibes the wave
Perfumed with lotus buds, and with his trunk
Sprinkles the fragrant dews upon her form,
Or rears the broad leaf of the lotus high
Above her head, to screen her from the sun.

Sítá. Well pleased, my Tamasá, I view this child
Of my affections; but, alas! the sight
Recalls the memory of far dearer sons.
How fare my boys?

Tam. In him you may behold them—
Such strength and courage as are his, are theirs.

Sítá. Ah me, unhappy! not alone condemned
To separation from my lord, but doomed
To live divided from my children!

Tam. Fate has so willed it.

Sítá. How have I deserved
A doom so harsh—what sins have I committed,
That the sweet faces of my lovely boys,
Shaded with curling locks and bright with smiles,
Where the red lips the budding teeth display,
Should never know the kisses of a father?

Tam. If fate be gracious, they may know them yet.

Sítá. As they recur to memory, my bosom
Swells with a mother's passion, and their sire
Full in my gaze, I seem once more to live
Blest amongst mortals.

Tam. Truly it is said,
The love that children waken is the bond
That binds their parents strongest to their faith;
And even when the wedded pair are held
By fond affection, still there needs this tie

To make their happiness complete and lasting.*

Vás. Be seated, prince. Here in this plantain grove
Behold the marble which in happier days
Supported thee and Sítá. Here she sat,
And from her hands gave fodder to the deer
That boldly crowded round their gentle mistress.

Ráma. I cannot bear to look upon it. [*Weeps.*

Vás. (*Aside.*) Oh, that my lovely friend could now behold
The altered state of her once beauteous lord,
His manly form, whose graces, ever new,
Were once the grateful objects of her sight,
Now shrunk and withered, and by ceaseless grief
Now pale and haggard his once blooming cheeks.
(*Aloud.*) Put forth your brightest fruits and flowers, ye trees
Ye breezes, breathe the perfume of the lotus;
And ye soft choristers, pour all your voices
In sweet continuous song, for Ráma comes;
Once more he visits his erst-loved domains.

Ráma. Here let us rest awhile.

Vás. Permit me ask,
How fares the prince, brave Lakshmańa?

Ráma. (*Not hearing her, apart.*)
'Twas in these scenes
The gentle *Maithilí* delighted fed
The innocent animals confiding round her.
Where'er I turn, sad recollections rise,
And my hard heart resolves itself in dew.

Vás. The *Mahárája* does not speak of Lakshmańa.

Ráma. (*Apart.*) Her cold respectful manner, and her voice
With starting tears, broken and indistinct,
I comprehend; she knows the tale: (*To her.*) The prince
Is well. [*Weeps.*

* A few speeches of the dialogue are here, and in some following passages, omitted, merely to compress a scene which, being devoid of action, is extended to a disproportionate length in the original, especially as the speeches of Sítá and Tamasá sometimes suspend the conversation of Ráma and Vásantí through an inconvenient interval.

Vás. Then why these tears?

Sítá. Vásantí, this is cruel:
My lord demands respect from all, and most
From those who love me.

Vás. How hadst thou the heart
To drive that gentle being from thee? Once
She was thy love, thy other, dearer life,
Light of thine eyes, and nectar of thy soul—
How can such deed be credited of Ráma?

Ráma. The world compelled it.

Vás. Why?

Ráma. It knew no cause.

Vás. Obdurate man, to heed the world's reports
Alone, nor reck the scorn that waits the cruel!
Hast thou forgotten what disastrous fate
Befell the fawn-eyed Sítá, when she dwelt
Before in lonely woods? What then occurred
May make thee tremble for what since has chanced.

Ráma. What horrible suggestions! Yes, I see
My Sítá once again the spoil of fiends.
In vain her slender form and lovely looks
Demand compassion; vainly do those eyes
Roll wild with terror, fearful as the glance
Unsteady of the yearling fawn, and vain
The tender burden that she graceful bears,
To move the savages to pity. Where,
O where, abandoned Sítá, art thou now?

Sítá. Alas! he weeps aloud.

Tam. 'Tis better thus
To give our sorrows way. Sufferers should speak
Their griefs. The bursting heart that overflows
In words obtains relief; the swelling lake
Is not imperilled, when its rising waters
Find ready passage through their wonted channel.*

* *Lit.* "By those who are in sorrow their sorrows should be uttered, as the heart in the agitation of grief is upheld by words." The sen-

Mark *Rámabhadra*—little cause has he
To thank mankind; yet, faithful to his duty,
He labours for their good, who oft have been
The source of ill to him, though still affliction
Unceasing for thy loss preys on his life,
As scorching summers parch the fragile flower.
He knows no pleasures, nor partakes the joys
Of social converse,—'tis to him relief
To-day to give a vent to sighs and tears.

Ráma. Alas!

Affliction rends my heart, and yet it breaks not;
Sorrow unnerves my frame, but leaves me conscious;
Though fires internal burn, they not consume me;
And fate, that tortures, yet forbears my life.
Ah, people of *Ayodhyá!* ye refused
Your queen a home amongst ye, and remorseless
Drove her to wander in the lonely wilds.
Be satisfied. The memory of the virtues
I loved so long now overpowers my strength,
And I too, homeless, melt away in tears.

Vás. Nay, nay, my lord, be firm.

Ráma. Be firm, Vásantí!

Alas! the twelve long years the world has been
Deprived of Sítá, have to me been nothing.
I have not lived: there has not been a Ráma.
Yet still I have endured—though sharp the pain
As if a burning brand or venomed sting
Were lodged within my breast—I have endured it.
But now the firmness of my heart is broken,

timent is familiar to the dramas of Shakespeare. Thus, in *Richard the Third*:—

"*Eliz.* Why should calamity be full of words?

"*Duch. of York.* Let them have scope, though what they do impart
Help nothing else, yet do they ease the heart."

And in *Macbeth*:—

"Give sorrow words; the grief that does not speak
Whispers the o'erfraught heart, and makes it break."

As round me rise so many sad memorials
To call my Sítá once again to view.
In vain I struggle with my inward passion,
And check the growing sorrows that distract me.
The anguish of my mind will force expression
More vehement, because so long repressed.
The rushing river, for a while impeded,
First saps the barrier, and at length its current
Impetuous sweeps the opposing sands away.

Vás. (*Aside.*) He is much moved; I will divert his thoughts
To other objects. Look around you, prince,
And mark the scenes that *Janasthána* offers.
Behold the spot, where in yon shady bower
Of twining creepers wove, you often sate,
To watch, impatient, Sítá's homeward course
From the *Godávarí's* pure stream; and she,
Who coming marked remote your fond anxiety,
As fearful of rebuke for long delay,
Bowed sportively her head, and with closed palms,
Touched her fair front to deprecate your anger.

Sítá. Cruel Vásantí! this is unmerciful,
Thus with heart-piercing shafts, incessantly
To wound the bosom of my lord and mine.

Ráma. Relentless Jánakí, where'er I gaze
I view thy charms—in vain, for thou art pitiless.
My heart is bursting—all my vigour flies me.
The world is a wide desert; I am burnt
With inward fires—deep, deep, in thickest gloom
My soul is plunged, and all is night around me.

[*Faints.*

Sítá. Alas! his senses fail him; as his thoughts
Revert to me, unhappy, his existence,
The hope of all, is thus again endangered.

Tam. Fear not, your hand revives him.

[*Sítá acts as before.*

Vás. He recovers.

Ráma. Once more, ambrosia,
Spread o'er each limb by that celestial hand,
Restores my parting spirit, and converts
My sorrows to ineffable delight.
Joy, joy, Vásantí, thou wilt share my joy!

Vás. Whence is this transport?

Ráma. Sítá, she is found!

Vás. Where?

Ráma. Here—before us—dost thou not see her?

Vás. Why mock my sorrows? why thus rend a heart
Already broken by my Sítá's loss?

Ráma. I mock thee not; I could not be deceived.
Too well I know the touch of that dear hand,
The marriage rite first placed in mine; even now,
Cool as the snow-drift to my fevered palm,
And soft as jasmine buds I grasp it—here—
[*By a sudden effort he catches hold of Sítá's hand.*

Sítá. Alas! I yield. [*Struggling.*

Ráma. Vásantí, it is real!
This rapture is too much; it quite unmans me;
'Tis no delusion; touch, and be convinced.

Vás. Alas! he raves. [*Sítá gets away.*

Ráma. 'Tis gone again! I feared it.
From my cold touch the cool palm shrinks; my grasp,
Trembling, ill held the tremulous prisoner,
And it has slipped away. What! no where! Speak,
Pitiless *Vaidehi!*

Sítá. I am rightly called,
To mark this agony and live.

Ráma. Oh, where—
Where art thou, dearest? Hear my call! appear!
Be not unmerciful! oh, fly me not!
'Tis strange; it must be phantasy, or else
Vásantí would have seen her. Do I dream?
Does Ráma sleep? or doth the mighty power
That framed the universe, and oft delights

To spread delusion, fabricate a phantom,
To cheat me of my senses?

Sítá. Nay, loved Ráma,
'Tis I who play a phantom, and deceive thee.

Ráma. My friend Vásantí, those who love me still,
Can gather little pleasure from my presence;
Why should I longer cause thy tears to flow?
Forgive me; let me hence.

Sítá. (*To Tamasá.*) Again I lose him.

Tam. Yield not to despair. Seek we the feet
Of *Bhagavatí*, to perfect the rites,
That will for Kuśa and for Lava win
Auspicious days to come.

Sítá. Oh, let me look,
A little moment longer, on a form
I never, never, may behold again!

Ráma. I go to finish, now, my *Aśwamedha.*
I have my bride.

Sítá. What is it that I hear?

Ráma. The image of my Sítá,
Wrought of pure gold, will grace the festival.*

Sítá. Thou art, indeed, the son of *Daśaratha!*
My past affliction all is now effaced;
Thrice happy she whom my loved lord reveres,
Who glads his heart, and is the hope of nations.

Tam. You speak your own eulogium, love.

Sítá. Forgive me. (*Seems ashamed.*)
You must despise this weakness.

Tam. Let us depart.

* Thus in the *Alcestis* of *Euripides, Admetus,* in order to console himself for the loss of his spouse, declares that—

> "By the hand of skilful artists framed,
> Her image shall be placed upon my couch."

The spirit with which Ráma has the image of Sítá formed is much more worthy of a hero and king. In all his conduct, indeed, he is vastly superior to *Admetus;* and in the delineation of a situation in some respects similar, the Hindu poet is equally superior to the Grecian.

Sítá. I follow you.

Tam. But with averted eye,
Casting its languid looks, not to the path
The feet should tread ; the painful effort strivės,
In vain, to overcome the strong attraction.

Sítá. I bow me to the feet of my dear lord,
The source of every blessing. [*Fainting.*

Tam. Be of courage.

Sítá. Alas! how short an instant to behold
The bright moon gleaming through contending clouds.

Tam. How manifold the forms affection takes,
And yet is one unchanged ! as water, seen
In bubbles, eddies, billows, is the same
Unaltered element.

Ráma. (*In his car, to the Charioteer.*)
This way direct my rapid car.

All. (*Addressing mutually each other.*)
May holy mother Earth,
The empress of the floods, with all the spirits
Of forests and of streams, the bard inspired,
The sage *Vasishtha*, and his pious dame,
Protect your path, and guide you unto happiness !

END OF THE THIRD ACT.

ACT IV.

THE HERMITAGE OF VÁLMÍKI.

Enter SAUDHÁTAKI *and* BHÁŃḊÁYANA, *two Ascetic disciples.*

Bháń. Behold, Saudhátaki, our humble dwelling!
Válmíki's holy hermitage assumes
The face of preparation; he expects
Unwonted guests to-day; the wild deer feed
Upon unusual fragments, and the air
Is filled with savoury odours.*

Sau. There must be
Some wondrous cause, to make our grey-beards lay
Their lectures by to-day.

Bháń. There is a cause,
And that of no mean import.

Sau. Tell me, I pray you,
What venerable ox may we expect
To visit us?

Bháń. For shame! refrain from jests:
The great *Vasishtha* hither brings the queens
Of *Daśaratha*, with Arundhatí,
From *Ŕishyaśŕinga* to our master's dwelling.

Sau. *Vasishtha* is it?

Bháń. The same.

Sau. I crave his pardon. I had thought, at least,
It was a wolf or tiger we should look for.

Bháń. How so?

* The text deals more in particulars. The deer is said to drink the scum of the water in which the ordinary sort of rice, as well as wild rice, has been boiled, and the air is charged with the smell of ghee, boiled rice, and vegetables, mixed with the fruit of the *jujube*, in the course of culinary preparation.

Sau. Why else was there provided
The fatted calf for his regale?

Bhúń. Why, know you not,
The *Vedas*,* which enshrine our holy law,
Direct the householder shall offer those
Who in the law are skilled, the honied meal,
And with it flesh of ox, or calf, or goat,
And the like treatment shall the householder
Receive from *Bráhmans* learned in the *Vedas*? †

* He quotes the text *Samáṁso madhuparkaḱ*, a rather extraordinary liberty in such a place.

† Some texts of Manu would seem to authorise the eating of animal food at all seasons, observing merely the preliminary ceremony of offering a portion of it to the gods or manes, like the heroes of Homer, with whom a sacrifice is only the prelude to a feast. Thus,

"Having bought flesh himself, or obtained it by aid of another, he who eats it, after worshipping the gods or manes, commits no sin."—(*Manu*, v. 32.)

"He who eats animals which may be eaten, is not defiled by the daily practice of the act: for animals which may be eaten and those who eat them were alike created by *Brahmá*" (v. 30). He admits, also, that animal food has been used by ancient sages, even as nourishment, without regard to sacrificial consecration. "Deer and birds were killed by *Bráhmańas* for sacrifice; also for the nutriment of dependants, as was formerly done by *Agastya*" (v. 22). However, *Manu* prohibits the expenditure of life for the gratification of the appetite, and restricts the use of animal food to the *Madhuparka* sacrifice and offerings to the manes and to the gods. "*Manu* has declared that animals may be killed in offerings to the gods in sacrifice and the *Madhuparka*, but not on any other occasion" (v. 41). The *Madhuparka* here implies the respectful reception of a guest, which included the presentation of a mixture of curds and honey (*madhu*, honey, and *parka*, aspersion). This is the ceremony alluded to in the text; and, agreeably to the law of *Manu*, meat was added to the offerings, comformably to the text: "Let him offer to a *Bráhmańa*, versed in the *Vedas*, a large ox or goat."—(*Miták*. p. 48.) Mr Colebrooke observes, that "It seems to have been anciently the custom to slay a cow on this occasion, and the guest was therefore called a *goghna* or cow-killer."—(*As. Res.* vii. 289.) Flesh was also distributed on public occasions, when *Bráhmańas* were assembled. Thus, *Yudhishṫhira*, on taking possession of the splendid hall of audience constructed for him by *Maya Dánava*, fed many thousand *Bráhmańas* with all sorts of viands, including the flesh of bears and deer. The great repugnance to animal diet that now exists amongst the Hindus in some provinces must have been of comparatively

Sau. You must mistake.

Bháń. How so?

Sau. Admit the meal of flesh
Was for *Vasishtha* dress'd; why was it not
Alike provided for the royal sage?
To Janaka were curds and honey given;
No flesh.

Bháń. 'Tis true; for though the sages use
To eat of flesh, yet Janaka foregoes
The practice. Sorrowing for his daughter's fate,
He leads an anchoret's abstemious life,
And in the woods of *Chandradwip* has spent
Long years of solitude and self-denial.

Sau. What brings him here?

Bháń. To see the sage Válmíki; and Kauśalyá
Is summoned by Arundhatí to meet
Her ancient friend *Vaideha.*

Sau. Let us leave
These elders to themselves, and join the youth,
Who make the utmost of their holiday.

Bháń. Agreed.

modern origin. We may be satisfied from the above, that the *Bráhmańas* seldom wanted excuses for partaking of it, and the other castes were not likely to be more scrupulous. In fact, the *Kshattriyas* were especially authorised to use it, and never hesitated to avail themselves of the permission. Thus Ráma, in his peregrinations, is described by Válmíki as catching, killing, and cooking the dinner of his spouse and himself:—

> Their thirst allayed, the princes ply the chase,
> And a fat stag soon falls beneath their arrows.
> A fire they kindle next, and dress their prize;
> Then, offering to the gods and manes made,
> With Sítá they the social banquet share.
>
> —(*Rámáyańa*, b. ii. sec. 40.)

The *Mahábhárata*, however, has in some places a leaning to the opposite doctrine, and in the *Dána-dharma* section, *Bhíshma* expatiates to *Yudhishthira* at considerable length upon the merit of abstaining from animal food, placing chariness of life amongst the first of virtues, a doctrine adopted apparently, or at least more rigidly professed, in order to compete upon an equal footing with the *Bauddhas* and *Jainas*.

See from the dwelling of Válmíki comes
The royal sage, and rests beneath the tree
That shades the cell. A deep and ceaseless sorrow
Preys on his heart, like a destroying fire,
That, lighted in the trunk of some tall tree,
Consumes unseen its sap. Let us withdraw.

[*Exeunt.*

Enter JANAKA.

My anguish, like a sharp-toothed saw, corrodes
Incessantly my heart. Whene'er I think
Upon my child, my sorrows freshly flow,
Like the continuous current of a river.
How hard it is, that neither age nor grief,
Nor penances austere, release my spirit
From this consuming frame—nor dare I loose
The vital spark myself, for deepest hell,
Where the sun never shines, awaits the wretch
Who lifts his hands against his own existence.
By recollection every hour renewed,
In spite of fleeting years, my griefs survive.
Daughter of sacrifice, alas! my Sítá,
That such should be the sad vicissitude
Thou shouldst have suffered, that it shames thy sire
To weep thy destiny as he could wish.
My child, my child! to memory still recur
Thy infant charms, thy lotus countenance,
Chequer'd with smiles and tears, where starting teeth
Like young buds shone, and thy sweet childish prattle
Tripping in utterance. Earth, mighty goddess,
Whose glory fire, and holy sages witness,
And *Gangá*, and the god of *Raghu's* race,
The sun, why cruel hast thou sought the death
Of thine own daughter? She to whom thou gavest,
As eloquence to wisdom, birth, and ever
Wast worshipped by her as her guardian deity.

Arundhatí approaches; with her comes
The queen of *Dasáratha*, my dear friend
Kauśalyá. Who shall put his trust in life?
Once in the royal mansion did she shine
The goddess of prosperity—I shame her
By such comparison—yet, now, she bows
To tyrant destiny, and pines in anguish.
Why should I heed my sufferings, when I mark
The sad reverse she feels? alas! her sight,
That once was bliss, is now as painful to me
As brine to a raw wound.

Enter KAUŚALYÁ, ARUNDHATÍ, *and* ATTENDANT.

Arun. You must comply. The sage commands you come
To meet the king; he is already here.
Why this reluctance, lady?

Atten. Be advised.
Arouse your firmness, madam, and obey
The orders of the sage *Vasishtha.**

Kau. I obey.
Yet hard the task to face mine ancient friend.
His grief and mine are one, and mine already
O'erpowers my heart—its fibres must give way.

Arun. Such pain is unavoidable; the griefs
Man feels, when absent from a faithful friend,
Renew at his encounter, and again
Extend, and deepen through a thousand channels.

Kau. Alas! how can I meet his gaze, deprived
Of his beloved child?

Arun. Think, you behold
In him a venerable relative,
To whom the great preceptor of his race,†

* The attendant has one or two speeches more, which are omitted in the translation.

† *Yájnavalkya,* a sage and legislator, and teacher of one portion of the *Yajur-Veda.*

The sacred knowledge of the *Vedas* gave.

Kau. I see in him a royal sage,-the friend
Of an illustrious sovereign, and the sire
Of her I called my daughter. Ah! I dream
Of other days and joys, that destiny
Has now, alas, unsparingly destroyed.

Jan. All hail! Arundhatí, to whom the earth
At twilight bends its waving head in homage:
Whom the three worlds revere, and who enjoyest
The love of him, of sages first and best,
Who lives the source exhaustless of pure light.

Arun. May light supreme illume thee—may the sun
That shines eternal hallow thee! *

Jan. My friend,
How fares the noble mother of the king?

Kau. Alas! [*Faints.*

Jan. What's this?

Arun. Your sight too well recalls
Her lord, her children, and the long past days
Of happiness, now gone—the fond remembrance
O'ercomes her strength—the matron's heart is still
As soft and delicate as the tender flower.

Jan. Alas! that I should be the cause of suffering
To one I have not seen so long, the wife
Of my still cherished friend—united with me
In closest bonds—dear as my heart, my peace,
Dear as my person, or my life itself,
The present fruit and object of my being,
Or whatsoever else were dearest to me.

* The salutation and reply are both very curious. The first is a little unintelligible, but both are precisely in the spirit of the *Gáyatrí*, or sacred verse of the *Vedas*, and indicate a system very different from the common Hindu polytheism. The text of Janaka's speech is corrupt, but *Arundhatí's* reply is, *param jyotis te prakáśatám, ayam twám punátu devaḥ paro rájá ya esha tapati:*—May supreme light enlighten thee, may this divine light who glows, purify thee.

And is not this his wife? and can I give
Her pain, that does not equally afflict
My friend?—for she was ever one with him
In joy and sorrow. Fate is here alone
To blame: then let me, as I think of him,
Forbear to agonise her sinking heart.

Kau. Where art thou, dearest Jánakí? Methinks
I still behold thy graceful limbs, as light
As lunar rays, and mark thy lotus face,
Budding with playful smiles, and shedding pride
And fortune on thy marriage celebration,
As the delighted monarch called thee child,
And bade thee sit upon his knee, and termed thee
The pride of *Raghu's* loftiest hope, the bond
Of Janaka's exalted house, and his.

Jan. Imperial *Daśaratha*, every way
Within my heart thy memory is secured.
Fathers in social life but rarely prize
Their daughters, and confine their fond regard
To those who wed them; but not thus didst thou,
For Sítá ever was to thee a daughter,
And cherished as thy child; but thou art gone,
And the dear seed of our alliance blighted.
Fie upon life! the world is now a hell.

Kau. My child, my Jánakí! in vain I mourn thee;
Nor will my life, enfeebled by despair,
Yet bound in chains of adamant, release me.

Arun. Take comfort, princess; give your tears some respite,
Recall the words your pious teacher uttered,
Who prophesied at *Ŕishyaśŕinga's* dwelling,
The dews of happiness would yet descend,
And cheer the last days of your closing life.

Kau. I have no relish, now, for worldly happiness.

Arun. You cannot doubt the seer's prophetic sight.
Trust me, what he hath said will surely be:
Whate'er is uttered by the holy *Bráhman*,

Who is the light divine made manifest,
Must come to pass—the blessing which invoked
Propitious *Lakshmí* to the nuptial rite,
Was not unmeaning, nor pronounced in vain.

[*A noise behind.*

Jan. The boys amidst their sports.

Kau. Little suffices to the joys of youth. (*Looks out.*)
But who is yonder—strong, and light, and active?
He bears the noble port of *Rámabhadra:*
Who should this be, that he so charms my sight?

Arun. (*Apart.*) This must be one that *Bhágirathí* named
To me in secrecy; which should it be,
Kuśa or Lava?—we will ascertain.

Jan. In sooth, he bears a strong similitude:
His parted locks, dark as the lotus leaf,
Denote the warrior tribe, and 'mongst his fellows
He shows a proud pre-eminence. It seems
That Ráma once more has become a boy—
Who is this youth that thus delights our sight?

Arun. Some *Kshattriya* lad, who here awhile pursues
His sacred studies.

Jan. You have rightly judged
His birth: for see, on either shoulder hangs
The martial quiver, and the feathery shafts
Blend with his curling locks: below his breast,
Slight tinctured with the sacrificial ashes,
The deer-skin wraps his body: with the zone
Of *Murvá* bound, the madder-tinted garb
Descending vests his limbs; the sacred rosary
Begirts his wrist, and in one hand he bears
The *pípal* staff, the other grasps the bow.*
Arundhatí, whence comes he?

* These insignia of the military student are according to *Manu*, with the addition of the ashes of the fuel used in sacrifice, and the bracelet or rosary of the seeds of the elœocarpus, which are not indispensable accompani-

Arun. You forget;
I came here but to-day.

Jan. (*To the attendant.*) My worthy friend,
Go to Válmíki, and of him inquire
Who is this boy: and tell the boy himself,
Some aged persons wish to talk with him.

Atten. As you command. [*Exit.*

Kau. What think you?—will he come?

Arun. What busy fancies has his sight suggested?
Dismiss them; they are idle.

Kau. He hears our messenger respectfully;
Dismisses him, and hither comes the youth.

Jan. The natural graces of expanding youth,
Though lost to fools, familiar to the wise,
Shed not the virtue that in him resides.
As he advances, he attracts my mind,
Firm though it be, as sways the slender rod
Of magnet force the ponderous mass of iron.

Enter LAVA.

Lava. To talk with me; and yet I know them not.
How am I to address them—ignorant
What claims their birth, or tribe, or name may give them
To my respect? yet, to the aged, this
At least is due. (*Approaches.*) Conceive the brow of Lava
Is bent to do you reverence.

Arun. and Jan. Long life await you!

Kau. Long be thy days, my child!

Arun. Come hither, child. (*Embraces him; then apart.*)
This dear embrace, so long delayed,
Fulfils at length my every wish.

Kau. Come hither, youth. (*Embraces him.*)
He is, indeed, most like,

ments, and indicate a bias to the *Śaiva* faith. The *pípal* staff is a staff made of the wood of the *pípal* or holy fig-tree. The zone of *murvá* is a girdle fastened over one hip and hanging loosely over the other, made of the fibres of a kind of creeper, *Sanseviera zeylanica.*

Not only in his stature, nor in hue
As jetty as the sable leaves that float
Upon the stream, nor in his mellow voice,
Deep as the wild duck's cry when gathering pleased
The fibres of the lotus stalk; but most
His firm flesh is like Ráma's to the touch,
Hard as the seed-cup of the water-lily;
Then in his countenance—there well I see—
Dost thou not note it? (*To Janaka.*) Look attentively—
The features of my daughter, beauteous Sítá.

Jan. I mark it well.

Kau. My heart misgives me: hast thou a mother, child,
Or lives thy father in thy recollection?

Lava. Neither.

Kau. Whose art thou?

Lava. Wise Válmíki's.

Kau. Say on.

Lava. I know no more.

(*Behind.*) Warriors take heed, 'tis Chandraketu's order,
That none disturb the holy hermitage.

Arun. The prince is here; he leads the martial escort
That guards the consecrated steed; haply
We may behold him; this is fortunate.

Kau. The son of Lakshmańa commands—those sounds
Descend like drops of nectar in my ears.

Lava. Reverend sir, who is this Chandraketu?

Tam. Hast thou ever heard, brave youth,
Of Ráma and of Lakshmańa?

Lava. The heroes
Of the *Rámáyańa*?

Jan. The same.

Lava. How, should I not know it?

Jan. The son of Lakshmańa is Chandraketu.

Lava. The son of *Úrmilá*: the grandson thus
Of *Mithilá's* pious king.

Arun. He knows the history.

Jan. Since you are so well skilled in this, dear boy,
Tell us what other offspring had the sons
Of *Daśaratha*?

Lava. So much of the tale
Is not yet taught us.

Jan. Is it not composed?

Lava. It is, but not imparted; save a portion
For *Bharata*, the master of the drama,
To be performed, prepared, and, by the Sage
Himself, transcribed for an especial purpose.

Jan. What purpose?

Lava. To be taught by *Bharata*
To the *Apsarasas.* *

Jan. All this excites our curiosity.

Lava. Our reverend master
Is much engaged in this, and has despatched
His pupils with his work. Along with them,
Their guide and guard, in arms my brother went.

Kau. Hast thou a brother, child?

Lava. I have; his name is *Kuśa.*

Kau. Is he the elder?

Lava. In that his birth had just the start of mine.

Jan. Twin brethren are you then?

Lava. Grave sir, we are.

Jan. Tell us how far the tale of Ráma comes.

Lava. To Lakshmańa's return, when he had left
The delicate Sítá in the pains of travail,
Amidst the lonely woods, deserted thus,
To still the foul aspersions of the people.

Kau. Alas, my lovely child! that such a change,
The cruel work of destiny, should fall
Upon thy tender frame—and thou alone!

Jan. Poor helpless queen!
Disgrace, the forest terrors, and the pains

* The nymphs and actresses of *Indra's* paradise.

Of child-birth, all at once assail thy life;
The fiends impure close round their fated prey.
No refuge in thy fears. I cannot cease
To recollect thy sufferings.

Lava. Dame, who are these? (*To Arundhatí.*)*

Arun. Janaka and Kauśalyá.

Jan. Shame on the thankless race that wronged thy fame,
And Ráma's haste to listen to their calumnies.
The cruel blow that has o'erwhelmed my child
Arouses all my soul, and tempts my wrath
To deal with arms, or direr imprecations,
Destruction on my Sítá's persecutors.

Kau. Preserve us, dame, appease the royal sage.

Arun. Such expiation still must be performed
By all whom public calumny assails.
Remember Ráma is thy son: he claims
Thy love; the helpless people, too, demand
A king's compassion.

Jan. I indulge no hate
To either; Ráma ever is my son;
And for the citizens, I call to mind
Women and children, men infirm with years,
And sacred *Bráhmans* form the varied throng.

Enter PUPILS.

Pup. The horse, the horse!—so often in the *Vedas*
Read of—unseen, comes living in our sight.

Lava. The horse, the horse!—the mighty beast of war—
The beast of sacrifice. How looks he? tell me.

Pup. With four firm hoofs he spurns the ground: erect
He bears his arching neck; behind he lashes
His flowing tail, and scatters wide the grain.—
But whilst we chatter here he bounds away.
Come and behold. [*Lay hold of Lava.*

* The stage direction here is expressed with German precision. *Lava* surveys them with respectful and painful curiosity.

Lava. Elders, they drag me from you. [*Exeunt.*

Arun. Follow your pleasure.

Kau. Let us accompany him;
I live but in his sight.

Arun. His speed defies
Our tardy steps; we cannot keep in view
So fleet a runner.

Enter ATTENDANT.

Mess. I have seen Válmíki,
And to your questions thus replies the sage:—
That which is fit for you to know, in time
Shall be made known.

Jan. His answer is mysterious.
Come, matron and my friend; seek we, ourselves,
The venerable sage.

[*Exeunt.*

ANOTHER PART OF THE GROVE.

Enter LAVA *and the* PUPILS.

Pup. See, prince, is it not wonderful?

Lava. I see,
And recognise the *Aśwamedhik* steed.

Pup. How know you him?

Lava. Have you not read
The section that describes him? See, the guards
In mail arrayed, with spears and maces armed,
A hundred each, attend upon his course.
If you believe me not, go ask of them.

Pup. Ho! Soldier! tell, why is this steed so guarded?

Lava. (*Apart.*) The *Aśwamedha* is the glorious rite
Of all subduing monarchs; 'tis the mark
Of high pretension, and inflicts discredit
On every other of the warrior race.

Guard. The horse! brave youths. Upon the banner look,
And listen to the herald's cry: the steed
Is his who triumphed o'er the ten-necked fiend,
The only hero of the seven-fold world.

Lava. This is unbearable.

Pup. The prince is wise. What is it that he talks of?

Lava. Is earth deserted by the *Kshattriya* tribe,
That such proud vaunts are hazarded?

Guard. Compared
With our great prince, who can be called a *Kshattriya?*

Lava. Babblers! If there be such, they are, and know
No fear. Enough; away with idle words.
I, even I, will hurl that banner down,
Though guarded by your arrows. Hear me, friends
And fellows of my sports, drive off the horse
With clods of turf, and let him scamper hence
To gambol with the deer.

[*The boys run off.*

Enter a SOLDIER.

How now, imp of mischief, what would you do?
Away; a line of ruthless troops advance
To punish such mad pranks. The prince, with bow
Prepared, but gazing on yon lovely forest,
Awhile perceives you not; then haste away,
And hide yourselves amidst those clustering trees.

The Boys return.

(*To Lava.*) 'Tis done, as you desired.
The soldiers raise their bows, and point their shafts
Against you, and the hermitage is still
Remote. Fly; fly with the speed of deer.

[*Run off.*

Lava. Let the shafts fall, and the wide yawning bow
Expand its monstrous jaws, bristling with teeth

Innumerous and vast, round which the string
Laps like a tongue, impatient to distend
Its mighty stomach with its prey, and roaring
Loud as the clang of thunder-clashing clouds.

[*Exeunt.*

END OF THE FOURTH ACT.

ACT V.

Behind.

Ho, soldiers! haste, or we are put to shame!
See, hither speeds the prince: his charioteer
Urges the fiery steeds: Sumantra whirls
The lash, and on they bound, whilst o'er the head
Of Chandraketu his red banner floats
Loose to the breezes.

Enter CHANDRAKETU *in his Car, driven by* SUMANTRA.

Chan. What marvel 's this, Sumantra, what brave hero
Thus from his ceaseless-sounding bowstring rains
A shower of countless shafts upon our host?
Like a bright crest upon the brow of battle
The warrior shines, and as the mantling glow
Of scorn and anger kindles on his cheeks,
He wears a more than human loveliness.
Strange, that a lad, the son of some recluse
Or holy sage, should with such desperate valour
Singly defy a multitude of foes,
As if he was a scion yet unknown
Of *Raghu's* stock. With wonder I behold
His fiery darts that roar along the sky,
Like some wild elephant that cries with anguish,
When on his front the cleaving falchion falls.

Sum. Like thine his person; and his lofty bearing
Defies both gods and demons. As I gaze on him,
I call to memory Ráma, when, in youth,
He aimed his arrows at the host impure
That harassed *Kuśika's* exalted son.

Chan. I feel abashed when I observe his prowess.
Unmoved he stands, though round him madly rages

The storm of battle—through the murky air,
With clouds of dust obscured, the whirling sword
Flashes like lightning—rattle the rushing cars,
With jangling bells harsh pealing; onward roll
Like thunder-clouds the ponderous elephants,
Dark-laden with the tempest of the war.
He shouts defiance, and his clanging bow
Is heard above the rattling drums, more loud
And more reiterated than the din
Which mountain bowers reverberate to the roar
Of the wild elephant. The hero heaps
The earth with trunkless, tossing heads, as offerings
To satisfy the hungry king of death.

Sum. (*Apart.*) I dread to bring these daring youths together.
Should Chandraketu fall—and yet his birth
Demands the danger—if *Ikshwáku's* heir
Be wanting in the hour of peril, where
Shall man expect protection?

Chan. On every side the cowards yield. Oh, shame!

Sum. Prince, we are now within the hero's hail.

Chan. What name has by the heralds been proclaimed?

Sum. Lava.

Chan. Lava! Hero, hear!
Forbear these foes unworthy. Here am I.
On me exhaust thy daring, as on thee
My prowess longs to satisfy its craving.

Sum. He hears you, prince, and for a nobler enemy
Suspends pursuit: e'en so the lion's cub
Foregoes the flying elephant herd, and turns
To brave the falling thunderbolt.

Enter LAVA.

Lava. Hail, valiant prince! your words proclaim you worthy
Your lofty lineage, and of my encounter.
See, I obey your call! ——— (*Noise without.*)

What! do the slaves, once scattered from the field,
Return to seek the fight, and bar my way?
Though louder were their shouts than ocean's roar,
When o'er the wreck of worlds the blasts of fate
Drive his tumultuous waves, their clamours yield
Fresh fuel to my wrath, whose rising fires
More uncontrollable and fiercely glow,
Than the dread flames deep caverned in the earth,
And fed with splintered rocks.

Chan. Regard them not.
Esteem me as thy friend, for I admire
Thy merits; and consider thou as thine
Whate'er to me belongs. Thine are these troops,
And should not move thy anger; be thy prowess
Tried by the test of mine, and mine alone.

Lava. (*Turning back.*) This is indeed an honour, to receive
Such high encomium for this royal youth,
The bravest of the children of the sun.
Why measure him with these? Yet can I bear
These clamorous menaces, that from the crowd
Defy me? no; I thus efface my shame.

[*Rushes out.*

Chan. Behold him, where he speeds: with high disdain
He draws his bow against the crowds in front,
Whilst others press his rear. So central gleams
The bow of *Indra*, 'midst divided clouds,
Tossed in dissevered masses by the gale.
Ho! warriors, hear me: shall we thus be shamed
By such unequal fight?—shall valiant men
Attack a slender youth?—shall plaited mail
Oppose the deer-skin?—and the rattling car,
And horse, and elephant, combine to crush
A single foeman, as on foot he braves ye?

Lava. (*Returning.*) He pities me. Indeed, this waste of time
Shall cease. With heavenly arms I fight,

And they no more impede me.

[*Stands in the attitude of meditation.**

Chan. What is this?

The shouts are stilled.

Lava. Now for a nobler foe.

Sum. This is no common deed: the youth must wield
Celestial weapons.

Chan. It is true; for see,

In fearful change that equal pains the eye,
Alternate gloom to flashing lightning yields.
How like a painted army stands our host,
As the resistless charm subdues their senses;
And now along the sky dark vapours float
In masses, ponderous as the peaks of *Vindhya*,
And blackness gathered from the depths of hell;
Like molten brass, red sullen flames by fits
Glow through the gloom, and loud the breeze awakes,
As 'twere the wind of final dissolution.

Sum. Whence could he gain such power?

Chan. From whom,
But his great master, wise *Prachetas'* son?

Sum. Not his the gifts: *Kriśáśwa's* progeny
By him on *Viśwámitra* were bestowed,
And he to Ráma gave them.

Chan. Yet, perchance,
Others, who equally the light of truth
Within themselves possess, may of themselves
Obtain possession of the self-same powers.

Sum. Enough! Be on your guard: he comes.

Chan. and Lava. (*Together.*) 'Tis strange:
Some hidden cause my heart with rapture fills
At sight of this fair youth. Is it the hope
Of future converse—is it his lofty worth—

* This is a specimen of the use of the heavenly arms of which mention was made in the First Act. The weapon here employed is the *Jŕimbhaka*, or that which causes drowsiness; its influence is the result of *dhyána* or mediation.

Is it the fond transmission of regard
Felt in a former being—or does some tie
Of kindred undiscovered wake delight?

Sum. From various sympathies affection springs
In living beings. Oft the world's report,
The aspect of the stars, the eye's caprice,
Engenders love ere merit wins regard.
The sudden friend exacts no pledged requital;
For pure attachment is a bond sufficient
To knit two hearts together.

(*Looking at Lava, then aside.*)

Can it be?
Ah no! fate in the germ destroyed
The lovely plant. The parent stem cut down,
What flower shall blossom more?

Chan. I quit the car.

Sum. Why so?

Chan. To pay my homage to this valiant youth,
And do a soldier's duty. To assail
At such advantage one who fights on foot
The god of arms* forbids.

Sum. (*Apart.*) What shall I do?
The prince's will is worthy of his race,
And must not be opposed. Yet—can I bear
To witness such a conflict?

Chan. What will you say,
When men shall ask my father's honoured friend,
If Chandraketu did his duty?

Sum. Right.
War is the *Kshattriya's* duty, and thy race
Has never shrunk from contest: then proceed,
And shew thee worthy thy illustrious sires.†

* The *Sastra-devatá*, literally rendered in the text; but the Hindu Pantheon recognises no such personage, except *Kárttikeya* be intended. Perhaps merely the authorities or inspired teachers of the military art are intended.

† Several speeches of little interest are here omitted.

Lava. What mingled feelings rise as I approach him?
Dear to the night-flower as the rising moon,
His presence offers rapture to my sight;
But, as I grasp the heavy-clanging bow,
I feel my ardour for the fight revive,
And all my soul on fire.

Chan. (*Descending from the car, and bowing to Sumantra.*)
Accept, my friend,
The lowly reverence of Chandraketu,
Born of a race that boasts the Sun their sire.

Sum. May your great sire defend the sons he loves
In the dread hour of battle; may *Varáha*,*
All mighty and eternal, grant you fame,
And victory, and virtue, till you equal
The founder of your house;† may the great sage,
Your race's guardian, aid you; may the gods
Of air, and fire, and heaven, and may *Suparńa*‡
And *Vishńu's* self, infuse into thy heart
Their own celestial daring. Be the clang
Of Ráma's bowstring and of Lakshmańa's
The charm of potency to win thee victory.

Lava. Prince, you well become
The glittering car; this courtesy exceeds—

Chan. Do you, then, mount
An equal chariot.

Lava. (*To Sumantra.*) Honoured sir, persuade
The prince to keep his seat.

Sum. So you assent
To Chandraketu's wishes.

Lava. That would I do
Most cheerfully; but we are foresters,
The untaught tenants of the wood, and want
The princely skill to guide the car of battle.

* The incarnation of *Vishńu* as a boar.

† *Kakutstha*, the son of *Bhagíratha* and father of *Raghu*.

‡ *Garuda*, the monarch of the birds.

Sum. It is more strange that you so well are skilled
In dignity and courtesy. Trust me, youth,
Could *Rámabhadra* but behold thee thus,
His heart would melt with tenderness towards thee.

Lava. His fame has reached me, and I honour him;
And though I have presumptuously disturbed
The royal sacrifice, yet not the less
I feel deep reverence for the pious chief.
His vaunting followers alone provoked me,
To wipe away the infamy they heaped
On all the *Kshattriya* tribe.

Chan. Is it so hard
To own a sire's pre-eminence?

Lava. Not so:
But knows the prince the duties of a soldier?

Sum. You do not know the mighty *Rámachandra.*
Then speak not of him; you may boast, 'tis true,
You mastered feeble hearts like those in fight;
But when a foe like *Jámadagnya** bends
Beneath your arm, then you may vaunt your prowess.

Lava. A mighty triumph, truly! Is it not granted
A *Bráhman's* weapons are his words, and when
He wields a warrior's arms, his inexperience
Bears them inert? To conquer such a champion—
And such was *Jámadagnya*—is, methinks,
But scanty matter for a hero's praise.

Chan. Enough, enough! what hero, heavenly-born,
Descends on earth to hold in disesteem
The son of *Bhŕigu*, and who disregards
The might resistless that restored security
To all the universe?†

* The son of *Jamadagni, Paraśuráma.*

† He destroyed the *Kshattriya* or military race, except, it is said in some accounts, those in the solar line. Other statements aver that he exterminated all except some of the females who were married to *Bráhmans*, and thus continued the warrior tribe. As, however, many princes of both the solar and lunar dynasties are long subsequent to *Paraśuráma*, we must under-

Lava. (*In an ironical tone.*) I know the deeds
Of *Raghupati.* Long may he enjoy
His well-earned honours ; long may listening worlds
Admire the tale of his heroic exploits.
Still, glory wait upon the overthrow
Of a weak woman ; the advance that showed
No sign of fear when *Khara* felt his valour ;
And the bold scheme that conquered *Indrajit.**

Chan. Injurious youth, thy pride indeed is vast.

Lava. Away, great prince, I do not heed thy frown.

Sum. They burst with rage, and every limb is shook
With furious passion ; glows each sanguine eye
Like the red lotus ; the discoloured cheek,
And agitated brow are like the moon

stand his extermination of the *Kshattriyas* with a certain reservation. This is evidently necessary from the ordinary tenor of the story, which represents him as exterminating them twenty-one times : a succession of destructive feats he could scarcely have achieved, unless he "seven times thrice slew the slain."

* The destruction of *Táraká*, the disturber of the sacrifices of *Viśwámitra*, is related in the first book of the *Rámáyańa*, and the death of a woman is forbidden to a soldier. The backwardness of Ráma, or as it is described in the original, the three steps that were not in advance, does not so occur in the ordinary copies of the *Rámáyańa*, and the passage may have undergone some modification, as derogatory to the hero. Nothing about Ráma's retiring three paces has been met with in that part of the *Rámáyańa* which describes the death of *Khara* in the *Áraňya-Káńda ;* but it is admitted that Ráma felt alarm upon the approach of a mace hurled at him by the *Rákshasa :* "Seeing that weapon, like the mace of death, approaching, the prince was alarmed, considering that its flight could not be equalled or opposed by common arrows, the mace of the demon being of celestial origin." The attack upon *Indrajit*, which proved fatal to him, was the result of *Vibhíshańa's* advice, who was aware of a prophecy announced by *Brahmá*, that whoever should interrupt by force of arms a certain sacrifice commenced by that chieftain, would prove his destroyer. *Indrajit* was engaged in the rite, when, by the recommendation of *Vibhíshańa*, Lakshmańa and a party of Ráma's host were sent to attack the *Rákshasas*, who guarded him. The latter were routed. *Indrajit* abandoned the unfinished ceremony to come to their rescue, and was ultimately slain by Lakshmańa ; the exploit, therefore, added little to the glory of Ráma, as he took no part in the conflict, and as its result was predestined.

Stained with strange spots, or, like the water-lily,
When o'er its ruffled leaves the black bee spreads
His fluttering wings.

Lava and *Chan.* (*Together.*) Hence to the field of fight.

[*Exeunt.*

END OF THE FIFTH ACT.

ACT VI.

Enter a VIDYÁDHARA *and* VIDYÁDHARÍ *(a Male and Female Spirit of Air) in their Car.*

M. Sp. A fearful fight: less fierce the blows
When gods and Titans meet as foes.
See, love, what bright achievements grace
The warriors of the solar race.
Strained to each breast the bow is bent,
The shaft unintermitted sent;
The jangling bells incessant ring,
And frequent twangs the rattling string,
Whilst an alarum, long and loud,
Is sounded by yon thunder-cloud,
Inflated by supernal power,
In honour of such battle hour.
Quick, on each youthful champion's head,
A shower of heavenly blossoms shed,
Culled from the nectar-breathing tree
Of youth and immortality.

F. Sp. But what is this? o'er all the sky
The sudden streaks of lightning fly.

M. Sp. 'Tis *Maháadeva's* eye of flame
That opens on this battle game;
And from between the awful lashes,
Terrific in its glory, flashes
Such sparks, as scattered from the sun
On *Twashtri's* * whirling circle spun.

* *Twashtri*, the artist of the gods, the same with *Viśwakarman*, the father-in-law of *Súrya*. When *Sanjná*, unable to endure the splendours of her lord, fled from his embraces, the sun had recourse to her father, who, in order to temper his fierceness, put the planet on the grindstone and took off the edge of his rays.

Ah, no! I see the fiery blaze *—
'Tis Chandraketu's arm displays;
Around his car, with banneret,
And spears, and waving chowries set,
The fatal radiance rapid dances,
And on the chieftain's armour glances.
The warrior glows with yellow light,
The car is pale with ashen white—
'Tis all in flame—the god of fire
Puts forth his dread resistless ire,
And crackling, sparkling, roaring, strong,
His lambent furies curl along.
Now with the force of falling thunder
They rive the firmest rocks asunder.
The air is parching, love; beneath
My sheltering robe more coolly breathe,
And let us to a distance haste.

F. Sp. No further need; the peril 's past;
The scorching vapour glows no more,
The clouds distil their gelid store,
And pond'rous through the ether float,
As murky as the peafowl's throat,
Save where along their skirts entwine
The lightnings, like a wavy vine.

M. Sp. The shafts of *Varuńa* † arrest
In Lava's hand the fiery pest;
Yet still in vain; for now the wind,
From every quarter unconfined,
Comes sweeping forth, as 'twould displace
The world from off its solid base;
And swift along the lowering sky
The clouds before its fury fly:
And nature shakes, as if the gloom

* The *Ágneya* weapon, one of celestial armoury, or the weapon of fire.

† The deity of water, which element is wielded in the conflict.

Were Time's profound and yawning tomb,
Devouring all; or fated slumber
Were now preparing to encumber
The movements of the world, and close
Náráyań's senses in repose,
That, lost in him, the things of earth
Should cease awhile to issue forth.
'Twas wisely done, with *Váyu's* * force
To stem the torrent's gathering course,
And chase the clouds on Nature's breast,
Whence first they sprang, again to rest.

F. Sp. But who is this, that from his car
Alights to intercept the war,
And with his gentle speech controls
The fury of these daring souls?

M. Sp. 'Tis *Raghupati*; † he has slain
The fierce ascetic, and again
He seeks his realm. His voice they hear,
And cast aside the sword and spear:
Lava is calm; and lowly bends
The prince, as the great chief descends.
May fate conclude, as now begun,
This meeting of the sire and son. [*Exeunt.*

Enter RÁMA, LAVA, *and* CHANDRAKETU.

Ráma. Come, Chandraketu, to my breast, and cool
With thy embrace the fervour of my heart.

Chan. Receive my humblest homage.

Ráma. Fate, assuredly,
That gives thee power to wield celestial arms,
Auspicious smiles upon thy course.

Chan. My sire,
In this does fortune smile, that I have found

* The deity of wind, the element opposed to that of water.

† The lord, or chief, of the house of *Raghu*—Ráma.

A friend in this brave youth : may *Raghu's* lord
Behold him with the same complacent eye
He turns on me.

Ráma. This is indeed a presence
Of loftiest promise, active and robust,
As made a soldier's duty to fulfil,
To guard religion, and protect mankind.
Nor is there vigour only ; lighter graces
Are there concentred, and apparent virtues,
As if each excellence the world admires
Assumed a visible and human form.

Lava. (*Apart.*) Is this the mighty chief, the friend of virtue,
The stay and trust of men, the comforter,
The living shape of worth—embodied excellence ?
His sight subdues me—all my enmity
At once subsides—a new and strong affection
Grows in my bosom—all my pride is gone,
And shame o'ercomes me. First of the first is he—
As holiest shrines have oft a holier still.

Ráma. 'Tis strange a single glance should soothe my sorrow
And fill my breast with passionate regard !
What should the cause be ? for, without a cause,
How should affection ever be engendered ?
When no exterior motives can be traced,
Some secret spring must influence the heart.
Such are the sympathies that nature prompts,
When to the rising sun the flower expands,
And melts the moon-gem in the lunar ray.*

Lava. Instruct me, prince, who is this glorious chief ?

Chan. The elder of our house.

* The doctrine of sympathies was once very familiar to the philosophy of Europe. The moonstone, sunstone, and ironstone are three gems, according to the Hindus, the properties of which are analogous to the nature of the objects whence they are named. The latter is the magnet, the other two are fanciful : but probably the idea of them is derived from some natural substance.

Lava. How, *Raghunátha!*
Blest be the hour that I behold this deity.
(*Advances and bows down to the feet of Ráma.*)
Accept the veneration, prince, of Lava,
The lowly scholar of *Prachétas'* son.

Ráma. Arise, brave youth, forego this prostrate homage,
And find an equal welcome in my arms.
[*Embraces him.*

Lava. I merit not such graciousness; the less
That blind presumption led me here in enmity.
Forgive, my sire, the foolishness of Lava.

Ráma. What faults require forgiveness for my son?

Chan. Those of his native valour; for disdaining
The proud pretensions of the guards who followed
The sacrificial steed, he has displayed
Himself a hero.

Ráma. It was bravely done,
And like a *Kshattriya.* The true warrior brooks not
The vain assumptions of superior glory:
Fierce as the sun may dart his rays, he finds
The sunstone give them back in fiercer fire.

Chan. His brave disdain approves my friend a *Kshattriya;*
But more—he wields no common arms; observe,
Our troops are motionless, struck thus by him.

Ráma. (*To Lava.*) My son, undo the charm; and, Chandraketu,
Go forth and range them in array again,
And soothe their disappointed valour.

Chan. I obey. [*Exit.*

Lava. (*After meditating.*) The weapon is withdrawn.

Ráma. My son, these arms
Are of celestial origin; their use,
A mystery. The gods themselves obtained them
By ages of devotion, and the *Ŕishis*
Of primal days and powers supernal, saw them,
Self-radiant and endowed with wondrous virtue.
The holy texts that should enforce their service

The great *Kriśáśwa* taught * to *Viśwámitra*,
Through countless centuries his pious pupil;
And I from him received the sacred weapons,
Bound to attend for ever on my race.
Then tell me, Lava, by what potent means,
Whence, and from whom, didst thou obtain these arms?

Lava. Of themselves, uncalled, unsought-for, did they come
To me and to my brother.

Ráma. Thy brother?

Chan. We are twin.

Ráma. Where is he?

Kuśa (behind).

What say you, Lava is engaged alone
With Chandraketu's train? Then shall to-day
The pride of empire set in ignominy,
The towering crest of *Kshattriya* shall be humbled.

Ráma. Whom have we here? of deepest jet his hue,
And at his voice each hair upon my body
Starts up erect, like flowers that lift their heads
When hollow murmurs tell the coming storm.

Lava. 'Tis even he, my elder brother, Kuśa,
Returned from *Bharata's* abode.

Ráma. My son,
Invite him hither.

Lava. I obey; behold him!

Enter KUŚA.

This bow, whose string emits such vivid radiance
As gleams from heavenly arms, is fit for combat
With any of the mighty chiefs that trace
Their royal lineage, through the high descent
Of *Manu*, *Vaivaswata*, from the sun,

* Literally, "he declared to *Viśwámitra* the *Upanishad* containing the *Mantra*." It is clear, therefore, that by the use of these weapons, we are to understand the employment of charms, and the command over the elements, with which we are familiar in the magic of all countries.

Although of prowess to protect the gods
And tame the fiercest of the foes of heaven.

Ráma. What lofty daring does this youth display!
What brave defiance sparkles in his eye!
He seems to hold confederated worlds
As grass to trample on; he shakes the earth
With his proud tread; and though of tender years,
He shows of mountain stature. Is he mortal,
Or is it the spirit of valour that assumes
A mortal form?

Lava. Glory to your arms!

Kuśa. Rather to thine;
How now! I hear glad news—what's this?—war! war!

Lava. Restrain this swelling port, and hither come
With due humility.

Kuśa. Why so?

Lava. The godlike lord
Of *Raghu's* lineage deigns to give you welcome.

Kuśa. The godlike hero of our master's verse,
The guardian of the universal world?

Lava. The same.

Kuśa. How may I dare approach such majesty?
His presence awes me.* Justly has the bard
That sings his deeds entitled him divine.
Great sire, the scholar of *Prachetas*, Kuśa,
Bows thus in veneration.

[*To Ráma.*

Ráma. Rise, my child,
And yield me thy embrace. (*Embraces him.*) It is most strange:
Alike from either of these youths, the touch
Spreads rapture through my frame; from every pore
The dews, affection-born, distil, as if

* A few short speeches of no importance are omitted.

External consciousness were manifest;
And as my heart dissolves with ecstasy,
My form in waves of nectar seem to float.

Lava. Please you, sire,
To rest beneath the shelter of this tree.
The sun is high, and on my father's brow
Darts fiercely.

Ráma. As you will. (*They sit under a tree.*)
(*Apart.*) In every look and act, these youths display
The majesty that would become an empire.
Upon their forms has nature set the signs,
Like rays of light within a costly gem,
Or drops of nectar on a lovely lotus,
That indicate such glorious destiny,
As should alone to *Raghu's* sons pertain.
Dark as the dove's blue neck is their deep hue;—
Such shoulders has themonarch of the herd;—
Their dauntless looks are like the angry lion's;—
And, like the deep-toned music of the drum
Of holy sacrifice, each mellow voice.
I see in each my own similitude;
And not alone my likeness, but in much
They wear the lovely semblance of my Sítá.
The lotus countenance of Jánakí
Is even now before me;—such those teeth
Of pearly whiteness;—such the pouting lip,
The taper ear, and such the expressive eye,
Although 'tis tempered with a manly fierceness.
Their dwelling in these groves, the very same
Where Sítá was abandoned, and so like—
And then the heavenly weapons, self-presented,
That, as the sages say, would never quit
Our line without due cause—my queen's condition,
Burthened with promised joys—these thoughts distract
My heart, and fill my soul with hope and terror.

How can I learn the truth?—how ask these youths
The history of their birth?

Lava. What should this be? the countenance that sheds
Delight on all is now suffused with tears,
Like the bright lotus stained with drops of dew.

Kuśa. Remember, brother, of his queen bereft
The mighty Ráma cannot choose but sorrow.
Torn from the heart beloved, the world becomes
A dreary waste, and this sad separation
Is doomed to know no term. How could you utter
Such simple doubts, who know the song of Ráma?

Ráma. I am afraid to ask them. Let me hush
These fancies—my emotion has excited
Their notice and their pity—let me be firm.
Have you perused, my sons, Válmíki's verse?
I fain would hear something of his description
Of the bright glories of the solar race.

Kuśa. We have perused the poem. I retain
Some passages; please you, I will repeat them.

Ráma. Let me hear them.

Kuśa. "She formed for love; and Ráma's tender breast
To love, the prince was now supremely blest;
Nor less her lord did Sítá's thoughts inspire,
And mutual passion crowned each heart's desire."

Ráma. I cannot check my tears—so true this strain.
Alas! the uses of the world are now
Stale and unprofitable—a disordered chaos,
Involved in care, and closed by separation.
Where is the happiness on which our hopes
May rest with confidence? where is the worth
That mutually delights? where is that firm
And lasting union of two loving hearts,
Inseparably one in joy and sorrow?
Life ever blooms, but error ever blights it.
Blest be the verse that calls again to mind
The least of all the thousand excellences

That time, the foe of memory, would rob me of.
I see my Sítá now—when budding youth,
Expanded day by day into the bloom
Of woman, and when full-blown beauty joined
With ardent passion to subdue my heart,
And animate my every thought with love.
'Tis past,—how wonderful!

[*Sinks into meditation.*

Lava. How lost in thought he seems! not even a sigh
Steals forth, a sign of life: so silent lies
Some sacred statute in its holy shrine.*

(*Behind.*) The sages of the hermitage—the queen
Of *Daśaratha*, and Arundhatí,
Alarmed to hear the violence the youths
Have offered to the steed, are coming hither;
Yet slow their progress—age retards their flight,
Their limbs are tardy though their minds are fleet.

Ráma. What! are Arundhatí and Janaka,
Vasisht'ha, and my honoured mother, here?

[*Rising and looking out.*

Yes, I behold the monarch; like a thunderbolt
His sight affects me: with the holy priests
Who joined our hands; with so much to recall
The hopes that all have perished; thus to meet him,
And not to fall into a thousand fragments!
What task remains for Ráma to perform!

(*Behind.*) Alas! the unexpected sight of Ráma
O'ercomes the aged king; and now the queen,
Hastening to aid her ancient friend, beholds
Her son and senseless falls.

Ráma. Revive, my sire!
My dearest mother! oh, how ill deserved

* The Calcutta edition follows a different reading here in some passages.

This tenderness of all that either house
Yet boasts for one so pitiless as I!—
Yet let me haste to them.

Kuśa and *Lava.* This way—this way!

[*Exeunt rapidly.*

END OF THE SIXTH ACT.

ACT VII.

AN AMPHITHEATRE ON THE BANKS OF THE GANGES.*

Enter LAKSHMAŃA.

I have obeyed the sage, and have arranged
A theatre to hold this vast assemblage
Of gods, and men, and spirits of earth, air, ocean,
The serpent deities, and all the forms
That move and breathe—called hither by Válmíki,
On Ganga's sacred banks, that they may hear
His inspirations, with dramatic art,
Recited by the nymphs of *Indra's* heaven.
All is prepared, and the assembly waits—
And lo! the prince, who in his palace bears
The hardships of the anchorite, approaches.

Enter RÁMA.

Now, Lakshmańa, is the assembly gathered
For this performance?

Lak. All is ready.

Ráma. Be the youths,
Lava and Kuśa, stationed with the prince,
Your son.

Lak. Your wishes are foreseen—they sit together.
This is the royal seat.

* A play in a play is a device familiar to our theatre; that in Hamlet need scarcely be mentioned. Beaumont and Fletcher go further, and combine four plays in one. They are not so essential to the plot, however, as this and the play in Hamlet, both which representations indicate the opinion entertained by the authors of the moral efficacy of such performances.

Ráma. (*Sitting.*) Let them begin.

Enter MANAGER.

The sage *Prachetas'* son, the oracle
Of truth, thus issues his commands: let all
Assembled here, attend to the high tales
Of wonder and of holiness, related
As by the eye of saintly prescience seen.

Ráma. Enough! we know the *Ŕishis* are all holy;
Their wisdom is exempted from the stain
Of passion, and with immortality
Impregnate; and their words can never fail
Our reverence and attention.

Sítá. (*Within.*) Alas, alas! where art thou, dearest lord?
Brave Lakshmańa, where thou? The beasts of prey
Press round me to devour me—me—alone,
Unsheltered, undefended, in the forest.
What dreadful pangs!—I can no more sustain
This agony—these fears.—I will devote
My life to *Bhágírathí.*

Lak. This is piteous!

The Manager. The daughter of the earth, the helpless queen,
Her lord abandons to the lonely woods—
Now, as the pains of travail agonise her,
Consigns herself to Ganga's sacred wave. [*Exit.*

Ráma. (*Starting up.*) Dear love, forbear!
I fly to thy assistance.

Lak. Does my lord
Remember, what he views is but a fiction?

Ráma. Alas! that such a portion should have been
The gift of Ráma to his tender bride,
The dear companion of his forest dwelling!

Lak. Suppress these thoughts—let us attend the story.

Ráma. I am armed! pierceless as adamant.
[*Sits down.*

Enter SÍTÁ, *supported by* PŔITHIVÍ (*the Earth*) *and* GANGÁ (*the Ganges*), *each bearing a new-born Child.*

Ráma. Lakshmańa, I am lost; my senses stray
In sudden and bewildering gloom,—support me.

Gan. Revive, *Vaidehí!* Fate is now thy friend.
Amidst the waves, in safety hast thou given
Two hopes to *Raghu's* line.

Sítá. Can this be true?
Are these my infants? ah, my loved lord!
[*Fainting.*

Gan. Resume thy fortitude; my child, revive.

Sítá. Who art thou?

Pŕi. 'Tis *Bhágírathí*, the protecting goddess
Of your lord's line.

Sítá. (*Bowing to Gangá.*) Receive my adoration.

Gan. May the reward of virtue ever wait thee!
Behold thy mother, reverend goddess, earth.

Sítá. Am I so blest?

Pŕi. Let this embrace assure thee. [*Fainting.*

Lak. The queen is fondly cherished by the deities.

Ráma. Their love for this, their child, o'ercomes their spirits.
This passion of the soul, the common attribute
Of sentient beings, is the knot that binds
The cord that holds the universe, and till
The end of all perpetuates the race.

Gan. (*To Sítá.*) Dear child, earth's progeny, console thy parent.

Pŕi. What comfort can I know, being her parent,
Whose days, first blighted by the cruel fiend,
Are now by calumny unjust assailed?

Gan. 'Tis true; but subject to the will of fate,
What living thing may hope to bar its way?

Pŕi. But yet what plea can be devised for Ráma,
Who would not trust to me, to Janaka,
To holy fire, nor past, nor future knowledge,

Nor credited this tender hand, the pledge
Of faith and love, in youth to him consigned?

Sítá. Ah! does my husband still remember me?

Pŕi. Thy husband! who is he?

Sítá. Even he whom now my mother spoke of.

Ráma. And spoke of as he merited.

Gan. Queen, reflect. (*To Ṕrithiví.*)
Thou art the stay of all; and shalt thou share
The passions of the ignorant? Consider,
What he has done, the honour of his race
Imperatively willed; for wide and far
The stain upon his name was spread:—the test
In *Lanká* undergone, not elsewhere witnessed,
Was little credited, and it has been
The triumph of his high and royal race,
To claim the homage free and unreserved
Of all the world; what, then, remained for Ráma,
In this dilemma, else than to pursue
The course that he has trod?

Pŕi. Goddess, I hear
Your censures with delight; but strong affection
Controls my thoughts and language. Well I know
The love of Ráma, and the grief he feels
For loss of this dear child; yet, still he lives
For the sole benefit of his subject tribes,
For which, in other worlds, rewards await him.

Sítá. Oh, let my mother take
And hide me in her bosom!

Gan. Child, forbear.
Yet many years thy presence shall dispense
Delight upon mankind.

Pŕi. And for the present
These infants claim thy care.

Sítá. A widow I.

Pŕi. How should this be, whilst yet thy husband lives?

Sítá. I shall not live! how then have I a lord?

Prí. Think not so lightly of thyself, whose nature,
Pure as it is, still purer from communion
With us, shall shed new blessings on the world.

Lak. Heard you the queen?

Ráma. Let all the world receive
This testimony. (*A noise without.*) Hark! what wonders more?

Sítá. The heavens are overcast.

Gan. 'Tis true; observe,
The heavenly arms are visible, the ministers
Of Ráma, from *Kríśáśwa* first descended,
To *Viśwámitra* next, and last to him.

(*Behind.*) Great queen, all hail!
Behold the faithful servants of thy children—
As *Raghupati* erst to thee announced,
His servants we, the servants of thy sons.

Sítá. Oh, I am blest! the weapon gods appear
In all their glory.

Gan. Hail! celestial ministers,
Devoted to the race of *Raghu*—still to work
The will of his descendants—hail! all hail!
They disappear. Now, daughter, turn thine eye
On these infantine pictures of thy lord.

Sítá. Ah! who shall minister the holy rites
Their birth demands, that great *Vasishtha's* care
Has ever solemnised for *Raghu's* race?

Gan. This, daughter, need not dwell upon thy thoughts.
When they no more exact a mother's charge,
We will convey them to Válmíki's bower.
Prachetas' son, equal in power and knowledge
To *Angiras* or to *Vasishtha*, shall
Become their mighty master, and perform
The ceremonial rites their years require.

Ráma. This was well thought.

Lak. Does not the prince perceive,
In this, the birth of Kuśa and of Lava
Is covertly apprised him? From their infancy
Have they been masters of the heavenly arms;
They have received each sacred ordinance
From great Válmíki, and their vigorous youth
Numbers the years that now have passed away
Since the fair queen was sentenced to the woods.

Ráma. My heart beats high. I cannot speak my thoughts.

Pŕi. Come, daughter, with thy presence hallow earth.

Sítá. Most gladly; I am weary of the world.

Pŕi. Discharge thy dues maternal; when these boys
No more require thee, thou shalt be contented.

Sítá. Let it be so.

[*Exeunt Sítá, Gangá, and Pŕithiví.*

Ráma. Lo, earth receives her in its hollow caves!
Dear queen, fond partner of my forest dwelling,
Whose every thought is virtue, does, indeed,
Another world divide us, and for ever?

[*Faints.*

Lak. All-wise Válmíki, grant us thy protection—
For, such the purpose of thy sacred poem.

(*Behind.*) Remove the instruments of harmony—and let
All present mark the marvels that are wrought
By great Válmíki's will.

Lak. The waters of the Ganges are upheaved
With sudden agitation—all the sky
Is crowded with divinities; behold,
Where rising from the depth, the queen appears,
By Gangá and by Pŕithiví supported:
Hither she comes rejoicing.

(*Behind.*) Receive from us, Arundhatí, the pure
And faithful Sítá.

Lak. Prince, behold these wonders:
Alas! he still is senseless.

Enter ARUNDHATÍ *and* SÍTÁ.

Arun. Why thus bashful?
Haste thee, my child, and let the consciousness
Of that dear hand restore thy lord to life.

Sítá. (*Touching Ráma.*) He wakes.

Ráma. (*Reviving.*) My queen, my love!
My honoured mother, pure Arundhatí,
With *Ŕishyaśŕinga* and the pious *Śántá.*—
All here—all happy.

Arun. Prince, awhile attend;
The goddess of thy race in favour speaks.

Gangá. (*Without.*) Lord of the world, remember thy appeal.*
Thou hast invoked my cares for this thy queen,
That as a mother I should guard her ever,
Even as would Arundhatí. Behold,
I have obeyed thy will; my debt is paid.

Arun. Again attend; thy mother earth addresses thee.

Ṕrithiví. (*Without.*) Lord of the world, remember thy appeal;
Thou hast committed *Sítá* to my charge,
And called upon me to protect my child.
I have obeyed thy will; my debt is paid.

Ráma. (*Prostrating himself.*)
How have I, sinful as I am, deserved
Such heavenly favour?

Arun. People of *Ayodhyá,*
Receive your queen, whom the great goddesses,
Gangá and Ṕrithiví, thus highly honour,
And now by me, Arundhatí, presented you.
The gods themselves have testified her purity,
And fire borne witness to her spotless virtue.

* See the First Act.

From sacrifice she draws her birth,* and reigns
Wife of the greatest of the Sun's descendants.
Recall these things, and yield her veneration.

Lak. They feel the matron's censure : all the crowd
Is bent in prostrate homage to the queen,
Whilst from above, the guardians of the spheres,
And rulers of the planets, shed delighted,
A shower of heavenly flowers.

Arun. Lord of the world, imperial *Rámabhadra*,
In place of her similitude, be *Sítá*
Herself the partner of your sacred rite.

Ráma. Most joyfully.

Lak. (*To Sítá.*) Lady and queen, the shameless Lakshmańa
Is bold enough to offer you his homage.

Sítá. May length of days reward such worth as thine.

Arun. Now may the sage lead forth the lovely twins,
Kuśa and Lava, to embrace their parents.

Ráma. This is joy indeed!

Sítá. Where are my children?

Enter VÁLMÍKI *with* KUŚA *and* LAVA.

Vál. Behold your parents, children ; the prince Lakshmańa,
And there your grandsire—this your father's mother.

Sítá. My dear father, too!

Kuśa and *Lava.* Dear father! dearest mother!

Ráma. (*Embracing them.*) This is a recompense for all our sorrows.

Sítá. Come hither, Kuśa—hither, Lava—come
Embrace your mother, now indeed restored
To life.

Kuśa and *Lava.* We are most blest.

Sítá. Lord, I salute thee (*to Válmíki*).

Vál. May thy days be many.

Sítá. My dear father! thus, with all I love encompassed,
How can I bear so vast a weight of happiness.

* Sítá was born of the earth at a sacrifice performed by Janaka.

(*A noise behind.*)

Vál. (*Looking out.*) The demon *Lavaña* is slain, and here
The prince of *Mathurá* advances.

Lak. All
Conspires to make our happiness complete.

Ráma. I scarce can credit what I see—yet thus
Does fate oppress the prosperous.

Vál. Ráma,
Is there ought else that may require our aid?

Ráma. Nought, holy sire, but this:
May that inspired strain, whose lines impart
This tale, delight and purify the heart;
As with a mother's love, each grief allay,
And wash, like Gangá's wave, our sins away.
And may dramatic skill and taste profound
Pourtray the story and the verse expound,
So that due honour ever shall belong
To the great master of poetic song,
Alike familiar with a loftier theme,
The sacred knowledge of the ONE SUPREME.*

[*Exeunt.*

* The poet acquainted with the *Brahma-Śabda*, the inspired and uncreated *Vedas*, as identifiable with *Brahman* or the Supreme Being.

REMARKS ON THE UTTARA-RÁMA-CHARITRA.

THIS drama labours under the disadvantage of a subject drawn from national mythology; and although the more interesting on that account to those to whom it was originally addressed, it must lose much of its merit in the eyes of those to whom the mythos of the Hindus is unattractive or unknown.

Another defect, consequent upon the choice of its subject, is the want of action. The incidents are few, and although not unconnected with each other, nor independent of the *denouement*, they occur abruptly, and are separated by intervals of time and place, which trespass a little too strongly upon dramatic probabilities, and impair the interest of the story.

Apart from these defects, however, the drama has much to recommend it, and has more pretension to genuine pathos than perhaps any other specimen of the Hindu theatre. The mutual sorrows of Ráma and Sítá in their state of separation are pleasingly and tenderly expressed, and the meeting of the father and his sons may be compared advantageously with similar scenes with which the fictions of Europe, both poetical and dramatic, abound.

Besides the felicitous expression of softer feelings, this play has some curious pictures of the *beau ideal* of heroic bearing, and of the duties of a warrior and a prince. A higher elevation can scarcely be selected for either. The true spirit of chivalry pervades the encounter of the two young princes; and the quiet devotedness with which Ráma sacrifices his wife and domestic happiness to the prosperity of his subjects, is a worthy counterpart to the immolation of natural affections to public interest, which is so frequent in the early history of Greece.

The characters of the drama are individualised by the features just noticed as belonging to those of the heroic class, and by the sentiments of piety and the tone of authority which animate the religious personages introduced upon the scene; amongst whom, that females bear so important a part, may be regarded as another characteristic peculiarity. The incidents, as already noticed, are not numerous; but they are dramatic and interesting, and upon the feelings of a Hindu must have exercised a powerful influence. To a belief that vivifies all objects, and gives to mountains and rivers divine forms and sentient natures, the representations of this play must have been awful and sublime. The most inferior of the personages exhibited are the spirits of air, or of the forest, or the flood, who mingle familiarly and affectionately with demigods and deified sages. Earth, the mother of all beings, and Gangá, the river of the three worlds, are introduced in person; and the final reunion of Ráma with his family is witnessed, not only by the people of Ayodyhá and the elders of either race, but by the congregated deities of earth and heaven.

The language of the beings of fictitious existence is either narrative or descriptive, and in the former is simple, and in the latter picturesque. That of the human characters is, as usual with our author, rather passionate than poetical; but some brilliant thoughts occur, the justice and beauty of which are not surpassed in any literature. The comparison of Chandraketu to a lion's cub turning to brave the thunderbolt is one of these; and another is the illustration of the effects of education upon minds possessed or destitute of natural gifts. It is needless to specify other passages. The general tone of the piece is imaginative and elevated, and it is entitled at least to the designation of a dramatic poem.

SELECT SPECIMENS
OF THE
THEATRE OF THE HINDUS

SELECT SPECIMENS
OF THE
THEATRE OF THE HINDUS

TRANSLATED FROM
THE ORIGINAL SANSKRIT

BY

HORACE HAYMAN WILSON
BODEN PROFESSOR OF SANSKRIT IN THE UNIVERSITY OF OXFORD

IN TWO VOLUMES

VOL. II

Third Edition

GYAN

Published by

Gyan Publishing House
5, Ansari Road
Daryaganj, New Delhi-110002
Phone: 011-47034999, 9811692060
E-mail: books@gyanbooks.com

Distribution Network
gyanbooks.com
India, USA, Canada, UK, Australia, France

ISBN : 978-81-212-3992-9 (Set)
ISBN : 978-81-212-4906-5 (HB)
First Published, 1871

2nd Impression 2020

Printed at: Gyan Press, Delhi.

The book at your disposal is the edition of an old book originally published long back. The Text quality of this book may not be at par as compared to our other books but many readers approached us to reprint this important book so that it could satiate their hunger. We request all the readers of this book to help us to improve its quality by providing the necessary text of those pages which are not properly visible. Your valuable support in this case will be highly appreciated and acknowledged and our future readers will be benefitted immensely.

SELECT SPECIMENS

OF THE

THEATRE OF THE HINDUS

TRANSLATED FROM

THE ORIGINAL SANSKRIT.

BY

HORACE HAYMAN WILSON, M.A., F.R.S.,

BODEN PROFESSOR OF SANSKRIT IN THE UNIVERSITY OF OXFORD,

IN TWO VOLUMES.

VOL. II.

Third Edition.

LONDON:

TRUBNER & CO., 60 PATERNOSTER ROW.

1871.

CONTENTS OF VOL. II.

APPENDIX,

CONTAINING SHORT ACCOUNTS OF DIFFERENT DRAMAS.

MÁLATÍ AND MÁDHAVA,

OR

THE STOLEN MARRIAGE.

A Drama,

TRANSLATED FROM THE ORIGINAL

SANSCRIT.

INTRODUCTION.

Málatí and Mádhava; or, The Loves of the Youth Mádhava and the Maiden Málatí, has been already introduced to the knowledge of European readers, as an outline of the plot and a translation of part of the fifth Act were published by Mr. Colebrooke in his Essay on Sanscrit and Prakrit Prosody,* p. 51. The specimens then given were calculated to convey a favourable impression of the merits of the drama, which the perusal of the entire piece will probably confirm.

The story of *Málatí* and *Mádhava* is one of pure invention, and the piece belongs to the class of compositions termed *Prakarana*. It is referred to as an example of the class by all the works on *Rhetoric,* the oldest of which it consequently precedes. The history of the drama, however, or more correctly of its author, is attended with more certainty than most of the topics of the literary history of the Hindus.

By the introductions to *Málatí* and *Mádhava,* and the other dramas of the same writer, the *Uttara Rama Cheritra* and the *Vira Cheritra,* we are made fully acquainted with his origin and family. It appears from these accounts that Bhavabhúti, also named Sríkantha, or he in whose throat eloquence resides, was the son of a native of the South of India, a Brahman of Berar or Beder, and a member of the tribe of Brahmans who pretend to trace their descent from the sage Kasyapa, of whom it is said that some are still to be found in the vicinity of Condavir. The site of Bhavabhúti's birth-place is fully cor-

* *Asiatic Researches,* vol. x.

roborated by the peculiar talent he displays in describing nature in her magnificence, a talent very unusual in Hindu bards, who delight to pourtray her minuter beauties, and one which he no doubt derived from his early familiarity with the eternal mountains and forests of Gondwana.

It appears, however, that the place of Bhavabhúti's nativity was not the scene of his literary triumphs, and that these were attained under the patronage of the princes of Hindustan. The precision with which he delineates the topographical features of Ujayin and its vicinity, leaves little doubt of his having spent some time at that city, for accuracy in this respect could have been obtained at any time in India only by actual observation. The *Bhoja Prabandha,* indeed, includes Bhavabhúti amongst the writers at the Court of Bhoja at Dhár, but as intimated elsewhere,* this work can only be received as an authority for the priority of the writers described in it to the date of its own composition; the grouping, whether as regards place or time, being altogether fanciful. A preferable authority, the text of the *Dasa Rúpaka,* refers Bhavabhúti to some period anterior to Munja, the predecessor of Bhoja, by its alluding clearly to *Málatí* and *Mádhava,* and from it therefore we gather that the play was composed before the eleventh century. How long anterior to that date we have also evidence to substantiate, and from the History of Cashmir we learn that Bhavabhúti flourished in the eighth century, being patronised by Yasovermá, the sovereign of Kanoj, who reigned about A.D. 720.

The date thus given to the compositions of Bhavabhúti is quite in harmony with their internal evidence. The manners are purely Hindu without any foreign admixture. The appearance of women of rank in public, and their exemption from any personal restraint in their own habitations, are very incompatible with the presence of Mohammedan rulers. The licensed existence of *Bauddha* ascetics, their access to the great, and their employment as teachers of science, are other peculiarities

* Sanscrit Dictionary, Preface.

characteristic of an early date, whilst the worship of SIVA in his terrific forms, and the prevalence of the practices of the *Yoga*, are indications of a similar tendency. The *Linga* worship of SIVA, we know, was every where the predominant form of the Hindu faith when the Mohammedans first invaded India. With respect to the *Yogis*, by whom mystical rites were mostly cultivated, it may be observed, that there are many reasons for giving them a remote date: the excavations at Elephanta and Ellora appear to be their work; the sect is now almost extinct in Hindustan; and the *Kásí Khand*, a work probably of seven or eight centuries remote, states that the *Yoga* cannot be practised in the present age. Mysticism, in fact, gave way first to the philosophy of SANKARA ACHÁRYA in the seventh or eighth century, and was finally expelled by the new doctrine of *Bhakti*, or faith, which was introduced by RÁMÁNUJA and the *Vaishnavas* in the eleventh century, and has since continued to be the ruling dogma of every sect of Hindus.

The style of *Málatí* and *Mádhava* may also be referred to the period at which we may conclude that it was written. It is free from the verbal quibbling and extravagance of combination which the compositions of the time of BHOJA offer, but it comes very near to them: although classical it is highly laboured; although forcible it is diffuse, and is not unfrequently obscure. It abounds in the most complicated prosody, and is cited by Mr. Colebrooke for a specimen of the measure called *dandaka*, or a verse of fifty-four syllables, and a stanza consequently containing two hundred and sixteen. The author is also fond of an unreasonable display of learning, and occasionally substitutes the phraseology of logic or metaphysics for the language of poetry and nature. At the same time, the beauties predominate over the defects, and the language of the drama is in general of extraordinary beauty and power. The blemishes of the composition have materially affected the translation; and while it is very probable that the obscurity of some passages has led to an inexact interpretation of their import, the prosaic prolixity of others has involved the necessity of considerable compression and occasional omissions. The latter, when of any importance, will be particularized as they occur.

Málatí and *Mádhava* divides with *Sakuntalá* the honour of being still occasionally, although not very commonly, read by the Pandits; copies of it therefore are not very scarce. That used for the present translation was transcribed from Mr. Colebrooke's as being singularly free from errors. It had the advanvantage also of being illustrated by two excellent commentaries. The most copious of these is the work of JAGADDHARA, the son of RETNADHARA, described as a learned teacher, the prince of Pandits and poets, and administrator of law; the other is by a royal hand, the *Rájádhirája* MALANKA. We have no further particulars of these commentators, except that the first is known to have been a *Maithila* Brahman, and not very ancient.

DRAMATIS PERSONÆ.

Men.

Mádhava.—The son of *Devaráta*, studying at *Padmavátí*, in love with *Málatí*.

Makaranda.—His friend, in love with *Madayantiká*.

Kalahansa.—*Mádhava's* servant.

Aghoraghanta.—Priest of *Chámundá*, a terrific goddess.

A Messenger.

Women.

Málatí.—The daughter of the Minister of State *Bhúrivasu*, in love with *Mádhava*.

Madayantiká.—The sister of *Nandana* and friend of *Málatí*, in love with *Makaranda*.

Kámandakí.—Priestess of *Buddha*, nurse of *Málatí*, and Preceptress of *Mádhava*.

Kapála Kundalá.—Priestess of *Chámundá*.

Saudáminí.—Disciple of *Kámandakí*, and possessor of magical powers.

Lavangiká.—Foster sister of *Málatí*.

Mandáriká.—Attendant on *Kámandakí*, beloved by *Kalahansa*.

Buddharakshitá
Avalokitá } Disciples of *Kámandakí*.

Female Attendants.

Persons spoken of.

The Sovereign of *Padmávatí.*

Nandana.—His favourite, the brother of *Madayantiká.*

Bhúrivasu.—His minister, the father of *Málatí.*

Devaráta.—The father of *Mádhava,* and minister at *Kundinípura.*

Scene.—*Ujjayini* (*Ougein*), designated most usually as *Padmávatí,* and its vicinity.

Time.—A few days.

PRELUDE.

BENEDICTION.

MAY the trepidations of *Vináyaka's** countenance, attended by the cry of terror, long preserve you! those trepidations which at the dance of *Súlapáni*† proceeded from the entrance into his nostrils of the Lord of serpents with contracted hood, frightened at the cry of *Kumára's*‡ peacocks, upon hearing the sound of the tabor struck by the delighted *Nandi*,§ and whence the regions were filled with the buzzing of bees flying away from his temples.

May the tresses interwoven with a circular garland of serpents for flowers, where the waters of the *Mandákiní*|| are flowing over the lower chaplet of skulls worn in the crest, luminous with the light of the eye of the forehead, sparkling like lightning, and of which the young moon is confounded with the point of the *kétaka* flower, preserve thee!¶

* *Gánésa.*

† *Siva*, or the god who holds a trident in his hand.

‡ *Kártikéya*, the son of *Siva* and *Párvati*, the deity of war, represented as riding on a peacock.

§ *Nandi* is an attendant upon *Siva.*

|| The Ganges of heaven, supposed to trickle through the tresses of *Siva.*

¶ The perusal of the preceding dramas will have partly prepared the reader to understand this benediction; but it involves a number of Hindu common places, and may require explanation to be rendered intelligible.

Siva, for the amusement of *Párvatí* his bride, originated a particular dance, to the musical accompaniment of the tabor, struck by his attendant *Nandi.* His sons were present: *Kártikéya* mounted on his peacock, and *Ganésa* with the head and trunk of an elephant. *Siva* is embellished with a collar

Enter MANAGER.

Enough! what need of prolixity. (*Looking to the East.*) Ha! the celestial luminary, enlightening all the divisions of the world, is completely risen. I salute him.* (*Bowing.*) Oh thou, the universal form, who art the vessel of all auspicious light, be propitious to me, and enable me to support the burthen of the drama: remove from me, Lord of the world, thus prostrate, every sin, and augment all that is favourable to success. (*Looking off the Stage.*) Ho! *Márisha!*† the auspicious preparations are complete; from all quarters persons of distinction have come to celebrate the festival of *Kálapriyanáth*,‡ and I have been

---

a collar of the hooded snake twining round his neck and surmounting his head. The peacock is supposed to be particularly delighted by the approach of the rainy season, and the bird of *Kártikéya*, mistaking the deep sound of the drum for the rolling of thunder indicative of a storm, screams with delight. The peacock is considered the natural enemy of snakes, and the snake of *Siva*, alarmed at the approach of his mortal foe, deserts his place on the neck of the deity, and makes for the first hiding place he can find. This happens to be the tip of *Ganésa's* elephant trunk; his entrance into which disturbs the bees that are supposed to settle on the temples of an elephant. This is the purport of the first verse.

In the second, the author refers to the mode in which the hair is delineated in the figures of *Siva*, and as it is worn by the ascetics who profess his worship. It is allowed to grow long, and is then divided into three or four tresses, which are braided together and coiled upon the anterior part of the crown of the head, the apex of the coil projecting forwards a little on the right side. *Siva* also wears round his head a braid of snakes and a chaplet of skulls, and he has a half moon on his forehead; in the centre of his forehead is his third eye whose glances are of flame, and over his head flows the Ganges.

In these allusions the author refers to the popular personification of *Siva*, untinged with any references to his mystical worship.

* We may infer from this that the Hindu dramas were represented early in the morning.

† One term by which an actor is to be addressed.

‡ Who this deity is, is not known to the Pundits of the present day. *Malanka* takes no notice of the name; *Jagaddhara* is content to say it is that of a sort of divinity worshipped in that country. It is probably the appellation of a *Siva Linga*. In the *Varáha Purána*, *Kála Priya* is said to be a form

commanded by these wise and learned auditors to represent to them some new dramatic tale. How now! are the actors lazy?

Enter ACTOR.

Actor. We are not informed, sir, of the kind of piece required by the audience.

Man. Say, *Mârisha,* what are those qualities which the virtuous, the wise, the venerable, the learned, and the Brahmans require in a drama?

Actor. Profound exposition of the various passions, pleasing interchange of mutual affection, loftiness of character, delicate expression of desire, a surprising story, and elegant language.

Man. Then I recollect one.

Actor. What is it, sir?

Man. There is in the South, and in the province of *Viderbha,** a city named *Padma nagara,* where dwelt certain Brahmans of the family of *Kasyapa,* and followers of the *Tittiri* portion of the *Vedas* according to the teacher *Charana;* taking precedence at festivals, maintaining the five fires, observers of religious obligations, drinkers of the *Soma* juice, possessing names of note, and learned in the *Vedas.*† These Brahmans

---

a form of the sun worshipped to the south of the *Yamuná,* and *Kálapriya Náth,* his lord or god, implies a *Linga,* the construction of which is attributed to the sun. The more usual word in these compounds is *Iswara,* as *Someswara, Rámeswara, Visweswara,* &c.; but *Náth* is the term more especially employed by a particular sect, that of the *Yogis* or *Pásupatas,* the oldest sect probably now existing amongst the Hindus, and with whose tenets and practices *Bhavabhúti* appears to have been thoroughly acquainted.

* *Viderbha* is always identified with Berar, but the limits of the province in that case included the adjoining district of Beder, in which the name of *Viderbha* or *Biderbha* is traceable. Local traditions also assert, that the ancient capital, still called Beder, is the same as *Viderbha.* We do not find a *Padmanagar* in the maps: it is said to be called also *Padmávati.*

† The various allusions contained in this short description require explanation. *Kasyapa* was a sage, the son of *Marichi,* the son of *Brahmá,* and one of the *Prajápatis* or progenitors of created things. His share in creation was no unimportant one, as he was the father of the gods and demons, beasts,

constantly reverenced the study of holy writ, for the knowledge of truth; wealth, for the celebration of religious

---

beasts, birds, reptiles, and man. He is supposed by some modern writers to be a personification of the remains of the antediluvian race, who took refuge in the central Asiatic chain, in which traces of his name so plentifully abound, as in the *Koh-kas* or Caucasus, the Caspian, and Cashmir. It is asserted that the thirteen *Gotras* or families of Brahmans owe their origin to as many divine sages called after their names. *Kasyapa* is one of the number. The *Aswaláyana Sútra* of the *Rig Veda* contains the enumeration of the *Gotras* and their sub-divisions, but in a very involved and unintelligible style. The popular enumeration of them, however, is not uncommon; but it is nearly, if not wholly, confined to the South of India, where several of the reputed representatives of these tribes yet exist; especially about *Gooty* and *Condavir*. *Nandavaram*, it is said, was a grant made to the thirteen *Gotras* by the sovereign of India, *Nanda*, in the year of *Kali* 980; but if there is any foundation for the grant, it is of much more recent date, *Nanda* having lived in the fourth century before the Christian era. The *Vedas*, as explained by different teachers, branch out into innumerable schools, to which different tribes of Brahmans in the south of India are hereditarily attached: in upper India every classification of the kind has long been forgotten. A very principal division of the *Vedas* is that named in the text—the *Taittiriya* or white portion of the *Yajur*. It derives its name from *tittiri*, a partridge, in which shape, according to the *Vishnu Purána*, the sage *Vaisampáyana*, the first teacher of the *Yajur*, swallowed the fragments of this work, which he had compelled his disciple *Yajnavalkya*, who had offended him, to disgorge. This portion of the *Veda* was thence named *Taittiriya*. The legend seems to have been invented by the *Pauranic* writers to disguise their ignorance of the real purport of the designation. *Charana* is supposed by one commentator to be either a branch of the *Vedas* or some particular teacher, and by the other to imply a verse or foot, meaning that they were familiar with the metres of the *Vedas*. We are already familiar with the three fires a Brahman should maintain (*Vikrama* and *Urvasi*, Introduction, vol. i. p. 190); the other two, as mentioned in a *Súkta* of the *Rig Veda*, and the *Apastamba Sútra*, are the *Sabhya* and *Avasathya*, the precise purport of which names is not known to the Pundits, nor explained in the *Bháshya*. The literal sense would be the fire of the assembly and the fire of the village, as if a sacrificial fire was sometimes maintained in common. Religious obligations are certain fasts and penances, as the *Chandráyana*, &c. The *Soma* juice is the juice of the acid Asclepias, drinking which is an essential part of the ceremonial of the *Vedas*. The term rendered, taking precedence at festivals, is *Pankti Pávana*, a purifier of the row, or range, or assembly: that is, *Jagaddhara* says, in the place where there is food; or, in other words, they were *Agrabhojinah*, the first-served at a feast. He also quotes

rites;* wives, for the propagation of offspring; and life, for the practice of devotion.

Of this family the grandson of one, whose well-selected name was *Bhatta Gopála*, and the son of the pure in fame *Nilakantha,* whose auspicious appellation was *Bhavabhúti*, surnamed *Srikantha,* and whose mother was *Játukarní*, a poet familiar through friendship with actors, has given us a drama composed by him, replete with all qualities. To which indeed this sentence is applicable: "How little do they know who speak of us with censure? This entertainment is not for them. Possibly some one exists, or will exist, of similar tastes with myself, for time is boundless and the world is wide."

Again: what avails it to boast a knowledge of the *Yoga*,* of the *Sánkhya*,† of the *Upanishads*,‡ or of the *Vedas*? no benefit accrues from them in a dramatic composition. Fertility of imagination, melody of expression, and richness of meaning, are the indications of learning and of genius. Such a drama

quotes a text, without mentioning his authority, to show that the term implies a Brahman who has read the *Yajur*, *Sáma*, and *Atharva Vedas*, and the word is similarly explained by *Menu*, iii. 184.

"Those priests must be considered as the purifiers of a company who are most learned in all the *Vedas*, and all their *Angas*, together with their descendants, who have read the scriptures." The *Vedas* are well known; they consist of an infinite number of distinct tracts, classed under four heads, as the *Rig*, *Yajur*, *Sáma*, and *Atharva Vedas*. They comprehend a practical and philosophical portion. The ritual of the former is little known or practised.

* One of the schools of philosophy teaching the eternity of matter and spirit as well as of God, and the obtaining of final liberation from life by ascetic practices.

† Another system of philosophy, teaching the eternity of matter and spirit independent of God, founded by *Kapila*.

‡ The *Upanishads* are treatises on the unity of God and the identity of Spirit, forming part of the *Vedas*. Some of the shortest have been translated into English by Rammohun Roy, Dr. Carey, and Sir W. Jones. They were rendered also into Persian by order of Dara Shekoh, the son of Shah Jehan, and were thence rendered into Latin by Anquetil du Perron, a summary of whose work in the French has been published by Mons. Lanjuinais.

has been entrusted to us by the friendly and venerable *Bhavabhúti*, entitled Málatí and Mádhava, one written by himself. Let all the actors, prepared to represent this with their best abilities in the presence of the divine *Kálapriyanáth*, appear before me in the parts I have assigned them.

Actor (*after a pause*). Your orders shall be obeyed, but it is necessary to exhibit it with becoming decorations, and first, our chief actor in the costume of Kámandakí, an old female *Saugata** beggar, is to appear, together with Avalokitá, one of her disciples, for whose character I am cast.

Man. Very well; what more?

Actor. Then the semblance of Mádhava, the hero of the fiction, and lover of Málatí, is to be assumed: how is this to be effected?

Man. That is described after Makaranda and Kalahansa enter.

Actor. We are ready then to exhibit our performance in the presence of the assembly.

Man. Very well, I take the character of Kámandakí.

Actor. I am Avalokitá.

[*Exeunt.*

* A worshipper of *Sugata*, a form of *Buddha*.

END OF THE PRELUDE.

ACT I.

SCENE I.—KÁMANDAKÍ'S HOUSE.

Enter KÁMANDAKÍ *and* AVALOKITÁ.

Kám. Daughter, Avalokitá.

Ava. Mistress, your commands?

Kám. I have a task in hand: connubial rites
Must join the amiable progeny
Of Bhúrivasu and of Devaráta,
Long cherished friends: fair Málatí the maid,
And Mádhava the youth. Auspicious signs
Forerun a happy fate, and even now
My throbbing eye-ball tells* propitious destiny
Shall crown my schemes.

Ava. In truth an anxious care
This business proves; and much it moves my wonder,
How it should happen, one in rank and power
High raised, as Bhúrivasu, should require
To wed his child, the services of one
Arrayed in tattered weeds, whose humble food
Is the scant dole of charity, and whose thoughts
Disdain the obstacles that worldly troubles
Oppose to sanctity and final bliss.

Kám. Thou errest, daughter. That the minister
Appoints me to such duty, is the fruit
Of his regard and confidence, and with prayers

* We have already had occasion to notice this superstition. The left side is the lucky side in a woman, the right in a man. The purport of these palpitations seems to have been similarly understood by the Greeks.

And penances, and life, I am prepared
All that my friend ordains me to fulfil.
Recall you not, when from far-distant realms
Assembling students crowded to our school
To gather science? Then, before my friend,
Saudáminí and me, it was convened
By these two statesmen—at that time associate
In amity and study—that their children,
When ripe in years, in love should be united.
Hence Devaráta, *Viderbha's* king,
The pious councillor, sends from the capital,
Kundinipur,* to study in our schools,†
His son the blooming Mádhava, a youth
Of more than common merit, to acquit
The troth erst plighted, thus by him recalled
To the remembrance of his ancient friend.

Ava. But why this mystery? Why should not wed
The youth and maiden as their state becomes them;
And why to you their stolen loves entrusted?

Kám. The favourite of the sovereign, Nandana,
Sues him for Málatí. The king demands
The maiden of her father. To evade
His anger if the suit should be rejected,
Is this ingenious device adopted.

Ava. Yet why thus strange to Mádhava? his name
Seems even to the minister unknown.
Small proof of his regard.

Kám. A mere pretext. He knows youth indiscreet,
And fears to trust the lovers with his councils.
Let the world deem their union was the work
Of mutual passion only; so the king

* *Kundinipur* is placed by tradition as well as similarity of name in the modern district of Condavir.

† Literally, he comes to study logic; a very appropriate study, the commentator *Jagaddhara* observes, for one who requires sufficient craft to effect a stolen match.

And Nandana are foiled, nor we to blame.
A wise man veils his projects from the world;
Silent effects his schemes; whilst all his acts
Bespeak indifference, and his cheerful manners
Shew to suspicion's eye a heart at ease.

Ava. I comprehend your plans—'tis for this cause,
That by your orders I so often Mádhava
Have sent on various pleas along the road
By Bhúrivasu's palace.

Kám. True; and as I learn,
The princess from her casement has beheld
The youth—he graceful as the god of love,
Herself love's blooming bride—nor seen in vain.
Her waning form too faithfully betrays
The lurking care she now first learns to suffer.

Ava. To soothe that care, then, has her skill pourtrayed
The lineaments of Mádhava, to-day
Left by her foster sister with Mandáriká.*

Kám. In sooth not ill devised. Lavangiká
Knows that the youth's attendant, Kalahansa,
Doth love Mandáriká, and shrewdly deems
That from her hands he will obtain the portrait
To shew his master.

Ava. I have borne my part;
And to the garden of love's god directed
The steps of Mádhava at early dawn.
It is the festival of Madana. The princess
And damsel train will to his groves proceed,
And thus the youthful pair to-day will meet.

Kám. Thanks, daughter, for your kindly zeal to aid
The object of my wishes. But now inform me,
If you have tidings of Saudáminí,
Mine ancient pupil?

* The servant of the convent; or, as Kámandaki terms her, *Vihára Dási.*

Ava. I learn that upon mount *Sri Parvata**
She now resides, where, won by desp'rate penance,
Power more than earthly waits upon her will.
Kám. Whence is this information?
Ava. The formidable deity *Chámundá*
Is worshipped near the city cemetery.
Kám. She whom her miscreant votaries aver
Delights in living sacrifice?
Ava. The same.
From one of these, Kapála Kundalá,
I learnt the news, as I encountered her
By chance at eve. She is the pupil
Of a skull-bearing seer, Aghoraghanta,
A wandering mendicant, but dwelling now
Amidst the neighbouring forest. He has late
Come from *Sri Parvata.*
Kâm. 'Tis like Saudáminí.
Ava. Of her enough.
More pleasing themes attend, for Makaranda,
The early friend of Mádhava, adores
The lady Madayantiká, the sister
Of the king's favourite, and to secure
His happiness will yield to Mádhava.
Scarce less delight than to ensure his own.
Kâm. It has not been forgotten. Buddharakshitá
Attends that charge.
Ava. This, mistress, was well done.
Kám. Come, daughter, let us forth, and having learnt

* *Sri Parvata* means the same as *Sri Saila*, the mountain of *Sri* or *Lakshmi*, a place of sanctity in the Dekhin, near the Krishna river. It still retains its sanctity, but has lost the splendour it formerly seems to have possessed by the extensive remains of sculptures on the mountain, and the great labour and cost bestowed on the causeways by which it is approached. It is described by Col. Mackenzie in the 6th vol. of the *Asiatic Researches*, and was more recently visited by the late Dr. Voysey. The penance referred to is called in the text the *Kápálika vrata*, worship of the terrific forms of *Siva* and *Durgá*.

How Mádhava has fared, repair to Málatí.
I know her spirit lofty: we must proceed
With prudence if we would obtain success.
May mighty *Brahmá*, whose consummate skill
With sympathizing merit has endowed
The graceful pair, perfect his high design.
May our devices prosper: may the youth
Obtain his wishes, and his love be crowned
With the fair maid's affection: as the lotus
Buds in full beauty to the tender light
The moon autumnal sheds upon its leaves.*

[*Exeunt.*

Scene II.—A Garden.

Enter Kalahansa (*with a picture*).

I wonder where my master is to be found: he may well think his person equal to that of love himself, since it has made an impression upon the heart of Málatí. I feel rather weary, and shall take the liberty of reposing myself in this grove till I see my master and his friend. [*Retires.*

Enter Makaranda.

I learn from Avalokitá, my friend
Is in the grove of Madana, and thither
I go to seek him. Ha! he comes this way:
Yet something sure disturbs him, for his step
Has not its wonted nimbleness—his eyes
Are fixed on vacancy—his whole attire
Is disarrayed, and heaves his frequent sigh.
Has love been busy here, whose potent will,

* This is a very matter-of-fact of scene; but it is precisely according to rule, and does not very badly prepare for the appearance of the persons alluded to, the entrance of some of whom is considerably delayed. No character is to be introduced that has not previously been announced. This is a canon of the Hindu dramatic code, and was formerly one of our own laws. Massinger is remarkable for his precision in this respect; Beaumont and Fletcher are not unobservant of the rule.

By every lovely attribute administered,
Pervades the world, and on the form of youth,
Works sad and wondrous change?

Enter MÁDHAVA.

'Tis strange—'tis passing strange, my vagrant thoughts
No more return to me. Deserting shame,
Or self-respect, or fortitude, or judgment,
They dwell perverse upon one fond idea,
The lovely image of the moon-faced maid.
Wonder alone each faculty engrossed
As rapt I gazed upon her, and my heart,
As if immersed in heavenly nectar, glowed
Delusive extacy: too late I feel
I nursed a burning coal within my bosom.

Mak. (*coming forward*). Mádhava!
The sun is high, and darts his fiercest rays
Upon the aching brow: here let us enter,
And rest awhile beneath the garden's shades.

Mád. Even as you please. [*Exeunt.*

KALAHANSA *advances.*

My master and his friend are undoubtedly the two greatest ornaments of this garden. Well; shall I now take him this picture of himself—the delight of the eyes of Málatí and solace of her amorous pain; perhaps I had better let him repose himself awhile. It shall be so. [*Exit.*

Another part of the Garden.

Enter MÁDHAVA *and* MAKARANDA.

Mak. Here, at the foot of this wide-spreading tree,
Amidst the fragrance that the breezes waft
Abroad from every bud, let us recline.
[*They lie down.*
To-day was one of peril, Mádhava.
You could not sure behold the num'rous concourse
Of all our city's beauty, bound to pay

Their annual homage at the shrine of love,
And scape unharmed. In sooth, to me it seems
The shaft has lighted, and has grazed thy heart.
Nay, never droop the lotus of thy face :
If struck, reveal thy hurt: why shame to bear it.
Who can resist the heart-born deity?
Creatures of passion, all confess his power,
And gods themselves are impotent as we.*

Mád. I own my weakness—listen to its cause.
By Avalokitá advised, I went
To *Kámadeva's* temple, where I strayed,
Till weary I reclined beside a fountain
That laves the deep roots of a stately tree,
Whose clustering blossoms wooed the wanton bees
To cull their sweet inebriating fragrance.
Lulled by their songs, and tempted by the shade,
I laid me down, and in pure idleness,
To while away the time, I gathered round me
The new fall'n blossoms, and assiduous wove
A flowery garland. Whilst I was thus employed
There issued from the fane a beauteous maid.
Stately her gait—yet graceful as the banner
Love waves in triumph o'er a prostrate world.
Her train bespoke a princely rank—her garb
With youth's appropriate ornaments was graced—
Her form was beauty's shrine, or of that shrine
Radiant she moved the guardian deity.
To mould her charms, whatever nature offers
Fairest and best, had surely been assembled,†

* Literally, the same sentiment was evinced in the creation of the world in *Brahmá* and in *Siva*. *Káma* was scarcely created before he thought proper to make *Brahmá* enamoured of his own daughter. Inspiring *Siva* with love for *Párvati* was a more dangerous feat, and the archer god, although he succeeded, was reduced to ashes by the object of his triumph.

† Or literally, the moon, ambrosia, the stalk of the lotus, moonlight, &c., types severally of her face, her lips, her arms, her gracefulness, or beauty.

And love omnipotent was her creator.
Led by her maidens to collect the flowers
That thickly hung on my o'ershadowing tree,
She neared the spot. Ah! then too plain I noted
The signs of passion, for some happy youth
Long entertained, the lovely maid revealed.
As slender as the lotus stalk her shape;
Her pallid cheeks, like unstained ivory,
Rivalled the beauty of the spotless moon;
And still her prompt compliance with the wishes
Of her attendant damsels showed herself
Indifferent to all. I scarce had gazed
Upon her, but my eye felt new delight,
As bathed with nectar, and she drew my heart
As pow'rfully as attracts the magnet gem*
The unresisting ore, at once towards her.
That heart, though causeless be its sudden passion,
Is fixed on her for ever, chance what may,
And though my portion be henceforth despair.
The goddess destiny decrees at pleasure
The good or ill of all created beings.

Mak. Nay, Mádhava, this cannot be, believe me,
Without some cause. Behold! all nature's sympathies
Spring not from outward form, but inward virtue.
The lotus buds not till the sun has risen;
Nor melts the moon-gem till it feels the moon.
What then ensued?

Mád. When her fair train beheld me, they exchanged
Expressive looks and smiles, and each to each,
As if they knew me, murmured—This is he!
The music of their tinkling zones was stilled,
Repressed the silver echo of their anclets
Sharp clanging to their undulating motion.

* *Ayaskánta mani Saláheva,* "Like a rod of the ironstone gem." It should seem possible that artificial magnets, as well as the properties of the loadstone, were known to the Hindus.

Hushed was the melody their bracelets made,
Whilst their fair lotus palms, in sportive mood,
Were beating measure to their merriment.
Silent they stood, and with extended fingers,
As if they said, "The fates have favoured us,
Lady, behold *him* here!"

Mak. (*to himself*). This is indeed
A proof of preconceived regard.

Kal. (*advancing*). What is all this about: some pleasing story of which woman is the object?

Mak. Proceed, my friend.

Mád. What words shall picture what those looks conveyed;
The lore of love those lotus eyes revealed.
What firmness could resist the honest warmth
Of nature's mute expressiveness, nor fall
Before those orbs, that now like opening buds,
Beneath the creeper of the tremulous brow
Expansive bloomed, and now retiring shrunk
But half averted from the answering gaze,
Then dropped the veiling lashes o'er their brightness.
I felt their influence, and those looks of love,
Beaming with mild timidity, and moist
With sweet abandonment, bore off my heart—
Nay plucked it from my bosom by the roots
All pierced with wounds.
Incredulous of my happiness, I sought
To mark her passion nor display my own,
Though every limb partook the fond emotion.
Thence I resumed my task, and wove my wreath,
Seeming intent, till she at length withdrew
Attended by her maidens and a guard
Of eunuchs armed with staves and javelins.
A stately elephant received the princess
And bore her towards the city. Whilst they moved,
As winds the lily on its slender stalk,
So turned her head towards the grove of *Káma*,

And from her delicate lids she shot retiring
Glances with venom and ambrosia tipped.
My breast received the shafts. A mingled flame
And deathly chillness, since alternate spread
Throughout my form, and doom me to such agony
Words cannot paint, the world has never witnessed.
Perception dimly pictures present objects,
And past perceptions fade from recollection!
Vain were the lunar ray or gelid stream
To cool my body's fever, whilst my mind
Whirls in perpetual round, and knows not rest.

Kal. The object of this passion must assuredly be Málatí.

Mak. (*to himself*). My friend is lost, my counsels were but vain:
And e'en the wish were idle, that the deity,
Self-born, should spare his years, nor with sad change
Soil his pure mind. The flow'ry bow is strung,
And ardent youth is reckless of the peril.
(*To Mádhava.*) Know you the name and race of that fair lady?

Mád. Hear how I learnt them. Ere she had departed,
One of her train, apparently intent
On gathering flowers, privately approached me,
And borrowing from the garland I had woven
A covert for her meaning, thus addressed me—
"Well has been strung this string of blooming beauty,
And pleasing is it in our lady's sight,
Who in like excellence herself excels—
May then success reward such high desert,
And this bright produce of creative art
Bear richest fruit, exalted to that station
It's merit claims—suspended round the neck
Of Bhúrivasu's daughter, Málatí,*

* This piece of *double entendre* is much more precisely followed in the original and every word has a double import. The figure is termed *Akshara sangháta*, combination of letters.

Whose foster sister, and whose nearest friend,
Lavangiká, now stands before you."

Kal. This is as we wish, and fortune favours the design of the flower-armed deity.

Mak. Málatí, the daughter of the minister,
A mark for elevated rank, her name
Is ever in the mouth of our preceptress;
And rumour adds, the king solicits her
In marriage for his favourite, Nandana.

Mád. Requested by Lavangiká, I gave her
The flow'ry wreath. She took it with respect,
As 'twere a precious gift, and all the while
The eyes of Málatí were fixed on her.
Bowing with reverence, she then retired,
And quickly disappeared amidst the throng.
The princess and the people left the grove
And I directed hitherward my steps.

Mak. Your story, Mádhava, most plainly shews,
That Málatí's affection is your own;
And the soft cheek, whose pallid tint denoted
Love preconceived, is pale alone for you.
She must have seen you, though we know not where;
But maidens of her rank do not allow
Their eyes to rest on one to whom they have not
Already given their hearts: and then those looks
That passed among her maidens, plainly shewed
The passion you had wakened in their mistress.
Then comes her foster sister's clear enigma,
And tells intelligibly whose her heart.

Kal. (*advancing*). Look at this picture.

Mak. Mádhava's counterfeit—whose work is this?

Kal. Her's who has stolen his heart.

Mak. What, Málatí?

Kal. The same.

Mád. This gives me faith, dear friend, in your conjectures.

Mak. But, Kalahansa, how came you by this?

Kal. Mandáriká gave it to me. She had it from Lavangiká.

Mak. And what induced the princess to delineate
This picture? did Mandáriká inform you?

Kal. She painted it to amuse and relieve her distress.

Mak. What say you, Mádhava?—this lovely maid,
The soft light of your eyes, assuredly
Regards you bound to her in love's alliance.
What should prevent your union? Fate and love
Combined seem labouring to effect it. Come,
Let me behold the wondrous form that works
Such change in yours,—you have the skill; pourtray her.

Mád. To please you I will try. Bring me the pencil.
(*To Kalahansa.*)

(*Draws.*)

Hard is the task you have assigned me.—
A chilly tremor spreads through all my frame,
Damp dews distil from every opening pore,
And starting fast, my tears repeatedly
Dim the faint outline that my trembling hand,
Oh, how unworthily! attempts to picture:
Yet with what skill I have, 'tis done.

Mak. (*taking the drawing*). Most excellent and worthy of your passion.

It may be said of her— (*Writes on the drawing*)
" Whatever nature's loveliness displays
" May seem to others beautiful and bright;
" But since these charms have broke upon my gaze,
" They form my life's sole exquisite delight."

Enter MANDÁRIKÁ *hastily.*

Man. Ha! Kalahansa, you are at last overtaken. Makaranda, Mádhava, sirs, I salute you.

Mak. Approach, Mandáriká; what brings you hither?

Man. I followed Kalahansa to recover a picture.

Kal. (*gives her the one Mádhava has*). Here it is, take it.

Man. Málatí's picture, I protest. How came this here; who has painted it?

Kal. He whom she delineated, and with much the same intention.

Mak. He tells you truth; and now do you be honest.
Inform us how, and where, first Málatí
Saw Mádhava?

Man. She was called to the lattice by Lavangiká to look at him as he passed the palace.

Mak. So I supposed. We frequently have passed
In that direction.

Man. With your permission, I will communicate these events to my friend Lavangiká.

Mak. You have free leave.

(*Exit Mandáriká.*)

Mak. The monarch of a thousand beams now darts
His hottest rays; 'tis noon, let us go home.

Mád. Willingly—
The day's warm influence surely washes off
The careful labours of the morning toilet,
And steals those sandal marks, so neatly laid
In graceful lines across the flowery cheek.
Play o'er my limbs, ye soft refreshing breezes,
Whose previous homage has been paid to beauty,
And wrap in soft embrace my fair one's charms,
Diffusing o'er her form the honied fragrance
Shook from the jasmine's scarce-unfolded blossom.

Mak. Alas! the flow'r-armed and resistless deity
Has sadly changed the person of my friend;
Like the young elephant, when fever preys
On his yet tender frame. Our only hope
Is now Kámandakí.

Mád. 'Tis strange, most strange!
Where'er I turn, the same loved charms appear
On every side. Bright as the golden bud
Of the young lotus gleams her beauteous face,
Though oft averted from my fond regards.
Alas! my friend, this fascination spreads

O'er all my senses, and a feverish flame
Consumes my strength—my heart is all on fire,
My mind is tossed with doubt—and every faculty
In one fond thought absorbed, I cease to be
Myself, or conscious of the thing I am.

[*Exeunt.*

END OF THE FIRST ACT.

ACT II.

The Dwelling of Málatí.

Enter two Female Attendants *meeting.*

First Att. Hey, friend, I saw you just now near the music-room,* in deep conversation with Avalokitá: what were you two talking about?

Second Att. The whole story of the grove of *Káma* has been carried to Kámandakí by Mádhava's friend; and she being desirous of seeing Málatí, sent Avalokitá to her, who was telling me, that she had left Lavangiká and the princess together.

First Att. Why, Lavangiká said she wanted to gather *bakula* flowers in the grove of *Madana*, and has not since returned: has she been heard of?

Second Att. Yes, the princess saw her coming, on which she dismissed her attendants at the door of her apartments, but detained Lavangiká.

First Att. She had some very agreeable news to tell Málatí, I suppose, of the youth Mádhava.

Second Att. It is a hopeless passion I am afraid, and to-day's interview will only add to her distress. To-morrow the king gives the princess to Nandana; her father has consented to the match.

First Att. Consented!

Second Att. Yes, he told the king that he was "lord over his own daughter." This passion of Málatí and Mádhava will only yield them misery as long as they live.

* The *Sangita satá*, which we had occasion to notice in the preceding drama.

First Att. Now, then, we shall see what Kámandakí can do, and whether she will put forth her power.

Second Att. You talk idly. Come, let us depart.

[*Exeunt.*

Enter MÁLATÍ *and* LAVANGIKÁ.

Mál. Proceed, my dear Lavangiká, proceed.

Lav. This flow'ry wreath then did he send by me.

Mál. (*taking it*). 'Tis strung unevenly.

Lav. The fault is yours.

Mál. How should that be?

Lav. Where, deem you, were his thoughts:
Who caused that dark-hued youth's deep agitation?

Mál. Dearest Lavangiká,
You ever speak me comfort.

Lav. There might be better comfort. He, himself,
Here in your presence—gazing rapt upon you
With look intent, from eyes that tremulous glow,
Like the blown lotus shaken by the zephyr,
Forced, from the timid plea of weaving chaplets,
To dart upon you glances of delight,
From underneath the arching brow, that waves
In curve as graceful as the bow of *Káma.*

Mál. How can I credit this—how should I know,
From such brief interview, if the graceful youth
Be true, or if he only seek to mock me?

Lav. You have no need to fear in this, believe me.

Mál. Well, well; complete your story.

Lav. When I received the garland, I departed
And mingled with the crowd; thence to Mandáriká
I hastened, to receive again the picture
That in the morning had been left with her.

Mál. With her!—With what intent?

Lav. She has a lover, Kalahansaka,
A follower of Mádhava, and I knew
To him the picture would be shewn, and all
That thence ensued would be revealed to me.

Mál. (apart). Then Mádhava has seen it?
(Aloud.) What is your dearest wish, Lavangiká?
Lav. That he, whose heart now pines in hopeless passion,
May soothe his sorrows with this bright resemblance
Of the fair cause of his distress.

(Shews Máldti the picture drawn by Mádhava.)

Mál. (contemplating it). Yet still
My heart is ill at ease. I doubt me much
That this will prove a treach'rous comforter.—
What have we here?

(Reads Makaranda's lines.)

Oh, Mádhava! the graces of thy form,
Thy flattering tongue, and fascinating gaze,
Are all alike resistless—happy she
Who never has beheld them. On my heart
They, cruel, shed interminable anguish. *(Weeps.)*
Lav. Why, dearest friend, despond?
Mál. What should I hope!
Lav. Be sure of this, that he on whose account,
Like the young blossom from its slender stem
Plucked rude, you droop, and taste no more the fragrance
Of the sweet jasmine—he too, has been taught,
By love's relentless god, how hard it is
To bear such agony.
Mál. May happiness
Await his youth; for me, I dare not hope.
This is a day of strange and changeful feeling.
Love spreads through every vein like subtlest poison,
And like the fire that brightens in the breeze
Consumes this feeble frame—resistless fever
Preys on each fibre—fatal is its fury.
No one can bring me aid, nor tender mother
Nor father, nor Lavangiká can save me.
Lav. Such mutual passion may, in sooth, bestow

Delight when lovers meet; but when apart
Condemns them to affliction. From a brief
And passing gaze, thy life was brought in peril;
And now to-day his nearer presence sheds
A fiercer fever on thy delicate frame.
What now is to be said? We must admit,
The rarest and most difficult attainment
Of all on earth, is union with a lover,
Of equal excellence and like affection.

Mál. Life is distasteful to me: leave me, friend:
And yet I wrong thy gentleness. Repeatedly
Recurring to the anguish of my heart,
I lose all fortitude, and in my grief
Become capricious and unjust—forgive me.
Let the full moon blaze in the nightly sky:
Let love rage on, death screens me from his fury.
What should exact my love and veneration?
My father, and my mother, and my race,
Of still unblemished honour—not my life:
No! nor the mortal who subdues my heart.

Lav. (*apart*). What is to be done?

(*An* Attendant *enters, but without advancing far.*)

Att. The venerable Kámandakí.

Both. What would she?

Att. She seeks admission to the princess.

Both. What should delay her?

(*Attendant retires,* Málátí *conceals the picture.*)

Lav. (*aside*). In good time she comes.

Enter Kámandakí *and* Avalokitá.

Kám. (*soliloquises*).
So far, my friend, respected Bhúrivasu,
So far is well: in either world, assent
Awaits thy answer to the king. He, of his own,
Is the undoubted lord. Fate is our friend,
In all that chanced to-day in *Káma's* grove,

And in the interchange of tender tokens,
The garland and the picture, all conspires
To crown our sanguine-wishes with success.
Best pledge of blissful union is the bond
Of mutual love; and well the sage* has said,
"The marriage rite shall prosper, when the eye,
The tongue, and heart, unite the wedded pair."

Lav. The lady Málatí.

Kám. (*surveying her*).
I view her with affliction and delight.
Slender her frame, and delicate and pale,
Like the young plaintain, or the waning moon.
Soothing and pleasant is she to the eye,
Though thin and pallid be her cheek, and all
Declare the fires of love have triumphed here.
The hope of union with the youth engrosses
Her every thought. Loose and untied her zone,
Her soft lip quivers—starting drops suffuse
Her gentle lips—her bosom palpitates,
And her dark eye in soft abandonment
Moist, languid floats. Each look and gesture speaks
The fond desires that agitate her youth.
(*Approaches.*)

Lav. (*to Málatí*). Behold!

Mál. Priestess, I salute you. (*Bows.*)

Kám. May you enjoy, dear lady, in due season,
The fruit of all your wishes.

Lav. Pray be seated.

Mál. Is all propitious with the priestess?

Kám. (*sighing*). All.

Lav. (*aside*). That sigh is but the prelude to our play;
I have my cue. (*Aloud.*) And yet, respected lady,
Methinks that sigh, that struggling makes its way

* *Angiras.*

Through starting tears, is with your words at variance.
What can its import be?

Kám. Behold these weeds:
Sorts such a garb with one you call your friend?

Lav. What follows?

Kám. I am grieved, like unmeet union
Should sentence youth and charms innumerable,
Born to no profit, to a worthless bridegroom.

Lav. You do not grieve alone; the common voice
Condemns the minister's assent, and blames
His yielding Málatí to be the bride
Of Nandana, because the king requests it.

Mál. (*aside*). Alas! I am an offering to the monarch
Presented by my father.

Kám. 'Tis most strange
How he could overlook the vast defects
Of such alliance. But how can those
Feel natural affection for their offspring,
Whose souls are sunk in schemes of policy?
His only thought is clearly to secure
The friendship of the monarch's chosen friend
And boon companion, by his daughter's person.

Mál. (*apart*). The king's regard is all in all with him;
His Málatí is nothing.

Lav. 'Tis as you say, dame;
Or why should our young mistress thus be sacrificed
To age and ugliness?

Mál. (*apart*). Ah, luckless wench!
A thunderbolt has struck me to the ground.

Lav. To you she ever has been like a daughter;
Save her, dear lady, from this living death.

Kám. What can I aid? Fate and her sire alone
Exact obedience from a daughter. True,
Sakuntalá, of *Kusika's* high race,
Bestowed her love on a self-chosen lord—
The king *Dushyanta*. A bright nymph of heaven

Espoused a mortal monarch, *Pururavas,**
And the fair princess, *Vásavadattá,* scorned
The husband of her father's choice, and fled
With prince *Udayana.*† So poets tell.
But these were desperate acts, and must not be
Proposed for imitation. Let the minister
Complete his will—secure his master's favour
With the rich off'ring of his daughter's peace,
And yield this maiden to the sovereign's friend,
Like the pale moon, to *Ráhu's* foul embrace.

Ava. Mistress, time passes, it were well to think
Of Mádhava, who needs your aid.

Kám. 'Tis well.
Permit me, princess, to depart.

Lav. One moment. (*Aside to Málatí.*)
Say, shall I ask the dame who is the youth,
And what his origin?

* Although it is possible that reference may be here made to the *Puránas,* in which the stories alluded to are contained, it seems more likely that *Bhavabhúti* had in his thoughts the dramas of his predecessor *Kálidás.* The term used for the narrators is *A'khyána Vida,*—those who know stories, the events of past times,—*Purávritta,* which would scarcely have been applied to the inspired author or compiler of the *Puránas.*

† The story of *Udayana's* carrying off *Vásavadattá* makes a very distinguished figure in the lighter literature of the Hindus, and is very fully detailed in the *Vrihat kathá*; but in the popular version of the story *Udayana* carries off the princess by her father's connivance, and no mention is made of a rival for her hand,—king *Sanjaya,* as he is termed in the text, who was the husband of her father's choice. Neither is the circumstance mentioned by *Subandhu* in his poem of *Vásavadattá,* and indeed he seems to have given the story a new form altogether. My own inquiry confirms the remark of Mr. Colebrooke (*Asiatic Researches,* X. 451.) on the passage in the text, that no other trace has been yet found of the story to which *Bhavabhúti* alludes. I am better pleased to bear this testimony, because, in consequence of misunderstanding the exact purport of Mr. Colebrooke's remark, I considered him to have overlooked an allusion to the story of *Udayana* in the *Megha Dúta,* which, however, is merely general, and therefore throws no light on the passage. It seems probable that the story of *Vásavadattá* underwent some alterations subsequent to the time of *Bhavabhúti,* and the original form is lost.

Mál. Do so; I long to hear it.

Lav. Inform us, pious dame, what youth is this
In whom you shew such interest?

Kám. The story, though of import, needs no preface:—
The sovereign of *Viderbha* boasts for minister
The sage and long-experienced Devaráta,
Who bears the burthen of the state, and spreads
Throughout the world his piety and fame.
Such as himself your father knows him well,
For in their youth they were in study joined,
And trained to learning by the same preceptor;
And rarely in this world do we behold
Such characters as theirs; whose lofty rank
Is the abode of wisdom and of piety,
Of valour and of virtue; and whose fame
Spreads white and spotless through the universe.

Mál. I have often heard my father speak of him.

Kám. Bright as the rising moon, whose silver rays
First streaming o'er the eastern mountain, charm
The eyes of all mankind, a son from him
Has sprung, whose opening virtues early give
Occasion of rejoicing to the world.
Now, in his bloom, assiduous to collect
Ripe store of knowledge, has this youth been sent
From his paternal mansion to our city.
Here as he passes, many a lotus eye
Shoots from each casement soul-subduing glances,
But reckless he, along with Makaranda,
His friend and fellow of like years and worth,
Pursues his toils;—his name is Mádhava.

Mál. (*apart to Lavangiká*). Heard you, my friend?

Lav. In truth you have escaped
The perilous ocean, and the tree of heaven
Is now within your reach.

(*The conch is sounded without.*)

Kám. These echoing tones,

That through the deep recesses of the palace
Resounding spread, proclaim the evening hour.

(*They all rise.*)

Mál. (*apart*). Alas, my father! thy ambition spurns
A daughter's happiness—yet in my grief,
Some hope I borrow from the youth's descent,
And trust we meet again.

Lav. This is our way.

Kám. (*apart*). So far so well. An unsuspected messenger,
I have discharged my duty. Málatí
Is tutored to our wishes, and inspired
With hatred of the bridegroom—taught to question
Her father's love, reminded of examples
That vindicate the free choice of a husband.
Her admiration of her youthful lover
Is now approved by his illustrious birth
And my encomium of his high descent:
All this must strengthen and confirm her passion,
And now their union may be left to fate.

[*Exeunt.*

END OF THE SECOND ACT.

ACT III.

The House of Kámandakí.

Enter Buddharakshitá *and* Avalokitá *meeting.*

Budd. Ho, Avalokitá! where is our dame?

Ava. Do you not know? Disregarding the season for collecting alms,* she is ever with the princess.

Budd. And where have you been?

Ava. I have been to Mádhava by her orders, to tell him to repair to the public garden of the temple of *Sankara,* and place himself in the grove of red *asoka* trees, that extends to the *Kantaki* bower.

Budd. For what purpose?

Ava. This is the fourteenth day of the dark fortnight. Persuading the princess that the god *Sankara* is to be propitiated with offerings of flowers gathered by oneself, the dame takes her and Lavangiká thither, and whilst the former is collecting her oblation, she and Mádhava will, as it were by accident, again encounter. But where are you going?

Budd. I am on my way to my friend Madayantiká, to accompany her to the temple of *Sankara* also. I looked in to pay my respects to the priestess.

Ava. And how speed you in what you have in hand?

Budd. As our mistress could wish. I have won the entire confidence of Madayantiká, and by expatiating on the suitable-

* Literally the *Pindapáta vélá*, explained to signify the hour of going round to collect the *Pinda*, which is the name given, the commentator says, to the food collected by the *Saugata*, or *Bauddha* mendicant. The word means a lump or ball of any viands, usually of rice or meal. The same authority adds, the time is the seventh *gheri*, which will be one hour after noon.

ness and merit of Makaranda, have excited in her bosom the most lively affection for him and anxious wish to see him.

Ava. This is well. Now to our several duties.

[*Exeunt.*

Scene II.—The Garden.

Enter Kámandakí.

Kám. Poor girl! the lesson I have lately hinted
Has bowed her lofty spirit, and she seeks
To win me to her: mournfully she pines
When I am absent; brightens in my presence;
Whispers her secret thoughts to me; presents me
With costly gifts: when I depart she clings
Around my neck, and only lets me leave her
When I have vowed repeatedly return:
Then on my knee she sits, and bids me tell her
Again the stories of the nymphs that loved;
And questions o'er and o'er, with flimsy plea,
Their fate and conduct, then she silent pauses
As lost in meditation,—'tis enough:
To-day they meet. Daughter, this way; approach.

Enter Málatí *and* Lavangiká.

Mál. (*apart*). Alas! my father loves his child no more,
But offers her a victim to ambition;
One hope alone sustains me.

Lav. Taste, my friend,
The freshness of the breeze, that sweeps the blossoms,
And wafts around the *champaka's* perfume,
Breathing melodious with the buzz of bees
That cluster in the buds, and with the song
The *koïl* warbles thick and hurried forth,
As on the flow'ry mangoe's top he sits,
And all inebriate with its nectar sings.
The garden gale comes wooingly to sip

The drops ambrosial from thy moonlike face.
Come on, those shades invite us. (*They retire.*)

Enter MÁDHAVA.

The pious dame is here—her presence fills
My heart with rapture. So the peafowl hails
The flash that heralds the approaching shower.
Lavangiká—the third—'tis she—
'Tis Málatí! Ah me! a sudden chill
Pervades my heart and freezes every faculty,
To marble turned by her moon-beaming countenance,
Like mountains ice-bound by the gelid ray
Shot on their summits from the lunar gem.
How lovely she appears, as o'er her frame,
Like a fast-fading wreath, soft langour steals,
And heightens every beauty. Now mine eyes
Are conscious of their being. As I gaze
My heart consumes, and love lights all his fires.
(*Approaches unobserved.*)

Mál. (*advancing*). Come, Lavangiká, let us pluck flowers
From this delightful arbour.

Kám. Nay, rest my child;
Thy faltering tongue and languid frame evince
Fatigue: upon thy face the moist drops start,
And those bright eyes are shut—one might suspect,—
Thy form such soft abandonment betrays—
A lover's gaze were dwelling on thy beauties.
Come sit thee here, I have a tale to tell thee.

Mál. You are obeyed.*—(*Sits down by Kámandakí, who passes her hand under Málatí's chin so as to hold up her face towards Mádhava.*)

Kám. There was a youth, named Mádhava, who shared
With you an equal portion of my heart.

Lav. So we have heard.

* Two or three short speeches are here omitted.

Kám. He, from the luckless day
Of *Káma's* festival, has ceased to be
The master of himself, and though he told not
His sorrows to the moon or faithful friend,
His changing form, still lovely in decay,
Revealed the anguish he disdained to utter.
I hastened to his aid, and quickly guessed
The cause of his distress, when I was told
He had beheld this lovely countenance,—
The moon that swayed the heaving of his heart,
Like the deep waters of the tossing main.

Mád. (*behind*). How well she penetrates my secret !*

Kám. Reckless of life, his only pleasures now
Are tasks that feed and aggravate his flame.
He gazes on the mango buds; he listens
Attentive to the *koïl's* song; he breasts
The breeze impregnate with the flowery fragrance;
He hugs the lotus blossoms to his heart,
And basks beneath the deadly lunar beam—
This first fond passion preys upon my son,
And soon, I fear, cuts short his gentle being.†

Mál. (*to Lavangiká*).
Why does the dame alarm me thus with fear
For life so dear to all: what can I say?

Lav. (*to Kámandakí*).
You are not terrified alone—like fears
Pervade us for the princess. She has often
Beheld the youth, as by the palace walls
His course has frequent chanced, since when she pines,
As droops the lotus on its slender stem
Beneath the scorching sun: her youthful sports

* Mádhava's eulogy is rather more protracted; but it interrupts the business, and is more technical than poetical.

† Two short speeches of Mádhava and Málatí are here omitted, and other curtailments occur in this scene, in which some of the interlocutors are rather prolix.

Delight no more: pensive apart she sits
Whole days, her cheek upon her hand reclined.
We fondly hoped those looks that were exchanged
In *Káma's* grove, when like the present god
The youthful Mádhava appeared to grace
Love's festival, amidst his blooming votaries,
Would dissipate this melancholy mood,
And cheer her heart with hope, but passion since
Intenser rages in her tender heart,
And threatens her existence. Oh, befriend us!
If but a moment she could view the youth,
E'en that were such relief as earth receives
When, parched by sultry suns, she drinks revived
The bland and life-bestowing dews of heaven.
The hapless state of Málatí affrights us,
Unfit to struggle with the sports of destiny.
Do thou exert thy powers, and then the pair,
Who claim alike thy pity and regard,
Redeemed from death, shall prosper in their loves.*

Kám. My heart is filled with sorrow and delight.
I pity her sad state, even whilst I joy
To find her justly conscious of desert.

Lav. Behold these proofs, this picture of her lord!
(*Opening the garment over her breast.*)
And this decaying weath, strung by his hands,
Dear as her life, thus cherished in her bosom.

Mád. How enviable, dear garland, is thy fate,
Thus to be cherished like a friend, and waving
A graceful banner o'er that lovely bosom.

(*A noise behind.*)

" What ho! beware! in youthful strength and sport,
The tiger, in the temple's porch confined,
Has burst his iron cage, and roams at large,

* Lavangiká's speech is in the original so extremely diffuse, and contains so many repetitions and obscurities, that by much the most considerable portion of it has been omitted.

With tail high waving like a banner, vast
And mighty limbed, he stalks along the groves.
Now in the midst of mangled forms his paw,
As pond'rous as the thunderbolt, has felled,
The monster stands, and in his maw engulphs,
Wide as a cave, the quiv'ring flesh, or grinds
The cracking bones with hard, sharp-pointed teeth;
From his deep throat he roars in thunder loud,
And men and beasts fly trembling from the echo;
Begrimed with blood and dust he follows fast,*
And plies insatiate his death-dealing talons—
Look to your lives—as best you may, avoid him."

Budd. (*without*). Alas, alas! my dear friend Madayantiká!

(*Rushes in.*)

Oh, save us, save us! Madayantiká,
Our friend, the sister of the minister,
Is singled out and hunted by the tiger.

Mál. Oh, horror!

Mád. (*rushing forward*). Where is the savage!

Mál. (*with delight, apart*). He here!

Mád. Now I am blessed indeed; her gaze surprised
Dwells greedily upon my presence, and enchains me
In flow'ry bonds, falls on my heart like balm,
And sheds a show'r of heavenly nectar o'er me.

Lav. Can we not quit the garden?

Mád. Follow me. (*Going.*)

Kám. Beware, my son: though valiant, be not rash.

Mál. (*apart to Lavangiká*). I tremble now.

Mád. A moment pause. I mark the savage spread
Dismay, his course is marked with carcases,
And all his steps sink deep in mire and gore.

* This description is also somewhat compressed: the original *Prákrit* is very powerful, although too much laboured, and abounding more than enough in alliteration, *ex. gr. Nara turanga jamgaluggarabhrida gata guhá gabbha gambhíra ghaggharovalli,* "roaring with a loud roar from the depth of the cavern of a throat filled with the flesh of men and steeds."

Oh, horror! we are distant;—now he views
A maid—she flies—he follows.

All. Madayantiká!

Kám. Behold, a youth advances, now he stoops
To grasp a fallen sword.

Mád. He throws himself,
Brave youth, before the tiger: 'tis my friend!
'Tis Makaranda.

All. Noble, valiant youth!

Mád. Alas! the beast has wounded him.

Kám. Joy, joy! the savage falls.

All. What fate have we escaped!

Kám. My generous son, he bleeds profusely:
Supported by the trembling maid, he rests
Upon his sword, along whose ruddy blade
The trickling torrent reddens to the ground.

Mád. He faints; help, holy dame, preserve my friend.*

Kám. Fear not, fear not; but hasten to his succour.

[*Exeunt.*

* In the original "preserve me."

END OF THE THIRD ACT.

ACT IV.*

THE SAME SCENE.

MÁDHAVA *and* MAKARANDA *brought on by the women insensible.*

Mada. (*to Kám*). Befriend him, pious dame; oh, sâve this youth!

Who to preserve my life has risked his own.

(*The others*). What should we do?

Kám. Sprinkle o'er their limbs

The water of this ewer, and fan their faces

With your light robes.

(*They fan the youths and cast water from the Dame's kamandalu, or waterpot carried by an ascetic.*)

Mak. (*sighs and looks up*).

Why thus alarmed, my friend?—I am well,

Quite well.

Mada. (*with delight*). Ah me! he is restored.

Mál. (*puts her hand to Mádhava's forehead*). Lavangiká,

How happy you, your friend again is conscious!

Mád. (*reviving*). Rash youth, where are you? here to my heart.

(*They embrace; Kámandakí hangs over them.*†)

* An act is therefore constituted by the exit of all the performers after a sufficient interval, and not by mere change of scene.

† Literally, smells their heads, a mode of expressing intense affection, parental yearning, still common in India, and a very ancient oriental practice, however odd it may appear to European notions. It was perhaps rather the result of this practice than chance that Isaac notices the smell of Jacob's person: " And he came near and kissed him, and smelled the smell of his raiment, and blessed him and said; see, the smell of my son is as the smell of a field which the Lord hath blessed."

Kám. I revive. (*They all express delight.*)

Lav. We all partake your joy!

Budd. (*apart to Madayantiká*). This is the youth.

Mada. That, that is Mádhava I know, and this
Is he you mean.*

Budd. Have I not spoke him truly?

Mada. Were his worth
Less than it shews, you had not so described him.
And Málatí, as rumour runs, has fixed
Her heart upon his friend.

(*Turns to look at Makaranda*).

Kám. (*observing them apart*).
Approving destiny has wrought to-day
The interview of yonder pair.
(*Aloud to Makaranda.*) Tell us, my son, by what propitious chance,
Conducted to this grove, you came to save
The life of this dear maid?

Mak. I came to seek
My friend, directed to the grove of Káma
By Avalokitá, and charged with news
I gathered in the city, which I feared
Would add to his affliction, when I saw
This noble maiden flying from the wrath
Of yon ferocious animal.

Kám. (*apart*). 'Tis time
To pledge the faith of Málati. (*Aloud.*) My son,
(*To Mádhava*)
The joy your friend's escape must needs afford you,
Is fit occasion for you to present
Some token of regard to Málatí.

Mád. I willingly obey, and since to her
I owe my own recovery from the mist,
The peril of my friend spread o'er my senses;

* Her avoiding his name indicates her regarding him as a husband.

Here for returning consciousness, I pledge her,
A free-will offering each,—my heart, my life.

Lav. I answer for my friend: she deems the gifts
Deserving her acceptance.

Mada. (*apart*). On my word
The youth knows when to proffer what is sure
To meet with willing ears.

Mál. (*apart*). But this news;
What should it be to render him unhappy?

Mád. Now, Makaranda, tell us what you heard,
That threatened to afflict me?

Enter a MESSENGER.*

Mess. (*to Maday*). Lady, the minister, your brother Nandana,
Desires your presence. It has pleased the king
In person to announce, that Bhúrivasu
Consents this day to give him Málatí:
He wills you therefore come and share his happiness.

Mak. He brings you my intelligence.

(*Málatí and Mádhava express their despair.*)

Mada. (*embracing Málatí*).
My dearest friend, this is indeed delightful.
One city saw our birth; our infant sports
And opening youth have ever found us friends;
And now you are my sister, and the pride
Of our illustrious house.

Kám. In truth, my child,
Fate is propitious when she grants your brother
A bride like this.

Mada. We rather thank your prayers.
My friend Lavangiká, our every wish
Is gratified, now we obtain your princess.

* The order is given behind the scenes in the original.

Lav. It may be: we have no concern with it.

Mada. Come, wench (*to Buddharakshitá*), let's hasten and get every thing
In order for the bridal.

Budd. I attend you. (*They rise.*)

Lav. (*apart to Kám.*). This interchange of looks, from eyes that roll
Like the soft tremulous lotus, and express
The dear emotions and the new delights
That fill and agitate the heart, reveal
This couple conscious of the like desire.

Kám. No doubt, they taste like pleasure from the look
So oft repeated, and the furtive glance
Tells a plain story; sidelong and slow the eye
Glides to the angle of the drooping lids,
Half closed by passion's birth; the brow is raised
In gentle curve, and the loose veiling lashes
Tremble in soft abandonment: all speaks
The inward consciousness of new delight.

Mád. (*to Budd.*). Sure I shall see again this graceful youth,
The saviour of my life?

Budd. If fate so pleases.

[*Exeunt with Attendant.*

Mád. (*apart*). Now let the thread of hope, long idly cherished,
Snap like the fibre of the lotus stem.
Come, boundless anguish, but by death relieved,
And frantic grief, avowed despair possess
My every thought! be destiny appeased,
And love work all his vengeance. Adverse fate
Delights to aggravate my woes, and mocks me
With disappointment, after I have won—
No common prize—affection like my own.
I marked her as she heard her father's will:
Pale as the moon before the morning sun,

Her lovely countenance revealed her sorrows,
And added sharper poignancy to mine.

Kám. (*apart*). I cannot bear their grief; and hope destroyed,
Life is a burthen. (*Aloud.*) Mádhava, my son,
Tell me, have you indulged the expectation,
The minister would give his daughter to you?

Mád. (*bashfully*). No, never, never!

Kám. Then were you ill apprized
Of past occurrences.

Mak. We know this, dame,
That Málatí already is betrothed.

Kám. You know what you have heard; to all 'tis known,
That when the monarch for his favourite sued,
The minister replied, "Your majesty
Is master of your own———"

Mál. So rumour goes.

Kám. To-day we learn the king has given Málatí
As if she were his own. But mark me, son;
The bond of human actions is good faith,
And promises control the acts of men:
In speech, the seeds of good and ill reside,
And all events are upon words dependent.
Do you not see in *Bhúrivasu's* answer
A covert import lies?—for Málatí
Is not the daughter of the sovereign;
Nor law, nor social decency, acknowledges
A monarch's will as the authority
To regulate a daughter's bridal compact.
Fie on it! It is not to be thought of—
And more, my son,—doubt you my vigilance?
Why, then, alarm the tender child with fears
Of such a fate I would not wish your foes?—
Confide in me,—I will not spare my pains,
Nor life, if it be needed, to secure
Your union with the maiden.

Mak. Well resolved.

Their union is most suitable. Your heart,
Most holy dame, though from the world estranged,
Is softened still with pity and affection
Towards these thy children; and thy active love,
Howe'er opposed to penance and devotion,
Shall like the will of destiny prevail.

Enter a MESSENGER.

The queen commands you, dame, with speed conduct
The lady Málatí to the palace.

Kám. Daughter come.

(*Mád. and Mál. interchange looks and sighs.*)

Mád. (*apart*). Out on the world's vicissitudes!
Fate, like a friend, first shews my blooming maid
With tender passion like my own inspired;
Then with capricious fickleness afflicts
My heart with deeper anguish.

Mál. (*apart*). Come what may,
This happiness is mine,—I have beheld him.

Lav. This barbarous minister has taught my friend
To hate her being.

Mál. (*apart*). Love of life has borne
Its fruits mature:—my father's cruelty,
Stern as the offerer of human sacrifice,
And fate, alike relentless, have achieved
Their task. Ah me, unhappy! to what friend,
To what kind refuge, can I now repair!

[*Exit with Kâmandakí and Lavangiká.*

Mád. I fear me much, the hope the dame encouraged
Sprang from the dread she entertained for her
Whom she has loved from birth. My luckless days
Will bear, I doubt, no fruit. What's to be done?

(*Thinking.*)

Apply to horrid mysteries,—what else
Remains! (*To Makaranda.*) How now, my friend! methinks you grieve
For Madayantiká?

Mak. 'Tis even so:
My mind recalls her timid wild embrace.
When, fearful as the tender fawn, she clung,
With limbs diffusing nectar on my wounds,
Around me, heedless of her loose attire.

Mád. She will be yours, for Buddharakshitá
Your friend is hers; and whom should she affect
But you, whom she embraced as her preserver;
Snatched by your prowess from the monster's fangs?
Nor did her looks proclaim you were a stranger.
The fond regard those lotus eyes expressed
Was clearly no new lesson.

Mak. Let us hence.
Bathe where the *Sindhu* and the *Pára* meet,
And then reseek the town.

(*They rise and proceed.*)

This is the spot.
The union of the streams, whose favoured bank
Beholds our maidens, in the frequent bath,
Forego their robes, and with their tender hands
Veiling imperfectly their charms, commit
Their lovely bosoms to the friendly wave.

[*Exeunt.*

END OF THE FOURTH ACT.

ACT V.

SCENE.—THE FIELD IN WHICH DEAD BODIES ARE BURNED IN THE VICINITY OF A TEMPLE.

Enter in the air in a heavenly car and in a hideous garb,
KAPÁLAKUNDALÁ.

Glory to *Saktináth,** upon whose steps,
The mighty goddesses attend,† whom seek
Successfully alone the firm of thought.
He crowns the lofty aims of those who know
And hold his form, as the pervading spirit,
That, one with their own essence, makes his seat
The heart, the lotus centre of the sphere‡

* The lord of *Sakti*, or the divine energy under a female personification. In this sense *Sákti* is applicable to every goddess, but it is more especially the name of *Bhavání*, and her lord or husband is *Síva*.

† Surrounded by the *Saktis*, or by the eight goddesses so termed, or *Bráhmí*, *Maheswarí*, *Kaumárí*, *Vaishnaví*, *Váráhi*, *Máhendrí*, *Chámúndá*, and *Chandíká*, hideous goddesses, who attend upon *Síva* as *Bhairava*, the terrific and destructive deity, who is propitiated by offerings of wine and flesh.

‡ The *Nári chakra*, the heart, as the centre of the circle of the different organs and tubular vessels along which the vital air or spirit is conveyed, and this spirit being one with *Siva* (*Sarvam Siva mayam*) his form or nature (*Rúpa*) may be said to be seated in the heart. The six organs are the ear, the navel, the heart, the throat, the palate, and the eye-brow. The *Náris* or tubes are one hundred and one in number, but ten are principal, *Ilá*, *Pingalá*, *Sushumná*, *Gandhárí*, *Hastijihwá*, *Púshá*, *Aruná*, *Alambushá*, *Guhá*, *Sankiní*: these all unite in the heart. These notions belong to the *Yoga*. According to other doctrines, and the more obvious meaning of the original text, there are sixteen principal *Náris*. To those who have thus discovered the actual presence of divine spirit in themselves, the deity *Síva* gives the eight *Siddhis*. *Mahimá*, the faculty of enlarging the bulk; *Laghimá*,

Sixfold, by ten nerves circled. Such am I.
Freed from all perishable bonds, I view
The eternal soul embodied as the God,
Forced by my spells* to tread the mystic labyrinth,
And rise in splendour throned upon my heart.
Hence through the many channelled veins I draw†
The grosser elements of this mortal body,‡
And soar unwearied through the air, dividing
The water-shedding clouds. Upon my flight,
Horrific honours wait ;—the hollow skulls,
That low descending from my neck depend,
Emit fierce music as they clash together,
Or strike the trembling plates that gird my loins.
Loose stream on every side my woven locks
In lengthening braids ;—upon my pond'rous staff,
The string of bells, light waving to and fro,
Jangles incessantly ;—my banner floats
Upborne upon the wailing breeze, whose tone
Is deepened by the echoes it awakes
Amidst the caverns of each fleshless skull,
That hangs in dread array around my person.

(*Alights and looks about.*)

Laghimá, that of making it light; *Animá*, that of making it small or atomic; *Prákámya*, the power of gratifying passion; *Vasitá*, that of subjecting all; *Isitá*, supreme sway; *Prápti*, the faculty of reaching or grasping objects, however remote; and *Kámávasáyitwam*, the accomplishment of every natural desire.

* Fixed by the *Nyása*, which is a form of gesticulation made with a short and mystic prayer to the heart, the head, the crown of the head, and the eye, as *Om Sirase Namah. Om;* salutation to the head, with the addition of the *Kavacha*, the armour or syllable *Phat*, and the *Astra*, the weapon or syllable *Hum*. The entire *Mantra*, the prayer or incantation, is then, *Om Sirase Namah, Hum, Phat.*

† Agreeably to the text, *Abhyását pasyate Suryam paramátmánam átmánam*. By practice (*of the Yoga*) he (*the adept*) beholds his own soul, the supreme soul, as the sun.

‡ According to some, the five senses, or sight, smell, hearing, taste, and touch, or the five elements, earth, air, water, fire, and *akás*, or ether.

I scent the temple of *Karálá,* near
The cemetery, and perfumed of old
By fetid odours from the funeral pile—
It is my present object—for to-day,
My wise preceptor, great Aghoraghanta,
Calls me to aid him in the powerful rite
That terminates his toils—to-day he offers
The promised gift, the gem of woman kind,
A victim to the goddess. In this city
The damsel dwells, and I must make her mine.

Looking out.

But who comes hitherward, of pleasing form,
With braided hair, and in one hand a sword;
The other—ha! it braves the world's restraints,
And soiled with blood, determinately grasps
A lump of human flesh! And now I look
I know the youth; 'tis Mádhava, the son
Of the old dame Kámandakí's dear friend.
What makes him vender of the flesh of man?—
It matters not. Now to my work; for see,
The hour of twilight hovers o'er the west;
Along the skirts of the horizon steal
The winding glooms like dark *Tamála* blossoms;
And earth's far bounds are lost, as if immersed
In nascent waters; to the woods young night
Her own yet gentle shade imparts, as if
A wreath of smoke were wafted through the air,
And spread abroad in mist before the breeze.

[*Exit.*

Enter MÁDHAVA.

May those endearments yet be mine, that spring
From young affection and the dawn of passion,
Now first awakened in my Málatí;
Which for an instant only to imagine,
Inspires my heart with extacy unsullied
By all impure admixture. 'Twere enough

To be enfolded in her arms, to lean
My face upon her cheek, or to be prest
Against her firm and palpitating bosom,
Fragrant with perfume, and with pearls adorned.
Yet this is too remote ; I will but ask
To see her face, the shrine of love once more.
Once more ! Ah, no ! for ever in my view
She lives ; assiduous memory constant turns
To cherished hopes, and fed by hourly thoughts,
One sole idea engrosses every sense,
Till all my inmost soul is Málatí.*

(*A noise behind.*)

Now wake the terrors of the place,† beset
With crowding and malignant fiends ; the flames
From funeral pyres scarce lend their sullen light,
Clogged with their fleshy prey, to dissipate
The fearful gloom that hems them in. Pale ghosts

* The obvious purport of this passage is clear enough, but reference is intended by the original to the practice of identifying the individual spirit with the Supreme Spirit by the intensity of abstract meditation, agreeably to the *Yoga* philosophy, and without having corresponding terms to those employed, an intelligible translation is impracticable. Part of the preceding and a subsequent verse have been omitted, as weakening the general effect of passage. The first describes Málatí's face in the customary strain, and in the latter Mádhava observes that Málatí is as firmly united with his heart as if sewed to it—1. With the strong threads of recollection ; 2. Pinned to it with the shafts of *Káma* ; 3. Melted in it ; 4. Reflected by it ; 5. Inscribed or engraven on it ; 6. Set or planted in it ; Or, 7. Fixed to it by diamond glue (*vajra lepa*). The verse is curious as illustrative of the progress of the arts. The last is said to be a union of all valuable articles externally, as diamonds, &c., so that they cannot be detached, but how this is effected is not explained. Each of these terms is said by Jagaddhara to bear also a metaphysical sense, and to refer to the different scholastic notions of the mode in which the mind that perceives, and the object of perception, are combined, so as to produce consciousness.

* The *Smasán*, the place where bodies are burnt ; temples of *Durgá* in some of her terrific forms were usually erected in or near it, and monuments of stone or brick were not unfrequently reared where the pile had stood.

Sport with foul goblins, and their dissonant mirth
In shrill respondent shrieks is echoed round.
Well, be it so. I seek, and must address them.
Demons of ill, and disembodied spirits,
Who haunt this spot, I bring you flesh for sale;
The flesh of man* untouched by trenchant steel,†
And worthy your acceptance. (*A great noise.*)
How the noise,
High, shrill, and indistinct, of chattering sprites
Communicative fills the charnel ground!
Strange forms like foxes flit along the sky:
From the red hair of their lank bodies darts
The meteor blaze; or from their mouths, that stretch
From ear to ear thick set with numerous fangs,
Or eyes, or beards, or brows, the radiance streams.
And now I see the goblin host: each stalks
On legs like palm-trees, a gaunt skeleton,
Whose fleshless bones are bound by starting sinews,
And scantly cased in black and shrivelled skin;
Like tall and withered trees by lightning scathed
They move, and as amidst their sapless trunks
The mighty serpent curls, so in each mouth
Wide yawning rolls the vast blood-dripping tongue.‡
They mark my coming, and the half-chewed morsel
Falls to the howling wolf,—and now they fly.
(*Pauses, and looking round.*)
Race, dastardly as hideous! All is plunged
In utter gloom. (*Considering.*) The river flows before me,
The boundary of the funeral ground, that winds

* This was a necessary condition; for the goblins, to the great discredit of their taste we must presume, would not condescend to eat female flesh.

† Flesh cut off with a weapon was in disrepute, on account of its being too common, in consequence of the number of men killed in battle. It does not appear how our hero comes by his merchandize.

‡ The author indulges here in a strain of powerful but disgusting description, too revolting to European taste to be faithfully followed.

Through mouldering bones its interrupted way.
Wild raves the torrent as it rushes past
And rends its crumbling banks; the wailing owl
Hoots through its skirting groves, and to the sounds
The loud long moaning jackall yells reply.

(*Behind.*)

Ah, cruel father! she you meant an offering
To the king's favour, now deserted dies.

Mád. (*alarmed*). What voice was that, so musical and wild,
That sounds like the affrighted osprey's cry!
It bursts not unfamiliar to mine ear,
And penetrates my soul;—my throbbing heart
Faint dies within me, and a lifeless chill
Steals along every limb;—my tottering steps
Can scarce sustain their load. What should this be?
The dreadful sound came from *Karálá's* fane,
Fit scene for deeds of horror. Be it so—
I must be satisfied. [*Rushes off.*

SCENE.—INSIDE OF THE TEMPLE OF CHÁMUNDÁ.*

AGHORAGHANTA, KAPÁLAKUNDALÁ.

MÁLATÍ *dressed as a victim.*

Mál. Unpitying sire, thy hapless daughter dies!
Mother beloved, remorseless fate consigns

* *Chámundá* was an emanation of the goddess *Durgá*, springing from her forehead to encounter the demons *Chanda* and *Munda*, detached to seize the latter by the sovereign of the *Daityas*, *Sumbha*, as related in the *Durgá Máhátmya*, and her appearance, which is thus described in the *Márkandeya Purána*, accords in most respects with the allusions in the text: "From the forehead of *Ambiká*, contracted with wrathful frowns, sprang swiftly forth a goddess of black and of formidable aspect, armed with a scymitar and noose, bearing a ponderous mace, and decorated with a garland of dead corses, robed in the hide of an elephant, dry and withered, and hideous with yawning mouth and lolling tongue and bloodshot eyes, and filling the regions with her shouts." Having slain the demons, she bore their heads to her parent goddess, who told her that having slain *Chanda* and *Munda*, she should thenceforth be known on earth as *Chámundá*. She is also termed *Kálí* from her black colour, and *Karálá* or *Karálavadaná* from her hideous countenance.

Thy gentle heart to agony. Revered
And holy dame, who lived but for thy Málatí,
Whose every thought was for her happiness,
Thy love will teach thee long and bitter anguish.
Ah, my dear friend, Lavangiká, to thee
But in thy dreams I henceforth shall appear!

Mád. (*enters behind*). My fears were true—'tis she! but still she lives.

Aghor. (*running round quickly as in worship**).
Hail! hail! *Chámundá*, mighty goddess hail!
I glorify thy sport, when in the dance†
That fills the court of *Síva* with delight,
Thy foot descending spurns the earthly globe.
Beneath the weight the broad-backed tortoise reels;‡
The egg of *Brahmá*§ trembles at the shock;
And in a yawning chasm, that gapes like hell,
The sevenfold main‖ tumultuously rushes.

The elephant hide that robes thee, to thy steps
Swings to and fro;—the whirling talons rend

* The stage direction is *Twaritam parikrámati*, which may also mean only proceeding quickly; but the limits of the stage must restrict this motion, and the act of circumambulating an object of worship or respect is an essential part of the homage to be offered.

† This dance is the counterpart of that which *Siva* himself is supposed to perform, and of which notice was taken at the opening of the play. In this rite the bride of *Siva* is described only in her terrific form as *Chámúndá*, in which she is invested with a garb, ornaments, and attributes, similar to those of *Siva* himself, or with those of *Kálí*.

‡ The earth is in some legends supposed to rest upon the back of a tortoise.

§ The egg of *Brahmá* is the world, the orphic or mundane egg which floated amidst the water before creation, and from which *Brahmá*, the first-born, emerged according to some legends, but which, according to others, merely resolved itself into the upper and lower spheres.

‖ According to the geography of the *Puránas*, the earth consists of a series of a central circle and six other annular continents, separated from each other by as many oceans of different fluid substances.

The crescent on thy brow;—from the torn orb
The trickling nectar falls, and every skull
That gems thy necklace laughs with horrid life.*
Attendant spirits tremble and applaud;
The mountain falls before the powerful arms,
Around whose length the sable serpents twine
Their swelling forms, and knit terrific bands,
Whilst from the hood expanded frequent flash
Envenomed flames.

As rolls thy awful head,
The low'ring eye that glows amidst thy brow†
A fiery circle designates, that wraps
The spheres within its terrible circumference:
Whilst by the banner on thy dreadful staff,
High waved, the stars are scattered from their orbits.
The three-eyed god exults in the embrace
Of his fair spouse, as *Gauri* sinks appalled
By the distracting cries of countless fiends
Who shout thy praise. Oh, may such dance afford
Whate'er we need—whate'er may yield us happiness!‡

Mád. (*behind*). What luckless chance is this, that such a maid,
With crimson garb and garland like a victim§

* In the different terrific forms of *Síva* and *Durgá*, a necklace of skulls forms an invariable decoration, as does the crescent or half-moon on the forehead; and as we have before had occasion to observe, the moon is considered to be the peculiar reservoir of *Amrita* or the beverage of immortality.

† The eye in the forehead is one peculiar characteristic of *Síva* and of his consort when armed with his terrors.

‡ *Jagaddhara* is rather shocked to think that these praises of *Chámundá* should fail of producing their due effect, but consoles himself by the reflection that the worshippers were disappointed of their object, either on account of their wickedness or their inaccurate pronunciation of some part of the ritual.

§ We had occasion to notice these paraphernalia more particularly in the *Mrichchakati*. In like manner the ordinary victims of the Greeks were adorned

Adorned for sacrifice, should be the captive
Of impious wretches,* like a timid fawn
Begirt by ravenous wolves: that she, the child
Of the all-powerful minister, should lie
Thus in the jaws of death. Ah, cruel destiny,
How ruthless are thy purposes!

Kap. Fair maid,
Think upon him whom thou in life hast loved,
For pitiless death is near thee.

Mál. Ah, Mádhava,
Lord of my heart! Oh, may I after death
Live in thy memory! They do not die,
Whom love embalms in long and fond remembrance.

Kap. Poor child! her heart is Mádhava's.

Aghor. (*raising his sword*). No matter—
Come what come may, we must delay no longer.
This offering vowed to thee, divine *Chámundá*,
Deign to accept.

adorned with crowns and garlands, as were human victims: as thus in the *Clouds*, in the scene between *Socrates* and *Strepsiades*:—

"*Socr.* Now take this chaplet—wear it.
"*Strep.* Why this chaplet?
Wouldst make of me another *Athamas*,
And sacrifice me to a cloud?"

So also in the *Heraclidæ*; *Macaria*, when offering herself as a victim to secure the triumph of the Athenians, exclaims,

"To the scene of death,
Conduct, with garlands crown me."

The translator of Euripides also observes, that human sacrifices at their first origin appear to have consisted of virgins or young men in the state of celibacy, and in this respect the selection of Málatí offers another analogy.

* *Páshanda* and *Chandála*, heretics and outcasts. These epithets indicate little respect for the worshippers of *Durgá*, and their application so publicly declared, would lead us to infer that the author's sentiments were those of his age. *Jagaddhara* states that in the rite two legal prohibitions are violated, of which he gives the text; they are, "Let him not eat from the leaf of the asclepias, nor slay a female nor child;" and, "Females of every description of being, it is well known, are not to be slain."

Mád. (*rushes forward and snatches Málatí up in his arms*).
Vile wretch, forbear!
Kap. The term
Profane is thine.
Mál. Oh, save me, save me! (*Embraces Mádhava.*)
Mád. Princess, do not fear.
A faithful friend, who in the hour of death
Finds courage to declare his love, is near thee—
Be of good courage—on this impious wretch,
The retribution of his crimes descends.
Aghor. What sinful youth is this that interrupts
Our solemn rite?
Kap. The lover of the maiden,
The pupil of Kámandákí, who treads
These precincts for unholy purposes,
And vends the flesh of man.
Mád. Inform me, princess,
How has this chanced?
Mál. I know not. I reposed
At eve upon the terrace: when I woke
I found myself a prisoner.—But what led
Your steps to this retreat?
Mád. (*ashamed*). By passion urged,
Incited by the hope my life might be
Yet blest by this fair hand, I hither came
To invoke the unclean spirits of the dead.
Your cries I heard, and instant hurried here.
Mál. And wert thou thus regardless of thyself,
And wandering here for me?
Mád. Blest was the chance
That snatched my love from the uplifted sword,
Like the pale moon from *Ráhu's** rav'nous jaws.
My mind is yet with various passions tossed,

* The node or dragon's head, whose attempt to swallow the moon is the supposed cause of eclipses.

And terror, pity, wonder, joy, and rage,
By turns possess my soul.

Aghor. Rash Brahman boy,
Thou seek'st thy fate. The pitying stag defies
The tiger in the rescue of his doe,
And both are made the forest monarch's prey—
So shalt thou perish, who dar'st hope to save
The victim of my sacrifice. Thy blood,
As flies the severed head before my scymitar,
Shall stream an offering to the mighty mother
Of all created beings.

Mád. Wretch accursed,
Impious and vile! Couldst thou raise thy sword
Against this delicate frame, that timid shrunk
Even from the flowers her fond companions cast
In sportive mood upon her—but my arm
Like *Yama's* mace* now falls upon thy head.

Mál. (*to Mádhava*). Lord of my life, refrain from violence:
His crime is baffled, let him be. Avoid
All needless peril.

Kap. (*to Aghor.*). Holy sir, be firm;
Destroy the culprit.

Mád. and Aghor.† (*to the women*). Banish your alarms;
The villain dies. What other chance should wait
The issue of the contest, when the lion,
Whose talons light upon the elephant's brow,
As falls the thunderbolt upon the mountain,
Raises their might against the feeble deer.

(*A noise behind.*)

What ho! ye who are now in search of Málatí,

* *Yama* is the regent of hell and judge of the dead; he rides upon a buffalo, and is armed with a ponderous mace.

† We are familiar with such consentaneous declaration in the Italian opera, but not in the recited drama. It is common, however, in Spanish plays for two or three characters to speak together in the same words, with such trifling modifications as may be necessary to render them applicable to the speaker.

The venerable priestess, whose commands
Are ever wise, enjoins ye to surround
The temple of *Kerálá*. This can be
The act of none but him who ministers
To the terrific goddess, and the princess
Can be an offering for no other shrine.

Kap. We are surrounded!

Aghor. Greater is the need
Of manly resolution.

Mál. My dear father!
My venerable mistress!

Mád. I will place
The princess out of peril with her friends,
Then swift return for vengeance.

(*He carries Málatí off, and returns confronting Aghoraghanta.*)

Now let the falchion piecemeal hew thy form,
Ring on thy bones, and cleave thy sinewy joints,
Sport in the yielding marrow, and divide,
Resistless in its fury, limb from limb.

[*Exeunt fighting.**

* The Hindu theatre is as particular as the French in prohibiting the exhibition of death upon the stage. The commentator observes, the combatants disappear *Nátaké sákshád badhánabhidánat* from its not being allowed to represent slaughter visibly in a drama, agreeably to the Horatian precept—"*Nec pueros coram populo Medea trucidet.*"

END OF THE FIFTH ACT.

ACT IV.

A Public Place.

Enter Kapálakundalá.

Alas! the cruel Mádhava has slain
My venerable master in the cause
Of Málatí. In vain, I strove to stay
His ruthless hand; he spurned my supplications.
What now remains—vengeance! Yes, Mádhava,
Thou yet shalt feel my fury—no repose
Can the destroyer of the serpent brood
Expect to taste—the mother snake retains
Her wrath unmitigated, whets her fangs,
And hoards her venom, wakeful for revenge.

(*Without.*)

Ho, warriors! haste, be quick in preparation
Appointed by the elders. Let the Brahmans
Recite auspicious strains. Let all devise
Ingenious shows and fitting invocations
Propitiating fate—for near at hand
The bridegroom train approaches. Till they come,
Obedient to the holy dame's injunctions,
The matrons of her father's household send
The maiden to the temple of the deity*

* According to the Hindus, every city has its own *Sri*, its own fortune or prosperity, which in former times seems to have been represented by an image with a temple of its own. The practice amongst the ancients of considering a city under the protection of some well known divinity is more familiar to us, but an analogous superstition with that of the Hindus also prevailed amongst the polytheists of Europe. Thus in the seven chiefs before *Thebes*; the *Theban* women seek their shrines of the gods who are the guardians of the city.

That guards our walls, to pray that nought molest,
No evil interrupt the happy rite.
Quick, let a guard, in rich caparison
Arrayed, upon the briliant train attend.

Kap. 'Tis well—I will keep vigilant watch,
And in the bustle of this marriage feast,
I may perchance some fit occasion seize
To wreak my vengance upon Mádhava.

[*Exit.*

SCENE II.—INSIDE OF THE TEMPLE.

Enter KALAHANSA.

I was ordered by my master, who is concealed within the shrine here with his friend Makaranda, to go and see whether the lady Málatí leads the procession to this temple. I shall delight him.

Enter MÁDHAVA *and* MAKARANDA.

Mád. How will this end! from the first day I saw
The lovely maid, events succeeding add
Fresh fuel to my passion, and to-day
The crisis comes. Will the sage dame's device
Secure me bliss, or end in disappointment?

Mak. Fear not, my friend, her wisdom cannot fail.

Kal. (*approaches*). My lord, you are favoured by fortune. The lady Málatí is on the road, at the head of the procession.

" Yet, therefore, to the ancient images,
Confiding in their sacred power, I ran,
When at the gates sharp sleet of arrowy shower
Drove hard; my fears impelled me to implore
The blest gods to protect the city's strength."

And *Virgil* states, that on the fall of Troy the deities who had protected the empire departed from the shrines,

" *Excessere omnes adytis arisque relictis*
Dii, quibus imperium hoc steterat."—Æn. 2.

The gods that *Æneas* carried with him to Rome appear to have been of this order, the Penates of Troy.

" *Effigies sacræ divum Phrygiique Penates.*"

The public penates were those who presided over fortresses and cities.

Mád. Can it be true?

Mak. Why should you doubting question?
They are at hand; for hark, a hollow murmur,
Like that of rushing clouds, before the gate
Comes sudden on the ear, and now the drums
That peal in joy drown every other sound;
Here from the lattice we may see their march.

Kal. Look, master, see how the white umbrellas float like trembling lotuses in the lake of the atmosphere. The numerous banners undulate like waves as they play before the wind of the Chowris, which hover about like swans; and now the elephants advance, their golden bells tinkling as they stride; they are mounted by merry bevies of damsels singing songs of rejoicing, uttered indistinctly as interrupted by the betel that perfumes their mouths, and blazing like rays of light with glittering jewels of variegated tints, as if they were so many portions of the heavens decorated with fragments of *Indra's* bow.

Mak. The state of *Bhúrivasu* is, in sooth,
Most princely. As the countless jewels shoot
Their blaze into the sky, the heavens reflect
The countless hues, as if the peacock's plumage,
Or the mixed colours of the painted jay,
Played through the air, or China's gorgeous silks
Vested the atmosphere, or *Indra's* bow
Displayed throughout its many coloured radiance.

Kal. The throng of attendants hastily forming a circle, fall off to a respectful distance, and keep back the crowd with staves covered with silver and gold. Her elephant painted with vermilion resembles the ruddy dawn, or with the starry garland* on her brow, looks like the brilliant night. But she herself, the lovely object of all eyes, as pale and delicate as the new moon, advances from the ring.

Mak. The beauteous damsel well becomes the grace

* The *Nakshatra málá*, a garland of twenty-seven pearls, the number of the *Nakshatras* or lunar mansions.

Of bridal honours. Her emaciate form
And pallid cheek, although they plainly shew
Deep-rooted grief, heighten her loveliness,
Like some fair plant just budding into flower
And withered at the core. Behold! my friend,
The elephant kneels.

Mád. And Málatí descends,
And with the priestess and her faithful friend
Lavangiká, comes hither. (*They withdraw.*)

SCENE III.—INSIDE OF THE TEMPLE.

Enter MÁLATÍ, KÁMANDAKÍ, *and* LAVANGIKÁ.

Kám. (*to herself*). May fate assist the wishes of our hearts,
And may the just gods crown them with completion:
May I attain my aim, and this device,
That binds the children of my friends in love,
Secure their future happiness.

Mál. (*apart*). Ah me!
What blest occasion will afford the means
Of death to free me from the world;—but no,
Death comes not to the wretch who prays his aid.

Lav. (*apart*). This final parting from her love has plunged
My poor friend in despair.

Enter a FEMALE ATTENDANT *with a basket.*

Att. (*to Kámandakí*). His Excellency, dame, desires me to inform you, that his Majesty has sent this bridal dress and these ornaments, that Málatí may put them on in presence of the deity.*

Kám. 'Tis rightly judged—the place is most propitious.
Let us behold the gear!

* It was customary also amongst the Greeks for the intended bride to pay her adoration to some divinity before her marriage, usually to *Diana*; but at *Athens* no virgin was allowed to be married before worshipping *Minerva*, who, as in the present instance, was the tutelary deity of the city.

Att. This is the corset of white silk; this is the red muslin mantle—these are the ornaments; this the necklace—this is sandal, this the chaplet of flowers.

Kám. (*apart*). It were a pleasant trick, and Madayantiká
Will not be sorry to behold the youth.
(*Aloud.*) Inform the minister it shall be done
As he directs. (*Exit Servant.*) Daughter Lavangiká,
Attend the princess to the inner shrine.

Lav. Where tarry you meanwhile?

Kám. I would remain
Alone, and leisurely investigate
The value of these jewels. [*Exit.*

Mál. (*apart*). Left with Lavangiká alone!

Lav. This is the door. Here let us enter.

(*They enter. Scene changes to the interior of the Temple.*)

MÁDHAVA, MAKARANDA, *and* KALAHANSA *discovered.*

Mák. They come; let us conceal ourselves awhile,
Behind this pillar. [*They hide.*

Enter MÁLATÍ *and* LAVANGIKÁ.

Lav. Here is the perfume for the person—here
The flowery garland.* (*Offering them.*)

Mál. What are they to me!

Lav. Consider, my dear friend, you are sent here
By your respected mother to propitiate
The deity, and thus invoke good fortune
On the commencement of the marriage rite.

Mál. Why thus distract a wretch whose heart is torn

* Garlands made part of the bridal as well as sacrificial ornaments amongst the Greeks. Thus in *Agamemnon*, Clytemnestra, in addressing Achilles:

"Offspring of Thetis, pity my distress;
Succour a virgin named, tho' falsely named,
Your bride: yet I with flowers adorned her brow,
And fancied that I led her to your arms;
But now I to the bloody altar lead."—*Iphigenia in Aulis.*

With pangs intolerable, and whose mind
Is tortured by the wanton cruelty
Of unrelenting fate!

Lav. Alas! what would you say?

Mal. Whatever he, whose fortunes are, like mine,
Blighted by unavailing hopes, might counsel.

Mak. Heard you?

Mád. I heard—what little cheers my heart.

Mál. (*embracing Lavangiká*). My dearest friend, the sister of my soul,
Your hapless Málatí, about to die
Unwedded, begs one proof of your affection.
From earliest infancy you have replied
Unvarying to my confidence—ah! now,
Do not the first time disappoint my hopes—
Bear still my image in your heart, and see
The lotus lovely countenance of Mádhava,
The shrine of each auspicious excellence.

(*Weeps.*)

Mád. (*behind.*) Delightful words, that fortunately shed
Their nectar through my heart, and o'er my frame
Diffuse the powerful medicine that restores
The vigorous bloom of life's decaying flower.

Mál. Then tell the brave preserver of my life,
He must not, if he ever prized my love,
When he shall hear that I am dead, attempt
His days, but live to cherish my remembrance.
Tell him, I hope he will not wholly lose
The recollection of this life's events:
Although the tenant of another world,
I here shall live in memory alone.
Do this, and all your Málatí's desires
Your kindness will bestow.

Mak. Alas, poor girl!

Mád. The sad yet sweet tones of her fond despair
Awake contending sentiments—her grief

Excites both joy and pain, and fills my mind
With anguish and delight.

Lav. I am overcome
With horror! let me hear no more, my friend,
Words of such evil omen.

Mál. Ah, Lavangiká,
You love the life of Málatí alone—
Not Málatí.

Lav. What mean you?

Mál. I have borne
Thus long a hateful life, sustained alone
By flattering promises I yet might wed
The lord of my election. This is past;
But 'tis my firm resolve to end my days,
Free from the stain of violated faith,
To the divinity whom I have served—
Then do not thou oppose me in my purpose.

(*Falls at her feet.*)

Mak. Her love is boundless.

(*Lavangiká beckons to Mádhava.*)

Go take her place.

Mád. I tremble.

Mak. 'Tis a sign
Of coming happiness!

Mád. I go. (*Approaches gently and takes the station of Lavangiká who retires.**)

Mál. (*kneeling*). Speak your assent, my friend!

Mád. Forego such desperate purpose, simple maid:
My heart, dear girl, will never bear thy loss.†

Mál. Behold me prostrate till you give consent!

* The situation that ensues is rendered extravagantly improbable by the dialogue. If the discovery were natural, it would not be undramatic.

† This verse is both Sanscrit and Prakrit, according to the commentator. *Saralé sáhasa rágam parihara Rembhohru muncha samrambham. Virasam viraháyásam sohrum tava chittam asahamme.*

Mád. What can I say! desponding as thou art,
Do as thou wilt, but first this fond embrace.

Mál. Now I am blest!
(Rises and throws herself into Mádhava's arms.)
I have but half my friend;
For my fast-flowing tears obscure my sight.
Firm as the lotus cup, and smooth with down,
Thy form recalls a contact that allays
The fever of my grief; oh, bear its owner,
With hands thus elevated to your brow,
My farewell message.* 'Tis long since these eyes
Have lost the sight of thy engaging countenance,
As brilliant as the broad bright-beaming moon,
And lovelier than the full blown lotus flower.
The sufferings of my frame, which not the rays
Of the mild lunar orb, nor the cool breath
Of Malaya could appease, have long distressed
My friendly train with bitterest affliction.
My heart, whose firmness by incessant cares
Still growing more unbearable assailed,
Had sunk, was yet by hope sustained; but now
I hope no more. Let me still live, dear friend,
In your remembrance, and when I am gone,
May this, the work of Mádhava, preserved
Next to your heart, whene'er it meet your gaze,
Bring to your mind the Málatí you loved.
(Goes to hang the garland round the neck of Mádhava, and discovering her mistake, starts back in alarm.)

Mád. (*apart*). The gentle pressure of her heaving bosom
Has spread delightful coolness through my frame,
As if combined upon my skin were strewed
Sandal and camphor—*saivala*† and pearls—
The lotus fibre or the moonstone's dew.

* The gesture here adopted has the effect of partly covering the eyes, and is intended to give probability to Málatí's prolonged error.

† An aquatic plant (*vallisneria*) of supposed cooling powers.

Mál. Lavangiká betrays me!

Mád. Gentle maid,
Your own experience only cannot teach you
What others have endured—but this believe,
Such days as you have passed, such have I known,
Whose fevered flames have raged in every vein,
And anguish wrung conscious existence from me—
Thy love alone preserved my fleeting life.

Lav. You are ensnared, my friend, as you deserved.

Kal. This mutual confession is pleasant enough.

Mak. Princess, you are merciful, it is true,
My friend has undergone so sad a time,
And yet exists—now may his hopes be crowned,
And with that plighted hand the golden thread
Shall gird, be happiness his future portion.

Lav. How can you name the golden thread that girds
The bridal hand? Observe you not, her heart
Is agitated with the apprehension
Of an immediate and unwelcome marriage.

Mál. (apart). Out on it—what is this? it ill becomes
A maiden's honour.

Kám. (entering). How now,
My gentle child!

(*Málatí throws herself into her arms.*)

Kám. Look up, behold the youth who shared your sufferings,
Whose eyes first caught the flame; whose heart was next
To thee alone devoted; and whose frame,
Like thine emaciate, equal passion shews.
Behold him here! Dismiss this weak timidity—
Be love obeyed and destiny fulfilled.

Lav. What marvel, dame, our friend should be alarmed!
This is, to say the truth, a fearful personage—
The conqueror of the fierce and impious wretch
Who braved his fatal arm, when on the night
No moon illumes, and with no good intent,
He trod the confines of the funeral ground.

Mak. (*to himself*). Well said, Lavangiká, the double bond
Of love and gratitude is well suggested.

Mál. Alas, my parents!

Kám. Mádhava, my son.

Mád. Command me.

Kám. This is this dearest gem of *Bhúrivasu,*
The mighty minister, whose feet are blazoned
With the bright diadems of prostrate princes.
Fate, pleased congenial merit to unite,
And love and I their instrument, confer
This treasure to your care. (*Weeps.*)

Mak. Our hopes are gratified
By your kind aid.

Mád. But why these tears?

Kám. My son, long cherished friendship has endeared
The interests of your house to me, and now
That love is consummated, for mine old
And tried affection, and for other causes,
I may demand, you listen to my counsels.
Then heed my words, and pledge your faith to me,
You cherish this dear child most tenderly,
When I no more behold her.
(*About to fall at the feet of Mádhava.*)

Mád. (*preventing her*). Forbear! forbear! your kindness overpowers me.

Mak. Why should you need assurance, dame, of this—
The object of your praise—the living festival
Of human eyes—replete with warm affection
And brilliant worth—why, one were irresistible—
Their union is your surety.

Kám. My son (*to Mádhava*).

Mád. Behold me!

Kám. Málatí, my child.

Lav. She waits upon your will.

Kám. Remember children—
A virtuous wife and a respected lord

Are each to either all—kindred and friends,
Wealth, love, and life, and all the heart should covet.

Mak. 'Tis justly said.

Lav. What further has the dame
To order?

Kám. Makaranda, take these robes
And dress you for the bridal.

Mak. As you will.
Behind this curtain* I can make my toilet. (*Retires.*)

Mád. But will not this expose my friend to peril?

Kám. Out on thee—what hast thou to do in this?

Mád. I trust me to your judgment.

Enter MAKARANDA *in female attire.*†

Mak. My friend, behold your Málatí.

Mád. (*embracing him*). In truth,
The priestess highly favours Nandana,
To yield his admiration, for an instant,
A bride like this.

Kám. Now, my dear children (*to Málatí and Mádhava*), leave
This temple by the sacred grove, and pass
Quick to the garden of my sanctuary.
In the pavilion Avalokitá
Awaits your coming, with all means prepared
To celebrate the nuptial ceremony.
The rite accomplished, to the grove retire,
Where round the areka-trees the betel vine
Curls its pale leaves, as pallid as the cheek
Of the fair dames of *Kerala* who mourn

* *Chitra Javaniká*, a painted cloth, a screen or veil suspended in a temple before the adytum; according to *Malanka* it is rather arras or tapestry; he describes it as cloth covering the walls of a temple.

† A rather expeditious affair; but as the dress consists almost solely of one long wrapper, not so unmanageable as some of the transformations of a Mathews.

Their absent lords.* The beauties of the scene,
Begirt with waving oranges, and musical
With the sweet tone of numerous choristers,
Who sip delightedly the jujube's juice,
Shall breathe a warmer rapture on your loves.
There loiter till your friend and his fair maid,
The princess Madayantiká, shall join you.

Mád. This were indeed to crown my happiness.

Kal. If luck befriend us this will surely be.

Mád. There cannot be a fear.

Lav. Heard you, my friend?

Kám. Lavangiká
And Makaranda, we must now depart.

Mál. What, must you go, Lavangiká?

Lav. (*smiling*). I must.
This is our way.

[*Exeunt Kámandakí, Lavangiká, and Makaranda.*

Mád. Like some fair lotus is this trembling hand,
Along whose slender stalk the downy filaments
Erect extend, and from whose leaflet fingers
The pearly drops from love engendered fall.
I clasp it now in mine—as with his tusk
The elephant enwines the tender flower,
And gently wrests it from its native lake.

[*Exit with Málatí.*

* Malabar. They are often alluded to in this strain, and it is to be supposed, therefore, that the women of this province are of a fairer complexion than usual in India.

END OF THE SIXTH ACT.

ACT VII.

THE PALACE OF NANDANA.

Enter BUDDHARAKSHITÁ.

So far so well. Makaranda well became his disguise as Málatí, and by the instructions and good fortune of the dame has played his part unsuspected, and has been wedded to Nandana in the palace of the minister. Kámandakí then took leave, and has gone home, anticipating that the attendants will all be wearied with the bustle of the festival of bringing the bride to her husband's house, and that the evening will be favourable to the execution of our design. In the mean time Nandana, impatient to possess his bride, first endeavoured to sooth her alarms, and humbled himself at her feet. Finding this in vain he had recourse to violence; but he was so severely handled by the supposed maiden that he was compelled to desist. Enraged at the treatment, the tears starting from his eyes with pain and vexation, and his speech inarticulate with fury, Nandana vowed he would have no more to say to one, who was no better than the wanton of a boy. With this determination he left the apartments, and with this opportunity we may bring Madayantiká and Makaranda together.

[*Exit.*

SCENE II.—LAVANGIKÁ *and* MAKARANDA *on a couch in woman's attire discovered.*

Mak. You are confident that Buddharakshitá
Will make no blunder, and so disappoint
The project of the priestess?

Lav. Never fear:
And hark! the tinkling foot-bells, that proclaim

Their near approach: quick, spread this mantle over you,
And seem to sleep. (*He lies down as she covers him.*)

Enter MADAYANTIKÁ *and* BUDDHARAKSHITÁ.

Mada. Is indeed my brother
So grievously displeased with Málatí?
Budd. No doubt.
Mada. But this is unbecoming—let us go
And take to task this rude ill-mannered girl.
Budd. This is her chamber door.
Mada. Lavangiká,
Sleeps your fair friend?
Lav. Yes, do not break her slumbers.
She has been sadly vexed of late, and now,
Her cares awhile forgot, she tastes repose.
Here gently seat you on the couch.
Mada. (*sits down*). Indeed
She may be vexed; that she is rude I'm sure.
Lav. How, should she not be fretted—with a husband
So gently kind, affectionate and mild,
So skilled to win a maiden's confidence,
As is your brother?
Mada. Hey, Buddharakshitá,—
We blame her strange perverseness.
Budd. Perverse may not on all occasions be
Perverseness.
Mada. How so?
Budd. 'Tis true she treated with but scant respect
The husband prostrate at her feet; still this
Was maiden bashfulness, and might be pardoned.
You cannot deem so of your brother's anger,
Who in resentment of a coy resistance,
Such as became a virgin bride to offer
To boisterous violence, forgot all sense
Of his own dignity, and had recourse
To sheer abuse—such conduct is disgraceful

To you, not us. The poets well observe,
Women like flowers are of tender fabric,
And should be softly handled—they detest
The furious passion that would force their love
Impatient, ere their confidence be won.

Lav. Alas! who ever heard of such behaviour!
In many a house, men of exalted rank
Are wedded unto maids of gentle birth;
But who, like fire the breeze blows into flame,
Is rendered furious by the chaste reluctance
Of his young, fair, and unoffending bride.
A husband's harshness renders home distasteful
To the desponding wife, tortures her heart
With poisoned shafts, and makes her wish for death.
Occurrences like these compel a family
To murmur sorely when a girl is born.

Mada. (*to Budd.*). Our friend Lavangiká seems sadly grieved.
What fault so heinous is my brother charged with?

Budd. Did we not hear his words?

Mada. What were they?

Budd. "I will nought
Of one no better than a stripling's wanton."

Mada. Folly, insanity, my friend Lavangiká,
It is with shame I look you in the face.
But I should have some voice in this affair,
So hear what I advise.

Lav. I am attentive.

Mada. Dismiss the memory of my brother's rudeness.
Remember only that he is the husband
Of our friend Málatí; and to confess
The truth, you must admit there was some cause
For this intemperate language, though unmeet
For female ears.

Lav. I know no cause.

Mada. It has been noised abroad,
That Málatí had plighted her affection

To the youth Mádhava. This is no mystery.
But now, dear friend, exert your utmost skill,
That such ill-starred aversion to her husband
May utterly be rooted from her heart:
If not, a grievous shame will light upon her,
For wives resentful and ungentle plague
The hearts of men—this fear that I have hinted
You will not speak of.

Lav. Hence, you heedless girl,
To be beguiled by loose report so easily:
I hold no further talk with you.

Mada. Nay, nay,
Be not displeased: you need not hesitate
To own the truth—what, I suppose we knew not,
That Málatí had nearly pined to death
On Mádhava's account. We did not mark
The delicate beauty of her wasting form,
Like the young tender *ketaki*—we saw not
The animating influence of the wreath
Of *vakula* flowers, wove by the hand of Mádhava;
Nor did we note the evident sympathy
Each frame expressed, when either shewed as wan
As the moon's pallid disk when morning dawns.
You may forget, that I beheld their glances,
When in the garden of the flower-armed god
The youth and maiden met: their eyes encountering,
Swam with delight, and brilliant flashes shot
From each soft orb, uttering intelligibly
The language prompted by the soft emotion
That played through every agitated limb.
Then, when the news arrived the king had given her
In marriage to my brother—was not a change,
As if the hand of adverse fate had scorched
Her charms, and rudely from its living bands
Had wrung her heart, that moment manifest?
Nay, I remember too—

Lav. What more?

Mada. When, by the shrewd suggestion of the dame,
The youth was counselled to give Málatí
Some token of his happiness, that his friend,
The brave preserver of my life, was brought
Again to conscious being; he presented her
His heart, and life; and, if I heard aright,
Lavangiká replied, "my friend esteems
These liberal gifts most worthy her acceptance."

Lav. And who was he—the saviour of your life?
I have forgotten him.

Mada. Think, think again.
When I was chased by the ferocious beast,
And had no hope—that guardian youth appeared,
And heedless of a person which enshrines
The worth of all the world, quick interposed
His powerful arm to snatch me from destruction.
For me he braved the monster's mighty blows,
Falling like thunder strokes; his manly breast
Was scored with wounds, and ruddier than a wreath
Of crimson roses. But the tiger plied
His fangs and claws in vain—the hero triumphed—
The furious savage fell beneath his sword.

Lav. Ah, I remember now—'Twas Makaranda.

Mada. Whom, say you?

Lav. Makaranda. (*Taking hold of her.*)
How now!
What, are we all alike? How chances it,
That one so free from passion should betray,
Without apparent cause, this agitation,
And blossom like the round *kadamba* flower?*

Mada. Why laugh at me? I own I often think

* The *kadamba* flower when full blown is invested with projecting anthers like the erect bristles of a hedge-hog. Delight, according to the Hindus, gives a bristly elevation to the down of the body: the phenomenon here alluded to.

Of that brave youth who, reckless of his safety,
Rushed to my aid and snatched me from the jaws
Of all-devouring fate. I frequent view him,
As the sharp pain of his innumerous wounds
Forced the big drops from his exhausted limbs,
And leaning on his sword, awhile he stood,
Then closed his lotus eyes and fainting fell—
Content to leave this glorious living world
For Madayantiká, and in her presence.
Should I think less of one who saved my life?

Budd. All this is in your person plainly told.

Mada. Away, away! I have betrayed myself,
Depending on your faith.

Lav. Nay, dear girl,
We know that which we know. Come, be composed,
Confess the truth; there should be no disguise
Amongst such friends as we are. Let us taste
The pleasure mutual confidence bestows.

Budd. Lavangiká is right.

Mada. Well, I must need
Obey my friend.

Lav. Come, tell us how of late
You pass your time?

Mada. Hear me:
Before I saw the youth I frequent heard
His praise from Buddharakshitá, and pleased
By her description, let my fancy dwell
Upon his absent image, till my heart
Was filled with anxious longing to behold him.
At length 'twas willed by fate that we should meet,
Though for brief interval. Oh, then I found
How deep a wound had Madana* inflicted.
Life was distateful to me—on my form
The scorching flames of passion fiercely preyed,

* The Hindu Cupid.

And filled my kind attendants with affliction.
The only remedy I saw was death;
And anxious sought such welcome liberation.
Still Buddharakshitá opposed my purpose,
Assuaged my growing sorrows, and persuaded me
Still to endure this transitory world.
My dreams since come to animate my hopes;
Place in my eyes the object of my wishes,
Bring to my ears the music of his voice,
Fold me within his grasp, and picture more
Than I dare tell you—till I wake and view,
Ah me, the world a lone and dreary waste.*

Lav. 'Tis honestly avowed; and well I know,
It costs our friend here no small pains to hide
Some of these feelings from your tittering train.

Mada. You chatter giddily—I have done with you.

Budd. Regard her not, be sure that Málatí
Has for her ear some similar confession.

Mada. Nay, nay, you must not laugh at Málatí.

Budd. Well, I have done; and now, my tender friend,
I have a question for you, if you promise me
Inviolate secrecy.

Mada. What breach of trust
Have I committed, that there needs such promise?
My heart is wholly yours and Lavangiká's.

Budd. If Makaranda cross your sight again
By any accident, what would you do?

Mada. My eyes would rest unwearied on his form,
And on my heart would heavenly rapture fall.

Budd. And if, by love directed, he should offer
Such gentle violence as *Rukmini*
Endured from *Purushottama*,† and wrung
Your bridal vows from you?

* The latter part of this speech is somewhat compressed from the original.

† A name of *Krishna*. According to the *Harivansa*, *Rukminí* was the daughter of *Bhíshmaka*, king of *Kundina*, and was solicited in marriage by *Krishna*,

Mada. (*sighing*). Why tease me
With such vain hopes?

Budd. Nay, answer me.

Lav. Those sighs
Deep drawn, betray the secrets of her heart,
And give you plain reply.

Mada. What do you think of me?
He bought this body when he risked his own
And snatched me from the tiger—I am his.

Lav. 'Tis generously and gratefully resolved.

Budd. You will remember what you have now said.

Mada. Hark! (*Drums without.*)
The drum proclaims the second watch begun;
I must disturb my friend, and try to soothe
Her indignation at my brother's conduct,
And then to rest. Why, Málatí, asleep?

(*Goes to the couch, Makaranda shews his face and catches hold of her hand.*)

Hey, who is this?

Mak. Fear nothing, gentle maid;
Let not that palpitating breast distress
Your slender waist. In me, behold your slave!

Krishna, of whom she was enamoured; but the son of *Bhishma*, *Rukmi*, jealous of *Krishna's* fame, and being incensed by the death of *Kansa*, his friend, was hostile to the match, and negociated his sister's marriage with *Sisupala* king of *Chedi*, likewise inimically disposed towards *Krishna*. All the kings of India were invited to the wedding, and amongst them came *Krishna*, who seeing *Rukmini* proceed to offer her devotions at a temple, waylaid her on her return, and with the assistance of his brother *Balaráma* and his kinsmen carried her off to *Dwáraká*. A hot pursuit followed, and an engagement took place in which *Rukmi* was struck to the ground by *Kesava*, but his life was spared at his sister's intercession, and *Krishna* remained possessed of his prize. The marriage was solemnized at *Dwáraká*, and *Rukminí* remained the chief of *Krishna's* wives. He had ten sons by her, of whom *Pradyumna* is the most celebrated. The rape of *Rukminí* is also narrated nearly in the same words, as in the *Harivansa*, in the 5th Section of the *Vishnu Purána*, and more in detail in the tenth book of the *Bhágavat*, and in the *Krishna Janma Khanda* of the *Brahmavaivertta Purána*.

By your avowed affection elevated
To highest ectasy.

Lav. (*holding up Madayantiká's face*).
Behold your lover!
The object of your hopes. Within the palace
The servants soundly sleep—the night is dark.
Now shew your gratitude, let us take off
Our tinkling anclets, and depart.

Mada. Where should we go?

Budd. Where Málatí has gone.

Mada. What! has she fled?

Budd. She has; now let me see,
What I must think of you. (*Madayantiká weeps.*)
(*To Maka.*) Noble youth,
My dear friend gives to you—herself.

Mak. This is
A glorious conquest, and to-day I reap
The harvest of my youth—upon whose festival,
In proof of friendship, the fish-bannered god*
Presents me in his bounty this dear maid.
Come, by this private entrance let us fly.†
Our nightly journey will not want its pleasures.
The breeze that cool and fragrant sweeps along
The lofty terrace or the palace top,
Reveals the joyous scenes it has surveyed,
As with the camphory balm, and flowery perfume,
And winy odours, redolent it blows. [*Exeunt.*

* *Káma*, or Cupid, who bears upon his banner the *makara*, an aquatic monster something like the sign of the Zodiac Capricornus.

† The original here directs their exit, and the following lines are supposed to be spoken in the street.

END OF THE SEVENTH ACT.

ACT VIII.

The Mansion of Kámandakí.

Enter Avalokitá.

Whilst my mistress has gone to the palace of *Nandana*, I will seek Mádhava and Málatí. Ah, there they sit, upon the marble platform crowning the steps of the lake, refreshing themselves after the heat of the day. I will join them.

[*Exit.*

The Grove.

Málatí *and* Mádhava *discovered.—To them,* Avalokitá.

Mád. Night, ever friend to love, now spreads its shades.
Faint in the east the gentle moonlight gleams,
Pale as the palm's sear leaf, and through the air
The slowly rising breezes spread around
The grateful fragrance of the *ketaki.**
How shall I win this maid to confidence?
My dearest Málatí; whilst I retain
The cooling influence of the evening bath,
You are oppressed with heat: the trembling drops
Steal from your hair and quiver on your bosom,
And o'er your graceful form the down erect
Profusely rises. Whilst you suffer thus,
Come to my breast, let me but once embrace thee.
Why thus averse? Let those confiding arms,
Upon whose taper length the sudden dews
Start with alarm, as if the living gem
Kissed by the moon distilled its gelid moisture,

* A strong scented flower (*Pandanus odoratissimus*).

Twine round my neck; and if this may not be,
Why may I not be blessed with your discourse?
What, if this frame, long scorched by southern gales
And by the lunar beams, may not aspire
To your embrace, yet let mine ear, distressed
By the wild *koïl's* song, be now regaled
By your melodious voice, more musical
Than are the choirs of heaven.

Ava. (*advancing*). What folly, this—
What inconsistency—late, in my presence,
When Mádhava but a brief interval
Had disappeared, you were most miserable,
And thus exclaimed: "Where can my lord delay!
Would he were come, that I might gaze upon him
With eyelids never veiled, and all reserve
Discarded wholly, I might fly to him
And clasp him in my arms!" those were your words;
And now, what contrast.

(*Málatí looks at her spitefully.*)

Mád. (*apart.*) The dame's disciples
Are all endowed with clear intelligence
And eloquence of speech. (*Aloud.*) How, Málatí,
Speaks Avalokitá the truth?

(*Málatí shakes her head.*)

Or are you sworn to silence, by the lives
Of those whom best you love?

Mál. (*in a hesitating manner*). How should I know, my lord?

(*Pauses.*)

Mád. Delightful, though imperfect sounds! But see,
What should this mean! The starting tear-drop steals
From those fawn eyes, and glisten on that cheek,
Upon whose pallid hue the moon-beams play,
As if the lunar orb desired to quaff
The nectar of its beauty.

Ava. Why is this?
Why start these tears?

Mál. (*to her*). How long must I regret
The absence of Lavangiká: is it
Not possible to gather tidings of her?

Mád. (*to Avalokitá*). What says my love?

Ava. You have recalled the memory of Lavangiká,
And she is anxious for some news of her.

Mád. It was but now, I ordered Kalahansa
To go, and secretly collect intelligence
At Nandana's abode. Surely the plan
That was to win my friend a lovely bride
Cannot have failed?

Ava. Be sure of it.
But tell me, Mádhava:
You gave your life and heart to Málatí,
When brought again to consciousness—suppressed
By fear for Makaranda's bleeding wounds.
Now, if that friend beloved should win the maid,
And thus your happiness should be increased,
What gift remains to speak your gratitude
To him who may impart the pleasing tidings?

Mád. She tells me what to do. (*Looking at his bosom.*)
This garland, wove
Of the sweet flowers of that beauteous tree
That graced the grove of Madana, beneath
Whose conscious shade I first saw Málatí,
Shall be my free-will gift. It has been prest
Already to her bosom—from my hands
Conveyed by her dear friend Lavangiká;
And in her error, thinking that she gave
The garland to Lavangiká again
To bear to me, it came to me once more
From her, by whom all that I prize is given me.

Ava. Málatí, this garland ought to be
Something in your esteem—be on your guard
It do not pass into a stranger's hands.

Mál. You counsel well.

Mád. (*looking out*). 'Tis Kalahansa.
Mál. (*approaching*). Fate favours you, and Madayantiká
Is won.
Mád. (*embracing her*). The news is ecstasy.
(*Takes the garland from his neck and throws it on Málatí's.*)
Ava. The charge consigned to Buddharakshitá
Is well accomplished.
Mál. And I see
Lavangiká again.

Enter hastily KALAHANSA, MADAYANTIKÁ, BUDDHARAKSHITÁ. *and* LAVANGIKÁ.

Lav. Help, prince! the city guard have stopped midway
Your gallant friend; he checks pursuit alone,
That we with Kalahansa might escape.
Kal. And as we fled, we heard on every side
The gathering tumult; so that I fear fresh force
Has joined the guard.
Ava. Alas! how sad a chance!
One hour produces happiness and terror.
Mád. Come Madayantiká, my dwelling
Is honoured by your presence—for my friend,
His prowess is well known—be not alarmed;
Dread not, though singly he contend with multitudes.
To such as he, odds are of little moment—
He needs no succour but his own right arm,
Resistless as the lion, when delightedly
He rings his clashing claws, and cleaves asunder
The elephant's broad temples, from whose hollows
The trickling dew flows over the shattered cheek.
Ambitious to pursue the glorious path
A hero treads, I haste to aid my friend.
[*Exit with Kalahansa.*
Ava. Assuredly these heroes will return
Unhurt.
Mál. Do you and Buddharakshitá

Apprise Kámandakí of this mischance.
Lavangiká, overtake my lord ; intreat him
That he and his brave friend will think of us,
And shun all needless danger—go, be speedy.

[*Exeunt the three.*

After a pause.

Mál. Lavangiká delays—why comes she not?
This is a fearful interval ; dear girl (*to Madayantiká*)
I will go forth along the road, and meet
Lavangiká returning.

Mada. My right eye throbs.* (*Retires.*)

As MÁLATÍ *is going, enter* KAPÁLAKUNDALÁ.

Kap. Hold !

Mál. (*screams*). Ah ! husband (*in an under tone—stops terrified*).

Kap. Yes, call upon him.
Where is your love, the murderer of the pious,
The youthful paramour of wanton girls !
Let him, your husband, save you if he can.
Bird of the wild, that tremblest to behold
The hovering hawk, what canst thou hope, long marked
My prey. I bear thee with me to *Sri Párvata*,
There to consign thee to a painful death,
Torn piecemeal—victim of my just revenge.

(*Carries off Málatí.*)

Mada. (*coming forward*). I will even follow Málatí ;
Ha ! Málatí.

Lav. (*enters*). 'Tis I, Lavangiká.

Mada. How, have you seen the princess?

Lav. I have not.
Scarce had we left the garden's boundaries,
When hearing the increasing noise, the youth
Sprang speedily away, and in an instant

* An unlucky omen in a female—a lucky one in men.

Was lost amidst the throng: in vain I followed,
And thought it better to retrace my steps.
As I returned, I heard from every house
Regret for Makaranda and his friend—
The citizens were grieving for their fate.
The king, they said, had been informed the youths
Had borne away the daughter of the minister,
And furiously incensed, had sent his guards
To seize the fugitives—himself awaiting
Upon the palace terrace their return.

Mada. Ah me unhappy, I have heard my death.

Lav. But where is Málatí?

Mada. She went to watch
The road you should return. I then pursued
Her steps, but have not seen her since. Most likely
She has gone into the garden.

Lav. Let us seek her. Hold! who comes here?
'Tis Kalahansa: quick, your news.

Enter KALAHANSA.*

Kal. We have got well out of the scuffle! Oh dear me. I think I now see the glittering gleam of the polished sabres flashing in the moonlight—a pretty but awful appearance: and then what a tumult from the hostile force: assailed by the irresistible, merciless, and active Makaranda, they fled in dismay and confusion, with a clamour which filled the whole space of heaven, like that emitted by the tossing waves of *Kálindi*† when they were turned from their course by the mighty plough of *Balaráma,* in fulfilment of the menace

* In the original the women quit the stage searching for Málatí, and Kalahansa enters and tells the story to the audience, which is a very clumsy and Chinese mode of conducting the plot. A short speech or two has therefore been introduced to connect his narrative with the business of the piece.

† The *Yamuná* or *Jumná.*

that wine had dictated.* I shall not forget either the prowess of my master Mádhava; he soon cleared the road of the soldiers: they ran with no little speed, those who could, while covering the road with heaps of various weapons thrown away in their flight, from the concentrated thunder-stroke of his formidable arm. The king has truly a regard for merit. His eye dwelt with complacency on the lovely countenances of Mádhava and Makaranda, as they stood before him on the terrace, whither, after the affray was composed by the monarch's attendants, they had been respectfully conducted. Having heard their rank and connexions from me, the youths received every honour, and his majesty turning to Bhúrivasu and Nandana, who stood nigh, their faces as black as ink with rage and disappointment, said to them very condescendingly: "How now, are you not content with kinsmen such as these, ornaments of the world, eminent in worth and descent, and handsome as the new moon?" So saying he withdrew to the interior, and Mádhava and Makaranda were dismissed. They are now coming, and I have been sent on before to carry the tidings to the pious dame.

Lav. (*to Madayantiká*). Delightful news for you, nor less acceptable
To our dear Málatí: let us haste to find her.

[*Exeunt severally.*

Enter MÁDHAVA *and* MAKARANDA.

Mád. I cannot choose but marvel at thy prowess,
So more than mortal—breaking thy way resistless
Through all opposing ranks; scattering the timid,

* *Balaráma* having paid a visit to his friends and relations at *Gokula*, spent two months there chiefly in the society of the *Gopis* or nymphs of that district. On one occasion, being desirous of bathing in the *Jumná* from which he was a little way remote, he summoned the river to his presence. *Yamuná* refused to come, on which *Balaráma*, being elevated with wine, vowed he would compel her, and accordingly dragged her to him with his plough-share, the weapon he usually wielded, and only let the river go again upon the promise of future good behaviour.—*Bhágavat*, x. 65.

And levelling the fiercest with thy arm.
On either hand the frightened troops retired,
As forced my friend a path amidst the wave
Of battle, tossing with innumerous heads.

Mak. I do foresee the valiant will lose credit
With their fair nymphs, who in these festal nights,
Irradiated with the lunar beam,
Pledge deep the wine-cup, and impatiently
Court amorous dalliance from their lords returned.
They will declare that men are pithless grown,
When they shall find how ill the limbs are tuned
To love, crushed, bruised, and mangled by thy vigour.

Mád. We must not be unmindful of the clemency
The king displayed, whose favour overlooked
So readily our offences. Come, I long
To hear the story Kalahansaka
Has told, I know full well, to both the damsels.
You must prepare to tell the tale again,
Whilst Madayantiká declines her head,
Veiling her eyes with modesty, afraid
To meet the sidelong smiling glance of Málatí.*
Here is the garden gate.

[*They enter.*

Mád. How, all deserted!

Mak. Alarmed, no doubt, at hearing our return
Was intercepted, they must have dispersed,
And hid themselves amid the garden shades.
Search we about.

They search, and enter LAVANGIKÁ *and* MADAYANTIKÁ.

Lav. Ho, Madayantiká!
Here's Málatí. Ah no! yet fate is favourable;
The princely youths return.

* Laughing at Madayantiká, say the commentators, as the cause of so much disturbance. There is some confusion in the text and comment with regard to the speakers of this and the preceding speech.

Mak. and Mád. But where is Málatí?

Lav. Where Málatí! alas, we thought the tread
Of feet bespoke her here.

Mád. My heart misgives me—
My mind, on that dear maid alone intent
Desponds, and all my inmost soul gives way.
My left eye throbs, and then these words—ah me
What hope remains, she's lost to me for ever!

Mada. When you had left us, Málatí dispatched
The dame's attendants to their pious mistress—
Lavangiká she bade convey her prayers
To her loved lord, to shun all needless peril.
Next, anxious for your tidings, she herself
Went forth to watch the road, and since that time
I saw her not. We were even now engaged
In quest of her, amidst the shady groves,
When we encountered you.

Mád. My dearest Málatí,
How many thoughts of evil omen crowd
Upon my spirit! If 'tis in sport thou hidest,
Forego the barbarous pastime; if in anger,
Behold me humbled. If thou woudst try my love,
The test is undergone: oh, yield reply,
My heart can bear no more—now thou art cruel!

Women. Oh, dearest friend, where art thou!

Mak. (*to Mádhava*). Do not yield
Thus to despair—uncertain of her loss.

Mád. Oh think what agony she must have suffered,
In terror for my safety.

Mak. That may be.
But we have not yet thought to seek
The venerable priestess.

Women. Let us fly to her.

Mád. Yes, let us haste.

Mad. (*apart*). If we should find the damsel with the dame,
'Tis well: if not, I tremble for her life.

Alas! too often is the happiness,
That kindred, friends, or lovers taste, as brief
As lightning's transient glare.*

* So Shakspeare says of the happiness of lovers: it is,

"Brief as the lightning in the collied night."

And again, of the interchange of vows between *Romeo* and *Juliet*, it is

"Too like the lightning, which doth cease to be
Ere one can say it lightens."

END OF THE EIGHTH ACT.

ACT IX.

THE VINDHYAN MOUNTAINS.

Enter SAUDÁMINÍ.

From the tall mount *Sri Saila,** I, Saudámini,
Have sought the royal city *Padmávati,*
And now the steps of Mádhava pursue.
Unable to endure the scenes where late
His Málatí was lost, the youth is wandering,
Attended by his ever faithful friend,
Amidst these rugged paths and rocky vallies.

Alights.

How wide the prospect spreads—mountain and rock,
Towns, villages, and woods, and glittering streams.
There, where the *Párá* and the *Sindhu* wind,
The towers and temples, pinnacles and gates,
And spires of *Padmávati,*† like a city

* This is precisely in the style of one of the prologues of Euripides, who, as Brumoy observes, thought is expedient that a leading character should announce himself to the audience as speedily as possible, or, according to Boileau, *Qu'il declarat son nom. Et dit, Je suis Oreste ou bien Agamemnon.* The Hindu writer is, however, less minute than the Grecian, who makes his characters not only introduce themselves, but their connexions, to the audience. The Chinese historical drama offends by the same self-enunciation of the person and purposes of the character, much more extravagantly and constantly than the Hindu.

† I have in other places identified *Padmávati* with *Ujayin*, but I fear upon insufficient grounds, and there are some serious objections to their identity. If they were the same, the city must have been situated much nearer to the mountains than at present from the description here given. The old city, however, lay two miles north of the present, according to Sir J. Malcolm; Dr. Hunter says one; and there must consequently have been a still

Precipitated from the skies, appear,
Inverted in the pure translucent wave.
There flows *Lavana's* frolic stream, whose groves,
By early rains refreshed, afford the youth
Of *Padmávati* pleasant haunts, and where
Upon the herbage brightening in the shower
The heavy-uddered kine contented browze—
Hark! how the banks of the broad *Sindhu* fall,
Crashing, in the undermining current.
Like the loud voice of thunder-laden clouds
The sound extends, and like *Heramba's** roar,
As deepened by the hollow echoing caverns,
It floats reverberating round the hills.
Those mountains coated with thick clustering woods
Of fragrant *sandal*† and the ripe *málúra*,‡

a still older Ougein in a more southerly direction, if not more to the east also. The *Párá* and the *Madhumatí* named below appear to be the same, as each unites with the *Sindhu* or *Sindh*. If either, or both, intend the *Sipra*, the river that now washes Ougein, it is difficult to conceive how that could have united with the *Sindh*, if by that river the *Kali Sindh* of the present day be intended. The only confluence in the vicinity of Ougein now is that of the *Seerexepty* (*Saraswatí*), and *Sipra*, about five miles to the south. The *Chota Sindh* falls into the *Sipra* a long way to the north, and the larger *Sindh* flows into the *Chumbul*. It is probable, however, that the situation of *Padmávatí* must be looked for more to the south, somewhere in the modern Aurungabad or Berar. It may be intended for the *Padma-nagara*, the place of the poet's nativity, but none of the names of the rivers in its vicinity are traceable in modern maps.

* A name of *Ganesá*, who having the head, is supposed to have the voice of an elephant.

† The tree specified in the text is the *chandana* which usually signifies *sandal*; but the commentators intimate, what Dr. Roxburgh (*Flora Indica*) confirms, that the white or true *sandal* only grows on the mountains of Malabar or the Malaya mountains. The commentators suppose the *Rakta Chandana* may be the red sanders (*Pterocarpus santalinus*); but perhaps the tree intended may be the *santalum* or *syrium myrtifolium*, which grows in the Northern Circars, and which Dr. Roxburgh considers a strongly marked variety of the Malabar *sandal* tree.—*Flora Indica*, 2. 464.

‡ A fruit-tree commonly called *bel*—(*Ægle marmelos*).

Recall to memory the lofty mountains
That southward stretch, where the *Godáveri*
Impetuous flashes through the dark deep shade
Of skirting forests, echoing to her fury—
Where meet the *Sindhu* and the *Madhumati,*
The holy fane of *Swernavindu** rises,
Lord of *Bhaváni,* whose illustrious image
Is not of mortal fabric. (*Bowing.*) Hail! all hail!
Creator of the universal world. Bestower
Of all good gifts. Source of the sacred *Vedas;*
God of the crescent-crested diadem. Destroyer
Of love's presumptuous power. Eldest lord
And teacher of mankind, all glory be to thee!

Going.

This mountain is, in truth, a grateful scene.
The peaks are blackened with new dropping clouds,
And pleased the peafowl shriek along the groves.
The ponderous rocks upbear the tangled bowers,
Where countless nests give brightness to the gloom.
The inarticulate whine of the young bears,
Hisses and mutters through the caverned hills;
And cool, and sharp, and sweet, the incense spreads,
Shed from the boughs the elephant's tusk has sundered.

Looking.

'Tis noon: the lapwing† for the cassia's‡ shade,

* This was likely to be a *Linga,* for which form of worship *Ujein* was particularly celebrated about the period of the Mohammedan invasion, and probably long before. Of the particular deity or *linga,* however, here alluded to, no mention elsewhere has been traced, nor are the Pundits acquainted with any legend relating to it. The name implies the drop (*Vindu*) of gold (*Swerna*).

† The *kóyashthika,* which as the commentators say, is a synonime of the *tittibha* or lapwing. It is also said to imply the *kowa,* meaning perhaps the crow.

‡ The *cassia fistula.*

From the *Gambhári** wings its way. The pelican,†
Whose beak has sipped the acid fruit‡ beside
The stream, hastes now to plunge amidst its waters.
The *gallinule* creeps panting to the hollow
The *Tinisa*§ presents, and lower down,
Amidst the woods, the wild fowl make reply
To the soft murmuring of the mournful dove,
As in her nest she pours her frequent song.
Enough! I now will to the youths, and offer them
Such consolation as I may. [*Exit.*

Enter MÁDHAVA *and* MAKARANDA.

Mak. How dreary is the state, when nor the mind
Dare cherish hope, nor may indulge despair.
Like helpless brutes, fate whirls us round at will,
And ever plunges us in new misfortune.

Mád. Ah Málatí, where art thou! How so soon
Couldst thou desert me, ere my truth was known!
Remorseless maid, relent—behold my sorrows!
How canst thou prove thus cruel to that Mádhava,
Once so beloved! Behold me! I am he,
On whom thy hand, bound with the golden thread,‖

* The *gambhári* is a tree (*Gmelina arborea*).

† The *púrniká*, which is considered by some to be the same with the *panikauri*, which according to Buchanan, as quoted in Carey's Bengali Dictionary, is a kind of pelican (*Pelecanus fusicollis*). In the vocabularies it appears as a synonime of *násachinná*, or the cleft-nose, commonly *Nakchhali*. But what bird is intended by that appellation is not known unless it be a kind of Toucan, or horn-bill. According to some authorities *Púrniká* is considered synonimous with *Kumbhira makshiká*, the crocodile fly, commonly *Pankhi* or *Patavinga*—a large moth or butterfly.

‡ The name in the text is *Asmantaka*, which is one synonime of *Spondias mangifera*, or hog-plum. It is also a synonime of *Virana*, *Andropogon muricatus*, and of other plants; but that intended by the author is a leguminous plant, as the bird is said to have tasted the *simbi* of the plant, the pod or legume. Another synonime is the *Sinsapa* or *Sisu*, *Dalbergia ougeiniensis*.

§ The *Tinisa* is a tree the name of which has not been ascertained: carriage-wheels are made of its wood.

‖ Part of the marriage ceremony consists in tying a string or thread round the wrist of the bride.

Conferred in other days embodied bliss.
Alas! my friend, where in the world again
Shall equal tenderness be found? I long
Endured with withering limbs, like drooping flowrets,
The feverish pangs of love, till in the end,
Unable further to sustain the conflict,
I was content to cast away my life
Like worthless grass. What then remained for me
But to secure with gentle violence
That precious hand. Before the marriage rite,
Ere I had dared to hope, you may recall
My still increasing passion, sealed with tears,
Emaciate limbs, and heart-distracting anguish.
Such as I was, I am, and still my mind
Is tossed with agony. How strange it is,
This heart, that sorrow lacerates, does not break;
This frame, that sinks with anguish, cannot lose
Its conscious being—on my vitals preys
A burning fire, yet turns them not to ashes;
And fate, that piecemeal tears me, spares my life.*

Mak. As fierce as destiny, the flaming sun
Accords but ill with your exhausted strength:
Let us here rest awhile upon the marge
Of this wide lake, across whose shallow waters,
Cool with the spray, and fragrant with the odours
Gleaned from the yet young lotus, gently blows
The fresh and friendly breeze. It will revive you.

(*They sit—Makaranda continues, to himself.*)

I will endeavour to divert his thoughts.
(*Aloud.*) My friend, a moment interrupt your tears.
Behold awhile the beauties of this lake,
Where on its slender stem the lotus trembles,
Brushed by the passing swan, as on he sails,
Singing his passion. (*Mádhava jumps up.*)

* This passage occurs word for word in the original, in the *Uttara Ráma Cheritra.* See translation, p. 334.

Mak. He heeds me not, and now would hence. My friend,
One instant pause—taste the delightful perfume
That o'er the wave the bending *bayas** scatters,
Or jasmine† clustering round the flowery shore.
Observe, how smile the mountains, thickly set
With budding *kutajas*,‡ up to the very peaks,
Where stretches dark the canopy of clouds,
Inspiring rapture in the dancing peafowl.
Thick on the hill's broad bosom the *kadamba*§
Shews bright with countless blossoms: on the summit
Rest the black clouds in lengthening line: the streams
Descend through rows of budding *ketakas*,‖
And all the waving woods now laugh, emblazoned
With the *silindhra*¶ and the *lodhra*** flowers.

Mád. I mark, my friend, the distant woods present
A beauteous sight—but what of that. Ah me,
What else should thought suggest—the days approach
When the long line of clouds shall shed on earth
Their amaranthine drops—trembling in the breeze
That from the east comes powerful, and embued
With the rich odours of the *sál*†† and *arjuna*.‡‡

* The *bayas* or *bent*, a kind of cane (*Calamus Rotang*).

† *Yuthiká*, great-flowered jasmine (*J. grandiflorum*). It is also a name of a creeping kind of jasmine (*J.auriculatum*).

‡ The *kutaja* is a small tree (*Wrightea antidysenterica*).

§ The *kadamba* has been before alluded to as the *naudea cadamba*, a large and ornamental tree. The corollets of the flower are numerous, forming a large perfectly globular beautiful orange-coloured head, with the large white clubbed stimas projecting. *Flor. Indica*, 2. 121.

‖ The *ketaka* or *ketaki* has been already noticed as a flower with a strong odour. (*Pandanus odoratissimus*).

¶ The *silindhra* is a tree the name of which is not yet to be found in Botanical works on Indian plants.

** The *lodhra* or *lodh* is a tree (*symplocos racemosa*) the astringent bark of which is used in dyeing and making ink.

†† The *sál* is a valuable timber-tree (*Shorea robusta*).

‡‡ A kind of tree (*Pentaptera arjuna*).

Those days that boast the gateful interchange
Of heat and moisture, and the fragrant breath
The earth bestows, sprinkled with genial showers.
Ah! Málatí, how can I bear to contemplate
The stooping clouds, as purple as the blossoms
Of young *tamála** trees; the rain-drops trembling
Before the cooling gale; the joyful cry
That echoes round, as pleased the peafowl hail
The bow of heaven propitious to their loves.

(*Faints.*)

Mak. How hapless is the state of my dear friend!
My heart of adamantine mould could feel
Some taste of pleasure—now, alas, all hope
For Mádhava is lost. How void of sense
He lies. Ah! Málatí, how canst thou be
Thus unrelenting! Once for him you scorned
Your friends and ventured boldly. He has done
No wrong to thee, then why this stern desertion?
He does not breathe. Fate robs me of my happiness.
My heart is rent—my fibres fall apart.
The world is blank. I burn with inward fires—
My soul sinks plunged into the glooms of hell,
And dim obscurity veils every sense.
What shall I do! The gentle source of pleasure
To friendship's heart—the orb whose radiance shed
Ambrosia on the eyes of Málatí—the happiness
Of Makaranda—the bright ornament
Of all the world, now perishes. Alas!
My friend, my Mádhava, thou wast to me
The *sandal* of my form, the autumnal moon
Of these fond eyes, and rapture to my heart.
Now am I slain—untimely fate uproots
A life that knew no other wish than thee—
Remorseless, deign to smile upon thy friend.

* A tree remarkable for black flowers (*Xanthochymus pictorius*).

Speak to me, say, dost thou not know thy friend,
Thy fond and faithful friend, thy Makaranda?

(*Mádhava appears to recover.*)

Delightful shadows shedding on the world
New life—the cool refreshing drops that fall
From yon cærulean* cloud revive my friend.

Mád. (*recovering*). Where in this thicket may I hope to find
An envoy to my love. Ha, yonder winds
Around the mountain's brow, the gathering cloud;
Black as the tall *tamála*. As it stoops
From its high course, it pours its tribute down
Into the river bed, that gliding laves
The ebon *jambu* groves laden with fruit.

(*Rises and bows.*)

Thy form the lightning lovingly entwines;†

* The expression is *Achira dhauta Rájá patta ruchira chhavi*, shades of the tint of *Rájá patta* which has not long been cleaned. This, the commentators say, implies a light and clear blue; but why does not appear. The *Rájá patta* is properly a royal fillet or tiara. *Jagaddhara* says it means *Kheti*; and *Malanka* explains it *Ráyáti prastara* or *Rayati* stone. But neither of these words are found in any dictionary, Hindi or Bengali, nor can the pundits explain them.

† An address to a cloud as a messenger to a beloved object is a standing rule in Hindu poetry. A lengthened supplication of such a character I have given to the public in the *Megha Duta*, or Cloud Messenger, the celebrity of which poem probably made such kind of invocation commonplace. We have, however, a similar address in a poet of modern Europe; and although *Bhavabhuti* may have borrowed from *Kalidása*, we cannot suppose *Schiller* was under a similar obligation, when, in his Maria Stuart, Mary addresses the clouds:

Eilende wolken, segler der lüfte
Wer mit euch wanderte, mit euch schiffte,
Grüsset mir freundlich mein Jugendland.
Ich bin gefangen, Ich bin in banden,
Ach ich habe' kein andern gesandten
Frey in lüfter is eure bahn
Ihr seyd nich dieser königin unterthan.

Light clouds, ye barks of air,
Who with ye sails or flies?
To my youth's home, oh bear

My

Thy coming, thirsty *chátakas** proclaim;
The east wind fans thee with its gentle breath;
And *Indra's* bow irradiates thy course.
Hark! with deep voice he answers, and the sound,
Mixed with the peacock's raptured cry, reverberates
Along the echoing caves. He bids me speak.—
Majestic cloud—if haply as thou roamest
Free on thy airy path, thou shouldst behold
My love! allay the conflicts of her mind.
Tell her her Mádhava's distress; but heed,
You do not snap the slender thread of hope
That now alone sustains her fragile life.
He onward bends his course: I too will hence. (*Going.*)

Mak. Alas! the reason of my noble friend
Is clouded by insanity. Pious dame,
Observe his state, and lend thy guardian aid.

Mád. How now! the beauty of my love I view
In these young buds. Her eye the deer display—
The elephant has stolen her gait—her grace
The waving creeper shews—she has been slain,
And all her charms are scattered through the wild.
My love! my Málatí! (*He faints.*)

Mak. Obdurate heart, why break'st thou not, afflicted
By Mádhava's affliction—as my friend,
The shrine of all desert, lord of my life,
The fellow of my childhood's sports, in youth
My fond associate, thus laments his love.

Mád. (*sighing and rising*). Such close similitude the hand of *Brahmá*

My heart's recording sighs—
In captive bonds I lonely pine
Nor other envoy now is mine,
Save ye, who freely track your way,
Nor this tyrannic queen obey.

There are other obvious imitations of *Kalidása*, in the original text both of the *Megha Duta* and *Vikramorvaśí*.

* A bird which is said to drink no water but rain.

Creates but sparingly—it must be so.
Ho! ye, who tenant these high towering rocks
And leafy woods, I call to you; awhile
Grant me attention.* Tell me, have you seen,
Amidst these wilds a nymph of loveliest beauty,
Or know ye where she strays? I will describe
Her charms. Love rages tyrant in her bosom,
But lavishes his bounties on her form.—
Alas! the peafowl, as he dances wild
With rapture, drowns my sorrows with his cry—
With rolling eyeballs the *chakora*† flies
After his mate—the ape his female's cheeks
Besmears with flowery dust. Whom should I sue to;
Vain the request unseasonably proffered.
There, leaning on the *rohin's*‡ hollow stem, the elephant
Wearied supports his trunk upon his mate;
With the sharp points of his vast tusks he rubs
The corners of her eyes; he fans her form
With his broad ears, and thursts into her mouth
The broken fragments of the incense bough.
How blest the master of the forest herd!
But yon dejected animal bewails
His absent female. To the muttering clouds
He breathes no murmured echo—from the lake
He gleans no grateful fodder, and he roams
With humbled brow, where silent sits the bee,
Deprived the nectar of the frontal juice.—
Enough of this despondence! I will hence.
This is, indeed, the proud exulting monarch

* The commentator is prosaic enough to assert Mádhava addresses the animals of the forest. It may be so; but the Hindu system authorizes an appeal to the *Sthala Devatas* and *Vana Devatas*, *genii* of the soil and the forest, to the *Fauns* and *Dryads*, who preside over the mountain and the wood.

† The red-legged or Greek partridge (*Tetrao rufus*).

‡ A tree (*Andersonia rohitaka*).

Of the huge herd: his mighty roar invites
Grateful his willing mate; down his broad cheek
The viscid fluid sheds such cooling odour
As from the newly ripe *kadamba* breathes.
He rends away the lotus leaf, and stem,
And roots, and filaments, as in the lake
He madly plunges, frightening from their nests
The osprey and the heron,* and to the tune
Of his ferocious love, his ponderous ears
Waved dancing, lash the water into foam.
I will approach him.—Sovereign of the wild,
Thy youthful prowess merits praise no less
Than thine ingenuous fondness for thy mate;
With water fragrant with the rich perfume,
Drawn from the flowery lake, thou washest down
The savoury morsels of the lotus stalk,
With which thou erst hadst fed her—then in sport
Thou scatterest with thy trunk the silvery spray
Upon her brow?—Ah shame! why wav'st thou not
The straight stemmed lotus over her, as a shade
Against the sun?—Ah me! upon the brute
I waste the hours due unto my friend.
Yet Makaranda I lament the most
In this, I grieve alone—nor would I taste
Of any pleasure that thou couldst not share.
Perish the day that is not spent with thee
And with my Málatí! False are the joys
That spring from any source but her and thee.

Mak. Alas! amidst his wanderings he recalls
The fervour of his friendship, and some chord
Awakes his love, though reckless of my presence.
(*Advances.*) Behold me here! your faithful, sorrowing friend.

Mád. My friend, can it be true! Oh let me be

* Or more correctly the *sáras* or Indian crane.

Convinced by thine embrace. Alas, I die.
I have no hope, my Málatí is lost! (*Faints.*)

Mak. (*looking*). Alas! the consciousness that my embrace
Had waked, again has flown—what hope is left me!
Alone, the sad conviction now survives
My friend is lost to me. Ah, Mádhava,
I now may banish all those needless fears
For your tranquillity, my anxious heart
Has in its love unceasing entertained.
Ah, happier were the moments of distress
That still evinced perception. All is over,
And now this body is a barren load.
Life is congealed, the faculties are dim,
And all the world a blank. Time is the source
Of ceaseless anguish, and the living world
Cold, dead, and cheerless, now that thou art gone.
Now what have I to do, beholding thus
The fate of Mádhava! It shall be so—
From this tall mountain summit will I plunge
Into the stream, the herald of my friend,
And glad precede him to the shades below.*
(*Approaching and looking at Mádhava.*)
Is this the form I have so oft embraced
Insatiate, and whose grace the eye of Málatí,
Bewildered with a love till then unknown,
Delighted drank! How wonderful, combined
Such countless merits with such early years.
Upon the world's tiara didst thou shine
The glittering gem; and now thou falls't, a prey
To death—like the full moon to *Rághu*'s jaws
Consigned—or like the volumed cloud, thin scattered
Before the driving breeze; or like the tree,

* Although not in the text, this expression is perfectly justifiable; for the Hindu mythology accords precisely with the Greek in sending the souls of the dead to receive judgment in the infernal regions, and according to the sentence of their judge they are thence conveyed to *Tartarus* or *Elysium*, to *Naraka* or *Swerga*, according to their evil or good deeds.

That ere it puts its goodliest blossoms forth,
Consumes to ashes in the forest's bláze.
Let me once more embrace him, and address
My last farewell to my expiring friend.
Shrine of pure knowledge and of noblest worth,
Lord of the life of Málatí. Reflection
Of all surpassing loveliness. Divinity
Of female hearts. Autumnal moon, that swayed
The tide of friendship's main, and charmed the days
Of Makaranda and the pious priestess—
My friend, my Mádhava, accept this last,
This fond embrace, from him whose life begun
Before thou wast, and who now terminates
His blighted days. A little while he lives—
And do not thou forbid his fixed design.
Through life I have partaken of thy fortune,
And drank in childhood of thy mother's milk;
It must not be, that thou shalt quaff alone
The sad libations of thy sorrowing kin.

(*Leaves him and retires.*)

Deep underneath the precipice the stream
Flows rapid. Mighty lord of *Gauri*, hail!
Grant me with Mádhava such future birth,
That, as in this life, I again may be,
In that to come, his follower and friend.

(*Going to precipitate himself, is withheld by Saudáminí.*)

Forbear, my son! forego your desperate purpose.

Mak. And who art thou, that seek'st to stay my will?

Saud. Art thou not Makaranda?

Mak. Let me go,
I am that luckless wretch!

Saud. In me behold
The mistress of supernal power,* and see
The vestiges of Málatí. (*Shews the bakula garland.*)

* Or, I am a *Yoginí*, one who by the practice of the *yoga* has acquired supernatural powers.

Mak. How! lives she?
Saud. Do not fear. But what insanity
Is this, and how unwelcome to your friend—
Where is he?
Mak. With despair o'ercome, even now
I left him—let us seek him—haste!
Mád. (*recovering*). Who wakes
My soul to sorrow once again—the wind,
Scattering the new and heavy laden clouds,
Regardless of my woes, has broke my slumbers.
Mak. Blest sight, my friend revives!
Saud. (*looking at Mádhava, then apart*). The forms of both
These youths has Málatí with truth described.
Mád. Hail, eastern gale! dissolve the dropping clouds,
And gratify the longing *chátaka*—
Arouse the peafowl's rapture, and expand
The blossoms of the *ketaki*—awhile,
The absent lover, lost to sense, forgot
His misery; thou again hast called his soul
To conscious agony: what wouldst thou more!
Mak. The all-pervading wind diffuses life
To creatures animate.
Mád. Celestial breeze,
Bear, with the fragrant odours thou hast wrung
From the *kadamba* blossoms, to my love,
The life of Mádhava—or rather breathe
From her, impregnate with the cooling perfume
Of her delicious form—thou art alone
My hope.
(*Bows with joined hands applied to his forehead.**)
Saud. This is the season to present
The well-known garland. (*Throws it over his hands.*)
Mád. Ha! the wreath I wove

* In the *anjali*, or respectful obeisance, the head is slightly bowed, the palms of the hands are brought together and raised laterally to the middle of the forehead, so that the tips of the thumbs only are in contact with it.

Of *bakula* flowers, amidst the sacred shades
Of *Káma's* temple, and long fondly worn
Upon the bosom of my best beloved.
It is the same—this is the part
Lavangiká was pleased to hear my Málatí
Pretend was strung awry; a mere pretext,
To veil the irrepressible delight,
Her radiant countenance too plain revealed.

(*Jumps up.*)

Now Málatí behold! ah no, you heed not
My hapless state—my parting breath escapes,
My heart desponds—my body is on fire,
And darkness spreads around me—oh be quick;
You need not mock my sorrow—cast upon me
One bliss-diffusing glance—oh, be not pitiless.

(*Looking round, then at the garland.*)

How did she give me this—welcome, dear wreath,
The favourite of my love, and long her friend.
Oh, whencesoever borne, welcome, most welcome!
When on that gentle form, the scorching flame
Of love resistless preyed, and all her maidens
Despaired—thy grateful succour saved the days
Of Málatí,—she clasped thee to her bosom,
And dreamt she pressed her lover to her heart.
Well I recall thy various passages
Between my neck and that of my beloved,
Engendering tenderness, exciting hope,
And animating passion's glowing fires.

(*Puts his garland to his heart and faints.*)

Mak. Revive, my friend. (*Fanning him.*)

Mád. Ha, Makaranda!
Dost thou not see how Málatí's affection
Is sealed with her fair hand—how chanced it, say,
Dost thou not know?

Mák. This holy dame has brought
These traces of the maid.

Mád. (*bowing*). With favouring ear
Receive my prayers,—oh tell me, Málatí,
Say, does she live?
Saud. Be of good cheer my son;
She lives.
Mád. How, where,—oh speak!
Saud. Some while ago it chanced,
Aghoraghanta at *Karálá's* shrine
Fell by the arm of Mádhava, in rescue
Of his fair maid.
Mád. Enough! I know the whole.
Mak. How so?
Mád. Kapálakundalá, his partner.—
Mak. Is it e'en so?
Saud. My son conjectures rightly.
Mak. Alas! how beauteous did the union shew
Of the bright moonlight and the lotus bed,
Till, like a dark unseasonable cloud,
Fate frowning came to intercept their joys.
Mád. Into what dreadful hands has Málatí
Now fallen—to what exposed—oh lovely maid,
How couldst thou bear the grasp unpitying
Of the fierce fiend—like the pale struggling moon
By hideous meteor seized! Kápalakundalá,
Respect her tender form—repress thy spirit
Malign, and learn benevolence—the flowret
By nature delicate, should not be crushed
With blows, but gently twined around the brow.
Saud. Enough! be calm. Remorseless as she is,
She dares not harm the maid—I will prevent her.
Mád. and Mak. (*bowing*). Accept our thanks. Oh say, to what we owe
Thy friendly care?
Saud. It is enough, at present,
To learn, that in your cause I will exert
The powerful knowledge, mystic rites and prayers,

Devout observance, and a sainted teacher,
Have armed me with. Come Mádhava, attend me.
(Takes hold of Mádhava, and they disappear.)

Mak. Astonishing reverse! the fearful gloom
Yields to the lightning flash of hope, and instant
The cheated eye resumes its wonted faculty.
(Looks round.)
How now, my friend not here! what can this be:
The dame is powerful in her magic rites,
But this alarms me. From one fear escaped,
Another comes to agitate my heart;
My mind is tossed amidst delight and dread,
And doubts one moment caused, subside the next.
I'll seek the priestess, who amidst the woods
Is roaming with her friends, and to her ear
Impart these wondrous chances.
[*Exit.*

END OF THE NINTH ACT.

ACT X.

ANOTHER PART OF THE FOREST.

Enter KÁMANDAKÍ, MADAYANTIKÁ, *and* LAVANGIKÁ.

Kám. My pride, my child, my Málatí, where art thou?
Oh yield me a reply. Your countless graces,
Your modesty, your elegance, your gentleness
Rise to my memory, consume my frame,
And rend my heart asunder. Oh, my daughter,
I well recall your infant countenance,
Your pleasing prattle, and the transient tears
And smiles, that shewed the young teeth budding forth.

Mada. and Lav. Oh, dearest friend, more radiant than the moon,
Ah whither hast thou flown? can fate assail
Remorseless thus, thy form as delicate
As the *sirisha* blossoms, and pursue thee
Unfriended and alone! Oh Mádhava,
Thy promised joys are blighted in this world.

Kám. Alas, my children, in your fond embrace
And new delight, fate, like a rising gale,
That fells the tree and tender vine together,
Has struck ye to the ground.

Lav. Obdurate heart,
Despairing, still to torture me.
(*Beats her breast, and falls on the ground.*)

Mada. Nay, do not yet
Yield to despair.

Lav. Alas, my life is bound
With bonds of adamant, and will not leave me.

Kám. My dear child;

From birth, Lavangiká was dear to thee,
And dost thou not compassionate her now:
Disdaining life, deprived of thee, her days
Are fading into gloom, as fluttering sinks
The lamp no oil supplies—How can'st thou quit
Kámandakí, within whose garb enfolded,
Thy infant limbs to health and beauty grew?
From the maternal breast wast thou confided,
A delicate plaything,* to my guardian care;
At first to ply thy sports, but more advanced
To learn the duties of thy state: now grown
To years mature, I have beheld thee wedded
To a loved husband, picked from all the world.
More than a mother's claims upon thy love
Have I—Ingrate, thou leav'st me to despair.
Ah me, I vainly hoped I should behold
A beauteous boy hang fondly at thy breast,
Or sport upon thy lap, his brow and forehead
White with protecting flour,† his lovely face
Brightened with causeless smiles.

Lav. Most holy dame,
I can no more endure this load of life:
This precipice relieves me of the burthen.
Grant me your blessing, that in after-life
I may once more behold my friend.

Kám. My daughter,
Life is alike unwelcome to my bosom,
Deprived of my dear children, and despair
Invades my heart; but different merits claim
A different birth, and if we should not gain

* Literally, an ivory doll; *Danta panchálíká; danta* here meaning the tooth of the elephant.

† The powder of white mustard is applied to the top of the head and the forehead, and other parts of a new born child, as a protection against evil spirits. A mixture of the same with oil and rice is scattered about in every quarter upon the commencement of a sacrifice, to keep off ghosts and fiends.

Reunion with our friends in days to come,
Abandonment of present life would yield
No fruit but vain repentance.

Lav. Be it so.

Kám. Daughter, Madayantiká.

Mada. Your commands—
If they direct me lead the way to death,
Behold—I am prepared.

Lav. Dear friend, refrain
From self-destruction—Keep me in your memory.

Mada. Away, I am not subject to your will.

Kám. (*apart*). Alas! there is no hope.

Mada. (*apart*). Dear husband, fare thee well.

Lav. This is the loftiest point, and far below
The Madhumati twines its glittering zone.

Kám. Enough—our purpose brooks not of delay.

(*They are about to cast themselves down.*)

(*Without.*) Astonishing reverse—the fearful gloom
Yields to the lightning flash of hope.

Kám. Who comes,—
My son.

Enter MAKARANDA.

Without your friend—say how is this?

Mak. A dame of more than mortal powers has used
Her art in our behalf.

(*Without*). A fearful crowd is gathered—Bhúrivasu,
Despising life and spurning worldly hopes,
Since he has learned his daughter's death, repairs,
To cast himself into the raging flames
At Swernavindu's shrine—Alas, we all
Shall mourn his fate.

Lav. and Mada. How short an interval
Rejoiced those lovers in each other's sight.

Kám. and Mak. 'Tis most miraculous! what strange events
This day alternate! drops of fragrant sandal

And sharp-edged swords in the same shower commingle ;
And sparks of flame, and streams of heavenly nectar,
Descend together from unclouded skies.
The life-restoring drug with poison blends,
And light and gloom ; and destiny entwines
The thunderbolt and lunar rays together.

Mál. (*without*). Dear father hold ! Oh, let me view again
The lotus of thy countenance—oh turn
Thy gaze upon thy child. How, for my sake,
Can'st thou desert thyself, the brilliant boast
Of an auspicious race, whose fame pervades
Both earth and heaven ! Ah, wherefore purpose thus
Again to plunge me into bitterest woe ?

Kám. My daughter, how is this ? Art thou redeemed
From death, once more to be exposed to peril ;
As lurk the demons of eclipse, to seize
The feeble moon scarce struggling out of darkness ?

Lav. Behold our friend !

Enter MÁDHAVA *carrying* MÁLATÍ *senseless.*

Mád. Alas ! from danger rescued, has again
Fear fallen upon thee—who shall bar the gate
To shut out adverse destiny ?

Mak. My friend,
Where is the dame ?

Mád. With her we hither speeded
Swift from *Sri Párvata ;* but when we heard
The news the forester imparted to us,
I missed her suddenly.

Kám. and Mak. Oh, dame of power,
Befriend us still ; why hast thou disappeared ?

Mada. and Lav. My Málatí, I speak to thee, thy friend—
Priestess, preserve us, still she is insensible ;
She does not breathe, her heart is still. Alas !
The sire and daughter are to each other,
In turn, the instrument of death.

Kám. My dear child!

Mád. My love!

Mak. My friend!

Kám. (*looking up.*) What welcome drops are these
That fall from heaven to aid us.

Mád. She revives—
Long sighs relieve her labouring breast, her heart
Resumes its pulse; her gentle eye unfolds,
And from unconscious stillness that dear face
Once more expands, as at the dawn of day
The lotus bares its bosom to the sun.

(*Behind.*) Deaf to the king's entreaties, and the prayers
Of Nandana, though humbled at his feet,
Upon the flaming marge, the minister
By me has been prevented, and recalled
To life and joy.

Mád. and Mak. (*looking up.*) Mark, holy dame—From heaven,
The kind magician pours upon our hearts
The nectar of her tidings: they surpass
The virtue of the balmy shower.

Kám. Blest news!

All. Our happiness is now secure.

Kám. My child!

Mál. The priestess!
(*Falls at her feet, Kámandakí raises and embraces her.*)

Kám. Restored to life, my child, to life restore
Your friends, and with your fond embraces, cool
As lunar rays, reanimate existence
In those who live for you.

Mád. (*to Makaranda.*) My faithful friend,
This breathing world may now be well endured.

Mak. In sooth it may.

Mada. and Lav. Dear Málatí, confirm
The happiness we see, by your embrace.

Mál. My dearest friends! (*Embraces them.*)

Kám. Tell me, my sons, how chanced these strange events?

Mád. Our past misfortunes were the wrathful work
Kapálakundalá's revenge inspired ;
And that we 'scaped her toils, our thanks are due
To this propitious and all-powerful friend.

Kám. Aghoraghanta's death was then the source
Of these mischances !

Mada. and Lav. Strange vicissitude !
After repeated trials, adverse fate
In kindness terminates its chequered course.

Enter SAUDÁMINI.

Sau. (*to Kámandaki.*) Hail, holy dame—your scholar pays you homage!

Kám. Saudámini, most welcome.

Mád. and Mak. Then we owe
Our succour to the priestess: this, her first
Disciple—all is clear.

Kám. This is well done.
And many a life preserved has sanctified thee.
'Tis long since we have met, dismiss this reverence,
And let me grateful press thee to my bosom.

(*Embraces her.*)

Thou hast deserved the praises of the world,
Whose lofty powers, the harvest of the seed
By early study sown, are shewn by deeds
That shame the mightiest masters.*

Mada. and Lav. Is this Saudáminí ?

Mál. It is: by her,
The friend and pupil of my pious guardian,
The fierce Kapálakundalá was foiled.
She bore me to her dwelling, and there leaving me

* The expression is rather singular, " exceeding a *Bodhisatwa*—a pious person endowed with miraculous powers, and who is considered as an inferior incarnation of *Buddha*. It is, however, in harmony with the character of *Kámandakí*, whose sanctity, and the respectful allusions to the *Bauddhas*, shew that the play was composed before their decline.

Secure, conveyed the wreath of *bakula* flowers
To snatch you from despair.

Mada. and Lav. She has, indeed,
Been scarcely less propitious to us, than our old
And reverend preceptress.

Mád. and Mak. The bright gem
That grants whatever is desired, demands
The suppliant's prayer: the dame's assistance came
All unsolicited.

Sau. (*apart.*) These thanks oppress me—
Respected mistress, from the king I bear
A letter to the youth—it was inscribed
With Nandana's concurrence, and the assent
Of Bhúrivasu. (*gives her a letter.*)

Kám. (*Takes it and reads.*)
" Unto all be health—
" The king commands—We are well pleased to greet
" A son in you, of noble race descended;
" Amongst the worthiest eminent, and late
" From great calamity redeemed; and more,
" In love and grace to you, we do permit
" Your well-loved friend to wed the youthful maid,
" Whom first affection yielded to his hopes."
You hear, my son?

Mád. I do, and all I wished,
Thus hearing, have obtained.

Mál. The lingering dart
Of fear is now extracted from our hearts.

Lav. The loves of Málati and Mádhava
Will now no more be thwarted.

Mák. See, where come
Our other friends, and faithful Kalahansa.

Enter AVALOKITÁ, BUDDHARAKSHITÁ, *and* KALAHANSA.

All (*bowing.*) Glory to Kámandakí, the sage
Perfector of all aims! Glory to Mádhava,

The Moon that sheds delight on Makaranda!
Now Fate propitious smiles.

Lav. Who does not share
This general joy!

Kám. And that our story,
Full of strange varied incidents, is closed
In happiness, deserves congratulation.

Sau. And Devaráta and his ancient friend,
Will see with joy their children now are joined
In that affiance they so long projected.

Mál. (*apart.*) Hey—how is this?

Mak. and Mád. (*to Kámandakí.*) How sorts the dame's discourse
With past events?

Lav. (*apart to Kám.*) What's to be said?

Kám. (*to her.*) We need no longer fear
The wrath of Nandana, now we obtain
His sister's aid. (*Aloud*) 'Tis even as you have heard.
Whilst yet I taught your fathers, they agreed,
That when their children came to years mature,
Their hands should be united, and they left
Saudaminí and me to take those cares
That might secure your union, hoping thus
To shun the anger of exalted rank.

Mál. (*apart*). What marvellous secrecy!

Mád. and Mak. It moves our wonder.
Yet must the schemes of the illustrious, planned
For virtuous ends, and prudently conducted,
Ever enjoy success.

Kám. My son, what more remains?
The happiness that was your earliest hope,
By my devotions, and the skilful pains
Of my disciples, is at last ensured you.
The king and Nandana approve the suit
Of your dear friend, and hence no fear prevents
His union with his love. If yet there be
A wish ungratified, declare it, speak.

Mád. (*bowing*). My happiness henceforth is perfect: all
The wish I cherish more, is this; and may
Your favour, holy dame, grant it fruition.
Still may the virtuous be exempt from error
And fast to virtue cling—may monarchs, merciful
And firm in equity, protect the earth—
May in due season from the labouring clouds
The fertile showers descend—and may the people,
Blest in their friends, their kindred, and their children,
Unknowing want, live cheerful and content.

[*Exeunt all.*

REMARKS ON MALATI AND MADHAVA.

THE preceding drama requires less allowance for any peculiarity in national manners than most of the specimens of the Hindu theatre. It offers nothing to offend the most fastidious delicacy, and may be compared in this respect, advantageously, with many of the dramas of modern Europe, which treat of the passion that constitutes its subject.

The manner in which love is here depictured is worthy of observation, as correcting a mistaken notion of the influence which the passion exercises over the minds of the natives, of at least one portion of Asia. However intense the feeling, and it is represented as sufficiently powerful to endanger existence, it partakes in no respect of the impetuosity which it has pleased the writers of the West to attribute to the people of the East;

> The barbarous nations, whose inhuman love
> Is wild desire, fierce as the suns they feel.

The fierceness of their suns is a very efficient cause for the gentleness of their passions; and the hardy children of the north find their complicated system of social restraint insufficient to curb those impulses, which they derive from a less enervated frame and a more lofty spirit.

If, however, the love of the Hindus be less vehement than that of the Goth, Dane, or Norman of uncivilized days, it is equally remote from the extravagance of adoration which later times have learnt from those who never taught the lesson, the mirrors of Chivalry, who were equally vowed to the service of God and the ladies. There is no reason to think their love was a whit purer than that of any other people or time; but the fancy was favourable to poetical imagination, and has beneficially influenced the manners of modern Europe. The heroine of this drama is loved as a woman: she is no goddess in the estimation of her lover, and although her glances may inflame, no hint is given that her frowns can kill. At the same time, Mádhava's passion is as metaphysical as need be, and

> Málatí alone,
> Heard, felt, and seen, possesses every thought,
> Fills every sense, and pants in every vein.

The passion of Málatí is equally intense with that of Juliet; but her unconquerable reserve, even to the extent of denying her utterance to him she loves more than life, is a curious picture of the restraint to which the manners of Hindu women were subjected, even whilst they were in enjoyment, as appears from the drama, of considerable personal freedom.

The fervour of attachment which unites the different personages of the drama so indissolubly in life and death, is creditable to the national character. Unless instances of such disinterested union had existed, the author could scarcely have conceived, much less depictured it.

There is no great discrimination of character in the piece, nor could it be well expected as the business is so limited. It is not, however, wholly wanting, and Makaranda and Madayantiká are much less mere lovers than Mádhava and Málatí. The cautious, though devoted perseverance of Kámandakí is maintained throughout, and the benevolence of Saudámini is well contrasted with the malignity of Kapálakundalá.

The incidents of the story are varied, and some of them are highly dramatic—they are rather diffusely spread out, but they are all essential to the denouement, the concurrence of all parties in the union of the lovers.

There is more passion in the thoughts of *Bhavabhúti* than in those of *Kálidása*, but less fancy. There are few of the elegant similitudes in which the latter is so rich, and there is more that is common-place, and much that is strained and obscure. In none of his dramas does *Bhavabhúti* make any attempt at wit, and we have no character in either of his three dramas approaching the *Vidúshaka* of either of the two preceding pieces. On the other hand, he expatiates more largely in the description of picturesque scenery and in the representation of human emotions, and is perhaps entitled to even a higher place than his rival, as a poet.

THE MUDRÁ RÁKSHASA,

OR

THE SIGNET OF THE MINISTER.

A Drama,

TRANSLATED FROM THE ORIGINAL

SANSCRIT.

PREFACE.

The MUDRÁ RÁKSHASA is a drama of a very different description from either of the preceding, being wholly of a political character, and representing a series of Machiavelian stratagems, influencing public events of considerable importance. Those events relate to the history of CHANDRAGUPTA, who is very probably indentifiable with the *Sandrocottus* of the Greeks, and the drama therefore, both as a picture of manners and as a historical record, possesses no ordinary claims upon our attention.

The object of the play is to reconcile RÁKSHASA, the hostile minister of NANDA, the late king of *Palibothra*, to the individuals by whom, or on whose behalf, his sovereign was murdered, the Brahman CHÁNAKYA and the prince CHANDRAGUPTA. With this view, he is rendered by the contrivances of CHÁNAKYA, an object of suspicion to the prince with whom he has taken refuge, and is consequently dismissed by him. In this deserted condition he learns the imminent danger of a dear friend whom CHÁNAKYA is about to put to death, and in order to effect his liberation surrenders himself to his enemies —they offer him, contrary to his expectations, the rank and power of prime minister, and the parties are finally friends. It is unnecessary to describe the plot more fully in this place.

Simple as is the subject of the drama there is no want of action in its development. The stratagems of CHÁNAKYA are varied, numerous, and well connected, and although there is occasionally some want of probability in their execution, yet they are made to contribute very successfully and ingeniously towards the production of their combined result. It must be acknowledged, that the political code from which they emanate, exhibits a morality not a whit superior to that of the Italian school; but a remarkable, and in some respects a redeeming principle, is the inviolable and devoted fidelity which appears as the uniform characteristic of servants, emissaries, and friends: a singular feature in the Hindu character which it has not yet wholly lost.

The author of the play is called in the prelude *Visákhadatta,* the son of *Prithu,* entitled *Mahárájá,* and grandson of the *Sámanta* or chief *Vateswara Datta.* We are not much the wiser for this information, as we can scarcely venture to conclude, although it is not impossible, that the *Chouhan* chief of Ajmer, *Prithu Rai,* who was killed at the end of the twelfth century by the Mohammedans, is here intended. There is nothing unusual in a prince's being an author, or at least a reputed one, and the closing speech of the drama clearly refers to the victorious progress of a foreign foe, whom it may not be unreasonable to connect with the *Ghorian* invasion.*

The late Major Wilford has called the author of the MUDRÁ RÁKSHASA, *Ananta,* and quotes him as declaring that he lived on the banks of the *Godáverí* (*As. Res.* vol. v. p. 280.) This however must be an error, as three copies, one of them a *Dekhini* manuscript in the *Telugu* character, have been consulted on the present occasion, and they all agree in the statement above given.

There is a commentary on the drama by *Vatéswara Misra,* a *Maithila Brahman,* the son of *Gauripati Misra,* who has laboured with more pains than success to give a double interpretation to the composition, and to present it as a system of policy as well as a play. Another commentary by *Guhasena* is said to exist, but it has not been met with; and the one referred to, owing to the commentator's mystification of obvious meanings, and the exceedingly incorrect state of the manuscript, has proved of no advantage.

It may not here be out of place to offer a few observations

* At the same time it is to be observed, that according to the *Prithwi Rai Ráyasa,* the father of Prithu the king of Ajmer, was named *Someswara,* and his grandfather *Ananda.*

on the identification of CHANDRAGUPTA and SANDROCOTTUS. It is the only point on which we can rest with any thing like confidence in the history of the Hindus, and is therefore of vital importance in all our attempts to reduce the reigns of their kings to a rational and consistent chronology. It is well worthy therefore of careful examination, and it is the more deserving of scrutiny, as it has been discredited by rather hasty verification and very erroneous details.

Sir William Jones first discovered the resemblance of the names, and concluded CHANDRAGUPTA to be one with SANDROCOTTUS. (*As. Res.* vol. iv. p. 11.) He was, however, imperfectly acquainted with his authorities, as he cites "a beautiful poem" by *Somadeva*, and a tragedy called the coronation of *Chandra*, for the history of this prince. By the first is no doubt intended the large collection of tales by *Somabhatta*, the *Vrihat Kathá*, in which the story of NANDA's murder occurs: the second is, in all probability, the play that follows, and which begins after CHANDRAGUPTA's elevation to the throne. In the fifth volume of the *Researches* the subject was resumed by the late Colonel Wilford, and the story of CHANDRAGUPTA is there told at considerable length, and with some accessions which can scarcely be considered authentic. He states also that the *Mudrá Rákshasa* consists of two parts, of which one may be called the coronation of CHANDRAGUPTA, and the second his reconciliation with RÁKSHASA, the minister of his father. The latter is accurately enough described, but it may be doubted whether the former exists.

Colonel Wilford was right also in observing that the story is briefly related in the *Vishnu Purána* and *Bhágavat*, and in the *Vrihat Kathá*; but when he adds, that it is told also in a lexicon called the *Kámandakí* he has been led into error. The *Kámandakí* is a work on *Niti*, or Polity, and does not contain the story of NANDA and CHANDRAGUPTA. The author merely alludes to it in an honorific verse, which he addresses to CHÁNAKYA as the founder of political science, the Machiavel of India.

The birth of NANDA and of CHANDRAGUPTA, and the circumstances of NANDA's death as given in Colonel Wilford's account, are not alluded to in the play, the *Mudrá Rákshasa*, from which the whole is professedly taken, but they agree generally with the *Vrihat Kathá* and with popular versions of the story. From some of these, perhaps, the king of *Vikatpalli*, *Chandra Dás*, may have been derived, but he looks very like an amplification of *Justin's* account of the youthful adventures of *Sandrocottus*. The proceedings of CHANDRAGUPTA and CHÁNAKYA upon NANDA's death correspond tolerably well with what we learn from the drama, but the manner in which the catastrophe is brought about (p. 268) is strangely misrepresented. The account was no doubt compiled for the translator by his pundit, and it is therefore but indifferent authority.

It does not appear that Colonel Wilford had investigated the drama himself, even when he published his second account of the story of CHANDRAGUPTA (*As. Res.* vol. ix. p. 93), for he continues to quote the *Mudrá Rákshasa* for various matters which it does not contain. Of these, the adventures of the king of *Vikatpalli*, and the employment of the Greek troops, are alone of any consequence, as they would mislead us into a supposition, that a much greater resemblance exists between the Grecian and Hindu histories than is actually the case.

Discarding, therefore, these accounts, and laying aside the marvellous part of the story, I shall endeavour, from the *Vishnu* and *Bhágavat Purános*, from a popular version of the narrative as it runs in the south of India, from the *Vrihat Kathá*,* and from the play, to give what appear to be the genuine circumstances of CHANDRAGUPTA's elevation to the throne of *Palibothra*.

A race of kings denominated *Saisunágas*, from *Sisunága* the first of the dynasty, reigned in *Magadhá*, or *Behar*: their

* For the gratification of those who may wish to see the story as it occurs in these original sources, translations are subjoined; and it is rather important to add, that in no other *Purána* has the story been found, although most of the principal works of this class have been carefully examined.

capital was *Pátaliputra,* and the last of them was named NANDA or MAHÁPADMA NANDA. He was the son of a woman of the *Súdra* caste, and was hence, agreeably to Hindu law, regarded as a *Súdra* himself. He was a powerful and ambitious prince, but cruel and avaricious, by which defects, as well as by his inferiority of birth, he probably provoked the animosity of the Brahmans. He had by one wife eight sons, who with their father were known as the nine NANDAS; and, according to the popular tradition, he had by a wife of low extraction, called *Murá,* another son named CHANDRAGUPTA. This last circumstance is not stated in the *Puránas* nor *Vrihat Kathá,* and rests therefore on rather questionable authority; at the same time it is very generally asserted, and is corroborated by the name *Maurya,* one of CHANDRAGUPTA's denominations, which is explained by the commentator on the *Vishnu Purána* to be a patronymic formative, signifying the son of *Murá.* It also appears from the play, that CHANDRAGUPTA was a member of the same family as NANDA, although it is not there stated that he was NANDA's son.

But whatever might have been the origin of this prince, it is very likely that he was made the instrument of the insubordination of the Brahmans, who having effected the destruction of NANDA and his sons, raised CHANDRAGUPTA, whilst yet a youth, to the throne. In this they were aided by a prince from the north of India, to whom they promised an accession of territory as the price of his alliance. The execution of the treaty was evaded, very possibly by his assassination, and to revenge his father's murder, his son led a mingled host against *Magadhá,* containing amongst other troops, *Yavanas,* whom we may be permitted to consider as Greeks. The storm was averted, however, by jealousies and quarrels amongst the confederates. The army dispersed, and MALAYAKETU, the invader, returned baffled and humbled to his own country. CHANDRAGUPTA reigned twenty-four years, and left the kingdom to his son. We have now to see how far the classical writers agree with these details.

The name is an obvious coincidence. *Sandrocottus* and CHANDRAGUPTA can scarcely be considered different appellations. But the similarity is no doubt still closer. Athenæus, as first noticed by Wilford (*As. Res.* vol. v. p. 262.) and subsequently by Schlegel (*Indische Bibliothek*), writes the name, *Sandrakoptus*, and its other form, although more common, is very possibly a mere error of the transcriber. As to the *Andracottus* of Plutarch, the difference is more apparent than real, the initial sibilant being often dropped in Greek proper names.

This name is however not the only coincidence in denomination that may be traced. We find in the play that CHANDRAGUPTA is often called *Chandra* simply, or the moon, of which *Chandramas* is a synonime; and accordingly we find in *Diodorus Siculus*, the king of the *Gangaridæ*, whose power alarms the Macedonian, is there named *Xandrames*. The *Aggramen* of *Quintus Curtius* is merely a blundering perversion of this appellation.

There are other names of the prince, the sense of which, though not their sound, may be discovered in classical writers. These are *Vrishala*, and perhaps *Maurya*. The first unquestionably implies a man of the fourth or servile caste; the latter is said by Wilford to be explained in the *Játi Viveka* the offspring of a barber and a *Súdra* woman, or of a barber and a female slave. (*As. Res.* vol. v. p. 285.) It is most usually stated, however, to mean the offspring of *Murá*, as already observed, and the word does not occur in any of the vocabularies in the sense attached to it by Col. Wilford.* It is sufficient, how-

* Colonel Tod considers *Maurya* a probable interpolation for *Mori*, a branch of the *Pramára* tribe of Rajputs, who in the eighth century occupied Chitore. He observes also, that Chandragupta in the *Puránas* is made a descendant of *Sehesnag* of the *Takshak* tribe, of which last no other mention has been found, whilst instead of *Sehesnag* the word is *Sisunaga*; and with respect to the fact of the princes belonging to the *Pramára* tribe no authority is cited. Colonel Tod, like the late Col. Wilford, is sparing of those specific references, which in all debateable points are indispensable. See *Transactions Royal Asiatic Society*, vol. i. p. 211. Also, *Account of Rájást'han*, p. 53.

ever, to observe, that the term *Vrishala,* and frequent expressions in the drama, establish the inferior origin of CHANDRAGUPTA, a circumstance which is stated of the king of the *Gangaridæ* at the time of Alexander's invasion by Diodorus Siculus, Quintus Curtius, and Plutarch.

According to the two former of these writers, *Xandrames* or *Chandramas* was contemporary with Alexander. They add, that he was the son of the queen by an intrigue with a barber, and that his father being raised to honour and the king's favour, compassed his benefactor's death, by which he paved the way for the sovereignty of his own son, the ruling prince. We have no indication of these events in the Hindu writers, and CHANDRAGUPTA, as has been noticed, is usually regarded as the son of NANDA, or at least a relative. It may be observed that his predecessors were *Súdras,* and the character given to MAHÁPADMA NANDA in the *Vishnu Purána,* agrees well enough with the general tenour of the classical accounts, as to his being of low origin and estimation, although an active and powerful prince. If NANDA be the monarch alluded to, there has been some error in the name; but, in either case, we have a general coincidence in the private history of the monarch of the *Gangaridæ,* as related by the writers of the east or west.

If the monarch of Behar at the time of Alexander's invasion was NANDA, it is then possible that CHANDRAGUPTA, whilst seeking, as the Hindus declare, the support of foreign powers to the north and north-west of India, may have visited Alexander, as asserted by Plutarch and Justin. We cannot, however, attach any credit to the marvellous part of the story as told by the latter, nor can we conceive that a mere adventurer, as he makes *Sandrocoptus* to have been, should have rendered himself master of a mighty kingdom, in so brief an interval as that between Seleucus and Alexander, or by the aid of vagabonds and banditti alone.

Although, therefore, the classical writers had gleaned some knowledge of CHANDRAGUPTA's early history, it is very evident that their information was but partially correct, and that they have confounded names, whilst they have exaggerated some circumstances and misrepresented others. These defects, however, are very venial, considering the imperfect communicatien that must have subsisted between the Greeks and Hindus, even at the period of Alexander's invasion, and the interval that elapsed before the accounts we now possess were written. These considerations rather enhance the value of both sets of our materials. It is more wonderful that so much of what appears to be the truth should have been preserved, than that the stories should not conform in every particular.

However questionable may be the contemporary existence of Alexander and *Sandrocoptus,* there is no reason to doubt that the latter reigned in the time of Seleucus Nicator, as Strabo and Arrian cite the repeated declarations of Megasthenes, that he had often visited the Indian prince. Seleucus is said to have relinquished to him some territories beyond the Indus, and to have formed a matrimonial alliance with him. We have no trace of this in the Hindu writers, but it is not at all improbable. Before the Christian era the Hindus were probably not scrupulous about whom they married; and even in modern days, their princesses have become the wives of Mohammedan sovereigns. CHANDRAGUPTA, however, had no right to be nice with respect to the condition of his wife, and in whichever way the alliance was effected, it was feasible enough, whilst it was a very obvious piece of policy in CHANDRAGUPTA, as calculated to give greater security to his empire and stability to his reign. The failure of Seleucus in his attempt to extend his power in India, and his relinquishment of territory, may possibly be connected with the discomfiture and retreat of MALAYAKETU, as narrated in the drama, although it may be reasonably doubted whether the Syrian monarch and the king of *Magadhá* ever came into actual collision. It is very unlikely that the former ever included any part of the Punjab within his dominions, and at any rate it may be questioned, whether CHANDRAGUPTA or his posterity long retained, if they ever held possession of the north-western provinces, as there is no conjecturing any resemblance between the names of the *Maurya* princes (*As. Res.* vol. ix. table) and the *Amitrochates* and *Sophagasenas*, who reinforced the armies of Antigonus the son of Seleucus, and of Antigonus the Great, with those elephants that were so highly prized by the successors of Alexander (Wilford, *As. Res.* vol. v. p. 286, and Schlegel, *Indische Bibliothek*), although, as shewn by Schlegel, the names are undoubtedly Sanscrit and Hindu.

All the classical writers agree in representing *Sandrocoptus* as king of the nations which were situated along the Ganges, which were the *Gangaridæ* and *Prasii*—called, however, indifferently, but no doubt inaccurately, *Gargaridæ*, *Gandaridæ*, and *Gandarii*, and *Prasii*, *Parrhasii*, and *Tabresii*. The first name was probably of Greek origin, expressing, as *Raderus* and *Cellarius* justly observes, the situation of the nations in the neighbourhood of the Ganges; but in truth there was a nation called the *Gandhari* or *Gandaridæ* west of the Indus, whom the classical authors often confound with the *Gangetic* nations, as has been shewn in another place. (*As. Res.* vol. xv.) The other appellation, which is most correctly *Prasii*, is referable to a Hindu original, and is a close approximation to *Práchí*, the eastern country, or *Práchyá*, the people of the east, in which division of *Bharata Khanda*, or India, *Mithilá*, the country opposite to *Behar*, and *Magadhá*, or South *Behar*, are included by Hindu geographers. Both Greek and Hindu accounts are therefore agreed as to the general position of the people over whom CHANDRAGUPTA reigned.

Finally; the classical authors concur in making *Palibothra* a city on the *Ganges*, the capital of *Sandrocoptus*. Strabo, on the authority of Megasthenes, states that *Palibothra* is situated at the confluence of the *Ganges* and another river, the name of which he does not mention. Arrian, possibly on the same authority, calls that river the *Erranoboas*, which is a synonime of the *Sone*. In the drama, one of the characters describes the trampling down of the banks of the *Sone*, as the army approaches to *Pátaliputra*; and *Pátaliputra*, also called *Kusumapura*, is the capital of CHANDRAGUPTA. There is little question that *Pátaliputra* and *Palibothra* are the same, and in the uniform estimation of the Hindus, the former is the same with Patna. The alterations in the course of the rivers of India, and the small comparative extent to which the city has shrunk in modern times, will sufficiently explain why Patna is not at the confluence of the *Ganges* and the *Sone*, and the only argument, then, against the identity of the position, is the enumeration of the *Erranoboas* and the *Sone* as distinct rivers by Arrian and Pliny: but their nomenclature is unaccompanied by any description, and it was very easy to mistake synonimes for distinct appellations. *Rájamahal*, as proposed by Wilford, and *Bhágalpur*, as maintained by Franklin, are both utterly untenable, and the further inquiries of the former had satisfied him of the error of his hypothesis. His death prevented the publication of an interesting paper by him on the site of *Palibothra*, in which he had come over to the prevailing opinion, and shewn it to have been situated in the vicinity of Patna.*

It thus appears, that the Greek and Hindu writers concur in the *name*, in the *private history*, in the *political elevation*, and in the *nation* and *capital* of an Indian king, nearly, if not exactly cotemporary with Alexander, to a degree of approximation that cannot possibly be the work of accident; and it may be reasonably concluded, therefore, that the era of the events described in the following drama is determined with as much precision as that of any other remote historical fact.

* *Asiatic Researches*, vol. xiv. p. 380.

APPENDIX TO PREFACE.

1.

PAURANIC ACCOUNTS OF *CHANDRAGUPTA.*

The son of *Mahánandi*, born of a *Súdra* woman, a powerful prince named *Mahápadma,* shall put an end to the *Kshetriya* rule, and from his time the kings will be mostly *Súdras* void of piety. He will bring the earth under one umbrella, his rule being irresistible, and he will reign like another *Bhárgava.* He will have eight sons, *Sumálya* and others, who will be kings of the earth for one hundred years. A Brahman will destroy these nine *Nandas,* and after their disappearance the *Mauryas* will reign in the *Kali* age. That Brahman will inaugurate Chandragupta as king.—(*Bhágavat,* 12th *Skandha.*)

Mahánandi will be the last of the ten *Saisunága* princes, whose joint reigns will be three hundred and sixty-two years. The son of *Mahánandi* or *Nanda,* named *Mahápadma,* will be born from a *Súdra* mother. He will be avaricious, and like another *Parasuráma* will end the *Kshetriya* race, as from him forwards the kings will be all *Súdras.* He, *Mahápadma,* will bring the whole earth under one umbrella, his rule being irresistible. He will have eight sons, *Sumálya* and others who after him will govern the world. He, and these sons will reign for a period of one hundred years, until *Kautilya,* a Brahman, shall destroy the nine *Nandas.*

After their destruction the *Mauryas* will possess the earth, *Kautilya* inaugurating Chandragupta in the kingdom.—(*Vishnu Purána.*)

The comment explains *Maurya* thus;—so named from Chandragupta, the first, who derived this name from his mother *Murá,* one of the wives of Nanda.

2.

STORY OF *NANDA*, AS RELATED BY *VARARUCHI* IN THE *VRIHAT KATHA*.

I now returned from my sojourn in the snowy mountains, where by the favour of *Síva* I had acquired the *Páninéya* grammar. This I communicated to my preceptor *Versha*, as the fruit of my penance; and as he wished to learn a new system, I instructed him in that revealed by *Swámí Kumára*. *Vyári* and *Indradatta* then applied to *Versha* for like instructions, but he desired them first to bring him a very considerable present. As they were wholly unable to raise the sum, they proposed applying for it to the king, and requested me to accompany them to his camp, which was at that time at *Ayodhyá;* I consented, and we set off.

When we arrived at the encampment we found every body in distress, Nanda being just dead. *Indradatta*, who was skilled in magic, said; "This event need not disconcert us: I will transfuse my vitality into the lifeless body of the king. Do you, *Vararuchi*, then solicit the money: I will grant it, and then resume my own person, of which do you, *Vyári*, take charge till the spirit returns." This was assented to, and our companion accordingly entered the carcase of the king.

Story of Yogananda.

The revival of Nanda caused universal rejoicing. The minister *Sakátala* alone suspected something extraordinary in the resuscitation. As the heir to the throne, however, was yet a child, he was well content that no change should take place, and determined to keep his new master in the royal station. He immediately, therefore, issued orders that search should be made for all the dead bodies in the vicinage, and that they should forthwith be committed to the flames. In pursuance of this edict the guards came upon the deserted carcase of *Indradatta*, and burning it as directed, our old associate was compelled to take up his abode permanently in the tenement which he had purposed to occupy but for a season. He was by no means pleased with the change, and in private lamented it with us, being in fact degraded by his elevation, having relinquished the exalted rank of a *Brahman* for the inferior condition of a *Súdra*.

Vyári having received the sum destined for our master, took leave of his companion *Indradatta*, whom we shall henceforth call *Yogananda*. Before his departure, however, he recommended to the latter to get rid of *Sakátala*, the minister, who had penetrated his secret, and who would, no doubt, raise the prince CHANDRAGUPTA to the throne as soon as he had attained to years of discretion. It would be better, therefore, to anticipate him, and, as preparatory to that measure, to make me, *Vararuchi*, his minister. *Vyári* then left us, and in compliance with his counsel I became the confidential minister of *Yogananda*.

A charge was now made against *Sakátala*, of having, under pretence of getting rid of dead carcases, burnt a Brahman alive; and on this plea he was cast into a dry well with all his sons. A plate of parched pulse and a pitcher of water were let down daily for their sustenance, just sufficient for one person. The father, therefore recommended to the brothers to agree amongst themselves which should survive to revenge them all, and relinquishing the food to him, resign themselves to die. They instantly acknowledged their avenger in him, and with stern fortitude refusing to share in the daily pittance, one by one expired.

After some time *Yogananda*, intoxicated like other mortals with prosperity, became despotic and unjust. I found my situation therefore most irksome, as it exposed me to a tyrant's caprice, and rendered me responsible for acts which I condemned. I therefore sought to secure myself a participator in the burthen, and prevailed upon *Yogananda* to release *Sakátala* from his captivity and reinstate him in his authority. He therefore once again became the minister of the king.

It was not long before I incurred the displeasure of *Yoga-*

nanda, so that he resolved to put me to death. *Sakátala,* who was rejoiced to have this opportunity of winning me over to his cause, apprised me of my danger, and helped me to evade it by keeping me concealed in his palace. Whilst thus retired, the son of the king, *Hiranyagupta,* lost his senses, and *Yogananda* now lamented my absence. His regret moved *Sakátala* to acknowledge that I was living, and I was once more received into favour. I effected the cure of the prince, but received news that disgusted me with the world, and induced me to resign my station and retire into the forests. My disappearance had led to a general belief that I had been privately put to death. This report reached my family. *Upakosá,* my wife, burnt herself, and my mother died broken hearted.

Inspired with the profoundest grief, and more than ever sensible of the transitory duration of human happiness, I repaired to the shades of solitude and the silence of meditation. After living for a considerable period in my hermitage, the death of *Yogananda* was thus related to me by a Brahman, who was travelling from *Ayodhyá* and had rested at my cell.

Sakátala brooding on his plan of revenge, observed one day a Brahman of mean appearance digging in a meadow, and asked him what he was doing there. CHÁNAKYA, the Brahman, replied: "I am rooting out this grass which has hurt my foot." The reply struck the minister as indicative of a character which would contribute to his designs, and he engaged him by the promise of a large reward and high honours to come and preside at the *Sráddha* which was to be celebrated next new moon at the palace. CHÁNAKYA arrived, anticipating the most respectful treatment; but *Yogananda* had been previously persuaded by *Sakátala* to assign precedence to another Brahman, *Subandhu,* so that when CHÁNAKYA came to take his place he was thrust from it with contumely. Burning with rage, he threatened the king before all the court, and denounced his death within seven days. NANDA ordered him to be turned out of the palace. *Sakátala* received him into his house, and persuading CHÁNAKYA that he was wholly innocent of being instrumental to his ignominious treatment, contributed to encourage and inflame his indignation. CHÁNAKYA thus protected, practised a magical rite, in which he was a proficient, and by which on the seventh day NANDA was deprived of life. *Sakátala* on the father's death effected the destruction of *Hiranyagupta*, his son, and raised CHANDRAGUPTA, the son of the genuine NANDA, to the throne. CHÁNAKYA became the prince's minister; and *Sakátala* having attained the only object of his existence, retired to end his days in the woods.

3.

STORY OF *NANDA* AND *CHANDRAGUPTA*, BY A PUNDIT OF THE DEKHIN.

(From a Manuscript in the collection of the late Col. Mackenzie, *Sanscrit*, *Telinga* character.)

After invoking the benediction of *Ganesa* the writer proceeds: In the race of *Bharadwája*, and the family of the hereditary councillors of the *Bhosala* princes, was born the illustrious and able minister *Bhávájí*. He was succeeded by his son *Gangádhara* surnamed *Adhwari* (a priest of the *Yajur Véda*), who continued to enjoy the confidence of the king, and was equal to *Vrihaspati* in understanding.

By his wife *Krishnámbiká*, *Gangádhara* had two sons, who were both employed by the *Raja*, *Sahuji*, the son of the preceding prince. The favour of the *Raja* enabled these ministers to grant liberal endowments to pious and learned *Brahmans*.

The elder of the two, *Nrisinha*, after a life passed in prayer and sacred rites, proceeded to the world of *Brahma*, leaving three sons.

Of these, the elder was *Ananda Ráya Adhwari*. He was noted for his steadiness and sagacity from his childhood, and in adult years deserved the confidence of his prince, *Sáhuji*. He was profoundly versed in the *Vedas*, a liberal benefactor of the *Brahmans*, and a skilful director of religious rites.

Upon his death and that of the youngest brother, the survivor, *Tryambaka Adhwari*, succeeded to the reputation of his ancestors, and cherished his nephews as his own children.

Accompanied by his mother he proceeded to the shores of the *Ganges*, and by his ablutions in the holy stream liberated his ancestors from the ocean of future existence.

He was solicited by *Sáhu*, the king, to assume the burthen of the state, but regarding it incompatible with his religious duties he was unwilling to assent. In consideration of his wisdom and knowledge he was highly venerated by the *Rájá* and presented with valuable gifts, which he dedicated to pious rites or distributed to the *Brahmans*. Having on a particular occasion been lavish of expenditure in order to gratify his sovereign, he contracted heavy debts, and as the prince delayed their liquidation, he was obliged to withdraw to seek the means of discharging them. On his return he was received by *Sáhu* and his nobles with high honours, and the prince by the homage paid to him obtained identification (after death) with *Tyágésa*, a glory of difficult attainment to *Yayáti*, *Nata*, *Mándhátá*, and other kings.

The brother of the prince, *Sarabhaji*, then governed the kingdom and promoted the happiness of all entrusted to his care by *Sáhu*, for the protection of piety, and rendering the people happy by his excellent qualities: the chief of the *Brahmans* was treated by him with increased veneration.

The land of *Chola* is supplied at will by the waters of the *Káverí*, maintained by the abundant showers poured down constantly by *Indra*, and in this land did the illustrious *Sarabhaji* long exercise undisturbed dominion and promote the happiness of his people.

Having performed with the aid of his reverend minister the late rite to his brother, he liberally delivered *Tryambaka* from the ocean of debt, and presented him with lands on the bank of the *Káveri* (the *Sahyagirijá*), for the preservation of the observances enjoined by religion and law.

And he diffused a knowledge of virtue by means of the *Tantra* of the son of the foe of *Káma* (*Kártikeya*), as communicated by *Brahmá* to *Náreda* to relieve his distress, and whatever learned man takes up his residence on the hill of *Swámi* and worships *Skanda* with faith, will undoubtedly obtain divine wisdom.

Thus, on the mountain of *Swámi*, enjoying the favour of *Girísa*, does *Tryambaka* reside with uninterrupted prosperity, surrounded by his kinsmen, and sons, and grandsons, and *Brahmans* learned in the *Vedas*, engaged in the performance of the holy rites and the worship of *Iswara*. May he live a thousand years!

An object of his unbounded benevolence, and one to be included in those cherished by his bounties, having worshipped the lord of *Srí* (*Vishnu*), and acquitted himself of his debt to the Gods and Manes, is rewarded by having it in his power to be respectfully obedient to his (*Tryambaka's*) commands. This individual, named *Dhúndí*, the son of the excellent Pundit *Lakshmana*, of the family of *Vyása*, had in his possession, and expounded, the new and wonderful drama entitled the *Mudrá Rákshasa*, and in order to convey a clear notion of his drama, the composition of *Visákha Datta*, he relates as an introduction the following particulars of the story.

Story of Nanda and Chandragupta.

According to the *Purúnas* the *Kshetriya* sovereignty was to cease with Nanda. In the beginning of the *Kali* age the *Nandas* were kings so named.

Amongst them Sarvárthasiddhi was celebrated for his valour; he was monarch of the earth and his troops were nine crore and one hundred. *Vaktranása* and others were his hereditary ministers, but amongst them the most famous was the Brahman, Rákshasa.

He was skilled in government and policy, and the six attributes of princes; was eminent for piety and prowess, and was highly respected by Nanda. The king had two wives, of whom *Sunandá* was the elder—the other was of

Súdra extraction; she was the favourite of the king, of great beauty and amiable character—her name was *Murá*. On one occasion the king in the company of his wives administered the rights of hospitality to a venerable ascetic, and after washing his feet sprinkled the queens with the water: nine drops fell upon the forehead of the elder, and one on *Murá*. This she received with reverence, and the Brahman was much pleased with her deportment.

Murá accordingly was delivered of one son, of most excellent qualities, who was named *Maurya*. *Sunandá* was delivered of a lump of flesh.

This RÁKSHASA divided into nine portions, which he put into a vessel of oil, and carefully watched.

By his cares nine infants were in time evolved, who were brought up by RÁKSHASA and called the nine *Nandas* after their progenitor.

The king when he grew old retired from the affairs of state, consigning his kingdom to these nine sons, and appointing *Maurya* to the command of the army.

Maurya had a hundred sons, of whom CHANDRAGUPTA was the best, and they surpassed the *Nandas* in merit.

The *Nandas* being therefore filled with envy, conspired against his life, and inviting him and his sons into a private chamber put them to death.

At this time the *Raja* of *Sinhalá* sent to the court of the *Nandas* a lion of wax in a cage, so well made that it seemed to be alive. And he added this message, "If any one of your courtiers can make this fierce animal run without opening the cage, I shall acknowledge him to be a man of talent."

The dullness of the *Nandas* prevented their understanding the purport of the message; but CHANDRAGUPTA, in whom some little breath yet remained, offered, if they would spare his life, to undertake the task, and this being allowed, he made an iron rod red-hot, and thrusting it into the figure, the wax soon ran, and the lion disappeared.

Although they desired his death, CHANDRAGUPTA was taken

by the *Nandas* from the pit into which he had been cast, and continued to live in affluence. He was gifted with all the marks of royalty: his arms reached to his knees; he was affable, liberal and brave; but these deserts only increased the animosity of the *Nandas*, and they waited for an opportunity of compassing his death.

Upon one occasion CHANDRAGUPTA observed a Brahman of such irascible temperament, that he tore up violently a tuft of *kusa* grass, because a blade of it had pierced his foot: on which he approached him, and placed himself under his protection through fear of incurring the Brahman's resentment.

This Brahman was named *Vishnugupta*, and was deeply read in the science of government taught by *Usanas* (*Saturn*), and in astronomy: his father, a teacher of *niti* or polity, was named *Chanaka*, and hence the son is called CHÁNAKYA.

He became the great friend of CHANDRAGUPTA, who related to him all he had suffered from the *Nandas*.

On which CHÁNAKYA promised him the throne of the *Nandas*; and being hungry, entered the dinner-chamber, where he seated himself on the seat of honour.

The *Nandas*, their understanding being bewildered by fate, regarded him as some wild scholar of no value, and ordered him to be thrust from his seat. The ministers in vain protested against the act; the princes forcibly dragged CHÁNAKYA, furious with rage, from his seat.

Then, standing in the centre of the hall, CHÁNAKYA, blind with indignation, loosened the lock of hair on the top of his head, and thus vowed the destruction of the royal race:—"Until I have exterminated these haughty and ignorant *Nandas*, who have not known my worth, I will not again tie up these hairs."

Having thus spoken, he withdrew, and indignantly quitted the city, and the *Nandas*, whom fortune had deserted, made no attempt to pacify him.

CHANDRAGUPTA being no longer afraid of his own danger, quitted the city and repaired to CHÁNAKYA, and the Brahman

Kautilya, possessed of the prince, resorted to crooked expedients for the destruction of the *Nandas.*

With this view he sent a friend, *Indrasermá,* disguised as a *Kshapanaka,* as his emissary, to deceive RÁKSHASA and the rest, whilst on the other hand he excited the powerful *Parvatendra* to march with a *Mlechchha* force against *Kusumapura,* promising him half the kingdom.

The *Nandas* prepared to encounter the enemy, relying on the valour of RÁKSHASA. He exerted all his prowess, but in vain, and finding it impossible to overcome the hostile force by open arms, attempted to get rid of *Maurya* by stratagem; but in the mean time all the *Nandas* perished like moths in the flame of CHÁNAKYA's revenge, supported by the troops of *Parvatendra.*

RÁKSHASA, being worn in body and mind, and having lost his troops and exhausted his treasures, now saw that the city could no longer be defended; he therefore effected the secret retreat of the old king SERVÁRTHASIDDHI, with such of the citizens as were attached to the cause of the *Nandas,* and then delivered the capital to the enemy, affecting to be won to the cause of CHANDRAGUPTA.

He prepared by magic art a poisoned maid, for the destruction of that prince; but *Kautilya* detected the fraud, and diverting it to *Parvatésa* caused his death; and having contrived that information of his share in the murder of the monarch should be communicated to his son, MALAYAKETU, he filled the young prince with alarm for his own safety, and occasioned his flight from the camp.

Kautilya, though master of the capital, yet knowing it contained many friends of NANDA, hesitated to take possession of it, and RÁKSHASA, taking advantage of the delay, contrived with *Dáruvermá* and others, machines and various expedients to destroy CHANDRAGUPTA upon his entry: but *Kautilya* discovered and frustrated all his schemes.

He persuaded the brother of *Parvateswara,* VAIRODHAKA, to suspend his departure, affirming with solemn asseverations, that

RÁKSHASA, seeking to destroy the friends of CHANDRAGUPTA, had designed the poisoned maid for the mountain monarch. Thus he concealed his own participation in the act, and the crafty knave deceived the prince, by promising him that moiety of the kingdom which had been promised to his brother.

SERVÁRTHASIDDHI retired to the woods to pass his days in penance, but the cruel *Kautilya* soon found means to shorten his existence.

When RÁKSHASA heard of the death of the old king he was much grieved, and went to MALAYAKETU and roused him to revenge his father's death. He assured him that the people of the city were mostly inimical to CHANDRAGUPTA, and that he had many friends in the capital ready to co-operate in the downfall of the prince and his detested minister. He promised to exhaust all his own energies in the cause, and confidently anticipated *Malayaketu's* becoming master of the kingdom, now left without a legitimate lord. Having thus excited the ardour of the prince, and foremost himself in the contest, RÁKSHASA marched against *Maurya* with an army of *Mlechhas*, or barbarians.

This is the preliminary course of the story—the poet will now express the subject of the drama. It begins with an equivoque upon the words *Krúra graha*, in the dialogue of the prelude. This ends the introduction.

4.

EXTRACTS FROM CLASSICAL WRITERS RELATING TO THE HISTORY OF SANDRACOTTUS.

He (Alexander) had learned from Phigæus that beyond the *Indus* was a vast desert of twelve days' journey, and at the farthest borders thereof ran the Ganges. Beyond this river dwell the *Tabresians*, and the *Gandaritæ* whose king's name was *Xandrames*, who had an army of 20,000 horse, 200,000 foot, 2,000 chariots and 4,000 elephants. The king could not believe this to be true, and sent for *Porus*, and inquired of him whether it was so or not. He told him all was certainly true, but that the present king of the *Gandaritæ* was but of a mean and obscure extraction, accounted to be a barber's son; for his father being a very handsome man, the queen fell in love with him, and murdered her husband, and so the kingdom devolved upon the present king.—*Diodorus Siculus.*

At the confluence of the Ganges and another river is situated *Palibothra*: it is the capital of the *Prasii*, a people superior to others. The king, besides his birth-name and his appellation from the city, is also named *Sandracottus*. *Megasthenes* was sent to him.

Megasthenes relates that he visited the camp of *Sandracottus*, in which 400,000 people were assembled.

Seleucus Nicator relinquished the country beyond the *Indus* to *Sandracottus*, receiving in its stead fifty elephants, and contracting an alliance with that prince (contractâ cum eo affinitate).—*Strabo.*

Phegelas informed him, that eleven days from the river the road lay over vast deserts to the Ganges, the largest stream in India, the opposite bank of which the *Gangaridæ* and *Parrhasii* inhabited. Their king was named *Aggramen*, who could bring into the field 20,000 horse and 200,000 foot, 2,000 chariots and 3,000 elephants. As these things appeared incredible to the king, he referred to *Porus*, who confirmed what he heard. He added, however, that the king was not only of low, but of extremely base origin, for his father was a barber, whose personal merits recommended him to the queen. Being introduced by her to the king then reigning, he contrived his death, and under pretence of acting as guardian to his sons, got them into his power and put them to death. After their extermination he begot the son who was now king, and who, more worthy of his father's condition than his own, was odious and contemptible to his subjects.—*Quintus Curtius.*

Megasthenes tells us he was at the court of *Sandracottus*.

The capital city of India is *Palembothra* on the confines of the *Prasii*, where is the confluence of the two great rivers, *Erranoboas* and *Ganges*. The first is inferior only to the *Indus* and *Ganges*.

Megasthenes assures us he frequently visited *Sandracottus* king of India.—*Arrian*.

Sandracottus was the author of the liberty of India after Alexander's retreat, but soon converted the name of liberty into servitude after his success, subjecting those whom he rescued from foreign dominion to his own authority. This prince was of humble origin, but was called to royalty by the power of the gods; for, having offended Alexander by his impertinent language, he was ordered to be put to death, and escaped only by flight. Fatigued with his journey he laid down to rest, when a lion of large size came and licked off the perspiration with his tongue, retiring without doing him any harm. The prodigy inspired him with ambitious hopes, and collecting bands of robbers he roused the Indians to renew the empire. In the wars which he waged with the captains of Alexander he was distinguished in the van, mounted on an elephant of great size and strength. Having thus acquired power, *Sandracottus* reigned at the same time that *Seleucus* laid the foundation of his dominion, and *Seleucus* entered into a treaty with him, and settling affairs on the side of India directed his march against Antigonus.—*Justin*—15—4.

The kings of the *Gandarites* and *Prasians* were said to be waiting for them there (*on the Ganges*) with 80,000 horse, 200,000 foot, 8,000 chariots and 6,000 elephants. Nor is this number at all magnified, for *Androcottus*, who reigned not long after, made *Seleucus* a present of 500 elephants at one time, and with an army of 600,000 men traversed India and conquered the whole.

Androcottus, who was then very young, had a sight of

Alexander, and he is reported to have said, that Alexander was within a little of making himself master of those countries: with such hatred and contempt was the reigning prince looked upon, on account of his profligacy of manner and meanness of birth.—*Plutarch.*—Life of Alexander.

DRAMATIS PERSONÆ.

MEN.

Chandragupta, also called *Vrishala* and *Maurya*.—The young king of *Pátaliputra*.

Chánakya, or *Vishnugupta*.—A Brahman, chiefly instrumental to *Chandragupta's* accession to the throne and now his minister.

Rákshasa.—The minister of the last king, the enemy of *Chandragupta*, and whom it is *Chánakya's* policy to win over to an alliance with his protegé.

Malayaketu.—Son of the king of the Mountains, leading an army against *Pátaliputra*.

Bhágurávana.—His supposed friend.

Nipunaka,
Siddhártha,
Jivasiddhi,
Samiddhártha,
A Man.
} Agents and emissaries of *Chánakya*.

Sárangarava.—*Chánakya's* Pupil.

Chandana Dás,
Sakata Dás.
} Friends of *Rákshasa*.

The son of *Chandana Dás*.

Virádhagupta,
Priyamvadaka,
Courier.
} Servants and agents of *Rákshasa*.

Vaihínara.—An attendant on *Chandragupta*.

Jajáli.—An attendant on *Malayaketu*.

Officers and attendants.

Women.

The wife of *Chandana Dás.*

Sonottará.—An attendant on *Chandragupta.*

Vijayá.—An attendant on *Malayaketu.*

Persons spoken of.

Nanda.—King of *Pátaliputra,* slain by *Chánakya's* contrivance.

Párvataka or *Parvateswara.*—King of the Mountains, at first the ally of *Chandragupta* but afterwards slain privily by *Chánakya.*

Servárthasiddhi.—Placed on the throne by *Rákshasa,* after the death of *Nanda,* but retired to a life of devotion.

Vairodhaka.—The brother of *Párvataka,* and killed by *Rákshasa's* emissaries by mistake for *Chandragupta.*

Various Princes, Chiefs, Bards, &c.

The Scene is laid partly at *Pátaliputra,* or *Palibothra,* and partly at the capital, or subsequently at the camp of *Malayaketu.*

The time of each Act is that of the action—the intervals of the acts are uncertain,

PRELUDE.

Enter the MANAGER.

May the craft of that *Síva* protect you, who desirous of concealing *Ganga** thus evaded the inquiries of his Goddess—what is this, so brilliant that decorates thy brows†—a digit of the moon—has it no name—you know the name, it is impossible that you should have forgotten it—I talk of a woman not of the moon—let *Vijayá*‡ tell you then, if the moon does not satisfy you.

May the dance of the victor of *Tripura*§ protect you—that dance to which space is wanting. Lightly treads the god lest he should overset the earth—he cramps his action lest his arms reach beyond the limits of the three worlds, and he bends his spark-emitting glances on vacuity, lest they should consume the objects on which they gaze.‖ Enough.

I am commanded by this assembly to represent the drama entitled *Mudrárákshasa,* the work of *Visákha Datta,* the son of *Prithu Mahárája,* and grandson of the chieftain *Vateswara*

* As a goddess, *Gangá,* or the deified Ganges, is usually viewed as an object of jealousy by Durgá the wife of *Siva.*

† On her descent from heaven by the prayers of *Bhagírath, Siva* received the falling river upon his head.

‡ *Vijayá* is one of the attendants upon *Durgá.*

§ *Siva,* from his destruction of the three cities of a demon, thence named *Tripura* or *Tripurásura,* the supposed origin of the modern *Tippera.*

‖ The dance of *Siva,* and that of his consort, its exact counterpart, have already been fully adverted to in the *Málatí* and *Mádhava.*

Datta;* and it is a great satisfaction to me to perform this drama before an audience so capable of appreciating its merits. Justly is it said, the tillage of a blockhead will rear a harvest in a fertile soil; the luxuriant growth of the grain does not depend upon the talents of the sower. Having therefore gone home and summoned my wife† I shall proceed with my company to the representation. Here is my house: I will enter.

How now! what festival have we here to-day that all the domestics are so busy? One is bringing water, another grinding perfumes, a third weaves a chaplet of many colours, and a fourth is sighing over a pestle. I must call one of them and ask the meaning of all this. Here, you clever, sharp, sensible, hussy, come hither; you sum of all wishes and decorum, come hither.‡

Enter ACTRESS.

Here am I, Sir; what are your commands?

Mana. Tell me what is going on here; have any Brahmans been invited to do honour to my race, or have any welcome guests arrived that there is such preparation?

Act. The Brahmans have been invited, Sir, by me.

Mana. What for, pray?

Act. There is an eclipse of the moon to-day.

Mana. Who says so?

Act. The people of the city.

* According to other authorities, however, the father of *Prithu*, *Prithwi*, or *Prithivi Rája*, was named *Somesa* or *Vigraha Deva*, and his grandfather *Sarnga Deva* or *Visála Déva*. The term *Datta* is also more appropriate to a man of the *Vaisya* tribe than a *Rajput*; but then *Vatéswara* is called a *Sámanta*, a term especially implying a warrior and a chief, and as in the case of the *Játs*, the agricultural tribes occasionally follow a military life. These considerations, however, leave the individuality of the author very doubtful.—*Asiatic Researches*, vol. xv, p. 407. *Transactions of Royal Asiatic Society*.

† He calls her the *Griha Kutumbiní*, literally, the head of the house or of the family; but by the authority she exercises she should scarcely be less than his wife.

‡ This is obviously imitated from the *Mrichchakati*.

Mana. Stop your preparations, dame, for the Brahmans you have invited: there is no eclipse to-day. Trust to one who has laboured diligently in the sixty-four divisions of astronomy; for observe, when *Ketu,* the angry planet, labours to depose from his high throne the mighty *Chandra*—

(*Behind.*) Who talks of deposing the king?*

Mana. The friendly Sage† is active in his defence.

Act. But who was that, who so readily noticed on earth the peril of the monarch?

Mana. I need not heed particularly, but we will find out. I will repeat what I said, and if he repeat his exclamation we may know his voice. Observe, "when the angry *Ketu* endeavours to depose *Chandra*—"

(*Behind.*) Who threats the king though I am yet alive?

Mana. Ha! I know;—it is *Kautilya,* as crooked in nature as in name,‡ the flames of whose anger have burnt up the family of *Nanda.* He has caught but part of my speech, and confounds it with an allusion to hostility towards his pupil.

Act. Here he comes: we had better get out of his way.

[*Exeunt.*

Enter CHÁNAKYA *with his top-knot*§ *untied.*

Where is this babbling wretch, that idly threatens
The monarch I have raised?—lives there the man
That does not trembling pray he may behold
These tresses bound again, whose length dishevelled
Hangs an envenomed snake to Nanda's race;
A smoky wreath, engendered by the fires

* The original plays upon two words, *Ketu* the planet, or *Malayaketu* a prince, enemy of the present king, and *Chandra* his name, or the moon.

† The planet *Budha* or Mercury, or in the text the *Budha Yoga*; but there is no *Yoga* so named, and unless a different system be alluded to, simple conjunction or propinquity must be implied. The term has a double import here: *Budha,* Mercury, or a wise man, referring to *Chánakya.*

‡ *Kautilya,* implies crookedness, both physical and moral.

§ The single lock of hair left on the shaven head of a Brahman.

Of my consuming wrath ? The fool, unwitting
Of his own weakness, would he play the moth,
And heedless plunge into the deadly flame
Of my resentment, blazing like a meteor,
Fierce o'er the prostrate forest of my foes ?
What ho ! Sárangarava.

Enter PUPIL.

Your commands, Sir.

Chán. A seat.

Pup. It waits you in the porch, Sir.

Chán. Bring it here ; affairs of weight disturb me.
It is not fit the teacher should endure
A scholar's disobedience.

(*Pupil brings him a seat—he sits.*)

What should this rumour be, so general noised
Amongst the citizens ? They say that Rákshasa,
In stern resentment of the total fall
Of Nanda's race, stirs up th'aspiring son
Of Parvatéswara ; who would avenge
His father's death, to join him, and has vowed
To make him lord of Nanda's former realm.
With these designs, they have implored the aid
Of the great monarch of the *Mlechcha* tribes ;*
And now, against the sway of *Vrishala*
These fierce and formidable foes combine.
It may be thus—'Tis known to all the world,
I vowed the death of Nanda, and I slew him.
The current of a vow will work its way
And cannot be resisted. What is done
Is spread abroad, and I no more have power
To stop the tale. Why should I ? Be it known,
The fires of my wrath alone expire,
Like the fierce conflagration of a forest,

* Literally, by the great *Mlechcha Rajá*, *Mahatá Mlechcharajéna.*

From lack of fuel—not from weariness.
The flames of my just anger have consumed
The branching ornaments of Nanda's stem,
Abandoned by the frightened priests and people.
They have enveloped in a shower of ashes
The blighted tree of his ambitious councils:
And they have overcast with sorrow's clouds
The smiling heavens of those moon-like looks
That shed the light of love upon my foes.
Now may *they* triumph—*they*, who late beheld
With downward looks and struggling indignation,
Scarce smothered by their terrors, my dishonour,
Thrust from my seat, and banished from the presence,
Disgraced but not dejected—now they see me
Spurn Nanda and his offspring from their throne,
As from the mountain's crest the lion hurls
Incensed the lordly elephant.
My vow is now accomplished, but I bear,
In *Vrishala's* defence, the fatal arms
That have uprooted Nanda's tyrant race,
Like fond affections from the breast of earth;
And now, in him, his fortune must implant,
Firm as the fragrant lotus in the lake.
Such is the equal fruit of love and hatred,
And friends and foes confess alike the power
That works their elevation or their fall.
Yet, what avails it, to have rooted out
The stem of Nanda; what to have allied
Fortune with Chandragupta, unsubdued
Whilst Rákshasa remains? His faith inflexible
Survives their ruin, and whilst yet exists
The most remote of kindred to their house
He is our foe. Well; be it so!
We must devise with craft to break the league
We cannot face. The sole remaining shoot
Of Nanda's stem, the pious anchorite,

Sarvárt'ha siddhi, tranquil lies in death;
Even in the instant Rákshasa had promised
Malayaketu, that more vigorous means
Should be pursued to overturn our empire.

(*Addressing vacancy.*)

'Tis bravely done, thou worthy minister,
Thou saintly priest, thou human *Vrihaspati.**
The mercenary herd obey their lords
For their own profit: should they hold their faith
In time of adverse fortune, they expect
That future days will give back power and wealth.
How few, like thee, regardless of reward,
And animated by remembered kindnesses,
Unwearied labour in the perilous service
A master no more lives to recompense?
How shall I change the enmity of such
As thou to friendship? It but little profits
To court alliance with a fool or coward;
Nor do the brave and wise claim our dependance,
Unless fidelity confirm their worth.
They, who to intellect and courage join
Devoted faith, are wedded to their lords,
In adverse ever as in prosperous fortune.
I must not sleep in this. To win the chief
Demands my utmost care. Thus far, success
Befriends our cause, and on his head revert
His hostile councils. Whilst he designed
One of the princes to destroy, and drive
Me hence, I gained his minister, directed
The shaft against Parvataka, and spread
The rumour, Rákshasa had done the deed.
So runs the general credence; but his son,
Malayaketu, knows the truth. To him

* The regent of the planet of Jupiter, and preceptor and councillor of the gods.

'Twas purposely revealed; and with the aid
Of Bháguráyana, he frightened fled.
Now he is leagued with Rákshasa, and may
Defy our arms whilst aided by his policy.
Yet some discredit must attend his union
With one the world conceives his father's murderer,
A stain no skill nor craft can wipe away.
I have my spies abroad—they roam the realm,
In various garb disguised, in various tongues
And manners skilled, and prompt to wear the shew
Of zeal to either party, as need serves.
At home, my agents, versed in every shift
And quaint device, maintain assiduous quest
Amongst the people of the capital,
And instant note amidst the multitude
The covert friends of Nanda and his minister.
The chiefs, whose ready aid placed Chandragupta
Firm on his throne, are faithful to his cause,
And careful servants keep unwearied watch
To baffle those who would administer
Envenomed draughts and viands to the king.
There is a fellow of my studies, deep
In planetary influence and policy,*
The Brahman, *Indusermá*; him I sent,
When first I vowed the death of Nanda, hither;
And here repairing as a *Bauddha* mendicant,†
He speedily contrived to form acquaintance
And friendship with the royal councillors.
Above them all, does Rákshasa repose

* Literally, "Having obtained great proficiency in the *Dandaníti* political system of *Usanas*, and the sixty-four *Angas*, or branches of the *Jyotish Sástra*, the science of astronomy or astrology."

† Having the marks of a *Kshapanaka*, which usually designates a *Bauddha* mendicant; but, as hereafter shewn, the individual is a *Jain* not a *Bauddha*, and the confusion of terms is worthy of notice, as characteristic of a period subsequent to the disappearance of the *Bauddhas* in India.

In him implicit confidence. 'Tis well (*rises*).
We triumph in his aid. Then none shall dare
Deride our purposes. The kingly burthen
Unbending, Chandragupta shall sustain,
And vigilantly guard his regal prize.
He must not hope for indolent delights
Whose daring wins a throne. The king of men
And monarch of the woods, alike must vanquish
Frequent and fierce aggression, to enjoy
In peace the prey their prowess has achieved. [*Retires.*

Enter NIPUNAKA, *a spy in the service of Chánakya, disguised, and carrying a scroll, or cloth with figures of Yama on it.**

Devotion to *Yama*† alone be selected,
For only by him is existence protected:
Their servants all other gods leave in the lurch,
When *Yama* his messengers sends in their search,
But trust we to *Yama*, and well are we sped,
With a friend whilst alive, and a friend when we're dead.
I'll enter here, show my pictures and chaunt my song.

(*Entering Chánakya's house.*)

Pup. Stop, stop! you must not enter here.

Nip. No!—pray, whose house is it?

Pup. It belongs to my preceptor, of well-selected name.‡

* A *Yama* Pata. It should seem to be a sort of raree show. The showman probably held something of a religious character; the person and his accompaniment are now unknown.

† The *Hindu Pluto.*

‡ *Sugrihita námna Arya Chánakyasya.* This phrase is of constant occurrence in the preceding dramas, as well as this, and indicates the importance attached, not to well-sounding, but to lucky or propitious appellations. This superstition was common amongst the nations of antiquity; and, according to Cicero, care was taken in the lustration of the people, that those who conducted the victims, and on the formation of the army that the first soldier on the muster-roll should have auspicious names. Cum imperator exercitum, censor populum lustraret, bonis nominibus qui hostias ducerent, eligebantur, quod idem in delectu consules observant, ut primus miles fiat bono nomine.

Nip. Then it belongs to a brother professor, so let me pass. I must have some talk with him, and let him see what I know.

Pup. What can you teach my master, pray?

Nip. Don't be wroth. One man cannot know every thing; he may know some things, to be sure, and so may even such as I am.

Pup. How dare you detract from my master: he knows every thing?

Nip. Does he know, think you, by whom *Chandra** is disliked?

Pup. What has he to do with such knowledge?

Nip. He will know what is to be known, I dare say; but you only understand thus, that the lotus cannot bear *Chandra*, its disposition is counter to its shape and beauty: the place abounds with such.

Chán. (*overhearing*). He means, the minds of men are yet averse
To Chandragupta.

Pup. What nonsense do you chatter?

Nip. I talk very good sense, if—

Pup. What?

Nip. Those who hear me understand me.

Chán. (*aloud*). Advance, you will find one, friend
Willing to hear and understand.

Nip. Long life to your Excellency!

Chán (*apart*). Amidst my many missions I forget
What was assigned Nipunaka. Oh! I remember,
He was to gather and report the state
Of public feeling. Welcome, friend; sit down.

Nip. As your honour commands. (*Sits on the ground.*)

Chán. Now for your news. What say the citizens—
How do they stand affected?

Nip. Your Excellency has removed all their grievances,

* The moon, or Chandragupta.

so that they cannot choose but be well affected to the auspicious Chandragupta. There are, however, in the city three men attached personally to the minister Rákshasa, who cannot bear his Majesty's prosperity.

Chán. They weary of their lives then—who are they?

Nip. The first is a *Bauddha* beggar.

Chán. (*apart*). A *Bauddha* beggar—excellent. (*Aloud*) His name?

Nip. Jivasiddhi.

Chán. (*apart*). My own true emissary. (*Aloud*) Well, who next?

Nip. Rákshasa's very particular friend, the scribe Sakata Dás.

Chán. (*apart*). A scribe—a matter of light moment; yet

'Tis well not to despise a foe though humble:
He has been noted—and Siddhárthaka
Fastened upon him as a friend. (*Aloud*) The third?

Nip. Is also the friend of Rákshasa, an inhabitant of Pushpapur, the head of the jewellers, named Chandana Dás. In his house the wife of the minister was left when he fled from the city.

Chán. (*apart*). This man must be, in truth, his friend:

To one, alone, he valued as himself,
Would Rákshasa commit so dear a charge.
(*Aloud*) How know you, that the wife of Rákshasa
Was left in trust of Chandana Dás?

Nip. This seal-ring will apprize you.

Chán. (*taking the ring* and reading the name*) Rákshasa—Rákshasa is in my grasp! (*Aloud*) How got you this?

* *Angulíya mudrá*, a finger-ring seal. Seals or signets of this kind were from the earliest periods commonly used in the East. Ahasuerus takes his signet off his hand and gives it first to Haman and again to Mordecai; and Herodotus notices that each of the Babylonians wore a seal-ring. The Greeks and Romans had their rings curiously engraved with devices, and that cast by Polycrates into the sea was the work of an engraver whose name the historian has not thought unworthy of commemoration. Thus also in the Demagogues of Aristophanes:—

" *Demus.*

Nip. I will tell your Excellency. It was your pleasure that I should take note of the sentiments and conduct of the citizens. To gain free access to their habitations I assumed this disguise, and amongst other houses I entered that of Chandana Dás. Exhibiting the *Yama* show, I commenced my ballad, when a little boy of about five years of age, of a most lovely appearance, his eyes sparkling with the curiosity common at his years, ran out from a viranda in the court. Cries of, "He is gone out—he is gone out!" uttered by female voices proceeded instantly from the apartment adjoining, and a woman

" *Demus.* This is no ring of mine, it tallies not
With my device, or much my eyes deceive me.
" *Sausage Seller.* Allow me, Sir. What might be your impression?
" *Dem.* A roasted *thrium* in thick fat enclosed.
" *Saus.* I see no *thrium.*
" *Dem.* What the impression then?
" *Saus.* A wide-mouthed gull, high seated on a rock.
In act to make a speech."

The use of the seal amongst the ancients, as amongst the Orientals to the present day, was not, as with us, to secure an envelope, but to verify letters and documents in place of a written signature. Amongst the natives of Hindustan, both Mohammedan and Hindu, the seal is engraved with the name of the wearer, and the surface being smeared superficially only with ink, the application of the seal to the paper leaves the letters which are cut in the stone, white on a black ground. Such also was the manner in which the seals of the Greeks and Romans were applied. It might be suspected that the translator of Euripides was thinking of a seal of wax on the outside of a letter, in the following passage in Iphigenia in Aulis:

" *Attendant.* But how, if I speak thus, shall I find credit,
Or with your daughter, or the royal dame?
" *Agamemnon.* The seal which on that letter I have stamped,
Preserve 'unbroken.' "

It is literally "Take care of the seal which you bear on that letter." The stage direction should be probably "giving his ring to the messenger," a mark of confidence, and a confirmation of the previously impressed signature, which would induce Clytemnestra to trust him implicitly. There could be no need to charge the messenger not to break, or not to efface a mere impression within a folded letter, as it is previously described; and if that impression alone were sufficient to inspire belief, it was unnecessary for the messenger to require of Agamemnon to grant any further token. *Sphragis*, the word used in all these places, is placed by Julius Pollux amongst the synonimes of finger-ring seals, *Episêmoi daktylioi.*

coming to the door caught hold of the child and dragged him in with some little resistance. She exposed her person with evident caution, so that little more of her was distinguished than a pair of very beautiful arms. In the struggle with the child, however, this ring, which as it is a man's ring was probably too large for her finger, slipped off, and rolling near my foot stopped there, like a modest woman stooping to make a bow. I took an opportunity of picking it up unobserved, and finding that it bore the name of Rákshasa I brought it to your honour.

Chán. Sárangarava.

Enter PUPIL.

(*To Nipunaka.*) You may withdraw, now I have heard the story:
But before long your toils shall be rewarded.

Nip. As you command. [*Exit.*

Chán. Paper and ink! What shall I write? By this
Is Rákshasa to be subdued.

Enter a FEMALE SERVANT.

Serv. Victory to your Excellency!

Chán. (*apart*). I accept the omen.* (*Aloud.*) Sonottará, what news?

* Great importance is attached to the fortuitous expressions of individuals throughout these dramas, and a prosperous or unprosperous result anticipated from the thoughts or the words, by the person to whom they are addressed. The Greek plays are full of similar instances, and they are sufficiently abundant in every other department of classical literature. Cicero cites various curious examples in his book "De Divinatione." That related of Lucius Paulus is very analogous to the instance in the text. "Lucius Paulus the consul had been appointed to conduct the war against Perseus. On returning to his house in the evening he found his little daughter Tertia full of grief, and on asking her what was the matter, replied '*Persa (a puppy so named)* is no more.' Taking her up in his arms, and kissing her, the consul exclaimed, 'I accept the omen,' and the event corresponded with the expression." The effect of the omen seems also with the Hindus, as well as the Greeks and Romans, to have depended in a great measure upon a person's applying it, and signifying his acceptance of it. The phrase addressed to Chánakya is a customary one to princes and ministers, *Jayatu árya*, and it is

Son. His Majesty Sri Chandra has sent me, with his profound respects, to request your assistance in paying the final honours to Parvateswara; and it is his wish to make an offering to learned Brahmans of the jewels and valuable articles worn by that prince.

Chán. (*apart*). In all he meets my wishes. (*Aloud*) Go, Sonottará,

Inform the king his purpose is most fitting,
And should be speedily performed. As for the gems,
They are no doubt of cost, and should be given
Only to Brahmans of repute. Those I will send
When I have put their merits to the test,
To take the presents at his hands.

Son. I obey. [*Exit.*

Chán. Sárangarava, seek out Viswavasu,
Bid him and his two brothers from the king
Receive those gifts, and then repair to me.

[*Exit Pupil.*

What further purpose shall I give the letter?
My spies inform me, of the *Mlechcha* princes,
The chiefest five, or Chitravermá king
Of Kuluta—the king of Malaya, Nrisinha,
The lion-voiced—the monarch of Cashmir,
Brave Pushkaráksha—Sindhusena, prince
Of Saindhava, for enemies o'erthrown
Renowned; and powerful with his hordes of horse,
Meghák'hya—Párasika's sovereign;* these
Are friends of Rákshasa. I write their names;
Let Chitragupta† wipe them from the record.—

is rendered prophetic by Chánakya's assent, *Gríhítoyam Jaya sabda.* The word *jaya* (victory) is accepted. *Oionon* dekesthai, Omen arripere, and Sabdam Grihítum, are terms of similar import in the three languages.

* The position of Kuluta is not known; that of Malaya, the western Ghats, is very oddly introduced as a kingdom other than Hindu. *Saindhava,* is Sindh and Balochisthan; and *Párasíka,* Persia.

† The registrar of *Yama,* or the recorder of the dead.

No, not their names. It were as well to leave
Some indistinctness. Ho, Sárangarava.

Enter PUPIL.

I have bethought me—learned Brahmans write
Not always clearly. To Siddhárthaka
Convey these my instructions. (*Whispers.*) I myself
Will tell him for what purpose, and for whom
The note is meant, and who the writer is.
Let it be copied by Sakata Dás, and folded
In fashion of a letter, but not addressed;*
Nor let the writer know he writes for me.

Pup. As you direct. [*Exit.*

Chán. Malayaketu is o'erthrown!

Enter SIDDHÁRTHAKA.†

Sid. Victory to your Excellency! the letter is prepared.

Chán. Let me peruse it—Right,
Now sign it with this seal. (*Gives Rákshasa's seal-ring.*)

Sid. It is done. What else?

Chán. I would assign you
A business of great import.

Sid. I hold myself much honoured by the trust.

Chán. Go to the place of execution, give
The executioner a signal privily,
And then put on a most ungoverned fury.
Attack the officers, and they, prepared,
Will fly in seeming terror. They dispersed,
Untie the bonds that fasten Sakata Dás,
And with him shape your flight to Rákshasa.
He, for the preservation of his friend,
Will give you ample recompense, which you
Accept, and for a time remain his follower,

* Literally, "without any name being seen externally."

† In the conduct of the business this piece is inferior to its immediate predecessors, and bears most resemblance to the *Mrichchakati*.

Until the foes approach the city, when
This end must be contrived. (*Whispers.*)

Sid. As you command.

Chán. Sárangarava!

Enter PUPIL.

Bear the chief officers of justice* these,
The king's commands:—Arrest the *Bauddha* mendicant
Named Jivasiddhi; let it be proclaimed
He was commissioned here by Rákshasa,
And by the poisoned maiden has destroyed
The prince Párvataka. Be this duly cried,
And then he must be banished with each mark
Of contumely from the capital.
The scribe, too, Sakata Dás, whom Rákshasa
Stirs up to plot against the royal person,
Let him be seized! his crime proclaimed abroad;
Then bear him to the stake, and into bonds
Conduct his family.

Pup. It shall be done. [*Exit.*

Chán. Now shall Rákshasa be taken.

Sid. (*advancing*). I have taken—

Chán. (*apart*). Rákshasa; most true. (*Aloud*) Whom?

Sid.—Your highness's commands, and now depart
To give them action.

Chán. It is well. (*Giving him the letter and the ring.*)
Success attend you!

Sid. Such are your commands. [*Exit.*

Enter PUPIL.

Pup. The officers obey the orders of the king.

Chán. Now, child, go call the provost of the jewellers,
Chandana Dás his name.

Pup. I shall obey. (*Exit and returns with him.*) This way,
Provost,

* The *Kálapásika* and *Dandapásika*, the bearers of the noose of death and of punishment.

Chand. (*apart*). Chánakya's cruel nature gives alarm
To those who are not conscious of offending—
I have offended—what can I expect!
I have desired my friends, lest that my house
Be seized on by this tyrant, to remove
The family of Rákshasa, and now
I am prepared—what may befall me, may be.

Pup. Here, sir, is Chandana Dás.

Chand. Glory to your Excellency!

Chán. Provost, you are welcome: sit.

Chand. Excuse me, sir,
This ceremony suits not with the sorrow
In which the sufferings of my friends
Have left me. I will sit me down,
So please you, on the ground.

Chán. It must not be;
This distance needs not when with such as I am.
Here, take this seat.

Chand. If you will have it so.
(*Apart.*) What does he purpose?

Chán. Now, Provost, does your trade
Yield you due profit?

Chand. With your honour's patronage,
All trade must flourish, so of course must mine.

Chán. And do the people still recall to mind
The many virtues of their former lords,
When they comment on Chandragupta's vices?

Chand. I cannot hear such words. (*Stops his ears.*)
The virtues of his majesty afford
The soothing pleasures that autumnal moons
Diffuse.

Chán. It may be; but all kings expect
To meet from those they cherish some requital.

Chand. You need but speak it, sir, and any sums—
What monies may be needed?

Chán. You forget;
This is the reign of Chandragupta, not
Of Nanda. To his avaricious soul
Your treasures were acceptable; but now,
Your king esteems your happiness his wealth.

Chand. I joy to hear it.

Chán. You should rather ask
How best such happiness may be evinced.

Chand. Command.

Chán. 'Tis easy—let no man presume
To offer opposition to his sovereign.

Chand. What luckless wretch exists, who would pretend
To think of opposition! Does your grace
Know such a man?

Chán. Thou art the man.

Chand. Alas!
How should a blade of straw encounter flame?

Chán. Yet thus it is. Why, even now your house
Gives shelter to the family of Rákshasa,
The open enemy of Chandragupta.

Chand. This is untrue. Some base and secret foe
To me has brought this story to your ears.

Chán. You need not be alarmed. The miscreant servants
Of the late sovereign, when they fled the state,
Compelled by force the honest citizens
To give unwilling shelter to their families.
In this *they* are unblamed—the only act
That makes it an offence is its concealment.

Chand. I do admit that formerly, indeed,
The family of Rákshasa was thus
Lodged in my house.

Chán. This is again untrue:
Your former declaration would imply
They never found asylum in your mansion.

Chand. I own I was in this not quite sincere.

Chán. Such insincerity will now obtain

Its proper estimation—but deliver
The family of Rákshasa, and you may yet
Be held excused.

Chand. I have already said—
They *were* in my abode.

Chán. Where are they gone?

Chand. I do not know.

Chán. You do not know! Beware:
The hooded snake hangs over you, and far
Your hope of safety lies. As Vishnugupta
Will Nanda—(*checking himself*). What! merchant, can you be
So idle, as to cherish hopes that Rákshasa
Will triumph over Vrishala? Have you forgotten,
Fortune deserted Nanda in his life,
With all his power and warlike friends to back him?
Now she is steadily affianced—bound
To Chandra, as is moonlight to the moon;
And who shall think to sunder them? who so rash,
To thrust his arm into the lion's jaws,
And seek to tear away his pointed fangs,
Red as the twilight moon, stained with the blood
Of the fresh-slaughtered elephant?

Chand. (*apart*). These words,
Alas! too well events have justified.

(*A noise behind.*)

Chán. How now, Sárangarava, what has chanced?

Pup. The Bauddha beggar, Sir, named Jivasiddi, is banished from the city by order of the king.

Chán. A holy man—I mourn his fate: yet such
The treatment that the prince's foes deserve.
You mark, good Provost,—Vrishala resolves
To treat his enemies with just severity.
Take a friend's counsel, and give up the family
Of Rákshasa, then Chandragupta's favour
Will long be your's.

Chand. They are not in my dwelling.

(*A noise behind.*)

Chán. Again!—Sárangarava, what is this?

Pup. The scribe, Sir, Sakata Das, is led forth to be impaled.

Chán. So let him reap the fruit of disobedience.—
You see the king is stern. Believe me, Provost,
He will not brook your giving an asylum
To those who are his enemies. Resign them—
So you and yours shall yet escape with life.

Chand. What signs of fear do you behold in me,
To think I should be moved to sacrifice
Those I had sheltered, by the dread of death?
But I have said it—those you seek of me
I have not in my power. What more remains?

Chán. You hold to this?

Chand. I do.

Chán. (*apart*). 'Tis bravely spoken.
Who in this selfish world would lose the hope
Of affluence, and like *Sivi*,* thus discharge
The arduous task of generous self-devotion!
(*Aloud.*) This is your last resolve?

Chand. It is.

Chán. Expect the king's displeasure.

Chand. I am prepared—do with me as you please.

Chán. Sárangarava, bid the officers
Secure this miscreant. Hold! let them seize †
His house and family, and keep them close,
Till I impart this matter to the king:
He will, I know, command the forfeiture
Both of his wealth and life.

Pup. I shall obey—this way Provost.

* *Sivi* was a prince who, to save a dove from the pursuit of a hawk without prejudice to the latter, gave it a piece of his own flesh.

† This duty is assigned to the *Durga pálaka* and *Vijaya pálaka*, who should be military officers, if not proper names.

Chand. I attend. (*Apart.*) Happy that friendship's claim,
Not mortal frailty, terminates my life.
[*Exit.*

Chán. Now Rákshasa is safe; for when he learns
The faith and imminent danger of his friend,
Imperilled in his cause, he will, I know,
Be eager to prevent the sacrifice;
And ere he suffer that this merchant lose
His life for him, will offer up his own,
As much less precious than so dear a friend. (*Noise.*)
How now!

Enter PUPIL.

Pup. Siddhart'háka has rescued Sakata Dás, Sir, as he was about to suffer death, and they are fled together.

Chán. (*apart*). Our work is well begun. (*Aloud.*) Fled, say you?
Quick! boy, and order Bhágaráyana
To overtake and seize them.

(*Pupil goes out and returns.*)

Pup. Alas! Sir, he too has disappeared.

Chán. (*apart*). For our advantage. (*Aloud.*) Let him be pursued.
Where are the officers?*

Pup. They are overcome with terror; and Bhadrabhata and many other chiefs, I learn, Sir, were off this morning long before daylight.

Chán. (*apart*). They will promote our triumph. (*Aloud.*) Let them go.
We shall not miss them. Those who now have fled,
Had in their hearts deserted us. Let all
Who would abandon us be free to go:
I heed them not, whilst yet the mind is firm

* In the original, *Chánakya* names them: *Bhadrabhata, Purushadatta, Dingiráta, Balagupta, Rájasena, Rohitáksha, Vijayavermá;* and it may be observed, that they are names not of present currency, although Sanscrit. *Chánakya* also sends out to dispatch them after *Bhágaráyana* as before, a ceremony dispensed with in the translation.

That plucked down Nanda, and in which I feel
More powerful far than in a hundred hosts.
Let not my spirit fail, though left alone,
And we shall conquer. As for the fugitives,
They shall be seized and meet with their reward.
(*Apart*) Now, Rákshasa, I have you—I shall see you
Tame and submissive to my sovereign's will,
Caught by superior craft, though now you roam
Unshackled like the elephant, whilst yet
He ranges, high in blood, amidst the shades
And cooling torrents of his native woods.

[*Exeunt.*

END OF THE FIRST ACT.

ACT II.

Street before Rákshasa's House.

Enter Virádhagupta, *an agent of Rákshasa, disguised as a Snake-catcher.*

Those who are skilled in charms and potent signs may handle fearlessly the fiercest snakes.

Passenger. Hola! what and who are you?

Vir. A snake-catcher, your honour—my name is *Jírnavisha.* What say you, you would touch my snakes? What may your profession be, pray? Oh! I see, a servant of the Prince—you had better not meddle with snakes—A snake-catcher unskilled in charms and antidotes, a man mounted on a furious elephant without a goad, and a servant of the king appointed to a high station and proud of his success, these three are on the eve of destruction. Oh! he is off.

2d Pass. What have you got in your basket, fellow?

Vir. Tame snakes, your honour, by which I get my living. Would you wish to see them? I will exhibit them here, in the court of this house, as this is not a convenient spot.

2d Pass. This, you blockhead, is the house of Rákshasa, the prince's minister—there is no admittance for us here.

Vir. Then go your way, Sir: by the authority of my occupation I shall make bold to enter. So—I have got rid of him.

* 'Tis very strange—and what will be the end?
The efforts of my master, Rákshasa,
To shake the power of Chandragupta, fail,
Defeated by Chánakya's foresight: yet, methinks,

* In the original he changes his style from a low and difficult Prakrit to Sanscrit.

When I observe Malayaketu aided
By Rákshasa's high wisdom, I behold
The sovereign sway wrested from Chandragupta.
Fortune is bound to Maurya's cause with cords
Fast woven by Chánakya, yet the hand
Of Rákshasa seems often on the point
To snatch her from her bands. Between such foes,
Such masters of their craft, the cause of Nanda
Hangs in suspense, and fortune wavers—
Like a young female elephant, whose love
Two lordly males dispute, between these ministers,—
Doubting on which she shall confer her favour.
Well, time determines. Now to visit Rákshasa.

[*Exeunt.*

SCENE.—AN APARTMENT.

RÁKSHASA *with Attendants.*

Alas! my cares are vain: my anxious days
And sleepless nights are all of no avail,
Since like the house of *Yadu,** Nanda's race
Has perished utterly, exterminated
By powerful foes and unrelenting fate.
Now a new master claims my zealous service,
Not for the mercenary hope of fortune,
Nor coward apprehensions for my safety;
Not for the idle love of brief authority,
Nor in forgetfulness of former faith.
I serve this Lord, the better to effect
The fall of Nanda's enemies, and pay
The tribute of revenge his fame demands.
Oh Goddess lotus-throned!† dost thou so lightly

* The members of the family of *Yadu*, in which *Krishna* was born, were all destroyed upon the eve of his death or return to heaven, by intestine division and an affray amongst themselves, in which all the combatants were slain.

† *Lakshmi*, the Goddess of Fortune, appeared at the creation seated on a lotus amidst the waters.

Esteem desert, that Nanda is forgotten
And all thy favour lavished on his foe,—
On Maurya's ignominious son?*
Why, like the frontal juice, didst thou not perish,
That dries when falls the royal elephant.
Was there no chief of noble blood to win
Thy fickle smiles, that thou must elevate
A base-born outcast to imperial sway,—
And thus, with truly feminine caprice,
(For women are unsteady as the buds
That float in air), fly from exalted worth?
But I shall cure thee of this fleeting fancy,
By levelling the mansion of thy choice.
For this have I consigned my wife and child
To my friend's care, and when I fled the capital
Left them behind, that men may therefore deem
I cherish confident purpose to return
To them and to my home, and thus, the zeal
Of those who yet are faithful to the cause
Of Nanda, may not slacken by despair.
To Sakata Dás is ample wealth entrusted
To recompense our emissaries, sent
To work by craft the death of Chandragupta,
Or foil the secret malice of the foe;
And Jivasiddhi and some other friends,
Are nominated to convey intelligence
Of all that chances every instant to me.
What else can be devised? mine ancient lord,
Who for his own destruction kindly reared
A tiger's cub, and his illustrious race,
Are ever in my thoughts. I yet may strike
The savage that destroyed them to the heart,
With wisdom's shaft, if fate be not his shield.

* *Chándragupta* is here therefore the grandson, not the son of *Murá*.

Enter Jajáli, *the Chamberlain of* Malayaketu.

Health to your Excellency!

Rák. Jajáli, welcome: what has brought you hither?

Jaj. I come a messenger from the prince. Malayaketu grieves to see your Excellency so regardless of personal appearance; and without desiring you to be unmindful of your ancient monarch, he requests you will pay regard to his wishes. He therefore sends you these jewels, taken from his own person, and entreats your Excellency will wear them.

Rák. My worthy friend, apprise the noble prince,
The virtues of my former gracious lord
Are all forgotten in his highness' merits;
But that I must not decorate my person
Whilst I endure the deep humiliation
Of late discomfiture—nor till his foes
Are all exterminated, and I rear
His golden throne within the regal palace.

Jaj. This is an easy matter to your Excellency, therefore respect this first favour of the prince.

Rák. I do respect his orders, and your message:
The prince's will in this shall be accomplished.

Jaj. I take my leave.

Rák. I bow to you.

[*Exit Jajáli.*

Priyamvadaka, who waits to see me?

Priyamvadaka *enters with* Virádhagupta.

Rák. Who is this?

Priy. A snake-catcher, your Excellency.

Rák. (*feeling his left eye throb*).
What should this import? the sight of snakes, too—*
I have no pleasure in the exhibition;
Give him a donation, and let him go.

Priy. Here is for your pains; for not seeing—not for seeing.

Vir. Inform the minister, I beg of you, that besides exhi-

* An equally unlucky omen as the throbbing of the left eye.

biting snakes, I am a bit of a poet in the vulgar tongue. If I cannot have the honour of seeing him, request he will favour me by perusing this. (*Gives a paper.*)

Priy. He says, Sir, he is a poet as well as a snake-catcher, and requests your perusal of this paper. (*Gives it.*)

Rák. "The busy bee, that from each flower,
Extracts the nectary juice,
To fragrant honey all its store
Converts for others' use."*

(*Apart*) He means by this, he brings news from the capital,
The city of flowers. Who should this be—it is
Virádhagupta—such was his disguise.

(*Aloud*) Bid him approach—he is no vulgar bard,
And merits our encomium.

PRIYAMVADAKA *brings* VIRÁDHAGUPTA *forward.*

Rák. Priyamvadaka, I will see these snakes.
In the mean time, do you and your companions
Discharge your several duties.

Priy. We obey, Sir.

[*Exit with attendants.*

Rák. My friend Virádhagupta, sit you down.

Vir. As you command, Sir.

Rák. It grieves me to behold you thus;—how hard
A fate pursues the friends of Nanda!

Vir. Heed it not, Sir;
Your wisdom will ere long restore us all
To former fortune.

Rák. What news from Pushpapur?

Vir. I have much to tell, Sir: where shall I commence?

Rák. With Chandragupta's entry in the city.
Whate'er my agents since have done inform me.

Vir. You will remember, Sir, when in close league
United by Chánakya, Parvatéswara
And Chandragupta in alliance, led

* Sic vos non vobis mellificatis apes.

Their force against our city—a wild multitude
Of *Sakas, Yavanas,* and mountaineers ;
The fierce *Kámbojas,* with the tribes who dwell
Beyond the western streams,* and Persia's hosts,
Poured on us like a deluge.

Rák. Who shall dare
Assail the city whilst I breathe? Quick! line the walls
With archers—plant the elephants at the gates :
Let those who scorn a feeble foe, who thirst
For martial glory, and who fear not death,
Attend me to the field!

Vir. Compose yourself :
I merely speak of what has some while passed.

Rák. I had forgot myself; I deemed it present.
Yes,—well I recollect the inspiring trust
That Nanda then reposed in me. On me
His every hope relied ; and his affection,
Converting me to many like myself,
To every quarter threatened by the foe

* The *Sakas* of the Hindus cannot be other than the *Sacæ* or *Sakai* of classical geography. They are perpetually named in various works, and seem to have been known on the borders of India or in its western districts in the first century preceding Christianity. *Vikramáditya* king of Ougein being known as the *Sakári* or enemy of the *Sacæ,* his era dates B.C. 56, and it should appear that about this date, some northern tribes had settled themselves along the Indus, constituting the Indoscythi of Arrian. Their attempt to penetrate further to the east, by way of Kandesh and Malwa, was not improbably arrested by *Vikramaditya,* whence the epithet *Sakárí.* The term of *Yavanas* is in modern times applied to Mohammedans of every description, but in this instance, and in works prior to the Mohammedan era, some other people must be intended. The interpretation of the word by Sir W. Jones is, Ionians or Asiatic Greeks, and there are some considerations in its favour, although the chief argument in its behalf is the difficulty of attaching it to any other people. The mountaineers, or *Kirátas* may come from any part of India. They are known in classical geography as the *Cirrhadæ* or the *Cirrodes,* the latter in *Sogdiana,* near the Oxus. The *Kámbojas* are the people of the Arachosia, or north-eastern province of Persia. For the site of the *Báhíkas,* as they are termed in the text, we are indebted to the *Mahabhárat,* and the *Párasikas* speak for themselves.

His orders sent me—" Rákshasa, behold
Yon troop of elephants, like a black cloud,—
Disperse them.—Rákshasa, lead on those horse,
That bound like waves, and charge the foe's advance.—
Rákshasa, draw up the foot in firm array,
And drive them back."—Your pardon—pray proceed.

Vir. Beholding Pushpapura thus beleaguered,
And grieving for the sufferings of the people,
Servárthasiddhi, quitting further thought
Of opposition, private left the city,
And thence assumed the life of an ascetic.
Lorn of their lord, the warriors soon relaxed
Their efforts, and resistance ceased; and soon
The trumpets of the enemy proclaimed
Their triumph to unwilling ears. You, then,
Departed to maintain the realm of Nanda
In other provinces; devising means*
Intended Chandragupta to remove,
Which failing him, the mountain king destroyed.

Rák. So fate decreed, and turned aside the blow;
As *Vishnu* craftily contrived to ward
The shaft of *Karna* from the breast of *Arjuna*,
And speed it to *Hirimba's* son.† What then?

Vir. The prince Malayaketu was alarmed

* These means are designated in the text here, as well as in other places, and in other books, the *Visha Kanyá*, the Poison-Maid, which it would be more consonant to our ideas to consider as an effigy, but it appears to mean a female whose nature was charged with venom so that her embraces should prove fatal. The *Hitopadesa* says, Chánakya killed Nanda by means of a fatal emissary; and the author of the *Purusha Paríkshá*, a modern collection of tales in Bengali, taken chiefly from the Sanscrit, in giving a version of this story adds, that the damsel was so venomous that flies alighting on her person instantly perished.

† *Kerna* had received a lance from *Indra* which was fated to kill one individual, and which he kept, intending it for *Arjuna*. But *Ghatotkacha*, the son of *Bhima* by the *Rákshasí*, *Hirimbá*, having by the counsel and aid of *Krishna* become so formidable to the *Kuru* host as to threaten their destruction, *Kerna* was compelled to hurl the lance against him, and *Arjuna* thus escaped the peril.—(*Mahábhárat, Kerna Parva.*)

By this, his father's death, and quickly left
The camp. His father's brother, whom Chánakya
Persuaded that the monarch's death was not
His deed, or Chandragupta's, still remained
Confiding, and the entry of the foe
Of Chandragupta into Nanda's palace
Was solemnly proclaimed.

Rák. What then befell?

Vir. Chánakya called the architects together,
And gave them orders to prepare the palace,
With all expedient haste, for the reception
Of Chandragupta at the hour of midnight,
As by the aspect of the stars determined.
To this they answered, all should be made ready,
And that anticipating his desires,
Their provost, Dáruvermá, had completed
The decorations of the outer gateway;
The rest would soon be done. Chánakya praised
Their ready zeal, and promised Dáruvermá
His promptitude should meet its due reward.

Rák. Whence was Chánakya's satisfaction?
I deem that Dáruvermá's project failed
To work its end, or wrought an end unwished.
For such simplicity, such hasty service,
That would not wait the orders of Chánakya,
Could not have failed to rouse his strong suspicion.

Vir. At the hour of midnight
All was prepared; and at the moment fixed,
Vairodhaka and Chandragupta, seated
On the same throne, installed as equal kings,
Divided Nanda's empire.

Rák. Then to Vairodhaka the like partition
That bought the aid of Parvateswara
Was pledged?

Vir. It was.

Rák. A shrewd contrivance, truly!

To banish all suspicion, they had wrought
The death of Parvateswara, to quit
An ill-judged contract: other means were found,
No doubt, to rid them of this second dupe.

Vir. At the appointed hour,
Vairodhaka, as first inaugurated,
Entered the city. He was clothed in mail,
O'er which were thrown robes of rich dye, and strewn
With snow-white pearls* profuse; his brow was radiant
With the imperial fillet; the fragrant wreath
Flowed o'er his breast, and costly ornaments,
Cumbrous adorned at once and masked his person.
All thought him Chandragupta. He was mounted
On Chandragupta's elephant, and attended
By Chandragupta's guards to do him honour.
As he approached the gateway, Dáruvermá,
True to his faith and sharing in the error
That fancied Chandragupta present, stood
Prepared to let the temporary arch,
Contrived for such a purpose, fall upon him.
The princes who composed his train now reined
Their steeds and chariots, and alone Vairodhaka
Advanced upon his elephant. The driver,
Alike your servant, poor Berberaka,
Attempted then to draw from it's concealment
Within his golden stick the hidden dagger,
Provided for his need, and with the weapon
To stab him he supposed was Chandragupta.

Rák. Alas, untimely efforts both!

Vir. As forth
He stretched his hand to grasp the staff that hung
Suspended by a chain of gold, the elephant,

* *Hima vimala muktáguna*, "a string of pearls as pure as snow." This comparison is of too rare an occurrence to be looked upon as common-place, and it is an idea not likely to have occurred to a native of the South of India.

Who marked his arm extended, and imagined
The blow was meant for her, sprang quickly forward.
Her entrance in the gateway gave the signal
To loose the spring that stayed the impending arch—
It fell !—but crushed Berberaka, in act
To strike the blow, which shaken, missed his aim.
When Dáruvermá saw the driver slain,
The prince unharmed, and all the fraud revealed,
Despairing of his own escape, he seized
The iron bolt that had secured the arch,
And with it dashed Vairodhaka to earth.

Rák. Fruitless despair !—what was his fate ?

Vir. He fell
Beneath a shower of stones the prince's followers
O'erwhelmed him with, incensed.

Rák. We lose in him
A faithful friend—and what of our physician,
Abhayadatta ?

Vir. His tasks are all accomplished.

Rák. Is Chandragupta dead ?

Vir. No, Fate has saved him.

Rák. What meant your words ?

Vir. I will apprise your Excellency—
The poisoned draught had duly been concocted,
And would have been administered, but Chánakya,
In pouring it into a golden goblet,
Observed the colour change, and thus detected
The venomous admixture—then forbidding
The prince to taste it, ordered the physician
To swallow his own dose—and thus he died.

Rák. A learned man has perished. What has chanced
The chamberlain, Pramodaka ?

Vir. The same—
The sums you had entrusted to his charge
He lavished with unbounded prodigality,
Till such expenditure drew observation.

He answered incoherently the questions
Put to him as to his immense possessions,
And thus suspicion gaining confidence,
He was condemned, by order of Chánakya,
To suffer cruel death.

Rák. Fortune still balks our schemes.
What news of the brave men who were concealed
In the subterrene avenue that led
To Chandragupta's sleeping chamber—thence
To steal by night, and kill him as he slept?

Vir. They have sustained the fortune of the rest.

Rák. How so: were they discovered by Chánakya?

Vir. Even so—before the king retired to rest,
The watchful minister was wont to enter
The chamber, and with diligent scrutiny
Inspect it—thus he saw a line of ants
Come through a crevice in the wall, and noticed
They bore the fragments of a recent meal;
Thence he inferred the presence of the feeders
In some adjoining passage, and commanded
That the pavilion should be set on fire
That moment. Soon his orders were obeyed,
And our brave friends, in flame and smoke enveloped,
Unable to escape, were all destroyed.

Rák. 'Tis ever thus.—Fortune in all befriends
The cruel Chandragupta. When I send
A messenger of certain death to slay him,
She wields the instrument against his rival,
Who should have spoiled him of one-half his kingdom;
And arms, and drugs, and stratagems, are turned
In his behalf, against my friends and servants,
So that whate'er I plot against his power,
Serves but to yield him unexpected profit.

Vir. Yet let us on, Sir. What is once begun,
Is not to be abandoned. Obstacles foreseen
Deter the poor of spirit from an enterprize—

Some, more adventurous but not all resolved,
Commence, and stop midway; but noble minds
Like thine, by difficulties warmed, defy
Repeated checks, and in the end prevail.
A weary burden is the cumbrous earth
On *Sesha's** head, but still he bears the load.
Day after day the same fatiguing course
The sun pursues, yet still he travels on.
Shame mocks the man of elevated rank,
Who holds his promise light, like meaner creatures:
To him a law inflexible proclaims,
His faith once pledged, he can no more recede.†

Rák. You speak the truth—that which is once begun
Should never be relinquished. Well, what else?

Vir. Chánakya's vigilance was now increased
A thousand-fold, and every one suspected
Of enmity to Chandragupta, all
Your friends and kindred, found in Pushpapur,
Have been arrested.

Rák. Whom has he seized?

Vir. First, Jivasiddhi, the religious mendicant,
Him he has banished.

Rák. (*apart*). This is a slight affliction; one who owns
No children nor dependants. (*Aloud*) But what plea
Was urged for such a sentence?

Vir. That he supplied,
Employed by you, the poisoned emissary
That killed Párvataka.

Rák. (*apart*). Well done, *Kautilya*,
One seed bears double fruit with you--you lose
A sharer of your spoil, and heap on us
The infamy of his death. (*Aloud*) What more?

Vir. He then

* The many-headed snake on which the Earth is supposed to rest.

† It may be doubted if perseverance is any where recommended in a more manly and spirited tone.

Proclaimed, that Dáruvermá and the rest
Were bribed by Sakata Dás to kill the king,
And he was sentenced therefore to the stake.

Rák. Alas, how little fitting to my friend
So vile a death! Yet less art thou, who perishest
In a loved master's cause, to be lamented,
Than I, who still in vain survive the fall
Of Nanda's race—Go on, I am prepared
To hear the worst—what other friends have suffered?

Vir. In dread of what might happen, was your family
Removed to a more safe asylum.

Rák. Why were they not delivered to Chánakya?
Chandana Dás in this is much to blame.

Vir. He had been more to blame, had he betrayed
His friend.

Rák. Go on—

Vir. He faithfully refused
To yield his charge: Chánakya, then, incensed—

Rák. —Put him to death?

Vir. Not so; he had him seized,
With all his family, and thrown in prison.

Rák. Why then rejoicing tell me, that my family
Is in a safe asylum—rather say,
That I and mine are held in captive bonds.

Enter ATTENDANT.

Victory to your Excellency!—Sakata Dás is at the gate.

Rák. Is it possible?

Att. It is not possible for your Excellency's servants to imagine an untruth.

Rák. Virádhagupta, what is this?

Vir. Fortune relents, and has preserved our friend.

Rák. Why do you hesitate—admit him quick.

[*Exit Attendant, and returns with Sakata Dás followed by Siddhárthaka.*

Sak. Victory to the minister!

Rák. Welcome, my friend. I little hoped to see you,
Since you were honoured with Kautilya's notice.
(*Embraces him.*
How chanced this happiness—inform me?

Sák. This,
My friend Siddhárthaka dispersed my guard,
And bore me off in safety from the stake.

Rák. 'Twas bravely done. These ill repay such merit,
But favour us, and take them.
(*Gives him the jewels and ornaments off his person.*)

Sid. (*apart*). I must obey my lord Chánakya's orders. (*Falls at the feet of Rákshasa.*) Sir, I am grateful; but I am here a stranger, and know not what I shall do with these valuables. If your Excellency will allow it, I should wish to leave them in your treasury—they can be sealed with my seal.

Rák. Let it be so.

Sak. (*taking the seal*). What is this—your name, appears
Engraved upon the seal (*to Rákshasa*).

Rák. (*apart*). Alas! what's this I hear!
When I departed from the capital,
I left my wife this seal, to comfort her
Under my absence—how should it now have fallen
Into this man's possession! (*Aloud*) Say, Siddhárthaka,
How got you this?

Sid. I found it at the door of one Chandana Dás, a jeweller of Kusumapur.

Rák. 'Tis probable—

Sid. What, Sir?

Rák. —That seals like this are found
At rich men's doors.

Sak. My friend Siddhárthaka,
The name of Rákshasa appears engraved
Upon this ring; present it to the minister,
And be assured the gift will be rewarded.

Sid. Its acceptance is all the reward that I desire.

(*Gives.*)

Rák. My friend, this ring must be employed
In our affairs.

Sak. It shall be as you wish it.

Sid. May I presume?

Rák. Speak boldly.

Sid. I have deserved, as your Excellency knows, the enmity of Chánakya; I dare not return to Pátaliputra, and I should therefore hope to be allowed to remain at the feet of your Excellency.

Rák. I am well pleased you have forerun my purpose.

Sid. I am highly favoured.

Rák. Withdraw my friend (*to Sakata Dás*). Go, taste repose awhile,
With this your fellow traveller. [*Exeunt.*

Rák. Now then, Virádhagupta, to the rest
Of thine intelligence. How thrive the schemes
That we have set on foot to sow dissension
'Twixt Chandragupta and his followers?

Vir. Well—the chief accomplished, all the rest succeeds.

Rák. How so; what mean you?

Vir. This especially,—
That since Malayaketu was removed,
Chánakya has been slighted by the prince:
Whilst haughty with his triumphs, and disdaining
Superior rule, he frequent disobeys
The will of Chandragupta, who thence cherishes,
I much suspect, deep and augmenting anger.

Rák. Return, my friend, in this disguise. There dwells
At Pushpapur, the minstrel Stanakalasa;
He is with us—tell him, that Chandragupta
Should be informed, by stanzas well designed
To rouse his wrath, yet covert in expression,
Chánakya contravenes his high commands,
And spurns the king's authority. Should aught

Ensue, despatch a courier straight,
To bring me tidings here.

Vir. It shall be done. [*Exit.*

Enter ATTENDANT.

Att. Victory to your Excellency! Sakata Dás sends word, these three sets of jewels are arrived for sale. Will your Excellency examine them?

Rák. (*looking at them*). They are jewels of great price,
Tell him to make the purchase, at what cost
The seller may demand. [*Exit Attendant.*
I will send a courier to Kusumapur.
Chánakya and his prince will surely sever,
And then we reach our aim. Full well I know
That Maurya, in his pride, conceives himself
Supreme o'er all the monarchs of the world.
With equal arrogance, Chánakya vaunts.
This is my deed.—I made this man a king.
The one has gratified his vowed resentment,
The other reaped the fruit of his ambition.
No mutual interest now cements their council;
No acts of friendship bind them now together;
And once a breach, however slight, be made
In their alliance, 'tis dissolved for ever.

END OF THE SECOND ACT.

ACT III.

The Palace of Chandragupta at Pataliputra.

Enter Vaihínara, *one of the Royal Attendants.*

Ah—I feel I am no longer young!—Desire, you torment me in vain. Age has set his stamp upon my forehead: my limbs afford but tardy obedience to my will, and should the objects of sense be presented to my senses, their functions are disappointed by their incompetence to perform them. What ho!—Warders of the *Sugánga* palace, prepare the apartments for the reception of his Majesty, who is coming hither, to view from the lofty turrets, the city decorated as suits the festival of the autumnal full moon. What say you—the celebration is prohibited! By whom, I pray you? Why, you unlucky rogues, hold ye your lives so cheap?—away, despatch—suspend bright *chounris* from the glittering pillars, and let festoons of flowers, and wreaths of curling incense twine round the lofty columns. Sprinkle the earth with flowers and perfumed waters, to recover her from her fainting fit, as it were, at being so long debarred the lion-mounted throne. Quick, quick! the king approaches. He who in his tender years, faltering sometimes through humanity, but never failing through fatigue, now supports the weighty burthen of the earth, which has been hitherto sustained by his mighty and unquailing preceptor with nervous strength through the most arduous paths.

Enter Chandragupta *with Female Attendant.*

Chandra. How irksome are the toils of state to those
Who hold their tasks as duties.—Kings must leave
Their own desires, and for the general good,

Forego their own advantage. But to lose
My own for others' benefit makes me a slave;
And what should slaves know of sincere regard?
Fortune makes kings her sport, and vain the hope
To fix the fickle wanton in her faith.
She flies the violent, disdains the mild,
Despises fools, the wise she disregards,
Derides the cowardly, and dreads the brave.
My honoured minister and friend commands me
To wear the semblance of displeasure towards him,
And rule awhile without his guiding aid.
How can I act a part my heart disowns?
Yet 'tis his will, and he must be obeyed.
The pupil, worthy of the name, conforms
In all to his preceptor; if he stray
It is unwillingly—his teacher's voice
The goad that brings him back. Differing at once
From those who have no power of self-election,
And those who heed no pleasure but their own,
The wise and virtuous never know restraint,
For all they wish a sage preceptor sanctions.—
Vaihínara, conduct us to the palace.

Vai. This is it; please your majesty ascend;
Be careful.

(*Chandragupta mounts the terrace.*)

Chandra. How beauteous are the skies at this soft season!
Midst fleecy clouds, like scattered isles of sand,
Upon whose breast the white heron hovers, flows
In dark blue tides the many-channelled stream;
And like the lotus blossoms, that unfold
Their petals to the night, the stars expand.
Below is *Gangá* by the autumn led,
Fondly impatient, to her ocean lord,
Tossing her waves as with offended pride,
And pining fretful at the lengthened way.
But how is this? as city-wards I gaze,

I mark no note of preparation
That speaks the festive time. Vaihínara,
Did we not issue orders, that the capital
Should hold this festival with due solemnity?

Vai. Such were your Majesty's commands.

Chandra. Why disobeyed, then?

Vai. They demand obedience
From all the world—how should the citizens
Withhold compliance?

Chandra. What, then, is this I view!
Why is the city thus immersed in gloom:
Why do not sportive bands of either sex
Spread mirth and music through the echoing streets:
Why are not all the citizens with their wives
Abroad and merry making: why shine not
Their dwellings emulous with rival splendour,
No longer dreading public to display
Their affluence to their sovereign, not their tyrant?

Vai. The truth———

Chandra. Speak out.

Vai. —Your majesty has spoken.

Chandra. What mean you? be intelligible.

Vai. There is no merry making—'tis forbidden.

Chandra. Forbidden! How—by whom?

Vai. Forgive us, Sire;
Your servants have not courage to inform you.

Chandra. It could not be Chánakya?

Vai. Who should else
Have set so little value on his life,
As to oppose your Majesty's commands?

Chandra. A seat, Sonottará.

Vai. So please your Majesty,
This is the royal throne.

Chandra. Away, away—
I must this instant see Chánakya;—call him.

Vai. As you command. [*Exit.*

SCENE II.—CHÁNAKYA'S HOUSE,

Chánakya discovered seated.

It will not be—though Rákshasa persist
To thwart our projects and attempt to cast
The king, as I hurled Nanda, from his throne,—
His efforts are in vain. He does forget
That Chandragupta is not Nanda, cursed
With evil counsellors, proud and unjust.
Neither is Rákshasa, though rank and title
Confer similitude, Chánakya's equal.
I may discard these anxious thoughts. The prince
Malayakétu is enclosed with toils
That only wait the signal to secure him;
And Rákshasa himself is close surrounded
By friends supposed, in truth my spies and creatures.
There wants but this—the semblance of dissension
'Twixt me and Maurya's son.—His own device
Shall catch himself; his craft to disunite
Our league shall scatter ruin midst the foe.

Enter VAIHÍNARA.

The situation of a king's servant is one of no little vexation: he is not to stand in awe of his master alone, but of his master's minister; of the prince's noble associates and friends, and even of the companions of his lighter hours. Learned men call a life of servitude a dogged life,* and very justly; for a servant like a dog fawns and whimpers, and all for a morsel of meat. Tnis is Chánakya's house—a splendid mansion for a minister and sumptuously furnished. Here is a bit of stone for bruising cow-dung fuel; here is a bundle of holy grass† collected by the disciples—and the old walls, from which a thatched roof projects, are covered by a parcel of fuel stuck up to dry. Chandragupta merits such a minister. False

* *Sevám lághavakarmim Swavrittim viduh*—The term is applied by *Menu* to the service of a Brahman for hire.

† *Kusa, Poa Cynosuroides.*

flatterers laud a prince though he be good for nothing, and poverty compels many honest men to become false flatterers. Desire is a despotic emperor. Those who have no wants are your only freemen, and to them a monarch is no more than a whisp of straw. Ah! there is the minister. Glory to your grace! (*Kneels.*)

Chán. Vaihínara, what brings you hither?

Vai. His majesty whose feet are touched by gems
That gleam on regal diadems, declines
His forehead to your sacred feet, and begs
You will attend him speedily.

Chán. Indeed!
Attend him speedily! Has he heard, believe you,
That I forbade the purposed festival?

Vai. He has.

Chán. (*angrily*). Who had the daring to inform him?

Vai. Pray you, Sir, be patient:
The king himself perceived it from the terrace
Of the *Sugánga* palace.

Chán. By you he was inflamed to wrath against me.

Vai. (*remains silent*).

Chán. Yes; well I know, the servants of the monarch
Bear me but little love. Where is the king?

Vai. At the *Sugánga* palace.

Chán. Lead me thither. [*Exeunt.*

Scene III.—The Palace again.

Chandragupta seated on the throne.

Enter Chánakya *and* Vaihínara.

Vai. So please your grace, ascend.

Chán. (*ascending the terrace sees Chandragupta. Apart*)
He fills the seat of kings.—Why, this is well:
The throne, the race of Nanda has abandoned,
Now bears a prince who well becomes the state
Of king of kings—my cares are all rewarded,
(*Chandragupta descends and falls at Chánakya's feet.*)

Chán. Arise, my son.
And may thy regal feet absorb the beams
Shot from a thousand diadems, as bend
Before thee in subjection and humility,
The crowned brows of tributary kings—
Whether they sway the shores of southern seas,
Whose depths are rich with many coloured gems,
Or rule the realms where Gangá falls in showers,
Cold on Himála's ice-encrusted brow.

Chandra. So will it be whilst I retain your favour,
Whate'er my wish affect.—I pray you sit.

Chán. (*seated*). Now, Vrishala, what means this urgent summons?

Chandra. To gain the pleasure of your honoured presence.

Chán. Enough of this—kings do not call their servants
From weighty cares on insufficient grounds:
Declare the cause.

Chandra. Your excellency's orders
Inhibiting our festival.

Chán. For this
You would reprove me?

Chandra. Nay, not so, Sir;
I merely seek to be informed.

Chán. 'Tis well.
But 'tis a pupil's duty, to be ready
To acquiesce in acts that he may think
Demand inquiry.

Chandra. No doubt. But I am sure,
The measures that must claim my acquiescence
Are not without their reason, and 'tis that
I beg to know.

Chán. You rightly judge me, Vrishala;
Chánakya never acts, even in his dreams,
Without due motives.

Chandra. Those I wish to hear.

Chán. Have you not read, all public acts possess
A threefold source, and from the king, the minister,
Or both conjointly emanate. What I have done,
Is done by virtue of the state I hold;
And to inquire of me why I did it,
Is but to call my judgment or authority
In question, and designedly affront me.
(*Chandragupta turns away as if offended.*)

Music behind.

First Bard. Like *Siva's* ashen whiteness, autumn bears
The budding grass,* and like the foul hide wears
The dun clouds,† scattering from the silver beams
Of the bright moon—that in mid azure gleams,
As on his polished brow‡—
Above, below,
O'er all, they twine;
More brilliant than around his neck the line
Of the skull-woven chaplet§—see—on high,
Yon row of swans sail laughing through the sky,

* *Siva* is represented with his person powdered with the greyish white ashes of burnt cow-dung, termed *Vibhuti*, which is consequently used in a similar way by all the *Saiva* and by many of the *Vaishnava* ascetics. The season of autumn, or that following the rains, is said to be invested with a similar whiteness, from the *kása* grass, or *saccharum spontaneum*, with which the country along the Ganges, and the banks of rivers in general, are overspread at this period. This grass grows from ten to fifteen feet high, and the base of the flowers is surrounded with an immense quantity of bright silver-coloured wool, which whitens all the fields.

† Part of *Siva's* scanty raiment is the skin of an elephant, or more properly of an *Asura* or Titan killed by him under that form, and thence named *Gajásura*. To this the autumnal clouds, no longer deeply laden with the dews of a tropical climate nor yet wholly discharged of their waters, are not unaptly compared.

‡ *Siva*, as has been mentioned on various occasions, wears the crescent moon upon his forehead.

§ A necklace of sculls adorns the neck of *Siva* in his terrific forms.

The Godhead's pearly smile.*—May Autumn,† clad
In *Siva's* semblance, thus like him make glad
The hearts of men. May *Vishnu's* shrinking glance
Yield peace and joy—as, waking from his trance,
His opening eyes are dazzled by the rays
From lamps divine, that blaze,
And from the gems
That burn upon their stems:
Those eyes, that with long slumber red,
Ambrosial tear-drops shed,
As pillowed on his snake-couch mid the deep
He breaks reluctant from his fated sleep.‡

Second Bard. Shall monarchs mighty o'er innumerous bands
Allow their slaves their hests to disobey?
Shall the gaunt lion suffer puny hands
To rend his talons and his fangs away?
Is that god-given strength to be reviled
From *Brahmá* that proceeds,
And upon earth on kings alone conferred;
Or on the monarch of the wild,
The elephant, who leads
Through shady groves and dells his fierce, yet subject herd?
What makes a monarch, not his throne, his crown—
But men to work his will—to tremble at his frown.

* It is a curious common-place in Hindu poetry, to compare a smile to objects of a white colour, originating perhaps in the striking contrast between the teeth and the complexion, which give to the former when displayed in a laugh additional whiteness.

† The season of *Sarat*, or the two months *Aswin* and *Kártik* (from September to November), which follow the periodical rains.

‡ At the intervals of the minor destruction of the world *Vishnu* is represented as reposing himself upon the serpent *Sesha*, amidst the waters by which the earth is overspread. He also takes a nap of four months' duration from the 11th of *Ashárh* to the 11th of *Kártik*, or about the middle of June to the middle of October, or from the time the periodical rains usually commence till their termination, and it is to his awakening from this last slumber, as most apposite to the season, that the *Vaitálika*, or Bard, alludes.

Chán. (*meditating.*) What do these strains import? The first conveys
A simple benediction; but the second
Has deeper meaning. Ha! is it e'en so?
It must be: Rákshasa; thy hand is here:
But 'tis too palpable. Chánakya wakes!

Chandra. Vaihínara,
Reward those stanzas with a thousand pieces.*

Vai. I shall obey your majesty.

Chán. Hold, hold! Vaihínara. [*To Chandragupta.*
What has deserved such prodigal bounty?

Chandra. If thus my lightest mood is to be canvassed
And thwarted by your excellency, my kingdom
Is but a prison to me.

Chán. It is ever thus
When monarchs reign with delegated sway.
If I displease you, take into your hands
Your own authority.

Chandra. We shall do so.

Chán. I am content, and gladly shall return
To humbler cares.

Chandra. Yet we would first be told
Why you forbade the wonted festival;
Or whether worthier motives prompted you,
Than the proud thought to contravene our will.

Chán. Why deem I wish to contravene your orders?
What other hands have hung them, as a wreath
Of newly-gathered flowers, upon the neck
Of prostrate princes—those, whose rule extends
As far as to the boundaries that girt
The black and tossing waters of the main.

Chandra. What else could urge you?

Chán. I shall inform you.
Sonottará, request the scribe to give you

* In the original, a hundred thousand *suvernas:* the number is a favourite donation, and is put, in fact, for any considerable sum.

The scroll I trusted to his care.

[*Exit Sonottará and returns with the paper.*

Son. 'Tis here, Sir.

Chán. Your Majesty will please to pay attention.
(*Reads*) "The chieftains late attached to Chandragupta
And now deserted to Malayaketu.—
First, Bhadrabhatta, governor of the elephants;
Purushadatta, master of the horse;
Then Hingaráta, nephew of the chamberlain;
His highness Balagupta, the king's cousin;
The tutor of the young prince, Rájaséna;
The general's younger brother, Bhágaráyana;
His highness Rohitáksha, prince of Malwa;
And lastly, Vijayavermá, chief by birth
Of all the warrior tribe."

Chandra. Why have they fled?

Chán. The masters of the elephants and horse,
Neglecting their high charge for wine and wassail,
Had been displaced, and though allowed such means
As their late rank demanded, such reduction
But little pleased the chieftains, and they left us
To seek the service of the enemy.
'Twas avarice urged the nephew of the chamberlain,
And even your Majesty's kinsman, to desert:
They sold their faith. The tutor of the prince,
Whom with most lavish benefits your Majesty
Had ever recompensed, conceived a dread,
The bounties showered upon him would ere long
Be by your hand resumed; and, to retain
The wealth he merited so ill, he fled.
For Bhágaráyana, friendship of old
Attached him to the sire, and this regard
Extending to the son; his councils snatched
Malayaketu timely from our grasp.
Awhile he tarried; but of late observing
Your highness' policy secured your foes,

His conscious treason warned him of his peril
And counselled his escape; he fled, and now
Is high in favour with Malayaketu,
Who grateful for his aid, and in remembrance
Of that affection which he showed his father,
Has nominated him his minister.
The prince of Malwa, and the Kshetriya chief,
Disdained the elevation of your kin
To rank competing with their own, and hence
Their flight. Your doubts are now, I trust, removed.

Chandra. And yet methinks 'tis strange—the principles
That influenced these nobles known so well,
Nought was devised to stop their purposed flight.

Chán. What means could prudent policy suggest?
Favour already had been tried in vain,
And vainly would have bribed their future faith;*
While force had brought your new-got power in peril,
Opposed to their adherents, joined by those
Who lurk the covert enemies of your reign.
'Tis well they are from hence—but thus assisted,
And further aided by barbaric hosts,
Malayaketu purposes to march
And storm us in our capital. Is this
A time for frivolous merriment?—a time
To muster men, repair our shattered walls,
To toil in arms, not idle in festivity.

Chandra. I marvel much, that foresight so profound
As still your councils evidence, allowed
The only cause of all these causeless fears,
Malayaketu, to escape our power.

Chán. Why needed it prevention? Our sole means
To countercheck his flight, had been to cast
His person into bonds, or to have yielded him,
As plighted to his sire, your kingdom's moiety.—

* This passage is compressed, the original again particularizing each individual.

His thraldom had exposed us to men's censure,
For violence and deep ingratitude:
And to but little purpose had our hands
Removed the mountain monarch from his claim,
Had we conceded empire to his son.—
These reasons moved me to permit his flight.

Chandra. And yet you suffered, seemingly unnoted,
The stay of Rákshasa within our capital.

Chán. I would not give it public note. His friends
Were many, of fidelity approved,
Devoted to his will, inflexibly attached
By his own worth and by long service to him.
All, too, that cherished Nanda's memory,
Made common cause with him, and his vast wealth
Secured adherents numerous and brave.
Provided with these hostile means, he long
Maintained a dangerous ferment in the capital,
But like a barbed arrow from a wound
By dexterous sleight extracted, he was driven
At length to quit the city, and remote,
Wage an avowed and less alarming enmity.

Chandra. Why not arrested and by force detained?

Chán. The act had led to blood—and Rákshasa
Had perished in the desperate attempt
To make him captive living, or had wrought
Escape by the destruction of your friends:
Either alike to be lamented. No!
'Tis craft that snares the monarch of the woods,
And stratagem alone must win us Rákshasa.

Chandra. 'Tis shrewdly argued, but the truth is clear,
And you must own in Rákshasa a master.
Although the city was our own, this foe
Abandoned not his home: treading disdainfully
Upon our very throats, he echoed back
Our clamorous shouts of triumph with defiance,
And laughed all threats and stratagems to scorn.

Oh! none but those who boast unquestioned worth
Deserve our trust—not the mere partial friends,
Whom prosperous fate attaches to our cause.

Chán. 'Twere wise in you to give your trust to Rákshasa;
He, who would drive you from your throne, as I
Expelled the sons of Nanda,—who would raise
Malayaketu to that throne, where I
Have seated you.

Chandra. 'Tis fate I thank—no mortal—for my sceptre.

Chán. Illiberal and ungrateful! Who but I
Vowed and achieved the downfall of my foes?
Whose hand but mine unloosed these angry locks
Portending wrath and fate? What other arm
Destroyed inexorable all the race
Of Nanda, o'er a hundred kings supreme?
Like beasts I felled them; and this vaunted statesman,
This Rákshasa, looked on.
From numerous pyres, and undisturbed, the smoke
Spread a long veil of clouds beneath the sky,
And blurred the light of day; expectant flights
Of vultures hovering o'er the darkness, clapped
Their wings with hope, and gibbering spectres snuffed,
Exultingly, the exhalations borne
Aloft by flames, whose sullen fierceness fed
Upon the marrow and the flesh of kings.

Chandra. The hapless race of Nanda were destroyed
By adverse destiny.

Chán. Thus, shallow mortals
Ascribe whatever ill betide to fate.

Chandra. Wise men refrain from idle vaunts.

Chán. Enough!
I understand you. Vrishala, you seek
To trample on me as a slave. My hand
Hurries to set my braided locks at liberty,
And my impatient foot again would stamp
The confirmation of a second vow.—

Beware how you arouse those slumbering flames
That Nanda's fall has scarcely yet appeased.

Chandra. (*apart*). Is he indeed incensed! Methinks the earth
Shakes, apprehensive of his tread, recalling
The trampling dance of *Rudra*; from his eye,
Embrowned with lowering wrath, the angry drops
Bedew the trembling lashes, and the brows
Above are curved into a withering frown.

Chán. Here break we off; I will no more contend.
If Rákshasa be better worthy trust,
If he be my superior give him this.

[*Throws down his ministerial dagger.**

This is indeed his triumph! Well he knew,
Could he remove Chánakya, he should soon
Achieve a victory over Maurya's son.
His ends are all accomplished: the dissension
He sought to rouse has risen. Yet, miscreant, yet
Thy scheme malign shall only yield thee shame!

[*Exit.*

Chandra. Vaihínara, apprise our court, the Brahman
Chánakya is dismissed, and we ourselves
Henceforth conduct the functions of the state.

Vai. (*apart*). Chánakya out of office! this is strange:
Not mine however to condemn his majesty.
'Tis a sufficient fault in any minister
To be dismissed. The elephant is termed
A vicious beast who frequent quits his path,
Although his awkward driver goads him from it.

Chandra. What do you murmur?

Vai. Nothing, your Majesty. I but observed,
That now your Majesty is king indeed. [*Exit.*

Chandra. (*apart*). Our own immediate followers deceived,
My great preceptor's project cannot fail.

* The original has simply, weapon, "*sastram.*" A dagger of a particular shape is the official weapon, however, in modern Hindu courts.

(*Aloud*). Sonottará, this wearisome contention
Has quite o'erpowered me—lead me to my chamber.
(*Apart*) Although 'tis in obedience to his will
I have put on this show of disrespect,
My mind is ill at ease.
Oh, how can those, who have indeed provoked
The awful anger of their sacred guide,
Survive the terrors of such dread displeasure!

[*Exeunt.*

END OF THE THIRD ACT.

ACT IV.

THE HOUSE OF RÁKSHASA.

Enter COURIER.

A hundred *yojanas* and more, out and back again, are no slight matter, and no one would have thought of such a thing, only that my master's commands were peremptory to travel without stopping. Now, then, to the minister's residence. Holoa! where is the warder, to apprise his excellency that his courier Karabhaka, like a camel in speed, has returned from Pátaliputra?—What ho!

Enter WARDEN.

Gently, gently, my friend!—his excellency, exhausted with fatigue and watching, is troubled with a violent headache, and is not yet risen—so, wait awhile, till I find an opportunity of informing him you are returned.

Cour. Very well, take your own time. [*Exeunt.*

RÁKSHASA *discovered on his couch—Sakata Dás asleep on a chair.*

Rák. It will not be—sleep flies me—nor the change
Of night or day short intermission brings
From wakeful care; whilst fate continues adverse,
And aids the crooked projects of Chánakya.
Such task is mine as on dramatic bard
Devolves—to fix the object of the action,
Develope fitting incidents, uprear
Fruit unexpected from self-pregnant seeds,
Dilate, condense, perplex, and last reduce
The various acts to one auspicious close.

Enter WARDEN.

Glory to your excellency !*

Rák. Your news ?

War. The courier, Karabhaka, from Pátaliputra is returned, and is desirous of being admitted to your presence.

Rák. Haste, bid him enter.

War. (*without and returns*). He is here, Sir.

Rák You are welcome—sit.

Cour. As you command. [*They retire.*

Enter an ATTENDANT *on Malayaketu, bearing a staff.*

Stand apart : stand out of the way. Know you not, my masters, the vulgar are not admitted to the sight of kings and Brahmans of high rank. Out of the way !—his Highness the prince Malayaketu approaches, on his road to visit the minister Rákshasa who is indisposed. Away, away ! [*Exit.*

Enter MALAYAKETU *with* BHÁGURÁYANA *and an Attendant.*

Mal. Nine months have o'er us passed, since that sad day
My father perished, and his spirit still asks
His funeral honours—the revenge I vowed,
But which, scarce meriting the form of man,
I hesitate to pay. To beat the breast
To rend the vesture, to discard all ornament,
To scatter ashes on the humbled head,
And utter groans and sighs,—these are the shows
Of feminine despair, to be exacted
From the afflicted partners of my foes,
As a fit offering to my father's ghost—
This were a proof of filial grief and love,
And still withheld, admits no more delay.
I will take up the brave man's load, and tread
The fatal path my sire has gone, or dry

* There is some inauspicious juxta-position of expressions here between Rákshasa and the Door-keeper, which cannot well be translated even if worth translating.

My mother's tears, exchanged for bitter showers
The wives of slaughtered enemies shall shed.
Jajáli, let the princes who attend us
Here halt awhile; alone, we would receive,
And unannounced, the welcome of our minister.

Jajáli. (speaking as to persons without).
Princes and potentates, his Highness orders
That none shall follow him; here halt awhile.
(To the Prince)
They have obeyed, Sir, and like ocean's waves,
Pass not the bounds assigned. The steed short-reined
Curves his proud neck and paws the passive air,
As if to spurn the skies: the stately elephant
Stops sudden, and the music of his bells
Is on the instant mute.

Mal. You and my train
Fall off, and none but Bhágaráyana
Attend me to the minister.

Jajáli. Your Highness is obeyed. [*Exit with followers.*

Mal. My valued friend, the nobles who have late
Abandoned Chandragupta, and transferred
To us their faith and service, have declined
The mediation of our minister Rákshasa;
And rather by the surety of our general
Proffer their fealty. They justify
Their flight from Chandragupta, that they found him
The puppet of his minister Chánakya,
Whose arrogant sway they longer scorn to brook,
And therefore with their followers withdrew
From an unworthy lord, to choose us worthier
Their plighted troth. This I can comprehend;
But that they should refuse the guarantee
Of one so wise, so brave, and so approved
A servant and a friend, as Rákshasa,
Does somewhat, I confess, move my surprise.

Bhag. And yet, methinks, their motives are not hard

To scan, and haply may be thus expounded.
'Tis true, that Rákshasa has ever seemed
Your Highness' faithful friend; but 'tis well known,
Chánakya is the object of his emnity,
Not Chandragupta. Should, then, the prince
Discard the haughty minister, no more
Might Rákshasa affect your Highness' interests.
Nay, 'tis surmised, should such event betide,
That from the love he bears the stock of Nanda,
Of which this Chandragupta is a scion,
He may be tempted to desert our cause
And join the enemy, who, in regard
Of old hereditary ties,* no doubt,
Will gladly welcome Rákshasa again.
In prudent fear of such vicissitude,
These valiant chieftains have declined the surety
Of Rákshasa, lest from his veering faith
Their own fidelity become suspected.
'Tis thus that I conceive of their objections.

Mal. 'Tis plausibly interpreted.—Let us on
And seek the minister.

Bhag. This is his dwelling:
So please your Highness enter.

RÁKSHASA *and the* COURIER—MALAYAKETU *and* BHÁGURÁYANA *behind and unobserved.*

Rák. Now tell me, friend; you went to Kusumapur,
And saw the bard to whom you were addressed?

Cour. I did, Sir.

Mal. They talk of Kusumapur. Hold back awhile,
And listen to them unobserved; for courtiers
Disguise unwelcome truths, when to their masters

* The history of modern India, and the records of inscriptions some centuries back, shew that the office of minister was frequently hereditary, and that the lines of king and premier ran collaterally through several generations. It is this connexion to which the original refers.

They bear intelligence, but when in private
They speak their honest thoughts.

Rák. And have we speeded?

Cour. Such is your grace's fortune.

Rák. How, let me hear?

Cour. Agreeably to your Excellency's commands, I set off with all speed for Kusumapur; there finding Stanakalasa the Bard, I communicated to him my instructions.

Rák. Proceed.

Cour. It so chanced, that at the period of my arrival, Chandragupta purposing to win popularity with the citizens, issued orders that the autumnal festival should be held with usual celebration. The gratifying tidings spread rapidly throughout the capital, and the people welcomed it with as much rapture as a man feels when he meets with a kinsman.

Rák. Alas, lamented Nanda, moon of monarchs,
How, reft of thee, should autumn's moonlight shed*
Delight upon the nations!—What ensued?

Cour. Whilst the expectation of the people was at its height, the festival was suddenly prohibited by the villainous Chánakya, much to their disappointment; and Stanakalasa availed himself of this opportunity to recite some stanzas, calculated to rouse Chandragupta's indignation.

Rák. 'Twas seasonably done. The seed is sown,
And in due time shall bear the fruit of discord.
The very vulgar brook impatiently
The sudden interruption of their pastimes;
And shall a king, of nature uncontrolled
And spirit lofty as his state, submit
To such degrading check? impossible!
He must and will resent it.—Pray proceed.

Cour. Chandragupta was highly incensed at this opposition to his commands, and after bestowing many praises on your excellency's merits, he dismissed Chánakya from his station.

* The original has some quibbling upon the words Chandra and Chandratwa, the moon and its nature, or Chandragupta and moon-like lustre.

Mal. (*behind.*) Indeed, does Chandraguptá prize so high
The worth of Rákshasa?

Bhag. He shews much less
The rate at which he holds it, by his praise,
Than by his thus discarding so abruptly
His minister Chánakya.

Rák. Yet, methinks,
The prohibition of a popular festival,
Were insufficient reason to exite
The wrath implacable of Chandragupta
Towards Chánakya.

Mal. It is enough, methinks—
Why seeks he other motives?

Bhag. He opines,
Chánakya were too wise to be displeased
With Chandragupta for a trivial cause,
And that the prince would scarce prove so ingrate
To one whom he may thank for his dominion,
As to forget the deference that is due
To his preceptor; therefore, if the breach
Be cureless, it must spring from graver source.

Cour. There were other causes, your excellency, that moved Chandragupta to wrath.

Rák. What were they?

Cour. The escape of the prince Malayaketu, and the evasion of your excellency, with both which the prince reproached Chánakya.

Rák. (*to Sakata Dása*).
What ho, my friend, awake, awake, we triumph:
I have my hand on Chandragupta now.*

Sak. (*awaking.*) How, are your family arrived, your friend
Chandana Dás at freedom, and the rest
Escaped from apprehension?

Bhag. (*apart.*) It is true—
They now indeed are free from all anxiety.

* The expression is literally, he is now under my hand.

Mal. "I have my hand on Chandragupta now"—
What should these words of Rákshasa import?

Bhag. What else, but that Chánakya now removed,
He counts the regency of Chandragupta
Already in his grasp.

Rák. Heard you, my friend,
Whither the minister, dismissed, retired?

Cour. At present, Sir, he remains in Pátaliputra.

Rák. He has not sought the forest dwelling then?
What, does he meditate another vow?

Cour. It was rumoured, that he purposed to depart and end his days in the woods.

Rák. I deem this little probable.
What think you, friend? (*to Sakata Dás.*) Will he, who so resented
Removal from his seat, though by a king,
Who like an earthly *Indra* ruled, commanded,
Patient endure expulsion from authority
By one whom he himself created king?

Mal. What is to him Chánakya's forest dwelling?

Bhag. Methinks 'tis much—he holds his aim secure,
As long as lives Chánakya far removed
From Chandragupta.

Sak. (*to Rákshasa.*) What need further doubt:
It cannot be that Maurya, who has placed
His foot on prostrate kings, and proudly trod
On moony diadems, should bear contempt
And insult from a servant; and though Chánakya
Be of obdurate temperament, he knows
What pains one vow has cost him, and may pause
Ere he again indulge his fiery nature
To weigh the turns of ever slippery fortune.

Rák. You rightly judge—I will be satisfied.
Go, lead this faithful messenger within,
And let him taste repose.

Sak. I shall obey. [*Exit with Courier.*

Rák. Now to the prince.

(*Going he is met by* MALAYAKETU *and* BHÁGURÁYANA *advancing*).

Mal. Behold him here, my lord.
I come to save your excellency trouble.

Rák. To do me honour. Please your highness sit.

Mal. I trust the indisposition that ere while
Afflicted you is now subdued?

Rák. Impossible,
Until the style of Highness, howe'er graced
By your high bearing, be exchanged for that
Of Majesty, more fitted to your worth.

Mal. Tis long
Your excellency has promised such a change
Is feasible—when will it be effected?
We gather here a formidable host,
Who burn to march against the foe.

Rák. Proceed.
The hour is come—conduct them forth to conquest.

Mal. What are our hopes—what tidings of the enemy?

Rák. He has sustained a heavy blow.

Mal. Explain.

Rák. Discord has risen 'twixt the prince and minister,
And severs Chandragupta from Chánakya.

Mal. No mighty loss, methinks, to lose a minister.

Rák. To other princes none—but a main wound
To Chandragupta.

Mal. Less to him than others.

Rák. How so?

Mal. The proud deportment of Chánakya
Excited general disaffection. Now,
He gone, the minds of men will reassume,
With whetted zeal, affection to their prince.

Rák. Not so—there are two parties in the state,
The friends of Chandragupta or of Nanda.
The arrogance of Chánakya may have proved
Distasteful to the former; to the latter

It nought imported. They beheld alone
The base ingratitude of Chandragupta,
Who could abet and aid the murderous plot,
That his own kinsmen and his benefactors
Consigned to death. For this their scorn and hate
Pursue him unrelenting, though he boast
The name and sway of king, and though the many
Conceal their sentiments, whilst unassured
Of safety from his power. Let them observe
A prince of potency advance his arms
Against the tyrant, they will not be tardy
To join his banners, and proclaim their enmity
By overt acts. Such they behold in you,
Their hope and their protector, and already
They frequent seek asylum in your tents.

Mal. Yet, is the minister's disgrace the sole
Inducement to advance? I apprehend
There may be other reasons.

Rák. Such there are:
But this the chief.

Mal. Has Chandragupta none
Among his servants, able to supply
The vacant charge; or if upon himself
He take the load, may he not still defy us?

Rák. He cannot.

Mal. How so?

Rák. Be pleased, Sir, to take note:
The weighty cares of state are jointly borne
By ministers and kings—or kings alone.
Not so with Chandragupta: inexpert
Of wordly business, he devolved all charge
Upon his minister—all in all to him,
As to a blind man is his trusty guide.
Fortune, impatient of divided pains,
Must, where a king and minister dispute
Her favours, one for other wholly fly.

And the unpractised prince, who nothing knows
Of kingly rule, can no more hope to govern
His empire with prosperity, deprived
Efficient counsel, than the babe receive
Due nutriment, denied his nurse's breast.

Mal. (*apart*) 'Tis well I am not so dependent. (*Aloud.*) Yet,
To an invader, you must be aware,
Some weightier motives need, than the dismissal
Of the most sapient minister.

Rák. In this
There needs no more. But let your highness weigh
These circumstances also, which concur
To urge your march—your forces are collected;
Yourself, the heir legitimate of kings;
Your adversary but a base usurper.
His very capital is hostile to him.
In me you have—(*checking himself*) a faithful guide at least;
And all appliances and means to boot
Provided; nought remains but your command.

Mal. Then let us march. Our mighty elephants
Shall drink the Soan's dark waves, and echo back
The roaring of its waters—spread through the groves
That shade its bordering fields, intenser gloom;
And faster than the undermining torrent,
Hurl its high banks into the boiling stream;
Then rolling onwards like a line of clouds
That girts in rain and thunder Vindhya's peaks,
Environ with portentous storm the city,
And lay its proud walls level with the ground.

[*Exit with Bháguráyana.*

Rák. Who waits?

(*Enter* ATTENDANT.)

Whatever Soothsayer* attend,

* A belief in judicial astrology has prevailed throughout the East from the earliest periods on record to the present day.

Command approach.

(*The Attendant goes out and returns.*)

So please you, Sir, the *Bauddha* mendicant
Is here.

Rák. A *Bauddha* mendicant the first encountered !*

Att. 'Tis Jivasiddhi, Sir.

Rák. Let him assume a not revolting semblance,
And bid him enter.

The Attendant goes out and returns with JIVASIDDHI, *a Kshapanaka.*

Jiva. The precepts of the holy Saints† should ever be obeyed,
By virtue of whose cooling drugs is passion's heat allayed:
Whose healing skill a bitter portion here on earth has given,
That afterwards a sweet succeed, and man find health in heaven.
May the faithful ever know
Virtuous increase here below.

Rák. Now tell me, Sage,—is this a day auspicious
For men to undertake a distant journey ?

Jiva. (*after meditation*).
The aspects are viewed.
The conjunctions are good:
Or by noon will decline

* An unlucky omen; to deprecate which is the purpose of Rákshasa's next speech.

† Of the *Arhats.* By this and by his salutation of *Srávaka* addressed to those whom he speaks to, it is clear that, although the author calls this character a *Kshapanaka*, a *Bauddha* mendicant, he means a *Jain.* The *Bauddha* salutation is *Upásaka* or *Buddhopásaka*, worshipper of *Buddha*, (see *Mrichchakatika*). *Srávaka* is the generic term of the *Jain* laity, and *Sávaga Dhamma láho hodu* for *Srávaka Dherma lábha bhavatu* as used by *Jivasiddhi* in one place, is still the ordinary salutation a Jeti, or religious Jain, proffers to the laity. From the introduction of the *Jains* the antiquity of the drama cannot be very great. The mendicant speaks *Paisáchi Prákrit*, it is said by the commentator: it differs not much from *Mágadhi.*

The Star that's malign.
But the way must go forth
To the South from the North,
As the full moon is bright
In the East on the right.
And the Sun sinks to rest
On the left in the West;
Whilst Virgo displays
Before you her rays,
And Mercury hies
To her house in the skies;
And in front too appears
The pale gleaming star,
That spreads through the spheres
Fear, famine, and war.

Rák. The day, as reckoned by the moon, I find
Is unpropitious.

Jiva. And what of that? The day no more
Than one is counted—planets, four:
And mansions are thrice twenty told
And four. If friendly these, be bold;
For save when through the dark eclipse
The moon with difficulty slips,
The lunar influence shall bestow
Whate'er you seek, where'er you go.

Rák. Consult with other learned soothsayers—

* The astrological purport of these passages can scarcely be made intelligible without conversancy with the original system. It is considered favourable to set out on a journey when certain divisions of the lunar day or *Karanas* do not occur, and when the moon is rising on the one hand, and the sun setting on the other, and when the *Lagna*, or point of rising of Mercury in that portion of the Zodiac appropriated to Virgo, occurs in front of the traveller. Rákshasa objects that it is the day of full moon, which as well as the 6th, 8th, and 12th lunar days, are considered unpropitious. The astrologer replies, that it is decidedly so only when an eclipse occurs, and that if other aspects are propitious the journey may be undertaken.

Jiva. Not I—Do you consult them,* I shall go home.

Rák. Nay, be not offended.

Jiva. I know of no offence—but some one does.

Rák. Who?

Jiva. Fate, who drives you blindfold on your way,
To join the foe, and your own friends betray.

[*Exit.*

Rák. (*to the servant.*) See—what is the hour?

Att. Near sunset, Sir.

Rák. Indeed—so near the time, when like the slaves
That fly a lord whom fortune has abandoned,
The trees that cast their shadows at the dawn
With servile speed before the rising sun,
Now turn them backward from his downward course.

[*Exeunt.*

* This reply has nothing strange to those who know the sturdy self-importance of Hindu ascetics, and especially of the Jetis, when of any consideration with their own sect.

END OF THE FOURTH ACT.

ACT V.

THE CAMP OF MALAYAKETU.

Enter SIDDHÁRTHAKA, (*with a Letter and Packet*).

The creeper of Chánakya's policy will put forth fruit undoubtedly, watered as it is with the dews of wisdom, shed by the clouds of place and time.*—This letter is intrusted to me by the illustrious statesman, signed with the seal of Rákshasa, and this packet with the ornament he presented to me is sealed with the same. With these I will return to Pátaliputra—(*Going—stops*) How! a heretic approaches this way—an unpropitious encounter! It cannot now be helped; I will counteract its effects by looking at the sun.

Enter JIVASIDDHI.

All glory be paid to the *Arhats,* who shew
The only true path to perfection below.

Sid. Soothsayer, I salute you.

Jiva. Be of good faith, son, for in hand
Designs thou hast that faith demand,
A task as full of fear and pain
As traversing the boundless main.

Sid. How do you know?

Jiva. That which I know I know, and thou
Upon a journey travellest now:
Such purpose thy appearance shows;
What else, that letter will disclose.

Sid. As it seems you know my intention, and that I am

* This metaphorical style is not natural to the compositions of the period to which the drama belongs: the Hindus were perhaps beginning to borrow it from their neighbours.

travelling to another country, tell me, I beg of you, whether this be a lucky day.

Jiva. What think'st thou that thy shaven pate
May from the planets learn its fate?

Sid. You know, so speak at once. If it be lucky I will go; if not, I will tarry.

Jiva. It unpropitious is to steal
From hence without the prince's seal.

Sid. How so?

Jiva. I will tell you in plain words—It was lately free to all to pass at pleasure to and from the camp, but now we approach Kusamapura, no person is allowed ingress or egress without a passport signed by Bháguráyana with the prince's seal. If you have such, proceed—if not, hide yourself close, or you will be seized by the guard, and brought back bound hand and foot.

Sid. You do not know, I fancy, that I am the friend of his excellency the minister Rákshasa. Who shall stop me, though I have not a pass?

Jiva. The friend of the devil you may be,* it weighs nought: there is no other means of going forth but the prince's seal.

Sid. How then can I effect my purpose?

Jiva. I trust you may succeed, go on—I shall to Bhágaráyana, and solicit a passport for myself to go hence to Pataliputra.

[*Exeunt severally.*

A PAVILION NEAR MALAYAKETU'S TENT.

Enter BHÁGURÁYANA *and* ATTENDANT.

Bhág. Chánakya's policy is most surprising,
And whether he succeed or fail, improve
Success or screen discomfiture, extract
Fair fruit from seeds sown in ungrateful soil,
He proves himself the statesman, and still triumphs
As sure and irresistible as fate.

* The literal phrase is, friend of *Rákshasa* or *Pisácha,* those words implying literally a fiend, a goblin.

Bring me a seat here, Bhásura, the Prince
Commands me to attend in his pavilion:
Should any seek my signet give them entrance.

Att. I shall observe, Sir.

[*Exit Attendant.*

Bhág. It grives me much this prince, whose honest thoughts
Affect me with regard, should from me reap
Requital so unmeet as treacherous friendship.
And yet what else is in my gift? Who owns
Dependence on another, must resign
All claim of kindred, friends, the world's esteem,
And equal weigh disgrace or reputation.
He sells his soul for perishable treasure,
Does as he's bid, nor longer has the privilege
To scan the difference betwixt right and wrong.

MALAYAKETU *enters behind with* VIJAYÁ, *an* ATTENDANT.

Mal. These doubts of Rákshasa perplex me strangely:
And whether I may venture to rely
Upon his faith, Chánakya now dismissed
From Maurya's entertainment, or it be
More prudent to regard him as an enemy
Hereafter dangerous, alternate moves
Conflicting thoughts, 'midst which my understanding
Whirls like a potter's wheel, nor finds
A point on which to settle in decision.
Where shall I meet with Bhágaráyana?

Vij. So please your Highness, yonder he sits,
Engaged in granting passports to those persons
Whose business calls them from the camp.

Mal. Approach him gently.
His head is downward dropped, and with his hands
He veils his eyes, as if in meditation.

Enter ATTENDANT.

So please your excellency, a mendicant requests admission for a pass.

Bhág. Let him enter

Attendant goes out and returns with JIVASIDDHI.

Jiva. Believer,* may you know increase of virtue!

Bhág. (*apart*) How, Jivasiddhi, the friend of Rákshasa?
(*aloud*) Sage, I salute you.

Jiva. May your virtue prosper.

Bhág. You go hence, I deem, on Rákshasa's affairs?

Jiva. Not so; I quit this place that I may hear
His name no more.

Bhág. How now! what grave offence
Against the seer has Rákshasa committed?

Jiva. None against me;
But I repent me of my past misdeeds.

Bhág. Repent of past misdeeds! You much exite
My marvel.

Mal. (*behind*) And mine too.

Bhág. I wish to hear
The secret import of your words.

Mal. So I.

Jiva. I cannot utter things, so all unfit
To be made known.

Bhág. The deeper seems the mystery,
The more my need to hear its explanation.

Jiva. There is no mystery, but much of shame.

Bhág. If there be nought mysterious, speak the truth.

Jiva. I will not.

Bhág. Then expect no passport from me.

Jiva. Perforce then I must make disclosure.—Hear!
Dwelling at Pátaliputra, I contracted,
Though poor, an intimcy with Rákshasa,
At that same season when his craft employed
The poison-maid his secret instrument
To work the murder of the mountain king.

* *Sávage, dhamma viddhi hodu,* for *Srávaka Dherma vriddhi bhavatu.* Srávaka is properly a hearer, but is applied to the Jains.

Mal. My sire destroyed by Rákshasa; and not,
As I have still imagined, by Chánakya!

Jiva. I after shared his fortunes, when ere long
I was exiled the city by Chánakya—
But now, with his own policy engrossed,
He plans some scheme by which I may be banished
From life.

Bhág. Yet, hitherto, the rumour runs,
The murderous act was by Chánakya wrought,
Not Rákshasa—its object, to evade
The resignation of the pledged gratuity
For friendly aid, a moiety of the kingdom.

Jiva. (*covering his ears*) Mark me, Believer—to this hour Chánakya,
Knows not the venomed-maid even by name.

Bhág. I seal your passport (*seals it*); but attend me now,
To bear these matters to his highness.

Mal. I am here;
And with deep-wounded ear have overheard
A friend impart—what better had become
An enemy's tongue. My father's hapless fate
To-day o'erwhelms me with redoubled anguish.

Jiv. (*apart*). The prince has overheard me! then
I gain my object.

[*Exit.*

Mal. Oh most unkind return! My father's heart
Was wholly Rákshasa's—of him, he said,
With confident energy, this is my friend,
And to this friend he owes his fall! so wept
By all our house, entrusted to the care
Of this deceitful fiend. Oh Rákshasa,
Thy devilish nature fits well to thy name.

Bhág. (*apart*). We must beware, the life of Rákshasa
Is not imperiled by the prince's fury—
Such are our master's most precise injunctions.
(*Aloud.*) Repress this agitation, Sir, be calm,

Be pleased to sit, and listen to the counsel
Your friend and servant would presume to offer.

Mal. Speak on, my friend.

Bhág. Then please your highness, think,
That those who govern kingdoms must compute
Of friend, or foe, or neutral, as suggested
By principles of state and not the pleas
Of private feeling, which teach love or hate,
To ordinary men. The aim of Rákshasa
Was first to crown Sarvárt'hasiddhi; but
To this your father, as a mightier prince
Than Chandragupta, was the main impediment,
And thence the deadlier foe. Such cause of enmity
Admitted as of weight, the act of Rákshasa
Was prudent policy not vulgar crime.
Again: consider, Sir;
Wisdom political turns foes to friends,
And changes friends to foes; like a new birth,
It razes out all memory of past deeds,
Which to remember nought advantages,
As utterly as if they were, indeed,
The long-past actions of a former being.
Then for events gone by, let Rákshasa
Escape your censure, or at least forbear him
Until the realm of Nanda be your own.
No more of need to your success, he then
May be disposed of as your highness pleases.

Mal. So be it as you counsel—you judge wisely:
His death or bondage might alarm our followers,
And make our triumph doubtful.

Enter AN OFFICER.

Off. Victory to your highness! The captain of the guards reports that a man has been apprehended attempting to retire secretly from the camp, and on his person this letter was found—will it please your highness to examine him?

Mal. Bring him in.

[*Exit Officer and re-enters with* SIDDÁRTHAKA.

Sid. (*To himself.*) Praise be to mother Fidelity, animating her children in virtue, and turning their faces away from faults.

Off. This is the man,

Bhág. Who should this be?—a stranger, or the servant
Of any of our host?

Sid. A servant, sir,
A humble follower of the minister.

Bhág. Why sought you, then, thus covertly to quit
The camp without the prince's seal?

Sid. I went
Upon affairs requiring speed.

Bhág. So urgent,
That for their need, his highness' strict commands
Were disregarded?

Mal. Look at the paper!

Bhág. It bears in truth the seal of Rákshasa.

Mal. Efface it not, and let me hear the letter.

Bhág. "All greeting, and as fits from whence and whom
"It comes, to him for whom these news are meant.
"The expulsion of our adversary proves
"The truth of one whose words are ever true.
"The season is propitious now to show
"The promised kindness, and discharge the price
"That buys the plighted transfer of attachment.
"Then will these friends be ours, and strenuous join
"To overturn the mansion, where till now
"They have sought refuge. To requite such service,
"We must remind you, though no doubt 'tis needless,
"To call to recollection their conditions.
"Some stipulate domains, some gold, and some
"Demand the elephants and spoils of war.
"The three invaluable jewels sent
"Have been received, and in return unworthy,
"This offering comes, perhaps not wholly valueless,

"But to enhance its worth, Siddhártha bears,
"In words, what else may claim your confidence."

Mal. What can this dark epistle mean?

Bhág. Siddhárthaka!
Who sends this letter?

Sid. I do not know, sir.

Bhág. You are the bearer, and you do not know
From whom it comes; but let that rest awhile.
Speak out; to whom were you to have conveyed
The intrepretation that this letter promises?

Sid. To whom, but to your Grace.

Bhág. To me?

Sid. This violence so bewilders me,
I know not what I utter.

Bhág. We shall amend your knowledge. Bhásura,
Conduct him forth, and scourge him till he find
His recollection.

(*Siddhárthaka is led out and presently brought back by the Attendants.*)

Off. So please your Excellency, whilst flogging the prisoner, this packet dropped from his person.

Bhág. This is impressed with the same signet.

Mal. 'Twas this that gave the letter value. Open it,
But injure not the seal.

(*Bhág. opens it, takes out a jewel, and gives it to the prince.*)

This gem I took from my own person,
And sent a friendly present to the minister.
This letter is no doubt for Chandragupta.

Bhág. We will not leave the inference for question.
Away with him, and scourge him, till he own
The truth without reserve.

Sid. Oh, pardon me,*
And I will speak the truth without reserve.

(*Falls at the feet of Malayaketu.*)

* In the original he is again led out to be scourged, and then agrees to confess.

Mal. Arise! speak boldly—thy dependent station
Pleads thy excuse—reveal whate'er you know.
Sid. Then thus it is—that letter was entrusted me
By Rákshasa, to bear to Chandragupta.
Mal. And what the interpretation you should add.
Sid. Thus he commanded me: The kings
Barbaric are my personal friends, and may
Be to your interests won. They of Kulúta,
Malaya, and Kashmir, desire territory
From the possessions of Malayaketu;
The chiefs of Sindh and Persia covet most
His elephants and treasures. For myself,
Cháńakya's exile will as fully crown
My wishes, as those spoils that I have named
Will satisfy the craving of these princes.
Such was my message.
Mal. What! can this be true,
That my allies are treacherously affected?
And yet why doubt it? they have ever followed
The guidance and the beck of Rákshasa.
Ho, Vijayá! command the minister's presence.
Vij. It shall be done, sir. [*Exit Vijayá.*

SCENE.—RÁKSHASA'S DWELLING, RÁKSHASA *discovered.*

Our martial preparations are complete;
But whether more reliance may be placed
Upon our strength or Chandragupta's host,
I feel not wholly confident.
The premises that lead to truth are sure,
If logically urged, and though opposed
By hostile disputants, confirm the cause
They advocate.* The object of discussion
Is to both parties common, and to admit
Position incompatible is often

* The original passage is somewhat obscure, from its referring wholly to a proposition in logic described in technical terms.

As fatal unto monarchs aş logicians.
Yet I will trust; especially that now
Amidst the foe such disaffection spreads,
And they are weakened by intestine strife.
I will not fear. Who waits? Go, Priyaṁvada,
And to the kings confederated bear
This message—"We approach Kusumapura,
The capital of the enemy—be vigilant—
Look well to your array. Let this be
The order of your march. The *Khaśa* troops,
The men of *Magadha*, and my contingent,
Lead in the van. The centre be composed
Of the *Gándháras*, with the *Yavana* chiefs.*
The *Kíras* and the *Śakas*, with the bands
Of *Chedi* and the *Húna* cohorts, form
Our rear battalia—whilst our royal friends,
With their choice warriors in firm phalanx knit,
Surround the prince and guard his sacred life."

Pri. I shall impart your orders.

[*Exit Priyaṁvadaka, and enter Vijayá.*

Vij. Victory to your Excellency!
His highness wills your presence.

Rák. But a moment—
Ho! there, who waits? Inform S'akata-Dás
That I am summoned by the prince, and need
Becoming decoration to appear
Before his highness, who but late presented me
With costly trinkets—let him send me either
Of those rich jewels which to-day he purchased—
Quick, despatch.

(*Attendant goes out and returns with an ornament.*)

Att. This is the jewel, sir.

Rák. 'Tis well. (*Puts it on.*)

* The Calcutta edition reads *patibhiḥ* not *pattibhiḥ*, and the metre requires the former; the former translation, *yavana foot*, was therefore incorrect.

Now, lead the way. What should this summons mean
Howe'er unconscious of committed error,
The guidance of grave matters cannot fail
To prompt uneasy thoughts. A life of service
Is still a life of dread, and those most elevated,
As objects most of envy and malevolence,
Should ever be prepared to fear a fall. (*They proceed.*)

Vij. Behold his highness!

Rák. I observe him.
Absorbed in thought he seems—his youthful head
Already bowed with care, and on his hand
Reclined, whilst on the ground his eye reposes,
Or gazes fixed upon vacuity.—
All triumph to the prince!

Mal. I greet you, minister;—sit.
We grieve to have so little of your presence.

Rák. 'Tis true, my frequent absence has deserved
Your highness' censure, but the preparations
Our march exacts prevents my due attendance.

Mal. If yet determined, I should wish to learn
The disposition of our march.

Rák. 'Tis this:
The *Khaśa* troops and men of *Magadha*
And my adherents are the van brigade:
The *Yavana* and *Gándhára* forces
March in the centre; and the *Húna* cohorts,
The troops of *Chedi*, *Kíras*, and *Śakas*, form
The rear. The bands of the confederate kings
Are ordered to protect your highness' person.

Mal. (*Apart.*) Palpable treason!—they are named my guards
Who have conspired to give me up a prisoner.
(*Aloud.*) Send you any one
Precursor of our march to Kusumapura?

Rák. There needs not any—in five days our host
Will lie before its gates.

Mal. What man is this, then,

Who with despatches from your Excellency
Goes thither even now?

Rák. From me? impossible! (*Sees Siddhárthaka.*)
Siddhártha—how is this?

Sid. Forgive me, sir,
The fear of punishment severe has wrung
The secret from me.

Rák. Secret—what secret?
I know of none—I understand you not!

Sid. I own, I have but ill-obeyed your orders;
But stripes and pain—(*Appears to hesitate.*)

Mal. He fears to speak the truth
Before his lord.—Do you apprize the minister
What he has told. (*To Bhágurâyańa.*)

Bhág. Your highness is obeyed. (*To Rákshasa.*)
This man avers, your Excellency sends him,
The bearer of a letter and a message
To Chandragupta.

Rák. And is it so, Siddhártha?

Sid. Stripes forced me to confess the truth.

Rák. 'Tis false!
What will not torture force the innocent
To own!

Mal. (*To Bhág.*) Let him behold the letter!
Show him the packet.

Bhág. Read this note. (*Gives it to Rákshasa, who reads and returns it.*)

Rák. A weak invention of the enemy.*

Bhág. Behold this jewel! (*Showing him the jewel.*)
Is this, too, but a hostile stratagem?

Rák. No: this I recognise—'twas given me,
Even by your highness; and in note of deep
Acknowledgment, I did present the same
To this Siddhártha for a most dear service.

* Lit.—Prince, this is an attempt of the enemy. *Kumára, śatroń prayoga eshań.*

Bhág. To such a man, methinks, but little fitted
This princely gift, and one that had been graced
By his own royal wearing.

Mal. "Siddhártha bears
In words, what else may claim your confidence!"
So writes your Excellency.

Rák. I sent no message, sir; I wrote no letter.

Mal. Whose is this seal?

Rák. The counterfeit of mine.

Mal. That may be true:
A seal, the fraudulent may imitate.

Bhág. 'Tis possible it may be; but the writing—
Whose characters are these, S'iddhárthaka?
(*Siddhárthaka looks at Rákshasa, and hesitates.*)
Speak, or expect fresh stripes.

Sid. S'akat́a-Dása's.

Rák. If it be his, I must admit it mine.

Mal. Let him be called.

Bhág. (*Apart.*) Cháńakya's emissaries
Nothing advance that may not be attested.
Should S'akat́a-Dás appear and own he wrote
This letter, then the whole is manifest,
And Malayaketu's rage o'erleaps restraint.
This were less perilous. (*Aloud.*) With your highness' leave,
A friend of Rákshasa will not confess,
At least before him, that he wrote such letter:
Were it not better to procure a specimen
Of his own handwriting, and with this compare it?

Mal. You are right.
Vijayá, you hear. (*To the Attendant.*)

Vij. I shall observe.
Will not his seal be also needed?

Mal. Bring it along. (*Vijayá goes out and returns.*)
This is the seal of S'akat́a-Dás, and this
His writing.

Mal. (*Comparing them.*) It is the very same,—compare it.

Rák. (*Examining the two papers, then apart.*)

'Tis true, the writing is in both the same.
What must I think—he has been still my friend;
But haply, pining for his absent family,
He proves at last a traitor to his lord.
The seal is his; Siddhártha his associate;
And this mysterious letter is his writing.
To purchase his indemnity, or tempted
By the allurements of a crafty foe,
He has fallen off from honour, and abandoned
His fair imperishable fame, and me.

Mal. Three costly gems, this letter writes, have been
Received, and one methinks adorns your person.
Let me behold it nearer. (*Rákshasa gives it to him.*)
What do I see? (*Apart.*)
If I am not deceived, this jewel once
My sire possessed. (*To Rákshasa.*) Whence did your Excellency
Obtain this ornament?

Rák. Of some merchants, sir,
By whom 'twas sold me.

Mal. Vijayá, look here.—
Know you this gem?

Vij. How should I not remember it?
For often have I seen it when 'twas worn
By your illustrious sire, the king Parvataka.

Mal. Father lamented, well thy splendid ornaments
Became thy princely person, so attired;
As glorious as the autumn's evening sky,
Bright with the moon, and set with radiant stars.

Rák. (*Apart.*) If this, indeed,
Was Parvateśwara's, the seeming merchants,
In truth Cháńakya's agents, were by him
Employed, to send them to me.

Mal. Is it likely?

Such royal gems Parvataka once owned,
And Chandragupta as the kingly share
Of plunder set apart, should have been sold
By pedlar traders, bartered for vile cost?
No; it is clear the treacherous Chandragupta
Was here the vendor, and ourselves the price.

Rák. (*Apart.*) The snare is deeply laid; and though I know
The letter and the message are not mine,
Yet mine the seal. The writer is my friend.
The jewels, which it were absurd to deem
Maurya would vend, are found in my possession.
These facts so strongly argue treason, vain
The hope to gain my innocence belief.
Why then prefer reply? 'Tis wiser far
To acquiesce in silence, than engage
In angry words and profitless contention.

Mal. Now, I would ask your Excellency.

Rák. Ask
Him who deserves such epithet, not me,
Degraded by these accusations.

Mal. Proofs—
For by what other name shall we denote
This packet, this epistle, and these gems?

Rák. They prove, indeed, the malice of my fate,
And not alone the cunning of Cháńakya.

Mal. Why censure destiny for faults that spring
From vulgar avarice? Base and ungrateful!
Thy murderous fraud repaid my sire's affection
And confidence, that knew no fear, with death;
And now, ourselves, to whose regard thou owest
Thy present power and rank, with like deceit
Thou wouldst betray, and for a paltry bauble
Wouldst sell our bodies, as they were mere carrion,
To our most deadly enemies, proud to be
The mercenary hireling of their hate.

Rák. This blow is heavier far than my disgrace.
Son of Parvataka, I here protest
My innocence!

Mal. Who killed my father?

Rák. Fate!

Mal. We know it was thy doing—by thy friend,
And penitent agent, Jívasiddhi owned.

Rák. Is he too but Cháńakya's instrument?
My very heart leagues surely with my foes.

Mal. Bhásuraka, convey our general word:
The foreign princes, our allies, have plotted
To seize our person, and deliver us
Captive to Chandragupta: let him, therefore,
Secure them, and defeat their foul intents.
The three who are ambitious of our lands
Cast in a pit and whelm them o'er with earth,*
Till their desires be satiated: the others,
Whose moderate pretensions are confined
To martial stores, treasure, and elephants,
Be by those elephants trampled under foot;
And so their craving will be gratified.

Att. I shall impart your highness' commands.

[*Exit.*

Mal. For you, sir, I shall violate no troth
Once plighted. Go, join Chandragupta;
Him, and his crafty counsellor, though aided
By your profound experience, we yet trust,
We have the strength to root out from the earth.

Bhág. Enough! time flies, my prince. March we at once
Against the capital of the enemy. Let the dust,
Rolling in volumes from the trampling tread
Of our fierce elephants and steeds, ascend
In clouds, and hover o'er the trembling foe,
Proclaiming our approach in wrath, and spreading

* Part of the answer made by the Athenians to the messenger of Darius, who demanded earth and water.

Intenser paleness o'er the maiden's cheeks,
That far outvie the lodh's pale blossom, graced
By locks more sable than the jetty bee. [*Exeunt.*

Rák. How horrible my fate! My love still works
The ruin of my friends, my foes escape!
What now remains? Shall I conceal my shame
Amidst the thicket's gloom? No, rankling hate
And unappeased hostility will never
Sleep at devotion's bidding. Shall I end
My being, and attend my fallen sovereign?
No; thus to fly the contest whilst a foe
Triumphs secure, were base and womanish.
What, if I grasp my trusty sword, and rush
Desperate to death amidst the hostile ranks?
No; yet I may not. If my heart be still
Conscious of grateful duty, I must first
Effect the freedom of that faithful friend,
Who welcomes bonds and death for mine and me.

[*Exit.*

END OF THE FIFTH ACT.

ACT VI.

SCENE.—PÁṬALIPUTRA.

Enter SIDDHÁRTHAKA (*ornamented*).

Now Keśava of cloudy hue, the destroyer of *Keśin*, triumphs: Chandragupta, the moon of the eyes of the virtuous, is victorious—the policy of Cháńakya is successful, and has discomfited the confiding army of the foe. I have not yet seen my old friend Samiddhárthaka, and will go seek him. Oh, here he comes!

Enter SAMIDDHÁRTHAKA.

Sam. The treasures of the heart that animate at festive assemblies, and inspire delight in family parties, are sources of affliction alone in the absence of our friends. Where now shall I find Siddhárthaka, who I hear is returned from Malayaketu's camp? Oh, there he is! Welcome, my dear friend, welcome.

Sid. Ha! my dear friend, all happiness! (*They embrace.*)

Sam. I have little cause to rejoice, methinks, when you could so long delay coming to my house after your return.

Sid. Excuse me; the truth is, I was ordered by Cháńakya to go immediately, and carry my intelligence myself to the auspicious prince Śríchandra. I went accordingly; was rewarded as you see (*showing the ornaments*), and am now on my way to your habitation.

Sam. Well, my friend, and what news had you to convey to His Majesty that proved so agreeable? may I hear it?

Sid. Why not?—what is there that you may not hear?—Beguiled by the policy of our master, Malayaketu dismissed Rákshasa from his service, and put to death the five foreign kings, his allies; upon which, this violent and imprudent man, being looked upon as one whom no good fortune could attend, was abandoned by his chief followers. They left his camp gradually, and returned to their own countries, till being left almost alone, he was made prisoner by Bhadrabhaťa and our other captains.

Sam. How could that be? for Bhadrabhaťa had deserted to him, having been dissatisfied with Śríchandra. This is like the drama of a bungling writer, in which the catastrophe is inconsistent with the beginning!

Sid. So much the more honour to the never-failing policy of Cháńakya; a policy as certain as the decrees of destiny. Well, after that, Cháńakya with great state went forth, and secured the whole barbarian host with all its chiefs.

Sam. Where are they now?

Sid. Look yonder; observe those elephants, roaring aloud with passion, and vast and black as the rain cloud:—see those horses, richly caparisoned, plunging in fear of the lash.

Sam. I see, I see. Now let them rest, and tell me how it is that Cháńakya resigned the administration, who publicly now resumes his post?

Sid. Ha, ha! do you think you can fathom the intentions of Cháńakya? Rákshasa himself was unequal to the task.

Sam. And where is Rákshasa?

Sid. He quitted the enemy's camp during the confusion that ensued upon the retirement of the chiefs, and privately entered Kusamapura; not unobserved, for his steps were followed by a diligent spy, and due notice of his coming has been given to Cháńakya.

Sam. Why should he come hither again, disappointed in all his schemes to recover the city for the race of Nanda?

Sid. Affection for his friend Chandana-Dása brings him, I suspect.

Sam. Do you expect Chandana-Dása's liberation?

Sid. His liberation! how is that possible? for you and I are to conduct him to the place of execution and put him to death.

Sam. How so? Has not Cháńakya executioners enough, that he must put us upon such a cruel duty?

Sid. Gently, my friend. If you intend remaining a little longer in this world, you will not call Cháńakya's orders in question: so, come along, we will put on the *cháńdála* dress, and lead Chandana-Dása to execution. [*Exeunt.*

A GROVE.

Enter a man with a rope in his hands.

This is the place which *Undura* described, and where I am ordered by the sagacious and successful Cháńakya to throw myself in the way of Rákshasa. Here he comes, I fancy, avoiding notice apparently.—I will hide amongst these trees and observe where he stops. (*Retires.*)

Enter RÁKSHASA.

Alas, the harlot Fortune, to whom change
Is ever welcome, now transfers her favours
To a new dynasty—whilst the multitude,
No less inconstant, and of former benefits
Regardless, follow in her fickle train.
The burthen of the state, by those abandoned
Who failed to reap the harvest of their virtues,
Is now with daring confidence assumed
By weak and worthless hands; and without head
Not long the body politic subsists.
Base-born and vile, Fortune with Vrishala,
A partner meet, associates,—her great lord,
The monarch of mankind, forgotten quite:
And for the present she appears immovable.
What's to be done—whatever I devise,
Inflexibly adverse, Fate counteracts,
And still implacably pursues my course,
Wherever I direct my hopes. Too soon,
To heaven transported my lamented lord.

I lent assistance to the mountain king—
In vain; his death came hard upon our union.
Then did I aid his son's projected vengeance,
But still in vain—I wrought my own disgrace.
Fate, not the indignant Bráhman, is the enemy
Of Nanda's race. Ill-judging, rash barbarian,
Who on such baseless charges could mistrust
My faith, and deem that one who had maintained
Devotion to a fallen lord unshaken,
Would from his truth be tempted, or would cease
His just and stern resentment but with life.
This, the untutored savage could not see—
Or haply, when a man is doomed to fall,
Fate first perverts his intellect.* He now
Is held in captive bonds: well—let him perish;
Not therefore will I harbour thought of peace
With Chandragupta. Be it said, I failed
In all my projects, this shall be my fame,—
Foiled as I was, I yet was unsubdued.
These gardens mark the city's pleasant confines,
And oft were honoured by my sovereign's presence,
When with abandoned curb and loosened rein,
He urged his rapid steed, and in mid course
Struck with unerring shafts the distant targe.†
These scenes are hateful to me now. But whither
Shall I repair? Here I may lurk unnoted,
Till I can gain some tidings of my friend.
Alas, how rarely seen by mortal prescience
The strange vicissitudes of human life!
Once when I came abroad, like the new moon,
The people paused to gaze and point at me,
As in resplendent state I moved along,

* Quem Deus vult perdere, prius dementat. *Daivenopahatasya buddhir athavá púrvam viparyasyati*; or rather, the understanding of one struck by fate will first become perverted.

† This is Medic, Persian, or Parthian.

And in my train great potentates esteemed it
An honour to be numbered. Now, alone,
Covered with shame, and dreading to be marked,
I shrink from every eye, and like a thief
Who apprehends detection, cowering, creep
Into the darkness of these ancient groves;
And those my benefactors to whose favour
I owed my former greatness, are no more.
This garden too has lost its former splendour!
The shattered walls are like a noble race
By poverty reduced: the lake is dry,
Like a kind heart that pines for luckless friends;
As destitute of fruit the trees, as schemes
Of policy by fate opposing blighted;
And rank grass chokes the fertile soil, like vice
And ignorance, the rude uncultured mind.
These hoarse resounding murmurs of the dove,
Varied alone by the harsh ringing strokes
Of the destroying axe, seem to bewail
The ruin of these shades, whose naked trees,
Leafless and sear, are destined soon to fall
And yield their limbs to feed funereal fires.
Here on this marble, fractured as my fortunes,
I will sit down and rest. (*Sits and listens.*)
What mean those sounds?
The mingled bray of horn and beat of drum,
These shouts of multitudes, given back redoubled
In echoes from the palace towers, afflict
The listening ear, and fill the bounds of space.—
Sounds of rejoicing are they? Yes, they tell
Of Maurya's victory, and the captive son
Of the brave mountain king. Where'er I roam,
The foe's superiority assails
Mine eye and ear, and destiny compels me
Despitefully to contemplate their triumph.

The Man. (*Coming forward.*) He sits, and does not see me—

Now to practice
The orders of Chánakya. (*He advances so as to be seen by Rákshasa, and fastening the rope round his neck, pretends to purpose hanging himself.*)

Rak. Who should this be, whom misery extreme,
Like mine, enforces to such desperate act?
Hold, friend—what means this recklessness of life!
Who art thou, speak?

Man. A wretch, deprived of all
That life held dear.

Rák. If not to thee too painful
Nor secret be thy sorrows, let me hear,
Who am a fellow in thy miseries,
The cause of such rash purpose.

Man. Thou may'st hear it.
I cannot bear one instant to survive
A dear loved friend.

Rák. (*apart*). A censure of the apathy
With which I view the sufferings of my friends.
(*Aloud.*) Proceed.

Man. A wealthy banker, Jishnu Dás,
Resided here.

Rák. I know the name: an old and valued friend
Of Chandana. (*Apart.*) What has befallen him?

Man. I lose in him whom most I love. His wealth
Upon the indigent he now bestows,
And yields his life an offering to the flame:
Even now he goes to sacrifice. Unable
To view, or to outlive so sad a blow,
I hither come, at the same time to end
Those days, that would be misery without him.

Rák. What are his motives? pines he under anguish
Or bodily pain no medicine can assuage?

Man. Not so.

Rák. Then is he by the tyrant king
Compelled to choose his fate by fire or poison.

Man. Stranger—in Chandragupta's happy reign
We know not tyranny.

Rák. It may be so;
Perhaps his aims ambitious may affect
Some object unattainable; or perchance
He woos some damsel, who repays his love
With scorn?

Man. Such sorrows would but ill become
A sober burgher.

Rák. What then should it be
But loss of some dear friend?

Man. You name his motive

Rák. (*apart*). Too well my heart assured me it was so.
I scarcely dare know more—yet must enquire
His fate. (*Aloud.*) Go on—the friend of Jishnu Das—
Who is he—tell me?

Man. I can no longer parley.

Rák. One moment—answer me?

Man. The banker, Chandan Dás.

Rák Fate has at last descried a spot defenceless,
A passage for a wound—Be firm my heart,
You have no heavier blow to fear. (*Aloud.*) Proceed.

Man. With him was Jishnu Dás combined in bonds
Of amity; and when his friend incurred
The prince's anger, to preserve his life,
He offered all the accumulated wealth
He and his prudent ancestors had gathered:
In vain. The Prince replied: " Not for his wealth
The prisoner is in durance; let him yield
The family of Rákshasa, whom 'tis known
He secretly protects, and he is free—
If he persist to hide them from our search,
His forfeit life alone allays our wrath."
So persevering, Chandana is now
Led forth to execution. His firm friend

Enters the final fire, and I conclude
My miserable being.

Rák. Hold awhile;
Return and seek thy friend—bid him forbear
His fearful purpose—Chandana shall live;
I go to save him.

Man. By what means?

Rák. This sword,
Friend of my trust, oft tried in time of peril,
Bright as the heaven's clear azure when the clouds
Disparted vanish—and whose keen edge bites,
Remorseless, when the stone of battle whets
Its sharpness—now it prompts me to defy
Opposing multitudes to guard a friend.

Man. His safety is ensured, if, as I guess,
I see illustrious Rákshasa before me.

Rák. You see in me, the servant of a race
I could not save—the friend whose friendship yields
Ruin—the ill starred and humbled Rákshasa.

Man. Such as thou art, accept my veneration.

(*Falls at his feet.*)

Rák. Arise—time hastes—quick to thy friend repair,
And tell him what has chanced.

Man. Yet may I, Sir,
Thus humbly counsel. Sakata Dás, ere while
Condemned by Chandragupta to impalement,
Was at the place of execution rescued.
And to a distant region safe conveyed.
The king, by his evasion much incensed,
Commanded that the executioners
Should suffer death. Since then more vigilant,
The officers of justice, should they see
An armed man approach and dread a rescue,
Proceed not to the place of execution,
But instant put their prisoner to death.

Therefore be cautious, Sir, or your attempt
Will but accelerate your friend's destruction. [*Exit.*

Rák. The politic expedients of Chánakya
Are yet to me inexplicable. Why,
If his contrivances sent Sakata,
His emissary, to effect my downfall,
Should those who suffered his escape incur
Such bloody retribution, and acquit
Their negligence or treachery with death?
From this I might infer the letter found,
A forgery—but how?—here all is dark.
This at the least is clear, not now the season
To use the sword. Forewarned by past events,
The ministers of justice were in vain
Again assailed—yet something must be tried—
Inaction were a crime. In deadly plight
My friend now stands for me, and can I less!
No; I will cheerfully confront the danger,
And with my own redeem his dearer life. [*Exit.*

END OF THE SIXTH ACT.

ACT VII.

SCENE.—PATALIPUTRA.

Enter SIDDHÁRTHAKA *as a Chandála or public executioner.*

Out of the way, out of the way, my masters, and let every one who values his life, his wealth, his family, avoid the displeasure of the king as he would poison. Sickness is a simple demolition of man's life, and unwholesome diet noxious only to himself; but he, and all his, perish, if he incur regal indignation. If you doubt what I say, behold this Chandana Dás led to execution, and followed by his wife and child. What is that you say—is there no chance of his escape? Yes, if he give up the family of Rákshasa. How! say you, give up those whom he is pledged to shelter for the sake of his life—he will never be guilty of so base an action! Very well, do you mark his unhappy lot, lest such should be your fate.

(*Enter* CHANDANA DÁSA *dressed for execution, bearing the stake upon his shoulder, followed by his wife and child, and by* SAMIDDHÁRTHAKA *as second executioner, with attendants and guards.*)

Wife. Ah, woe is me—that such disgraceful fate,
A felon's doom, should close a life of credit!
Ah ruthless destiny—that barbarous man
Should persecute alike both friend and foe,
The guilty and the innocent confounding!
A savage hunter, who in thickets spares not
The beautiful and inoffensive deer.

Chand. Where is my faithful friend: will none reply
To my last supplications? Ah, how few

Approach in adverse season! Those alone
Are friends who hold on with us to the last,
And follow us with eyes suffused with tears.

Sid. This is the place, so now dismiss your family.

Chand. Withdraw, my love, and lead our boy along.

Wife. Forgive me, husband. To another world
Thy steps are bound, and not to foreign realms,
Whence in due time they homeward will return.
No common farewell our leave-taking now
Admits, nor must the partner of thy fate
Leave thee to trace thy solitary way.

Chand. What dost thou mean?

Wife. To follow thee in death.

Chand. Think not of this—our boy's yet tender years
Demand affectionate and guardian care.

Wife. I leave him to our household gods, nor fear
They will desert his youth. Come, my dear boy,
And bid thy Sire a long and last farewell.

Boy. (*falling at his feet*). What must I do, my father, when deprived
Of thee.

Chand. Go, dwell where'er Chánakya is not.

Sid. Come, Sir, the stake is planted.

Wife. Oh save us, save us!

Chand. Yield not thus to grief.
Exalted princes, Nanda's glorious sons,
Who stooped to solace misery from the throne,
Have gone before me to the realms of heaven:
And that I die by no infirmity
Of frail humanity, but for a friend,
Is subject of rejoicing, not of tears.

Sid. Come, come, we have delayed too long—bring him and raise him on the stake—his family will retire of their own accord fast enough.

Chand. One moment only—let me kiss my boy.
Loved child, adieu! Remember, all that lives

Must die; but he that to preserve his friend
Expires, dies with honour.

Son. Such a lesson
There scarcely needed; for full well I know,
Faith to a friend is still our house's fame.

Sid. Bring him along (*they lead Chandana Dás towards the stake*).

Wife. Oh, mercy, mercy!

Enter RÁKSHASA *hastily.*

Rák. Lady, dismiss your fears.
Hold! officers—your prisoner must not suffer.
He, who in safety long unmoved surveyed
His sovereign's fall, the danger of his friends,
And calmly, as if seated at a festival,
Looked down upon their sufferings, comes at last,
To claim of right his own, these marks of shame,
These garlands and insignia of the grave.

Chand. Oh, what is this!

Rák. The feeble imitation
Of your exalted virtue.

Chand. No; our ruin—
What hast thou done—think'st thou thy destruction
A grateful sight to me?

Rák. Hear me, my friend—
Life is to every living creature dear—
In saving thine, I have performed my duty,
And do not heed thy censures. (*To the Officer.*) Hence, report
These welcome tidings to your ruthless lord.

Sid. (*to Samiddh*). Hark ye, comrade, do you lead Chandana Dás under the shade of those trees; I will go and inform his Excellency that Rákshasa is secured.

[*Exeunt severally.*

SCENE.—CHÁNAKYA'S HOUSE.

Enter SIDDHÁRTHAKA *with* RÁKSHASA.

Sid. Ho, Warder, inform Chánakya, that destructive thunderbolt to the host of Nanda, that elevation of the house of Maurya, and aggregate of every virtue—

Rák. Must I hear this!

Sid. That the minister Rákshasa is secured; his wisdom and valour bound by the chains his Excellency's policy provided.

Enter CHÁNAKYA (*wrapped up in a mantle concealing his person*).

Chán. What are these tidings! Tell me, who has brought,
Safe in his robe, this fire unquenchable;
Who bound in bonds the circumambient wind?
Who craftily encaged the roaring lion,
Foaming with fury, from his hard-won strife
With the fierce elephant; or who has forded
The bottomless main, unharmed amidst its monsters?

Sid. What, but your honour's sagacity!

Chán. Not so, my friend, but fate, the constant foe
Of Nanda's race.

Rák. (*aside*). This must be himself,
The vile Chánakya. Rather, let me own,
The wise Chánakya; and exhaustless mine
Of learning—a deep ocean stored with gems
Of richest excellence. Let not my envy
Deny his merits.

Chán. This then is Rákshasa,
Whose enmity so long has held at bay,
And doomed to sleepless nights, the friends of Vrishala,
And furnished me with theme of ceaseless thought!
(*Discovering himself.*)
Hail minister, most welcome! Vishnugupta*
Pays thee his homage.

* The proper name of Chánakya.

Rák. Minister! the title
Is now my shame. Reverence to Vishnugupta!
Approach me not—a Sudra's touch defiles me.*
Chán. You are deceived; no Sudra your attendant,
But one whom you before have seen, Siddhártha,
A servant of the king, and equal rank
That other seeming Sudra holds. The first,
You may remember, was the venturous friend
Of Sakata Dás, the bearer of the letter,
Written indeed at my request by Sakata,
But with entire unconsciousness of what
Its purport or intended destination.
Rák. This is indeed most welcome news, assured
My friend was not unfaithful.
Chán. You shall hear:—
The chieftains who deserted to your army—
That letter—this Siddhártha—the three jewels,
Your purchase—your astrologer—the man
Whom you this morning in the garden met—
The imminent peril of your friend the jeweller—
Were all expedients to win your alliance,
Devised by me; or rather, say by Vrishala,
Who hither comes, impatient to behold you.
Rák. (*apart*). How shall I act!

Enter CHANDRAGUPTA *attended.*

Chandra. A mighty host o'erthrown without a conflict,
Exposes me to shame. Of what avail
The feathery shafts, that indolently lie
With downward points recumbent in the quiver,
Not launched with force against the destined aim!
And yet, what need of prowess, whilst alert,
My holy patron's genius is, alone,

* Which would have made him impure. The following speech explains that such disgrace was not incurred, and shews why the office of Chandála was intrusted to such hands.

Able to bend the world to my dominion?
Tutor and guide, accept my lowly reverence!
(*To Chánakya.*)

Chán. Your every hope is now accomplished. Vrishala,
Salute this honourable minister—
Rákshasa, hereditary councillor
Of your imperial house.

Rák. (*apart*). A bond of union
His promptness has created.

Chandra. (*to Rákshasa*). Chandragupta
Greets you, exalted Sir, with veneration.

Rák. (*apart*). This, Chandragupta! yet so young—so raised
To mighty empire, as the forest monarch,
Over subjected herds. (*Aloud*) King, may you triumph!

Chandra. Triumph is certain—now to the guidance
Of my preceptor I may add your vigilance.

Rák. (*apart*). What, does the pupil of Kautilya scoff me?
I wrong him, and my stubborn enmity
Misdeems his graciousness.

Chán. Say, wishes Rákshasa
The life of Chandana?

Rák. A needless question.

Chán. But how can Vrishala consent to grant
Such generous proof of grace, whilst Rákshasa
Yet holds aloof, and menaces defiance!
If it be true, that you desire his safety,
Forego the sword, and in its stead assume
This weapon. (*Offering him the ministerial dagger.*)*

Rák. Pardon me, I am not fit
To bear what you so worthily have wielded.

Chán. Not fit! how so? Why then these elephants
Incessantly caparisoned, till their backs
Are fretted by the burthen, and they pine,
Of needful rest and sustenance curtailed?

* A drawing of this dagger occurs in the last volume of Duff's History of the Mahrattas.

Or why these steeds, of rider never eased,
Chafed by the constant curb and whip, and jaded
By labour unrelaxed? Whom may they thank
For this but Rákshasa, whose valour humbles
The pride of the most haughty? To be brief,
The life of Chandana, and your acceptance
Of ministerial conduct, are conditions
Which we cannot disjoin.

Rák. (*apart*). Mine ancient faith,
And grief for Nanda's race, still closely cling,
And freshly, to my heart; and yet perforce
I must become the servant of their foes!
The plants so long I tenderly have cherished,
And watered with assiduous love, must now
By my own hands be levelled, to preserve
A dearer friend. Not Brahma's self foresees
The devious current of this world's events.
(*Aloud*) I yield me, Vishnugupta. Friendship triumphs!
Friendship, who works strange metamorphosis
Of human sentiments, controls my purposes,
And I submit. (*Takes the dagger.*)

Chán. (*to Chandra*). Fate, prince, is now made sure.

Enter an Officer.

Off. Victory to your grace! for Bháguráyana
And the accompanying chiefs, conduct the prince
Malayaketu to the city's confines,
There to await your Excellency's orders.

Chán. Impart their coming to the noble Rákshasa,
Who now directs the state, and ask of him
Their meet instructions.

Rák. If it be so,
Permit me, prince, to crave a boon. You know,
How in Malayaketu's dwelling long
I found asylum—in return, I beg
His forfeit life.
(*Chandragupta looks interrogatively at Chánakya*).

Chán. (*to Chandra*). The minister's first suit
Exacts compliance. (*To the Officer*) Go, inform the chiefs,
His majesty, by Rákshasa's request,
Is moved to clemency, and to the prince
Extends forgiveness—rendering back to him
His liberty and patrimonial lands—
And order them forthwith to lead him hence,
Home to his native country.

Att. I obey. (*Going.*)

Chán. Hold! this message to the governor of the city
Likewise convey. His Excellency, Rákshasa,
Being now admitted to the royal favour,
His friend the banker, Chándana, is named
The provost of the merchants. And this order
Bear to the captain of our host: in proof
Of the high satisfaction that the king
Receives from his new minister, he wills
That all the captives and the martial stores,
Coursers and elephants excepted, gain
Enfranchisement. Nay, free them too;
We need them not, strengthened by such alliance.
All shall be free—the only thing condemned
To lasting bondage, be this lock of hair.
My vow is all fulfilled. Say, Rákshasa,
Is there aught else the aim of your desires?

Rák. My only wish is now my sovereign's glory.
Long graced by virtue, and beloved by friends
Of eminent faith and merit, may he guard
From harm this nurse of elemental life.
Now harassed by barbarians,* earth repairs

* This allusion to *Mlechchas* is corroborative of the Drama's being written in the eleventh or twelfth century, when the Patan princes were pressing upon the Hindu sovereignties. The boar alluded to is the third incarnation of Vishnu in the *Varáha Avatára*, the delineations of which manifestation of that divinity represent the figure of a man with the head of a boar, and the earth, recovered from the waters of the deluge, resting on the points of his tusks.

For refuge to the bosom of true royalty,
So to escape second annihilation.
As erst, by strength divine upstaid, she rode
Safe on the tusks of that celestial boar,
Who snatched her from the o'er incumbent floods,
And reared her green hills once again to heaven.

[*Exeunt.*

REMARKS ON THE MUDRA RAKSHASA.

THE peculiarities of this play have already been adverted to. It is a historical or political drama, and represents a curious state of public morals, in which fraud and assassination are the simple means by which inconvenient obligations are acquitted, and troublesome friends or open enemies removed. It is not, however, that such acts are not held in themselves as crimes, or that their perpetrators, if instigated by vulgar vice or ferocity, are not condemned as culprits; it is only when the commission of the crime proposes a political end that it is represented as venial, and is compatible with the possession of great virtues, and even with an amiable character. The principle is one which has long pervaded Asiatic courts, and has proved no unimportant instrument in working their downfall.

In delineating the operation of this system, the author of the drama has evinced considerable dexterity, and has contrived to invest his chief personages with interest and dignity; an effect produced, in a great measure, by shewing them wholly unmindful of personal advantage. Chánakya has to fulfil a vow, but, that accomplished, relinquishes rank and power; and Rákshasa, whilst he pursues Chandragupta with hostility, seeks only to revenge the death of his former sovereign, without the thought of acquiring fortune or dignity for himself.

The author has also been fortunate in the delineation of these two statesmen, who although of the same depraved school of politics, are of very different characters. Chánakya is violent and inexorable; Rákshasa gentle and relenting. Chánakya's ruling principle is pride of caste; Rákshasa's, attachment to his friends and sovereign. Chánakya revenges wrongs done to himself; Rákshasa, those offered to them he loves. Chánakya with his impetuous passions combines deep design; Rákshasa, notwithstanding his greater temperance, is a bungler in contrivance, and a better soldier than a plotter.

Another redeeming feature in Hindu treachery is devoted fidelity to an employer. Although some of the personages cannot help expressing a disgust for the duty they have to discharge, they never think of betraying their trust; and they never intimate any relaxation of purpose, although treated with indignity or blows.

The plot of the drama singularly conforms to one of the unities, and the occurrences are all subservient to one action, the conciliation of Rákshasa. This is never lost sight of from first to last, without being made unduly prominent. It may be difficult, in the whole range of dramatic literature, to find a more successful illustration of the rule.

The conduct of the action is open to some objections, but rather on the score of stage management than dramatic probability. The chain of evidence by which Rákshasa is separated from Malayaketu is ingeniously connected.

The succession of incidents is active and interesting, although women form no part of the Dramatis Personæ, except in the episodical introduction of Chandana Dása's wife, a peculiarity that would be scarcely thought possible in the dramatic literature of Europe.

The author of the Mudrá Rákshasa was not a poet of the sphere of Bhavabhúti or Kálidas. His imagination rises not to their level, and there is scarcely a brilliant or beautiful thought in the play. As some equivalent for the want of imagination, he has a vigorous perception of character, and a manly strain of sentiment, that are inferior only to elevated conception and delicate feeling. He is the Massinger of the Hindus.

The language of the original partakes of the general character of the play; it is rarely beautiful or delicate, but always vigorous, and occasionally splendid.

RETNAVALI;

OR

THE NECKLACE.

A Drama,

TRANSLATED FROM THE ORIGINAL

SANSCRIT.

PREFACE.

THE RETNÁVALÍ is a play of a different character from any of those which we have hitherto examined. Although the personages are derived from Hindu history, they are wholly of mortal mould, and unconnected with any mystical or mythological legend; and the incidents are not only the pure inventions of the poet, but they are of an entirely domestic nature. In this latter respect the RETNÁVALÍ differs from the *Mrichchakatí, Múlati Mádhava,* and *Mudrá Rákshasa,* whilst its exemption from legendary allusion distinguishes it from the *Vikramórvasi* and *Uttara Ráma Cheritra.*

Although, however, the RETNÁVALÍ differs from its predecessors in these respects, and in others of still greater importance, it is well entitled to attention, as establishing an era in the history of both Hindu manners and literature, of which we are able to fix the date with precision.

The story of this drama appears to have been not wholly the invention of the author, but to have enjoyed very extensive popularity, at a period to which we cannot refer with confidence. The loves of VATSA, prince of *Kausámbi,* and VÁSAVADATTÁ, princess of *Ujayin,* are alluded to in the *Megha Dúta,* and are narrated in the *Vrihat Kathá* of *Soma Deva.* The last is a writer of the same period as the drama, but he does not pretend to have invented the story; and the manner in which the tale is adverted to * in the *Megha Dúta,* the date of which work is unknown, but which is no doubt anterior to the

* The author terms *Avanti* or "Ougein," great with the number of those versed in the tale of *Udayana* (Vatsa).

Vrihat Kathá, seems to indicate a celebrity of some antiquity.* The second marriage of VATSA, which forms the business of the RETNÁVALÍ, appears to be the invention of the writer, as it is very differently told in the *Vrihat Kathá*; the heroine being there named *Padmávati*, and being a princess of *Magadhá*, not of Ceylon. The circumstances under which the marriage is effected are altogether distinct.†

From whatever source, however, the plot of the drama may have been derived, it is very evident that the author is under considerable obligation to his predecessors, and especially to *Kálidás*, from the *Vikrama* and *Urvasí*, of which writer several situations, and some of the dialogue even, are borrowed. At the same time, the manners described are very different, and the light and loose principles of VATSA are wholly unlike the deep, dignified passion of *Purúravas*. If we compare the RETNÁVALÍ with the *Mrichchakatí*, or with the dramas of *Bhavabhúti*, the difference is still more striking, and it is impossible to avoid the conviction, that they are the productions of different ages, and different conditions of society; the RETNÁVALÍ indicating a wider deviation from manners purely Hindu, more artificial refinement, and more luxurious indulgence, and a proportionate deterioration of moral feeling.

The RÉTNÁVALÍ, considered also under a purely literary point of view, marks a change in the principles of dramatic composition, as well as in those of social organization. Besides the want of passion and the substitution of intrigue, it will be very evident that there is in it no poetic spirit, no gleam of inspiration, scarce even enough to suggest a conceit in the ideas. The only poetry of the play, in fact, is mechanical. The structure of the original language is eminently elegant,

* The *Vásava Dattá* of *Subandhu*, the nephew of *Vararuchi*, and as well as his uncle patronized by *Bhoja*, has nothing in common with the story of Vatsa and his bride, except the name of the latter. The *Megha Dúta*, therefore, does not refer to that work. *Subandhu* also alludes to the *Vrihat Kathá*, to which he is consequently subsequent.

† The story is translated from the *Vrihat Kathá*, in the *Quarterly Oriental Magazine*, Calcutta, vol. ii. p. 198.

particularly in the Prákrit. This dialect appears to equal advantage in no other drama, although much more laboured in the *Málati Mádhava:* the Sanscrit style is also very smooth and beautiful without being painfully elaborate. The play is, indeed, especially interesting on this account, that whilst both in thought and expression there is little fire or genius, a generally correct and delicate taste regulates the composition, and avoids those absurdities which writers of more pretension than judgment, the writers of more recent periods, invariably commit. The RETNÁVALÍ, in short, may be taken as one of the connecting links between the old and new school; as a not unpleasing production of that middle region, through which Hindu poetry passed from elevation to extravagance.

The place to which the RETNÁVALÍ is entitled in the dramatic literature of the Hindus is the more interesting, as the date is verifiable beyond all reasonable doubt. It is stated in the prelude to be the composition of the sovereign, *Sri Hersha Deva.* A king of this name, and a great patron of learned men, reigned over Cashmir: he was the reputed author of several works, being however in fact only the patron, the compositions bearing his name being written, the author of the *Kávya Prakás* asserts, by *Dhávaka* and other poets. That it was fashionable in his reign to take the adventures of VATSA for the subject of fictitious narrative, we may infer from their being the groundwork of the *Vrihat Kathá,* the author of which was a native of Cashmir, and a cotemporary of the prince. *Somadeva,* the author, states that he compiled his collection of tales for the amusement of the grandmother of *Hersha Deva,* king of Cashmir, the son of *Kalasa,* the son of *Ananta,* the son of *Sangráma.* His genealogy is nearly identifiable with that of *Abulfazl,* which runs in Gladwin's translation of the *Ayin Akbeti, Sungram, Haray, Anunt, Kulusder, Ungrus, Hurruss.* The two additional princes, *Huray* and *Ungruss,* reigned conjointly but forty-four days, and they are for all chronological purposes non-entities.* But we have fortunately a better

* See also the *Quarterly Oriental Magazine* for March 1824, p. 64.

authority than either of the preceding, in the history of Çashmir by *Kalhana Pandit.* The first portion of this work, down to the reign of *Sangráma Deva,* in A.D. 1027, is translated summarily in the fifteenth volume of the Asiatic Researches. Since its publication, the subsequent portion of the original has been procured in Cashmir, and presented to the Asiatic Society by the late enterprizing traveller, Mr. Moorcroft. From this we are enabled to trace the successors of *Sangráma* with precision.

Sangráma reigned twenty-five years, and was succeeded by his son *Hari,* who enjoyed his elevation but twenty-two days, having been removed, it was supposed, by the practices of his mother, who aspired to the regency during the minority of a younger son. She was set aside by the chief officers of the state, under whose ministry *Ananta,* the next prince, reigned interruptedly fifty-three years, when he was succeeded by his son *Kalasa. Kalasa* reigned eight years, and being displeased with his son *Hersha,* left the crown to a kinsman, *Utkersha.* That prince, however, enjoyed his authority but twenty-two days, having been defeated, and invested in his palace, by the partisans of the legitimate heir, and putting an end to his existence rather than fall into their hands. *Hersha* succeeded. He consequently ascended the throne A.D. 1113, and the play must have been written between that date and A.D. 1125, the termination of his reign. No mention is made of the composition by the author of the history: but he dwells at much length, and with some acrimony, on *Hersha's* patronage of poets, players, and dancers, and the prince's conversancy with different dialects and elegant literature. *Hersha's* propensities, indeed, were not likely to be regarded with a favourable eye by a Brahmanical historian, for, in order to defray the expenses into which he was led by them, he made free with the treasures of the temples, and applied their gold and silver vessels, and even the images of the gods, to his necessities. These measures, and others of an equally imprudent character, distracted the latter period of his reign with civil broils, and he perished in an insurrection which transferred the crown to a different dynasty. The date thus assigned for the composition refers to a period, which Mohammedan history and Hindu literature sufficiently establish, as pregnant with important changes in the political situation and national character of the natives of Hindustan.

The RETNÁVALÍ has been translated in prose for the same reasons that the preceding dramas have been rendered in measured language: the fitness of the vehicle for the thoughts, and adaptation of the style to the pitch of the original ideas. Prose would have done scant justice to the merits of *Kálidás* or *Bhavabúti*, for with them it would have had to translate lofty imaginings: it is perfectly applicable to the level conceptions of *Sri Hersha*. It may also form a not unacceptable variety, and it may likewise serve to convey some idea, how far the translator may be suspected of widely deviating from his text in the preceding dramas.

DRAMATIS PERSONÆ.

Men.

Vatsa.—The king of *Kausámbí.*

Yaugandaráyana.—His chief minister.

Vasantaka.—The king's confidential companion.

Vasubhúti.—The ambassador of the king of *Sinhala.*

Bábhravya.—An envoy from *Vatsa* to the king of *Sinhala.*

Samvarana Siddha.—A Magician.

Vijaya Vermá.—An officer of *Vatsa's* army.

Women.

Vásavadattá.—The queen of *Vatsa.*

Retnávalí, or *Ságariká.* } The princess of *Sinhalá.*

Kánchanamálá.—The Queen's principal attendant.

Susangatá.—The friend of *Ságariká.*

Nipuniká, *Madaniká*, *Chutalatiká*, *Vasundhará.* } Female attendants.

Persons spoken of.

Vikramabáhu.—The king of *Sinhalá* or *Ceylon*, father of *Retnávalí*, and maternal uncle of *Vásavadattá.*

Rumanwán.—The general in chief of *Vatsa.*

Scene.—The palace of *Vatsa* in *Kausámbí.*

Time, Three Days.

PRELUDE.

BENEDICTION.

MAY that presentation of the flowery offering made by the mountain goddess to her mighty lord, preserve you! Trembling she raised herself to reach his brows; but agitated by his triple glance, and bowed downwards by her heaving bosom, she missed her aim, and dropped the fragrant wreath.

May *Gaurí* ever be propitious to you! She who after new nuptials, yet scarce confiding, first hastened to her husband as remotely he advanced, then turned averse from him as he approached, till gently forced to the embraces of the smiling god by her persuading damsels.

May *Síva* ever be your trust! He who laughingly narrated to his goddess, how the sacrifice was disturbed, the holy fires were quenched by his flaming glances; how the Brahmans in terror were dragged by their turbans to the ground by his mischievous goblin legions; how *Daksha*'s* spouse implored in

* *Daksha* was the son of *Brahmá* and father of *Satí*, whom at the recommendation of the *Rishis* or sages, he espoused to *Siva*, but he was never wholly reconciled to the uncouth figure and practices of his son-in-law. Having undertaken to celebrate a solemn sacrifice, he invited all the gods except *Siva*, which so offended *Satí*, that she threw herself into the sacrificial fire. To avenge her fate, *Siva* created *Vírabhadra* and other formidable beings, and sent them to the scene of action, where they disturbed the rites, beat and mutilated the assistants, and even maltreated the gods, till *Siva* was appeased, and arrested their excesses. *Daksha*, who had been decapitated in the scuffle, was restored to life, but the head of a ram was substituted for his own. *Satí* was born again as the daughter of the mountain *Himálaya*, and was again married to *Siva*. From this, her second birth, she is called *Párvatí* the mountaineer, or *Girijá* the mountain-born. The disturbance of *Daksha's* sacrifice appears to have been a favourite legend with the Hindus who excavated the cavern temples of Ellora and Elephanta, the leading incidents appearing sculptured in both.

tears his pardon, and the gods, frightened, fled. Glory to the moon! Reverence to the gods! Prosperity attend illustrious Brahmans! May the earth be fertile, and may the king of moon-like loveliness shine ever resplendent as the monarch of the night.*

Enter MANAGER.

Enough! I have been desired by the princes here assembled from various realms, recumbent at the feet of our illustrious monarch, *Sri Hersha Deva*, and who are collected together at this vernal festival;† to represent for their entertainment the unequalled drama entitled Retnávalí, the elegant composition of our sovereign. "We have heard of this drama," they remark, "but have not yet witnessed its

* The extension of the *Nándí*, or benediction, to four stanzas, in the original, is unusual, and although sanctioned by the writers of systems, is evidently a modern innovation, not an improvement upon ancient practice.

† According to the *Bhavishyottara Purána*, the *Vásantaki Yátrá*, or festival of Spring, extended from about the middle of *Chaitra* to the full moon in the same month, and comprised three festivals: the *Damana Pujá*, in which the *dona* or *artemisia* flower was worshipped; the *Dola Yátrá*, or swinging of the gods; and the *Ratha Saptamí*, on which the gods came in cars to witness the frolics of man and nature under the influence of spring. The *Damana Yátrá* occurred on the 14th of the dark half of the month: the day of the *Dola Yátrá* is not specified, but it must have been on or about the new moon; the *Ratha Yátrá* occupied seven days, but they are not particularized. From the third to the full moon, every day had its separate divinity. *Gaurí* was to be worshipped on the 3d, *Ganesa* on the 4th, *Indra* on the 5th, *Skanda* on the 6th, the *Sun* on the 7th, *Siva* on the 8th, *Chandá* and *Chámundá* on the 9th, *Vyása* and the *Rishis* on the 10th, *Vishnu* on the 11th, *Brahmá* on the 12th, *Siva* again on the 13th and 14th, and all the gods on the 15th. All this, however, looks very like *Saiva* innovation, and probably the original festival, beginning with the *Holiká* on the full moon of *Phálguna*, was devoted to *Vasanta* alone, or conjointly with his friend *Káma Deva*, the god of love, whose especial festival, on the 13th and 14th of *Chaitra*, terminated the whole. Nothing of the kind is now known, from the *Holiká*, which is now termed the *Dola Yátrá*, to the *Madanotsava* on the thirteenth of *Chaitra*, light half, which latter is rarely observed. The *Dola Yátrá* and *Rath Yátrá* have also been displaced, and in Bengal, at least, transferred to festivals appropriated to *Krishna* alone, in the months of *Jyeshth*, and *Asharh*; June—July.

performance; and in compliance therefore with our wishes, and with deference to the king, who is the delight of all hearts, we request you to perform the piece as you best may." Very well: as soon as the decorations of the stage are ready I shall fulfil your desires.

That this whole assembly will be highly gratified I make no doubt. *Sri Hersha* is an eminent poet; the audience are judges of merit; the story of *Vatsa** is current in the world; and we, the actors, are experienced in the histrionic art; and I hope, therefore, that with so precious a poem, and such means of doing it justice, the opportunity afforded me of appearing before so distinguished an assembly will yield me the fruit of all my desires. Now then to my mansion, to call forth my dame. What ho, mistress, come hither!

Enter ACTRESS.

Your commands, Sir?

Mana. The drama of Retnávalí is to be represented before this princely audience—go, dress for your character.

Actr. Ah, Sir, you forget my only daughter has been betrothed by you to a husband who is abroad, and that the matrimonial rites cannot be performed in consequence of my son-in-law's absence in a foreign country: with so much anxiety on this account, how shall I be able to act?

Mana. Oh, never sorrow for the absent. Propitious fate restores them to us from distant isles, from ocean's central waves and earth's extremest bounds.

* *Lokachári cha Vatsa Raja Cheritam,* "The story of *Vatsa* current in the world." The *Vrihat Kathá* describes *Vatsa* or *Udayana,* as the son of *Sahasránika,* the son of *Satánika,* the son of *Janamejaya,* the son of *Parikshit,* the son of *Abhimanyu,* the son of *Arjuna*: but the *Purans* do not confirm this descent. We do not find the name at all in the *Bhágavat,* but in the *Vishnu Purána, Udayana* is the son of a second *Satánika,* the 19th in succession from *Janamejaya.* How far he is the celebrated prince of this name is doubtful. In the *Mahábhárat,* we have a *Vatsa* named among the princes, but no specification of the individual.

Behind. Son of *Bharata*, most truly uttered.

Mana. (*listening*). Away, child, away, no longer hesitate: here comes my brother as the noble Yaugandharáyana. Come, come, we have no time to lose. [*Exeunt.*

END OF THE PRELUDE.

ACT I.

SCENE.—THE PALACE OF VATSA.

Enter YAUGANDARÁYANA.*

'Tis true! fate, if propitious, soon restores the absent, and from remotest isles, the wastes of ocean, and the bounds of earth, safe gives them to us again—else how chanced it, that the fair daughter of the king of Lanká, whom, as directed by the seer, we had sent to obtain, and who was by her father, with rich gifts, consigned a bride to our illustrious prince, escaped annihilation? Borne on a plank, the relique of her shattered bark, a merchant of Kausámbí found her floating in mid sea. Her costly necklace spoke her of no common rank, whence with all honour she was treated, and to our capital conveyed. Fate still smiled upon our sovereign. I have transferred the maiden to the honourable keeping of the queen; and now I hear our chamberlain, Bábhravya, and Vasubhúti, the minister of Sinhalá, who had accompanied the princess, having by some means reached the shore, are on their way hither, having been encountered by Rumanwán on his march to chastise the king of Kosalá.† I have little need to fear the end of this; but faithful service ever has its cares. The eleva-

* Wherever Vatsa is introduced the same personages are assigned to him as associates, or Vásavadattá his wife, Yaugandharáyana his minister, Vasantaka his companion and *buffo*, and Rumanwán his general.

† *Kosalá*, according to the *Rámáyana*, is the country along the bank of the *Saryu*, and consequently formed part, at least, of the modern province of Oude. At different periods, however, it was much more extensive. The *Vishnu Purána* and *Bhágavat*, apparently speak of it by the name of *Sapta Kosalá*, the seven *Kosalas;* and in the ninth century, the authority of the king of *Kosalá* extended into *Gondwana*, as appears from inscriptions.

tion of my master's power is my aim, and destiny co-operates with my design—neither can the seer prophetic err. The king himself alone I doubt, for still he loves to follow where his own inclinations lead—(*a noise behind*). Hark! the mellow drum, accompanied with song and shouts, indicates the clamorous rejoicings of the multitude. I suspect the king has come forth to behold from his palace the frolic merriment with which his subjects celebrate the festival of *Kámadeva.** Ah, yes, I see him on the terrace: wearied of tales of war, and seeking most his reputation in his people's hearts, he issues forth attended by his companion Vasantaka, like the flower-armed deity himself, descended to take a part in the happiness of his worshippers. I will retire to my dwelling, and meditate in tranquillity the measures best adapted to ensure us a fortunate termination of the task we have begun. [*Exit.*

(VATSA RÁJÁ *discovered seated, dressed as for the Spring festival, and attended by* VASANTAKA.)

Vats. My friend!

Vas. Your majesty!

Vats. I scarcely can express the content I now enjoy. My kingdom is rid of every foe, the burthen of my government reposes on able shoulders, the seasons are favourable, and my

* This *Vasantotsava, Madhútsava,* or *Kámotsava,* is a festival held on the thirteenth and fourteenth of *Chaitra,* at which *Kámadeva,* the god of love, was formerly worshipped. The season was one of much merriment, and the genial influence of returning spring was hailed with music and jollity. Part of the amusement of the people consisted in throwing over each other, by means of syringes, water or fine powder, coloured with saffron or with other yellow or red pinguents, and scented with perfumes. A more elegant missile commonly used in some places is rose leaves, large baskets and trays of which are prepared for that purpose. The festival of *Kámadeva* holds its place in the kalendar, but its observance is restricted to a few places. In fact, it seems to have merged into the *Phálgunotsava* or *Holi,* celebrated a month before, when the like merriment and affusion of coloured powder or water takes place. In the south of India *Káma* is worshipped at this period also, which still further identifies the origin of the festival, although it has undergone some important modifications in date and purpose.

subjects prosperous and happy. In the daughter of Pradyota* I have a wife whom I adore, and in thee, Vasantaka,† a friend in whom I can confide. Attended by thee, thus, at such a season, and so disposed, I might fancy myself the deity of desire, and this vernal celebration held in honour of myself.

Vas. Excuse me. Since you admit me to be a part of it, I shall even claim the whole; and, so highly exalted by your regard, I shall maintain that the festival is mine. Observe the general joy. As if intoxicated with delight, the people dance along the streets, sporting merrily with each other's persons, and mutually scattering the yellow tinted fluid. On every side, the music of the drum and the buz of frolic crowds fill all the air. The very atmosphere is of a yellow hue, with clouds of flowery fragrance.

Vats. Yon lofty mansion opposite to us is occupied by a merry band. I knew not that Kausámbí ‡ was so wealthy!—She outvies the residence of the God of wealth. Her numerous sons are clad in cloth of gold, sprinkled with the fragrant dust

* According to the *Vrihat Kathá, Pradyota* is the king of *Magadhá,* the father of *Padmávatí,* Vatsa's second wife, whose place is assumed by Retnávalí in the drama: the father of Vásavadattá is named in the same work *Chandasena.*

† Either the spring, or like the spring, the affix *ka* being pleonastic, or implying similitude.

‡ *Kausámbí* always appears as the capital of Vatsa. According to the *Rámáyana,* it was built by *Kusámba,* the son of *Kusa,* a descendant of *Brahmá.* Buchanan, upon the authority of the *Bhágavat,* ascribes its foundation to *Chakra,* a descendant of *Arjuna;* but neither the *Bhágavat* nor *Vishnu Purána* states that *Nimi Chakra* built *Kausámbí.* They say, that when *Hastinapur* shall be washed away by the Ganges, *Nimichakra* will reside at *Kausámbí.* From which it is to be inferred, that *Kausámbí* existed at the time that *Hastinapura* was destroyed. The site of *Kausámbí,* Buchanan supposes to have been that of the ruins ascribed to *Hastinapur,* but it was more probably lower down in the *Doab,* bordering upon *Magadhá* on one side, and *Kosalá* on the other. It is elsewhere (*Oriental Magazine,* Calcutta, No. I. p. 67) intimated, that it was possibly about *Kurrah,* which according to the inscription found there (*As. R.* ix. 433), was comprised within *Kausámba Mandal,* or district of *Kausámbí.* The city so termed was probably not far from Allahabad.

of the colour of dawn, or tinted with the saffron dye, decked with glittering ornaments, and tossing their heads proudly with splendid crests, fit for Káma himself. The soil, plashy with the frequent shower and tread of numerous feet, is converted into vermilion paste, as the artificial bloom is washed down from the cheeks of the maidens and mingled with the ground.

Vas. See where a coloured shower falls on a thick and struggling crowd, shrinking in vain from the mischievous pipes of those mirthful maids.

Vats. I should compare the city to the subterranean world, where the snake gods dwell.* The mischievous pipes are crested snakes—the scattering dust of yellow fragrance sheds unearthly dimness, and the gleaming tiaras dart through it such radiance as beams from the serpent jewels.

Vas. Look, Sir, where Madaniká and Chútalatiká approach us: their gestures indicate the influence of the divinity of the season.

Enter MADANIKÁ *and* CHÚTALATIKÁ, *two of the Queen's Attendants, dancing and singing.*

Mad. Cool from southern mountains blowing,
Freshly swells the grateful breeze,
Round with lavish bounty throwing
Fragrance from the waving trees;
To men below, and Gods above,
The friendly messenger of love.

Chút. Lightly from the green stem shaken,
Balmy flowrets scent the skies—
Warm from youthful bosoms waken
Infant passion's ardent sighs.
And many a maid around is roaming,
Anxious for her lover's coming.

Both. Nor alone the tender blossom

* *Pátála*, the region below the earth, inhabited by the *Nágas* or serpent demigods.

Opens to the smiling day,
Lordly man's expanding bosom
Buds beneath the genial ray,
Offering to the flowery dart,
Of love, a soft and yielding heart.

Vats. I perceive, indeed, the influence of the season expressed in their appearance. The fillet of the one is loosened, and her long tresses float dishevelled to the air: the necklace of the other seems too weighty for her languid frame, though she plies her tinkling anklets with more than wonted activity.

Vas. I will gird up my garb and join them, shall I, in compliment to the festival?

Vats. If you please.

Vas. (*descends*). Come, Madaniká, teach me your poem.

Mad. A poem, you simpleton! it is no poem.

Vas. What is it then?

Mad. A ballad.

Vas. Oh, a ballad! if that is the case, I wish you good bye.*

Mad. You must not leave us.

Vas. Consider my character. (*They hold him and sprinkle him with yellow powder, till he breaks away.*) Here I am at last my good friend: I have been in jeopardy.

Chút. Come, we have amused ourselves long enough, let us bear the queen's message to his majesty.

Mad. Come on (*approaching Vatsa*). Glory to your majesty! So please you, the queen commands—I crave pardon, requests.

Vats. Nay, Madaniká, you are quite correct; the queen

* In the original Vasantaka says, "Teach me your *Charchari;*" to which the reply is, "It is not *Charchari* but *Dwipadi khanda,*" a form of metre; but *khanda,* meaning granulated sugar, Vasantaka asks if it is the *khanda* of which sweetmeats are made? Madaniká replies, 'It is not made but is recited (*patíyadi*):' to which Vasantaka, with surprise, rejoins, 'Oh, if it is recited, I had better go back to my friend.' It is not easy to discover the wit of this passage, although some puns are probably designed throughout.

commands, particularly at a season sacred to the god of love. What are her orders?

Mad. She is bound to-day to offer homage to the image of the flower-armed deity, which stands at the foot of the red *asoka* tree in the garden of the palace, and requests your majesty's presence at her devotions.

Vats. You see, my friend, how one festival begets another.

Vas. Let us go thither. I will officiate as your priest, and I hope my benediction will not be wholly unproductive.

Vats. Go, Madaniká, and let the queen know that we shall meet her in the garden.

Mad. As your majesty commands. [*Exeunt.*

Vats. Come, my friend, lead the way to the garden. (*They descend and proceed.*)

Vas. This is the place, Sir. Behold the rich canopy of the pollen of the mango blossoms, wafted above our heads by the southern breeze, and the chorus bursts from the *köils* and the bees to hail your approach.

Vats. The garden is now most lovely. The trees partake of the rapturous season—their new leaves glow like coral, their branches wave with animation in the wind, and their foliage resounds with the blythe murmurs of the bee. The *bakula* blossoms lie around its root like ruby wine; the *champaka* flowers blush with the ruddiness of youthful beauty; the bees give back in harmony the music of the anclets, ringing melodiously as the delicate feet are raised against the stem of the *asoka* tree.*

Vas. No, no; it is not the bees who mimic the ringing of the anclets; 'tis the queen with her train approaching.

Vat. You are right; they are at hand. [*They retire.*

Enter VÁSAVADATTÁ *the Queen,* KÁNCHANAMÁLÁ, SÁGARIKÁ, *and other damsels attending.*

Vásava. Now, Kánchanamálá, where is the garden?

Kánch. This is it, madam.

* The contact of the stem of the *asoka* tree by the foot of a woman of superior beauty is supposed to make it blossom.

Vásava. And where the red *asoka* tree, at the foot of which I am to pay my offerings to Madana?

Kánch. It is in sight. This is the *mádhaví* creeper, your majesty's own plant; it is now rich with blossoms. This is the plant his majesty takes such care of, the jasmine that he expects to blossom out of season:—now we pass it, and this is the tree.

Vásava. Very well; where are the offerings?

Ságar. Here, madam. (*Presenting them.*)

Vásava. (*looking at her, then aside*). What carelessness! an object I have hitherto so cautiously concealed, thus heedlessly exposed: it shall be so. (*Aloud.*) How now, Ságariká, what make you here; where is my favourite starling, that I left to your charge, and whom it seems you have quitted for this ceremony? Away! deliver the oblations to Kánchanamálá, and return.

Ságar. As your majesty pleases. (*Gives the offerings and withdraws to a short distance.*) The bird is safe with my friend Susangatá. I should like to witness the ceremony. I wonder if *Ananga** is worshipped here as in my father's mansion! I will keep myself concealed amongst these shrubs and watch them, and for my own presentation to the deity I will go cull a few of these flowers. [*Retires.*

Vásava. Now, place the divine *Pradyumna*† at the foot of the tree.

Kánch. (*arranges the offerings*). It is done, madam.

Vatsa. Come, Vasantaka, they are ready, let us join them. The queen stands by the side of the god of the fish-emblazoned banner,‡ as slight and graceful as his own bow, and as delicate as the flowers that tip his shafts. My love, Vásavadattá!

* The bodiless deity, either metaphorically, as applied to his influence on the mind, or with reference to the legend of his being reduced to ashes by the angry look of *Siva* when pierced by *Káma's* arrows, and thus inspired with love for *Párvatí.*

† *Pradyumna*, the son of *Krishna*, was an incarnation of *Kámadeva.*

‡ The banner of *Kámadeva* bears the *Makara*, or marine monster.

Vásava. My lord! Victory attend him: let him honour our rites by his presence!—That is his regal seat.

Kánch. Now, let her majesty commence the ceremony, and to the god, whose station is the red *asoka* tree, present the accustomed gifts of sandal, saffron, and flowers.

Vásava. Give them to me.

Kánch. (*presents them severally to the Queen, who offers them to the Image*).*

Vatsa. Whilst thus employed, my love, you resemble a graceful creeper twining round a coral tree; your robes of the orange dye, your person fresh from the bath. As rests your hand upon the stem of the *asoka*, it seems to put forth a new and lovelier shoot. The unembodied god to-day will regret his disencumbered essence, and sigh to be material, that he might enjoy the touch of that soft hand.

Kánch. The worship of the divinity concluded, be pleased, madam, to pay adoration to your lord.

* According to the *Bhavishyottara Purána*, the worship of *Kámadeva* was instituted by *Siva* in pity of the fate to which he had consigned him. On the thirteenth of *Cháitra*, the worshipper having bathed, was to adore the portrait, or as it was practised apparently in most places, the image of *Kámadeva* either in person, or as in the present instance, in one of his manifestations, attended by his wives *Rati* and *Priti*, his friend *Vasanta*, and a train of nymphs and choristers, represented in a grove of *asoka* trees, or placed in the shade of one of them with flowers, fruits, and perfumes. It was in a grove of *asoka* trees that *Káma* incurred *Siva's* wrath, whence the selection of that tree. The prayer addressed to the divinity, which the author does not give, perhaps either because it was well known, or because its repetition might be thought profane, is "Salutation to *Kámadeva* the destroyer, the god of gods, endowed with a form, to thee who disturbest the minds of *Brahmá*, *Vishnu*, *Siva*, and *Indra*." A rather longer prayer is addressed to the same god in the *Tithi Tatwa*, cited from the *Bhavishya Purána*, where it is not found; "God, armed with a flowery bow, salutation be to thee! Salutation be to thee, who bearest a fish on thy banner! Salutation to thee, who shakest the firmness of divinities and saints! Son of *Mádhava*, *Kandarpa*, the foe of *Samvara*, the lord of *Rati*, glory to thee, the mind-engendered, the subduer of the whole universe! May all the infirmities and frailties of my birth perish, and may my fortunes ever enjoy desired prosperity! Glory to the destroyer, to *Káma*, the embodied form of the god of gods, the agitator of the hearts of *Brahmá*, *Vishnu*, *Siva*, and *Indra!*"

Vásava. Where are flowers and unguent?

Kánch. Here, madam.

(*Vásavadattá worships the King.**)

Ságar. (*returns*). I have idled my time whilst gathering these flowers, so that I fear the ceremony is over; behind this tree I can observe them undiscovered. What do I see! can this be true. Does then the deity, whose effigy only we adore in the dwelling of my father, here condescend to accept in person the homage of his votaries! I, too, though thus remote, present my humble offering. (*Throws down the flowers.*) Glory to the flower-armed God: may thy auspicious sight both now and hereafter prove not to have been vouchsafed to me in vain! (*Bows down, then rising looks again.*) The sight, though oft repeated, never wearies. I must tear myself from this, lest some one should discover me. [*Withdraws a little.*

Kánch. Approach, Vasantaka, and receive your portion.

Vásava. Accept, most worthy Sir, these propitiatory presents. (*Gives Vasantaka sandal, flowers, and jewels.*)

Vasan. May prosperous fortune ever be your fate!

(*The Bard† behind.*)

The sun from his diurnal road declines,
And in the west with flaming radiance glows—
Like some illustrious prince, whose glory shines
Intensest, as his days approach their close.
The moon comes forth amidst the evening sky,
With aspect as our youthful monarch's bright,
To soothe the night flower's love-empassioned sigh,
And at thy feet to shed his sacred light.

Ságar. How! (*returning*). Is this Udayana, to whom my father destined me a bride! The sight of him has purified my person from the contaminating gaze of others.

* This is also conformable to the *Bhavishyottara Purána*, which directs, "Having offered adoration to the mind-born divinity, let the wife worship her husband, with ornaments, flowers, and raiment. Thinking internally with entire complacency, 'this is the god of love.'"

† Hindu princes, as we have had previous occasion to notice, always retained a sort of poetic bellman to announce the time of day.

Vatsa. The twilight has drawn in, and we have been insensible of the course of time, our minds engrossed by holy and delightful duties. Look, madam, where the pale eastern sky, like a love-lorn damsel, seems to sicken with impatience for the coming of her lord. Let us rise, and return to the palace.

[*They rise.*

Sâgar. They come! I must fly hence. Ah me, unhappy! no longer to behold him, whom I could gaze upon for ever.

Vatsa. Come, love, thou puttest the night to shame. The beauty of the moon is eclipsed by the loveliness of thy countenance, and the lotus sinks humbled into shade—the sweet songs of thy attendant damsels discredit the murmur of the bees, and mortified, they hasten to hide their disgrace within the flowery blossom. [*Exeunt.*

END OF THE FIRST ACT.

ACT II.

The Garden of the Palace.

Enter Susangatá *with a Sáriká, or talking bird, in a cage.**

What can have become of Ságariká? she left this bird in my charge, and went I know not whither. Here comes Nipuniká!

Enter Nipuniká.

These tidings his majesty has charged me with, I must use dispatch in conveying to the queen. [*Going.*

Sus. How now! Nipuniká, what engrosses your thoughts, that you pass as if you saw me not—whither, in such haste?

Nip. I will tell you. We have a great sage come to court, the venerable Srikhanda Dás, from *Sri Parvat.*† He has taught the king the craft of making flowers blossom at any season, and his majesty being about to exercise his new art upon his favourite jasmine, sends me to request the queen's presence. But where are you going?

* The *Sáriká* is the same as the *Maina*, the Indian Grakle, *Gracula religiosa*, about the size of a jackdaw, having violet black plumage, with a naked yellow occipital band. As Shaw observes, "These birds are of a lively docile disposition, and when kept in a state of a confinement, imitate with great facility the various sounds within hearing, and even learn to speak with greater distinctness than most of the parrot tribe;" so also Bontius, speaking of this bird, which he calls the Indian starling, observes: "It imitates man's voice much more accurately than a parrot, so that oftentimes it is troublesome with its prattle."

† The temple of *Siva* in the upper part of the peninsular, visited and described by Captain Mackenzie (*As. Res.* vol. v.). This was one of the twelve great Lingas, the worship of which seems to have flourished particularly about the period of the first Mohammedan invasion. Prior to the some date, also, it seems to have been a place of great resort for *Yogis* or *Saiva* ascetics. Mention of *Sriparvat* has been made before in *Málatí and Mádhava*.

Sus. To look for Ságariká.

Nip. I passed her just now; she had a brush and pallet as if about to paint a picture, and went into the plantain bower: you will find her there, I dare say. Adieu! I must to our mistress. [*Exeunt severally.*

A PLANTAIN BOWER OR HALL.*

Enter SÁGARIKÁ, *with a picture.*†

Be still, my foolish heart, nor idly throb for one so high above thy hopes. Why thus anxious again to behold that form, one only view of which has inspired such painful agitation? Ungrateful, too, as weak, to fly the breast that has been familiar to thee through life, and seek another, and as yet, but once beheld, asylum. Alas! why do I blame thee: the terror of *Ananga's* shaft has rendered thee a fugitive;—let me implore his pity. Lord of the flowery bow, victor of demons and of gods! dost thou not blush to waste thy might upon a weak defenceless maiden, or art thou truly without form or sense? Ah me! I fear my death impends, and this the fatal cause (*looking at the picture*). No one approaches; I will try and finish the likeness I am here attempting to pourtray (*looking at the picture*). My heart beats high, my hand trembles, yet I must try, and, whilst occasion favours me, attempt to complete these lineaments, as the only means to retain them in my sight. [*Draws.*

Enter SUSANGATÁ.

This is the plaintain bower. Ha! she is here, and apparently so intent upon some painting, that she does not notice my approach. I will keep out of her sight and look at what she is doing. (*Approaches gently and looks over Ságariká.*) How!

* The term on this and similar occasions is *Griha (Hara, Ghara)* or *Sálá*, literally a house or hall. It is not improbable that green-houses or analogous buildings were known to the Hindus. In general, however, these places appear to have been pavilions, with particular plants and flowers planted both within and without.

† More correctly, a leaf or sheet for a picture—*Chitraphalaka.*

—the king's picture! well done, Ságariká! but so it is: the royal swan leaves not the lotus-crowded lake to sport elsewhere.

Ság. It is finished, but in vain, my tears veil the picture from my sight. (*Raises her head, and beholding Susangatá hides the picture.*) How, Susangatá! sit down.

Sus. (*sits down and puts her hand upon the picture*). Who is this you have delineated?

Ság. The deity of this festival, *Ananga.*

Sus. It is cleverly done, but there wants a figure to complete it. Let me have it, and I will give the god his bride. (*Takes the paper and draws.*)

Ság. (*angrily*). Hey, Susangatá! what mean you; you have sketched my likeness?

Sus. Do not be offended without cause. I have given your *Kámadeva* my *Retí,* that is all. But come, away with disguise, and confess the truth.

Ság. (*apart*). My friend has discovered my secret. (*Aloud.*) My dear friend, I am overcome with shame—promise me that nobody else shall be made acquainted with my weakness?

Sus. Why should you be ashamed?—attachment to exalted worth becomes your native excellence. But be assured I will not betray you, it is more likely this prattling bird will repeat our conversation.

Ság. Alas! my friend, my agitation overpowers me.

Sus. (*placing her hands on Ságariká's heart*). Be composed, be composed! I will bring some leaves and fibres of the water-lily from this lake. (*Brings some leaves and fibres of the lotus, and binds the former with the latter upon Ságariká's bosom.*)*

Ság. Enough, enough, my friend, take away these leaves and fibres,—it is vain to offer me relief. I have fixed my heart where I dare not raise my hopes. I am overcome with shame —I am enslaved by passion—my love is without return—death my only refuge. [*Faints.*

* The lotus leaves and fibres are supposed to be of great cooling efficacy in allaying the fever of passion.

A noise behind.

The monkey has escaped from the stable, and rattling the ends of his broken chain of gold, he clatters along as if a number of female feet, bound with tinkling anklets, were in sportive motion. Chased by the grooms and frightening the women, he has bounded through the inner gate. The unmanly eunuchs, lost to shame, fly from his path, and the dwarf takes shelter in the jacket of the chamberlain. The *Kirátas* who guard the surrounding walls are true to their designation,* and bowing themselves lowly through fear, are ashamed to look each-other in the face.

Sus. Up, up, my dear friend! the wild brute is coming hither.

Ság. What shall we do?

Sus. Hide in the shade of this *tamála* grove: haste, he comes! [*Exeunt.*

SCENE.—ANOTHER PART OF THE GARDEN.

Enter SÁGARIKÁ *and* SUSANGATÁ.

Ság. What has become of the drawing: did you leave it behind? some one will discover it.

Sus. Never heed the picture now. The ape has broken the cage to get at the curds and rice, and let the *sáriká* fly: let us endeavour to recover her, or she will repeat what has passed between us.

Behind. Astonishing, astonishing!

Ság. Hey, Susangatá, is that the ape coming?

Sus. No, coward; it is the worthy Vasantaka, our royal master's friend. Let us hence, the *sáriká* is far away.

Ság. I attend you. [*Exeunt.*

* Perhaps a pun is here intended, *kiráta* a mountaineer being derived from the roots, *kri* to scatter and *ata* to go, that is, they scattered or ran away: or the joke lies in their stooping low, they being of low caste. The monkey's escape from the stable is another instance of the practice alluded to in the Persian and Hindustani Proverb: "The misfortune of the stable be upon the monkey's head.—*Bilai Tahila ba ser i maimun.*"

Enter VASANTAKA.

Very strange indeed! most marvellous! the power of Srikhanda Dás is most surprising, by whose simple will the jasmine has been covered with countless buds, as if smiling disdainfully upon the queen's favourite *mádhaví*. I will go and tell my friend what has happened. Ah! yonder he comes, looking quite confident of his hopes, and as pleased as if he looked upon the jasmine blossoming in his presence. His eye sparkles with pleasure: I will join him. [*Exit*.

SCENE.—ANOTHER PART OF THE GARDEN.

Enter VATSA.

I shall make the queen turn pale with anger. She will look upon the creeper like a rival beauty, as the delicate shrub displays the brilliance of its nascent buds, and swells, as gently inflated with the zephyr's sighs.

Vas. (*approaches*). Victory to your majesty!—fortune is propitious.

Vatsa. I doubt it not, my friend; for inconceivable is the virtue of drugs, and charms, and gems. Lead the way, and let these eyes this day obtain by the sight the fruit of their formation.

Vas. This way.

Vatsa. Precede.

Vas. (*advances and stops to listen: he turns back in alarm*). Fly, fly, Sir!

Vatsa. Why?

Vas. There is a goblin in yonder *bakula* tree!

Vatsa. Away, simpleton, go on, and fear not! how should any such being have power at this season to harm?

Vas. He speaks quite distinctly—if you disbelieve me advance and listen.

Vatsa. (*advances*). I hear a distinct voice, and a sweet one, too, like that of a woman: from its small and sharp tone it must be a starling. (*Looking up*) Ah! there she sits.

Vas. A starling?

Vatsa (*laughing*). A starling, look there!

Vas. And so, my good friend, your fears made you fancy a starling to be a goblin.

Vatsa. Out on you, blockhead! would you accuse me of what you have done yourself.

Vas. Well, now do not you interfere. (*Holds up his staff.*) You impertinent bird, have you no more respect for a Brahman: stop a moment, and with this crooked staff I will bring you down from the tree like a ripe wood-apple.

Vatsa. Forbear, forbear! how prettily she talks.

Vas. Yes, now I listen again, she says, give this Brahman something to eat.

Vatsa. Something to eat, is ever the burthen of the glutton's song. Come, say truly, what does she utter?

Vas. (*listening and repeating*). "Who is this you have delineated? Do not be offended without cause; I have given your *Kámadeva*, my *Reti*." Hey, Sir! what should this mean?

Vatsa. Oh, I suppose some female has been drawing her lover's portrait, and passing it off on her companion as the picture of the god of love: her friend has found her out, and ingeniously exposed her evasion, by delineating her in the character of *Káma's* bride.

Vas. Very likely.

Vatsa. Be still, she speaks again. (*They listen.*)

Vas. (*repeating*). "Why should you be ashamed; attachment to exalted worth becomes your native excellence."

Vatsa. Likely, likely!

Vas. Nay, do not you presume upon your scholarship; I will expound all she says, when she has finished. The lady that is pictured is very handsome.

Vatsa. We shall have leisure to satisfy our curiosity; let us now listen.

Vas. Very well; do you hear what she says: "Take away these lotus leaves and fibres—it is in vain you strive to offer me relief."

Vatsa. I hear and understand.

Vas. How the jade chatters to-day! but I will explain all I hear.

Vatsa. Very likely, but now listen.

Vas. Hey!—I declare she speaks in measure, like a Brahman skilled in the four *Vedas*.

Vatsa. What said she, I did not hear?

Vas. "I have fixed my heart where I dare not raise my hopes;—I am overcome with shame and despair, and death is my only refuge."

Vatsa. With the exception of yourself, my worthy friend, what learned Brahman would call this speaking in measure?

Vas. Why, what is it?

*Vatsa.** Prose.

Vas. Prose! Oh, very well, and what does it mean?

Vatsa. Some young female may be supposed to have spoken the sentence, indifferent to life, because uncertain of her affection being returned.

Vas. (*laughing loudly*). You may as well drop these evasive interpretations: why not say at once, "The damsel doubts my returning her passion." Who but yourself could have been delineated as the god of the flowery bow. (*Claps his hands and laughs.*)

Vatsa. Peace, simpleton! your obstreperous mirth has frightened the bird away; see! there she flies.

Vas. She has perched on the plantain bower: let us follow her.

Vatsa. Oppressed by the shafts of *Káma,* the delicate maid entrusts her companions with the sorrows of her breast: the tattling parrot or imitative starling repeats her words, and they find a hospitable welcome in the ears of the fortunate.

[*Exeunt.*

* Vasantaka says, "It is a *richa* that the bird has repeated," or a verse peculiar to the *Vedas*: the *Raja* says, "No; it is a *gáthá*," which is correct, the verse consisting of four lines of 12—15—12—15 mátras or short vowels.

The Plantain Bower.

Enter Vatsa *and* Vasantaka.

Vas. Here is the bower; let us enter: but what has become of the starling? No matter; let us rest on this bench, where the breeze breathes cool and soft amidst the waving leaves of these *bananas*.

Vatsa. As you please. (*They sit.*)

Vas. What is yonder? It looks like the cage of the starling—broken to pieces most probably by the monkey.

Vatsa. See what it is.

Vás. I will. (*Looking about.*) What's here, a picture—(*takes it up*). Ha, ha! my friend, you are in luck.

Vatsa. What is that?

Vas. Just what I said: here is your likeness. Who but yourself could have been delineated as the god of the flowery bow?

Vatsa. Give it me.

Vas. Stop a little. What! is such a jewel of a girl, as is here pictured, to be seen for nothing?

Vatsa. Take this—(*gives him a golden bracelet, and Vasantaka delivers the picture.*) Ha! behold, my friend; what lovely swan is this that wings her flight to *Mánasa,* in whose sports the lotus trembles, who declares such auspicious fortune shall befall us, and whose face might be taken for the full moon by *Brahmá,* when he first emerged from his lotus throne—(*looking at the picture*).

Enter Susangatá *and* Ságariká.

Sus. It is hopeless to follow the bird; let us get the drawing again, therefore, and go in.

Ság. By all means.

Vas. (*to the king*). Well, my friend, who is this damsel, think you, that seems to bend her head so humbly?

Sus. Hark! I hear Vasanta talking—I suspect to the king; let us conceal ourselves amongst the plants and hear what they are talking of—(*they hide behind the plantain trees*).

Vatsa. *Brahmá,* when he first emerged from his lotus throne, had taken such a face for the unrivalled orb of the moon.

Sus. (*to Ságariká*). You are in luck, girl; your lover is dwelling upon your praises.

Ság. How can you make so light of me as to treat me as matter for your mirth?

Vas. Why should she hang down her head in this manner?

Vatsa. Has not the starling told us all?

Sus. There! I told you so; that bird has repeated our conversation.

Ság. (*to herself*). What will he reply? I hang between life and death!

Vas. Well, and does she please your eyes?

Vatsa. Please my eyes, say you? My sight insatiate rests upon her graceful limbs and slender waist: reluctantly it rises to her budding bosom, and thence ascending, fixes on those soft expressive orbs, where tremulously hangs the crystal tear.

Sus. Did you hear?

Ság. Did you hear? he praises the artist's skill!

Vas. Well, Sir, and what dulness must there be in you, not to perceive that in this, the object of the damsel's affection, your resemblance is exhibited?

Vatsa. I cannot deny that she has flatteringly delineated my likeness, nor doubt her sentiments,—for observe the traces of the tear that has fallen upon her work, like the moist dew that starts from every pore of my frame.

Ság. (*to herself*). Heart, be of good cheer! your passion is directed to a corresponding object.

Sus. My friend, you are fortunate; we must treat you now with the deference due to her whom our master loves.

Vas. (*looking round*). Here are other traces of her passion: the lotus leaves she has applied to her heart whilst revealing her affection to her friend.

Vatsa. You have guessed well. Where it has been in contact with her form the leaf has faded, but is still green where the contour of her well proportioned shape has interposed an interval between the verdure and her person. The central freshness of the lotus leaf that has reposed upon her bosom reveals not the fervour of her love, but these two pallid circles on either side betray the violence of her affection.

Vas. (*picking up the fibre*). Here is another vestige—it has bound the lotus leaf upon her bosom.

Vatsa (*applying it to his heart*). It still dispenses its cooling freshness. Say, fibre, art thou withered, because thou art no longer cherished between those palpitating orbs, whose friendly contiguity scarce leaves room for the lodgment of a silken thread, much less for thee.

Sus. (*apart*). His grace must be violently affected to talk thus incoherently. It will not become me to leave him to these fancies. (*To Ságariká.*) Well, my friend, what you came for is before you.

Ság. Why, what did I come for, pray?

Sus. The picture, what else? there it is—take it.

Ság. (*angrily*). As I don't understand what you say, I shall leave you. [*Going.*

Sus. How now, impatient! stop a moment, and I will recover the drawing before we leave this place.

Ság. Do so.

(*Susangatá comes forward, so as to be seen by Vasantaka.*)

Vas. Hide the picture, here, in this plantain leaf—here comes one of the queen's damsels. (*Vatsa covers it with his mantle.*)

Sus. (*advancing*). Glory to the king!

Vatsa. Welcome, Susangatá; sit down. How knew you that I was here?

Sus. That is not all my knowledge; I am acquainted with the secret of the picture, and some other matters, of which I shall apprize her majesty. [*Going.*

Vas. (*apart to Vatsa*). It is all blown—she is a great tattler—better bribe her to be silent.

Vatsa. Stay, Susangatá; accept these ornaments. (*Takes

off his bracelet, &c.) This is but a matter of sport, not to be mentioned to the queen.

Sus. Your grace is bountiful, you need not fear me. I was but in jest, and do not want these jewels. The truth is, my dear friend, Ságariká, is very angry with me for drawing her picture, and I shall be much obliged to your majesty to intercede for me and appease her resentment.

Vatsa (springing up). Where is she? lead me to her!

Vas. Give me the picture—I will take care of it; it may again be wanted.

Sus. This way. *(They advance.)*

Ság. He is here—I tremble at his sight.——I can neither stand nor move—what shall I do?

Vas. (seeing her). A most surprising damsel, truly; such another is not to he found in this world. I am confident that when she was created *Brahmá* was astonished at his own performance.

Vatsa. Such are my impressions. The four mouths of *Brahmá* must at once have exclaimed in concert, bravo, bravo! when the deity beheld these eyes more beauteous than the leaves of his own lotus, and his heads must have shaken with wonder, as he contemplated loveliness, the ornament of all the world.*

Sag. (to Susangatá). This is the picture you have brought. [*Going.*

Vatsa. You turn your eyes upon your friend in anger, lovely maid; yet such is their native tenderness they cannot assume a harsh expression. Look thus, but do not leave us, for your departure hence will alone give me pain.

Sus. She is very angry, Sir, I assure you; take her hand and pacify her.

* *Ventidius* to *Antony:*

> " You ——
> Were sure the chief, and best of human race.
> So perfect that the gods who formed you wondered
> At their own skill, and cried, a lucky hit
> Has mended our design." " ALL FOR LOVE."

Vatsa. You advise me well. (*Takes Ságariká by the hand.*)

Vas. I congratulate you, Sir; you enjoy unprecedented fortune.

Vatsa. You say rightly—she is the very deity *Lakshmí* herself: her hand is the new shoot of the *párijáta* tree, else whence distil these dew-drops of ambrosia?

Sus. It is not possible, my dear friend, you can remain inexorable whilst honoured thus with his grace's hand.

Ság. (*frowning*). Will you not forbear, Susangatá?

Vatsa. Nay, you must not be angry with your friend.

Vas. Why, like a hungry Brahman, should you thus be out of humour, lady?

Sus. Very well, my friend, I will say no more.

Vatsa. This is not right, resentful girl, to be so unforgiving to your intimate companions.

Vas. Hey! here again is Madam Vásavadattá.

(*The Raja lets go Ságariká's hand in alarm.*)

Ság. (*to Sus*). What shall I do?

Sus. We can escape unperceived behind this *tamála* tree. (*They go off hastily.*)

Vatsa (*looking round*). Why, my friend, where is the queen, where is Vásavadattá?

Vas. I do not know. I said, here again is Madam Vásavadattá; I meant in testiness of temper.

Vatsa. Out on thee! thou hast rudely snapped the string of splendid gems, that fate and acknowledged love had hung around my neck. [*They retire.*

Enter VÁSAVADATTÁ, *the Queen, and* KÁNCHANAMÁLÁ, *an attendant.*

Vásava. Well, girl, how far from hence is my lord's favourite jasmine tree?

Kánch. It is but a little way farther: we shall see it after passing this plantain bower.

Vásava. Let us hasten.

Kanch. I think I see his majesty. Yes, there he is; will it please you join him?

Vásava. (*approaching Vatsa*). Glory to my lord!

Vatsa (*to Vasantaka*). Hide the picture—quick.

(*Vasantaka takes it and holds it under his arm.*)

Vásava. Has the jasmine budded yet, my lord?

Vatsa. I have been waiting your arrival, and have not yet seen it; we will now visit it together.

Vásava. Oh no—I see by your countenance that it has flowered: that is sufficient, I will go no further.

Vas. Then your grace acknowledges we have conquered! huzza! (*waves his hand and dances; the picture falls; the Raja observes it, looks at him angrily, and points to the picture*).

Vas. (*apart to Vatsa*). Be calm; I will manage it.

Kanch. (*picking up the picture and shewing it to the Queen*) See, madam, whose portrait is this?

Vásava. (*looking at it and apart*). This is my lord, and is not this Ságariká? (*Aloud to Vatsa*) Pray what is this, my lord?

Vatsa. (*to Vasanta*). What shall I say?

Vas. (*to Vatsa*). Fear not, leave it to me. (*Aloud to Vásavadattá.*) I was observing, madam, that it would be very difficult to hit my friend's likeness, on which his majesty was pleased to give me this specimen of his skill.

Vatsa. It is as Vasantaka tells you.

Vásava. And this female standing near you—I suppose this is a specimen of Vasantaka's skill?

Vatsa. What should you suspect? That is a mere fancy portrait, the original was never seen before.

Vas. I'll swear to this, by my Brahmanical cord, that the original was never before seen by either of us.

Kanch. (*To the Queen, apart*). Why should he speak evasively, madam? there is no need to be angry.

Vásava. (*To her*). My honest girl, you do not understand his prevarications. I know Vasantaka. (*Aloud*) My Lord, excuse me. Looking at this picture has given me a slight headache. I leave you to your amusements. [*Going.*

Vatsa. What can I say to you, dearest? I really am at a loss! If I ask you to forgive me, that is unnecessary, if you are not offended; and how can I promise to do so no more, when I have committed no fault—although you will not believe my assertions.

Vásava. (*detaching herself gently and with politeness.*) You mistake, my lord; I assure you my head aches; on that account I take my leave.

[*Exit with Kánchanamálá.*

Vas. Your majesty has had a lucky escape. The queen's anger has dispersed like summer clouds.

Vatsa. Away, blockhead, we have no occasion to rejoice: could you not discover the queen's anger through her unsuccessful attempts to disguise it? Her face was clouded with a passing frown. As she hung down her head, she looked on me with an affected smile. She gave utterance to no angry words 'tis true, and the swelling eye glowed not with rage—but a starting tear was with difficulty repressed; and although she treated me with politeness, struggling indignation lurked in every gesture. We must follow, and endeavour to pacify her. [*Exeunt.*

END OF THE SECOND ACT.

ACT III.

Scene I.—A Chamber in the Palace.

Enter Madaniká, *one of the Queen's Attendants.*

Ho, Kausámbiká! tell me if Kánchanamálá is with the Queen? (*Listening*) What say you; she came in some time since and went out again; where can she be? Oh, she comes.

Enter Kánchanamálá.

Kánch. Bravo, Vasantaka, bravo! you are a deeper politician than the prime minister himself.

Mad. How now, fellow Kánchanamálá, what has Vasantaka done to merit your praises?

Kánch. What occasion is there for your asking? you are not able to keep the secret!

Mad. I swear by the feet of the queen, I will not mention it to any body.

Kánch. On that condition you shall hear. As I was passing from the palace to-day, I overheard Vasantaka and Susangatá in conversation behind the door of the picture gallery.*

Mad. What was the subject?

Kánch. Vasantaka said, Ságariká alone is the cause of my friend's indisposition; do you, Susangatá, devise a remedy.

Mad. And what replied she?

Kánch. She said, the queen having discovered what was going forward by finding the picture, but not suspecting me, has placed Ságariká under my charge—giving me, to insure

* *Chitta sáli*, or *Chitra sálá*. So in the *Viddhasálá bhanjiká*, a chamber of this kind occurs hung with portraits of the women of the interior of the palace.

my vigilance, some of her own clothes and ornaments. With these I will equip Ságariká as the queen, and myself as Kánchanamálá, and thus disguised will meet his majesty at the *mádhava* bower about sunset: do you come to this place and conduct us thither.

Mad. Very well plotted, Susangatá; but you are mistaken, if you think to deceive a mistress so kind to her attendants.

Kánch. And where are you going?

Mad. I was coming to look for you. You were so long in bringing us an answer about his majesty's illness, that the queen was very anxious, and sent me to see what had become of you.

Kánch. Her majesty is too simple, to be so easily deceived. But the king, whose only illness is love, is sitting in the pavilion over the ivory gate. Come along, let us carry this news to the queen. [*Exeunt.*

THE PAVILION.

VATSA *discovered.*

Vatsa. Endure, my heart, the fever love has kindled, and which the maid I sigh for can alone allay. Why reproach me with my folly for seeking to subdue thy fervours with the cooling sandal, instead of that lovely hand which was awhile in my grasp! The mind from its natural unsteadiness should be a difficult mark to hit; how happens it that the archer-god has lodged all his shafts in mine! Deity of the flowery bow, innumerable are those who may be struck with thy five arrows, and such as I am are notoriously thy aim. But in this is the usual state of things reversed, that I, singly, am pierced with thy countless darts, and am about to perish. Yet I suffer less on my own account than for poor Ságariká. She shrinks from every gaze, suspecting that her secret is discovered. If she observe two of her companions in conversation, she fancies herself the subject; and if they laugh, she thinks she is the object of their mirth. Alas, my love! thy uneasiness excites my compassion, and I share the dread thou sufferest from the glances of the queen, as they bend on thee with ill dissembled indignation.—How long Vasantaka delays! I havé sent him to obtain some tidings of the maiden.

Enter VASANTAKA.

Vas. (*to himself*). Ha, ha! my friend, you will be better pleased to-day than when you ascended the throne of Kausámbí, when you hear the agreeable news I bring you. Oh, there he is: he seems expecting me. Joy, joy, my friend; fortune is propitious, and promises to accomplish your desire.

Vatsa. How is Ságariká?

Vas. In a little time you may judge for yourself.

Vatsa. What, may I hope to see her soon?

Vas. Why not, am not I your councillor; I who laugh at the wisdom of *Vrihaspatí?*

Vatsa. Admitted—there is nothing you cannot manage; but come, tell me, I long to hear the particulars.

Vas. (*whispers in his ear*).* There, you have the whole.

Vatsa. This merits reward. (*Gives him a bracelet.*)

Vas. (*takes it and puts it on.*) Very becoming; a golden bracelet suits my arm. I will go and shew it to my wife. [*Going.*

Vatsa. Stop, my friend, stop, another time will serve your purpose. How much of the day remains?

Vas. (*looking*). See, my friend, the lord of a thousand rays approaches the bowers of the western mountain.

Vatsa. True, the lord of the one-wheeled car having performed the circuit of the world, now purposes to suspend his labours till the morrow's dawn, and halting on the mountain's brow, he calls in his scattered rays, whose golden lines converging round his chariot, look like the radiant spokes that shoot to their centre from the wide circumference of the spheres. As with assembled beams he rests upon the summit of the

* A clumsy mode of avoiding the repetition of the plot. We have had it in other pieces, as the *Mrichchakati* and *Mudrá Rákshasa.*

western hill, the lord of day thus breathes his farewell to the lotus: "Adieu, my beloved, my hour is come and I must depart: sleep dwell upon thy lids, till I again disturb thy slumbers." Let us therefore away to the *mádhavi* bower, and be punctual to the time appointed by my fair.

Vas. I attend you. The interval that separates the trees of the grove is lost, and they seem to form one close compacted mass. A dusky hue, like that of the hide of the buffalo or wild boar besmeared with mire, extends over the garden, and thick glooms spreading above the east, obscure the horizon.

Vatsa. True: first gathering in the east, the deepening gloom successively obscures the other regions of the sky: becoming intenser as it proceeds, it steals the hue of *Siva's* neck, and mountains, trees, and towns, the heavens and the earth, are hidden from our sight. Let us to the garden.

[*Exeunt.*

THE GARDEN.

Enter VATSA *and* VASANTAKA.

Vas. This clump of trees should be the *makaranda* grove, but I am not quite certain: how shall we find the way?

Vatsa. Go on, we are right, I know the path. The *champaka* trees are here, I smell their fragrance; and now the *sindhuváras*; we now pass the cluster of *bakulas,* and here are the *pátali* trees: their various odour indicates their situation, and would enable us to track the walk were they concealed by twice the present gloom.

Vas. Ha! here we are, this is the *mádhavi* bower. I know it by the perfume of the buds so tempting to the bees, and the smoothness of the emerald pavement. Do you remain here whilst I go for Ságariká, I shall soon be back.

Vatsa. Do not be long.

Vas. Do not be impatient, my friend. I am back already.*

[*Exit.*

* A form of speech still in use in reply to the commands of a superior: a servant, on being directed to do any thing, commonly answering, 'it is done.'

Vatsa. I wait you on this emerald seat. Who will take part with the inconstant swain, that abandons his old love for a new? The timid damsel that comes to her first assignation, casts but a sidelong glance upon her beloved, and though she shrink not from his embrace, averts her countenance from his gaze. 'Let me go,' she murmurs repeatedly; 'I will leave you!' but still submits to the gentle violence that prevents her departure.' What heightened charms does a stolen interview bestow upon the amorous maid! How long Vasantaka delays! surely Vásavadattá has not heard of our design. [*Retires.*

A CHAMBER.

Enter VÁSAVADATTÁ *and* KÁNCHANAMÁLÁ.

Vásava. Can it be possible, wench, that Ságariká has promised to meet my lord disguised in my attire!

Kánch. I have told your majesty; but if we find Vasantaka at the door of the picture gallery, your doubts, I hope, will be removed.

Vásava. Let us thither. [*Exeunt.*

CHAMBER LEADING TO THE PICTURE GALLERY.

Enter VASANTAKA, *disguised.*

Vas. I thought I heard the tread of feet; Ságariká approaches. [*Retires.*

Enter VÁSAVADATTÁ *and* KÁNCHANAMÁLÁ.

Kánch. This the place, madam. Now to see if Vasantaka is here. (*Snaps her fingers.*)

Vas. (*approaching*). Ha, Susangatá! well done: I declare I should have taken you for Kánchanamálá. Where is Ságariká?

Kánch. (*pointing to Vásavadattá*). There.

Vas. Why, this is the very queen herself.

Vásava. (*alarmed and apart*). How! am I recognised!

Vas. Come, Ságariká, this way.

Kánch. (*to the Queen*). All's safe, madam. (*Pointing to

Vasantaka) Ah! rogue, you will have cause to remember your words.

Vas. Haste, haste, Ságariká! the deer-marked deity rises in the east. [*Exeunt.*

A GROVE.*—VATSA *discovered.*

Why is my heart so agitated when I expect an interview with my fair; or is it that the flame of love burns fiercest as it approaches its gratification, as the days are hottest when the rains are about to descend.

Enter VASANTAKA, VÁSAVADATTÁ, *and* KÁNCHANAMÁLÁ.

Vas. (*to Vasava*). Lady Ságariká, I hear my friend muttering to himself his anxiety for your appearance; I will announce your arrival. (*Vásavadattá nods assent.*) Fortune is propitious to your majesty; Ságariká is here!

Vatsa. (*approaching her*). My beloved Ságariká, thy countenance is radiant as the moon, thy eyes are two lotus buds, thy hand is the full blown flower, and thy arms its graceful filaments. Come thou, whose whole form is the shrine of ecstasy, come to my arms, and allay the feverish pangs inflicted by the shapeless god.

Vásava. (*weeping, apart to Kánch.*) Ah, girl! my lord now speaks his honest self—how soon will his tone be changed. Is not this incomprehensible?

Kánch. It is so, indeed, madam; there is nothing so bad, that it may not be expected from these abominable men.

Vas. Come, Ságariká, take courage; speak to his majesty. We have had the harsh tones of the angry queen Vásavadattá grating in our ears to-day; let them be now regaled with the melody of your sweet voice.

Vásava. (*to Kánch. apart*). Hey, girl! am I accustomed to speak harshly? The worthy Vasantaka is very complimentary.

Kánch. He will have cause to recollect this.

* As the parties in this scene are occasionally for short intervals invisible to each other, we must suppose the trees so arranged as to intercept the sight of them.

Vas. See, my friend, the moon is up, and casts on every thing his rays as pallid as the maiden's cheek that whitens with resentment.

Vatsa. See, love, the lord of night now stands upon the mountain's crest, and throws his scattered rays around to emulate the radiance of thy cheek. But idle is his coming—does not thy countenance shame the beauty of the lotus! do not thine eyes diffuse dearer delight! What aid can he bring to the influence of the fish-bannered god, which is not wrought by a single glance of thine? Why should the moon shew himself whilst thy resplendent charms are visible? And if he rises, proud of his store of nectar, does he not know thy lips may boast too of *ambrosia!*

Vásava. (*throwing off her veil*). Believe me still Ságariká, my good lord; your heart is so fascinated by her, you fancy you behold Ságariká in every thing.

Vatsa. (*apart*). How! the queen Vásavadattá! What is this?

Vas. My life is in jeopardy—that is—what it is.

Vatsa. (*to the Queen*). Forgive me, dearest.

Vásava. Address not this to me, my lord—the epithet is another's property.

Vas. (*apart*). What is to be done! (*Aloud.*) Nay, madam! you are of too generous a spirit not to forgive this first offence of my dear friend.

Vásava. Worthy Vasantaka, the offence is mine, who have presumed to interrupt this intended interview.

Vatsa. It is of no use to deny it. But hear me: I bow me to thy feet, and mark my forehead with their vermil dye, in hope to transfer thither the hue with which anger discolours thy moon-like countenance. (*Falls at her feet.*)

Vásava. Rise, my lord, rise! that wife must be unreasonable indeed, who with such evidence of her lord's affection can presume to be offended. Be happy, I take my leave. [*Going.*

Vas. Nay, madam, be merciful; I am sure, if you quit his majesty in this posture, you will hereafter repent it.

Vásava. Away, fool! I know no reason for mercy nor repentance. [*Exit with Kánchanamálá.*

Vas. Your majesty may get up, the queen is gone. What is the use of weeping in a wood?

Vatsa. What, gone, without relenting!

Vas. Not so either, for our limbs are whole.

Vatsa. Out, simpleton! do you make a jest of this; you, by whose blundering this untoward accident has happened! The genuine regard, our long and tender union has inspired, will now appear pretended, and the impression of my inconstancy may render her unable to endure existence. No pang is so intolerable as that of unrequited affection.

Vas. The queen is angry, that is a clear case; as to what she will do, that is by no means certain. In the mean time is Ságariká alive or not?

Vatsa. I was thinking of her. [*They retire.*

Enter SÁGARIKÁ (*behind*), *dressed as the Queen.*

Ság. I have luckily got clear of the music hall, and have come so far in this disguise without being observed. But, alas! what shall I do now?

Vas. Why thus lost in thought, something must be devised.

Vatsa. But what?

Ság. (*behind*). 'Twere better far, that I should put an end at once to my sufferings and my life: the queen will then know nothing of my purpose, and Susangatá and I shall both escape disgrace. This tree will do.

Vatsa. I see nothing left for it but to appease the queen. Come, let us go in.

Vas. Stop, I heard steps! perhaps she has thought better, and returns.

Vatsa. She is a woman of a generous spirit—it may be so. Quick, ascertain!

Ság. With the fibres of the *mádhaví* I will suspend myself to this bough. Alas! my dear friends, far, far away, alone and unfriended, I thus terminate my miserable existence. (*Fastening the noose around her neck.*)

Vas. Who is there?—Ha, the queen! Hey why, what! haste, haste, my friend, or Vásavadattá will destroy herself.

Vatsa. (*advancing hastily*). Where, where is she?

Vas. Behold!

Vatsa (*rushing to her and tearing off the tendril*). Intemperate woman! what horrid act is this! my own life trembles in my throat: existence is not yours to abandon: forego such desperate thought.

Ság. (*apart*). My lord! His presence inspires the love of life; at least my last wish is accomplished, and having seen him, I shall die content. (*Aloud*) Let me go, Sir, you forget my dependant station; I may not find again an opportunity to end this hated being. Beware how you displease the queen.

Vatsa. Can it be, my own Ságariká! No more of this despair; away with these fatal bands, and to arrest my fleeting life, twine round my neck the noose of these dear arms. (*Embraces her.*) My friend, it rains without a cloud.

Vas. Very true, if the queen does not return like a sudden squall, and spoil our fine weather.

Enter VÁSAVADATTÁ *and* KÁNCHANAMÁLÁ.

Vásava. I treated my lord too disrespectfully, girl, as he condescended to cast himself at my feet; I must therefore see him again, and behave to him with more temper.

Kánch. Who would think in this way but your grace? However, better the king fail in decorum than your majesty, so let us seek him.

Vatsa. Say, fair maid, may not our affection hope to be returned?

Kánch. I hear his majesty's voice, he is probably seeking for you in hopes to pacify your anger.

Vásava. Let us approach gently from behind; I will cast my arms round his neck, and tell him I forgive him.

Vas. Take courage, Ságariká, make my friend a reply.

Vásava. (apart). Ságariká here!—Keep back, let us listen; I will presently be of the party.

Ság. Why, Sir, will you thus pretend regard you do not feel, and wantonly risk the displeasure of the queen, who, I know, is dearer to you than your life.

Vatsa. You utter what is not quite true, my love. When her bosom swells with sighs I express concern; when she is sullen I soothe her; when her brows are bent, and her face is distorted with anger, I fall prostrate at her feet. These marks of respect are due to the queen's exalted station; but the regard that springs from vehement affection, that is yours alone.

Vásava. (coming forward). I believe you, my lord, I believe you.

Vatsa. How now, madam, is it you? Why then you need not be offended. Cannot you perceive that I have been attracted hither, and misled by this resemblance of your dress and person? Be composed, I beg you. [*Falls at her feet.*

Vásava. Rise, rise! let not my exalted station put you to such unnecessary inconvenience.

Vatsa. (aside). She has overheard me—there is no chance then of appeasing her.

Vas. It is very true, madam. I assure you, that deceived by the belief that you were attempting to destroy yourself, I brought my friend to this spot, to preserve, as I thought, your life. If you doubt me see this noose. [*Takes up the noose.*

Vásava. Kánchanamálá, girl, take the twisted tendril and secure that Brahman, and make this hussy go on before us.

Kánch. As you command. (*Puts the noose over Vasantaka's neck, and beats him with the other end of it.*) Now, Sir, see what is the consequence of your ingenuity. You have had the queen's harsh voice grating in your ears, have you? do you recollect this. Come, Ságariká, do you go on before.

Ság. Why did I not perish when I sought to die!

Vas. Think of me, my dear friend, who am thus carried off an unfortunate captive by the queen.

Exeunt all but VATSA.

What an unlucky business this is! What is to be done? how shall I dissipate the rage that clouds the smiling countenance of the queen! how rescue Ságariká from the dread of her resentment, or liberate my friend Vasantaka? I am quite bewildered with these events, and can no longer command my ideas.—At any rate it is useless to stay here: I will in, and endeavour to pacify Vásavadattá. [*Exit.*

END OF THE THIRD ACT.

ACT IV.

A Chamber.

Enter Susangatá *with a Diamond Necklace in her hand.*

Alas, alas! my dear friend Ságariká, my timid, my tender, my generous friend: whither, lovely maiden, are you gone? shall I not again behold you? Pitiless destiny, why shouldst thou have endowed her with such unrivalled charms, to consign her to so hapless a fate! Despairing of her life, she has begged me to give this necklace to some Brahman. Whom shall I present it to? Eh, here comes Vasantaka, I will give it to him.

Enter Vasantaka.

Vas. So, I am well out of that scrape. Appeased by my excellent friend's intercession, her majesty has not only restored me to freedom, but has regaled me with cates from her own fair hands, and presented me with a dress and these earrings. Now then to seek the king.

Sus. (*advances*). Worthy Vasantaka, one moment.

Vas. Hey, Susangata, what's the matter; why do you weep? no bad news, I hope, of Ságariká.

Sus. It is of her I wished to speak. It is said that the queen ordered her off to Ujayin, and she was taken away at midnight; but whither she is gone I know not.

Vas. Alas, poor Ságariká, a damsel of such unequalled charms, and of such a gentle disposition! I much fear the violence of the queen.

Sus. She herself despaired of life, poor girl, and left with me this diamond necklace, to be presented to the worthy Vasantaka. Pray you, accept it.

Vas. (*covering his ears*). Excuse me, I could not stretch out my hand to take so sad a memorial. [*Weeps.*

Sus. For her sake, let me entreat you.

Vas. I tell you what: I will take it to the king. It will relieve the sorrow into which the loss of Ságariká has plunged him. (*Susangatá gives it to him, he looks at it attentively.*) Why, where could she have procured such a valuable necklace?

Sus. That excited my curiosity, and I asked her.

Vas. And what replied she?

Sus. She looked me in the face, and sighed, and said, Ah, Susangatá, it is now of no avail to tell my sad story,—and then burst into tears.

Vas. Although she has not confessed it, yet such an ornament is a proof that she belongs to some distinguished family. —Where is the king?

Sus. He went from the queen's apartments to the crystal alcove. Do you go to him—I must to her majesty.

[*Exeunt severally.*

THE CRYSTAL ALCOVE.

VATSA *discovered, seated.*

Deceitful vows, tender speeches, plausible excuses, and prostrate supplications, had less effect upon the queen's anger than her own tears; like water upon fire, they quenched the blaze of her indignation. I am now only anxious for Ságariká. Her form, as delicate as the petal of the lotus, dissolving in the breath of inexperienced passion, has found a passage through the channels by which love penetrates, and is lodged deep in my heart. The friend to whom I could confide my secret sorrows is the prisoner of the queen; in whose presence can I now give vent to my tears?

Enter VASANTAKA.

Vas. Yonder is my friend, emaciate with care, but graceful still, radiant as the newly risen moon. Health to your grace! fortune favours you. I have got out of her majesty's clutches, and these eyes have again the pleasure of beholding you.

Vatsa. My friend Vasantaka, embrace me (*embraces him*). Your dress declares you restored to the good graces of the queen. Tell me, what news of Ságariká. (*Vasantaka hangs down his head.*) I pray you speak.

Vas. I cannot utter such unpleasant tidings.

Vatsa. What tidings, speak? Alas, it is too plain, she is no more! Ságariká! [*Faints.*

Vas. (*alarmed*). My friend, revive—revive!

Vatsa. (*recovering*). Leave me, existence—I willingly resign you—haste, or you will be forcibly expelled. Already is that graceful maid far off.

Vas. You are alarmed unnecessarily. I was about to tell you, the queen has sent her to Ougein:—this I called unpleasant tidings.

Vatsa. To Ougein! Ah, cruel Vásavadattá. Who told you this?

Vas. Susangatá:—and more, she gave me this necklace to bring to your majesty. She knows why.

Vatsa. To alleviate my despair; what else. Give it me. (*Vasantaka gives him the necklace which he applies to his heart*). This has once hung upon her neck, and is now far removed from her: it is a friend that shares a similar fortune with myself, and will speak comfort to my sorrows: wear it, my friend, that as it meets my gaze I may acquire fortitude.

Vas. As you command. (*Ties the necklace round his neck.*)

Vatsa. Alas, I shall never again behold my love.

Vas. Speak not so loud—some one approaches.

Enter VASUNDHÁRÁ, *a Female Attendant, with a Sword.**

Vasun. Glory to your majesty!—So please you, the nephew

* The accounts of the early travellers in India speak of the female guard of the *haram*. According to *Manouchi*, that of Shah Jehan consisted of a hundred Tartar women, armed with a bow, a poignard, and a scimetar. The practice has been noticed in former plays, and seems to have been originally Hindu, if it was not universally Asiatic.

of Rumanwán, Vijayavermá, desirous of communicating to you some acceptable tidings, is at the door.

Vatsa. Let him enter.

VASUNDHARÁ *goes out, and returns with* VIJAYAVERMÁ.

Vij. Glory to your majesty! Your majesty's fortune is propitious in the triumphs of Rumanwán.

Vatsa. Are the *Kosalás* subdued?

Vij. By your majesty's auspices.

Vatsa. Rumanwán has well performed his task, and speedily achieved an arduous labour. Let me hear the circumstances of our triumph.

Vij. On receiving your majesty's commands, the general of the state, Rumanwán, soon collected a mighty army of foot, and horse, and elephants,* and marching against the king of *Kosalá*, surrounded him in a strong position in the *Vindhya* mountains.†

Vatsa. Proceed.

Vij. Impatient of the blockade, the *Kosalá* monarch prepared his troops for an engagement.

Vas. Your slowness sets my heart in a flutter.

Vij. Issuing from the heights, the enemy's forces came down upon us in great numbers, and the points of the horizon were crowded with the array of mighty elephants, like another chain of mountains: they bore down our infantry beneath their ponderous masses: those who escaped the shock were transpierced by innumerable arrows, and the enemy flattered himself he had for once disappointed our commander's hopes.

* It is not unworthy of remark, as illustrative of the progress of military science, and the date of the drama, that chariots are not mentioned here.

† This would be a strange position for a king of *Kosalá*, if that were confined to the Oude provinces, the *Vindhya* mountains running across western and central Hindustan, and passing to the Peninsula. But some time previous to the date of the drama the king of *Kosalá's* authority extended into South Behar. The greater part, if not the whole of Oude was, at this time, when the play was written, subjugated by the princes of *Kanouj*.

Fire flashed from the blows of contending heroes, helmets and heads were cloven in twain—the broken armour and scattered weapons were carried away in torrents of blood, and the defiance of the king of *Kosalá,* in the van of his army, was heard by our warriors; when—

Vatsa. How! was our force discomfited?

Vij. Our chief alone confronted him, and slew the monarch on his furious elephant with countless shafts.

Vas. Victory! victory! we have triumphed!

Vatsa. And honour to our gallant foe, the king of *Kosalá;* for glorious is the warrior's death when his enemies applaud his prowess. What next?

Vij. Rumanwán then appointed my elder brother, Sanjayavermá, to govern the country of *Kosalá,* and making slow marches in consequence of the number of his wounded, returned to the capital. He is now arrived.

Vatsa. Vasundhará, go apprise Yaugandharáyana to distribute the treasures of my favour.

Vasund. You are obeyed. [*Exit with Vijayavermá.*

Enter KÁNCHANAMÁLÁ.

Kán. Glory to your grace! The queen sends you word, that Samvarana Siddha, the magician, is arrived from Ougein: will your majesty be pleased to see him?

Vatsa. By all means; I take much pleasure in this cunning —bring him hither. (*Kánchanamálá goes, and returns with the magician, Samvarana Siddha, carrying a bunch of peacock's feathers in his hands.*)*

Kan. Here is the king.

Sam. (*waving the feathers and laughing*). Reverence to Indra, who lends our art his name,† and on whom *Samvara* and

* A bunch of peacock's feathers is still the implement of conjuring, and is carried by mendicants in India who pretend to skill in magic: it is especially borne about by *Jaina* vagrants.

† Conjuring is called *Aindrajálika* from *Indra* 'the deity;' and *jála* 'a net.'

*Vivara** attend! What are your majesty's commands: would you see the moon brought down upon earth, a mountain in mid air, a fire in the ocean, or night at noon? I will produce them—command.

Vas. My good friend, be careful,—take heed what sort of a person this conjuror may be.

Sam. What need of many words? By the force of my master's spells I will place before your eyes the person whom in your heart you are most anxious to behold.†

Vatsa. Go, girl, to the queen, and tell her that as the magician is her servant, I do not wish to witness his performances alone, but will see them in her company.

Kánch. She is here.

Enter VÁSAVADATTÁ.

Vásava. (*apart to Kánchanamdlá*). Girl, this man is from Ougein: think you he is a friend to me?

Kánch. Fear not, madam, he is well disposed to your grace's family.

Vásava. (*advances*). Victory to my lord!

Vatsa. Come, madam, the sage promises much: let us behold his cunning. (*Leads her to a seat, and sits beside her.*) Now, sir, display your power.

Sam. You shall be obeyed. (*Waves his plume.*) *Hari, Hara, Brahmá,* chiefs of the gods, and thou their mighty monarch, *Indra,* with the host of heavenly spirits, *Siddhas* and *Vidyádharas,*‡ appear rejoicing and dancing in heavens. (*The King and Queen look up and rise from their seats.*)

* Some technicalities of conjuring perhaps personified, the terms mean literally, comprehension and disunion. *Samvara* is also the name of a *Daitya*, who was also an enchanter.

† We see by this and other allusions to the art of magic, that the pretensions of the necromancers of India were not inferior to those of their brethren of the west, nor of dissimilar purport.

‡ The persons, character, and offices of the different inferior races of divinities are very ill defined in the heavenly polity of the Hindus. The

Vatsa. Most wonderful!

Vas. Extraordinary indeed!

Vásava. Most strange!

Vas. See, love: that is *Brahmá* throned upon the lotus.—That, *Sankara* with the crescent moon, his glittering crest—that, *Hari* the destroyer of the demon race, in whose four hands the bow, the sword, the mace, and the shell are borne.—There, mounted on his stately elephant, appears the king of *Swerga*: around them countless spirits dance merrily in mid air, sporting with the lovely nymphs of heaven, whose anklets ring responsive to the measure.*

Vásava. It is very marvellous.

Vas. (*apart*). The son of a slave—this conjuror!—what do we want with gods and nymphs—if he would treat us with a pleasant sight. let him shew us Ságariká.

Enter VASUNDHARÁ.

Vasun. So please your majesty, the minister Yaugandharáyana begs to inform you, that the king Vikramabáhu has sent you, along with your messenger who returns, the councillor Vasubhúti: be pleased to receive him, as the season is auspicious. Yaugandharáyana will also wait upon you as soon as he is at leisure.

Vásava. Suspend this spectacle, my lord. Vasubhúti is a man of elevated rank: he is also of the family of my maternal

Siddhas and *Vidyádharas* are beings of an intermediate order between men and gods, tenanting the middle regions above the earth, and are usually described as attending upon *Indra*, although they have chiefs and kings of their own. The *Vidyádharas* have much intercourse with men, intermarrying with mortals, and often having earthly princes and heroes for their kings. The *Siddhas* are of a more retired cast, and are rarely the subject of fabulous or mythological legend. The printed copy has *Cháranas*, and *Suras*, in place of *Vidyádharas*, implying inferior demigods.

* This is something like the Masque in 'the Tempest.'

uncle, and should not be suffered to wait: let us first see him.

Vatsa. Learned sir, be pleased to repose awhile.

Sam. (*waves the brush*) I obey (*going*). But we have yet some sights for your majesty to behold.

Vatsa. We will see them.

(*Vásava.*) Make him a present, Kánchanamálá.

Kánch. I shall, madam. [*Exit with the Magician.*

Vatsa. (*to Vasantaka*). Go and conduct Vasubhúti hither.

(*Retires with the Queen: Vasantaka goes out, and returns with* VASUBHÚTI *and* BÁBHRAVYA.)

Vas. This way.

Vasu. The avenues of this palace do in truth present a splendid scene. The eye is bewildered amongst the stately steeds and mighty elephants of war: the ear is regaled with harmonious sounds, and the heart is gratified by mixing with the throng of attending princes. The state of the king of *Sinhalá* is here effaced, and the magnificence of the entrance into every court betrays me into rustic admiration.

Bábh. The idea of seeing my master again after so long an absence, diverts my thoughts from every other object. Age and agitation together make my limbs tremble, my eyes are dimmed with involuntary tears, and I stutter and stumble in my speech.

Vas. (*in advance of them*). Come on, sirs.

Vasu. (*observing the necklace*). Bábhravya, we should know that necklace: it was presented by the king to his daughter on her departure.

Bábh. It is very like—shall I ask Vasantaka where he got it?

Vasu. No, no; it is not very surprising that princely families should possess jewels of a similar appearance.

Vas. The king,—advance.

Vasu. Victory to your majesty!

Vatsa. I pay you reverence.

Vasu. Prosperity ever attend your highness!

Vatsa. A seat for the minister.

Vas. This is a seat, (*Spreads his upper garment* on the floor.*)

Bábh. Bábhravya pays his respects to your majesty.

Vatsa. (*puts his hand on his shoulder*). Bábhravya, sit here.

Vas. Minister, the queen Vásavadattá.

Vásava. I salute your excellency.

Vasu. May your highness have a son like his father!

Bábh. Madam, Bábhravya bows to you.

Vatsa. Now, Vasubhúti, how is it with the sovereign of Sinhalá?

Vasu. (*sighs*). I know not what reply to offer.

Vásava. (*apart*). Alas! what can he have to communicate?

Vats. What is the meaning of this concern?

Bábhr. (*apart to Vasubhúti*). It is useless to hesitate—say at once what must be said.

Vasu. It is with difficulty, sir, that I can relate what has chanced, but thus it is. In consequence of the prophecy of the seer, that whoever should wed Retnávalí, my master's daughter, should become the emperor of the world, your majesty's minister, as you are aware, solicited her for your bride: unwilling, however, to be instrumental to the uneasiness of Vásavadattá, the king of Sinhalá declined compliance with his suit.

Vatsa. (*apart to Vásavadattá*). What strange untruths are these, my love, your uncle's envoy relates!

* This seems rather inconsistent with royal magnificence: but we are to recollect the only seats used by Asiatics of rank, even in the present day, are carpets, or cloths and pillows spread on the ground, which is elsewhere uncovered. The Mogul Emperors used a sort of throne, but their courtiers sat on the ground. The Hindu Rajas, the Peshwa, and others, sat upon a cloth supporting themselves by pillows.

Vásava. I cannot pretend to judge, my lord, who is to be believed here.

Vas. (*to Vasubhúti*). Well, and where is the princess now?

Vasu. My master, understanding at last that the queen was deceased,* consented to give his daughter to Vatsa. We were deputed to conduct her hither, when, alas, our vessel was wrecked, and—(*weeps*).

Vásava. Alas, unhappy that I am! Loved sister Retnávalí, where art thou, hear me and reply.

Vatsa. Be composed: the fate that causes, may remove our sorrows. Have not these escaped? (*Pointing to Vasubhúti and Bábhravya.*)

Vásava. Oh, that it may prove so, but fate is no friend to me.

(*Behind.*) The inner apartments are on fire. The flames spread over the palace top a roof of gold; they wind around with clouds of smoke; they shed intolerable heat, and fill the female train with affright. Alas! the former false report, that at Lávanaka† the Queen was burnt, will now become a pitiable truth.

Vatsa. (*starting up wildly.*) Vásavadattá burnt to death! my queen, my love!

* That she was burnt: so in the *Vrihat Kathá*, in which a similar story is told, except that the person is made Padmávati, princess of Magadhá. The queen Vásavadattá is there a party to the project of which Vatsa is kept in ignorance, his love for Vásavadattá not permitting him to think of a second bride whilst she lives. With Vásavadattá's concurrence, his ministers persuaded him that she had perished in the conflagration of the palace, purposely set on fire, whilst he was out on a hunting excursion, by which the objections of Padmávati's father to his daughter holding the inferior rank of a second wife were removed, and Vatsa was prevailed upon, as a duty he owed to his people and family, to marry again. The author of the drama also intimates, that Vatsa was ignorant of his minister's projects, and evidently follows the *Vrihat Kathá*, or a common authority.

† The place where the former palace was burnt. It must have been somewhere on the south bank of the Jumna, near its confluence with the Ganges.

Vásava. What extravagance is this—behold me at your side. But ah! help, help, my lord.

Vatsa. (*embracing her*). Be calm, my love.

Vásava. I think not of myself, but poor Ságariká. She is in bonds: my cruelty has kept her captive, and she will be lost without some aid—haste, haste, and save her!

Vatsa. Ságariká in peril! I fly to her rescue.

Vasu. What desperate purpose is this, Sir? the fatal folly of the moth.

Bábhr. Hear Vasubhúti, Sir.

Vas. (*catching hold of his robe*). Forbear! this is madness.

Vatsa. Let me go, fool! Ságariká will perish—think you I shall survive her?

Bábhr. What! shall the race of Bharata be imperilled for such trifling cause? But be that as it may, I will do my duty.

Vatsa. Stop, thou devouring flame! withhold thy veiling smoke, as high in air thy circling brilliancy revolves—behold! I come to share the destiny of Ságariká. The fire nears the prison of the maid—I shall the more quickly discover her.

[*Rushes off.*

Vásava. My inconsiderate speech has inflicted this anguish on my lord. I cannot bear his loss, and will follow.

Vas. Wait, madam, I will lead the way.

[*Exit with the Queen.*

Vasu. Vatsa has precipitated himself into the flames. After having witnessed the fate of the princess, what remains but that I also offer up my life. [*Exit.*

Bábhr. And must the race of Bharata thus causelessly perish?—But why do I delay—I will at least give proof of my fidelity. [*Exit.*

THE PALACE ON FIRE.

SÁGARIKÁ, *in chains, discovered.*

The blaze encompassess me on every side: thanks, lord of flame, thou puttest a period to my sorrows.

Enter VATSA.

Vatsa. The light shews me Ságariká—'tis she, alone, without assistance.

Ság. The prince! The sight of him inspires with me the hope of life. (*Aloud.*) Preserve me, Sire!

Vatsa. Fear not: support one moment these investing vapours—ha! the scarf on your bosom is on fire. (*Snatches it off.*) Your fetters impede your path,—let me support you. Dearest, cling to me. (*Takes her in his arms.*) Already is the heat allayed,—be of good cheer: the fire cannot harm thee, love, whose very touch abates its intensity. (*Pauses—looks round—closes his eyes, and re-opens them.*) Why, what is this! where are the flames! they have disappeared, and there stands the palace unharmed! Ha! the daughter of Avanti's monarch!

Enter VÁSAVADATTÁ, *who runs into* VATSA'S *arms.*

Vásava. My dearest lord!

Enter VASUBHÚTI, VASANTAKA, *and* BÁBHRAVYA.

Vatsa. My friends!

Vasu. Fate is propitious to your majesty.

Vatsa. This must have been a dream, or is it magic!

Vas. The latter, no doubt: did not that conjuring son of a slave say he had still something for your majesty to see.

Vatsa. (*to the Queen*). Here, madam, is Ságariká, rescued in obedience to your commands.

Vásava. (*smiling*). I am sensible of your obedience, my lord.

Vasu. (*to Bábhravya*). That damsel is wonderfully like the princess.

Bábhr. So it struck me.

Vasu. Excuse me, Sire, permit me, ask—whence is this maiden?

Vatsa. You must ask the queen.

Vasu. (*to Vásavadattá*). Will your grace inform me?

Vásava. Yaugandharáyana presented her to me, and told me she had been rescued from the sea: 'twas hence we designated her, the Ocean Maid.*

Vatsa. (*apart*). Presented by Yaugandharáyana, and without mentioning it to me—what could have been his motive?

Vasu. (*apart to Bábhravya*). The likeness—the necklace—the recovery of the damsel from the sea—leave no doubt that this is the daughter of the king of Sinhalá, Retnávalí. (*Advances to her*) Lady Retnávalí, do I find you in this condition?

Ság. (*looking at him*). Ha! the minister Vasubhútí!

Vasu. I die! [*Faints.*

Ság. Unfortunate that I am, I perish: my beloved parents, hear me; reply to your child. [*Faints.*

Vásava. What! Bábhravya, is this my sister,† Retnávalí?

Bábhr. It is.

Vásava. Revive, dear sister, revive.

Vatsa. Is this the daughter of Vikramabáhu of the house of Udatta, the sovereign of Sinhalá.

Vas. (*apart*). I knew this necklace was the property of no ordinary person.

Vasu. (*recovering*). Revive, dear lady,—be composed; see how your elder sister grieves! Console her sorrows with your embrace.

Retná. (*or Ságariká*). I have offended the queen, how shall I look her in the face again!

Vásava. Come hither, unrelenting girl—behold in me a sister! come to my arms. (*As Retnávali goes to embrace the Queen, she stumbles. Vásavadattá apart to Vatsa*). My good

* The meaning of Ságariká is, 'born of, or produced from, the *ságara*, or ocean.'

† She calls her 'sister,' although such close affinity does not exist; they are cousins, the king of Ceylon being the maternal uncle of Vásavadattá.

lord, I blush for my cruelty. Quick! undo these horrible bonds.

Vatsa. Be composed, I will remove them. (*Takes the chains off Retnávalí's feet.*)

Vas. Yaugandharayána is most to blame in this; he must have known the truth, and yet said not a syllable to any one.

Enter Yaugandharayána.

The temporary absence of her husband, and the contraction of marriage bonds with another wife, cannot fail to be displeasing to the queen: she may thank me for these favours, and I am ashamed to face her. Yet I am confident she will forgive me, when she considers my motives, and will be well pleased that the king obtains by these means the sovereignty of the world. However, happen what may, duty to a master must be performed without regard to such considerations.—They are here: I will approach.—Glory to the king! Pardon me, Sire, if I have accomplished any object affecting your interest, without previously consulting you.

Vatsa. What have you done, inform us?

Yaugan. Please your majesty to be seated, and I will tell you. It was formerly announced to us by a holy Seer, that the husband of the princess of Sinhalá should become the emperor of the world: we therefore earnestly applied to her father to give her hand to our sovereign; but, unwilling to be the cause of uneasiness to the queen, the monarch of Sinhalá declined compliance with our request: we therefore raised a report that Vásavadattá had perished by a fire at Lavanaka, and Bábhravya was dispatched with the news to the court of Sinhalá.

Vatsa. I have heard what ensued. But why place the princess with the queen in so unsuitable a station?

Vas. I can guess his object; he expected you would see her in the inner apartments, and take pleasure in her sight.

Vatsa. Has Vasantaka stated your purpose correctly?

Yaugan. Your majesty has said.

Vatsa. I suppose, too, you had some concern in the appearance of the conjuror?

Yaugan. What other means remained of restoring the damsel to your presence, or how else was Vasubhúti to have seen and recognised the princess?

Vatsa. (*to Vásavadattá, laughing*). Well, madam, it remains with you to say how we shall dispose of the sister you have acknowledged.

Vásava. My lord, you might as well speak out, and say, make Retnávalí over to me?

Vas. Your majesty very accurately conceives the minister's design.

Vásava. Come, here, Retnávalí, appear as becomes my sister. (*Puts on her her own jewels, then takes her by the hand and presents her to Vatsa*). Accept Retnávalí, my lord.

Vatsa. (*taking her hand*). Who would not prize the favours of the queen?

Vásava. And remember, my lord, she is far away from her natural relations; so treat her, therefore, that she may never have occasion to regret them.

Vatsa. I shall obey.

Vas. Victory to your majesty! The world is now in the possession of my friend.

Vasu. Princess, pay respectful reverence to Vásavadattá. (*Retnávalí bows*). Madam, you justly possess the title of queen.*

Vásava. (*embracing Retnávalí*). Glory to your majesty.

Vatsa. My cares are all rewarded.

Yaugan. What else can we perform to gratify your highness?

* *Devi*, literally 'goddess,' but applied to a queen, as the masculine form, *Deva*, is especially the title of a king. The speech of Vasubhúti conveys a hint, which the following one of Vásavadattá shews she understands.

Vatsa. What more is necessary? Vikramabáhu is my kinsman. Ságariká, the essence of the world, the source of universal victory, is mine, and Vásavadattá rejoices to obtain a sister. The *Kosalás* are subdued: what other object does the world present for which I could entertain a wish? This be alone my prayer: may Indra with seasonable showers render the earth bountiful of grain; may the presiding Brahmans secure the favour of the gods by acceptable sacrifices; may the association of the pious confer delight until the end of time,* and may the appalling blasphemies of the profane be silenced for ever.

* Or of the *Kalpa*, the period of the world's duration.

REMARKS ON THE RETNAVALI.

THERE is but little occasion to offer any additional remarks on the preceding drama. It is chiefly valuable as a picture of Hindu manners in a sphere of life secluded from common observation, and at a period of some antiquity. The manners depictured are not influenced by lofty principle or profound reflection, but they are mild, affectionate, and elegant. It may be doubted whether the harams of other eastern nations, either in ancient or modern times, would afford materials for so favourable a delineation.

The story is romantic, the incidents are well contrived, the situations are eminently dramatic, and although the spectator is let into the secret of the plot from the beginning, the interest is very successfully maintained. The intrigue corresponds perfectly with the definition given by Schlegel: it is the union of unexpected combinations, resulting from the contending operation of accidental occurrences and premeditated designs.

In the circumscribed limits of the action, we have no right to expect much contrast or development of character, and it is enough that all the individuals introduced preserve their identity. This is true even of the chambermaids, and the obliging confidante of the heroine is distinguishable from the termagant adviser of the queen.

The merits of the language have already been the subject of remark. Its poetry is merely mechanical: we have no fanciful illustration, nor novel and beautiful similitudes; neither do any sentiments worthy of notice occur, except the generous remark made by Vatsa on the death of the king of Kosalá.

The belief in vulgar magic, or common conjuring, which is repeatedly expressed in the drama, is worthy of remark, as it is something new. The supernatural powers described in *Málati and Mádhava* are of a very different description from the art that makes a flower blossom out of season, or covers a building with illusory flame.

APPENDIX,

CONTAINING

SHORT ACCOUNTS OF DIFFERENT DRAMAS.

THE preceding dramas are the most celebrated specimens of the Hindu theatre, and deserve the distinction. They are the best. Of the number which remain, some have considerable merit, although inferior to those which have been translated: but a considerable portion would have ill repaid the labour of rendering them into the English language.

In order, however, to leave as little doubt as possible on this subject, as well as to furnish as extensive a view as practicable of the theatre of the Hindus, all the specimens procurable have been perused with greater or less care, and an outline, proportionably extended, given of their purport, with translations of a few occasional passages, and such verifications of their literary history as could be discovered. The real extent and value of the dramatic literature of the Hindus will now, it is hoped, be accurately appreciated.

MAHAVIRA CHERITRA;

A Drama in Seven Acts.

CHARACTERS.

Dasaratha.—King of Ayodhyá, father of Ráma.

Janaka.—King of Mithilá, father of Sitá.

Kusadhwaja.—King of Kási, brother of Janaka.

Ráma.—Prince of Ayodhyá.

Lakshmana. } Other sons of Dasaratha.
Bharata.

Parasuráma.—The demigod; son of Jamadagni.

Viswámitra.—A holy sage.

Satánanda.—The family priest of Janaka.

Vasishtha.—The family priest of Dasaratha.

Yuddhájit.—The charioteer of Dasaratha.

Rávana.—The demon king of Lanká.

Málvaván.—His grandfather and chief minister.

Vibhíshana.—The brother of Rávana, and friend of Ráma.

Kumbhakerna.—Another brother of Rávana, faithful to his cause; slain by Ráma.

Meghanáda.—The son of Rávana; slain by Lakshmana.

Báli.—The king of the monkies; slain by Ráma.

Sugriva.—His successor.

Angada.—The son of Báli.

Hanumán.—A monkey chief, and friend of Ráma.

Sampáti. } The two vulture chiefs, descendants of Kasyapa, and friendly to Ráma.
Jatáyu.

Indra.—King of the gods.

Chitraratha.—King of the Gandherbas.

Spirits, Demons, Attendants, &c.

Sítá.—Daughter of Janaka, married to Ráma.

Urmilá.—Her sister, married to Lakshmana.

Mahodarí.—The wife of Rávana.

Súrpanakhá.—The sister of Rávana.

Táraká.—A female fiend.

The tutelary goddess of Alaká, the city of Kuvera.

The tutelary goddess of Lanká, the capital of Rávana.

Kausalyá. }
Kaikeyí. } Wives of Dasaratha.
Sumitrá. }

Mándavi. }
Srutakírtí. } Daughters of Kusadhwaja.

Female Spirits, Fiends, Attendants, &c.

The preceding list of persons will sufficiently explain the general subject of this drama. It is the same with the *Rámáyana,* or the adventures of Ráma, commencing in the play with his visit to Viswámitra's hermitage, and ending in his return to Ayodhyá. The course of the story is much the same in the play as in the poem, although there are a few variations in some of the details, and the story is much more compressed.

That the *Mahávíra Cheritra* is the composition of Bhavabhúti, we have not only the usual assurance in the prelude, and the concurrence of general belief, but the evidence of internal structure. The same loftiness of sentiment, excellence of picturesque description, and power of language which mark the *Uttara Ráma Cheritra,* and *Málatí and Mádhava,* are the characteristics of the *Víra Cheritra.* If the style is less harmonious, and the expression of tender feelings less freqnent than in either of the other dramas, the difference in these respects is to be regarded as designed, for the three plays of our poet are written upon the principle adopted by the only great dramatist of our own day, the authoress of 'Basil and De Montfort,' and may be considered as 'Plays of the Passions,' the characteristic sentiment of the *Uttara Ráma Cheritra* being the *karúná ras*, or tenderness; that of the *Málatí and Mádhava*, the *sringára ras*, or love; and that of the *Víra Cheritra*, the *víra ras*, or heroism. Consistently with this latter purpose, the situations and sentiments of the drama are of a stirring and martial description, and the language is adapted with singular felicity to the subjects from which it springs. It is sonorous and masculine, more vigorous than musical, and although highly elaborate, and sometimes turgid, is in general chaste, and always classical and stately.

The drama opens with an address to the supreme light, the one and indivisible, pure, eternal, and invariable God. The occasion of the performance is then stated to be, as usual with this author's dramas, the festival of *Kálapriyanátha*, supposed to be the celebrated *Omkáreswara* of Ujayin: we have also the usual account of the family of Bhavabhúti.

The prologue contains this peculiarity, that the actor communicates to the audience the outline of the story introductory to the business of the drama, and announces the entrance of Kusadhwaja with his two nieces, Sítá and Urmilá. Kusadhwaja,* the brother of Janaka, is called king of Sankásya, and with the two girls enters the hermitage of Viswámitra on the borders of the Kausiki (Cosi), having been invited by the Muni.† He is met by the sage with the two youths Ráma and Lakshmana, and the young persons become mutually enamoured. Whilst engaged in conversation a messenger from Rávana arrives, who has followed them from Mithilá, and comes to demand Sítá as a wife for his master. They are

* Buchanan makes him the son of Siradhwaja. The *Vishnu Puran* however says, 'brother,' and calls him king of Kásí; the *Agni Purána* says also, 'younger brother of Janaka.'

† The presence of the damsels is not a singularity: all the *Rishis* invited to the same, it is afterwards stated, are there with their wives and children.

further disturbed by Táraká, a female fiend, the daughter of Suketu, wife of Sunda and mother of Marícha. Ráma, by command of Viswámitra, destroys her. Viswámitra then invokes the heavenly weapons, who attend, and pledge their services to Ráma whenever called upon, and the sage recommends Kusadhwaja to invite the bow of Siva for Ráma's present trial, and consequent obtaining of Sítá. The bow arrives, self-conveyed, being, as the weapon of so great a deity, pregnant with intelligence. This faculty does not, however, preserve it entire, for Ráma snaps it asunder behind the scene, in consequence of which feat it is agreed that Sítá shall be wedded to him; Urmilá, her sister, to Lakshman; and Mándaví, and Srutakírtí, the daughters of Kusadhwaja, to Bharata and Satrughna. The party is again disturbed by Suváhu and Marícha, two demons, who are slain by Lakshmana and Ráma. The saint and his visitors then retire into the hermitage.

The second act opens with a dialogue between Mályaván, the minister and maternal grandfather of Rávana, and the demon's sister, Súrpanakhá, who have heard the news from Siddhásrama, and discuss the consequences with some apprehension. A letter arrives from Parasuráma, partly requesting and partly commanding Rávana to call off some of his imps, who are molesting the sages in Dandakáranya. He writes from Mahendra Dwipa. Mályaván takes advantage of this to instigate a quarrel between the two Rámas, anticipating that Parasuráma, who is the pupil of Siva, will be highly incensed when he hears of Ráma's breaking the bow of that divinity. The scene then shifts rather abruptly to Videha, the palace of Janaka, to which Parasuráma has come to defy the insulter of his god and preceptor. He enters the interior of the palace, the guards and attendants being afraid to stop him, and calls upon Ráma to show himself. The young hero is introduced, as proud of Parasuráma's seeking him and anxious for the encounter, but detained awhile by Sítá's terrors: at last the chiefs meet. The dialogue contains some interesting and curious mythological allusion to the history of Parasuráma, who having overcome his fellow pupil, Kártikeya, in a battle-axe fight, received his axe from his preceptor, Siva, as the prize of his prowess. The combat between the two Rámas is suspended by the arrival of Janaka and Satánanda, and Ráma's being summoned to attend the Kánchana Mochana, the loosening of Sítá's golden bracelet.

As a specimen of the style of the sentiments we may select the following :—

Parasuráma to Ráma. How now! presumest thou to bend thy brow
In frowns on me? Audacious boy, a scion
Of the vile Kshetriya race, whose tender years,
And newly wedded bride, teach me a weakness
I am not wont to feel. Throughout the world
The story runs, I, Ráma, and the son
Of Jamadagni, with remorseless arm
Struck off a mother's head. This vengeful axe
Has twenty times destroyed the Kshetriya race,
Not sparing in its wrath the unborn babe
Hewn piecemeal in the parent womb. 'Twas thus
I slaked the fires of a wronged father's wrath
With blood, whose torrents, drawn unsparingly
From martial veins, fed the vast reservoir
In which I love to bathe. Enough! to all,
That—that I am—is known.

Ráma. Give o'er thy vaunts—
I hold thy cruelty a crime, not virtue.

In the third act, Parasuráma is represented as awaiting Rámachandra's return, and he is accosted in succession by Vasishtha, Viswámitra, Satánanda, Janaka, and Dasaratha, who first endeavour to sooth, and then to terrify him; but he out-bullies them all: at last Rámachandra is heard calling on Parasuráma, and the chief goes off to the combat.

The fourth act opens with the annunciation of Rámachandra's victory, and Mályaván and Súrpanakhá enter, more alarmed than ever. Mályaván now suggests the scheme of sowing dissension in Dasaratha's family, in order that Ráma may be driven forth alone, and be thus thrown into the power of the *Rákshasas*. He discusses various schemes of policy connected with this project, and with that of getting rid of Vibhíshana, the brother of Rávana, and his partizans. He withdraws to put his schemes in execution, and the two kings, Janaka and Dasaratha, and their holy councillors, succeed, congratulating each other on the victory of Rámachandra. The prince and his defeated foe then appear, and Parasuráma is now as humble as he was before arrogant: he calls upon the earth to hide his shame.

Whilst Ráma regrets Bhárgava's departure, Súrpanakhá, disguised as Manthará, the favourite of Kaikeyí, Dasaratha's second wife, arrives with a letter to Ráma, requesting him to use his influence with his father to secure Kaikeyí the two boons which Dasaratha was pledged to grant her; specifying one to be her son Bharata's inauguration, and the other, assent to Ráma's voluntary exile. In the mean time Dasaratha, who has determined to raise Rámachandra to the participation of regal dignity, communicates his intention to his son. Ráma replies by informing him of Kaikeyí's message, and is earnest with his father to accede to her request. Yuddhájit and Bharata arrive, and all are full of wonder and concern: however, as there is no help for it, Dasaratha consents. Lakshmana and Sítá are alone to accompany Ráma, on which her father Janaka exclaims, "My child, what happiness it will be to wait upon thy husband in the hour of trouble, permitted to partake and cheer his wanderings!" Bharata requests permission to go with them, but Ráma refuses his assent; on which his brother, with notions very characteristerically oriental, begs his shoes of him, promising to instal them in the kingdom, and rule thereafter as their representative. The seniors are led out in deep despondence, and Ráma with his brother and wife set off to the woods.

The next or fifth act lies in the forests of Dandakáranya, and here Bhavabháti is himself. There is some turgidity, but considerable magnificence, in the opening dialogue between the two birds, Jatáyu and Sampáti, the vulture-descendants of Kasyapa, who have seen successive creations. They relate Ráma's progress towards the south; and Sampáti, the elder, leaves his brother Jatáyu, with strict injunctions to assist Ráma if needed: he then goes to the ocean, and Jatáyu to Malaya. He there comes to

> Where, amidst Janasthána's frowning woods,
> The tall Prasravana uprears his head,
> Dark tinctured in the clouds, and bathes his brow
> With thin descending dews; thence through his caves,
> He culls the oozing moisture, and sends forth
> The pure Godaveri to win her way,
> Stately and clear, through ancient trees that shade,
> Impervious tangling, her majestic course.

This descriptive style we find more frequently in the *Uttara Ráma Cheritra*; and, as observed in the introduction to that drama, it is characteristic of our author.

Jatáyu perches on the mountain, and very dramatically carries on the business of the piece—

> Yonder I mark the hero in pursuit
> Of the swift deer; and thither Lakshmana
> Directs his course remote. There, to the bower
> A holy seer approaches, and the dame
> Gives him meet welcome.—Ha! his form expands,
> 'Tis he, the felon Rávana—his train
> Crowd from the groves; he seizes upon Sítá—
> He mounts the car. Shame to thy birth,—forbear!
> Await my coming, and the vulture's beak
> Shall rend thy limbs, and revel on thy gore. [*Exit.*

Jatáyu is, however, killed in the conflict, which, with the usual regard to stage decorum, takes place behind the scenes. Lakshmana informs us of his fate, and Ráma enters raving with indignation. The brothers set off in pursuit of the ravisher, when Sramaná, a female devotee sent by Vibhíshana to Ráma, calls for succour, being seized by Kabandha, a headless fiend. Ráma sends Lakshmana to her rescue: he goes off to kill the demon, and returns with the dame. She gives Ráma a note from Vibhíshana merely complimentary; but Ráma, learning that he is with Sugríva, Hanumán, and other monkey chiefs at Rishyamúka, and that they have picked up some of Sítá's ornaments in the forest, determines to go to them. Kabandah then appears, to thank Ráma for killing him, being thereby liberated from a curse and restored to a divine condition.

They then proceed towards Rishyamúka, the residence of Báli, watered by the Pampá. Near it is the hermitage of Mátanga, with the fire and all things just ready for oblation, although the saint has been long in heaven: he left them in that state, apparently, as we shall presently see, for the convenience of Ráma. When the brothers arrive at the mountain, Báli appears like a cloud upon its peak and descends to the encounter, regretting that he should be compelled by his friendship for Mályaván to destroy Ráma. The heroes meet and exchange civilities.

Báli. Ráma, with wonder and delight I view
Thy martial bearing,—yet with grief I meet thee:
My eyes were never satiate of thy presence,
And yet, I mark thy coming with affliction.
Enough! what need of words. Now let the arm,
That humbled Jamadagni's haughty son,
Ply thy strong bow again.

Ráma. Illustrious chief,
I thank the fates that grant me thy encounter;
Yet must I wave the fight. I cannot wield
My weapons against one, like thee, unarmed.

Báli. (*smiles*). In sooth, brave Kshetriya, I have ill-deserved
Such generous forbearance, but the world
Knows our high deeds, I need not now proclaim them.

Address thee to the struggle. Thou art brave,
But still a mortal, and with mortal arms
Com'st to the field: not such the arms we wield.
Look round the forest, mark these circling hills—
These are the weapons of our monkey race,
And well these hands can whirl their ponderous fury.
Come to more level ground.

Ráma. Lead on, I follow thee.

Báli and Ráma. (*Looking at each other.*)
The earth will mourn a hero in thy fall. [*Exeunt.*

They go to the conflict; the noise brings Vibhíshańa, Sugríva, and all the monkey chiefs to the place. Báli is overthrown, and returns mortally wounded. He recommends the monkies to choose Sugríva, and his own son Angada, for their joint sovereigns, and mediates an alliance between Ráma and them, as well as with Vibhíshańa: the poet deviating in this, as in many other places, from the Rámáyańa, and exonerating Sugríva from any share in Báli's overthrow. Ráma and Sugríva pledge themselves to eternal friendship, over the sacrificial fire in Matanga's hermitage.

We call this holy fire the saint prepared
For sacrifice, to witness to our vows
Of friendship: ever may thy heart be mine,
As mine shall ever be devote to thee.

Báli then repeats his request to the monkey chiefs, as they were attached to him, to acknowledge Sugríva and Angada as their joint leaders, and to follow them in aid of Ráma against Rávańa in the ensuing contest: he is then led off to die, and the act closes.

Mályavat, lamenting over these miscarriages, opens the sixth act; and Trijatá, a *Rákshasí*, adds to his despondence by news of the mischief inflicted by Hanumat: he goes off to set guards and gather news. We are then introduced to Rávańa himself, meditating on his love. His queen Mandodarí comes to bring him tidings of Rámá's approach, but he only laughs at her. She tells him of the bridge made by Ráma · he replies, if all the mountains of the earth were cast into the ocean, they would not furnish footing to cross it. His incredulity is terminated by a general alarm, and the appearance of Prahasta, his general, to announce that Lanká is invested. Angada comes as envoy from Ráma, to command Rávana to restore Sítá and prostrate himself and family at the feet of Lakshmana. Rávana, enraged, orders some contumely or punishment to be inflicted upon him, which we cannot venture to explain: the expression is *Mukha sanskára*, the cleaning of the face, as if he had ordered him to be shaved. Angada, according to the stage direction, puffs his hair out with rage. This part must be dressed in character, an absurdity not without a parallel in the classical drama, in the *Io* of Æschylus, and the *Birds and Wasps* of Aristophanes. The monkey tells Rávana, if he were not an ambassador he would tear off his ten heads, and he then springs away; the tumult increases, and Rávana goes forth to the combat. Indra and Chitraratha then come to see the battle, and describe its progress. At first the Rákshasas have the worst: but Rávana, with his brother Kumbhakerna and his son Meghanáda, turn the tide: the monkeys fly, leaving Ráma almost unsupported. Lakshmana attacks Meghanáda: Rávana quits Ráma to assist his son. Ráma kills Kumbhakerna, and then goes to the aid of Lakshmana: the whole of Ráma's party are then overwhelmed with magic weapons, hurled invisibly by Rávana upon them, and fall senseless. Whilst Rávana seeks to restore Kumbhakerna, Hanumán reviving, goes to fetch *amrit*, and tearing up the mountain that contains it, returns to the field: his very approach restores Lakshmana, who jumps up with increased animation.

As brighter glows the diamond from the lathe,
Or gleams the falchion flashing from its sheathe;
As starts the serpent from his shrivelled skin,
Or bursts from envious clouds the lord of day

So Raghu's youngest hope, by heavenly herbs
Restored, with more than wonted ardour burns;
A moment wonders what has chanced, then all
On fire for glory, rushes to the fight.

Ráma also revives, and being instigated by the *Munis*, exerts his celestial energies, by which the *Daitya*, Rávańa, and his host speedily perish.

The seventh and last act begins with what the author calls the mixed Vishkambhaka. The latter means an actor or interpreter who carries on the story, which office is here performed by the tutelary deities of Alaká and Lanká, the latter of whom is consoled by the former, who has come to Vibhíshańa's coronation. We learn amongst other things from them, Sítá's passing the fiery ordeal in triumph, and Ráma's approach with the car of Kuvera: the goddesses therefore disappear. Ráma, accompanied by Sítá, Lakshmańa, Vibhíshańa, and Sugríva, then enter, and ascend the car which is to transport them to Ayodhyá, and the progress of which they represent: how, is rather doubtful. (*Sarve vimánagatiḿ nirúpayanti.*) What ensues is more curious than dramatic or interesting, although interspersed with some fine passages of picturesque description, one or other of the party pointing out the places over which they are supposed to fly. These occur in the following succession: the Setu or bridge of Ráma, the Malaya mountain, the Káverí river, the hermitage of Agastya, the Pampá river, the residence of Báli and of Jat́áyu, the limits of the Dańd́aka forest, the Sahya or S'ailádri mountains, the boundaries of Áryavarta. They then rise and travel through the upper air, approaching near the sun, and are met and eulogized by a *Kinnara* and his bride; they then come to the peaks of the Himálaya, and descend upon Tapovana, whence they go towards Ayodhyá, where Ráma is met by his brothers and their mothers, by Vasisht́ha and Viśwámitra, and is consecrated king, with which ceremony the drama terminates.

Upon the whole, as a play, the *Víra Cheritra* is inferior to Bhavabhúti's other productions. The choice of the story is no doubt the cause, as its embracing a period of time, and a number of incidents, not compressible within the bounds of dramatic representation, has thrown an undue proportion of the drama into narrative and description, to the destruction of action and interest. As a poem, however, it ranks worthily with the other works of the same author, and as a play is infinitely superior to others in which the same subject is treated by less skilful hands, as we shall have several opportunities of observing.

VENI SAMHARA;

A Drama in Six Acts.

CHARACTERS.

Yudhishthira.—The elder of the Pándava princes, and their king.

Bhíma.—The brother of Yudhishthira.

Arjuna.—The third Pándava prince.

Sahadeva.
Nakula. } The two younger Pándava princes, twin brothers.

Krishna—The friend and ally of the Pándavas.

Dhriratdshtra.—The father of the Kaurava princes, and uncle of the preceding.

Duryodhana.—The elder of the Kaurava princes, the son of Dhritaráshtra.

Kerna.—The friend and ally of Duryodhanu.

Kripa.—An ally of Duryodhana.

Aswatthámá.—A martial Brahman and sage, the son of Drona and nephew of Kripa.

Sanjaya.—The charioteer of Dhritaráshtra.

Sundaraka.—An attendant on Kerna.

Chárváka.—A Rákshasa, in the disguise of a holy ascetic.

A Rákshasa, or male goblin.

The Charioteer of Duryodhana.

Attendants, Soldiers, &c.

Draupadí.—The wife of the Pándavas.

Bhánumatí.—The wife of Duryodhana.

Gándhári.—The mother of Dhritaráshtra.

Attendant on Draupadí.

Attendant on Bhánumatí.

The mother of Jayadratha, king of Sindhu.

A Rákshasí, or female goblin.

Attendants.

The *Vení Samhára* is a drama founded on the *Mahábhárat.* The name alludes to an incident described in the latter part of the *Sabhá Parva* of that poem, Draupadi's being dragged by the *vení*, or braid of hair, into the public assembly by the hand of Duhsásana, one of the Kaurava princes, a disgrace that weighed most heavily upon the Pándavas, and was most bitterly revenged.

The introduction of this play presents a *nándí* or preliminary benediction of six stanzas: an extravagance unwarranted by the practice of the best writers, and prohibited by positive rule. Two of these, indeed, are omitted by the commentator, and the last is censured by the author of the *Kávya Prakása*, as inconsistent with the reverence due to Hari and Lakshmí, whose amorous sports it describes in a style suitable to mere mortals alone.

The manager then informs the audience that the play is a novelty, the composition of the poet "Bhatta Náráyana;" also designated by the title *Mriga Rája* or *Sinha*, meaning the same thing, the lion. It is an odd grouping of names, however, and leaves the character and person of the bard rather doubtful, the termination *Sinha* being most correctly applicable to a man of the regal or military caste, whilst *Bhatta* is an adjunct belonging to a Brahman.

The occasion of the performance, which it is usual to mention, is not adverted to, and the manager and actor go off to prepare for an exhibition of song and dance in honour of Krishna's return to the Pándava camp from a visit to the Kaurava princes, as a mediator between the contending chiefs. The business of the play begins with a conversation between Bhíma and Sahadeva, in which the former expresses his refusal to have any share in the negociations instituted by Krishna, and his determination to make no peace with the enemy until the insult offered to Draupadí is avenged. He expresses his resolution, in case the dispute be amicably adjusted, to disclaim all connexion with his own brothers, and throw off obedience to Yudhishthira.

> Shall I not grind the Kauravas to dust,
> Nor drink the blood of arrogant Duhsásana:

Shall not my mace upon the breast descend
Of proud Suyodhana, and crush the wretch,
Because your monarch seeks the price of peace?

The price is the demand of five villages or towns, Indraprastha, Tilaprastha, Máḿsada, Várańávata, and another: the Mahábharáta gives different names, as Avisthala, Vŕikasthala, and Mákandí; the fourth is the same. Sahadeva attempts to calm the fury of Bhíma, but in vain; and Draupadí, with her hair still dishevelled, and pining over her ignominious treatment, comes to inflame his resentment. She complains also of a recent affront offered by the queen of Duryodhana, in an in jurious comment upon her former exposure, which serves to widen the breach. A messenger now arrives to announce that Kŕishńa's embassy has been unsuccessful, and that he has effected his return only by employing his divine powers against the enemy. All the chiefs are summoned by the trumpet to prepare for battle.

Draup. Yet ere you go attend to my request;
Let not my shame so far inflame your wrath,
That heedless of your lives, you headlong plunge
Into the conflict: the chieftains of the enemy
Are neither rash nor timorous.
Bhíma. True, warrior dame.
The sons of *Páńdu* are well skilled to ford
The ocean of the fight, amidst whose waves
Floats many a headless corse; and howling monsters,
Gorged with the sanguine beverage, re-echo
The trumpet's sound. Foremost they lead the troops
O'er crashing cars and dying elephants,
The fierce encounter of whose ponderous brows
Has strewed the floating field with brains and gore.

The second act commences before day-break, and introduces Bhánumatí, the queen of Duryodhana, repeating to her friend and an attendant, a dream, in which she has beheld a *Nakula* or *Mungoose* destroy a hundred snakes. This is very ominous, Nakula being one of the Páńd́avas, and the sons of Kuru amounting to a hundred. Duryodhana overhears part of her story, and at first imagines the hostile prince is the hero of the vision. He is about to burst upon her full of rage, and when he catches the true import of the tale, he is at first disposed to be alarmed by it, but at last wisely determines to disregard it. For,

> By Angiras 'tis sung;
> The aspect of the planets, dreams and signs,
> Meteors and portents, are the sports of accident,
> And do not move the wise.

Bhánumatí offers an *arghya* of sandal and flowers to the rising sun to avert the ill omen, and then the king appears and soothes her. Their dialogue is disturbed by a rising whirlwind, from which they take shelter in a neighbouring pavilion. The mother of Jayadratha, king of Sindhu, then appears, and apprises Duryodhana that Arjuna has vowed, if sunset finds Jayadratha alive, he will sacrifice himself in the flames. His wrath is especially excited by the death of his son Abhimanyu, in which that chieftain had borne a leading part. Duryodhana laughs at her fears and those of his wife, and despises the resentment of the Páńd́avas. He observes, that this was fully provoked by the treatment which Draupadí received by his command, when, in the presence of the court and of the Páńd́avas, she called out in vain for mercy. Duryodhana then orders his war-chariot and goes forth to the battle.

The third act opens with a scene of power, but of bad taste, being full of revolting images. A Rákshasí enters, and expatiates on the stores she has provided for her cannibalism, and that of her partner; and when he makes his appearance, hungry, thirsty, and wearied, she gives him on the stage a feast of flesh and brains, and a refreshing beverage of blood in the skull of an elephant just slain. It appears from their dialogue, that up to the period of the contest, the following chiefs have fallen: Bhagadatta, Sindhurája, Angádhipa, Drupada, Bhúriśravas, Somadatta, and Báhlíka. Ghaťotkacha is also slain, and Bhíma is about to avenge his fall, on which account Hiďimbá, the queen of the Rákshasas and mother of Ghaťotkacha, has ordered these goblins to be ready to assist Bhímasena. Whilst engaged in conversation and feeding, this couple see Dróńa seized by Dhrishťadyumna and slain, and they finally retire before Aśwattháman, the son of Drońa, who makes his appearance armed. He is overtaken by his father's charioteer, who tells him of the treachery by which Drońa was slain, having been induced to throw away his arms by a false report that his son Aśwatthaman had perished, and been then killed at a disadvantage. Aśwatthaman's distress is assuaged by his maternal uncle, Kŕipa, who recommends him to solicit the command of the host from Duryodhana. In the meantime, Karńa is represented as filling the mind of the Kuru chief with impressions hostile to Drońa and his son, persuading him that Drońa only fought to secure Aśwatthaman's elevation to imperial dignity, and that he threw away his life, not out of grief, but in despair at the disappointment of his ambitious schemes. Kŕipa and Aśwatthaman now arrive, and Duryodhana professes to condole with Aśwatthaman for his father's loss. Karńa sneeringly asks him what he purposes, to which he replies:

What is my purpose? Hear it, king of Anga:
Whoever confident in arms is ranked
Amongst the adverse host—whome'er the race
Of proud Pánchála numbers, active youth,
Weak age, or babes unborn, whoe'er beheld
My father's murder, or whoever dares
To cross my path, shall fall before my vengeance.
Dark is my sight with rage, and death himself,
The world's destroyer, should not 'scape my fury.
Pupil of Jámadagnya, Karńa, mark me:

Amidst these very plains, the wrath of Ráma,
Roused by a father's death, filled mighty lakes
With Kshetriya blood. Such formidable arms,
Burning for hostile life, I bear, and such
My cause of rage, a father's fall; nor less
Than Ráma's acts shall Drona's son achieve.

Kripa then requests Duryodhana to give the command of the army to Aswatthámá. The king excuses himself on the plea of having promised it to Kerna, to whom he transfers his ring accordingly. A violent quarrel ensues between Kerna and Aswatthámá, and Duryodhana and Kripa have some difficulty in preventing them from single combat. Aswatthámá at last reproaches Duryodhana with partiality, and refuses to fight for him more. They are disturbed by Bhíma's proclaiming without, that he has at last encountered Duhsásana, the insulter of Draupadí, and is about to sacrifice him to his vengeance. Kerna, instigated by Aswatthámá, foregoes his anger, and is about to resume his arms, when a voice from heaven prevents him. He is obliged, therefore, to remain an idle spectator of the fight, but desires Kripa to assist the king: they go off for that purpose.

The fourth act opens with Duryodhana's being brought in by his charioteer, wounded: Duhsásana has been killed, and the army of the Kauravas put to the rout. On his recovery, the charioteer announces Duhsásana's death, and Duryodhana gives vent to his sorrows. He is joined by Sundaraka, a follower of Kerna, who gives in Prákrit a long and tedious account of the conflict between Arjuna and Vrishasena, the son of Kerna, the death of the young prince, and his father's distress; he also brings a leaf on which Kerna has written to Duryodhana, with an arrow dipped in his own blood, a message for aid. Duryodhana orders his chariot, and prepares to seek the fight again, when he is prevented by the arrival of his parents, Dhritaráshtra and Gándhári, who with Sanjaya commence the fifth act.

The old couple and Sanjaya endeavour to prevail upon Duryodhana to sue for peace, but he refuses.

My fall has Partha vowed, when he has left
Me brotherless; and all his brethren slain,
How shall Duryodhana endure to live?
Nor will I hear of peace until my mace
Shall crush and scatter to the winds that foe,
Remorseless Bhíma, whose ferocious wrath
Drank my young brother's, brave Duhsásan's, blood.

A tumult behind, and the entrance of the king's charioteer, announce the death of Kerna. Duryodhana, after expressing his grief, determines to go and avenge him, and mounts the car of Sanjaya for that purpose, when Arjuna and Bhíma arrive in search of him. On finding the seniors there, Arjuna purposes to withdraw; but Bhíma insists on first addressing them, which they do, but in insulting terms.

Arj. Parents, the middle Pándava salutes you,
Who in the battle's front has, victor, slain
The son of Rádhá, he whose pride beheld
The world as grass, and by whose vaunted prowess
Your children hoped to triumph o'er their foes.

Bhím. Bhíma in reverence bows his head to you:
He, who has overthrown the sons of Kuru,
He who inebriate, has like nectar quaffed
The blood of vile Duhsásana, and soon
Shall lay the proud Duryodhana in dust.

Dhritaráshtra reproaching them for this language, is told they use it not in pride, but in requital of his having witnessed, without interfering to prevent, the oppression and barbarous treatment the Pándavas experienced from his sons. Duryodhana interferes and defies Bhíma, who is equally anxious for the combat; but Arjuna prevents it, and the brothers are called off by a summons from Yudhishthira, who orders the battle to cease for the day and the dead bodies of either party to be burnt. Aswatthámá then enters and is disposed to be reconciled to Duryodhana : but the prince receives his advances coldly, and he withdraws in disgust. Dhritaráshtra sends Sanjaya after him to persuade him to overlook Duryodhana's conduct. Duryodhana mounts his car, and the aged couple seek the tent of Salya, king of Madrá.

In the sixth act Panchála brings to Yudishthira and Draupadí an account of Duryodhana's having been discovered concealed in a swamp, and compelled to fight with Bhimasena, by whom he will be slain. Yudishthira orders public rejoicings on the occasion. Chárváka, a Rákshasa disguised as a Muni, then enters, requiring rest and water. He tells them that he has seen Arjuna engaged with Duryodhana, Bhíma having been previously slain by the latter, and Krishna forcibly taken away by Ráma, and gives them to understand that Arjuna also has fallen. Draupadí determines to mount the funeral pile, and Yudishthira to put an end to himself, when the Rákshasa, satisfied with the success of his scheme, which was intended to prevail on this couple to perish, departs. The pile is prepared, and Yudishthira and Draupadí are about to sacrifice themselves, when they are disturbed by a great clamour. Supposing it to precede the approach of Duryodhana, Yudishthira calls for his arms, when Bhíma, his club smeared with blood, rushes in. Draupadí runs away; he catches her by the hair, and is seized by Yudishthira—on which the mistake is discovered. The episode is very absurd and impertinent.

The braid of Draúpadí's hair is now again bound up. Arjuna and Vásudeva arrive, and announce that they have heard of the fraud of the Chárváka, and Yudishthira adds that the mendicant has been slain by Nakula, on which Krishna expresses great satisfaction. The author has introduced the Chárváka, apparently, merely to have a hit at the atheistical sect, possibly intending the Bauddhas.

There is much good writing in this piece, although the style is rather powerful than polished: there is also poetry in the thoughts, but it is the poetry rather of passion than fancy, and the pathos and horror in which it delights are relieved by no brilliancy of illustration: both too are overdone, and the pathos becomes tiresome and the horror disgusting. The chief merit of the drama is individuality of character; the ferocity of Bhíma, the pride of Kerna, the fiery but kindly temperament of Aswatthámá, and the selfish arrogance of Duryodhana, are well delineated. The chief defect of the play is its undramatic construction. The business is clumsily contrived; the situations are ineffective or ludicrous; the scenes are awkwardly put together, and much too considerable a portion of the piece is thrown into narrative for the interest to be successfully supported. With exception of the last defect, the Veni Samhára is calculated to remind us very forcibly of the early attempts of the French and English dramatists.

There is nothing in the play to furnish a clue to its date. It is frequently cited in the Kávya Prakás, the Dasa Rúpaka, and Sáhitya Derpana, to which works it is consequently anterior. According to tradition, the author, Bhatta Náráyana, was one of the Kanouj Brahmans invited into Bengal by Adi Sura, from whom the Brahmans of that province are descended: he was of the Sándilya family. Adi Sura is supposed to have reigned three centuries before our era; but if we may place any dependance on Abulfazl's list of Bengal kings, he was the twenty-second prince in ascent from Belál Sen, who it is well known reigned in the thirteenth century. Assigning then the moderate duration of about three hundred years to these intermediate princes, and admitting the tradition with respect to Bhatta Náráyana, the Vení Samhára might have been written about the eighth or ninth century: a period not at all incompatible with the comparative harshness of its style and the rudeness of its execution, particularly if we conclude, agreeably to the tradition, that it was amongst the early results of the introduction of Brahminical literature into Bengal. There are considerable varieties in the manuscripts of this drama, and the name is also differently given as the *Veni Samvarana* or *Veni Samhára:* the import is the same, "The Binding of the Braid." There is a commentary on the drama, by *Jagaddhara,* entitled *Mahopádhyáya,* implying a teacher; and *Dharmádhikárika,* which may be merely an honorific epithet, although it should signify a judge or administrator of the law.

MALAVIKAGNIMITRA, OR AGNIMITRA AND MALAVIKA.

A Comedy in Five Acts.

DRAMATIS PERSONÆ.

Agnimitra.—King of Vidisá.

Gotama.—His confidant, the Vidúshaka or Buffo.

Haradatta. }
Ganadása. } Professors of music and dancing.

Sarasa.—The queen's dwarf.

Dhárini.—The principal queen.

Irávatí.—The second queen.

Málaviká.—The heroine.

Kausikí.—A female ascetic.

Vakulávalí.—One of the queen's attendants, and the friend of Málaviká.

Jayasená.—Female chamberlain.

Kaumudí.—Attendant on the queen.

Madhukáriká.—Female gardener.

Nipuniká. }
Chandriká. } Attendants on Irávatí.

Samáhitiká.—Pupil of Kausiká.

Jyotsná. }
Ramanyá. } Female singers presented to Agnimitra.

The scene is at Vidisa, in the garden and inner apartments of Agnimitra's palace. Time about twelve hours.

The play is usually considered as one of the three composed by Kálidás, who is thus said in the prelude to be the author:

Manager. I have been desired by the assembly to represent the Málavikágnimitra of Kálidása at this vernal festival:

Actor. Why make such an election? Why should we neglect the works of celebrated writers, such as Bhásaka and Saumilla, to perform the play of a cotemporary.

Manager. Why not? all that is old is not therefore necessarily excellent; all that is new is not despicable on that account alone. Let what is really meritorious, be pronounced so by the candid judge after due investigation; blockheads only are influenced by the opinions of others.

There is no reason to question the nomenclature of the author here, and the play is probably the work of a Kálidása. Tradition alone identifies him with the poet of Vikramáditya's reign, who preceded the Christian era, and the internal evidence is adverse to the dramas being the work of the author of *Śakuntalá* and *Vikrama and Urvaśí.* There is neither the same melody in the verse nor fancy in the thoughts. The mention of poets earlier than Kálidása is of no help, as nothing is known of them: their names do not appear in the *Bhoja-Prabandha* nor *Śárngdhara-Paddhati*, two works that enumerate some hundreds of eminent authors. The latter has a Bhása, which may be the same as Bhásaka; and the former notices a Bháskara, which might be thought to bear some relation to the same. One manuscript of the play reads in place of Bhásaka, Dhávaka, who we know was contemporary with Raja-Harsha-Deva, king of Kashmir, the Kávya-Prakáśa declaring him to be the real author of the works bearing the name of that prince. It is not unlikely, indeed, to have been the work of the time of Srí-Harsha, but can scarcely have been the production of a later date, in which Dhávaka had become an ancient writer. The dramas written in more recent periods are invariably, as far as is yet known, mythological, and have some one of the forms or family of Vishńu for the hero. There is no such thing as a decidedly modern drama the business of which is domestic intrigue: such a subject, indeed, was wholly incompatible with Hindu feelings, as affected by intercourse with their Mohammedan masters, whether the effect of that intercourse was terror or imitation. In addition to these considerations, the style of the play is very unlike that most common amongst modern writers, and most highly esteemed, being free from all jingle of sounds and from metaphorical common-place: it does not even affect any thing like the uniform smoothness, which seems to have preceded and ushered in the extravagancies of modern composition. The piece of sound criticism urged by the manager is also the sentiment of a day long gone by.

There are other considerations corroborative of the conclusion, that this drama is of no recent date, derived from the history of its hero. Agnimitra the king of Vidisá, is the son of Pushpámitra, whose father is still alive, and who is rather unaccountably termed the Senání or general. The personages are little known to the pundits of the present day. It appears from the Vishnu Purána, however, that Pushpámitra was the founder of the Sunga dynasty of Magadha kings, having been the general of Vrihadratha, the last of the Maurya race, whom he deposed and put to death: he was succeeded by his son Agnimitra, and no doubt remains therefore of the identity of the personages. The first of the Maurya race was Chandragupta, whom all research continues to recognise in Sandracottus. The princes of this family were ten in number, to whose reigns the reasonable term of one hundred and thirty-seven years is assigned in the Vishnu Purána, which places Agnimitra and his father, about one hundred and sixty years before our era, above a century before the Kálidása of Vikramáditya's court, and such a period was quite sufficient to qualify Agnimitra to become the hero of a domestic drama. The events of his reign which are familiarly alluded to, were not of a character to have survived any very protracted interval in popular recollection; and it may be observed also, that his capital, Vidisá, has been long obliterated from the literary records of the Hindus, and that its precise situation is utterly unknown: its flourishing condition in the days of one Kálidása is also adverted to in his *Mégha Dúta*. The term of general, applied in the play to Pushpámitra, may perhaps correct the history as given in the *Purána;* and although he dispossessed his first master of the crown, it seems likely that he refrained from appropriating it to himself, being contented to retain the military power, whilst he invested his son with the title and name of king. There might seem reason therefore to infer, that the play was the work of the Kálidás of antiquity; but the manners described appear to be those of a degenerate state of Hindu society, and it can scarcely be thought earlier than the tenth or eleventh century. It may possibly have been the production of a somewhat later day, in some part of India which continued to preserve its political independence and Hindu character. We shall now proceed to an analysis of the drama itself.

The play opens with the entrance of Vakulávalí, a female attendant upon Dhárini, the principal queen, who has been sent by her mistress to the *sangíta sálá,* a theatre or music saloon, to inquire of Ganadása, the progress made by his pupil, Málaviká, in dancing and singing. Another female servant, Kaumudí, joins her, and from their conversation we learn that the Rájá has seen the picture of Málaviká, painted by order of the queen for her *chitra sálá,* or picture gallery, notwithstanding her anxiety to keep the original from Agnimitra's knowledge. The sight of the picture has, of course, inspired the prince with an ardent desire to view the original, whom he has never yet beheld. In the next scene Vakulávalí tells Ganadása, the preceptor, that Málaviká was sent as a present to the queen by her brother, Vírasena, governor of the Antapála, or barrier fortress on the Nermada.

In the scene that follows, we find hostilities are about to break out between Agnimitra and Yajnasena, king of Viderbha (Berar). The first, on some occasion, had detained captive the brother-in-law of the latter, and Yajnasena had retaliated by throwing into captivity Mádhavasena, the personal friend of Agnimitra, when about to repair to Vidisá to visit that monarch. Yajnasena sends to propose an exchange of prisoners, but Agnimitra haughtily rejects the stipulation, and sends orders to his brother-in-law, Virasena, to lead an army immediately against the Raja of Viderbha. This affair being disposed of, he directs his attention to domestic interests, and employs his Vidúshaka or confidant, Gotama, to procure him the sight of Málaviká.

To effect this, Gotama instigates a quarrel between the professors, Ganadása and Haradatta, regarding their respective pre-eminence. They appeal to the Raja, who, in consideration of Ganadása's being patronised by the queen, refers the dispute to her. She is induced to consent reluctantly to preside at a trial of skill between the parties, as shewn in the respective proficiency of their select scholars. The queen is assisted by a protegée, a *Parivrájiká*, or female ascetic and woman of superior learning. In general, a *Parivrájiká* denotes an ascetic female of the Bauddha faith, but there is nothing in the piece to assign the character to any particular sect.

The second act opens with the assemblage of the party in the chamber where the performance is to take place, fitted up with the *sangíta rachaná*, or orchestral decorations. The king's object is attained, for Ganadása brings forward Málaviká as the pupil on whom he stakes his credit. Málaviká sings an *upagána* or prelude, and then executes what is represented as something of extraordinary difficulty, the *chatushpáda vastu*, in the *madhya laya*, or andante time, which was composed by Sermishthá. Some air is most probably implied, adapted to a stanza of four *pádas* or lines. Sermishthá is known as the queen of Yayáti, but whether she be the same with the composer of the air is more than uncertain. Málaviká's performance is highly applauded, and the Vidúshaka detains her until the queen, who has all along suspected the plot, commands her to retire. The exhibition of Haradatta's pupil not being essential to the intrigue, is evaded dramatically enough, by the warder's crying the hour of noon, on which the party breaks up, and the queen, with more housewifery than majesty, hastens away to expedite her royal husband's dinner.

The scene of the third act is laid in the garden, where stands an *aśoka* tree (*Jonesia aśoka*). A curious superstition prevailed amongst the Hindus formerly, which is the frequent theme of poetical allusion: they believed that this tree, when barren, might be induced to put forth flowers by the contact of the foot of a handsome woman. The tree in question does not blossom, and being the favourite of Dháriń́í, she has proposed to try the effect of her own foot. Unluckily, however, the Vidúshaka, whilst setting her swing in motion, has tumbled her out of it and sprained her ankle, so that she cannot perform the ceremony herself: she therefore deputes Málaviká to do it for her, who accordingly comes to the spot attired in royal habiliments, and accompanied by her friend Vakulávalí. In the conversation that ensues she acknowledges her passion for the king, who with his friend Gautama has been watching behind the tree, and overhears the declaration; he therefore makes his appearance and addresses a civil speech to Málaviká, when he is interrupted by another pair of listeners, Irávatí, the second queen, and her attendant. She commands Málaviká's retreat, and leaves the king, in a violent rage, to inform Dháriń́í of what is going forward.

In the beginning of the fourth act the Vidúshaka informs the Rájá, that Málaviká has been locked up in the *sárabháń́ḍagriha* by the queen. What that chamber is we do not exactly know; it must be a store or treasure room, and no very enviable place, as the Vidúshaka compares it to *Pátála*, the infernal regions. He undertakes, however, to effect her liberation; and whilst he prepares for his scheme the Rájá pays a visit to the queen.

In the next scene, whilst the Rájá is engaged in tranquil conversation with Dháriń́í and the Parivrájiká, the Vidúshaka rushes in, exclaiming he has been bitten by a venomous snake, whilst gathering flowers to bring with him as a present on his visit to the queen, and he exhibits his thumb bound with his cord, and marked with the impressions made by the teeth of the reptile. The Parivrájiká, with some humour as well as good surgery, recommends the actual cautery, or the amputation of the thumb; but the Vidúshaka pretending to be in convulsions and dying, the snake-doctor is sent for, who having had his cue, refuses to come, and desires the patient may be sent to him: the Vidúshaka is accordingly sent. The queen is in great alarm, as being, however innocently, the cause of a Bráhman's death. Presently the messenger returns, stating the only hope is the application of the snake-stone to the bite, and requesting the Rájá to order one to be procured: the queen has one in her finger ring, which she instantly takes off and sends to the Vidúshaka. This is his object; for the female jailor of Málaviká has, as he has ascertained, been instructed to liberate her prisoner only on being shown the seal ring or signet of the queen; and having got this in his possession, he immediately effects the damsel's release, after which the ring is returned to the queen, and the Vidúshaka is perfectly recovered. The king then being summoned away by a concerted pretext, hastens to the Samudra pavilion, where Málaviká has been conveyed with her friend and companion, Vakulávalí. This pavilion is decorated with portraits of the king and his queens, and Málaviká is found by her lover engrossed with their contemplation. Vakulávalí retires. The Vidúshaka takes charge of the door, but no sooner sits down on the threshold than he falls asleep: the Rájá and Málaviká, consequently, have scarcely time to exchange professions of regard, when they are again disturbed by the vigilant and jealous Irávatí, who sends information of her discoveries to Dhárińí, and in the meantime remains sentinel over the culprits. The party, however, is disturbed by news, that Agnimitra's daughter has been almost frightened to death by a monkey, and Irávatí and the Rájá hasten to her assistance, leaving Málaviká to the consolation derived from hearing the *asoka* tree is in blossom, an omen of the final success of her own desires.

The fifth act collects the Raja, Dhárini, the Parivrájiká, with Málaviká and other attendants about the *asoka* tree, when some presents arrive from the now submissive monarch of Viderbha, against whom the troops of Virasena have been successful. Amongst the gifts are two female slaves, who immediately recognize in Málaviká the sister of Mádhavasena, the friend of Agnimitra, whom the armies of the latter have just extricated from the captivity to which the Viderbha sovereign had consigned him. It appears that when he was formerly seized by his kinsman, his minister, Sumati, contrived to effect his own escape, along with his sister and the young princess. That sister, Kausikí, now reveals herself in the person of the Parivrájiká, and continues the story of their flight. Sumati joined a caravan bound to Vidisá. On their way through the Vindhya mountains they were attacked by the foresters, who were armed with bows and arrows, and decorated with peacock's plumes: in the affray Sumati was slain and Málaviká was lost. Kausikí, left alone, committed her brother's body to the flames, and then resumed her route to Vidisa, where she assumed the character of a female ascetic. The Raja observes she did wisely, which if a Bauddha ascetic be here, as is usual, intended, is a tolerant expression of some weight with regard to the antiquity of the drama. Kausiki soon found out Málaviká, but forbore to discover herself, confiding in the prophesy of a sage, who had foretold that the princess, after passing through a period of servitude, would meet with a suitable match.

The story now pauses, whilst Agnimitra issues his orders respecting the terms to be granted to Yajnasena, the king of Viderbha, the half of whose territory he assigns to Mádhavasena, the brother of Málaviká, their dominions to lie respectively north and south of the Varadá river, the Wurda of modern times, and retaining till very lately its character of a boundary, separating the states of the Nizam from those of the Nagpore, the Vidarbha or Berar Raja. In this part of the play, also, is the allusion to the general, Pushpámitra. A letter arrives from him, giving an account of some transactions that have occurred upon the southern bank of the Indus. On his own behalf, or that of his son, he had undertaken to celebrate an *aswamedha*, or sacrifice of a horse, for which it was essential that the steed should have a free range for twelve months, being attended only by a guard to secure him. This guard had been placed by Pushpámitra under the command of Aginimitra's son, Vasumitra. Whilst following the victim along the Indus, a party of Yavana horse attempted to carry off the courser, but they were encountered by the young prince, and after a sharp conflict, defeated. Pushpámitra concludes with inviting his son to come with his family to complete the sacrifice. The queen, Dhárini, overjoyed by the news of her son's success and safety, distributes rich presents to all her train and the females of Agnimitra's establishment, whilst to him she presents Málaviká. Irávatí communicates her concurrence in this arrangement, and the Raja obtains another bride. The piece closes with his expressing his hope, that he may ever retain the regard of his first queen, Dhárini, and that his subjects may never suffer any calamity whilst he reigns over them.

VIDDHA SALABHANJIKA, OR THE STATUE.

A Comedy in Four Acts.

CHARACTERS.

Vidyádhara Malla.—King of Trilinga and Kalinga.

Chárâyana.—His confidential attendant.

Bhágurâyana.—The minister.

Kálidás.—A servant of the minister.

An Ambassador from the king of Láta.

Kurangaka.—An officer of Vidyádhara Malla.

The queen of Vidyádhara Malla.

Mrigánkávalí.—The daughter of Chandravermá king of Láta, passing for some time as his son; under the charge of the queen.

Kuvalayamálá.—Princess of Kuntalá, the intended bride of the supposed son of Chandravermá, also under charge of the queen.

Pingaliká.—The wife of Cháráyana.

Mekhalá.—The foster sister and chief attendant on the queen.

Sulakshaná.
Vilakshaná.
Kurangiká.
Tarangiká. } Female attendants.

Attendants.

The *Viddha Sálábhanjiká* is a comedy of domestic intrigue, like the *Retnávalí and Málavikágnimitra:* it has not, however, the elegance of the former nor the spirit of the latter, and although not devoid of imagination, is much less classical than either. It has more bustle, and a more complicated plot, and gives a not unentertaining picture of the interests and amusements of Hindu princes in the retirement of their harams.

The benedictory stanzas at the commencement are addressed to Kámadeva and Párvatí, indicating adherence to Saiva tenets. The manager then states that the play is the work of Rája Sekhara ; and the occasion of the performance, the pleasure of the Yuvarája, probably the installation of the heir in the joint administration of the government.

A short introduction by Haridás, tells the audience that the minister of Vidyádhara Malla, the hero of the play, has discovered that the king of Láta having no son, has endeavoured to pass off his only daughter as a boy, and has sent her in that capacity to be taken care of by Vidyádhara Malla's queen. The scene then discovers the Rája and the Vidúshaka just risen from repose. The prince has seen a fancied vision, which he relates to his confidant, "for the burthen of the heart is lightened by sharing it with a faithful friend." He proceeds :

"A glorious halo appeared before me in my dream, bright as the moon's resplendent disk ; within the orb a beauteous maiden moved as gently radiant as the lunar rays in autumn skies. Advancing near me, she inclined her head in reverence, and as if pouring ambrosia into my ears, pronounced in softest tones, 'Glory to the deity of love!' then sighing, she took up this string of costly pearls and placed it on my neck. The act awoke me. I started up and saw my vision realised. I caught the nymph by her scarf ; but she hastily extricated herself from my hands and fled, leaving me this necklace alone the evidence of her presence."

The Vidúshaka, however, treats the whole as a dream, and reproaches the prince with his fickleness, as he had just before fallen in love with Kuvalayamálá, the princess of Kuntalá, and recommends him to be content with the queen, as "a partridge in the hand is better than a peahen in the forest."

The king and the Vidúshaka then go into the garden, where, over the edge of a terrace, they see some of the fair tenants of the inner apartments amusing themselves with swinging, a favourite pastime with the natives of India. Amongst them the king recognizes the countenance he has seen in his dream, but the party disappear on the advance of the Raja and his friend.

The Raja then enters a pleasure-house or pavilion called the *Keli kailás*—the *Kailás* (or mountain so called) of sport. It is an apartment described as built of crystal, and decorated with statues and paintings. Amongst the latter is one which, by an artist familiar with Indian antiquities and costumes, might be wrought into an instructive and interesting composition; it is thus described:

"There is your majesty at *pása* (dice) with the queen: behind you stands one damsel with the betel box, whilst another is waving the *chownri* over your head: the dwarf is playing with the monkey, and the parrot abusing the Vidúshaka."

The chamber also contains the portrait of Mrigánkávalí, the damsel whom the Raja has really seen in his supposed dream, and who is in the haram in the character of a youth, though wearing female attire; there is also a statue of her, whence the piece is named *Viddha Sálá bhanjiká*, meaning a carved effigy. Finally the lady is herself beheld through the transparent wall of the pavilion, but runs away on being observed: the Raja and his friend follow her in vain; the bards proclaim it noon, and the two friends repair to the queen's apartments to perform the midday ceremonies.

A conversation between two of the female attendants opens the second act, and gives us the history of Kuvalayamálá, the object of the Raja's passion before encountering his new flame. She is the daughter of Chandramahásena, king of Kuntalá, and has been sent to Vidyádhara Malla's queen, as the betrothed bride of the supposed son of Chandravermá, who is the queen's maternal uncle. Then follows a frolic practised by Mekhalá, the queen's foster-sister, on the king's confidant, Chárâyana. He is promised a new bride by the queen, and the ceremony is about to take place when the spouse proves to be a "lubberly boy;" he is highly indignant at the trick, and goes off threatening vengeance.

The Raja having followed and pacified his companion, they go into the garden, where they see the damsel Mrigánkávalí playing with ball: she still however flies their advance. Presently they overhear a conversation between her and one of her companions, from which it appears, that notwithstanding her shyness she is equally enamoured of the Raja. Evening is now proclaimed, and the parties retire.

A similar dialogue with that which commenced the second, begins the third act, the parties only being different. We now learn that the dream was the contrivance of the minister, Mrigánkávalí having been persuaded by the speaker, Sulakshaná, at his instigation, to believe that she was to behold the present deity of love, and having been introduced by a sliding door into the king's chamber. The minister's object in effecting a marriage between the Raja and the nymph, is to secure to his master the station of universal monarch, which a seer has prophesied shall accompany the hand of Mrigánkávalí. The author here, therefore, is indebted, either to the *Retnávalí*, or perhaps in common with that, to the popular story of *Vatsa*, for his notions. The consequence of the interview has been to render Mrígánkávalí passionately enamoured of the king.

From this we proceed to Cháráyana's retaliation. He has induced one of the women to hide in a bush, and when Mekhalá passed, to announce to her, she would die on the next full moon, unless she prostrated herself at the feet of some Brahman and crawled between his legs. The plot has so far succeeded that Mekhalá and the queen, both overcome with concern, have entreated Chárâyana to be the Brahman that shall preserve the life of the former. The transaction takes place, and when Mekhalá crawls between his legs Chárá-yana proclaims the device, and triumphs in the humiliation he has inflicted on her—the queen is in her turn incensed, and goes off in a pet. The Raja and the Vidúshaka seek the garden, where it is now moonlight. Mrigánkávalí and her friend Vilakshaná also come thither, and the lovers meet: this interview is broken off by a cry that the queen is coming, and they all separate abruptly.

The fourth and last act begins again with the dawn, when we have Cháráyaṅa and his wife introduced, the latter asleep. In her sleep, however, she is very communicative, and repeats a supposed dialogue between the queen and the Raja, in which the former urges the latter to marry Mrigánkávalí, the sister of the supposed Mrigánkavermá, come on a visit, it is pretended, to her brother—this being a plot of the queen's to cheat the king into a sham marriage, by espousing him to one she believes to be a boy. On her own part she, it is pretended by the dreamer, professes no difficulty, referring to her conduct on similar occasions, from which it appears that the Raja already possesses a goodly assortment of wives, the princesses of Magadhá, Málavá, Pánchála, Avanti, Jalandhara, and Kerala. The Vidúshaka suspects the trick, however, and wakes his wife, who rises and goes to the queen. Sleeping on the stage is contrary to the canons of the Hindu drama, but the natives of India sleep with so little of the "pomp and circumstance" of the bed-chamber, that there is no violation of decorum in such a representation.

The Vidúshaka having joined the Rája, a rather tedious conversation ensues, in which the amatory emotions of the Rája and his new mistress are described. This is interrupted by the preparations for the marriage, and they are followed by the ceremony, Vidyádhara Malla being wedded on the stage to Mrigánkávalí, another violation of dramatic rule, which prohibits the exhibition of sacred rites. In this case the holy fire is introduced and circumambulated. As soon as this is done, a messenger arrives from Chandravermá to announce that his master has a son, that consequently no further necessity exists for his daughter's assuming a character not belonging to her, and Mrigánkávalí accordingly is to be recognised as his daughter. The queen now finds that she has taken herself in, and given herself another rival bride: as the matter is past remedy, however, she assents with a good grace, and allows Vidyádhara Malla to marry Kuvalayamálá into the bargain. To crown the king's happiness, a messenger arrives from the camp with the news that the allied army of Kernáta, Sinhalá, Pándya, Murala, Andhra, and Konkana has been defeated, and Virapála king of Kuntalá, the ally of Vidyádhara Malla, reseated on a throne, from which his kinsman, supported by those troops, had formerly expelled him. The authority of Vidyádhara Malla is now declared to extend from the mouths of the Ganges to the sea, and from the Narmadá to the Támrapernì in the Dekhin, he being the chief of the Karachuli race, a Rajput tribe.

Many circumstances prove this drama to be comparatively modern: the language is more ornate than classical, the ideas are more affected than poetical; allusions to current practices and modes of dress are frequent and conversational, and proverbial forms of speech are not rare. The state of manners, particularly as affects the multitude of wives, is not of ancient character, for although there was no restriction in this respect, it does not appear that any very great latitude was usually exercised. Dasaratha had three wives, but his son Ráma had but one, Pándu had two, Dhritaráshtra but one, and many of the traditionary kings of the Hindus, in like manner, contented themselves with the same number. According to the law, indeed, the first wife was considered to fulfil the moral end of the association, except in the case of sterility, and the marriage of other wives, unless for the sake of progeny, a culpable sacrifice to sensual passions. This law, indeed, became obsolete; but to judge from the dramas, there ever remained a peculiarity in the practice of the Hindus which distinguishes them from the Mohammedans, and in no case do we find any allusion to a system of concubinage established in their harams.

Besides internal evidence, however, the author is not regarded as a writer of any great antiquity, although of considerable merit: his precise date is not known, but as he is mentioned in the *Sárngdhara Paddhati*, a work of the fourteenth century, he is prior to that period. He was probably not later than the reign of Bhoja, for the *Vásavádatta* of Subandhu contains an evident allusion to the play, as it is there said that every house in Kusumapur possesses a *Sálábhanjiká* and *Vrihat Kathá*; and he is also named in the *Saraswati Kanthábharana*, a work on rhetoric, attributed to Bhoja himself. It is said in the prelude that he is the tutor of the king, Mahendrapála, but we have not yet met with any prince of that name. We shall presently have occasion to revert to this subject, and it is here sufficient to observe, that from the author's familiarity with the political distinctions and the domestic usages of the people of southern and western India, he was probably a native of some of the provinces bordering upon the Nerbudda.

PRACHANDA PANDAVA.

The *Prachanda Pándava*, or 'Offended Sons of Pándu,' is a *nátaka* in two acts, entitled also the *Bála Bhárata*. The subject is taken from the *Mahábhárat*. The first act describes the marriage of Draupadí; the second, the loss of every thing at play by Yudishthira, the injurious treatment of Draupadí, and the departure of the Pandava princes to the forest. The author has not hesitated to represent in action the circumstances of Draupadí's being dragged by the hair, almost naked, into the public assembly, an insult in revenge for which Bhíma vowed to slay Duhsásana and drink his blood, and ultimately fulfilled his vow.

The introduction of this little drama, which is written in a simple but powerful style, is valuable for the account it gives of the author, Rája Sekhara, and his patron or patrons, of whom some notice has been taken in the preceding analysis of the *Viddha Sálábhanjiká*. He is here described as a poet, who occupies that rank in the literature of the day which Válmíki, Vyása, Bhartriharí, and Bhavabhúti, have severally filled: he is also designated as the son of the *mahámantrí* or prime minister, and Mahendrapála, the king, of the family of Raghu, is called his *sishya* or disciple. The assembly, however, before which the representation takes place is collected by Mahípala Deva, who may be the same with Mahendrapála, or is possibly his father or paramount lord. Of Mahípála it is said, that he is the sovereign of Aryavertta or central India, and the subjugator of the Kuntalas, Kulutthas, Kerala (Malabar), Kalingas, Muralas, and Mekalas (tribes along the Nermada). He is also said to be of the race of Raghu, meaning no doubt a Raghubansi Rajput, and he is said to be the son of the king

Nirbhaya, or Nirbhaya Narendra. The Sutradhára observes of the assembly, that it is formed of the learned men of the great city of Mahodaya, or the great Udaya, possibly Udayapur, the princes of which city affect to trace their descent from Ráma. The modern city of Udayapur, however, was not founded before the sixteenth century, and the name must be applied to some other place, unless it be no more than a title meaning the very splendid or fortunate. We cannot doubt the long prior existence of the drama, from the mention made of it, or of its author, in the works to which reference is made in the preceding article, and to which we may add the Kávya Prakás, a work probably anterior to the foundation of the modern Udayapur. Mahodaya may be the origin of the name of Mahoba, a city of which extensive ruins remain, and of which the history is little known. In a verse cited from another work by the writer, the Karpúra Manjarí, his wife, is styled 'the chaplet of the crest of the Chouhan race,' from which it follows that he belonged to that tribe. We can only conclude therefore that Rája Sekhara was the minister of some Rajput prince, who flourished in central India, at the end of the eleventh or beginning of the twelfth century.

Besides the *Viddhá Sálabhanjiká*, Rája Sekhara is the author of the *Karpúra Manjarí*, a dramatic composition of the class called *Sattaka*, entirely in Prakrit. It is named as a specimen of the class in the *Sáhitya Derpana*. The *Bála Rámáyana* is another dramatic performance attributed to this author, and is named in the same work.

HANUMAN NATAKA, OR MAHANATAKA.

A Drama in Fourteen Acts.

THE *Hanumán Nátaka,* or as it is emphatically termed, the *Mahá* or great *Nátaka,* is evidently an imperfect performance and the work of various hands. The legendary tale which obscurely accounts for this will be hereafter noticed : it is only necessary to advert to it here, in order to understand the progress of the drama. As might be implied from the title, the story is connected with that of Ráma, the monkey-chief Hanumán being a very important character in the adventures of the prince. The subject of the play is, in fact, the story of the *Rámáyana,* and it follows the order of the poem from the birth of Ráma till his return to Ayodhyá, after the conquest of Lanká. It agrees, therefore, in its dramatis personæ, also with the *Víra Cheritra,* and it is unnecessary to repeat the list.

Two or more benedictory stanzas invoking the favour of Hari as Ráma open the piece, but there is no mention of the *Sutradhára,* nor is there any prelude. We have, indeed, both here and throughout, no notice of entrances nor exits, nor in general any indication of the speaker, being left to infer the appropriate persons from the business of the scene, or being directed to their specification by the conjectures of the commentator. It is very evident that the person who speaks is very frequently unconnected with the story, and is the poet himself. This is the case at starting, as it begins :

"There was an illustrious and powerful monarch, the subduer of foes and the renowned ornament of the exalted house of the sun, named Dasaratha, in whose family, for the purpose of relieving the earth of her burthen, Bhúrisravas (Vishṇu) deigned to incorporate his divine substance as four blooming youths. The eldest, endowed with the qualities of imperial worth, was Ráma, the descendant of Raghu."

The poet then cursorily notices the early exploits of the hero, and states his going with Lakshmana to the court of Mithilá, to try his strength in the bending of the bow of Siva, and thereby winning Sítá for his bride: we have this represented dramatically; and Sítá, Janaka, the messenger or Purohita of Rávana, Lakshmana, and Ráma, maintain a dialogue easily followed, which ends in Ráma's triumph—the bow is broken, and he wins his bride.

The consequences of breaking the bow are then narrated by an indifferent person or the poet, and Parasuráma's appearance on hearing the sound is also in description. We have here in the passages describing him, one stanza which belongs to the *Víra Cheritra,* and another said to occur in the *Prabodha Chandrodaya.* The dialogue that ensues is something like that in the *Víra Cheritra,* but it terminates in Ráma's trying the bow of Parasuráma, and shooting an arrow from it which flies to Swerga. Parasuráma acknowledges him to be his superior, and the poet then proceeds to state, that Ráma and his brother, with Janaka and different sages, went to the capital of that prince, and Ráma was married to Sítá. This ends the first act, called the *Sítá Swayambara.*

The second act has no pretension to a dramatic character, being a description by the writer of the loves of Sítá and Ráma, in a strain which is prohibited by a positive rule, and is an offence against decency as well as the drama. It is evidently the addition of a comparatively modern and corrupt period, prior indeed to the vitiation of style, but marked by the debasement of moral feeling amongst the Hindus, which led to the degeneracy of poetical taste and subversion of political existence.

The third act is less dramatic than the first, and is wholly descriptive; such speeches as do occur being conformable to the usual style of oriental composition, which assigns speeches to the speaker in the first, and not in the third person, rather than to their being actually part of a dramatic dialogue. The subjects are the exile of Ráma, his fixing his residence at Pancháváti, the appearance of Marícha as a deer, and the chase of the supposed animal by Ráma and Lakshmana at Sítá's request.

The act opens with a description of the portents that indicated Ráma's impending separation from his father, the cause of which is the curse denounced upon the latter by the father of the ascetic, whom whilst formerly hunting he had accidentally slain; but the passage, though a striking one, is an imitation of several similar descriptions in the *Mahábhárat.*

Whilst thus their hours the youthful pair devoted
To love, that with enjoyment grew, the term
When the stern curse the Muni's sire denounced
Upon the erring king should shed its influence,
Approached. The sun with radiance dimmed looked forth,
Whilst fiery torches waved along the sky,
And meteors darted headlong through mid heaven:
Earth shook; the firmament rained showers of blood:
Around, the horizon thickened. In the day,
The pale stars gleamed; eclipse unseasonable
Darkened the noon: day echoed with the howls
Of dogs and jackalls, whilst the air replied
With horrid sounds and strange, such as shall peal,
When the destroying deity, in thunder,
Proclaims the dissolution of the world.

The fourth act opens with a description of the chase, in which we have the gestures of the deer delineated in a stanza from *Sakuntalá*—the speech of Dushmanta to his charioteer, "There he runs with his neck bent gracefully," &c.

Rávana then comes disguised to see Sitá.

'Oh, give me food,' he muttered, 'pious dame!'
Heedless she overstepped the magic ring

That Lakshmana had traced, when by the hand
She stretched in charity the Rákshas seized her,
Calling in vain upon the sons of Raghu.

Jatáyu, the vulture, is represented as endeavouring to rescue Sítá, but he is slain by Rávana. Sítá encounters Hanumán, and begs him to carry her ornaments, which she casts to him, to Ráma. Ráma returns from the chase to his cottage and finds it deserted:

Now having slain the fraudful deer, the prince,
With his brave brother, to their bower returned.
Sítá he sought, but sought in vain. His steps
Three several quarters trod, the fourth he left,
O'ercome with grief and terror, unexplored.

The fifth act contains the prosecution of Ráma's search after Sítá, his encounter with Báli, his triumph, and the dispatch of Hanumán to Lanká; and the sixth describes Hanumán's visit to Sítá, the feats he performs at Lanká, and his return to Ráma.

The seventh act describes the advance of Ráma's host, the fruitless expostulation of Vibhíshana with his brother, and his consequent desertion to Ráma; the further advance of the monkeys, the construction of the bridge over the sea, and the crossing over it of the troops.

Where first the monkey bands advanced, they viewed
A watery belt smooth circling round the shore:
The following troops with labour ploughed their way
Through the thick mire; the chiefs who led the rear
Exclaimed, with wonder filled, 'Here ocean was.'

Ráma, in the beginning of the eighth act, sends Angada, the son of Bálí, to persuade Rávana to relinquish Sítá peaceably. Angada has some feeling of aversion to Ráma, who killed his father, but thinks he shall best fulfil his father's wishes by promoting the war between Rávana and Ráma; he therefore goes to the former and defies him in very haughty terms.

The dialogue is more steadily maintained in this part of the work than any other. In one passage we have a curious description of the menial offices which Rávana had compelled the gods to perform in his household, and of the notions entertained by the Hindus of the *mythological,* as distinct from the *apparent* character of various objects of their worship.

Ráv. Indra weaves garlands for me, at my gate
The thousand-rayed* keeps watch, above my head
Chandra† uprears the umbrella of dominion,
The wind and ocean's monarch are my slaves,
And for my board the fiery godhead toils.
Know'st thou not this, and can'st thou stoop to praise
The son of Raghu, whose frail mortal body
Were but a meal to any of my household?

Ang. (*laughs*). Is this thy wisdom, Rávana? Infirm
Of judgment, dost thou deem of Ráma thus—
A mortal man? Then Gangá merely flows
A watery stream; the elephants that bear
The skies, and Indra's steed, are brutal forms;
The charms of Rembhá are the fleeting beauties
Of earth's weak daughters, and the golden age
A term of years. Love is a petty archer;
And he whose fame gilds with celestial glory
The triform world, the mighty Hanumán,
In thy profound discernment is an ape.

The dialogue continues very regularly dramatic to the end of the act, when Angada having in vain endeavoured to persuade Rávana to restore Sítá, leaves him to expect the immediate advance of the monkey host.

The ninth act begins with narrative, but soon breaks into a string of moral and political sentences, supposed to be uttered by Virúpáksha and Mahodara, two of Rávana's ministers. Several of these sentences occur in the Hitopadesa. Rávana is not to be persuaded, but goes to Sítá to try

* The Sun. † The Moon.

the effect of his personal solicitations—first endeavouring to deceive her by two fictitious heads, made to assume the likenesses of Ráma and his brother. Sítá's lamentations are stopped by a heavenly monitor, who tells her the heads are the work of magic, and they instantly disappear. Rávana then vaunts his prowess in war and love, and approaches Sítá to embrace her. She exclaims,

> Forbear, forbear! proud fiend, the jetty arms
> Of my loved lord, or thy relentless sword,
> Alone shall touch my neck.

Thus repulsed, Rávana withdraws, and presently reappears as Râma, with his own ten heads in his hands. Sítá thinking him what he appears is about to embrace him, when the secret virtue of her character as a faithful wife detects the imposition, and reveals the truth to her. Rávana, baffled and mortified, is compelled to relinquish his design. Sítá's apprehensions, lest she should be again beguiled, are allayed by a voice from heaven, which announces that she will not see the real Ráma until she has beheld Mandodarí kiss the dead body of her husband Rávana. The acts ends with a verse of familiar application and double import, being a series of quibbles; but it does not belong to this place, for it alludes to Kusa and Lava, who were not born for many years.

The eleventh act proceeds with the preparation for the combat, going from one party to the other very abruptly and unmethodically. A female Rákshasí attempts to assassinate Ráma, but is stopped and slain by Angada. The army then advances to Lanká, and Rávana comes forth to meet it. Kumbhakerna, his gigantic and sleepy brother, is disturbed from his repose to combat. He is rather out of humour at first, and recommends Rávana to give up the lady, observing:

> Though the commands of royalty pervade
> The world, yet sovereigns ever should remember,
> The light of justice must direct their path.

Rávana bids him go to sleep again:

They who assist us with a holy text
Are but indifferent friends. These arms have dashed
Their golden bracelets on the polished peaks
Of the eternal adamantine rock,
Uprooted from its base, and wrested victory
From the opposing grasp of gods and demons.
Confiding in thy prowess, sure in thee
To triumph o'er my foes, I have relaxed
Their fibre, but again their neves are braced.
I need thee not; hence to thy cell and sleep.

Kum. King, do not grieve, but like a valiant chief,
Pluck from thy heart all terror of thine enemies,
And only deem of thy propitious fortune,
Or who shall foremost plunge into the fight—
I will not quit thee.

Kumbhakerna's advance appears to terrify Ráma's troops, as he thinks it necessary to address them:

Ho! chiefs and heroes, why this groundless panic,
The prowess of our enemy untried.
In closer conflict? Ocean's myriad fry
Would drain the fountain, and before the swarm
Of hostile gnats the mighty lion falls.

Kumbhakerna is killed by Ráma; on which Indrajit, the son of Rávana, proceeds against the brethren. By the arrow called *Nágapása*, presented him by Brahmá, he casts Ráma and Lakshmana senseless on the ground, and then goes to Nikumbhila mountain to obtain a magic car by means of sacrifice. Hanumán disturbs his rites. Ráma and Lakshmana revive, and on being sprinkled with drops of amrita brought by Garura, the latter with a shaft decapitates Meghanáda, and tosses the head into the hands of his father Rávana, which ends the twelfth act.

In the opening of the thirteenth act, Rávana levels a shaft at Lakshmana, given him by Brahmá, and charged with the certain fate of one hero. It should seem to be something of the nature of fire-arms, a shell or a rocket, as Hanumán snatches it away, after it has struck Lakshmana, before it does mischief. Rávana reproaches Brahmá, and he sends Náreda to procure the dart again and keep Hanumán out of the way. With the fatal weapon Lakshmana is left for dead. Ráma despairs:

> My soldiers in their caves shall find protection;
> With Sítá I can die, but thou, Vibhíshana,
> What shall become of thee?

Hanumán reappears and encourages him. Rávana has a celebrated physician, Sushena, who is brought away from Lanká in his sleep, and directs that a drug (*vishalyá*) from the Druhina mountain must be procured before morning, or Lakshmana will perish. This mountain is six millions of *yojanas* remote, but Hanumán undertakes to bring it bodily to Lanká, and call at Ayodhyá on his way. He accordingly roots up the mountain, and is returning with it to Ráma, viâ Ayodhyá, when Bharata, who is employed in guarding a sacrifice made by Vasishtha, not knowing what to make of him, shoots Hanumán as he approaches. He falls exclaiming on Ráma and Lakshmana, which leads Bharata to discover his mistake. Vasishtha restores the monkey, and he sets off for Lanka again. It may be observed, that the nocturnal performance of *homa*, or sacrifice with fire, as here described, is contrary to the ritual. On Hanumán's return the medicament is administered, and Lakshmana revives. There is more description than dialogue in these passages; and the utter want of connexion which characterises the latter, would render the speeches quite unintelligible, if the chasms were not filled up very liberally by the commentator.

The fourteenth and last act opens with an embassy from Rávana, offering to give up Sítá for the battle-axe of Parasuráma; but this, Ráma replies, must be reserved for Indra.

In all which, however, the author blunders sadly, for Parasu-ráma retained his axe (see *Víra Cheritra*). On this refusal, Rávana goes forth after a brief dialogue with his queen Mandodarí, who animates his drooping courage with the true spirit of the tribe to which she belongs.

Banish your sorrow, lord of Lanká, take
One long and last embrace : we meet no more.
Or give command, and by your side I march
Fearless to fight, for I too am a Kshetriya.

The progress of Rávana through the air appals all nature.

In timid murmurs through the rustling woods
Low breathed the winds ; the sun with slackened fires
Gleamed pale abroad, and from their rapid course
The streams relaxing, slowly crept along.

He defies Ráma with great disdain, and in derision of his modest demeanour, asks him whether he is not overcome with shame by the recollection of his ancestor, Anáranya, killed formerly by Rávana. Ráma replies:

I do not shame, my noble ancestor
Fell in the combat. Victory or death
The warrior seeks, and death is not disgrace.
It ill befits thee to revile his fame,
When vanquished, thou couldst drag an abject life
In great Haihaya's dungeons, till thy sire
Begged thee to freedom, as the scanty dole
The vagrant gleans from charity. For thee
Alone I blush, unworthy of my triumph.

Rávana falls under the arrows of Ráma, and Mandodarí, his bride, bewails his death. The poet moralises on his end.

The heads that once on Siva's breast sustained
With heavenly splendour shone, now lie beneath
The vulture's talons. Such, alas! the doom
That waits on mortal creatures: thus the fruit
Of crimes committed in a former life,
Evolves to ripeness in our after being.

Sítá is recovered, but Ráma is rather shy of his bride, until her purity is established by her passing through the fiery ordeal: a test she successfully undergoes, in description, not in action. Indeed, after the dialogue between Ráma and Rávana, the style is scarcely ever colloquial. Ráma returns with Sítá and his friends to Ayodhyá, when Angada challenges them all to fight him, as it is now time to revenge his father's death. A voice from heaven, however, tells him to be pacified, as Báli will be born as a hunter in a future age, and kill Ráma, who will be then Krishna: he is accordingly appeased. Allusion to these incidents is peculiar to this drama, not occurring in the *Rámáyana, Vira Cheritra,* or *Murári Nátaka.* Ráma is then described as seated on the throne of Ayodhyá, and a brief reference is made to his ultimate exile of Sítá, after which the piece concludes with a string of stanzas of obscure and difficult construction in general, in praise of Rámachandra. The last verse contains a brief statement of the history of the poem.

The *Mahánátaka* is said to be originally the work of Hanumán, who engraved or wrote it on the rocks. Válmíki saw it, and anticipated the greater sweetness of its style would throw his *Rámáyana* into the shade. When he complained to the monkey, the latter had so little of the author about him, that he told the bard to cast the verses into the sea. Válmíki obeyed the injunction, and the *Mahánátaka* remained concealed for ages under the waves. At last portions were discovered and brought to Bhoja, by whose command Dámodara Misra arranged the fragments, filled up the chasms, and formed the whole into an entire work. There is no reason to doubt as much of this story as is credible, or that the fragments of an ancient drama were connected in the manner described. Some of the ideas are poetical, and the sentiments just and forcible: the language is in general very harmonious, but the work itself is after all a most disjointed and nondescript composition, and the patch-work is very glaringly and clumsily put together.

The date of the play is established, by the mention of Bhoja, to be a work of the tenth or eleventh century; and it is in part corroborative of the correctness of the assertion, that the drama was the work of Dámodara Misra, that the poet Dámodara is named in the *Bhoja Prabandha* as one of the many writers patronized by that monarch. That work also records the anecdote of some verses attributed to Hanumán being discovered by a merchant in Bhoja's reign, engraved upon some rocks on the sea-shore; the merchant brings a copy of the two first stanzas of one verse, and Bhoja travels to the spot to obtain the other two. The verse when complete is one that occurs in the play, and is that last translated. "The heads that once," &c.

One comment of this drama is the work of Mohandás, a *Ráma bhakt,* and possibly by his name as well as that attribute, a *Vaishnava Vairágí.*

DHANANJAYA VIJAYA.

This is a drama in one act, the subject of which is taken from the *Viráta Parva* of the *Mahábhárat,* and describes the recovery of the cattle of the Raja Virát by Arjuna, after they had been carried off by Kerna and the Kuru princes. The different chiefs appear, and threaten each other and praise themselves, very much in the strain of Homer's heroes. The battle is thrown into narrative, being described in a conversation between Indra and some of his attendants as they contemplate it from the clouds. The drama belongs to the class termed *Vyáyoga.* It is the composition of Kánchana Achárya, the son of Náráyana, a celebrated teacher of the *yoga,* of the race of *Kapi muni,* or *Káppáyana* Brahmans. The drama is performed in the autumnal season at the close of the rains, upon Vishnu's waking from his slumbers, by the written order of Jagaddeva, or in one copy, Jayadeva, which is delivered to the manager on the stage, for the entertainment of Gadádhara Misra and others. We have a Jayadeva, king of Kanouj, in the end of the twelfth century, and Gadádhara Misra is said to be a writer of repute, but of what works has not been ascertained. He is not the same as the celebrated logician Gadhádhara Bhattácharya, who was a native of Bengal, as the affix *misra* indicates a native of Gangetic Hindustan.

ANERGHA RAGHAVA, OR MURARI NATAKA.

A Drama in Seven Acts.

This play is most usually known by the latter appellation, which it derives from the author; the former is its most legitimate title, implying the sacred descendant of Raghu, Ráma being the hero of the piece. The story is consequently the same with that of the *Víra Cheritra* and *Hanumán Nátaka*, and the characters therefore need no particular specification.

The subject of the prelude is of an unusual description. The *Sútradhára* states that the assembly is collected on occasion of the *Purushottama yátrá*; that all the world is well acquainted with the talents of Kahala Kandala, an actor from another island (one comment says, Sinhala or Ceylon), and that he himself is the scholar of the Professor Bahurúpa, and a native of the middle country (explained by another comment, Ayodhyá or Oude). The first-named actor then sends the *Sútradhára*, whilst on the stage, a challenge to try their skill, and the manager determines that it shall be put to the test in the *Anergha Rághava*, a new composition by Murári, the son of Tantumati, and Sri Verddhamána Bhatta, of the Maudgala family.

The first act opens with a conversation between Dasaratha and Vámadeva, which serves to introduce Viswámitra, who comes to request the aid of Ráma. The dialogue between him and the king is an effort to outdo each other in complimentary speeches, most of which are in the very worst taste. As, for example, Viswamitra says to the king:

Confiding in your surety, that earth
No longer has occasion of alarm,

> Indra but rarely waving in the clouds
> His bow, foregoes its practice, and forgets
> His skill. Nay, further; from the copious draughts
> Of ghee your ceaseless sacrifices offer,
> His every limb is grown of size unwieldy,
> And scarcely can he see out of his eyes.

However, the whole composition is not of this description, and it does contain a few redeeming passages. When Viswámitra urges Dasaratha to aid him by the intermediate agency of Ráma, he observes:

> The monarch of the day invests the dawn
> With delegated rays to scatter night,
> And ocean sends his ministers the clouds,
> To shed his waters o'er the wide-spread earth.

The king also considering, and being reminded by Vámadeva, that the race of Raghu never sent away a petitioner ungratified, sends for Ráma and Lakshmana, and allows Viswámitra to take them with him.

The second act opens at dawn with a dialogue between Sunassepha and Pasumedra, two of the disciples of Viswámitra, in which the former gives the latter several legendary tales, relating to Bálí and Rávana and the Rákshasas, and the interruption occasioned by Táraká to their rites, on which account Ráma and Lakshmana have been brought to the hermitage to protect them. Sunassepha goes to collect wood, and Pasumedra to see the princes. Ráma and Lakshmana now describe the situation of the hermitage, its tenants and their duties. The former is on the banks of the Kausiki or Coosy river: they then describe the noon, and are supposed to rest in the shade till towards evening, although they do not leave the stage, nor is the dialogue interrupted: they are then joined by Viswámitra, who gives a long description of sunset, until he is stopped by the cry that Táraká is abroad. Ráma, after some hesitation about killing a female, goes to destroy her: on his return he expatiates at great length on the rising of the moon:—

The sovereign moon not yet o'ertops the hills,
But his precursor rays, that waken all
The beauty of the lotus, spread through heaven,
And as they bright advance, they chase the vapours
Far to the bounds of earth, or banish them
Deep in the rocky caves, or else prepare
To seize them living captives, as they seek
A refuge in the shadows of the mountain.

This is well enough, but then comes ridiculous conceit.

The watery darkness by the lunar beams
Is cleansed, as by the purifying nut:
Clear gleams the air, and in the shadowy hollows
The cloudy mire precipitated falls.
Or by the glittering shears, the brilliant heaven
Is shorn, and piecemeal into fragments clipped;
The shadows like the dusky rind are peeled,
And here and there are scattered o'er the vale.

Upon his rejoining the sage, Viswámitra proposes that they shall visit Mithilá.

The third act opens with a dialogue between the chamberlain and one of Sítá's attendants, from which it appears that Sítá begins to be conscious of her youth, and that Rávana has sent to demand her in marriage. A conversation next ensues between Viswámitra, Janaka, and Satánanda, in which the two princes are introduced to the king, and Viswámitra urges Janaka to let Ráma try to bend the bow of Siva. Saushkala, the messenger of Rávana, now arrives, to demand Sítá in marriage for his master, refusing at the same time, on his part, to submit to the test of bending Siva's bow. Satánanda replies for Janaka, and desires Ráma to go and try his fortune. The princes obey, and Ráma is described by those on the stage as breaking the bow: he has therefore won the lady. The family connexion is extended by the promise of Urmilá, Mandáví, and Sruta Kírtti, to Ráma's brothers. Saushkala is highly indignant, and departs to carry the information to his master's minister.

Act fourth: Mályaván describes the rising of the sun, and his disappointment on Rávana's account. Súrpanakhá arrives from Videha, and announces that Ráma and Sítá are married. Mályaván anticipates that Rávana will carry her off; and to render the attempt less perilous, projects inveigling Ráma into the forests alone, for which he sends Súrpanakhá in the disguise of Manthará, the attendant of Kaikeyi. She tells him that she had heard of Parasuráma's approach to Mithilá, and Mályaván conjectures the possibility of some good being effected by the result. The next scene introduces Parasuráma, in the same strain as the Mahávíra Cheritra, but more extravagantly. Ráma's humility is more excessive, and the other characters carry on a vituperative dialogue with Parasuráma without appearing, speaking successively from behind the scenes. We shall not cite any of the dialogue beyond Ráma's reply to Parasuráma's boasts of his destruction of the Kshetriya race: "This flag of your fame is now worn to tatters, let us see if you can mount a new one." Ráma then calls for his bow, and Parasuráma presents him with his axe. They go forth to fight: a voice behind proclaims that Sítá is apprehensive that Ráma again draws the bow for a maiden prize, and that he cannot draw it in vain. This is all the reference we have to the combat, as the two Rámas return immediately, very excellent friends. Parasuráma takes leave of the Rishis, who are behind the curtain, and departs. Janaka and Dasaratha now enter, and the latter declares his purpose of relinquishing the kingdom entirely to his son. Lakshmana announces the arrival of Manthará, and presents a letter from Kaikeyí, the purpose of which is to urge Dasaratha's fulfilment of his promise, and grant her, as the two boons, the coronation of Bharata, and banishment of Ráma. The old gentlemen faint: Ráma sends Lakshmana to prepare Sítá, and recommending his father to

Janaka, departs. The author makes very short work with this part of his story.

In the fifth act, a conversation between Sravaná, a female ascetic, and Jambaván, the bear, briefly describes the progress of Ráma with his wife and brother till their arrival in the forests. Sravaná goes to prepare Sugríva for the friendly reception of the travellers, and Jambaván hears a dialogue carried on between Lakshmana and Rávana, disguised as a juggler. Jatáyu then appears, and tells the bear he has seen Rávana and Máricha in the forest, and anticipates mischief to Ráma. Jambaván goes to find the chief and put him on his guard, and Jatáyu beholds Sítá carried off; he follows the ravisher. The language here is generally plain and intelligible, but there is no poetry. Some of the attempts at description make but a poor figure by the side of Bhavabhúti's delineations of the same scenery, and the dialogue between Jatáyu and Jambaván is a sorry substitute for the scene between Jatáyu and Sampátí in the *Víra Cheritra*. Lakshmana now appears, and is soon after joined by Ráma, and both express their grief, but with more philosophy than pathos. Lakshmana observes:

> The worse the ill that fate on noble souls
> Inflicts, the more their firmness; and they arm
> Their spirits with adamant to meet the blow.

Ráma replies:

> The firmness I was born with or was reared to,
> And rage, that fills my heart, restrains my sorrows;
> But harder is the task to fit my soul
> To bear unmurmuring a husband's shame.

Whilst engaged in conversation a cry of distress is heard, and on looking out, the youths observe Guha, the friendly forest monarch, assailed by the demon Kabandha, or a fiend without a head. Lakshmana goes to his aid, and returns with his friend Guha. In the act of delivering him, Lakshmana has tossed away the skeleton of Dundubhí, a giant, suspended by Báli, and Báli deeming this an insult, presently appears. After a prolix interchange of civility and defiance, Ráma and Báli go off the stage to determine their respective supremacy by single combat: the result is described by Lakshmana and Guha: Báli is slain. Voices without announce the inauguration of Sugríva, and his determination to assist Ráma to recover Sítá, and Lakshmana and his friend leave the stage to join the party. The whole of this act is very flat and undramatic, and the same character may be given of the rest of the drama: we have nothing but sounding words and obscure mythology, with very few poetical ideas or rational reflexions.

The sixth act continues the business of description, and Savana and Suka, two of Rávana's emissaries, describe to his minister Mályaván, the formation of the bridge over the sea, and the advance of Ráma's army: they foretell, also, an unfortunate result from Ráma's celerity, as Mályaván observes: "The activity of an assailant is ever the best assurance of success." Voices behind announce, that Kumbhakerna and Meghanáda have gone forth to battle. Mályaván wishes them prosperity, in a phrase perfectly oracular: Utinam, Ramum et Lakshmanum, Kumbhakernum et Meghanadum, vincere posse. The clumsy contrivance of voices behind the scene proclaims the deaths of Kumbhakerna and Meghanáda, and announces the departure of Rávana to the field. Mályaván determines to follow him:

> Haste we to Rávana, 'tis all I can
> In battle pilgrimage to expiate
> The sin of feeble age, and on the sword
> Resign a life, now useless to my sovereign.

The remainder of the act is a very prolix and nerveless description of the final contest and overthrow of Rávana, in an extravagantly laboured dialogue between two Vidyádharas. Several pages here are so insufferably tedious, and at the same time so difficult of construction, that they are quite unreadable, there being nothing to repay the pains of making out the meaning.

The Seventh and last Act resembles the concluding Act of the *Víra Cheritra,* and describes the return of Ráma with his wife and brother, and accompanied by Vibhíshana and Sugríva, in the celestial car of Kuvera, to his capital Ayodhyá. It is, of course, an act of pure description, and as little dramatic as the similar act of the *Víra Cheritra,* but unenlivened by the picturesque beauties which relieve the want of action in that drama. It is also infinitely more prolix, and in the same proportion more tedious. The route is also very preposterously diversified. In the *Víra Cheritra,* the travellers proceed over the Dekhin, through Aryavertta, or India proper, to the Snowy Mountains, and then turn back at once to Ayodhyá. Murári takes them from Ráma's bridge into the upper regions, whence they descry the different holy portions of the mythological mountain Sumeru, and visit Chandraloka, or the region of the moon; the sole object of which absurd deviation is a laboured and obscure display of legendary lore, the mythological details relating to Sumeru, Kailás, and the Chandraloka, occupying several hundred verses. The author then descends within ken of the earth, and commences his terrestrial description with an account of Sinhalá, or Ceylon, distinguishing that island, like all modern Hindu writers, from Lanká. The reason is obvious enough, particularly in a writer of the south India, Sinhala, or Ceylon, being too well known to be made the seat of legendary personages, supposed, as is the case with Vibhíshana and his Rákshasas, to be still existing. From Sinhalá we then pursue a tolerably rational route, described more in detail than in the *Víra Cheritra.* The places named are the Malaya mountains, the forest, the mountain Prasravana, the Godáveri, mount Mályávan, Kundinipura in the Máháráshtra country, the shrine of Bhimeswara, the city of Kánchi, Ujayin, and the temple of Mahákála, Mahishmatí, the capital of Chedi, the Jumna and Ganga rivers, and Varánasi, Mithilá, or Tirhut, and Champa, near Bhagelpur. The travellers then proceed westward to Prayâga, and the Antarvedi or Doab, when they again follow an easterly course and arrive at Ayodhyá. Vasishtha, the priest, and the brothers of Ráma, await his arrival, on which he is crowned, and the piece concludes.

Enough has been said to convey a correct notion of the character of the Anergha Rághava. It has no dramatic merit, being deficient in character, action, situation, and interest. As a poem, it presents occasionally poetic thoughts, but they are very few, and are lost amidst pages of flat common-place, quaint conceit, hyperbolical extravagance, and obscure mythology. Yet this drama bears in general a much higher character with the pundits of the present day, than the truly poetical compositions of Bhavabhúti and Kálidás. The vitiation of taste and abjectness of sentiment prevalent amongst them, sufficiently explain this unjust preference. The Hindus of these days are little able to estimate purity of conception, delicacy of feeling, or brilliancy of fancy: they trouble themselves, indeed, very little with the thoughts, and bound their criticism to an author's style. The language of Murári is, of course, as far from good taste as his ideas, but it has merit. As a specimen of elaborate composition it is unsurpassed, and the intricate and not unmusical combination of the words evinces prodigious labour, and a wonderful command of the Sanscrit language. One consequence of this is a total want of perspicuity, and without being intently studied and learnt by rote, there is little chance that the Anergha Rághava will be understood throughout.

Besides the celebrity Murári Misra derives from his elaborate style, he is indebted to the author of the *Siddhánta Kaumudí* for no slender reputation. As he deals largely in unusual grammatical forms and combinations, Bhattoji Díkshita has not unfrequently recourse to the *Anergha Rághava* for the illustration of his grammatical rules.

The style of the drama is sufficient evidence that the *Anergha Rághava* is of modern date. It is not possible, however, to fix the period of its composition with any precision. It of course preceded the *Siddhánta Kaumudí,* a work about two centuries old. It is subsequent to the time at which public festivals were instituted at Cuttack in honour of Jagannáth, as it was represented at the *Purushottama Yátrá.* As, however, the choice of the hero was Ráma, and no allusion is made to Krishna or Rádhá, there can be little doubt that it preceded the enthusiasm excited in favour of those latter divinities, by the Bengali visionary Chaitanya, in the end of the fifteenth century, and which still influences the prevailing worship of Cuttack. The bad taste displayed in the work will not allow us to carry it much farther back, and it is possibly, therefore, a production of the thirteenth or fourteenth century.

In the present instance two commentaries have been consulted: one is short and without any name; the other is full to tediousness. It is the composition of Sri Ruchi Mahopádhyáya, by command of the king Bhairava Deva, son of Narasinha Deva. The country governed by the prince is not named. If Orissa be intended, as is probable, this comment may be the work of the latter part of the thirteenth, or beginning of the fourteenth century, Narasinha Deva, king of Orissa, ascending the throne in 1236.

SAREDA TILAKA.

This is a piece of the class called *Bháṇa,* or a monologue in One Act, although of considerable length.

Rasikasekhara, a man of licentious habits, gives an account of the different individuals he encounters in the streets of Koláhalapur, at the time of the vernal festival. By far the greatest portion of the piece is in description, but part is in a supposititious dialogue, in which Rasikaşekhara having addressed some individual whom he names, adds *kim bravíshi ?*' 'what do you say ?' and then repeats himself the reply. The persons thus interrogated are chiefly females and courtezans, and the dialogue very generally will not admit of translation; occasionally it should appear, also, that the male characters shew themselves for a short interval, and speak for themselves, but there is no stage direction for entrance or exit. It is possible, therefore, that the whole is the exhibition of a single performer, who varying his voice and appearance, adapts himself to the different personations: a feat not uncommonly nor badly accomplished by some of the Indian *Bhanrs,* or professional jesters and mimics of the present day, although they may fall short of the more cultivated talent of this class in Europe.

Of the individuals described the majority are women, and the following are some of the most characteristic notices given by Rasikasekhara, who here is supposed to address a companion:

"Look where the lotus-eyed damsels of Kankana approach; their slender waists decorated with tinkling bells, and their charms guiding the shafts of Káma into every bosom.

There goes the maid of Gurjara, blooming as with perpetual youth, having eyes like the *chakora,* of the complexion of the yellow *rochaná,* and a voice musical as that of the parrot. She wears anclets of silver, large ear-rings set with pearls, and her boddice is buttoned below the hips with gems.

The matron of Mahárásh*t*ra proceeds yonder, her forehead stained with saffron, and with silver chains upon her feet. She wears a coloured veil, and a girdle round her loins.

Here comes the damsel of Nepal, whose locks are blacker than the bee, whose bosom is fragrant with musk, and whose forehead bears a mark brighter than the new moon.

Behold that lotus-faced maiden of Pán*d*ya bearing offerings in her hand; her person is decorated with pearls, and her bosom perfumed with sandal.

A Chola female approaches, whose cheeks are tinted with saffron, and whose dress is embroidered with the buds of the lotus.

The bosoms of those Dravida women are as moonlight in the courts of the young, whilst those of others are like lamps in water-jars.

Observe the lovely form of the damsels of Karnáta, whose forehead is stamped with a mole of musk and tinted with safflower; whose ears are ornamented with rings of gold, and whose bosom attracts the hearts of men.

Look at that Andhra female, whose graceful ear is decorated by the scroll of gold, whose nose-ring set with pearls trembles to her breath, and over whose bosom spreads the saffron-dyed vest.

The female worshipper of Śiva advances, her forehead streaked with the double line of ashy whiteness, and from whose neck the string of cowries depends; her soft lips are ruddy with betel, and her curls are of darkest jet.

And mark where the damsel devoted to Vishńu proceeds, her forehead marked with the saffron crescent, her tresses playing upon her long neck, and her eyes beautiful as the lotus."

The personages next in frequency of description are religious characters, to whom the author shews no great favour, not only in his portraits, but in one or two piquant anecdotes related in the course of the piece, of which some pious vagrant is the hero.

"Eh! who are these I see? The Jangama covered with ashes, wearing his hair in a braid, carrying the type of Śiva round his neck, and having shoes on his feet; he bears in his hand the segment of a skull: and the Vaishńava, his forehead marked with an upright streak, carrying a bow decorated with bells and peacock's feathers, and a wallet at his side.

There go the readers of the Purānas, carrying under their arms the sacred volumes wrapped up in the cloth on which they take their seat. They have rosaries in their hands, and their foreheads are stained with sandal.

Here, the haughty Yetis approach, clad in vestments dyed with ochre, bearing bambu staves, round which their nether vesture is wrapped, and arrogantly promulgating false doctrines.

And there go the personifications of hypocrisy, the Yogis, who to impose upon the people are counting their rosaries, and have smeared their bodies with the ashes of burnt cowdung. They suffer their beards to grow, their garments are dyed with ochre, and they carry their wallets under their arms, covered with the skin of the black deer."

One of the most laboured descriptions is the following :—

" Here comes a Snake-catcher, with his serpent and monkey. Upon his head he wears a scanty plume of peacock's feathers, round one of his arms winds the tendril of a vine, and a bracelet of shells decorates the other. His braided locks project from above his forehead, whilst beneath them, from ear to ear, extends across his brow the single streak of ashes. Repeating the incantation of Garura, and meditating upon his spiritual teacher, he cautiously opens his basket, and draws forth the slowly-excited reptile. Whilst the exhibitor is shaking his knee with one hand, and with the other playing upon his pipe, the snake slowly raises his head and expands his hood. The monkey then darts upon the snake and grips him with his teeth, and then recedes from the fury with which he darts forth his venom. Wonderful are the works of Brahmá! and yet what marvel is there that men can tame venomous animals, when women can tame men!"

In the original, the quibble is upon the word *bhújanga*, which means a gallant or a snake.

Except a few such insignificant attempts, there is little wit or satire in the composition, and still less poetry, beyond that which is merely mechanical. The style is highly laboured and involved, abounds with verbal jingle, and is not unfrequently encumbered with rhyme. This is a sufficient proof of its comparatively recent date, and the same inference is authorized by the allusions to the Jangamas and Vaishnavas, who, as here described, are modern sectaries. The composition cannot therefore be earlier than the twelfth century, and it is probably later. The author is named Sankara, who could not have been the religious reformer so denominated, although he may possibly be the Sankara Kavi mentioned in the *Sárngdhara Paddhati*. According to the original he was a native of Benares, but the performance is said to have been held at Koláhalapur. *Koláhala*, properly speaking, means an uproar, and the city had most probably only an allegorical existence, being also the fancied scene of the events described in the piece.

YAYATI CHERITRA.

This is a drama in Seven Acts, by Rúdra Deva. It was first performed at the Spring Festival, but it does not appear at what place, nor does any mention of the author elsewhere occur. He is not likely to be the same as Rúdra Bhatta, the author of the *Sringára Tilaka,* who is amongst the writers named in the *Sárngdhara Puddhati.*

A prince, named Rúdra Deva, is praised highly for his liberality in some of the examples quoted by Apyáya Díkshita, in his *Kuvalayánanda.* Apyáya flourished in the reign of Krishna Deva of Vijayanagar, about A.D. 1526, and the prince alluded to may possibly be Pratápa Rúdra Deva, sovereign of Telingana in the beginning of the fourteenth century. We have also a Rúdra, the author, real or supposed, of a vocabulary, whose date appears to be about the same, the thirteenth or fourteenth century. The *Yayáti Cheritra* is not quoted by the writers of systems, and only one copy has been met with, which is so exceedingly inaccurate that it is nearly unintelligible. As far as the business of the piece can be decyphered, it relates to the intrigue of Yayáti with Sermishthá, terminating in his union with her, and reconciliation with his queen Devayání. The story is told as follows, in the first section of the *Mahábhárat* and several of the *Puranas.*

Sermishthá was the daughter of Vrishapervá, king of the Daityas, and Devayáni the daughter of Sukra, regent of the planet Venus and the spiritual preceptor of the Daitya race. Devayáni having incurred the displeasure of Sermishthá, the latter threw the former into a well, where she was found by Yayáti, the son of Nahusha. Devayáni, on returning to her father, excited his anger against Vrishapervá, who to appease Sukra consented to give his daughter to Devayáni as her servant, with a thousand other female attendants. Devayáni married the king Yayáti. At the time of her marriage Sukra obtained the king's promise that he would never take Sarmishthá to his bed; but after some interval the king meeting her, fell in love with, and espoused her privately. The intrigue continued secret, until Yayáti had two sons by Devayání and three by Sarmishthá, when it was discovered by the former, and excited her resentment as well as that of her father. The violation of the king's promise was punished by premature decay, as denounced upon him by Sukra, with permission, however, to transfer his infirmities to any one who would accept them. Yayáti appealed to his sons; of whom the youngest alone, Puru, consented to assume the burthen. After a sufficient period Yayáti took his decrepitude back again, and left the sovereignty of the world to Puru in reward of his filial piety. All the sons of Yayáti were the founders of distinguished races. Yadu gave birth to the Yádavas, Turvasu to the Yávanas, Druhya was the ancestor of the Bhojas, and Anu of the Mlechchas. The Pauravas were the descendants of Puru, in whose line the Kaurava and Pandava families were comprised.

DUTANGADA, OR THE MISSION OF ANGADA.

This piece is styled a *Ch'háyá Nataka,* the shade or outline of a drama, the subject of which is taken from the *Rámáyana.* It consists of but four scenes. In the first, Angada, the son of Báli, is sent to demand Sítá; in the second, he executes his mission, and on his departure Rávana goes forth to battle. Two Gandhervas then enter, and in a short speech each, announce that Rávana is slain, on which Ráma enters in triumph. The composition was perhaps intended to introduce a spectacle of the battle and procession, as it is otherwise difficult to conceive what object its extreme conciseness could have effected. It is said to have been written for the *yátrá* of Kumára Pála Deva, by order of Tribhuvana Pála Deva, by the poet Subhata.

MRIGANKALEKHA.

This is a piece of the class termed *Nátiká*, in four acts, by Viswanáth, the son of Trimala Deva, originally from the banks of the Godáverí, but residing at Benares, where the piece was represented at the *yátrá*, or festival, of Viswéswara, the form under which Siva is particularly worshipped at that city.

Mrigánkalekhá is the daughter of the king of Kámarúpa, or Asam: she has been beheld by Karpúratilaka, king of Kalinga, whilst hunting, and the parties are mutually enamoured. The obstacle to their union is the love of Sankhapála, a demon, to oppose whose supernatural agency the minister of the king of Kalinga, who alone is aware of the circumstance, invites to the palace a benevolent magician, Siddhayogini, and Mrigánkalekhá is also lodged in the palace as the friend of the queen Vilásavatí. Notwithstanding these precautions, she is carried off by Sankhapála to the temple of Kálí, when the Raja wandering disconsolate beyond his garden-bounds, comes to the spot, rescues her, and kills Sankhapála. He is then united to Mrigánkalekhá in the presence of her father and brother, and with the consent of his queen, killing also, before the conclusion of the rite, the brother of Sankhapála, who comes to revenge him in the form of a wild elephant, but is encountered and slain by the king.

The author of this play is largely indebted to his predecessors for the story, incidents, and the thoughts of his play. The union of the king and Mrigánkalekhá is effected through the secret contrivance of the minister Retnachúra, because the lady's husband is to become the master of the world. This is taken from the *Retnávalí*. The conveyance of the princess to the temple of Kálí, and her rescue by the king, are borrowed from the *Málati and Mádhava;* and the site of the temple, and the appearance of the goblins, are described to precisely the same purpose, but with inferior power. During the Rájá's peregrinations in his love-frenzy, he passes through a wood, in which he inquires of different animals if they have seen his mistress, in a strain evidently copied from the fourth act of the *Vikrama and Urvaśí.* We must give the writer, therefore, little credit for originality; nor has he made good use of his materials, but has diluted the incidents he has borrowed with much prolix and tedious description of the rising and setting of the sun and moon, and the genial influence of the seasons. The language is polished, but in the modern style, and is rather elaborate than elegant. The play is clearly a comparatively recent composition, but no clue is afforded for the precise determination of its date.

VIDAGDHA MADHAVA.

This is a play in seven acts, the subject of which is taken from the *Bhágavat*, and relates to the loves of Krishna and Rádhá. It is, in fact, the "Songs of Jayadeva" dramatised.

It may easily be supposed, that the jealous squabbles of two lovers furnish insufficient materials for a play of such length, and accordingly the *Vidagdha Mádhava* has little action, and is made up of dialogue that leads to nothing, and of uninteresting description. An attempt has been made to give some variety to it by the introduction of Chandrávalí, a nymph of Vrindávan, enamoured of Krishna, and by representing the Paurnamásí, the personified day of full moon, as interesting herself in the union of Krishna and Rádhá. The piece is also in its different portions supposed to be applicable to the different seasons of the year at which the chief festivals in honour of Krishna are held, or the festival of spring in *Chaitra* or *Vaisakh*, that of the birth of Krishna in *Srávan* or the rains, and the *Rás yátrá*, or dance of Krishna with the Gopis, in the season of autumn.

The want of dramatic incident is not relieved by the literary merits of the composition, as there is little poetry in the thoughts. The style, though not devoid of melody, is not remarkably musical, and as the greater part of the characters are females, much the most considerable portion of the language is Prákrit. The work does not rank very high in the estimation of the Hindus, except those of a particular sect, the *Vaishnavas*, who have followed the doctrines of Chaitanya. The play is recommended to them, not only by the subject, but by its being the work of Rúpa, one of their founder's first disciples, and one of the early teachers of the sect. His name does not appear in the manuscript, and the prelude presents one singularity in the *Sútradhára's* personating the author himself. The commentary, however, and the concurrent tradition of the *Vaishnavas,* leave no doubt as to Rúpa's being the writer of the drama ; and it is further established by the date of it, which is specified in the manuscript S. 1589 (A. D. 1533), at which period there is no doubt he flourished.

ABHIRAMA MANI.

This is a drama in seven acts, the subject of which is the history of Ráma. The business is related in much the same order as in the *Vira Cheritra* and *Murári Nátaka.* The piece was performed also like the latter of these two works at Jagannáth, at the festival of Purushottoma or Vishnu. The author is named Sundara Misra, but we have no further knowledge of him. Of two copies consulted, one bears what appears to be the date of the composition, Sáka 1521, or A. D. 1597. The composition possesses little dramatic, although it has some literary merit.

MADHURÁNIRUDDHA.

This is a drama in eight acts, the subject of which is the secret loves of Ushá, the daughter of the Asura Báńa, and Aniruddha, the grandson of Kŕishńa, and the defeat and death of the former by that divinity.

In the first act Nárada apprises Kŕishńa and Balaráma, that Indra is again in dread of the power of the demons, and especially of Báńa, who has acquired the particular favour of S'iva, and who is therefore not to be easily subdued. The conference ends by Nárada's going to S'ońapur, the capital of the demon, to endeavour to impair the friendship between Báńa and S'iva, whilst Kŕishńa and his brother await the result.

In the second act we learn from a conversation between Jayá and Vírabhadra, attendants on Párvatí and S'iva, that the excessive arrogance of Báńa, in his anxiety to match himself with Vishńu, has offended the latter, who has accordingly departed for Kailása, after announcing that Báńa's anxiety shall be alleviated whenever his banner falls. Párvatí also has gone to Kailása, after announcing to Ushá that she will shortly behold her husband. Ushá and Chitrángadá are presently afterwards introduced, and in the conversation that ensues, the former expresses her impatience for the boon conferred by the goddess.

In the third act Aniruddha and his friend Vakulánka inform the audience, that the former is violently enamoured of a damsel he has seen in his sleep, and despairs of discovering who she is, when Nárada comes opportunely to his aid, and informs him that she is the daughter of Báńa; on which Anniruddha determines to go to his capital, first propitiating

Jwálámukhi by penance, in order to obtain the means of entering a city surrounded by a wall of perpetual flame.

The fourth act is one of mere conversation again, between Bána, his minister, and his wife. The banner has fallen, and they endeavour to prevail on him to propitiate Siva, in order to avert the evil omen, but he refuses.

In the fifth act Aniruddha repairs to the shrine of Jwálámukhí, and upon the point of offering himself as a sacrifice, is prevented by the goddess, and receives from her the power of travelling through the air. Jwálámukhi is the form of Durga, worshipped wherever a subterraneous flame breaks forth, or wherever jets of carburetted hydrogen gas are emitted from the soil. A celebrated place of this description exists in India near Nadoun, and that this is the shrine intended by the author is apparent, from the direction taken by Bhringi, a servant of Durgá who precedes Aniruddha, to prepare the goddess to grant his request. As he proceeds in his aerial car, he notices the countries of Orissa, Bengal, Behar, Oude or Ayodhya, Prayága, Hastinapur or Delhi, and Kurujangal or Tahneser, whence he comes to Jwálámukhi. Aniruddha's visit to the goddess is something unusual in dramatic composition, and characteristic of a prevailing form of the Hindu religion some few centuries ago, that of the ritual prescribed by the *Tantras.* In his description of the shrine, and the sports of the goblins who surround it, the author has imitated the *Múlati and Mádhava.*

In the next act Ushá and Chitralekhá receive a visit from Náreda, in whose presence the latter unfolds a picture containing portraits of all the chief characters in Swerga Pátála, and on earth, or Indra, and other gods; Sesha, Takshaka and the Nágas, and different princes, as the kings of Magadhá, Mathurá, Avanti, Madra, Mahishmati, and Viderbha, Yudhishthira, Krishna, Baladeva, Pradyumna, and finally Aniruddha, whom Ushá recognizes as the individual seen in her dream, and of whom she is enamoured. Náreda recommends

Chítralekhá being sent to Dwárávatí to invite Aniruddha, whom he enables to fly thither, whilst he remains in charge of Ushá, whom he sends to the garden to await her lover's arrival.

The seventh act brings Aniruddha and Chítralekhá to Sonapur, and the former is united to his mistress.

The eighth describes the detection of Aniruddha by Bána and the engagement that ensues, in a dialogue between Náreda and Párvata. Krishna, Baladeva, and Pradyumna coming to the aid of the prince, the day is going ill with Bána, when Kártikeya, Ganesa, and Siva and Chandí come to his succour. The author, who is a *Saiva,* gives the advantage to the sons of Siva, but the *Vishnu* and *Bhágavat Puránas* tell the story very differently, and subject the *Saivas* to rather severe treatment; the legend being apparently founded on some hostile conflict between the followers of Siva and Krishna. The dramatist is obliged to admit, that notwithstanding the presence of his allies, Bána has all his thousand arms cut off by Krishna except four. Siva advances to the aid of his votary, when a combat ensues between the gods, which Brahmá descends to arrest. They embrace, whilst Párvatí and Brahmá support Bána to make his submission. The parties enter, when Vishnu declares he is less sensible of the wounds inflicted by Bána, than of the regret he feels at his presumption in contending with Siva. The latter consoles him by telling him he only did a warrior's duty, and that military prowess is independent of all motives of love or hatred. Párvatí then brings Ushá to the spot, and by her desire, and that of Siva, Bána gives his daughter to Aniruddha. Siva then elevates him to the rank of one of his attendants, under the name of Mahákála, and the piece concludes with the wish of Aniruddha, that the fame of the verses of the bard may endure as long as the universe.

The *Madhurániruddha* is the work of Chandra Sekhara, the son of Gopinátha, the religious preceptor of a prince who is celebrated for his encouragement of literature and his victories over the Mlechchas. His name is said to be Víra, with the epithet Kesari, which being synonimous with Sinh, the prince intended is probably Vira Sinh, the Raja of Bundlecund, who flourished in the beginning of the seventeenth century. The piece was represented at a festival in honour of Siva, and the author is a decided *Saiva* although he has chosen a *Vaishnava* hero. We have no further information respecting the writer. The piece abounds too much with description to be a good play: the style has considerable merit.

KANSA BADHA.

A drama in seven acts, the subject of which is the destruction of Kansa by Krishna.

In the first act, Kansa, king of Mathurá, alarmed by a voice from heaven, that the son of his sister, predestined to destroy him, has escaped the precautions taken against his birth, consults with his minister what he shall do, and upon his advice orders all Brahmans and holy and religious characters to be seized or slain, and all sacred and pious observance to cease. In the second act, Garga the Muni relates to Tálajangha, an emissary of the minister, the different exploits of the juvenile Krishna, and the latter also witnesses the destruction of the demon Kesi, one of those infernal beings who in vain attempted to kill the divine child, instigated by their prescience of their fate when he should reach maturity. The third act is occupied with a dialogue between Akrúra and his Charioteer, the former being on his way to Gokul, to invite Krishna to Mathurá. The fourth act opens with what the author terms a *Prastávana*, an introductory dialogue between a staff-bear and an astrologer, respecting the object of Akrúra's journey. Balaráma and Krishna then make their appearance, attended by Sudáma and Akrúra, and accompanied by their foster parents, Nanda and Yasodá, who take leave of the children. The latter play the part of mutes, and after bowing to the elders and receiving their benediction, depart. The seniors then express their grief for their loss, and quit the stage; after which we have the boys again, as proceeding on their journey, till they are overtaken by a messenger from Rádhá, in consequence of which Krishna determines to spend some time at Vrindávan. The fifth act conveys them to Kansa's palace at Mathurá, describing the different occurrences on the road as related in the *Bhágavat*, and similar works. The first part of the sixth act consists of a dialogue between a *Vetradhara* and the *Koshtapála*, a staff-bearer, and the chief of the police, describing the combat of the youths with the royal elephant of *Kansa*, after the death of which they retire to make way for Balaráma and Krishna, with Kansa's two wrestlers, Chánúra and Mushtika. After some conversation between them and a few specimens of their skill, the former speakers resume the dialogue, and describe the defeat and death of the *athletæ*, which they go off to report to Kansa. We have then partly in action, and partly in narrative, the death of that prince, which ends the sixth act. The seventh act re-unites the boys with their mortal parents, Vasudeva and Devakí; and to console the latter for her brother's death, Krishna installs her father Ugrasena in the sovereignty of Mathurá.

This drama is consequently nothing more than a re-set of the tenth section of the *Bhágavat Purána*, which gives an account of the early life of the last incarnation of Vishnu as Krishna. It is, in fact, little else than the same work thrown into dialogue, and the character of it is chiefly narrative and descriptive. There is little action, and what there is, is inartificially and disjointedly put together. The language is in general good, although highly elaborate. The compounds are interminable and of constant recurrence, which is sufficient to establish the comparatively modern date of the play. The same may be inferred from the conjectural identification of the persons connected with the composition of the drama.

The author is called Krishna Kavi, the son of Nrisinha; he is also termed Sesha Krishna Pandita, the first of which appellations indicates a Marhatta original. With respect to the latter, there is a Krishna Pandita, of the Benares school of grammar, author of a commentary on the *Prakriya Kaumudí*, an abridgment of which, the *Tatwa Chandra*, was completed by one of his pupils, Jayanta, in the year 1687 (A.D. 1631). The patron of the author and person who presides in the assembly is styled, 'the sovereign upholding Goverddhana, the son of Toder, the ornament of the race of Tandana, and whose Guru was Girdhári Náth.' Girdhar Náth was the grandson of Vallabha, the founder of the Gokulastha Gosains, who flourished early in the sixteenth century; and Todar may have been Akber's financial minister, Toder Mal. The drama was performed at a festival held at Benares in honour of Visweswara; and it seems not improbable, therefore, that it was written about two centuries ago, or in the beginning of the seventeenth century, when Krishna Pandita, the preceptor of Jayanta, might easily be cotemporary with the son of Toder Mal, and a grandson of Vallabha Acharya.

PRADYUMNA VIJAYA.

This is a drama in seven acts, the subject of which is the victory of Pradyumna, the son of Krishna, over Vajranábha, the sovereign of the Daityas. The story is, in fact, taken with servile fidelity from the *Harivansa*, the last section of the *Mahábhárat*, and the incidents as there narrated are dramatised without addition or omission.

The chief personages of the play, as of the poem, are demigods and demons, and the Yádavas, or kinsmen of Krishna and his son. We have also in the former, as in the latter, the pair of geese, the *Hansa* and *Hansí*, who inspire Prabhávatí, the daughter of Vajranábha, and Pradyumna, with a mutual passion before they have beheld each other, and who contrive their secret nuptials. The introduction of such performers on the stage must have had rather an extraordinary effect, although not more so than the *Birds* and *Wasps* of Aristophanes, or the *Io* of Æschylus, who, as the dialogue sufficiently proves, were dressed in character.

The stolen interviews of the lovers being communicated by Náreda to the father, Pradyumna is about to fall a victim to his vengeance, when Krishna and Baladeva with their followers come to his rescue, and a combat ensues, in which Vajranábha is defeated and slain. The whole of this engagement, occupying the entire last Act, is described by two Gandherbas, as supposed to be seen by them from their chariots in the air. Other portions of the piece are in narrative to a very considerable extent, the subject of which is foreign to the business; as the wars of the gods and demons, the rape of Rambhá by Rávana, and the destruction of Káma by Siva. The action is also frequently interrupted by laboured and tedious descriptions of the hours of the day and seasons of the year, in the usual hacknied strain. The style, although elaborate, is not remarkably beautiful, and there is no imagination in the thoughts. The play is the work of a Pandit, not of a poet.

The author of the *Pradyumna Vijaya* is named Sankara Díkshita, the son of Bála Kríshna Díkshita, the son of Dhundhi Raja. The date of the composition is fixed at about the middle of the last century, having been written for performance at the coronation of Sabha Sinh, the Raja of Pannah, who was the son of Hridaya Sinh, and grandson of the celebrated Chatra Sal, Raja of Bundelkand.

SRI DAMA CHERITRA.

This is a play in five acts, the subject of which is taken from the tenth section of the *Bhágavat*, and is the elevation of Sridáma, (or, as written more frequently, Sudáma,) the early companion and fellow-student of Krishna, to sudden and unexpected affluence, by the regard of that deity, and in requital of Sridáma's attachment. The story, which is not uninteresting in its original form, attracted the taste of Sir William Jones, and forms part of his Hymn to Lakshmí, the goddess of wealth and fortune.

The opening of the piece is in the style of our ancient moralities; and in the first act, Poverty and Folly are sent to assail Sridáma, who is obnoxious to Lakshmí for his attachment to Saraswati, or, in other words, who prefers learning to house and lands; for Fortune, it is said, will not even glance upon the pious and wise, but flies them in proportion as they are devoted to philosophy and virtue. On the other hand, Krishna or Vishnu employs the same agents to recover those whom Fortune has corrupted. Folly entering into their hearts, prepares the way for Poverty, and when reduced to distress their minds are weaned from worldly affections, and they are fitted for heaven. These allegorical personages effect their purpose with Sridáma, by demanding the rites of hospitality, and being accordingly admitted into his dwelling.

In the second act Sridáma is persuaded by his wife, Vasumatí, who has seen a propitious dream, to repair to Krishna, to see if his opulent friend will restore his broken fortunes. He takes with him a handful of rice, dried and cleaned after boiling, as a present.

The third act conducts Sridáma to the palace of Krishna,

where he is received with great respect by that divinity and his two principal wives, Rukminí and Satyabhámá ; the former washes his feet, the latter wipes them, and Krishna sprinkles the remaining water upon his own head. After re-calling some of the occurrences of their juvenile days, when they were fellow-students, Krishna leads his friend into the garden, where they remain till towards sun-set ; Krishna, Sridáma, the Vidúshaka, Gálava, and the gardener, striving who shall utter the most tedious descriptions of the beauties of the place and the decline of the sun, when they are summoned to join the queens and their attendants.

The greater portion of the next act is occupied with the representation of Krishna's frolics amongst his women, and the buffoonery of the Vidúshaka, partly in action, partly in description, Sridáma and Gálava his disciple being spectators, and occasionally taking a part in the dialogue. After some time spent in this manner, Sridáma takes his leave, and, although dismissed with great reverence, departs as poor as he came. He recollects this on his way back, and consoles himself with observing, that wealth intoxicates as well as wine, and that the affection of Krishna is a thing which no one can steal from him. His disciple is not so submissive, and reminds him that it was not to get mere civility that he was sent on this errand by his wife. When they approach their residence they find, instead of the miserable hovel of Sridáma, a splendid and extensive town, and Sridáma is in great affliction at the disappearance of his wife, when he is seen and solicited by a *Kanchukí,* or chamberlain, who calls himself his servant, to enter a stately palace. Sridáma thinking this is a jest upon his poverty, threatens to beat him if he does not depart, but the chamberlain perseveres, and tells him that whilst he was absent Krishna has converted his cottage into a town, named after him Sridámapur, and supplied it with every article of use or luxury. With much reluctance and unyielding incredulity Sridáma is prevailed upon to enter the palace.

The last Act brings Krishna to pay a visit to his friend. He arrives in his aerial chariot accompanied by Satyabhámá and the Vidúshaka, and his bounties are duly acknowledged by the object on whom they have been bestowed.

There is too much description and too little action in this piece to constitute a good play, but there is some vivacity in the thoughts, and much melody in the style. It is a modern work, the composition of Sáma Rája Díkshita, the son of Narahari Díkshita, and was written for the amusement of Ananda Raya, a petty Raja in Bundlecund. This family of the Díkshitas, a race of Mahratta Brahmans, has continued its dramatic studies to the present day; and to a descendant of the author of this drama, Lalla Díkshita, I am indebted for the manuscript of the *Mrichchakati,* and for very valuable assistance in the translation of that and several other pieces in this collection. Lalla Díkshita is the only Brahman I ever met with who might be considered conversant with the dramatic literature of the Hindus.

DHURTTA NARTTAKA.

A farce in one act, or two *Sandhis* or portions, by Sámaraja Díkshita, the author of the preceding play, written for performance at a festival in honour of Vishnu. The chief object of this piece is the ridicule of the Saiva ascetics, one of whom, Mureswara, is represented in love with a dancing-girl. His two pupils, to whom he communicates his passion after swearing them to secresy by making them swallow some sea-water, endeavour to anticipate him, and being prevented by his vigilance, seek to expose him, by bringing him before Pápáchára, a king. The king, however, makes light of his offence, and at the intercession of others of the fraternity, who are of great credit in his kingdom, allows him to retain possession of the damsel. The satire is levelled at the assumption of the ascetic character by improper persons, and the king's confidant proclaims Mureswara a *Yavana*, or Mohammedan. In a dialogue also with a brother saint the same idea is conveyed.

" *Muréswara (pointing to Papa).* Who is that?

Krishnánanda. My well beloved disciple.

Mur. His caste?

Krish. A weaver.

Mur. What other followers have you?

Krish. Many; but what need you enquire? Behold, Yavanas, Súdras, potters, weavers, plowmen, cowherds, venders of liquors, and harlots out of number, are accomplished in their course of pupillage by simply whispering into their ears."

The piece is, of course, of the same date as the preceding. The language is highly laboured, but there is little fancy or humour in the composition. It has, however, the recommendation of being exempt from gross indecency, the prevailing blemish of the class to which it belongs.

DHURTTA SAMAGAMA.

The only manuscript of this met with is incomplete at the beginning and end, and consequently the name of the author does not appear. It is somewhat indelicate, but not devoid of humour. Viswánagara, a Jangama or mendicant of a particular class, quarrels with his disciples for the possession of Anangasená, a courtezan. They refer the case to Asujjáti Misra, a Brahman, who lives by solving knotty points of law, and who decrees that until it can be decided to which the damsel belongs, she shall remain under the protection of himself as umpire

HASYARNAVA.

A Comic piece in two acts. It is a severe, but grossly indelicate satire upon the licentiousness of Brahmans assuming the character of religious mendicants. It satirizes also the encouragement given to vice by princes, the inefficacy of ministers, and the ignorance of physicians and astrologers. The king, Anasayindhu, in his progress through his city, regrets to find every thing subverted; that Chandálas, not Brahmans, make shoes; that wives are chaste and husbands constant; and that respect is paid to the respectable, not to the vile. He stops at the house of a courtezan, where the rest of the characters assemble; Viswábhanda, in the garb of a Saiva mendicant: Kalahánkura, his disciple, and who fights for the possession of a courtezan: Vyádhisinddu, the doctor, who cures the cholic by applying a heated needle to the palate, and perforates the pupil of the eye in order to restore vision. Sádhuhinsaka, the chief of police, who reports with great satisfaction that the city is completely in the hands of thieves: the commander-in-chief, Ranajambúka, who after putting on his armour has valiantly cut a leech in two: and Maháyátrika, the astrologer, who, in answer to a question of the time to take a journey, indicates hours and positions which, according to Hindu belief, proclaim approaching death. The king leaves the party at the end of the first act: the second is occupied with the dispute between the ascetic and his pupil, which they refer to the decision of Mahánindaka, another Brahman, who asserts that he composed the *Vedas* and visited *Swerga*, where he treated Vrihespati and Brahmá with contempt, and gave Siva a drubbing. These notices will convey some idea of the composition. It is the work of a Pundit named Jagaddísa, and was represented at the vernal festival; but where, or when, it is not known. The physician, amongst his authorities, names Bágbhatta, a medical writer, subsequent to those who may be considered the fathers of the science, and who is therefore perhaps comparatively modern. The class of Brahmans aimed at also is that of the Kaula, Kulína, or Vámáchari, or left-handed sect, the practices of which, as reduced to a system, are not likely to be of any antiquity.

KAUTUKA SERVASWA.

This is also a *Prahasana*, or Farce in Two Acts, and is especially a satire upon princes who addict themselves to idleness and sensuality, and fail to patronize the Brahmans. The hero is Kalivatsala, or the darling of the age of iniquity: he is sovereign of Dhermanásá, or the destruction of virtue, and he takes as his spiritual guide, Kukermapanchánana, the Sivá of iniquity. Satyácharya, a pious Brahman returned from Vrindávan, who is treated by the king and his courtiers with great indignity, holds the following conversation with his brethren in jail.

Satya. How now, holy Sirs, how fares it with ye?

Brahmans. We once had lands in free gift.

Satya. What then?

Brahmans. Why, know you not the customs of this country? If the god of wealth owned lands here that yielded but a grain of corn, the king would send him in three days to beg alms, clad in tatters and with a platter in his hand. The characteristics of our sovereign are love of untruth, passion for other men's wives, fondness for the intoxicating juice of *bhang*, esteem for the wicked, addiction to vice, and detestation of virtue.

Satya. You say right. What chance is there for the good. The king is unwise, his associates are wicked, his chief councillor is a knave, and his minister a scoundrel. Yet the people are many; why is not such misconduct resented?

Brahmans. The manners of the people are equally depraved: they are valiant in oppression, skilful in falsehood, and persevering only in contempt for the pious.

Satya. How are the scribes?

Brahmans. They collect the revenues by any expedient, and vigilantly inflict penalties on the wise. The Brahmans are not allowed to keep even the dust upon their bodies; the dust accumulated on their feet is claimed by the Kayeths. What can we say of this reign? The dumb alone can speak truth, the deaf hear the law, the sons of the barren are well behaved, the blind behold the observance of the Scriptures.

Satya. Why do not men of merit quit the country?

Brahmans. Our dwellings have been given to courtezans, our lands to drunkards, and we are detained in prison for what our ancestors expended.

Satya. I have heard enough. It is sinful to hold any communication with the profane. Better fortune attend you.

There is some bitterness in this, and there is also some humour in the piece, especially at the expense of the General, Samara Jambúka, the jackall of war, who boasts that he can cleave a roll of butter with his falchion, and is said to tremble from top to toe at the approach of a mosquito. There is also some rather bold censure of the immoralities of the *Purános.*

Dermánala. What says the law? 'Thou shalt not commit adultery.'

Kukerma. The language of fools. So much of the law as the sages and gods themselves observed, be our guide, not such commands as they contemned, like this. Indra deceived the wife of Gautama; Chandra carried off the bride of his Guru; Yama enjoyed the spouse of Pándu in her husband's shape; and Mádhava debauched the wives of all the cowherds of Vrindávan. Those conceited fools, the Pandits, imagining themselves sages, alone have made this a sin.

Dherm. But this is the precept of the Rishis. How answer you to that?

Kukerma. They were impostors. Becoming too old to relish pleasure, they condemned it, and out of envy forbade to others what they could no longer enjoy themselves.

All. Very true, very true! We never heard such orthodox doctrine before.

In consequence of this and similar decisions, the king orders vice to be proclaimed virtue by beat of drum, and the piece concludes with the perpetual banishment of all the Brahmans.

There is more humour in this than any of the other Farces, and less indecency, although it is not wholly free from the ordinary fault of these attempts at wit. Hindu Comedy, however, is not worse than the old Comedy of the Greeks in this respect; and the indelicacy is attributable, in some degree, to the constitution of society in both instances, and the exclusion of women from public entertainments.

The *Kautuka Servaswa* is the composition of a Pandit named Gopináth. The date is not known, but it is not likely to be ancient, as it was written for representation at the autumnal festival of the *Durgá Pujá*, a ceremony peculiar to the province of Bengal, and no doubt, as there practised, of comparatively modern institution.

CHITRA YAJNA.

A drama in five acts, the subject of which is the celebrated legend of Daksha. The First Act describes the assemblage of the gods and sages on the occasion of the sacrifice, and their reception by Daksha. The dialogue is curiously imperfect, being left to be supplied by the performer, partly after the fashion of the *Comedia a Soggetto* of the Italian Theatre before Goldoni. Thus, at the end of the first act, the stage direction is: "Daksha bows down to the feet of the gods, and puts the dust from under them upon his head, after which he propitiates them fully in the spoken dialect, and then proceeds to the place of sacrifice, reading or reciting the usual *formulæ*, and followed by the Rishis." And the second act opens with the stage direction; "Daksha enters, takes his seat, and orders the attendants to distribute rice to the Brahmans, for the purpose of invoking their benediction. They receive the rice, scatter it, and pronounce the *Swasti vachana*, or benedictory text."

The whole ceremonial of the oblation to fire is then represented, contrary to the received rule, which prohibits the dramatic exhibition of sacred rites. Even some of the *mantras* are given, as *Swáhá Agnayé*, oblation to Agni, or fire, &c. After these ceremonies, Dadhíchi comes to the sacrifice, when a dispute ensues between him and Daksha, upon the impropriety of omitting to invite Siva; and the dispute becoming rather warm, Daksha orders his guest to be turned out, which closes the second act.

The third act contains little more than directions for the business. The gods partake Dadhíchi's indignation at the disrespectful mention of Siva, and rise to depart. Daksha orders his servants to guard the door and prevent their going forth: the gods, however, force their way. The Munis then also withdraw, on which Daksha goes out, exclaiming he will give double the usual presents to those who remain. Náreda follows him, announcing his purpose of going to Kailás with the news. The next scene represents Siva and Bhaváni, to whom Náreda comes to tell them what has occurred. "He enters playing the *viná,* and singing hymns in honour of Mahádeva," one of which of some length is given. Náreda's communication is very brief.

Siva. Now, Náreda, whence come you?

Nar. Your godship is omniscient, you know all that has happened, but have asked me through a wish to hear it from my lips. We were all invited to Daksha's sacrifice. Dadhíchi finding that you were not included, took Daksha to task pretty sharply, and walked off, upon which I came to pay you my respects.

This having said, and prostrated himself on the ground, the Muni Náreda, with his lute hanging on his neck, again departed from Kailása mountain.

Passages of narrative being occasionally interspersed in this manner with the dialogue and stage direction. This ends the act. The author treats Siva and Bhaváni as Mr. Puff does the confidante, and leaves them to get off the stage as they can; or rather it is to be supposed that they remain on, as they begin the fourth act. The goddess asks leave to go and see her father. Siva replies, it is quite contrary to etiquette to go without an invitation. She replies, she need not stand on ceremony with her father; when Siva addresses her rather uncivilly, but to the usual purport of Pauranic mysticism. "How! would you impose upon me with falsehoods. Daksha is not your father, nor is his wife your mother. You are the father of all things, the mother of the universe. Those versed in the *Vedas* declare you male and female too." The discussion on this subject occupies the rest of the act, and ends, like most matrimonial debates, in the lady's being allowed to follow her own inclinations.

In the fifth act Sati comes to her father, and vainly endeavours to impress him with respect for her husband. She quits him to throw herself into the sacrificial fire, which of course is left to the language of description. Náreda then makes his appearance, and tells Daksha to prepare for the consequences of his folly. Vírabhadra, Siva's attendant, then enters and plays some antics, to represent the treatment this being is described to have inflicted on the assistants at the sacrifice. "Shaking the earth with his tread, and filling space with his extended arms, he rolls his eyes in wrath. Some of the gods he casts on the ground and tramples on them; he knocks out the teeth of some with his fists, plucks out the beards of some, and cuts off the ears, arms, and noses of others; some he smites double, and others he tosses into the sacrificial fire;" and ends by decapitating the cause of his master's indignation, the helpless Daksha.

This heterogeneous composition is the work of a Pandit of Nadiya, Vaidyanátha Váchespati, Bhattáchárya, and was composed for the festival of Govinda, by desire of Iswara Chandra, the Raja of Nadiya, about twenty or thirty years ago. It is so far valuable, as conveying a notion of the sort of attempts at dramatic composition made by the present race of Hindus in Bengal. The *Yátrás* or *Játrás* which are occasionally represented in the Bengal language follow the plan of the *Chitra Yajna*, with still less pretension to a literary character. They are precisely the *improvista commedia* of the Italians, the business alone being sketched by the author, and the whole of the dialogue supplied by the actors. The dialogue is diversified by songs, which are written and learnt by heart. Some improvements, however, have been made of late years in the representation of the performance: the details of the story are more faithfully and minutely followed, and part of the dialogue is composed and taught by the author to the actors.

THE END.